Frommer's®

Hawaii with Kids

3rd Edition

by Jeanette Foster

Here's what the critics say about Frommer's:

"Amazingly easy to use. Very portable, very complete."
—BOOKLIST

"Detailed, accurate, and easy-to-read information for all price ranges."
—GLAMOUR MAGAZINE

"Hotel information is close to encyclopedic."
—DES MOINES SUNDAY REGISTER

"Frommer's Guides have a way of giving you a real feel for a place."
—KNIGHT RIDDER NEWSPAPERS

Wiley Publishing, Inc.

Published by:

WILEY PUBLISHING, INC.

111 River St.
Hoboken, NJ 07030-5774

ISBN: 978-0-470-30639-0

Editor: William Travis
Production Editor: Eric T. Schroeder
Cartographer: Guy Ruggiero
Photo Editor: Richard Fox
Production by Wiley Indianapolis Composition Services

Front cover photo: Boogie boarding at Wailea Beach, Maui
Panoramic photo: The Kona coast, Big Island of Hawaii

For information on our other products and services or to obtain technical support, please contact our Customer Care Department within the U.S. at 800/762-2974, outside the U.S. at 317/572-3993 or fax 317/572-4002.

Wiley also publishes its books in a variety of electronic formats. Some content that appears in print may not be available in electronic formats.

Manufactured in the United States of America

5 4 3 2 1

CONTENTS

4 OAHU 66

5 THE BIG ISLAND OF HAWAII 155

6 MAUI 228

7 MOLOKAI 304

8 LANAI 326

9 KAUAI 342

APPENDIX: FAST FACTS, TOLL-FREE NUMBERS & WEBSITES 408

INDEX 417

LIST OF MAPS

ABOUT THE AUTHOR

A resident of the Big Island, **Jeanette Foster** has skied the slopes of Mauna Kea—during a Fourth of July ski meet, no less—and gone scuba diving with manta rays off the Kona Coast. A prolific writer widely published in travel, sports, and adventure magazines, she's also a contributing editor to *Hawaii* magazine, the editor of *Zagat's Survey to Hawaii's Top Restaurants,* and the author of the Hawaii Chapter of *1000 Places to See Before You Die—in the U.S. and Canada.* In addition to this guide, Jeanette is the author of *Frommer's Hawaii, Frommer's Maui, Frommer's Kauai, Frommer's Pocket Guide to the Big Island, Frommer's Hawaii from $80 a Day, Frommer's Honolulu, Waikiki & Oahu,* and *Frommer's Maui & Lanai Day by Day.*

AN INVITATION TO THE READER

In researching this book, we discovered many wonderful places—hotels, restaurants, shops, and more. We're sure you'll find others. Please tell us about them, so we can share the information with your fellow travelers in upcoming editions. If you were disappointed with a recommendation, we'd love to know that, too. Please write to:

Frommer's Hawaii with Kids, 3rd Edition
Wiley Publishing, Inc. • 111 River St. • Hoboken, NJ 07030-5774

AN ADDITIONAL NOTE

Please be advised that travel information is subject to change at any time—and this is especially true of prices. We therefore suggest that you write or call ahead for confirmation when making your travel plans. The authors, editors, and publisher cannot be held responsible for the experiences of readers while traveling. Your safety is important to us, however, so we encourage you to stay alert and be aware of your surroundings. Keep a close eye on cameras, purses, and wallets, all favorite targets of thieves and pickpockets.

FROMMER'S STAR RATINGS, ICONS & ABBREVIATIONS

Every hotel, restaurant, and attraction listing in this guide has been ranked for quality, value, service, amenities, and special features using a **star-rating system.** In country, state, and regional guides, we also rate towns and regions to help you narrow down your choices and budget your time accordingly. Hotels and restaurants are rated on a scale of zero (recommended) to three stars (exceptional). Attractions, shopping, nightlife, towns, and regions are rated according to the following scale: zero stars (recommended), one star (highly recommended), two stars (very highly recommended), and three stars (must-see).

In addition to the star-rating system, we also use **six feature icons** that point you to the great deals, in-the-know advice, and unique experiences that separate travelers from tourists. Throughout the book, look for:

Finds	Special finds—those places only insiders know about
Fun Facts	Fun facts—details that make travelers more informed and their trips more fun
Moments	Special moments—those experiences that memories are made of
Overrated	Places or experiences not worth your time or money
Tips	Insider tips—great ways to save time and money
Value	Great values—where to get the best deals

The following abbreviations are used for credit cards:

AE	American Express	DISC	Discover	V	Visa
DC	Diners Club	MC	MasterCard		

FROMMERS.COM

Now that you have the guidebook to a great trip, visit our website at **www.frommers.com** for travel information on more than 4,000 destinations. With features updated regularly, we give you instant access to the most current trip-planning information available. At Frommers.com, you'll find scoops on the best airfares, lodging rates, and car rental bargains. You can even book your travel online through our reliable travel booking partners. Other popular features include:

- Online updates to our most popular guidebooks
- Vacation sweepstakes and contest giveaways
- Newsletter highlighting the hottest travel trends
- Podcasts, interactive maps, and up-to-the-minute events listings
- Opinionated blog entries by Arthur Frommer himself
- Online travel message boards with featured travel discussions

1

How to Feel Like a Hawaii Family

Maybe the two of you visited Hawaii B.C. (Before Children), or maybe a trip to Hawaii has been the dream for years. There's no place on earth quite like this handful of sun-drenched mid-Pacific islands. The Hawaii of South Seas literature and Hollywood films really does exist. Here you'll find palm-fringed blue lagoons, lush rainforests, hidden gardens, cascading waterfalls, wild rivers running through rugged canyons, and volcanoes soaring 2 miles into the sky. And oh, those beaches—gold, red, black, and even green sands caressed by an endless surf. The possibilities for adventure—and relaxation—are endless. Each of the six main islands is distinct and infinitely complex. There's far too much to see and do on a 2-week vacation, which is why so many people return to the Aloha State year after year.

As a nearly lifelong Hawaii resident, I'm letting you in on some of the secrets that Hawaii families enjoy. We live here because of the beauty, culture, and lifestyle of these precious islands. You don't have to be rich to live in Hawaii (although, as my mother says, "it sure helps") to enjoy a quiet early-morning walk on the beach just as the sun lights up the turquoise water, to smell the sweet fragrance of just-blooming ginger, or to hear the thundering music of a waterfall. Hawaii can be a place that teaches your kids to enjoy the richness of their senses, from the vibrant colors of a rainbow to the smell of a bamboo forest just after an afternoon rainsquall.

Hawaii can also be a place of adventure, the opportunity for you and your children to try new things: Snorkel in warm tropical waters filled with neon-colored fish; coast down a dormant (but not extinct) volcano; silently glide over calm waters in a double kayak; or soar through the air, stopping to hover over an exploding volcano in a helicopter.

Even the word "Hawaii" conjures magic the world over, not only for the incredible beauty here but also for the culture and the lifestyle. This is a land founded by people who had immense respect for the island and the ocean. Their creed was a lifestyle of harmony and generous sharing. Millions of visitors flock to these islands every year because with all that's going on in the world today, they hunger for this harmony and generosity, which in Hawaii is referred to as the "aloha spirit."

All is not perfect in paradise. It is expensive in Hawaii: The islands sit in the middle of the Pacific, the most remote island chain in the world, and everything that is not grown or produced here has to be shipped or flown in—so be prepared to pay more. And despite being part of the United States, things are definitely done differently in Hawaii—that's why you've shelled out the money to give your family an opportunity to experience life here.

Part of raising a family is building memories that will last a lifetime. A trip to Hawaii will create memories not only of what you did, but of a lifestyle—the way people related to each other, the way the ocean smelled in the early morning, the way the stars glittered at night, the way the multicolored flowers looked in the full sun, and the time your family spent in a very special place.

When in Hawaii . . .

Hawaii loves travelers—they are the main industry, and a majority of Hawaii residents earn their living in the tourism industry or an industry closely connected to it. I love to pretend I'm a visitor when I travel around the state. Visitors are taken good care of and are treated like guests. Still, if you want to do as the Hawaiians do while you're in Hawaii, below are some helpful tips to help you blend in a little better:

- **Do not buy matching outfits.** It has always puzzled me that seemingly normal people come to Hawaii and feel that the entire family has to be dressed in a carbon-copy set of aloha wear: matching aloha shirts for the boys that perfectly match the baggy *muumuu* (Hawaiian-style dress) for the girls. Look around: Do you see troops of families in replica outfits? That's not to say that you can't outfit your family in aloha wear—just let each individual pick his or her own outfit.
- **Prepare for a variety of weather.** In addition to the shorts and T-shirts you throw in the suitcase, pack some clothes to keep you warm, especially if you plan to visit the mountains in Hawaii. Yes, even in summer, it is cold atop the mountains. At the ocean, after the sun sets, the temperature can drop and the wind can pick up. Whenever I'm at a sunset event on the ocean, I can always pick out the locals: They are the ones carrying sweaters because they know how the temperatures drop an hour after sunset.

GETTING THE MOST OUT OF THIS BOOK

The purposes of this book are to help visitors get the most out of their trip to Hawaii and to update local residents who want a refresher on all the activities for families. You won't find a lot of historical information or social commentary here. What you will find are opinions on the best places for families to stay, restaurants that welcome children, and a range of activities for all ages. I have purposely left out many chain restaurants and shops that your hometown may already have. You can go to them anytime—while you're in Hawaii, try to do things unique to Hawaii.

There are lots of islands in Hawaii, and each is unique. Read through each island chapter before you decide which island will best suit your family. ***Remember:*** Do not try to do more than one island a week; if you do, you'll have a vacation in interisland terminals instead of on beautiful beaches. The islands are far apart and it takes a full day to check out of your hotel, fly to another island, and check into a new hotel.

Once you decide which island you will explore, have a family planning session and choose the major things you want to see and do. Don't plan any more than one major activity a day, and leave at least a couple of days wide open. Pinpoint activities on a map—does your plan make sense or are you crisscrossing the island unnecessarily? If you're on Oahu and driving to the Polynesian Cultural Center, for example, perhaps you can plan a stop at the North Shore for a picnic lunch.

- **Drive with aloha.** Hawaiians probably drive slower than drivers elsewhere, give way to other drivers, and never, never *(never)* use horns to signal dissatisfaction with another driver. (The *only* time locals use their horns is to greet someone they know.) And one more thing: If you are sightseeing and driving slowly, look in your rearview mirror to see if you are holding up traffic—if so, please pull over and let the cars go by.
- **Be friendly.** Reach your hand out and greet everyone. Local residents say, "How-zit?" meaning "how are you?" Tell people your name and ask for theirs.
- **Get out of resort areas and explore.** Resorts are fabulous, but there is so much more to Hawaii. Rent a car and get out and drive. Stop along the way, talk to local residents, ask them what their favorite beach for snorkeling is, where they love to eat, and what they'd do if they had a day off.
- **Be appreciative.** Hawaii locals just love compliments. If you like the store, restaurant, activity, even your hotel room—tell the management. People in Hawaii are long on appreciation and admiration and short on criticism (even constructive criticism).
- **Smile.** You're in Hawaii and it's warm and beautiful—there's a lot to smile about.

When you arrive, allow yourself, especially the kids, time to recover from jet lag. Not only is Hawaii 2,500 miles and two time zones from the U.S. West Coast (three time zones during daylight saving time), but there's a huge change in climate and temperature. Plan nothing on the day you arrive, except checking into your hotel, maybe some beach time, an early dinner (remember the time change), and an early bedtime. Once you're ready to see the sights, be flexible.

So let's get started with planning the vacation of your dreams. For those too excited to page through from beginning to end, this chapter highlights the very best Hawaii has to offer.

1 THE BEST HAWAII EXPERIENCES

- **Hitting the Beach:** A beach is a beach is a beach, right? Not in Hawaii. With 132 islets, shoals, and reefs, and a general coastline of 750 miles, Hawaii has beaches in all different shapes, sizes, and colors, including black. The variety on the six major islands is astonishing; you could go to a different beach every day for years and still not see them all. For the best of a spectacular bunch, see "The Best Beaches for Families," later in this chapter.
- **Taking the Plunge:** Don mask, fin, and snorkel and explore the magical

world beneath the surface, where you'll find exotic corals and kaleidoscopic clouds of tropical fish; a sea turtle may even come over to check you out. Can't swim? That's no excuse—take one of the many submarine tours offered by **Atlantis Adventures** (✆ **800/548-6262;** www.atlantisadventures.com) on Oahu, the Big Island, and Maui. See chapters 4, 5, and 6.

- **Meeting Local Folks:** If you go to Hawaii and see only people like the ones back home, you might as well not have come. Extend yourself—leave your hotel, go out and meet the locals, and learn about Hawaii and its people. Just smile and say, "How-zit?"—which means "How are you?" ("It's good" is the usual response)—and you'll usually make a new friend. Hawaii is remarkably cosmopolitan; every ethnic group in the world seems to be represented here. There's a huge diversity of food, culture, language, and customs.
- **Feeling History Come Alive at Pearl Harbor** (Oahu): The United States could turn its back on World War II no longer after December 7, 1941, when Japanese warplanes bombed Pearl Harbor. Standing on the deck of the USS *Arizona* Memorial (✆ **808/422-0561;** www.nps.gov/usar)—the eternal tomb of the 1,177 sailors and Marines trapped below when the battleship sank in just 9 minutes—is a moving experience you'll never forget. Also in Pearl Harbor, you can visit the USS *Missouri* Memorial; World War II came to an end on the deck of this 58,000-ton battleship with the signing of the Japanese surrender on September 2, 1945. See p. 117.
- **Watching for Whales:** If you happen to be in Hawaii during humpback-whale season (roughly Dec–Apr), don't miss the opportunity to see these gentle giants. A host of boats—from small inflatables to high-tech, high-speed sailing catamarans—offer a range of whale-watching cruises on every island. One of my favorites is along the Big Island's Kona coast, where **Captain Dan McSweeney's Whale Watch Learning Adventures** (✆ **888/WHALE-76** [942-5376] or 808/322-0028; www.ilovewhales.com) takes you right to the whales year-round. (Pilot, sperm, false killer, melon-headed, pygmy killer, and beaked whales call Hawaii home even when humpbacks aren't in residence.) A whale researcher for more than 25 years, Captain Dan frequently drops an underwater microphone or video camera into the depths so you can listen to whale songs and maybe actually see what's going on. See p. 214.
- **Creeping Up to the Ooze** (Big Island): Kilauea volcano has been adding land to the Big Island continuously since 1983. If conditions are right, you can walk up to the red-hot lava and see it ooze along, or you can stand at the shoreline and watch with awe as 2,000°F (1,093°C) molten fire pours into the ocean. You can also take to the air in a helicopter and see the volcano goddess's work from above. See "Hawaii Volcanoes National Park" under "Exploring the Big Island with Your Kids," p. 203.
- **Greeting the Rising Sun from atop Haleakala** (Maui): Bundle up in warm clothing, fill a Thermos with hot chocolate, and drive to the summit to watch the sky turn from inky black to muted charcoal as a small sliver of orange light forms on the horizon. There's something about standing at 10,000 feet, breathing in the rarefied air, and watching the first rays of sun streak across the sky. This is a mystical experience of the first magnitude. See "House of the Sun:

Haleakala National Park" under "Exploring Maui with Your Kids," p. 270.

- **Taking a Day Trip to Lanai** (Maui): If you'd like to visit Lanai but have only a day to spare, consider taking a day trip. **Trilogy** (✆ **888/MAUI-800** [628-4800]; www.sailtrilogy.com) offers an all-day sailing, snorkeling, and whale-watching adventure. Trilogy is the only outfitter with rights to Hulopoe Beach, and the trip includes a minivan tour of the little isle (pop. 3,500). See p. 284. You can also take **Expeditions Lahaina/Lanai Ferry** (✆ **800/695-2624;** www.go-lanai.com) from Maui to Lanai, then rent a four-wheel-drive vehicle from **Dollar Rent-A-Car** (✆ **800/588-7808**) for a day of backcountry exploring and beach fun. See p. 285.
- **Soaring over the Na Pali Coast** (Kauai): This is the only way to see the spectacular, surreal beauty of Kauai. Your helicopter will dip low over razor-thin cliffs, flutter past sparkling waterfalls, and swoop down into the canyons and valleys of the fabled Na Pali Coast. The only problem is that there's too much beauty to absorb, and it all goes by in a rush. See "Helicopter Rides over Waimea Canyon & the Na Pali Coast" under "Exploring Kauai with Your Kids," p. 380.
- **Watching Rainbows at a Waterfall:** Rushing waterfalls thundering downward into sparkling freshwater pools are some of Hawaii's most beautiful natural wonders. If you're on the Big Island, stop by **Rainbow Falls** (p. 203) in Hilo, or the spectacular 442-foot **Akaka Falls** (p. 199), just outside the city. On Maui, the road to Hana offers numerous viewing opportunities. At the end of the drive, you'll find **Oheo Gulch** (also known as the Seven Sacred Pools), with some of the most dramatic and accessible waterfalls on the islands. (See "Tropical Haleakala: Oheo Gulch at Kipahulu" under "Exploring Maui with Your Kids," p. 277.) Kauai is loaded with waterfalls, especially along the North Shore and in the Wailua area, where you'll find 40-foot **Opaekaa Falls,** probably the best-looking drive-up waterfall on Kauai. (See "Wailua River State Park" under "Exploring Kauai with Your Kids," p. 383.) With scenic mountain peaks in the background and a restored Hawaiian village on the nearby riverbanks, the Opaekaa Falls are what the tourist-bureau folks call an eye-popping photo op.
- **Smelling the Flowers in a Tropical Garden:** The islands are redolent with the sweet scent of flowers. For a glimpse of the full breadth and beauty of Hawaii's spectacular range of tropical flora, I suggest spending a few hours at a lush garden. Two tropical havens not to be missed on the Big Island include the 40-acre **Hawaii Tropical Botanical Garden** (p. 199), featuring 1,800 species of tropical plants, and the **World Botanical Gardens** (p. 199), showcasing some 5,000 species. **Liliuokalani Gardens** (p. 200), the largest formal Japanese garden this side of Tokyo, resembles a postcard from Asia, with bonsai, carp ponds, pagodas, and a moon gate bridge. On lush Kauai, **Na Aina Kai Botanical Gardens** (p. 386), about 240 acres in size, is sprinkled with some 70 life-size (some larger than life-size) whimsical bronze statues, hidden off the beaten path of the North Shore.
- **Exploring the Grand Canyon of the Pacific—Waimea Canyon** (Kauai): This valley, known for its reddish lava beds, reminds everyone who sees it of Arizona's Grand Canyon. Kauai's version is bursting with ever-changing color, just like its namesake, but it's smaller—only a mile wide, 3,567 feet

deep, and 12 miles long. This grandeur was created by a massive earthquake that sent streams flowing into a single river, which then carved this picturesque canyon. You can stop by the road and look at it, hike down into it, or swoop through it by helicopter. See p. 379.

2 THE BEST WAYS TO ENJOY HAWAIIAN CULTURE

- **Experiencing the Hula:** For a real, authentic hula experience on Oahu, check out the **Bishop Museum** (p. 113), which has excellent performances on weekdays. The first week after Easter brings Hawaii's biggest and most prestigious hula extravaganza, the **Merrie Monarch Hula Festival** (p. 226), at Hilo on the Big Island; tickets sell out by January 30, so reserve early.
- **Buying a Lei in Chinatown** (Oahu): There's actually a host of cultural sights and experiences to be had in Honolulu's Chinatown. Wander through this several-square-block area with its jumble of exotic shops offering herbs, Chinese groceries, and acupuncture services. Before you leave, be sure to check out the lei sellers on Maunakea Street (near N. Hotel St.), where Hawaii's finest leis go for as little as $4. If you'd like a little guidance, follow the recommendations in "Shopping with Your Kids," p. 143.
- **Listening to Old-Fashioned "Talk Story" with Hawaiian Song and Dance** (Big Island): Once a month, under a full moon, "Twilight at Kalahuipua'a," a celebration of the Hawaiian culture that includes storytelling, singing, and dancing, takes place oceanside at Mauna Lani Resort (✆ **808/885-6622;** www.konafriends.com/maunalani-talkstory.html). It hearkens back to another time in Hawaii, when family and neighbors would gather on back porches to sing, dance, and "talk story." See "Old-Style Hawaiian Entertainment," on p. 227.
- **Visiting Ancient Hawaii's Most Sacred Temple** (Big Island): On the Kohala coast, where King Kamehameha the Great was born, stands Hawaii's oldest, largest, and most sacred religious site: the 1,500-year-old Mo'okini Heiau, used by kings to pray and offer human sacrifices. This massive three-story stone temple, dedicated to Ku, the Hawaiian god of war, was erected in A.D. 480. It's said that each stone was passed from hand to hand from Pololu Valley, 14 miles away, by 18,000 men who worked from sunset to sunrise.
- **Exploring Puuhonua O Honaunau National Historical Park** (Big Island): This sacred site on the south Kona coast was once a place of refuge and a revered place of rejuvenation. You can walk the same consecrated grounds where priests once conducted holy ceremonies, and glimpse the ancient way of life in precontact Hawaii in the re-created 180-acre village. See p. 192.
- **Visiting the Most Hawaiian Isle:** A time capsule of Old Hawaii, Molokai allows you to experience real Hawaiian life in its most unsullied form. The island's people have woven the cultural values of ancient times into modern life. In addition to this rich community, you'll find the magnificent natural wonders it so cherishes: Hawaii's highest waterfall, its greatest collection of fishponds, and the world's tallest sea cliffs, as well as sand dunes, coral reefs, rainforests, and gloriously empty beaches. The island is pretty much the same Molokai of generations ago. See chapter 7.

3 THE BEST HOTEL BETS

- **Most Family-Friendly:** There is no contest. On the Big Island, **Four Seasons Resort Hualalai at Historic Kaupulehu** (**© 888/340-5662**; www.fourseasons.com) offers a relaxing vacation in the lap of luxury, and the staff goes above and beyond its duties to pamper your kids. You can't get any better than this—everything from a complimentary children's program, something for the teenagers, and kid-friendly restaurants. See p. 163.
- **When Price Is No Object:** No question about it: the **Halekulani** (**© 800/367-2343**; www.halekulani.com) is an oasis of calm amid the buzz. This beach hotel is the finest Waikiki has to offer. (Heck, I think it's the finest in the state.) The complimentary children's program is tops, the rooms are practically suites, and the service is superb. See p. 82.
- **When Price Is Your Main Objective:** I recommend two places. On Oahu, the **Doubletree Alana Hotel–Waikiki** (**© 800/222-TREE** [222-8733]; www.alana-doubletree.com) is run by the Hilton Hawaiian Village and located within walking distance of Waikiki Beach. At this small boutique hotel, you get comfortable rooms and the kind of prompt service that you usually receive only at twice the price. (Rack rates here start at $189.) See p. 79. On the Big Island of Hawaii, the best deal is the oceanfront **Kona Tiki Hotel** (**© 808/329-1425**; www.konatiki.com). Its tastefully decorated rooms, with private lanais overlooking the ocean, start at just $69 a night! Although it's called a hotel, this small, family-run operation is more like a large B&B, with plenty of friendly conversation around the pool at the morning continental breakfast buffet. See p. 166.
- **Best Suite Deals:** The standout is **Fairmont Kea Lani Maui** (**© 800/659-4100**; www.kealani.com). This is the place to get your money's worth; for the price of a hotel room you get an entire suite—plus a few extras. Each unit in this all-suite luxury hotel has a kitchenette, a living room with entertainment center and sofa bed, an oversize marble bathroom with separate shower big enough for a party, a spacious bedroom, and a large lanai that overlooks the pools, lawns, and white-sand beach. See p. 246.
- **Most Peace and Quiet:** Head out to the North Shore on Oahu for the **Turtle Bay Resort** (**© 800/203-3650**; www.turtlebayresort.com). The resort is spectacular: an hour's drive from Waikiki, but eons away in its country feeling. Sitting on 808 acres, this place is loaded with activities and 5 miles of shoreline with secluded white-sand coves. All the rooms have great views, there are tons of activities for the *keiki* (children), and there's even a romantic restaurant for an adults' night out. See p. 94.
- **Most Hawaiian:** Nestled into the older section at the north end of the resort area, the **Kaanapali Beach Hotel** (**© 800/262-8450**; www.kbhmaui.com), on Maui, has an irresistible local style and a real Hawaiian warmth that's missing from many other, more modern hotels. Old Hawaii values and customs are always close at hand, and the service is some of the friendliest around. Children ages 5 and younger eat free and kids ages 6 to 12 can order from the special discounted kids' menu. As part of the hotel's extensive Hawaiiana program,

you and your kids can learn to cut pineapple, weave lauhala, or even dance the *real* hula. There's also an arts-and-crafts fair 3 days a week, a morning welcome reception on weekdays, and a Hawaiian library. Just opened is Kupanaha, a gourmet dinner show with world-renowned magicians. See p. 240.

- **Best Views:** Every view in Hawaii is terrific, but the **Princeville at Hanalei** (✆ **800/826-4400;** www.princeville.com) on Kauai is set in one of the most remarkable locations in the world, on a cliff between the crystal-blue waters of Hanalei Bay and steepled mountains; you arrive on the ninth floor and go down to the beach. This palace of green marble and sparkling chandeliers recalls Hawaii's monarchy period of the 19th century. Opulent rooms with magnificent views, a great children's program, and all the activities of Princeville and Hanalei make this one of Hawaii's finest resorts. See p. 360.
- **Best Beach:** A tough category with so many contenders, but I'm going with the golden sand and generally calm waters in front of Maui's **Four Seasons Resort Maui at Wailea** (✆ **800/334-MAUI** [334-6284]; www.fourseasons.com/maui). This is the ultimate beach hotel for latter-day royals, with excellent cuisine, spacious rooms, gracious service, and beautiful Wailea Beach. The most kid-friendly hotel on Maui not only offers a complimentary kids' program year-round and an everyday activities center (daily 9am–5pm), but also makes the children feel welcome with extras such as complimentary milk and cookies on their first day. Children's menus are offered at all resort restaurants and even from room service. See p. 247.
- **Best Fitness Center & Spa:** On Maui, **Spa Grande at the Grand Wailea Resort Hotel & Spa** (✆ **800/888-6100;** www.grandwailea.com) is Hawaii's biggest spa, at 50,000 square feet, with 40 treatment rooms. The spa incorporates the best of the Old World (romantic ceiling murals, larger-than-life Roman-style sculptures, mammoth Greek columns, huge European tubs); the finest Eastern traditions (a full Japanese-style traditional bath and various exotic treatments from India); and the lure of the islands (tropical foliage, ancient Hawaiian treatments, and island products). This spa has everything, from a top fitness center to a menu of classes, and is constantly on the cutting edge of the latest trends. See p. 247. On Kauai, the luxurious **ANARA Spa at the Grand Hyatt Kauai Resort and Spa** (✆ **800/55-HYATT** [554-9288; www.kauai.hyatt.com) is the place to get rid of stress and be soothed and pampered in a Hawaiian atmosphere, where the spirit of aloha reigns. An elegant 25,000-square-foot spa, ANARA (A New Age Restorative Approach) focuses on Hawaiian culture and healing, with some 16 treatment rooms, a lap pool, fitness facilities, lava rock showers that open to the tropical air, outdoor whirlpools, a 24-head Swiss shower, Turkish steam rooms, Finnish saunas, and botanical soaking tubs. See p. 350. And, on Oahu, **Ihilani Spa at the JW Marriott Ihilani Resort & Spa at Ko Olina** (✆ **800/626-4446;** www.ihilani.com) is an oasis by the sea. This free-standing 35,000-square-foot facility is dedicated to the traditional spa definition of "health by water." The modern, multistoried spa, with its floor-to-ceiling glass walls looking out on tropical plants, combines Hawaiian products with traditional therapies to produce some of the best water treatments in the

state. You'll also find a fitness center, tennis courts, and a bevy of aerobic and stretching classes. See p. 95.

- **Best Room Service:** Not only does Oahu's **Hilton Hawaiian Village Beach Resort & Spa** (✆ **800/HILTONS;** [445-8667] www.hawaiianvillage.hilton.com) on Waikiki Beach have a great menu and prompt room service, but the entire megaresort is kid-friendly. The Rainbow Express is the Hilton's year-round daily program of activities for children 5 to 12. Wildlife parades about the restaurants, where kids 4 to 11 eat free. See p. 79.
- **Best Lagoon:** My pick is Oahu's **Kahala Hotel & Resort** (✆ **800/367-2525;** www.kahalaresort.com). The lush, tropical grounds at this resort far from Waikiki include an 800-foot crescent-shaped beach and a 26,000-square-foot lagoon (home to two bottle-nosed dolphins, sea turtles, and tropical fish). Views from the floor-to-ceiling sliding-glass doors are of the ocean, Diamond Head, and Koko Head. The resort offers a "keiki club" for kids, with activities ranging from lei making to snorkeling. See p. 92.

4 THE BEST DINING BETS

- **Most Kid-Friendly Service: Hoku's** (✆ **808/739-8780**), at Oahu's Kahala Mandarin, is elegant without being stuffy, and creative without being overwrought. The staff at this fine-dining room treats kids like princesses and princes. See p. 109. On Maui, the kids will be graciously welcomed at **David Paul's Lahaina Grill** (✆ **808/667-5117**), a gourmet eatery which offers a great kids' menu with a kid's soup or salad of the day, fried chicken strips, corn dog, or mahi and shrimp, as well as desserts (ice cream and chocolate cake). See p. 254.
- **Best Kids' Menu:** Bev Gannon, one of the 12 original Hawaiian Regional Cuisine chefs, is raising the next generation of "foodies" at her gourmet haven in the pineapple fields of Maui at the **Haliimaile General Store** (✆ **808/572-2666**). Kids eat just as well as their parents when ordering from the creative kids' menu. See p. 261.
- **Best Views:** In Hawaii, views generally translate into "ocean views," and you can't get any closer to the ocean on the Big Island of Hawaii than **Huggo's** (✆ **808/329-1493**) or **Pahu i'a** (✆ **808/325-8000**) at the Hualalai Four Seasons Resort. It helps that both restaurants can hold your attention by their food alone without that distracting ocean view. See p. 176 and 175. On Kauai, **The Beach House** (✆ **808/742-1424**), which sits right on a promontory with a 180-degree ocean view, also serves excellent cuisine. See p. 363.
- **Best Decor:** On Oahu, the favorite decor from a kid's point of view has to be at **Sam Choy's Breakfast, Lunch, Crab & Big Aloha Brewery** (✆ **808/545-7979**), where an all-wood sampan (the centerpiece of the 11,000-sq.-ft. restaurant) commands attention. The kids can wash their hands in an oversize wok at the center of the room. Plus a 2,000-gallon live-crab tank lines the open kitchen with an assortment of crabs in season. See p. 105.
- **Best If You Have a Sitter:** The romantic, elegant dining room at **La Mer** (✆ **808/923-2311**) in Waikiki's

Halekulani is the only AAA Five-Diamond restaurant in the state. See p. 96. Also on Oahu, another great "date-night" rendezvous is **Chef Mavro Restaurant** (✆ **808/944-4714**), where wine pairings perfectly match the elegant cuisine of (James Beard award winner) Chef George Mavrothalassitis. See p. 105. It's worth a drive to the North Shore for the romantic atmosphere and first-rate food of **21 Degrees North** (✆ **808/293-8811**), in the Turtle Bay Resort. See p. 111. On Maui, I'd suggest **Vino** (✆ **808/661-VINO** [661-8466]), serving the best Italian food on Maui at an exquisite location overlooking the rolling hills of the Kapalua Golf Course. It is run by the team of D. K. Kodama, chef and owner of Sansei Seafood Restaurants and Sushi Bar (p. 98), and master sommelier Chuck Furuya. See p. 258. On Kauai, book **Dondero's** (✆ **808/742-1234**) in the Grand Hyatt Kauai Resort and Spa before you leave home to ensure a starlight table overlooking the ocean. See p. 366.

- **Best Burgers:** The winners of this highly competitive category are the juicy burgers at Oahu's two **Kua Aina locations** (✆ **808/591-9133** in Ward Village, or **808/637-6067** in Haleiwa); and Lahaina's **Cheeseburger in Paradise** (✆ **808/661-4855**) on Maui. See p. 103, p. 112 and 255. On Kauai, it's a tie between **Bubba Burgers** (✆ **808/823-0069**) and **Duane's Ono-Char Burger** (✆ **808/822-9181**). See p. 370 and 371.
- **Best Outdoor Setting:** You can't beat the beachside location under the spreading tree at the **Hau Tree Lanai** (✆ **808/921-7066**), at the New Otani Kaimana Beach Hotel on the outskirts of Waikiki. See p. 97. On Kauai, the lush garden setting in the Poipu Resort area at **Plantation Gardens** (✆ **808/742-2216**) beckons even the most jaded (seen-it-all) teenager. See p. 366.
- **Best Breakfast:** In Waikiki, there's no question that the winner is the quirky, late-night and morning eatery **Eggs 'n Things** (✆ **808/949-0820**), with huge, huge breakfasts and never-ending coffee refills. See p. 99. On the Big Island, the **Coffee Shack** (✆ **808/328-9555**), overlooking Kealakekua Bay and coffee fields, is the place for the most *ono* (delicious) breakfast. See p. 178.
- **Best Brunch:** Not only a winner in terms of best food, best display of food, and best variety of food, but also the winner of great views at brunch (Waikiki Beach) and best brunch decor is Oahu's **Orchids** (✆ **808/923-2311**), at the very plush Halekulani. See p. 96.
- **Best Milkshakes:** Kids will love the giant milkshakes at **Ken's House of Pancakes** (✆ **808/935-8711**) in Hilo on the Big Island, the only 24-hour restaurant on that island. See p. 185. On Kauai, the small roadside stand called **Banana Joe's** (✆ **808/828-1092**) offers creamy smoothies made of just-picked tropical fruit. See p. 403.
- **Best Japanese:** Pushing the envelope of Japanese food (and with a touch of Pacific Regional) is **Kenichi Pacific** (✆ **808/322-6400**), in Kona on the Big Island. The appetizers menu is so tempting, your kids might just want to graze from one dish to the next. See p. 177. For more traditional Japanese food, try **Miyo's** (✆ **808/935-2273**), in Hilo, where children's portions are half-price. See p. 185.
- **Best Chinese:** The kids will vote for **Panda Cuisine** (✆ **808/947-1688**) on Oahu every time. Quick, easy, and moderately priced, this dim sum, Hong Kong–style restaurant is perfect for a family lunch. See p. 103.

- **Best Hawaiian Regional Cuisine:** The masters of Hawaiian Regional Cuisine include **Alan Wong's Restaurant** (✆ **808/949-2526**) on Oahu; **Merriman's Market Café** (✆ **808/886-1700**) on the Big Island; and **Roy's Restaurant** (✆ **808/396-7697**) on Oahu, Kauai, Maui, and the Big Island. Any of these great places will introduce you to the unique blends of Hawaii's fresh produce, fish, and meats in this well-loved cuisine. See p. 106, 181, and 110, respectively.
- **Best Pizza:** This is another hotly contested category with many great places to choose from. On the Big Island, head to **Boston Basil's Pizzeria** (✆ **808/326-7836**), where sauce is the thing. See p. 177. On Maui, my two favorite picks are **Nicky's Pizza** (✆ **808/667-0333**) and **Shaka Sandwich & Pizza** (✆ **808/874-0331**) for perfect crusts. See p. 257 and 259. And on Kauai, **Brick Oven Pizza** (✆ **808/332-8561**) still makes pizza the old fashioned way. See p. 367.
- **Best Pasta:** There's great pasta in Hawaii, but the two standouts are **Buon Amici** (✆ **808/732-5999**) on Oahu and **Pomodoro** (✆ **808/332-5945**) on Kauai. See p. 108 and 367.
- **Best Mexican: Norberto's El Café** (✆ **808/822-3362**) on Kauai has been serving lard-free Mexican for nearly a generation. See p. 371. In Waimea on the Big Island, the tiny **Tako Taco Taquería** (✆ **808/887-1717**) pumps out healthy Mexican at wallet-pleasing prices. See p. 183. And on Maui, although **Mañana Garage** (✆ **808/873-0220**) can't really be classified as "true" Mexican (in fact, it defies classification in any category), the eclectic cuisine here (not to mention the very oddball decor) will make your kids smile. See p. 253.
- **Best for Feeding Large Families:** In terms of getting your money's worth of good food at bargain prices, head to the **Olive Tree Cafe** (✆ **808/737-0303**) on Oahu to take out or eat at the outdoor tables. See p. 110. On Maui, two fabulous budget-price eateries for large families are **AK's Cafe** (✆ **808/244-8774**) and **Moana Bakery & Cafe** (✆ **808/579-9999**). See p. 253 and 262.
- **Best Fresh Fish: Mama's Fish House** (✆ **808/579-8488**) in Kuau on Maui is synonymous with excellent fish. (Even the kids get fresh fish on the keiki menu.) See p. 262. But that's not all; at the other end of Maui (and also on Oahu) in Kapalua and in Kihei, **Sansei Seafood Restaurant** (✆ **808/669-6286**) has only the best fish, carefully prepared. See p. 258.
- **Best for Aspiring Gourmands:** Take your budding "foodies" to the Big Island, where, on the Kona side, the **Hualalai Club Grille by Alan Wong** (✆ **808/325-8525**) will serve them (from the kids' menu) the best in Hawaiian Regional Cuisine. See p. 175.
- **Best Ice Cream:** At stores, restaurants, and ice-cream parlors throughout the state, ask for **Roselani Ice Cream** (✆ **808/244-7951**), Maui's only made-from-scratch, old-fashioned ice cream. See p. 300. On the Big Island, be sure to try **Tropical Dreams Ice Cream** (✆ **808/889-5577**), another creamy taste treat. See p. 182.
- **Best Delivery:** On Oahu, you are no longer limited by the room service menu in your hotel room. **Room Service in Paradise** (✆ **808/941-DINE** [941-3463]; www.rsiponline.com) is the answer to a parent's prayers. They deliver almost a dozen different cuisines (from American/Pacific Rim to Italian

to sandwiches and burgers) from 50 different restaurants to your hotel room. See p. 96.

- **Best Takeout:** On Oahu, great grinds (food) can be had from Honolulu's **Kaka'ako Kitchen** (✆ **808/596-7488**). See p. 103.
- **Best Diner:** Maui has the best diners in the state. My two faves are **CJ's Deli and Diner** (✆ **808/667-0968**) in Kaanapali for the best food in a retro atmosphere, and **Peggy Sue's** (✆ **808/875-8944**) in Kihei for an upscale Maui-kinda diner the kids will love. See p. 256 and 259.
- **Best Shave Ice:** Like surfing, shave ice is synonymous with Haleiwa, the North Shore Oahu town where **Matsumoto Shave Ice** (✆ **808/637-4827**)—and other neighboring establishments—serves mounds of icy treats to long lines of thirsty takers. This tasty and refreshing cultural phenomenon is even better over ice cream and adzuki beans. See p. 126.
- **Best Plate Lunch:** For seasoned plate lunchers who favor the traditional "two scoop rice" lunches weighted with carbohydrates and hefty meats, **Zippy's** (21 locations throughout Oahu; visit www.zippys.com for the one nearest you) is a household word. On Kauai, **Pono Market** (✆ **808/822-4581**), **Fish Express** (✆ **808/245-9918**), and **Koloa Fish Market** (✆ **808/742-6199**) are at the top of the plate-lunch pyramid. See p. 365, 364 and 364, respectively.
- **Best Noodles:** Ramen, udon, saimin, pho, pasta, chow mein—Hawaii is the epicenter of ethnic noodle stands and houses, with many recommendable and inexpensive choices. **Jimbo's Restaurant** (Oahu; ✆ **808/947-2211**), a neighborhood institution, is tops for freshly made udon with generous toppings and a homemade broth. See p. 108.
- **Best Tropical Fruit: Mangosteen,** the queen of fruit in Indonesia, is the sensation at the Hilo Farmers' Market on the Big Island. Mangosteen's elegant purple skin and soft, white, floral-flavored flesh (like lychee, but more custard-like than translucent) make this fruit a sure winner. It joins the ranks of rambutan, durian, sapote, sapodilla, and other exotic Asian newcomers. The mango is always a much-anticipated feature of late spring and summer. **Hayden mangoes** are universally loved for their plump, juicy flesh and brilliant skins. Papaya lovers, take note: **Kahuku papayas**—firm, fleshy, dark orange, and so juicy they sometimes squirt—are the ones to watch for on menus and in markets; check out the supermarkets and the roadside stands in Kahuku on Oahu. **Sunrise papayas** from Kapoho and Kauai are also top-notch. White, acid-free, extra sweet, and grown on Kauai and the Big Island, **Sugarloaf pineapples** are the new rage. Hilo is the town for **lychees** (also known as litchis) in summer, but Honolulu's Chinatown markets carry them, too. Decidedly Hawaiian are **Ka'u oranges,** grown in the volcanic soil of the southern Big Island and available in supermarkets and health food stores. Don't be fooled by their brown, ugly skin—they're juicy, thin-skinned, and sweet as honey.
- **Other Mighty Morsels:** Poi biscotti from the **Poi Company,** available at supermarkets and gourmet outlets such as Hawaiian Regional Cuisine Marketplace (in Macy's in Ala Moana, Honolulu), is a new taste treat, the consummate accompaniment to another island phenomenon, Kona coffee. Highly

esteemed coffee growers (all based on the Big Island, of course), include **Bears' Coffee** (© 808/935-0708); **Kona Blue Sky Coffee** (© 877/322-1700 or 808/322-1700); **Waimea Coffee Company** (© 808/885-4472); and **Bad Ass Coffee Company** (multiple locations). The buttery, chocolate-dipped shortbread cookies of **Big Island Candies** (Big Island; © **808/935-8890**) are worth every calorie and every dollar. See p. 225. From Kauai, Hanapepe town's venerable **Taro Ko Chips** (© **808/335-5586** for the factory) are the crunchy snack that neighbor islanders drive long miles to find, then cart home in hand-carried bundles. See p. 403.

5 THE BEST BEACHES FOR FAMILIES

- **Lanikai Beach** (Oahu): Too gorgeous to be real, this stretch along the windward coast is one of Hawaii's postcard-perfect beaches—a mile of golden sand as soft as powdered sugar bordering translucent turquoise waters. The year-round calm waters are excellent for swimming, snorkeling, and kayaking. Completing the picture are two tiny offshore islands that function not only as scenic backdrops but also as bird sanctuaries. See p. 129.
- **Hapuna Beach** (Big Island): This half-mile-long crescent regularly wins kudos in the world's top travel magazines as the most beautiful beach in Hawaii—some consider it one of the most beautiful beaches in the world. One look and you'll see why: Perfect cream-colored sand slopes down to crystal-clear waters that are great for swimming, snorkeling, and bodysurfing in summer; come winter, waves thunder in like stampeding wild horses. The facilities for picnicking and camping are top-notch, and there's plenty of parking. See p. 212.
- **Kapalua Beach** (Maui): On an island with many great beaches, Kapalua takes the prize. This golden crescent with swaying palms is protected from strong winds and currents by two outstretched lava-rock promontories. Its calm waters are perfect for snorkeling, swimming, and kayaking. The beach borders the Kapalua Bay Hotel, but it's long enough for everyone to enjoy. Facilities include showers, restrooms, and lifeguards. See p. 279.
- **Papohaku Beach** (Molokai): One of Hawaii's longest beaches, these gold sands stretch on for some 3 miles and are about as wide as a football field. Offshore, the ocean churns mightily in winter, but the waves die down in summer, making the calm waters inviting for swimming, picnics, beach walks, and sunset watching. See p. 318.
- **Hulopoe Beach** (Lanai): This golden, palm-fringed beach off the south coast of Lanai gently slopes down to the azure waters of a Marine Life Conservation District, where clouds of tropical fish flourish and spinner dolphins come to play. A tide pool in the lava rocks defines one side of the bay, while the other is lorded over by the Manele Bay Hotel, which sits prominently on the hill above. Offshore, you'll find good swimming, snorkeling, and diving; onshore, there's a full complement of beach facilities, from restrooms to camping areas. See p. 335.
- **Haena Beach** (Kauai): Backed by verdant cliffs, this curvaceous North Shore

beach has starred as paradise in many a movie. It's easy to see why Hollywood loves Haena Beach, with its grainy golden sand and translucent turquoise waters. Summer months bring calm waters for swimming and snorkeling, while winter brings mighty waves for surfers. There are plenty of facilities on hand, including picnic tables, restrooms, and showers. See p. 390.

2

Planning a Family Trip to Hawaii

If you have enough trouble getting your kids out of the house in the morning, dragging them thousands of miles away may seem like an insurmountable challenge. But family travel can be immensely rewarding, giving you new ways of seeing the world through smaller pairs of eyes. This chapter will give you the nuts-and-bolts information you need to plan an affordable, safe, and memorably fun family vacation.

Hawaii has so many places to explore, things to do, sights to see—it can be bewildering to plan your trip with so much vying for your attention. Where to start? In the pages that follow, I've compiled everything you need to know to plan your ideal trip to Hawaii.

The first thing to do: **Decide where you want to go.** Each island offers a different experience for families, so be sure to read each destination chapter (especially each chapter introduction) before you make up your mind which island is perfect for your family vacation. I strongly recommend that you **limit your island-hopping to one island per week.** If you decide to go to more than one in a week, be warned: You could spend much of your precious vacation time in airports and checking in and out of hotels. Not much fun!

My second tip is to **fly directly to the island of your choice;** doing so can save you a 2-hour layover in Honolulu and another plane ride. Oahu, the Big Island, Maui, and Kauai now all receive direct flights from the mainland; if you're heading to Molokai or Lanai, you'll have the easiest connections if you fly into Honolulu.

For additional help in planning your trip and for more on-the-ground resources in Hawaii, please turn to the "Fast Facts, Toll-Free Numbers & Websites" appendix, on p. 408.

1 CHOOSING THE PERFECT ISLAND

Although Hawaii has eight islands, only six are available to visitors: Oahu (where Honolulu and Waikiki are located), Maui, the Big Island of Hawaii, Molokai, Lanai, and Kauai. The island of Niihau is privately owned and off-limits to nonresidents. Kahoolawe, used as a bombing target by the military, has been returned to the state of Hawaii and is still being cleared of bombs.

OAHU This island is home to world-renowned Waikiki and very urban Honolulu. Millions of tourists flock to these well-known areas every year. Here's the place of sand and sunshine, historical and cultural activities, the Honolulu Zoo, the Waikiki Aquarium, and the Bishop Museum. There's also another side to Oahu: On the North Shore, big waves roll ashore every winter into the tiny communities on the more rural part of the island. The Polynesian Cultural Center offers a day's worth of fun. Just being out in the country, hopping from beach to sandy beach, should be on every family's list.

MAUI Maui is one of Hawaii's more popular vacation spots, perfect for families. The "Valley Isle," as local residents call it, offers luxurious hotels and resort areas, bargain condos for large families, and plenty of activities for all ages (from watersports such as snorkeling and kayaking to coasting a bike down the 10,000-ft. dormant volcano Haleakala). Even the daylong ride along the windy, two-lane Hana Highway is an adventure. Maui does not have an urban center like Honolulu and Waikiki, but it offers a vacation for active families as well as a place just to kick back and relax.

MOLOKAI The "most Hawaiian island" is a small, slipper-shaped rural community of mainly Hawaiians. This is for families seeking a quieter, more relaxed vacation. Certainly not a place for shopping or fine dining, Molokai is country. Only one hotel on the island, plus a few condos and vacation rentals, makes this a get-away-from-everything vacation and definitely a make-your-own-fun place for the kids.

LANAI The smallest of the islands for visitors, this former plantation community now boasts two luxurious resorts, a tiny hotel, and a handful of B&Bs and vacation rentals. The resorts here are excellent for families, offering all the amenities for a fun vacation; those on a budget can still enjoy Lanai's beautiful beaches, remote hiking, and community spirit.

THE BIG ISLAND OF HAWAII The largest Hawaiian island (bigger than all the other islands combined), the Big Island offers families a diverse vacation, from the sunny shores of Kailua-Kona and the top of the nearly 14,000-foot volcanoes to the spouting lava flowing into the sea and the lush tropical jungle just outside of Hilo.

The Big Island is just as fabulous to first-timers as it is to repeat Hawaii visitors. It's not as urban as Oahu and not as crowded as Maui, but it offers its own unique vacation experience.

KAUAI The oldest of the Hawaiian Islands, Kauai is ringed with beautiful white-sand beaches. It is the site of the "Grand Canyon of the Pacific," Waimea Canyon, home to hundreds of waterfalls. Most of the island is accessible only via helicopter. Kauai offers families many outdoor activities, from watersports to biking. Not as urban as Maui, Kauai is a place to go for a quieter vacation.

2 VISITOR INFORMATION & MAPS

For information about traveling in Hawaii, contact the **Hawaii Visitors and Convention Bureau (HVCB),** Suite 801, Waikiki Business Plaza, 2270 Kalakaua Ave., Honolulu, HI 96815 (© **800/GO-HAWAII** or 808/923-1811; www.gohawaii.com). The bureau publishes the helpful *Accommodations and Car Rental Guide* and supplies free brochures, maps, and the *Islands of Aloha* magazine, the official HVCB magazine. If you want information about working and living in Hawaii, contact the **Chamber of Commerce of Hawaii,** 1132 Bishop St., Suite 402, Honolulu, HI 96813 (© **808/545-4300;** www.cochawaii.com).

INFORMATION ON HAWAII'S PARKS

Hawaii has several national parks and historic sites—four on the Big Island, and one each on Maui, Oahu, and Molokai. The following offices can supply you with hiking and camping information:

- On the **Big Island: Hawaii Volcanoes National Park,** P.O. Box 52, Hawaii National Park, HI 96718 (© **808/985-6000;** www.nps.gov/havo); **Puuhonua o Honaunau National Historical Park,** P.O. Box 129, Honaunau, HI 96726 (© **808/328-2326;** www.nps.gov/puho); **Puukohola Heiau National Historic**

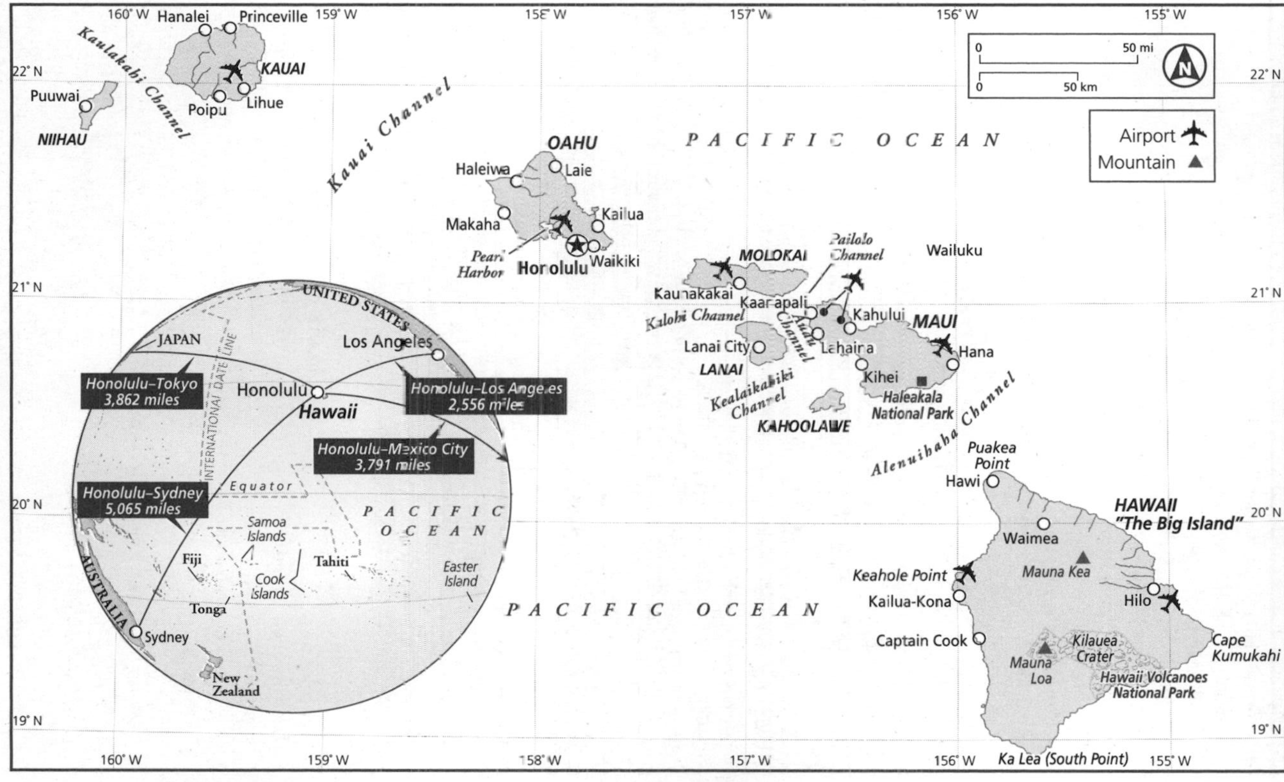
Hanalei
Princeville
KAUAI
Lihue
Poipu
Puuwai
NIIHAU
Kaulakahi Channel
Kauai Channel
OAHU
Haleiwa
Laie
Kailua
Makaha
Pearl Harbor
Honolulu
Waikiki
PACIFIC OCEAN
Airport
Mountain
50 mi
50 km
MOLOKAI
Kaunakakai
Pailolo Channel
Wailuku
Kaanapali
Kahului
MAUI
Kalohi Channel
Auau Channel
Lanai City
Lahaina
Hana
LANAI
Kihei
Kealaikahiki Channel
Haleakala National Park
KAHOOLAWE
Alenuihaha Channel
Puakea Point
Hawi
HAWAII
"The Big Island"
Waimea
Mauna Kea
Keahole Point
Kailua-Kona
Hilo
Captain Cook
Kilauea Crater
Mauna Loa
Cape Kumukahi
Hawaii Volcanoes National Park
Ka Lea (South Point)
PACIFIC OCEAN
UNITED STATES
JAPAN
Los Angeles
INTERNATIONAL DATE LINE
Honolulu
Hawaii
Honolulu–Tokyo 3,862 miles
Honolulu–Los Angeles 2,556 miles
Honolulu–Mexico City 3,791 miles
Honolulu–Sydney 5,065 miles
Equator
PACIFIC OCEAN
Samoa Islands
Fiji
Tahiti
Cook Islands
Easter Island
Tonga
AUSTRALIA
Sydney
New Zealand
22° N
21° N
20° N
19° N
160° W
159° W
158° W
157° W
156° W
155° W

Site, P.O. Box 44340, Kawaihae, HI 96743 (✆ **808/882-7218;** www.nps.gov/puhe); and **Kaloko-Honokohau National Historical Park,** 72-4786 Kanalani St., Kailua-Kona, HI 96740 (✆ **808/329-6881;** www.nps.gov/kaho).

- On **Maui: Haleakala National Park,** P.O. Box 369, Makawao, HI 96768 (✆ **808/572-9306;** www.nps.gov/hale).
- On **Molokai: Kalaupapa National Historical Park,** P.O. Box 2222, Kalaupapa, HI 96742 (✆ **808/567-6802;** www.nps.gov/kala).
- On **Oahu: USS *Arizona* Memorial at Pearl Harbor** (✆ **808/422-0561;** www.nps.gov/usar).

To find out more about Hawaii's state parks, contact the **Hawaii State Department of Land and Natural Resources,** 1151 Punchbowl St., No. 130, Honolulu, HI 96813 (✆ **808/587-0300;** www.hawaii.gov). The office can provide you with information on hiking and camping at the parks and will send you free topographic trail maps.

HAWAII ON THE WEB

Listed below are some of the most useful sites.

- **Hawaii Visitors & Convention Bureau:** www.gohawaii.com
- **Hawaii State Vacation Planner:** www.bestplaceshawaii.com
- **Planet Hawaii:** www.planet-hawaii.com
- **Oahu Visitors Bureau:** www.visit-oahu.com
- **The Hawaiian Language Website:** www.geocities.com/~olelo
- Big Island's **Kona-Kohala Resort Association:** www.kohalacoastresorts.com
- **Hawaii's Big Island Visitors Bureau:** www.bigisland.org
- **Maui Visitors Bureau:** www.visitmaui.com
- **Maui Net:** www.maui.net
- **Maui's Kaanapali Beach Resort Association:** www.kaanapaliresort.com
- **Molokai Visitors Association:** www.molokai-hawaii.com
- **Lanai Visitors Bureau:** www.visitlanai.net
- **Kauai Visitors Bureau:** www.kauaivisitorsbureau.org
- Kauai's **Poipu Beach Resort Association:** www.poipu-beach.org
- **Weather information:** http://weather.hawaii.edu or www.weather.com

WHAT TO PACK

So what kid gear should you bring with you to Hawaii? I would recommend bringing your own **stroller** from home, primarily because your child is used to the stroller (and it's one less thing to adjust to) and you're used to maneuvering it. You can rent a stroller, but many mothers are not happy with the rental selections. Bringing your own also means you'll have the stroller the second you get off the plane; after a long flight, you'll be happy to have a vehicle for baby as you round up your luggage and leave the airport.

Most hotels will supply cribs, often for free (and some even have strollers); I've noted the ones that do and any additional charges in the "Family-Friendly Accommodations" listings in the island chapters. Most hotels will childproof your hotel room, but condo and vacation rentals may not provide this service. Most baby products that you use at home can be found in the islands; if you are unsure, check with your hotel and they can help you find the items you need. If you're renting a car, bring a **car seat** (some car rental agencies will have them; but they are in short supply, so check when you book); if you don't bring your own, you will have to rent one when you arrive. **Baby's Away** (www.babysaway.com) rents cribs, strollers, highchairs, playpens, infant seats, and other children's gear on Maui (✆ **800/942-9030** or 808/875-9030), the Big Island

(✆ **800/996-9030** or 808/987-9236), and Oahu (✆ **800/496-6386** or 808/222-6041). The staff will deliver whatever you need to wherever you're staying and pick it up when you're done.

Clothing-wise, Hawaii is very informal. **Shorts, T-shirts,** and **tennis shoes** will get you by at most restaurants and attractions; **a casual dress** or a **polo shirt** and **khakis** are fine even in the most expensive places. Dinner jackets for men are required only in some of the fine dining rooms of a very few ultra-exclusive resorts, such as the Halekulani on Oahu, the Big Island's Mauna Kea Beach Hotel, Four Seasons Resort Lanai, and The Lodge at Koele—and they'll cordially provide you with a jacket if you don't bring your own. Aloha wear is acceptable everywhere, so you may want to plan on buying an aloha shirt or a *muumuu* (a Hawaiian-style dress) while you're in the islands.

So bring **T-shirts, shorts, long pants,** a **bathing suit, a long-sleeve coverup** (to throw on at the beach when you've had enough sun for the day), **tennis shoes,** and **rubber slippers** or **flip-flops.** If you plan on hiking, bring **hiking boots** and **good socks.**

The tropical sun poses the greatest threat to anyone who ventures into the great outdoors, so be sure to bring **sun protection:** a good pair of sunglasses, strong sunscreen, a light hat (like a baseball cap or a sun visor), and a **canteen** or water bottle if you'll be hiking—you'll easily dehydrate in the tropical heat, so figure on carrying 2 liters of water per day on any hike. Campers should bring **water-purification tablets or devices.**

You won't have to stuff your suitcase with 2 weeks' worth of shorts and T-shirts. Almost all of Hawaii's hotels and resorts—even the high-end ones—have **laundry facilities.** If your accommodations don't have a washer and dryer or laundry service, there will likely be a laundromat nearby. The only exception to this is Hana on Maui; this tiny town has no laundromat, so check with the place where you're staying beforehand.

One last thing: It really can get cold in Hawaii. If you plan to see the sunrise from the top of Maui's Haleakala Crater, venture into the Big Island's Hawaii Volcanoes National Park, or spend time in Kokee State Park on Kauai, bring a **warm jacket;** 40°F (4°C) upcountry temperatures, even in summer when it's 80°F (27°C) at the beach, are not uncommon. It's always a good idea to bring at least a windbreaker, a sweater, or a light jacket. And be sure to toss some **rain gear** into your suitcase if you'll be in Hawaii from November to March.

3 ENTRY REQUIREMENTS

PASSPORTS

New regulations issued by the Department of Homeland Security now require virtually every air traveler entering the U.S. to show a passport. As of January 23, 2007, all persons, including U.S. citizens, traveling by air between the United States and Canada, Mexico, Central and South America, the Caribbean, and Bermuda are required to present a valid passport. As of January 31, 2008, U.S. and Canadian citizens entering the U. S. at land and sea ports of entry from within the Western Hemisphere will need to present government-issued proof of citizenship, such as a birth certificate, along with a government-issued photo ID, such as a driver's license. A passport is not required for U.S. or Canadian citizens entering by land or sea, but you are highly encouraged to carry one.

For information on how to obtain a passport, go to **"Passports"** in the **"Fast Facts"** section of the appendix (p. 411).

VISAS

The U.S. State Department has a **Visa Waiver Program (VWP)** allowing citizens of the following countries to enter the United States without a visa for stays of up to 90 days: Andorra, Australia, Austria, Belgium, Brunei, Denmark, Finland, France, Germany, Iceland, Ireland, Italy, Japan, Liechtenstein, Luxembourg, Monaco, the Netherlands, New Zealand, Norway, Portugal, San Marino, Singapore, Slovenia, Spain, Sweden, Switzerland, and the United Kingdom. (***Note:*** This list was accurate at press time; for the most up-to-date list of countries in the VWP, consult www.travel.state.gov/visa.) Canadian citizens may enter the United States without visas; they will need to show passports (if traveling by air) and proof of residence, however. ***Note:*** Any passport issued on or after October 26, 2006, by a VWP country must be an **e-Passport** for VWP travelers to be eligible to enter the U.S. without a visa. Citizens of these nations also need to present a round-trip air or cruise ticket upon arrival. E-Passports contain computer chips capable of storing biometric information, such as the required digital photograph of the holder. (You can identify an e-Passport by the symbol on the bottom-center cover of your passport.) If your passport doesn't have this feature, you can still travel without a visa if it is a valid passport issued before October 26, 2005, and includes a machine-readable zone, or between October 26, 2005, and October 25, 2006, and includes a digital photograph. For more information, go to **www.travel.state.gov/visa**.

Citizens of all other countries must have (1) a valid passport that expires at least 6 months later than the scheduled end of their visit to the U.S., and (2) a tourist visa, which may be obtained without charge from any U.S. consulate.

As of January 2004, many international visitors traveling on visas to the United States will be photographed and fingerprinted on arrival at Customs in airports and on cruise ships in a program created by the Department of Homeland Security called **US-VISIT.** Exempt from the extra scrutiny are visitors entering by land or those that don't require a visa for short-term visits. For more information, go to the Homeland Security website at **www.dhs.gov/dhspublic**.

For specifics on how to get a visa, go to **"Visas"** in the **"Fast Facts"** section of the appendix (p. 413).

MEDICAL REQUIREMENTS

Unless you're arriving from an area known to be suffering from an epidemic (particularly cholera or yellow fever), inoculations or vaccinations are not required for entry into the United States.

CUSTOMS

What You Can Bring into the U.S.

Every visitor more than 21 years of age may bring in, free of duty, the following: (1) 1 liter of wine or hard liquor; (2) 200 cigarettes, 100 cigars (but not from Cuba), or 3 pounds of smoking tobacco; and (3) $100 worth of gifts. These exemptions are offered to travelers who spend at least 72 hours in the United States and who have not claimed them within the preceding 6 months. It is forbidden to bring into the country almost any meat products (including canned, fresh, and dried meat products such as bouillon, soup mixes, and so forth). Generally, condiments including vinegars, oils, spices, coffee, tea, and some cheeses and baked goods are permitted. Avoid rice products, as rice can often harbor insects. Bringing fruits and vegetables is not advised, though not prohibited. Customs will allow produce depending on where you got it and where you're going after you arrive in the U.S. Foreign tourists may carry in or out up to

$10,000 in U.S. or foreign currency with no formalities; larger sums must be declared to U.S. Customs on entering or leaving, which includes filing form CM 4790. For details regarding U.S. Customs and Border Protection, consult your nearest U.S. embassy or consulate, or **U.S. Customs** (www.cbp.gov).

What You Can Take Home from Hawaii

Canadian Citizens: For a clear summary of Canadian rules, write for the booklet *I Declare,* issued by the Canada Border Services Agency (✆ 800/461-9999 in Canada, or 204/983-3500; www.cbsa-asfc.gc.ca).

U.K. Citizens: For information, contact **HM Customs & Excise** at ✆ **0845/010-9000** (from outside the U.K., 020/8929-0152), or consult their website at **www.hmce.gov.uk**.

Australian Citizens: A helpful brochure available from Australian consulates or Customs offices is *Know Before You Go.* For more information, call the **Australian Customs Service** at ✆ **1300/363-263,** or log on to **www.customs.gov.au**.

New Zealand Citizens: Most questions are answered in a free pamphlet available at New Zealand consulates and Customs offices: *New Zealand Customs Guide for Travellers, Notice no. 4.* For more information, contact **New Zealand Customs,** The Customhouse, 17–21 Whitmore St., Box 2218, Wellington (✆ **04/473-6099** or 0800/428-786; www.customs.govt.nz).

4 WHEN TO GO

Most visitors don't come to Hawaii when the weather's best in the islands; rather, they come when it's at its worst everywhere else. Thus, the **high season**—when prices are up and resorts are often booked to capacity—is generally from mid-December to March or mid April. The last 2 weeks of December, in particular, are the prime time for travel to Hawaii. If you're planning a holiday trip, make your reservations as early as possible, expect crowds, and prepare to pay top dollar for accommodations, car rentals, and airfare.

The **off season,** when the best rates are available and the islands are less crowded, is spring (mid-Apr to mid-June) and fall (Sept to mid-Dec)—a paradox because these are the best seasons to be in Hawaii, in terms of reliably great weather. If you're looking to save money, or if you just want to avoid the crowds, this is the time to visit. Hotel rates and airfares tend to be significantly lower, and good packages are often available.

Note: If you plan to come to Hawaii between the last week in April and early May, be sure you book your accommodations, interisland air reservations, and car rentals in advance. In Japan, the last week of April is called **Golden Week** because three Japanese holidays take place one after the other. Waikiki is especially busy with Japanese tourists during this time, but the neighboring islands also see dramatic increases.

Due to the large number of families traveling in **summer** (June–Aug), you won't get the fantastic bargains of spring and fall. However, you'll still do much better on packages, airfare, and accommodations than you will in the winter months.

CLIMATE

Because Hawaii lies at the edge of the tropical zone, it technically has only two seasons, both of them warm. There's a dry season that corresponds to **summer** (Apr–Oct) and a rainy season in **winter** (Nov–Mar). It rains every day somewhere in the islands any time of the year, but the rainy season sometimes brings enough gray weather to spoil your tanning opportunities. Fortunately, it seldom rains in one spot for more than 3 days straight.

The **year-round temperature** doesn't vary much. At the beach, the average daytime high in summer is 85°F (29°C), while the average daytime high in winter is 78°F (26°C); nighttime lows are usually about 10° cooler. But how warm it is on any given day really depends on *where* you are on the island.

Each island has a leeward side (the side sheltered from the wind) and a windward side (the side that gets the wind's full force). The **leeward** sides (the west and south) are usually hot and dry, while the **windward** sides (east and north) are generally cooler and moist. When you want arid, sunbaked, desert-like weather, go leeward. When you want lush, wet, junglelike weather, go windward.

Hawaii is also full of **microclimates,** thanks to its interior valleys, coastal plains, and mountain peaks. Kauai's Mount Waialeale is the wettest spot on earth, yet Waimea Canyon, just a few miles away, is almost a desert. On the Big Island, Hilo is one of the wettest cities in the nation, with 180 inches of rainfall a year, but at Puako, only 60 miles away, it rains less than 6 inches a year. If you travel into the mountains, the climate can change from summer to winter in a matter of hours because it's cooler the higher you go. So if the weather doesn't suit you, just go to the other side of the island—or head into the hills.

On rare occasions, the weather can be disastrous, as when Hurricane Iniki crushed Kauai in September 1992 with 225 mph winds. Tsunamis have swept Hilo and the south shore of Oahu. But those are extreme exceptions. Mostly, one day follows another here in glorious, sunny procession, each quite like the other.

HOLIDAYS

When Hawaii observes holidays (especially those over a long weekend), travel between the islands increases, interisland airline seats are fully booked, rental cars are at a premium, and hotels and restaurants are busier.

Federal, state, and county government offices are closed on all federal holidays: January 1 (New Year's Day), the third Monday in January (Martin Luther King, Jr., Day), the third Monday in February (Presidents' Day, Washington's Birthday), the last Monday in May (Memorial Day), July 4 (Independence Day), the first Monday in September (Labor Day), the second Monday in October (Columbus Day), November 11 (Veterans Day), the fourth Thursday in November (Thanksgiving Day), and December 25 (Christmas).

State and county offices are also closed on local holidays, including Prince Kuhio Day (Mar 26), honoring the birthday of Hawaii's first delegate to the U.S. Congress; King Kamehameha Day (June 11), a statewide holiday commemorating Kamehameha the Great, who united the islands and ruled from 1795 to 1819; and Admissions Day (third Fri in Aug), which honors the admittance of Hawaii as the 50th state on August 21, 1959.

Other special days celebrated in Hawaii by many people but which involve no closing of federal, state, and county offices are the Chinese New Year (which can fall in Jan or Feb; in 2009 it's Jan 26), Girls' Day (Mar 3), Buddha's Birthday (Apr 8), Father Damien's Day (Apr 15), Boys' Day (May 5), Samoan Flag Day (in Aug), Aloha Festivals (in Sept and Oct), and Pearl Harbor Day (Dec 7).

KIDS' FAVORITE HAWAII EVENTS

Please note that, as with any schedule of upcoming events, the following information is subject to change; always confirm the details before you plan your trip around an event.

For an exhaustive list of events beyond those listed here, check http://events.frommers.com, where you'll find a searchable, up-to-the-minute roster of what's happening in cities all over the world.

JANUARY

Rockstar Games Pipeline Pro 2009, Banzai Pipeline, North Shore, Oahu. Competition is judged on the best wave selection and maneuvers on the wave. Call ✆ **732/528-0621;** www.usbatour.org. Early January.

Pacific Islands Arts Festival at Thomas Square, across from Honolulu Academy of the Arts, Honolulu, Oahu. Work from more than 100 artists and artisans, entertainment, food, and demonstrations fill the day. Admission is free. Call ✆ **808/696-6717.** Mid-January.

Ka Molokai Makahiki, Kaunakakai Town Baseball Park, Mitchell Pauole Center, Kaunakakai, Molokai. Makahiki, a traditional time of peace in ancient Hawaii, is re-created with performances by Hawaiian music groups and *halau* (hula schools), ancient Hawaiian games, a sporting competition, and Hawaiian crafts and food. It's a wonderful chance to experience the Hawaii of yesteryear. Call ✆ **800/800-6367** or 808/553-3876; www.molokai-hawaii.com. Late January.

Ala Wai Challenge, Ala Wai Park, Waikiki, Oahu. This all-day event features ancient Hawaiian games, like *ulu maika* (bowling a round stone through pegs), *oo ihe* (spear throwing at an upright target), *huki kaula* (tug of war), and a 1/4-mile outrigger canoe race. It's also a great place to hear Hawaiian music. Call ✆ **808/923-1802;** www.waikikicommunitycenter.org. Last weekend in January.

Hula Bowl Football All-Star Classic, Aloha Stadium, Honolulu, Oahu. An annual all-star football classic featuring America's top college players. Call ✆ **800/971-1232;** www.hulabowlhawaii.com. Ticket orders are processed beginning April 1 for the next year's game. Mid- to late January.

Chinese New Year, Maui. Lahaina town rolls out the red carpet for this important event with a traditional lion dance at the historic Wo Hing Temple on Front Street, accompanied by fireworks, food booths, and a host of activities. Call ✆ **888/310-1117** or 808/667-9175. Also on Market Street in Wailuku; call ✆ **808/244-3888.** On Oahu a big celebration takes place in Chinatown; call ✆ **808/533-3181** for details. January 26, 2009, ushers in the year of the ox.

Narcissus Festival, Honolulu, Oahu. Taking place around the Chinese New Year, this cultural festival includes a queen pageant, cooking demonstrations, and a cultural fair. Call ✆ **808/533-3181** for details.

FEBRUARY

NFL Pro Bowl, Aloha Stadium, Honolulu, Oahu. The National Football League's best pro players square off in this annual gridiron all-star game. Call ✆ **212/450-2000** or 808/486-9555; www.nfl.com. Early February (a week after the Super Bowl).

Whale Day Celebration, Kalama Park, Kihei. A daylong celebration in the park with a parade of whales, entertainment, a crafts fair, games, and food. Call

✆ **808/249-8811** or visit www.visitmaui.com. Early or mid-February.

Whale Quest Kapalua, Kapalua Resort. This weekend-long event celebrates whales through lectures, interactive displays and events, art and photo exhibitions, and walks. Mid-February.

Waimea Town Celebration, Waimea, Kauai. This annual 2-day party on Kauai's west side celebrates the Hawaiian and multi-ethnic history of the town where Captain Cook first landed. This is the island's biggest event, drawing some 10,000 people. Top Hawaiian entertainers, sporting events, rodeo, and lots of food are on tap during the weekend celebration. Call ✆ **808/338-1332;** www.wkbpa.org/events.html. Weekend after Presidents' Day weekend.

Sand Castle Building Contest, Kailua Beach Park, Oahu. Students from the University of Hawaii School of Architecture compete against professional architects to see who can build the best, most unusual, and most outrageous sand sculpture. Call ✆ **808/956-3518.**

Punahou School Carnival, Punahou School, Honolulu. This event has everything you can imagine in a school carnival, from high-speed rides to homemade jellies. All proceeds go to scholarship funds for Hawaii's most prestigious high school. Call ✆ **808/944-5753.** Early to mid-February.

Buffalo's Big Board Classic, Makaha Beach, Oahu. This contest involves traditional Hawaiian surfing, long boarding, and canoe-surfing. Call ✆ **808/951-7877.** Depending on surf conditions, it can be held in February or March.

March

Kona Brewer's Festival, King Kamehameha's Kona Beach Hotel Luau Grounds, Kailua-Kona, Big Island. This annual event features microbreweries from around the world, with beer tastings, food, and entertainment. Call ✆ **808/334-1133.** Second Saturday in March.

Annual Kona Chocolate Festival, Kona, Big Island. A 3-day celebration of the chocolate (cacao) that is grown and produced in Hawaii. Days 1 and 2 are filled with symposiums and seminars on chocolate and its uses. Day 3 features a Gala party with samples of chocolate creations by Big Island chefs, caterers, and ice-cream and candy makers. A chocoholic's dream! For information and tickets, call ✆ **808/324-4606** or visit www.konachocolatefestival.com. Mid- to late March.

Ocean Arts Festival, Lahaina. The entire town of Lahaina celebrates the annual migration of Pacific humpback whales with an Ocean Arts Festival in Banyan Tree Park. Artists display their best ocean-themed art for sale, and Hawaiian musicians and hula troupes entertain. Enjoy marine-related activities, games, and a Creature Feature touch-pool exhibit for children. Call ✆ **888/310-1117** or 808/667-9194, or visit www.visitlahaina.com. Mid-March.

Prince Kuhio Day Celebrations, all islands. State holiday. Various festivals throughout the state celebrate the birth of Jonah Kuhio Kalanianaole, who was born on March 26, 1871, and elected to Congress in 1902. Kauai, his birthplace, stages a huge celebration in Lihue; call ✆ **808/240-6369** for details. Molokai also hosts a 2-day-long celebration; call ✆ **808/553-3876** to learn more. March 26.

April

East Maui Taro Festival, Hana, Maui. Taro, a Hawaiian staple food, is celebrated through music, hula, arts, crafts, and, of course, food. Call ✆ **808/264-3336;** www.tarofestival.org. Varying dates in April.

Annual Ritz-Carlton Kapalua Celebration of the Arts, Ritz-Carlton Kapalua, Maui. Contemporary and traditional artists give free hands-on lessons. Call ✆ **808/669-6200.** The 4-day festival begins the Thursday before Easter.

Merrie Monarch Hula Festival, Hilo, Big Island. Hawaii's biggest hula festival features 3 nights of modern *(auana)* and ancient *(kahiko)* dance competition in honor of King David Kalakaua, the "Merrie Monarch" who revived the dance. Tickets sell out by January 30, so reserve early. Call ✆ **808/935-9168;** www.merriemonarchfestival.org. The week after Easter (Apr 13–20, 2009).

David Malo Day, Lahainaluna High School, Lahaina, Maui. This daylong event with hula and other Hawaiian cultural celebrations commemorates Hawaii's famous scholar and ends with a luau. Call ✆ **808/662-4000.** Mid-April.

May

Outrigger Canoe Season, all islands. From May to September, canoe paddlers across the state participate in outrigger canoe races nearly every weekend. Call ✆ **808/383-7798,** or go to www.y2kanu.com for this year's schedule of events.

Annual Lei Day Celebrations, various locations on all islands. May Day is Lei Day in Hawaii, celebrated with lei-making contests, pageantry, arts and crafts, and the real highlight, a Brothers Cazimero concert at the Waikiki Shell. Call ✆ **808/692-5118** or visit www.honolulu.gov/parks/programs/leiday for Oahu events (✆ **808/597-1888,** ext. 232, for the Brothers Cazimero show; ✆ **808/886-1655** for Big Island events; ✆ **808/224-6042** for Maui events; or ✆ **808/245-6931** for Kauai events). May 1.

World Fire-Knife Dance Championships and Samoan Festival, Polynesian Cultural Center, Laie, Oahu. Junior and adult fire-knife dancers from around the world converge on the center for one of the most amazing performances you'll ever see. Authentic Samoan food and cultural festivities round out the fun. Call ✆ **808/293-3333;** www.polynesianculturalcenter.com. Mid-May.

International Festival of Canoes, West Maui. Celebration of the Pacific islands' seafaring heritage. Events include canoe paddling and sailing regattas, a luau feast, cultural arts demonstrations, canoe-building exhibits, and music. Call ✆ **888/310-1117;** www.mauifestivalofcanoes.com. Mid- to late May.

Shinnyo-en Hawaii Temple Floating Lanterns Festival, Magic Island at Ala Moana Beach Park. A ceremonial floating of some 700 lanterns takes place at sunset, representing an appeal for peace and harmony. Hula and music follows. Call ✆ **808/947-2814;** ww.lanternfloatinghawaii.com. Memorial Day weekend.

June

Hawaiian Slack-Key Guitar Festival, Maui Arts and Cultural Center, Kahului, Maui. Great music performed by the best musicians in Hawaii. It's 5 hours long and absolutely free. Call ✆ **808/242-SHOW** (242-7469) or 808/226-2697; www.slackkeyfestival.com Late June.

King Kamehameha Celebration, all islands. This state holiday features a massive floral parade, *hoolaulea* (party), and much more. Call ✆ **808/586-0333** for Oahu and Kauai events, ✆ **808/886-1655** for Big Island events, ✆ **808/667-9194** for Maui events, or ✆ **808/553-3876** for Molokai events; or visit www.kamehamehadaycelebration.org. June 11.

Great Waikoloa Food, Wine & Music Festival, Hilton Waikoloa Village, Big Island. One of the Big Island's best food and wine festivals features Hawaii's top chefs (and a few mainland chefs) showing off their culinary talents, wines from around the world, and an excellent jazz concert with fireworks. Not to be missed. Call ✆ **808/886-1234** or visit www.hiltonwaikoloavillage.com or www.dolphindays.com. Mid-June.

Maui Film Festival, Wailea Resort, Maui. Five days and nights of screenings of premieres and special films, along with traditional Hawaiian storytelling, chants, hula, and contemporary music. Call ✆ **808/572-3456;** www.mauifilmfestival.com. Beginning the Wednesday before Father's Day.

King Kamehameha Hula Competition, Neal Blaisdell Center, Honolulu, Oahu. This is one of the top hula competitions in the world, with dancers from as far away as Japan. Call ✆ **808/586-0333** or visit www.hawaii.gov/dags/king_kamehameha_commission for information. Third weekend in June.

The Flavors of Honolulu, Civic Center Grounds, Honolulu. Formerly known as The Tastes of Honolulu, Hawaii's premier outdoor food festival features small samples from 25 restaurants, entertainment, beer and wine tasting, cooking demos, gourmet marketplace. Proceeds go to Abilities Unlimited. Call ✆ **808/532-2115;** www.abilitiesunlimitedhi.org. End of June.

Kapalua Wine and Food Festival, Kapalua, Maui. Famous wine and food experts and oenophiles gather at the Ritz-Carlton and Kapalua Bay hotels for formal tastings, panel discussions, and samplings of new releases. Call ✆ **800/KAPALUA** (525-2582) or go to www.kapaluaresort.com. End of June or early July.

July

Lanai Pineapple Festival, Lanai City, Lanai. Celebrates Lanai's history of pineapple plantations and ranching, and includes a pineapple-eating contest, a pineapple-cooking contest, entertainment, arts and crafts, food, and fireworks. Call ✆ **808/565-7600** or visit http://lanai.aloha-hawaii.com. First Saturday in July.

Bon Dance and Lantern Ceremony, Lahaina. This colorful Buddhist ceremony honors the souls of the dead. Call ✆ **808/661-4304.** Usually early July.

Prince Lot Hula Festival, Moanalua Gardens, Honolulu, Oahu. Authentic ancient and modern hula, as well as demonstrations and arts and crafts, are some of the things you'll encounter at this festival. It's a good alternative to April's much better-known (and much more crowded) Merrie Monarch Hula Festival. Call ✆ **808/839-5334** or visit www.mgf-hawaii.org. Third Saturday in July.

Ukulele Festival, Kapiolani Park Bandstand, Waikiki, Oahu. This free concert features a ukulele orchestra of some 600 students (ages 4–92). Hawaii's top musicians all pitch in. Call ✆ **808/732-3739;** www.roysakuma.net. Late July.

Queen Liliuokalani Keiki Hula Competition, Neal Blaisdell Center, Honolulu, Oahu. More than 500 *keiki* (children) representing 22 halau from the islands compete in this dance fest. The event is broadcast a week later on KITV-TV. Call ✆ **808/521-6905.** Late July.

Hawaii State Farm Fair, Aloha Stadium, Honolulu, Oahu. The annual state fair is a great one: It features displays of Hawaii agricultural products (including orchids), educational and cultural exhibits, entertainment, and local-style food. Call ✆ **808/682-5767** or visit www.ekfernandez.com. Late July or early August.

Quiksilver Molokai to Oahu Paddleboard Race, starts on Molokai and finishes on Oahu. Some 70 participants from an international field journey to

Molokai to compete in this 32-mile race, considered to be the world championship of long-distance paddleboard racing. Race begins at Kaluakoi Beach on Molokai at 7:30am and finishes at Maunaloa Bay, Oahu, around 12:30pm. Call ✆ **808/638-8208.** Mid- to late July.

AUGUST

Hawaii International Jazz Festival, The Hawaii Theatre, Honolulu, Oahu. This festival includes evening concerts and daily jam sessions, plus scholarship giveaways, the University of Southern California jazz band, and many popular jazz and blues artists. Call ✆ **808/941-9974**. Early August.

Maui Onion Festival, Whalers Village, Kaanapali, Maui. Everything you ever wanted to know about the sweetest onions in the world. Food, entertainment, tasting, and the Maui Onion Cook-Off. Call ✆ **808/661-4567,** or go to www.whalersvillage.com/onionfestival.htm. Early to mid-August.

Hawaii State Windsurf Championship, Kanaha Beach Park, Kahului. Top windsurfers compete. Call ✆ **808/877-2111.** Early August.

Tahiti Fete, Wailuku. Annual Tahitian dance competition, arts and crafts, and food, held in the War Memorial Gym, Wailuku. Call ✆ **808/244-8088. Puukohola Heiau National Historic Site Anniversary Celebration,** Kawaihae, Big Island. This is a weekend of Hawaiian crafts, workshops, and games. Call ✆ **808/882-7218.** Mid-August.

Duke's Ocean Fest Ho'olaule'a, Waikiki. Nine days of water-oriented competitions and festivities celebrating the life of Duke Kahanamoku. Events include the Hawaii Paddleboard Championship, the Pro Surf Longboard Contest, the International Tandem Surfing Championship, the Corona Extra Duke Volleyball Classic, a Surf Polo tournament, and a Hawaiian Luau (luau is $60 at the door). For specifics call ✆ **808/545-4880;** www.dukefoundation.org. Mid-August.

Hawaiian Slack-Key Guitar Festival Gabby Style, Queen Kapiolani Park Bandstand, Honolulu. The best of Hawaii's folk music—slack-key guitar—performed by the best musicians in Hawaii. It's 6 hours long and absolutely free. Contact ✆ **808/226-2697;** www.slackkeyfestival.com. Third Sunday in August.

SEPTEMBER

Waikiki Rough-Water Swim, from Sans Souci Beach to Duke Kahanamoku Beach, Waikiki. A popular 2½-mile, open-ocean swim. Early registration is encouraged, but they will take last-minute entries on race day. For information (no phone) go to www.waikikiroughwaterswim.com. Labor Day weekend.

Queen Liliuokalani Canoe Race, Kailua-Kona to Honaunau, Big Island. The world's largest long-distance canoe race draws hundreds of participants. Call ✆ **808/331-8849** or visit www.kaiopua.org. Labor Day weekend.

Parker Ranch Rodeo, Waimea, Big Island. This is a hot rodeo competition in the heart of cowboy country. Call ✆ **808/885-7311** or go to www.parkerranch.com. Labor Day weekend.

Hawaiian Slack-Key Guitar Festival, Sheraton Keauhou Bay Resort & Spa, Kona, Big Island. The best of Hawaii's folk music (slack-key guitar) performed by the best musicians in Hawaii. It's 5 hours long and absolutely free. Call ✆ **808/239-4336** or e-mail kahokuproductions@yahoo.com. Early September.

Aloha Festivals, various locations statewide. Parades and other events celebrate Hawaiian culture and friendliness throughout the state. Call ✆ **808/589-1771** or visit www.alohafestivals.com for a schedule of events.

Aloha Festivals Poke Recipe Contest, Hapuna Beach Prince Hotel, Mauna Kea Beach Resort, Kohala Coast, Big Island. Top chefs from across Hawaii and the U.S. mainland, as well as local amateurs, compete in making this Hawaiian delicacy, poke (pronounced po-*kay*): chopped raw fish mixed with seaweed and spices. Here's your chance to sample poke at its best. Call ✆ **808/880-3424** or visit www.pokecontest.com.

A Taste of Lahaina, Lahaina Civic Center, Maui. Some 30,000 people show up to sample 40 signature entrees from Maui's premier chefs during this weekend festival, which includes cooking demonstrations, wine tastings, and live entertainment. The event begins Friday night with Maui Chefs Present, a dinner/cocktail party featuring about a dozen of Maui's best chefs. Call ✆ **888/310-1117** or go to www.visitmaui.com. Second weekend in September.

Maui Marathon, Kahului to Kaanapali, Maui. Runners line up at the Maui Mall before daybreak and head off for Kaanapali. Call ✆ **866/577-8379,** or visit www.virr.com or www.mauimarathon.com. Mid- to late September.

October

Emalani Festival, Kokee State Park, Kauai. This festival honors Her Majesty Queen Emma, an inveterate gardener and Hawaii's first environmental queen, who made a forest trek to Kokee with 100 friends in 1871. Call ✆ **808/245-3971.** Second Saturday in October.

Aloha Classic World Wavesailing Championship, Hookipa Beach, Maui. The top windsurfers in the world gather for this final event in the Pro Boardsailing World Tour. If you're on Maui, don't miss it—it's spectacular to watch. Call ✆ **808/298-3560;** www.alohaclassicwindsurfing.com. Depending on weather, can be in October or November.

Ironman Triathlon World Championship, Kailua-Kona, Big Island. Some 1,500-plus world-class athletes run a full marathon, swim 2½ miles, and bike 112 miles on the Kona-Kohala coast of the Big Island. Spectators can watch the action along the route for free. The best place to see the 7am start is along the sea wall on Alii Drive, facing Kailua Bay; arrive before 5:30am to get a seat. The best place to see the bike-and-run portion is along Alii Drive (which will be closed to traffic; park on a side street and walk down). To watch the finishers come in, line up along Alii Drive from Holualoa Street to the finish at Palani Road/Alii Drive; the first finisher can come as early as 2:30pm, and the course closes at midnight. Call ✆ **808/329-0063** or visit www.ironman.com.

Halloween in Lahaina, Maui. There's Carnival in Rio, Mardi Gras in New Orleans, and Halloween in Lahaina. Come to this giant costume party (some 20,000 people show up) on the streets of Lahaina; Front Street is closed off for the festivities. Call ✆ **808/667-9175** or go to www.visitmaui.com. October 31.

Hana Ho'ohiwahiwa O Ka'ilulani. The Sheraton Princess Kaiulani Hotel commemorates the birthday of its namesake, Princess Victoria Ka'iulani, with a week of special activities: complimentary hula lessons, lei making, ukulele lessons, and more. The crowning touch is the Princess Ka'iulani Keiki Hula Festival. The festival showcases performances by more than 200 keiki from halau on the island of Oahu. The festival takes place mid-month and admission is free. Call ✆ **808/931-4524.**

NOVEMBER

Hula O Na Keiki, Ka'anapali Beach Hotel, Ka'anapali, Maui. This solo hula competition for children ages 5 to 17 is in its 18th year. Hawaiian dance, arts, and music round out the weekend festival. Call ✆ **808/661-0011;** www.kbhmaui.com. Early November.

Hawaiian Slack-Key Guitar Festival, Kauai Marriott Resort, Lihue, Kauai. The best of Hawaii's folk music (slack-key guitar) performed by the best musicians in Hawaii. It's 5 hours long and absolutely free. Call ✆ **808/226-2697** or e-mail kahokuproductions@yahoo.com. Mid-November.

Annual Kona Coffee Cultural Festival, Kailua-Kona, Big Island. Celebrate the coffee harvest with a bean-picking contest, lei contests, song and dance, and the Miss Kona Coffee pageant. Call ✆ **808/326-7820** or go to www.konacoffeefest.com for this year's schedule.

Hawaii International Film Festival, various locations throughout the state. This cinema festival with a cross-cultural spin features filmmakers from Asia, the Pacific Islands, and the United States. Call ✆ **808/550-8457** or visit www.hiff.org. First 2 weeks in November.

Annual Invitational Wreath Exhibit, Volcano Art Center, Volcano National Park, Big Island. Thirty-two artists, including painters, sculptors, glass artists, fiber artists, and potters, produce both whimsical and traditional "wreaths" for this exhibit. Park entrance fees apply. Call ✆ **866/967-7565** or 808/967-7565; www.volcanoartcenter.org. Mid-November through the first of January.

Triple Crown of Surfing, North Shore, Oahu. The world's top professional surfers compete in events for more than $1 million in prize money. Call ✆ **808/739-3965;** www.triplecrownofsurfing.com. Held between mid-November and mid-December, whenever conditions are best.

DECEMBER

Na Mele O Maui, Ka'anapali, Maui. Traditional Hawaiian song competition for children in kindergarten through 12th grade. $2 admission. Takes place in the ballroom of one of the Kaanapali resort hotels. Call ✆ **808/661-3271;** www.kaanapaliresort.com. First Friday in December.

Old-Fashioned Holiday Celebration, Lahaina, Maui. This day of Christmas carolers, Santa Claus, live music and entertainment, a crafts fair, Christmas baked goods, and activities for children takes place in the Banyan Tree Park on Front Street. Call ✆ **888/310-1117;** www.visitlahaina.com. Second Saturday in December.

Billabong Pro Maui, Honolua Bay at Kapalua Resort, Maui. The final Triple Crown women's surfing contest of the year, bringing together the best of the women's international surfing community. Call ✆ **808/669-2440** or visit www.kapalua.com. Early December.

Festival of Lights, all islands. On Oahu, the mayor throws the switch to light up the 40-foot-tall Norfolk pine and other trees in front of Honolulu Hale, while on Maui, marching bands, floats, and Santa roll down Lahaina's Front Street in an annual parade. Molokai celebrates with a host of activities in Kaunakakai; on Kauai the lighting ceremony takes place in front of the former county building on Rice Street, Lihue. Call ✆ **808/523-4385** on Oahu, ✆ **808/667-9175** on Maui, ✆ **808/552-2800** on Molokai, or ✆ **808/828-0014** on Kauai. Early December.

Honolulu Marathon, Honolulu, Oahu. This is one of the largest marathons in the world, with more than

30,000 competitors. Call ✆ **808/734-7200;** www.honolulumarathon.org. Second Sunday in December.

Aloha Bowl, Aloha Stadium, Honolulu, Oahu. A Pac-10 team plays a Big 12 team in this nationally televised collegiate football classic. Call ✆ **808/483-2500.** Christmas Day.

Rainbow Classic, University of Hawaii, Manoa Valley, Oahu. Eight of the best NCAA basketball teams compete at the Special Events Arena. Call ✆ **808/956-7523.** The week after Christmas.

First Light, Maui Arts and Cultural Center, Maui. Major films are screened at this festival (past films have included *The Lord of the Rings: Return of the King, Mystic River, Aviator, Hotel Rwanda,* and many others). Not to be missed. Call ✆ **808/573-3456** or visit www.mauifilmfestival.com. End of December and early January.

5 GETTING THERE

Most major U.S. and many international carriers fly to Honolulu International Airport. Some also offer direct flights to Kailua-Kona, on the Big Island; Kahului, Maui; and Lihue, Kauai.

United Airlines (✆ **800/225-5825;** www.ual.com) offers the most frequent service from the U.S. mainland, not only flying to Honolulu, but also flying nonstop from Los Angeles and San Francisco to the Big Island, Maui, and Kauai. **American Airlines** (✆ **800/433-7300;** www.americanair.com) offers flights from Dallas, Chicago, San Francisco, San Jose, Los Angeles, and St. Louis to Honolulu, plus several direct flights to Maui and Kona. **Alaska Airlines** (✆ **800/252-7522;** www.alaskaair.com) offers daily flights between Seattle and Kahului from late April to October and twice-a-week flights on the same run from November to late-April.

Continental Airlines (✆ **800/231-0856;** www.continental.com) offers the only daily nonstop from the New York area (Newark) to Honolulu. **Delta Air Lines** (✆ **800/221-1212;** www.delta.com) flies nonstop from the West Coast and from Houston and Cincinnati. **Hawaiian Airlines** (✆ **800/367-5320;** www.hawaiianair.com) offers nonstop flights to Honolulu from several West Coast cities (including new service from San Diego), plus nonstop flights from Los Angeles to Maui. **Northwest Airlines** (✆ **800/225-2525;** www.nwa.com) flies nonstop daily from Detroit to Honolulu.

Locally, **Hawaiian Airlines** (✆ **800/367-5320;** www.hawaiianair.com) flies nonstop to Sydney, Tahiti, and American Samoa.

Visitors arriving by air should cultivate patience and resignation before setting foot on U.S. soil. Getting through immigration control may take as long as 2 hours on some days, especially summer weekends. Add the time it takes to clear Customs, and you'll see that you should make a very generous allowance for delay in planning connections between international and domestic flights—an average of 2 to 3 hours at least.

AGRICULTURAL SCREENING AT THE AIRPORTS At Honolulu International and the neighbor-island airports, baggage and passengers bound for the mainland must be screened by agricultural officials. Officials will confiscate local produce like fresh avocados, bananas, and mangoes, in the name of fruit fly control. Pineapples, coconuts, and papayas inspected and certified for export; boxed flowers; leis without seeds; and processed foods (macadamia nuts, coffee, jams, dried fruit, and the like) will pass.

Flying with Kids

If you plan carefully, you can make it fun to fly with your kids.

- You'll save yourself a good bit of aggravation by **reserving a seat in the bulkhead row.** You'll have more legroom, your children will be able to spread out and play on the floor underfoot, and the airline might provide bassinets (ask in advance). You're also more likely to find sympathetic company in the bulkhead area, as families with children tend to be seated there.
- Be sure to **pack items for your kids in your carry-on luggage.**
- **Have a long talk with your children** before you depart for your trip. If they've never flown before, explain to them what to expect. If they're old enough, you may even want to describe how flight works and how air travel is even safer than riding in a car. Explain to your kids the importance of good behavior in the air—how their own safety can depend upon their being quiet and staying in their seats during the trip.
- **Pay extracareful attention to the safety instructions** before takeoff. Consult the safety chart behind the seat in front of you and show it to your children. Be sure you know how to operate the oxygen masks, as you will be expected to secure yours first and then help your children with theirs. Be especially mindful of the location of emergency exits. Before takeoff, plot out an evacuation strategy for you and your children in your mind's eye.
- Ask the flight attendant **if the plane has any special safety equipment for children.** Make a member of the crew aware of any medical problems your children have that could manifest during flight.
- **Be sure you've slept sufficiently** for your trip. If you fall asleep in the air and your child manages to break away, all sorts of sharp objects could cause injury. Especially during mealtimes, it's dangerous for a child to be crawling or walking around the cabin unaccompanied by an adult.
- **Be sure your child's seat belt remains fastened properly,** and try to reserve the seat closest to the aisle for yourself. This will make it harder for your children to wander off—in case, for instance, you're taking the red-eye or a long flight and you do happen to nod off. You will also protect your child from jostling passersby and falling objects—in the rare, but entirely possible, instance that an overhead bin pops open.

  In the event of an accident, unrestrained children often don't make it—even when the parent does. Experience has shown that it's impossible for a parent to hold onto a child in the event of a crash, and children often die of impact injuries.

  For the same reason, sudden turbulence is also a danger to a child who is not buckled into his own seat belt or seat restraint. According to *Consumer Reports Travel Letter,* the most common flying injuries result when unanticipated turbulence strikes and hurtles passengers from their seats.
- **Try to sit near the lavatory,** though not so close that your children are jostled by the crowds that tend to gather there. Consolidate trips there as much as possible.
- Try to **accompany children to the lavatory.** They can be easily bumped and possibly injured as they make their way down tight aisles. It's especially dangerous for children to wander while flight attendants are blocking passage with their service carts. On crowded flights, the flight crew may need as

Moments The Welcoming Lei

Nothing makes you feel more welcome than a lei. The tropical beauty of the delicate garland, the deliciously sweet fragrance of the blossoms, the sensual way the flowers curl softly around your neck—there's no doubt about it: Getting lei'd in Hawaii is a sensuous experience.

Leis are much more than just a decorative necklace of flowers—they're also one of the nicest ways to say hello, goodbye, congratulations, I salute you, my sympathies are with you, or I love you.

During ancient times, leis given to *alii* (royalty) were accompanied by a bow, since it was *kapu* (forbidden) for a commoner to raise his arms higher than the king's head. The presentation of a kiss with a lei didn't come about until World War II; it's generally attributed to an entertainer who kissed an officer on a dare, then quickly presented him with her lei, saying it was an old Hawaiian custom. It wasn't then, but it sure caught on fast.

Lei making is a tropical art form. All leis are fashioned by hand in a variety of traditional patterns; some are sewn of hundreds of tiny blooms or shells or bits of ferns and leaves. Some are twisted, some braided, some strung. Every island has its own special flower lei. Maui likes the *lokelani,* a small rose. Leis are available at the Kahului Airport, from florists, and even at supermarkets.

Leis are the perfect symbol for Hawaii: They're given in the moment, their fragrance and beauty are enjoyed in the moment, but when they fade, their spirit of aloha lives on. Welcome to the islands!

much as an hour to serve dinner. It's wise to encourage your kids to use the restroom when you see the attendants preparing to serve.

- Be sure to **bring clean, self-containing, compact toys.** Leave electronic games at home. They can interfere with the aircraft navigational system, and their noisiness, however lulling to children's ears, will surely not win the favor of your adult neighbors. Magnetic checker sets, on the other hand, are a perfect distraction, and small coloring books and crayons also work well, as do card games like Go Fish.
- Because most airlines no longer have free meals, **pack your kids' favorite picnic-type meals to eat on the plane and give them to the kids shortly after takeoff.** After all, if your kids have a happy flight experience, everyone else in the cabin is more likely to as well.
- You'll certainly be grateful to yourself for packing **tidy snacks** like rolled dried fruit, which are much less sticky and wet and more compact and packable than actual fruit. Blueberry or raisin bagels also make for a neat, healthy sweet and yield fewer crumbs than cookies or cakes. Gingersnaps, crisp and not as crumbly as softer cookies, will also help curb mild cases of motion sickness. And don't forget to stash a few resealable plastic bags in your purse. They'll prove invaluable for storing everything from half-eaten crackers and fruit to checker pieces and Matchbox cars.

Kids with Colds

It's even more difficult for kids to make their ears pop during takeoff and landing. The eustachian tube is especially narrow in children; the passage is even tighter when mucous membranes are swollen. This can make ascent and descent especially painful—even dangerous—for a child with congested sinuses. If your little one is suffering from a cold or the flu, it's best to keep him grounded until he recuperates. (If you must travel with your child as scheduled, give him or her an oral child's decongestant an hour before ascent and descent; or administer a spray decongestant before and during takeoff and landing.)

Long-Haul Flights: How to Stay Comfortable

- Your choice of airline and airplane will definitely affect your legroom. Find more details about U.S. airlines at **www.seatguru.com**. For international airlines, the research firm Skytrax has posted a list of average seat pitches at **www.airlinequality.com**.
- Emergency exit seats and bulkhead seats typically have the most legroom. Emergency-exit seats are usually left unassigned until the day of a flight (to ensure that someone able-bodied fills the seats); it's worth getting to the ticket counter early to snag one of these spots for a long flight. Many passengers find that bulkhead seating (the row facing the wall at the front of the cabin) offers more legroom, but keep in mind that bulkhead seats have no storage space on the floor in front of you.
- To have two seats for yourself in a three-seat row, try for an aisle seat in a center section toward the back of coach. If you're traveling with a companion, book an aisle and a window seat. Middle seats are usually booked last, so chances are good you'll end up with three seats to yourselves. And in the event that a third passenger is assigned the middle seat, he or she will probably be more than happy to trade for a window or an aisle.
- Ask about entertainment options. Many airlines offer seat-back video systems where you get to choose your movies or play video games—but only on some of their planes. (Boeing 777s are your best bet.)
- To sleep, avoid the last row of any section or the row in front of an emergency exit, as these seats are the least likely to recline. Avoid seats near highly trafficked toilet areas. Avoid seats in the back of many jets—these can be narrower than those in the rest of coach. Or reserve a window seat so you can rest your head and avoid being bumped in the aisle.
- Get up, walk around, and stretch every 60 to 90 minutes to keep your blood flowing. This helps avoid **deep vein thrombosis,** or "economy-class syndrome."
- Drink water before, during, and after your flight to combat the lack of humidity in airplane cabins. Avoid caffeine and alcohol, which will dehydrate you.
- If you're flying with kids, don't forget to carry on toys, books, pacifiers, and snacks and chewing gum to help them relieve ear pressure buildup during ascent and descent.

6 MONEY & COSTS

It's always advisable to bring money in a variety of forms on a vacation: a mix of cash, credit cards, and traveler's checks. You should also exchange enough petty cash to cover airport incidentals, tipping, and transportation to your hotel before you leave home, or withdraw money upon arrival at an airport ATM.

ATMS

Nationwide, the easiest and best way to get cash away from home is from an ATM (automated teller machine), sometimes referred to as a "cash machine" or "cashpoint." ATMs are everywhere in Hawaii—at banks, supermarkets, Long's Drugs, and Honolulu International Airport, and in some resorts and shopping centers. The **Cirrus** (✆ **800/424-7787;** www.mastercard.com) and **PLUS** (✆ **800/843-7587;** www.visa.com) networks span the country; you can find them even in remote regions. Go to your bank card's website to find ATM locations at your destination. Be sure you know your daily withdrawal limit before you depart.

Note: Many banks impose a fee every time you use a card at another bank's ATM, and that fee is often higher for international transactions (up to $5 or more) than for domestic ones (where they're rarely more than $2). In addition, the bank from which you withdraw cash may charge its own fee. To compare banks' ATM fees within the U.S., use **www.bankrate.com**. Visitors from outside the U.S. should also find out whether their bank assesses a 1% to 3% fee on charges incurred abroad.

CREDIT & DEBIT CARDS

Credit cards are the most widely used form of payment in the United States: **Visa** (Barclaycard in Britain), **MasterCard** (EuroCard in Europe, Access in Britain, Chargex in Canada), **American Express, Diners Club,** and **Discover.** They also provide a convenient record of all your expenses and offer relatively good exchange rates. You can withdraw cash advances from your credit cards at banks or ATMs, but high fees make credit card cash advances a pricey way to get cash.

It's highly recommended that you travel with at least one major credit card. You must have a credit card to rent a car, and hotels and airlines usually require a credit card imprint as a deposit against expenses.

ATM cards with major credit card backing, known as **debit cards,** are now a commonly acceptable form of payment in most stores and restaurants. Debit cards draw money directly from your checking account. Some stores enable you to receive cash back on your debit card purchases as well. The same is true at most U.S. post offices.

Why Oahu Is More Expensive

No, it's not your imagination—Oahu is more expensive than the other islands. That's the result of the Hawaii State Legislature passing a bill allowing the City and County of Honolulu (which is the entire island of Oahu) to add an additional .05% tax on to the state general excise tax of 4%. Everything you buy on Oahu will have this tax, and so will your hotel bill. The funds from this additional tax are earmarked for mass transit for Oahu.

7 HEALTH

STAYING HEALTHY

General Availability of HealthCare

Contact the **International Association for Medical Assistance to Travelers** (IAMAT; ✆ **716/754-4883** or, in Canada, 416/652-0137; **www.iamat.org**) for tips on travel and health concerns in the countries you're visiting, and for lists of local, English-speaking doctors. The United States **Centers for Disease Control and Prevention** (✆ **800/311-3435;** www.cdc.gov) provides up to date information on health hazards by region or country and offers tips on food safety. The website **www.tripprep.com**, sponsored by a consortium of travel medicine practitioners, **Travel Health Online,** may also offer helpful advice on traveling abroad. You can find listings of reliable clinics overseas at the **International Society of Travel Medicine** (www.istm.org).

Insects

Like any tropical climate, Hawaii is home to lots of bugs. Most of them won't harm you. However, watch out for mosquitoes, centipedes, and scorpions, which do sting and may cause anything from mild annoyance to severe swelling and pain.

MOSQUITOES These pesky insects are not native to Hawaii but arrived as larvae stowed away in water barrels on the ship *Wellington* in 1826, when it anchored in Lahaina. There's not a whole lot you can do about them, except to apply commercial repellent, which you can pick up at any drugstore.

CENTIPEDES These segmented bugs with a jillion legs come in two varieties: 6- to 8-inch-long brown ones and 2- to 3-inch-long blue guys. Both can really pack a wallop with their sting. Centipedes are generally found in damp, wet places, such as under wood piles or compost heaps; wearing closed-toe shoes can help prevent stings. If you're stung, apply ice at once to prevent swelling. See a doctor if you experience extreme pain, swelling, nausea, or any other severe reaction.

SCORPIONS Rarely seen, scorpions are found in arid, warm regions; their stings can be serious. Campers in dry areas should always check their boots before putting them on and shake out sleeping bags and bed rolls. Symptoms of a scorpion sting include shortness of breath, hives, swelling, and nausea. In the unlikely event that you're stung, apply diluted household ammonia and cold compresses to the area of the sting and seek medical help immediately.

Hiking Safety

In addition to taking the appropriate precautions regarding Hawaii's bug population, hikers should always let someone know where they're heading, when they're going, and when they plan to return; too many hikers get lost in Hawaii because they don't let others know their basic plans.

Always check weather conditions with the **National Weather Service** (✆ **808/973-4381** on Oahu; see individual island chapters for local weather information) before you go. Hike with a pal, never alone. Wear hiking boots, a sun hat, clothes to protect you from the sun and from getting scratches, and high-SPF sunscreen on all exposed areas of skin. Take water. Stay on the trail. Watch your step. It's easy to slip off precipitous trails and into steep canyons. Many experienced hikers and boaters today pack a cellphone in case of emergency; just dial ✆ **911.**

Vog

The volcanic haze dubbed *vog* is caused by gases released when molten lava—from the continuous eruption of Kilauea volcano on the Big Island—pours into the

Don't Get Burned: Smart Tanning Tips

Hawaii's Caucasian population has the highest incidence of malignant melanoma (skin cancer) in the world. And nobody is completely safe from the sun's harmful rays: All skin types and tones can burn. To ensure that your vacation won't be ruined by a painful sunburn (especially in your first few days in the islands), here are some helpful tips.

- **Wear a strong sunscreen at all times.** Use a sunscreen with a sun protection factor (SPF) of 15 or higher; people with a light complexion should use 30 or higher. Put sunscreen on as soon as you get out of the shower or at least 30 minutes before you go outside. Apply it liberally; 1 tablespoon per limb is recommended, and reapply every 2 hours.
- **Block UVA and UVB rays.** Wrinkles, sagging skin, and other signs of premature aging can be caused by ultraviolet A (UVA) rays. For years, sunscreens concentrated on blocking out just ultraviolet B (UVB) rays. The best protection from UVA rays is zinc oxide (the white goo that lifeguards wear on their noses), but other ingredients also provide protection. Read the label, and get another brand if your sunscreen doesn't contain one of the following: zinc oxide, benzophenone, oxybenzone, sulisobenzone, titanium dioxide, or avobenzone (also known as Parsol 1789).
- **Wear a hat and sunglasses.** The hat should have a brim all the way around, to cover not only your face but also the sensitive back of your neck. Make sure your sunglasses have UV filters.
- **Protect your children from the sun.** Infants 5 months and under should not be in the sun at all. Older babies need zinc oxide to protect their fragile skin, and all children should be slathered with sunscreen frequently. Remember that in strong tropical sun even limited sun exposure (including reflected sun) can lead to burns in infants and babies; always have sun protection on tender skin during daylight hours.
- **If you start to turn red, get out of the sun.** Contrary to popular belief, you don't have to turn red to tan; if your skin is red, it's burned, and that's serious. The best remedy for sunburn is to get out of the sun immediately and stay out of the sun until all the redness is gone. Aloe vera (straight from the plant or from a commercial preparation), cool compresses, cold baths, and anesthetic benzocaine also help with the pain of sunburn.

ocean. Some people claim that long-term exposure to the hazy, smoglike air has caused bronchial ailments, but it's highly unlikely to cause you any harm in the course of your visit.

There actually is a vog season in Hawaii: the fall and winter months, when the trade winds that blow the fumes out to sea die down. The vog is felt not only on the Big Island, but also as far away as Maui and Oahu.

One more word of caution: If you're pregnant or have heart or breathing problems, you should avoid exposure to the sulfuric fumes that are ever present in and around the Big Island's Hawaii Volcanoes National Park.

Ocean Safety

Because most people coming to Hawaii are unfamiliar with the ocean environment, they're often unaware of the natural hazards it holds. With just a few precautions, your ocean experience can be a safe and happy one. An excellent book is *All Stings Considered: First Aid and Medical Treatment of Hawaii's Marine Injuries* (University of Hawaii Press, 1997), by Craig Thomas and Susan Scott.

Note that sharks are not a big problem in Hawaii; in fact, they appear so infrequently that locals look forward to seeing them. Since records have been kept, starting in 1779, there have been only about 100 shark attacks in Hawaii, of which 40% have been fatal. Most attacks occurred after someone fell into the ocean from the shore or from a boat; in these cases, the sharks probably attacked after the person was dead. But there are general rules for avoiding sharks: Don't swim at sunrise, at sunset, or where the water is murky due to stream runoff—sharks may mistake you for one of their usual meals. And don't swim where there are bloody fish in the water, as sharks become aggressive around blood.

SEASICKNESS The waters in Hawaii can range from as calm as glass (off the Kona Coast on the Big Island) to downright frightening (in storm conditions), and they usually fall somewhere in between. In general, expect rougher conditions in winter than in summer. Some 90% of the population tends toward seasickness. If you've never been out on a boat, or if you've been seasick in the past, you might want to heed the following suggestions:

- The day before you go out on the boat, avoid alcohol, caffeine, citrus and other acidic juices, and greasy, spicy, or hard-to-digest foods.
- Get a good night's sleep the night before.
- Take or use whatever seasickness prevention works best for you—medication, an acupressure wristband, ginger root tea or capsules, or any combination. But do it ***before* you board;** once you set sail, it's generally too late.
- While you're on the boat, stay as low and as near the center of the boat as possible. Avoid the fumes (especially if it's a diesel boat); stay out in the fresh air and watch the horizon. Do not read.
- If you start to feel queasy, drink clear fluids like water, and eat something bland, such as a soda cracker.

STINGS The most common stings in Hawaii come from jellyfish, particularly Portuguese man-of-war and box jellyfish. Since the poisons they inject are very different, you need to treat each sting differently.

A bluish-purple floating bubble with a long tail, the **Portuguese man-of-war** causes some 6,500 stings a year on Oahu alone. These stings, although painful and a nuisance, are rarely harmful; fewer than 1 in 1,000 requires medical treatment. The best prevention is to watch for these floating bubbles as you snorkel (look for the

Everything You've Always Wanted to Know About Sharks

The Hawaii State Department of Land and Natural Resources has launched a website, www.hawaiisharks.com, that covers the biology, history, and culture of these carnivores. It also provides information on safety and data on shark bites in Hawaii.

Planning Your Outings

On Oahu—especially in Waikiki—everything is relatively close and walking is the preferred method of transportation, but on other islands you most likely will be driving. Be sure to pull out this guide's maps, so you can group all your sightseeing on one side of the island.

At the beginning of each island chapter is information on the various parts of the island, which will help you plan your daily jaunts. Be sure to allow plenty of time for driving, for finding a parking space (yes, Hawaii has parking problems), and for getting lost (and found again).

Finding a Restroom: Any restaurant or fast-food joint has restrooms. In Waikiki or other resort areas, the hotels all have restrooms off the lobby. Every park in Hawaii has restrooms, though some may be cleaner than others. When you enter an attraction (such as a museum, Sea Life Park, or even a sightseeing boat), ask where the restrooms are—then you can take the kids quickly when they suddenly decide that they need a bathroom *now.*

Nursing Moms and Infants: You'll be in good company everywhere in Hawaii. Nursing in public is legal, but you might want to have a blanket or diaper so you can cover the appropriate parts. Most restrooms also have changing areas and chairs for mothers who are a bit shy about nursing in public.

Hiring a Babysitter: The larger hotels and resorts can refer you to qualified babysitters. You can also contact **People Attentive to Children (PATCH),** which can refer you to babysitters who have taken a training course on childcare. On Oahu, call ✆ **808/839-1988;** on Maui, call ✆ **808/242-9232;** on Kauai, call ✆ **808/246-0622;** or visit www.patchhawaii.org.

hanging tentacles below the surface). Get out of the water if anyone near you spots these jellyfish.

Reactions to stings range from mild burning and reddening to severe welts and blisters. *All Stings Considered* recommends the following treatment: First, pick off any visible tentacles with a gloved hand, a stick, or anything handy; then rinse the sting with salt water or fresh water, and apply ice to prevent swelling and to help control pain. Avoid folk remedies like vinegar, baking soda, or urinating on the wound, which may actually cause further damage. Most Portuguese man-of-war stings will disappear by themselves within 15 to 20 minutes if you do nothing at all to treat them. Still, be sure to see a doctor if pain persists or a rash or other symptoms develop.

Transparent, square-shaped **box jellyfish** are nearly impossible to see in the water. Fortunately, they seem to follow a monthly cycle: 8 to 10 days after the full moon, they appear in the waters on the leeward side of each island and hang around for about 3 days. Also, they seem to sting more in the morning hours, when they're on or near the surface.

The stings can cause anything from no visible marks to red, hivelike welts; blisters; and pain lasting from 10 minutes to 8 hours. *All Stings Considered* recommends the following treatment: First, pour regular household vinegar on the sting; this will stop additional burning. Do not rub the area. Pick off any vinegar-soaked tentacles with a stick. For pain, apply an ice pack. Seek additional medical treatment if you experience shortness of breath, weakness, palpitations, muscle cramps, or any other severe symptoms. Most box jellyfish stings disappear by themselves without any treatment.

PUNCTURES Most sea-related punctures come from stepping on or brushing against the needle-like spines of sea urchins (known locally as *wana*). Be careful when you're in the water; don't put your foot down (even if you have booties or fins on) if you can't clearly see the bottom. Waves can push you into *wana* in a surge zone in shallow water. The spines can even puncture a wet suit.

A sea urchin puncture can result in burning, aching, swelling, and discoloration (black or purple) around the area where the spines entered your skin. The best thing to do is to pull any protruding spines out. The body will absorb the spines within 24 hours to 3 weeks, or the remainder of the spines will work themselves out. Again, contrary to popular wisdom, do not urinate or pour vinegar on the embedded spines—this will not help.

CUTS All cuts obtained in the marine environment must be taken seriously because the high level of bacteria present in the water can quickly cause the cut to become infected. The best way to prevent cuts is to wear a wet suit, gloves, and reef shoes. Never touch coral; not only can you get cut, but you can also damage a living organism that took decades to grow.

The symptoms of a coral cut can range from a slight scratch to severe welts and blisters. *All Stings Considered* recommends gently pulling the edges of the skin open and removing any embedded coral or grains of sand with tweezers. Next, scrub the cut well with fresh water. If pressing a clean cloth against the wound doesn't stop the bleeding, or the edges of the injury are jagged or gaping, seek medical treatment.

8 WORDS OF WISDOM & HELPFUL RESOURCES

Hawaii is paradise for children: beaches to run on, water to splash in, and unusual sights to see. Hawaiians love keiki, so don't be surprised if local residents smile and laugh at your baby or talk to your kids. People in Hawaii feel like aunties and uncles to all kids.

SOME PRACTICAL ADVICE

In addition to all the logistics of traveling with kids (from all the paraphernalia required for your infant to the sandwich bags of Cheerios and juice boxes for the preschool set to special items your 7-year-old cannot live without), here are some tips on how to make your trip happier for everyone.

- **Plan ahead.** It will help to have your time mapped out ahead; you can always adjust your schedule. Some activities must be booked in advance, and if you wait until you get here, it may be too late. You'd be surprised how quickly your vacation can fly by until you have only a couple days left and a long list of activities you and your kids want to do.
- **Don't try to do too much.** The whole idea of going to Hawaii is to slow down, so don't ruin your trip by trying to do everything and see everything in the time you have. Plan to see no more than one island a week (otherwise, you'll spend your time visiting the interisland airports). Don't jampack the days with activities; one activity or outing a day will be a good pace, with time off to do

nothing (or to return to an activity that your kids particularly enjoyed).

- **Allow twice the amount of time.** This will save not only your trip, but also your sanity. You're unlikely to get the kids up and going as quickly as you do at home. Restaurants in Hawaii move at a slower pace. You'll be driving to unfamiliar places, so allow extra time to get lost, look for parking, or stop on the way because a beautiful rainbow has bloomed across the sky and the kids want a photo.
- **Expect traffic.** Yes, Virginia, we do have traffic in Hawaii (with the exceptions of Molokai and Lanai): From 6 to 9am and 3 to 6pm, the roads will be filled with cars. Plan your outings accordingly or have plenty of "car games" at the ready.
- **Eat a good breakfast and plan your meals.** As my mom used to say, "You need breakfast for fuel." Feed your kids a good breakfast; then use this guide to figure out where you'll have lunch and dinner that day. Make it a game to look up restaurants and plan your meals. Otherwise, you may be stuck driving around with hungry kids looking for a place to eat in an area that has no restaurants, diners, fast-food places, nothing.
- **Watch your kids' energy level.** The climate change may make them a bit more tired than normal. Also, they may be hyped up and so excited that they crash sooner in the day than they usually do. Don't try to push them or you'll end up with very cranky children.
- **Be extra careful in the sun.** Put sunscreen on your kids (and yourself) first thing in the morning (the sunscreen will soak in better after a shower). When they are in the sun, apply a tablespoon of sunscreen to each limb every hour. Be sure that the keiki always have hats and sunglasses before you leave in the morning. Avoid direct sun from 10am to 3pm, the most intense part of the day. I suggest that you always carry a bag with extra sunscreen, insect repellent, and plenty of water. Make sure your kids are constantly drinking water (even if it means a bathroom stop every hour).
- **Set aside some time for yourself.** Plan to spend at least 1 night out on the town doing adult things without the kids—they will survive a night with a babysitter. If you're traveling with your sweetheart, don't miss the opportunity to enjoy the romantic atmosphere of Hawaii.

9 SPECIALIZED TRAVEL RESOURCES

FAMILY TRAVEL RESOURCES

For Single Parents

Online, the **Single Parent Travel Network** (www.singleparenttravel.net) offers excellent advice, travel specials, a bulletin board, and a free electronic newsletter. The **Family Travel Forum** (www.familytravelforum.com) also hosts a single-parent travel bulletin board for tips from fellow travelers.

For Grandparents

Discounts for seniors are available at almost all of Hawaii's major attractions, and occasionally at hotels and restaurants. The Outrigger hotel chain, for instance, offers travelers ages 50 and older a 20% discount off regular published rates—and an additional 5% off for members of AARP. Always ask when making hotel reservations or buying tickets. And always carry identification with proof of your age—it can really pay off.

Mention the fact that you're a senior when you make your travel reservations. Although all of the major U.S. airlines except America West have cancelled their senior discount and coupon-book programs, many hotels still offer discounts for seniors. In most cities, people over the age of 60 qualify for reduced admission to theaters, museums, and other attractions, as well as discounted fares on public transportation.

Members of **AARP,** 601 E St. NW, Washington, DC 20049 (✆ **800/424-3410** or 202/434-2277; www.aarp.org), get discounts on hotels, airfares, and car rentals. Anyone over 50 can join.

If you're 62 or older and plan to visit Hawaii's national parks, you can save sightseeing dollars by picking up an **American the Beautiful** pass from any national park, recreation area, or monument. This lifetime pass has a one-time fee of $10 and provides free admission to all the parks in the system, plus a 50% savings on camping and recreation fees. You can pick one up at any park entrance; be sure to have proof of your age with you. For more information, go to www.nps.gov/fees_passes.htm, or call ✆ **888/467-2757.**

For Gay & Lesbian Parents

Hawaii is known for its acceptance of all groups. The number of gay- or lesbian-specific accommodations on the islands is limited, but most properties welcome gays and lesbians like any other travelers.

The Center Hawaii's mailing address is P.O. Box 22718, Honolulu, HI 96823, but its physical location is at 2424 S. Beretania St., between Isenberg and University, Honolulu (✆ **808/951-7000;** fax 808/951-7001; www.thecenterhawaii.org). It's open Monday through Friday from 10am to 6pm and on Saturday from noon to 4pm and is a referral center for nearly every kind of gay-related service you can think of, including the latest happenings on Oahu. Check out their community newspaper, *Outlook* (published quarterly), for information on local issues in the gay community in the islands.

For information on Kauai's gay community and related events, contact the **Gay/Lesbian/Bisexual/Transgender Audio Bulletin Board** (✆ **808/823-6248**).

For the Big Island, Oahu, Maui, and Kauai check out the website for **Out in Hawaii,** www.outinhawaii.com, for vacation ideas and a calendar of events.

The International Gay & Lesbian Travel Association (IGLTA; ✆ **800/448-8550** or 954/776-2626; www.iglta.org) is the trade association for the gay and lesbian travel industry, and offers an online directory of gay- and lesbian-friendly travel businesses; go to their website and click on "Members."

Many agencies offer tours and travel itineraries specifically for gay and lesbian travelers. **Pacific Ocean Holidays** (✆ **800/735-6600** or 808/923-2400; www.gayhawaii.com) offers vacation packages that feature gay-owned and gay-friendly lodgings. Also on their website is *A Guide for Gay Visitors & Kamaaina.*

For Families with Special Needs

Travelers with disabilities are made to feel very welcome in Hawaii. There are more than 2,000 ramped curbs in Oahu alone, hotels are usually equipped with wheelchair-accessible rooms, and tour companies provide many special services. The **Statewide Independent Living Council of Hawaii,** 414 Kauwili St., Suite 102, Honolulu, HI 96817 (✆ **808/522-5400;** www.hisilc.org), can provide information.

The only travel agency in Hawaii specializing in needs for travelers with disabilities is **Access Aloha Travel** (✆ **800/480-1143;** http://accessalohatravel.com), which can book anything, including rental vans (available on Maui and Oahu only), accommodations, tours, cruises, and airfare. For more details on wheelchair transportation and tours around the islands, see "Getting Around" in the island chapters.

For travelers with disabilities who wish to do their own driving, hand-controlled cars can be rented from **Avis** (✆ **800/331-1212**) and **Hertz** (✆ **800/654-3131**). The number of hand-controlled cars in Hawaii is limited, so be sure to book at least a week in advance.

Vision-impaired travelers who use a Seeing Eye dog can now come to Hawaii without the hassle of quarantine. A recent court decision ruled that visitors with Seeing Eye dogs need only to present documentation that the dog has had rabies shots and is a trained Seeing Eye dog. For more information, contact the **Animal Quarantine Facility** (✆ **808/483-7171;** http://hawaii.gov/hdoa/ai/aqs/aqsbrochure.pdf). The **American Foundation for the Blind** (✆ **800/232-5463;** www.afb.org) also provides information on traveling with Seeing Eye dogs.

10 PACKAGES FOR THE INDEPENDENT TRAVELER

Package tours are simply a way to buy the airfare, accommodations, and other elements of your trip (such as car rentals, airport transfers, and sometimes even activities) at the same time and often at discounted prices.

One good source of package deals is the airlines themselves. Most major airlines offer air/land packages, including **American Airlines Vacations** (✆ 800/321-2121; www.aavacations.com), **Delta Vacations** (✆ 800/654-6559; www.deltavacations.com), **Continental Airlines Vacations** (✆ 800/301-3800; www.covacations.com), and **United Vacations** (✆ 888/854-3899; www.unitedvacations.com). Several big **online travel agencies**—Expedia, Travelocity, Orbitz, Site59, and Lastminute.com—also do a brisk business in packages.

Some packagers specialize in Hawaiian vacations. **Pleasant Holidays** (✆ **800/2-HAWAII** or 800/242-9244; www.pleasantholidays.com) is by far the biggest and most comprehensive packager to Hawaii; it offers an extensive, high-quality collection of 50 condos and hotels in every price range. **Travelzoo** (www.travelzoo.com) often has package deals to Hawaii as well.

Hawaii's **top hotel chains** offer package deals and special rates as well. Packages may be available for families, seniors, honeymooners, and golfers, and some offer discounts on rental cars or multinight stays. Check with **Outrigger**'s "Ohana" (Hawaiian for "family") Hotels (✆ **800/462-6262;** www.ohanahotels.com) and the more upscale "Outrigger" resorts and condominiums (✆ **866/956-4262;** www.outrigger.com), the ResortQuest chain (✆ **1800/GO-RELAX;** www.resortquest.com), **Marc Resorts Hawaii** (✆ **800/535-0085;** fax 800/633-5085; www.marcresorts.com), and **Castle Resorts and Hotels** (✆ **800/367-5004;** fax 800/477-2329; www.castleresorts.com).

Travel packages are also listed in the travel section of your local Sunday newspaper. Or check ads in the national travel magazines such as *Arthur Frommer's Budget Travel Magazine, Travel + Leisure, National Geographic Traveler,* and *Condé Nast Traveler.*

11 SPECIAL-INTEREST TRIPS

If all you want is a fabulous beach and a perfectly mixed mai tai, then Hawaii has what you're looking for. But the islands' wealth of natural wonders is equally hard to resist; the year-round tropical climate and spectacular scenery tend to inspire almost everyone to get outside and explore.

If you don't have your own snorkel gear or other watersports equipment, or if you just don't feel like packing it, don't fret: Everything you'll need is available for rent in the Islands. We discuss all kinds of places to rent or buy gear in the island chapters that follow.

SETTING OUT ON YOUR OWN VERSUS USING AN OUTFITTER

There are two ways to go: Plan all the details before you leave and either rent gear or schlep your stuff 2,500 miles across the Pacific, or go with an outfitter or a guide and let someone else worry about the details.

Experienced outdoors enthusiasts may head to coastal campgrounds or even trek to the 13,796-foot-high summit of Mauna Loa on their own. But in Hawaii, it's often preferable to go with a local guide who is familiar with the conditions at both sea level and summit peaks, knows the land and its flora and fauna in detail, and has all the gear you'll need. It's also good to go with a guide if time is an issue or if you have specialized interests. If you really want to see native birds, for instance, an experienced guide will take you directly to the best areas for sightings. And many forests and valleys in the interior of the islands are either on private property or in wilderness preserves accessible only on guided tours. The downside? If you go with a guide, plan on spending at least $100 a day per person. We've recommended the best local outfitters and tour-guide operators on each island in the chapters that follow.

But if you have the time, already own the gear, and love doing the research and planning, try exploring on your own. Each island chapter discusses the best spots to set out on your own, from the top offshore snorkel and dive spots to great daylong hikes, as well as the federal, state, and county agencies that can help you with hikes on public property; we also list references for spotting birds, plants, and sea life. We recommend that you always use the resources available to inquire about weather, trail, or surf conditions; water availability; and other conditions before you take off on your adventure.

For hikers, a great alternative to hiring a private guide is taking a guided hike offered by the **Nature Conservancy of Hawaii,** P.O. Box 96, Honolulu, HI 96759 (✆ **808/572-7849** on Maui, 808/621-2008 on Oahu, or 808/553-5236 on Molokai); or the **Hawaii Chapter of the Sierra Club,** P.O. Box 2577, Honolulu, HI 96813 (✆ **808/579-9802** on Oahu; www.hi.sierraclub.org). Both organizations offer guided hikes in preserves and special areas during the year, as well as day- to week-long work trips to restore habitats and trails and to root out invasive plants. It might not sound like a dream vacation to everyone, but it's a chance to see the "real" Hawaii—including wilderness areas that are ordinarily off-limits.

All Nature Conservancy hikes and work trips are free (donations are appreciated). However, you must reserve a spot for yourself, and a deposit is required for guided hikes to ensure that you'll show up; your deposit is refunded once you do. The hikes are generally offered once a month on Maui, Molokai, and Lanai, and twice a month on Oahu. For all islands, call the Oahu office for reservations. Write for a schedule of guided hikes and other programs.

The Sierra Club offers weekly hikes on Oahu and Maui. Hikes are led by certified Sierra Club volunteers and are classified as easy, moderate, or strenuous. These half-day or all-day affairs cost $1 for Sierra Club members and $3 for nonmembers (bring exact change). For a copy of the club newsletter, which lists all outings and trail-repair work, send $2 to the address above.

Local eco-tourism opportunities are also discussed in each island chapter. For more information, contact the **Hawaii Ecotourism Association** (✆ **877/300-7058;** www.hawaiiecotourism.org).

USING ACTIVITIES DESKS TO BOOK YOUR ISLAND FUN

If you're unsure of which activity or which outfitter or guide is the right one for you and your family, you might want to consider booking through a discount activities center or activities desk. Not only will they save you money, but good activities centers should also be able to help you find, say, the snorkel cruise that's right for you, or the luau that's most suitable for both you *and* the kids.

Remember, however, that it's in the activities agent's best interest to sign you up with outfitters from which they earn the most commission. Some agents have no qualms about booking you into any activity if it means an extra buck for them. If an agent tries to push a particular outfitter or activity too hard, be skeptical. Conversely, they'll try to steer you away from outfitters who don't offer big commissions. For example, Trilogy, the company that offers Maui's most popular snorkel cruises to Lanai (and the only one with rights to land at Lanai's Hulopoe Beach), offers only minimum commissions to agents and does not allow agents to offer any discounts at all. As a result, most activities desks will automatically try to steer you away from Trilogy.

Another important word of warning: Stay away from activities centers that offer discounts as fronts for timeshare sales presentations. Using a free or discounted snorkel cruise or luau tickets as bait, they'll suck you into a 90-minute presentation—and try to get you to buy into a Hawaii timeshare in the process. Because their business is timeshares, not activities, they won't be as interested, or as knowledgeable, about which activities might be right for you. These shady deals seem to be particularly rampant on Maui.

There are also a number of very reliable local activities centers on each of the neighbor islands. On Maui your best bet is **Tom Barefoot's Cashback Tours** (✆ **800/ 895-2040** or 808/661-8889; www.tombarefoot.com), 834 Front St., Lahaina. Tom offers a 10% discount on all tours, activities, and adventures if you pay using cash, a personal check, or traveler's checks. If you use a credit card, you'll get a 7% discount.

On the Big Island, check out the **Activity Connection,** Bougainvillea Plaza Suite 102, 75-5656 Kuakini Hwy., Kailua-Kona (✆ **800/459-7156** or 808/329-1038); it offers up to 15% off on various island activities.

Finally, you can book activities yourself and get the commission by booking via the Internet. Most activities offer from 10% to 25% off their prices if you book online.

OUTDOOR ACTIVITIES A TO Z

Here's a brief rundown of the many outdoor activities available in Hawaii. For our recommendations on the best places to go, the best shops for renting equipment, and the best outfitters to use, see the individual island chapters later in this book.

BIRDING Many of Hawaii's tropical birds are found nowhere else on earth. There are curved-bill honeycreepers, black-winged redbirds, and the rare o'o, whose yellow feathers Hawaiians once plucked to make royal capes. When you go birding, take along *A Field Guide to the Birds of Hawaii and the Tropical Pacific,* by H. Douglas Pratt, Phillip L. Bruner, and Delwyn G. Berett (Princeton University Press, 1987).

Kauai and **Molokai,** in particular, are great places to go birding. On Kauai large colonies of seabirds nest at Kilauea National Wildlife Refuge and along the Na Pali Coast. Be sure to take along a copy of *The Birds of Kauai* (University of Hawaii Press), by Jim Denny. The lush rainforest of Molokai's Kamakou Preserve is home to the Molokai thrush and Molokai creeper, which live only on this 30-mile-long island.

BOATING Almost every type of nautical experience is available in the islands, from old-fashioned Polynesian outrigger canoes to America's Cup racing sloops to submarines. You'll find details on all these seafaring experiences in the individual island chapters.

No matter which type of vessel you choose, be sure to see the Hawaiian islands from offshore if you can afford it. It's easy to combine multiple activities into one cruise: Lots of snorkel boats double as sightseeing cruises and, in winter, whale-watching cruises. The main harbors for visitor activities are Kewalo Basin, Oahu; Honokohau, Kailua-Kona, and Kawaihae on the Big Island; Lahaina and Maalaea, Maui; Nawiliwili and Port Allen, Kauai; and Kaunakakai, Molokai.

BODYBOARDING (BOOGIE BOARDING) & BODYSURFING Bodysurfing—riding the waves without a board, becoming one with the rolling water—is a way of life in Hawaii. Some bodysurfers just rely on hands to ride the waves; others use hand boards (flat, paddle-like gloves). For additional maneuverability, try a boogie board or bodyboard (also known as belly boards or *paipo* boards). These 3-foot-long boards support the upper part of your body and are very maneuverable in the water. Both bodysurfing and bodyboarding require a pair of open-heeled swim fins to help propel you through the water. The equipment is inexpensive and easy to carry, and both sports can be practiced in the small, gentle waves. See the individual island chapters for details on where to rent boards and where to go.

CAMPING Hawaii's year-round balmy climate makes camping a breeze. However, tropical campers should always be ready for rain, especially in Hawaii's winter wet season, but even in the dry summer season as well. And remember to bring a good mosquito repellent. If you're heading to the top of Hawaii's volcanoes, you'll need a down mummy bag. If you plan to camp on the beach, bring a mosquito net and a rain poncho. Always be prepared to deal with contaminated water (purify it by boiling, through filtration, or by using iodine tablets) and the tropical sun (protect yourself with sunscreen, a hat, and a long-sleeved shirt). Also be sure to check out "Health," earlier in this chapter, for hiking and camping tips.

There are many established campgrounds at beach parks, including Kauai's Anini Beach, Oahu's Malaekahana Beach, Maui's Waianapanapa Beach, and the Big Island's Hapuna Beach. Campgrounds are also located in the interior at Maui's Haleakala National Park and the Big Island's Hawaii Volcanoes National Park, as well as at Kalalau Beach on Kauai's Na Pali Coast and in the cool uplands of Kokee State Park. See "Beaches" or the hiking or camping sections in the individual island chapters, for the best places to camp. For more details on getting regulations and camping information for any of Hawaii's national or state parks, see the "Visitor Information & Maps" section at the beginning of this chapter.

Hawaiian Trail and Mountain Club, P.O. Box 2238, Honolulu, HI 96804, offers an information packet on hiking and camping throughout the islands. Send $2 and a legal-size, self-addressed, stamped envelope for information. Another good source is the *Hiking/Camping Information Packet,* available from **Hawaii Geographic Maps and Books,** 49 S. Hotel St., Honolulu, HI 96813 (© **800/538-3950** or 808/538-3952), for $7. The **University of Hawaii Press,** 2840 Kolowalu St., Honolulu, HI 96822 (© **888/847-7737;** www.uhpress.hawaii.edu), has an excellent selection of hiking, backpacking, and bird-watching guides, especially Stuart M. Ball, Jr.'s *The Hikers Guide to the Hawaiian Islands.*

GOLF Nowhere else on earth can you tee off to whale spouts, putt under rainbows, and play around a live volcano. Hawaii has some of the world's top-rated golf courses. But be forewarned: Each course features hellish natural hazards, like razor-sharp lava, gusty trade winds, an occasional wild pig, and the tropical heat. And greens fees tend to be very expensive. Still, golfers flock here from around the world and love every minute of it. See the individual island chapters for coverage of the resort courses most worth splurging on (with details, where applicable, on money-saving twilight rates), as well as the best budget and municipal courses.

A few tips on golfing in Hawaii: There's generally wind—10 to 30 mph is not unusual between 10am and 2pm—so you may have to play two to three clubs up or down to compensate. Bring extra balls: The rough is thick, water hazards are everywhere, and the wind wreaks havoc with your game. On the greens, your putt will *always* break toward the ocean. Hit deeper and more aggressively in the sand because the type of sand used on most Hawaii courses is firmer and more compact than on mainland courses (lighter sand would blow away in the constant wind). And bring a camera—you'll kick yourself if you don't capture those spectacular views.

See our coverage in each island chapter.

HIKING Hiking in Hawaii is a breathtaking experience. The islands have hundreds of miles of trails, many of which reward you with a hidden beach, a private waterfall, an Eden-like valley, or simply an unforgettable view. However, rock climbers are out of luck: Most of Hawaii's volcanic cliffs are too steep and brittle to scale.

Fun for Less: Don't Leave Home Without a Gold Card

Almost any activity you can think of, from submarine rides to Polynesian luau, can be purchased at a discount by using the **Activities and Attractions Association of Hawaii Gold Card,** 355 Hukilike St., No. 202, Kahului, HI 96732 (✆ **800/398-9698** or 808/871-7947; fax 808/877-3104; www.hawaiifun.org). The Gold Card, accepted by members on all islands, offers a discount of 10% to 25% off activities and meals for up to four people; it's good for a year from the purchase date and costs $30.

Your Gold Card can lower the regular $149 price of a helicopter ride to only $119, saving you almost $120 for a group of four. And there are hundreds of activities to choose from: dinner cruises, horseback riding, watersports, and more—plus savings on rental cars, restaurants, and golf.

Contact Activities and Attractions to purchase your card. You then contact the outfitter, restaurant, rental-car agency, or other proprietor directly; supply your card number; and receive the discount.

Hawaiian Trail and Mountain Club, P.O. Box 2238, Honolulu, HI 96804, offers an information packet on hiking and camping in Hawaii; to receive a copy, send $2 and a legal-size, self-addressed, stamped envelope. **Hawaii Geographic Maps and Books,** 49 S. Hotel St., Honolulu, HI 96813 (✆ **800/538-3950** or 808/538-3952), offers the *Hiking/Camping Information Packet* for $7. Also note that the **Hawaii State Department of Land and Natural Resources,** 1151 Punchbowl St., No. 131, Honolulu, HI 96809 (✆ **808/587-0300;** www.hawaii.gov), will send you free topographical trail maps.

The **Nature Conservancy of Hawaii** (✆ **808/537-4508** on Oahu, ✆ **808/572-7849** on Maui, or ✆ **808/553-5236** on Molokai; www.tnc.org/hawaii) and the **Hawaii Chapter of the Sierra Club,** P.O. Box 2577, Honolulu, HI 96803 (✆ **808/538-6616**), both offer guided hikes in preserves and special areas during the year. Also see the individual island chapters for complete details on the best hikes for all ability levels.

A couple of terrific books on hiking are Stuart M. Ball, Jr.'s *The Hiking Guide to the Hawaiian Islands*, published by the University of Hawaii Press, and his book on Oahu, *The Hikers Guide to Oahu,* also from University of Hawaii Press.

Before you set out on the trail, see "Health," earlier in this chapter, for tips on hiking safety, as well as "What to Pack," earlier in this chapter.

HORSEBACK RIDING One of the best ways to see Hawaii is on horseback; almost all the islands offer riding opportunities for just about every age and level of experience. You can ride into Maui's Haleakala Crater, along Kauai's Mahaulepu Beach, or through Oahu's remote windward valleys on Kualoa Ranch, or you can gallop across the wide-open spaces of the Big Island's Parker Ranch, one of the largest privately owned ranches in the United States. See the individual island chapters for details. Be sure to bring a pair of jeans and closed-toe shoes to wear on your ride.

KAYAKING Hawaii is one of the world's most popular destinations for ocean

kayaking. Beginners can paddle across a tropical lagoon to two uninhabited islets off Lanikai Beach on Oahu, and more experienced kayakers can take on Kauai's awesome Na Pali Coast. In summer, experts take advantage of the usually flat conditions on the north shore of Molokai, where the sea cliffs are the steepest on earth and the remote valleys can be reached only by sea.

SCUBA DIVING Some people come to the islands solely to take the plunge into the tropical Pacific and explore the underwater world. Hawaii is one of the world's top 10 dive destinations, according to *Rodale's Scuba Diving Magazine*. Here you can see the great variety of tropical marine life (more than 100 endemic species found nowhere else on the planet), explore sea caves, and swim with sea turtles and monk seals in clear, tropical water. If you're not certified, try to take classes before you come to Hawaii so you don't waste time learning and can dive right in.

If you dive, **go early in the morning.** Trade winds often rough up the seas in the afternoon, especially on Maui, so most operators schedule early-morning dives that end at noon. To organize a dive on your own, order ***The Oahu Snorkelers and Shore Divers Guide,*** by Francisco B. de Carvalho, from University of Hawaii Press.

Tip: It's usually worth the extra bucks to go with a good dive operator. Check the operators we've listed throughout the book, which will give you the most for your money.

SNORKELING Snorkeling is one of Hawaii's main attractions, and almost anyone can do it. All you need is a mask, a snorkel, fins, and some basic swimming skills. In many places, all you have to do is wade into the water and look down at the magical underwater world.

If you've never snorkeled before, most resorts and excursion boats offer snorkeling equipment and lessons. You don't really need lessons, however; it's plenty easy to figure out for yourself, especially once you're at the beach, where everybody around you will be doing it. If you don't

Tips Snorkel Bob's

If you're planning on visiting several islands and would like to rent snorkel gear on one island and keep it with you for your whole trip, try **Snorkel Bob's** (www.snorkelbob.com), which lets you rent snorkel gear, boogie boards, life jackets, and wet suits on any one island and return them on another. A basic set of snorkel gear costs $3.50 a day or $9 a week—a very good deal. The best gear is $6.50 a day or $29 a week; if you're nearsighted and need a prescription mask, it's $9 a day or $39 a week.

You can find Snorkel Bob's on **Oahu** at 702 Kapahulu Ave. (at Date St.), Honolulu (✆ **808/735-7944**); on **Maui** at 1217 Front St., in Lahaina (✆ **808/661-4421**), at Napili Village, 5425-C Lower Honoapiilani Hwy., Napili (✆ **808/669-9603**), and in South Maui at Kamole Beach Center, 2411 S. Kihei Rd., Kihei (✆ **808/879-7449**); on the **Big Island** at 75-5831 Kahakai St. (off Alii Dr., next to Huggo's and the Royal Kona Resort), in Kailua-Kona (✆ **808/329-0770**); and on **Kauai** at 4-734 Kuhio Hwy. (just north of Coconut Plantation Marketplace), in Kapaa (✆ **808/823-9433**), and in Koloa at 3236 Poipu Rd., near Poipu Beach (✆ **808/742-2206**).

have your own gear, you can rent it from one of dozens of dive shops and activity booths, discussed in the individual island chapters that follow.

While everyone heads for Oahu's Hanauma Bay—the perfect spot for first-timers—other favorite snorkel spots include Kee Beach on Kauai, Kahaluu Beach on the Big Island, Hulopoe Bay on Lanai, and Kapalua Bay on Maui. Although snorkeling is excellent on all the islands, the Big Island, with its recent lava formations and abrupt drop-offs, offers some particularly spectacular opportunities. Some of the best snorkel spots in the islands—notably, the Big Island's Kealakekua Bay and Molokini Crater just off Maui—are accessible only by boat.

Some snorkeling tips: Always snorkel with a buddy. Look up every once in a while to see where you are and if there's any boat traffic. Don't touch anything; not only can you damage coral, but camouflaged fish and shells with poisonous spines may surprise you. Always check with a dive shop, lifeguards, or others on the beach about the area in which you plan to snorkel and ask if there are any dangerous conditions you should know about.

WHALE-WATCHING Every winter, pods of Pacific humpback whales make the 3,000-mile swim from the chilly waters of Alaska to bask in Hawaii's summery shallows, fluking, spy hopping, spouting, breaching, and having an all-around swell time. About 1,500 to 3,000 humpback whales appear in Hawaiian waters each year.

Humpbacks are one of the world's oldest, most impressive inhabitants. Adults grow to be about 45 feet long and weigh a hefty 40 tons. Humpbacks are officially an endangered species; in 1992 the waters around Maui, Molokai, and Lanai were designated a Humpback Whale National Marine Sanctuary. Despite the world's newfound ecological awareness, humpbacks and their habitats and food resources are still under threat from whalers and pollution.

The season's first whale is usually spotted in November, but the best time to see humpback whales in Hawaii is between **January and April,** from any island. Just look out to sea. Each island also offers a variety of whale-watching cruises, which will bring you up close and personal with the mammoth mammals; see the individual island chapters for details.

Money-saving tip: Book a snorkeling cruise during the winter whale-watching months. The captain of the boat will often take you through the best local whale-watching areas on the way, and you'll get two activities for the price of one. It's well worth the money.

WINDSURFING Maui is Hawaii's top windsurfing destination. World-class windsurfers head for Hookipa Beach, where the wind roars through Maui's isthmus and creates some of the best windsurfing conditions in the world. Funky Paia, a derelict sugar town saved from extinction by surfers, is now the world capital of big-wave board sailing. And along Maui's Hana Highway, there are lookouts where you can watch the pros flip off the lip of 10-foot waves and gain hang time in the air.

Others, especially beginners, set their sails for Oahu's Kailua Bay or Kauai's Anini Beach, where gentle onshore breezes make learning this sport a snap. See the individual island chapters for outfitters and local instructors.

12 STAYING CONNECTED

TELEPHONES

Generally, hotel surcharges on long-distance and local calls are astronomical, so you're better off using your **cellphone** or a **public pay telephone.** Many convenience groceries and packaging services sell **prepaid calling cards** in denominations up to $50; for international visitors, these can be the least expensive way to call home. Many public pay phones at airports now accept American Express, MasterCard, and Visa credit cards. **Local calls** made from pay phones in most locales cost 50¢ (no pennies, please).

All calls on-island are local calls; calls from one island to another are long distance and you must dial "1," then the Hawaii area code, 808, then the phone number.

Most long-distance and international calls can be dialed directly from any phone. **For calls within the United States and to Canada,** dial 1 followed by the area code and the seven-digit number. **For other international calls,** dial 011 followed by the country code, city code, and number you are calling.

Calls to area codes **800, 888, 877,** and **866** are toll-free. However, calls to area codes **700** and **900** (chat lines, bulletin boards, "dating" services, and so on) can be very expensive—usually a charge of 95¢ to $3 or more per minute, and they sometimes have minimum charges that can run as high as $15 or more.

For **reversed-charge or collect calls,** and for person-to-person calls, dial the number 0 and then the area code and number; an operator will come on the line, and you should specify whether you are calling collect, person-to-person, or both. If your operator-assisted call is international, ask for the overseas operator.

For **local directory assistance** ("information"), dial 411; for long-distance information, dial 1, then the appropriate area code, and 555-1212.

CELLPHONES

Just because your cellphone works at home doesn't mean it'll work everywhere in the U.S. (thanks to our nation's fragmented cellphone system). It's a good bet that your phone will work in major cities, but take a look at your wireless company's coverage map on its website before heading out; T-Mobile, Sprint, and Nextel are particularly weak in rural areas. If you need to stay in touch at a destination where you know your phone won't work, **rent** a phone that does from **InTouch USA** (✆ **800/872-7626;** www.intouchglobal.com) or a rental-car location, but be aware that you'll pay $1 a minute or more for airtime.

If you're not from the U.S., you'll be appalled at the poor reach of our **GSM (Global System for Mobile Communications) wireless network,** which is used by much of the rest of the world. Your phone will probably work in most major U.S. cities; it definitely won't work in many rural areas. To see where GSM phones work in the U.S., check out www.t-mobile.com/coverage/national_popup.asp. And you may or may not be able to send SMS (text messaging) home.

INTERNET/E-MAIL

Without Your Own Computer

To find cybercafes in your destination, check **www.cybercaptive.com** and **www.cybercafe.com**.

Most major airports have **Internet kiosks** that provide basic Web access for a per-minute fee that's usually higher than cybercafe prices. Check out copy shops like **Kinko's** (FedEx Kinkos), which offer computer stations with fully loaded software (as well as Wi-Fi).

With Your Own Computer

More and more hotels, resorts, airports, cafes, and retailers are going Wi-Fi (wireless fidelity), becoming "hotspots" that offer free high-speed Wi-Fi access or charge a small fee for usage. Wi-Fi is even found in campgrounds, RV parks, and entire towns. Most laptops sold today have built-in wireless capability. To find public Wi-Fi hotspots at your destination, go to **www.jiwire.com**; its Hotspot Finder holds the world's largest directory of public wireless hotspots.

For dial-up access, most business-class hotels in the U.S. offer dataports for laptop modems, and a few thousand hotels in the U.S. and Europe now offer free high-speed Internet access.

Wherever you go, bring a **connection kit** of the right power and phone adapters, a spare phone cord, and a spare Ethernet network cable—or find out whether your hotel supplies them to guests.

For information on electrical currency conversions, see "Electricity," in the "Fast Facts" section of the Appendix.

13 GETTING AROUND HAWAII

For additional advice on travel within each island, see "Getting Around" in the individual island chapters that follow.

INTERISLAND FLIGHTS

Since September 11, 2001, the major interisland carriers have cut way, way, way back on the number of interisland flights. The airlines warn you to show up at least 90 minutes before your flight, and believe me, with all the security inspections, you will need all 90 minutes to catch your flight.

In 2008, Hawaii lost one of its three major interisland carriers, Aloha Airlines; two major carries remain, **Hawaiian Airlines** (✆ **800/367-5320;** www.hawaiian.com) and **go!** (✆ **888/IFLYGO2** (435-9462**;** www.iflygo.com).

Visitors to Molokai and Lanai have three commuter airlines to choose from: **go!Express,** which has a fleet of Cessna Grand Caravan 208B planes; **PW Express** (✆ **888/866-5022** or 808/873-0877; www.flypwx.com), part of the **Pacific Wings** discount airline, flies daily nonstop flights between Honolulu and Molokai and Lanai, plus flights from Kahului, Maui, and Molokai; and **Island Air** (✆ **800/323-3345** or 808/484-2222), which serves Hawaii's small interisland airports on Maui, Molokai, and Lanai. However, I have to tell you that I have not had stellar service from Island Air and recommend that you book on go!Express or PW Express if you are headed to Molokai or Lanai.

Overseas visitors can take advantage of the APEX (Advance Purchase Excursion) reductions offered by all major U.S. and European carriers. In addition, some large airlines offer transatlantic or transpacific passengers special discount tickets under the name **Visit USA,** which allows mostly one-way travel from one U.S. destination to another at very low prices. Unavailable in the U.S., these discount tickets must be purchased abroad in conjunction with your international fare. This system is the easiest, fastest, cheapest way to see the country.

BY CAR

Hawaii has some of the lowest car rental rates in the country. (An exception is the island of Lanai, where they're very expensive.) To rent a car in Hawaii, you must be at least 25 years of age and have a valid driver's license and credit card. ***Note:*** Foreign driver's licenses are usually recognized in the U.S., but you should get an international one if your home license is not in English.

At Honolulu International Airport and most neighbor-island airports, you'll find most major car rental agencies, including **Alamo** (© 800/327-9633; www.goalamo.com), **Avis** (© 800/321-3712; www.avis.com), **Budget** (© 800/572-0700; www.budget.com), **Dollar** (© 800/800-4000; www.dollarcar.com), **Enterprise** (© 800/325-8007; www.enterprise.com), **Hertz** (© 800/654-3011; www.hertz.com), **National** (© 800/227-7368; www.nationalcar.com), and **Thrifty** (© 800/367-2277; www.thrifty.com). It's almost always cheaper to rent a car at the airport than in Waikiki or through your hotel (unless there's one already included in your package deal).

Rental cars are usually at a premium on Kauai, Molokai, and Lanai, and may be sold out on the neighbor islands on holiday weekends, so be sure to book well ahead.

INSURANCE Hawaii is a no-fault state, which means that if you don't have collision-damage insurance, you are required to pay for all damages before you leave the state, whether or not the accident was your fault. Your personal car insurance may provide rental-car coverage; check before you leave home. Bring your insurance identification card if you decline the optional insurance, which usually costs from $12 to $20 a day. Obtain the name of your company's local claim representative before you go. Some credit card companies also provide collision-damage insurance for their customers; check with yours before you rent.

DRIVING RULES Hawaiian state law mandates that all car passengers must wear a **seat belt** and all infants must be strapped into car seats. You'll pay a $50 fine if you don't buckle up. **Pedestrians** always have the right of way, even if they're not in the crosswalk. You can turn **right on red** after a full and complete stop, unless otherwise posted.

BY FERRY

At the time of writing, the **Hawaii Superferry** (© **877-HI-FERRY** (443-3779); www.hawaiisuperferry.com) had just begun service between Honolulu and Maui, and had plans to extend service between Honolulu and Kauai and Honolulu and the Big Island.

The 3-hour trip from Honolulu to Maui or Kauai will be offered once daily 6 days a week (no Sat service). The one-way trip from Honolulu to the Big Island will be a 4-hour trip. If you are prone to seasickness, you might want to fly instead.

14 TIPS ON ACCOMMODATIONS

Hawaii offers all kinds of accommodations, from simple rooms in restored plantation homes and quaint cottages on the beach to luxurious oceanview condo units and opulent suites in beachfront resorts. Each type has its pluses and minuses, so before you book, make sure you know what you're getting into.

TYPES OF ACCOMMODATIONS

HOTELS In Hawaii, "hotel" can indicate a wide range of options, from few or no on-site amenities to enough extras to qualify as a miniresort. Generally, a hotel offers daily maid service and has a restaurant, on-site laundry facilities, a pool, and a sundries/convenience-type shop. Top hotels also have activities desks, concierge and valet service, room service, business centers, airport shuttles, bars and/or lounges, and perhaps a few more shops.

The advantages of staying in a hotel are privacy and convenience; the disadvantage is generally noise (either thin walls between rooms or loud music from a lobby lounge late into the night). Hotels are often a short walk from the beach rather than right on the beachfront (although there are exceptions).

RESORTS In Hawaii a resort offers everything a hotel does—and more. You can expect direct beach access, with beach cabanas and lounge chairs; pools and a Jacuzzi; a spa and fitness center; restaurants, bars, and lounges; a 24-hour front desk; concierge, valet, and bellhop services; room service (often round-the-clock); an activities desk; tennis and golf; ocean activities; a business center; kids' programs; and more.

The advantage of a resort is that you have everything you could possibly want in the way of services and things to do; the disadvantage is that the price generally reflects this. And don't be misled by a name—just because a place is called "ABC Resort" doesn't mean it actually *is* a resort. Make sure you're getting what you pay for.

CONDOS The roominess and convenience of a condo—which is usually a fully equipped, multiple-bedroom apartment—makes this a great choice for families. Condominium properties in Hawaii generally consist of several apartments set in either a single high-rise or a cluster of low-rise units. Condos usually have amenities such as some maid service (ranging from daily to weekly; it may or may not be included in your rate), a pool, and an on-site front desk or a live-in property manager. Condos tend to be clustered in resort areas. There are some very high-end condos, but most are quite affordable, especially if you're traveling in a group.

The advantages of a condo are privacy, space, and conveniences—which usually include a full kitchen, a washer and dryer, a private phone, and more. The downsides are the standard lack of an on-site restaurant and the density of the units (vs. the privacy of a single-unit vacation rental).

BED & BREAKFASTS Hawaii has a wide range of places that call themselves B&Bs: everything from a traditional B&B—several bedrooms in a home, with breakfast served in the morning—to what is essentially a vacation rental on an owner's property that comes with fixings for you to make your own breakfast. Make sure that the B&B you're booking matches your own mental picture. Note that laundry facilities and private phones are not always available. I've reviewed lots of wonderful B&Bs in the island chapters that follow. If you have to share a bathroom, I've spelled it out in the listings; otherwise, you can assume that you will have your own.

The advantages of a traditional B&B are its individual style and congenial atmosphere, with a host who's often happy to act as your own private concierge. In addition, B&Bs are usually an affordable way to go. The disadvantages are lack of privacy, usually a set time for breakfast, few amenities, and generally no maid service. Also, B&B owners usually require a minimum stay of 2 or 3 nights, and it's often a drive to the beach.

VACATION RENTALS This is another great choice for families and for long-term stays. "Vacation rental" usually means that there will be no one on the property where you're staying. The actual accommodations can range from an apartment to an entire fully equipped house. Generally, vacation rentals allow you to settle in and make yourself at home for a while. They have kitchen facilities (at least a kitchenette), on-site laundry facilities, and a phone; some also come with such extras as a TV, VCR, and stereo.

The advantages of a vacation rental are complete privacy, your own kitchen (which can save you money on meals), and lots of conveniences. The disadvantages are a lack of an on-site property manager and generally no maid service; often a minimum stay is required (sometimes as much as a week). If you book a vacation rental, be sure that you have a 24-hour contact to call if the toilet won't flush or you can't figure out how to turn on the air-conditioning.

15 SHOW & TELL: GETTING KIDS INTERESTED IN HAWAII

If your kids are 10 or younger, there are a couple of books they probably will like that explain Hawaii. *A Beautiful Hawaiian Day,* by Henry Kapono, is the story of a little Hawaiian girl named Kaleo who finds a magical seashell that jettisons her back in time to when King Kamehameha was a child. This future great chief teaches Kaleo about Hawaii's history and culture. *The Ancient Hawaii Color Book,* by Bellerophon, is entertaining for the entire family: It depicts original art and artifacts of Hawaiian gods and goddesses, and scenes of life when Europeans first reached the Hawaiian Islands. While the kids color the pages, you'll find yourself learning about Hawaii's cultural history. For preschoolers, get *Baby Honu's Incredible Journey,* by Tammy Yee. This locally popular and well-illustrated book tells the story of a baby green turtle's adventures through Hawaiian waters.

If you are planning a trip to Hawaii Volcanoes National Park, check out the video *VolcanoScapes 3 . . . Living on the Edge!—Hawaii's Kilauea Volcano.* Not only is the footage of the eruption spectacular, but the cultural historical information is entertaining as well as informative. For the Hawaii portrayed in the movies, the old favorite is *Hawaii,* made in 1966 with Julie Andrews and Max von Sydow and based on James Michener's book, which is not entirely accurate, but close enough for the movies. For pure entertainment there's *Blue Hawaii,* made in 1961 with Elvis Presley. It has a hokey plot, but it's Elvis, in Hawaii, with Angela Lansbury as his mom. Although Disney's *Lilo & Stitch* is fantasy, and not a true picture of Hawaii,

Teach Your Kids Hawaiian

Here are some basic Hawaiian words that you'll often hear in Hawaii and see throughout this book. For a more complete list of Hawaiian words, visit **http://hawaiianlanguage.com**.

akamai smart
aloha greeting or farewell
halau hula school
hale house or building
kahuna priest or expert
kamaaina old-timer
keiki child
lanai porch or veranda
mahalo thank you
malihini stranger, newcomer
mana spirit power
muumuu loose-fitting gown or dress
ono delicious
paniolo Hawaiian cowboy(s)
wiki quick

preschoolers and young elementary school–age kids will love it and look forward to seeing the “real” Hawaii. Older kids can get a primer on the bombing of Pearl Harbor with the films *Pearl Harbor,* a Hollywood blockbuster starring Ben Affleck; and *Tora! Tora! Tora!,* which depicts the famous December 7, 1941, incident from both the U.S. and the Japanese points of view.

If you would like to play Hawaiian music to get your kids in the mood, a couple of websites will guide you through the wonderful world of Hawaiian music: **www.hawaii-music.com** and **www.mele.com**. You can listen to different songs, order CDs, read about the history of Hawaiian music, and even track the trends of Hawaiian music over the years.

3

Suggested Hawaii Itineraries

What should I do in Hawaii? This is the most common question that readers ask me. The purpose of this chapter is to give you my expert advice on the best things to see and do on each island, and how to do them in an orderly fashion so you are not driving madly from one end of the island to the other.

First, **do not plan to see more than one island per week.** With the exception of the ferry between Maui and Lanai, getting from one island to another is an all-day affair once you figure in packing, checking out of and into hotels, driving to and from airports, and dealing with rental cars, not to mention time actually spent at the airport and on the flight. Don't waste a day of your vacation seeing our interisland air terminals.

Second, **don't max out your days.** This is Hawaii—allow some time to do nothing but relax. Remember that you most likely will arrive jet-lagged, so it's a good idea to ease into your vacation. In fact, exposure to sunlight can help reset your internal clock, so I include time at the beach on the first day of most of these itineraries.

Third, **don't try to see and do everything on this trip.** If this is your first trip to Hawaii, think of this as a "scouting" trip. Hawaii is too beautiful, too sensual, too enticing to see just once in a lifetime. You'll be back.

Finally, keep in mind that the following itineraries are designed to appeal to a wide range of people. If you're a scuba diver, check out chapter 2, "Special-Interest Trips," to plan your trip around your passion.

One last thing—**you will need a car to get around the islands.** Oahu has an adequate public transportation service, but even so, it's set up for Hawaii residents, not tourists carrying coolers and beach toys (all carry-ons must fit under the bus seat). So plan to rent a car. But also plan to get out of the car as much as possible. Hawaii is not a place to view from your car window. You have to get out to smell the sweet perfume of plumerias, to hear the sound of the wind through a bamboo forest, and to plunge into the gentle waters of the Pacific.

1 A WEEK ON OAHU

The island of Oahu is so stunning that the *alii,* the kings of Hawaii, made it the capital of the island nation. This itinerary assumes you are staying in Waikiki—if you are in another location, be sure to factor in the time for traveling.

Day 1: Arrival & Waikiki Beach ★★

After you get off the plane, lather up in sunscreen, grab your sunglasses and hat, and head for the most famous beach in the world—**Waikiki Beach** (p. 127). If you have kids in tow or you can't handle a whole afternoon in Hawaii's intense sun, you might consider checking out Hawaii's water world by dropping by the **Waikiki**

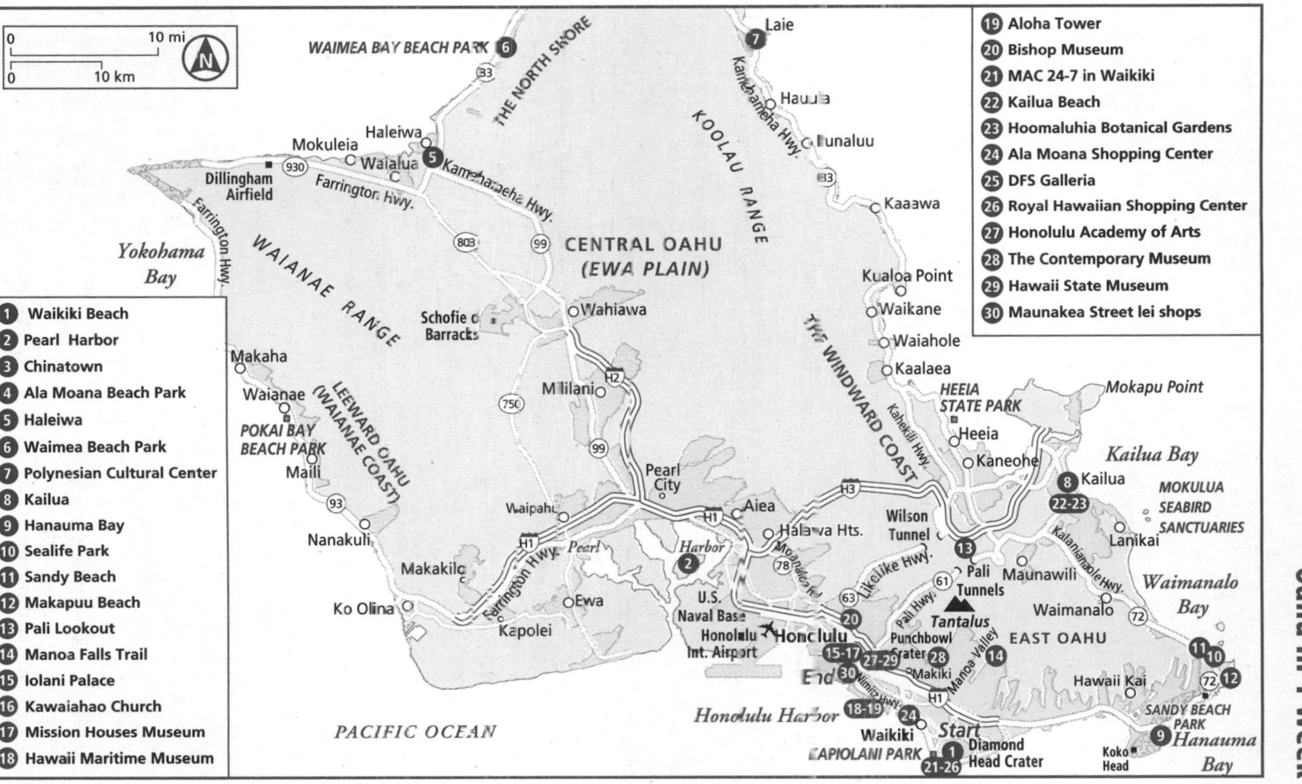
0 10 mi
0 10 km
N
WAIMEA BAY BEACH PARK
THE NORTH SHORE
Laie
Kamehameha Hwy.
Hauula
Punaluu
KOOLAU RANGE
Kaaawa
Mokuleia
Haleiwa
Waialua
Dillingham Airfield
Farrington Hwy.
Kamehameha Hwy.
Farrington Hwy.
Yokohama Bay
WAIANAE RANGE
CENTRAL OAHU (EWA PLAIN)
Wahiawa
Schofield Barracks
Kualoa Point
Waikane
Waiahole
Kaalaea
THE WINDWARD COAST
Kahekili Hwy.
HEEIA STATE PARK
Heeia
Kaneohe
Mokapu Point
Kailua Bay
Kailua
MOKULUA SEABIRD SANCTUARIES
Lanikai
Makaha
Waianae
POKAI BAY BEACH PARK
Maili
LEEWARD OAHU (WAIANAE COAST)
Nanakuli
Mililani
Pearl City
Waipahu
Aiea
Halawa Hts.
Wilson Tunnel
Pearl Harbor
Moanalua Fwy.
Likelike Hwy.
Pali Hwy.
Pali Tunnels
Maunawili
Kalanianaole Hwy.
Waimanalo
Waimanalo Bay
Tantalus
Punchbowl Crater
Makiki
Manoa Valley
EAST OAHU
Makakilo
Farrington Hwy.
Ko Olina
Kapolei
Ewa
U.S. Naval Base
Honolulu Int. Airport
Honolulu
End
Nimitz Hwy.
Honolulu Harbor
Waikiki
Start
KAPIOLANI PARK
Diamond Head Crater
Hawaii Kai
SANDY BEACH PARK
Hanauma Bay
Koko Head
PACIFIC OCEAN
1 Waikiki Beach
2 Pearl Harbor
3 Chinatown
4 Ala Moana Beach Park
5 Haleiwa
6 Waimea Beach Park
7 Polynesian Cultural Center
8 Kailua
9 Hanauma Bay
10 Sealife Park
11 Sandy Beach
12 Makapuu Beach
13 Pali Lookout
14 Manoa Falls Trail
15 Iolani Palace
16 Kawaiahao Church
17 Mission Houses Museum
18 Hawaii Maritime Museum
19 Aloha Tower
20 Bishop Museum
21 MAC 24-7 in Waikiki
22 Kailua Beach
23 Hoomaluhia Botanical Gardens
24 Ala Moana Shopping Center
25 DFS Galleria
26 Royal Hawaiian Shopping Center
27 Honolulu Academy of Arts
28 The Contemporary Museum
29 Hawaii State Museum
30 Maunakea Street lei shops

Aquarium (p. 118), or gaining insight into Waikiki's past on the **Waikiki Historic Trail** (p. 119), a 2-mile trail marked with bronzed surfboards. Be sure to catch the sunset (anywhere on Waikiki Beach will do), and get an early dinner.

Day ❷: Pearl Harbor ★★★ & Honolulu's Chinatown ★★★

Head to the **USS *Arizona* National Memorial at Pearl Harbor** (p. 117). Get there as early as possible—by the afternoon, the lines are 2 hours long. While you are there, be sure to see the **USS *Missouri* Memorial** (p. 112) and the **USS *Bowfin* Submarine Museum & Park** (p. 118). On your way back, stop in **Chinatown** for lunch and take a walk around this unique area. In the afternoon, take a nap or head for the beach at **Ala Moana Beach Park** (p. 127) or a shopping spree across the street at the **Ala Moana Center** (p. 146). Plan to have dinner in Honolulu or the surrounding area.

Day ❸: North Shore ★★★ & the Polynesian Cultural Center ★

Start your day with a drive to the **North Shore** (see "Central Oahu & the North Shore," in chapter 4). If you're up early enough, have breakfast in the quaint town of **Haleiwa;** if not, at least stop and get a picnic lunch before you beach-hop down the coast of the North Shore and choose from some of the world's most beautiful beaches, like **Waimea Beach Park,** which is calm for swimming in summer but gets pounded with 30- and 40-foot waves in winter. Any time after 12:30pm, head for the **Polynesian Cultural Center** in Laie (p. 116). Allow at least 2 hours to tour this miniglimpse of the Pacific. Continue driving down the coast road to the small town of **Kailua.** Stay for dinner here to avoid the traffic back to Waikiki.

Day ❹: Snorkeling in Hanauma Bay ★★ & Watching Marine Life at Sea Life Park ★

If it's not Tuesday (when the park is closed), head out in the morning for the spectacular snorkeling at **Hanauma Bay** (p. 128). After a couple of hours, wander down the coast to **Sea Life Park** (p. 117). If you have kids, this is a must-stop. Otherwise, you can continue beach-hopping down the coastline—check out **Sandy Beach** (p. 128) and **Makapuu Beach Park** (p. 128) to see which one appeals to you. Then turn back to take the Pali Highway back to Waikiki (be sure to stop at the **Pali Lookout,** p. 121).

Day ❺: Rainforest Hike ★★, Historic Honolulu & Hawaiian Culture

You probably could use a day out of the sun by now, so try a short hike into the rainforest, just a 15-minute drive from downtown Honolulu. Be sure to wear good hiking or trail shoes for the **Manoa Falls Trail** (p. 141), and bring mosquito repellent. Next, head for downtown Honolulu to see some of the city's historic sites, including the **Iolani Palace** (p. 119), **Kawaiahao Church**, **Mission Houses Museum,** and **Hawaii Maritime Center** (p. 116). For a view of where you've been, go to the top of the **Aloha Tower,** at the Aloha Tower Marketplace, for a bird's-eye view of Honolulu. Stop for lunch at either the Marketplace or one of the nearby restaurants. Spend the afternoon at the **Bishop Museum** (p. 113) to immerse yourself in Hawaiian culture.

Day ❻: Kailua Beach ★★★

On your last full day on Oahu, travel over the Pali Highway to the windward side of the island and spend a day at **Kailua Beach.** Before you leave Waikiki, drop by **MAC 24-7** (p. 98) and pick up a picnic lunch. Kailua is the perfect beach to just relax or snorkel or try something different, such as kayaking or windsurfing. You can spend the entire day here, or you can take an afternoon hike at the **Hoomaluhia Botanical Gardens** (p. 138).

Day ❼: Final Day: Shopping & Art

Been having too much fun to shop for gifts for your friends back home? You can find a great selection of stores in Waikiki at the **Ala Moana Shopping Center,** the **DFS Galleria,** and the **Royal Hawaiian Shopping Center.** If you're more interested in looking than buying, check out the **Honolulu Academy of Arts** (p. 122), **The Contemporary Museum**, or the **Hawaii State Art Museum.** On your way back to the airport, be sure to stop at one of the **Maunakea Street lei shops** (p. 148) in Chinatown to buy a sweet-smelling souvenir of your trip.

2 A WEEK ON THE BIG ISLAND OF HAWAII

A week is barely enough time to see the entire Big Island of Hawaii; 2 weeks would be better. But if your schedule doesn't allow more time, this tour will let you see the highlights of this huge island (twice the size of all the other islands combined). The itinerary is set up for people staying either in Kailua-Kona or on the Kohala Coast, and I suggest you spend at least 2 nights in Volcano Village to enjoy one of the stars of the Big Island, Hawaii Volcanoes National Park.

Day ①: Arrival & Beach Time

After you settle into your hotel, head for the beach: Snorkelers should go to **Kahaluu Beach Park** (p. 209); surfers to **White Sands Beach** (p. 212 privacy buffs to **Kekaha Kai State Park** (**Kona Coast State Park;** p. 212); and beach aficionados to **Anaehoomalu Bay, Hapuna Beach,** or **Kaunaoa Beach (Mauna Kea Beach),** depending on whether you want to snorkel, bodyboard, or just relax (see reviews starting on p. 212 to help you decide). When the sun starts to wane, head for old **Kailua-Kona** town and wander through the **Hulihee Palace, Mokuaikaua Church,** and **Kamchameha's Compound at Kamakahonu Bay** (p. 188). Find a spot to watch the sunset (either on the pier or along the seawall), and then head for dinner in either **Kailua-Kona** or **Keauhou.**

Day ②: Out on the Water, Then Drive to Hawaii Volcanoes National Park ★★★

Since you most likely will be up early your first day in Hawaii (and still on mainland time), take advantage of it and book a morning sailing/snorkeling tour on the ***Fair Wind*** (p. 214) to **Kealakekua Bay,** a marine-life preserve. Spend the morning floating in a rainbowed sea of fish and enjoy a terrific lunch onboard the sailing catamaran. After you return to Keauhou, start driving south. Great stops along the way are **Puuhonua O Honaunau National Historical Park** (p. 192), **South Point** (p. 174), and **Green Sand Beach (Papakolea Beach..** Then head up **Mauna Kea** to the **Hawaii Volcanoes National Park** (p. 186) and stay at one of the many quaint bed-and-breakfasts in the tiny village of **Volcano** (a list of recommended accommodations starts on p. 186).

Day ③: Exploring an Active Volcano ★★★

The highlight of your trip most likely will be the time you spend in the incredible **Hawaii Volcanoes National Park** (p. 203). I recommend spending the morning exploring the park and taking hikes. Your first stop should be the Kilauea Visitors Center. Then explore **Halemaumau Crater, Thurston Lava Tube, Devastation Trail,** and all the other sites in the crater. Find out from the rangers how to get to the current lava flow. In the afternoon, drive down to the current flow and walk out as far as the rangers will allow. Go eat a nice dinner in Volcano and return to the flow after dark, armed with a flashlight, water bottle, and jacket. Since you were

The Big Island in 1 Week

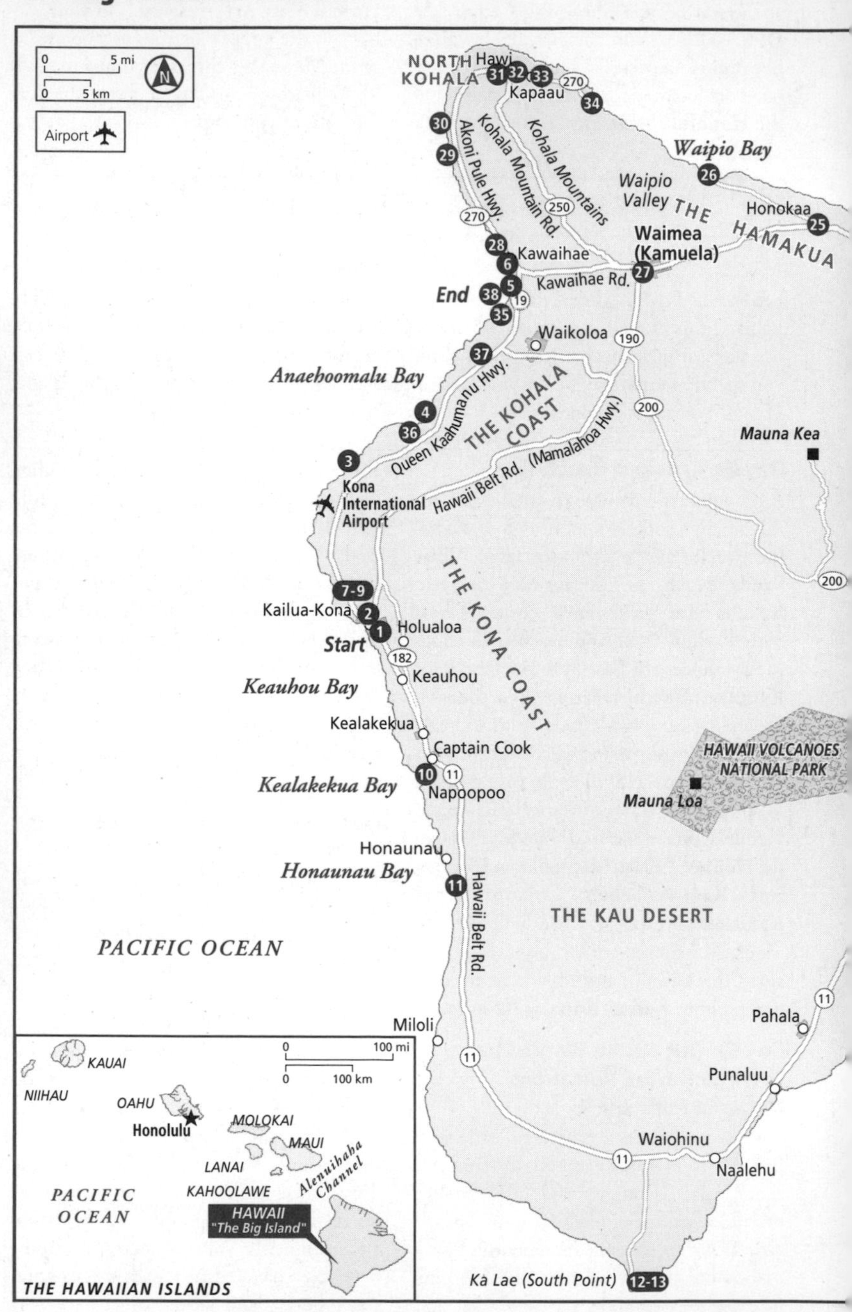

PACIFIC OCEAN
COAST
19
Laupahoehoe
Honomu
220
24
23
22
21
Hilo Bay
Saddle Rd.
Hilo
16-20
Hilo International Airport
Stainback Hwy.
Keaau
Mountain View
130
Pahoa
THE PUNA REGION
Volcano
15
KAHAUALEA NATURAL AREA RESERVE
Kilauea Caldera
14
Chain of Craters Rd.
132
130
137
HAWAII VOLCANOES NATIONAL PARK
1 Kahaluu Beach Park
2 White Sands Beach
3 Kekaha Kai State Park (Kona Coast State Park
4 Anaehoomalu Bay
5 Hapuna Beach
6 Kaunaoa Beach (Mauna Kea Beach)
7 Hulihee Palace
8 Mokuaikaua Church
9 Kamehameha's Compound at Kamakahonu Bay
10 Kealakekua Bay
11 Puuhonua O Honaunau National Historical Park
12 South Point
13 Green Sand Beach (Papakolea Beach
14 Hawaii Volcanoes National Park
15 Volcano
16 Bears' Coffee
17 Banyan Drive
18 Liliuokalani Gardens
19 Lyman Museum & Mission House
20 Pacific Tsunami Museum
21 Nani Mau Gardens
22 Hawaii Tropical Botanical Garden
23 World Botanical Garden
24 Akaka Falls
25 Honokaa
26 Waipio Valley
27 Waimea
28 Puukohola Heiau National Historic Site
29 Lapakahi State Historical Park
30 Mo'okini Luakini Heiau
31 Bamboo
32 Kohala Rainbow Café
33 The Original King Kamehameha Statue
34 Pololu Valley Lookout
35 Puako Petroglyph Archaeological District
36 Kona Village Luau
37 Mauna Kea
38 Kohala resorts

there during the day, the path to the volcano after dark will be familiar to you. Seeing the ribbon of red lava snake its way down the side of the mountain and then thunder into the ocean is a sight you will never forget. You are going to be tired after this full day, so I recommend spending another night in Volcano.

Day ❹: Touring Old Hawaii: Hilo Town ★★★, Akaka Falls ★★★, Waipio Valley ★★★ & Cowboy Country

It's just a 45-minute drive from Volcano to **Hilo** (p. 213), so plan to arrive early in the morning, grab a cup of coffee at **Bears' Coffee** (p. 223), and wander through the old town, being sure to see **Banyan Drive, nardens, Lyman Museum & Mission House,** the **Pacific Tsunami Museum,** and one of the wonderful botanical gardens such as **Nani Mau Gardens, Hawaii Tropical Botanical Garden** (p. 199), or **World Botanical Gardens** (p. 199). Head up the Hamakua Coast, stopping at **Akaka Falls** (p. 199) and planning a lunch stop in **Honokaa.** After lunch, be sure to see **Waipio Valley** (p. 199), the birthplace of Hawaii's kings, before heading for **Waimea** (p. 221). Spend some time in this cowboy town and at the **Parker Ranch Visitor Center and Museum** (p. 196). Spend the night along the Kohala Coast.

Day ❺: The Kohala Coast: Stepping Back in Time ★★★

Get an early start on your trip back in time. The first stop is just south of Kawaihae, at the **Puukohola Heiau National Historic Site** (p. 193), the temple Kamehameha built to the war god to ensure his success in battle. Allow at least an hour to view the temple and wander through the visitor center. Keep driving up Highway 270 to the **Lapakahi State Historical Park** (p. 194) for a view of a typical 14th-century Hawaiian village and the **Mo'okini Luakini Heiau** (p. 194). Plan a lunch stop in Hawi or Kapaau at either **Bamboo** (p. 182) or **Kohala Rainbow Cafe** (p. 182), and stop by **The Original King Kamehameha Statue** (p. 196) in Kapaau. The final stop on your northward journey is the **Pololu Valley Lookout** (p. 196). On your way back, in the late afternoon (the best time for viewing), be sure to stop at the **Puako Petroglyph Archaeological District** (p. 194). If it's Friday, make reservations at the **Kona Village Luau** (p. 226) for the perfect ending to your trip back in time.

Day ❻: Mauna Kea: Where the Gods Live ★★★

Sleep in, have a lazy morning at the beach, and, in the afternoon, plan to explore Hawaii's tallest mountain (and dormant volcano), **Mauna Kea** (p. 197). You need a four-wheel-drive vehicle to climb to the top of the 13,796-foot Mauna Kea, so I recommend you book with the experts, **Mauna Kea Summit Adventures** (p. 198), for a 7- to 8-hour visit to this mountain, sacred to the Hawaiians and treasured by astronomers around the globe.

Day ❼: Relaxing or Shopping

Depending on how much time you have on your final day, I recommend either relaxing on the beach or being pampered in a spa. Spa-goers have a range of terrific spas among the **Kohala resorts** (reviews start on p. 169) to choose from. Shoppers have lots to choose from—see my recommendations starting on p. 220.

3 A WEEK ON MAUI

I've outlined the highlights of Maui for those who just have 7 days and want to see everything. Two things I suggest: First, spend 2 nights in Hana, a decision you will not regret, and second, take the Trilogy boat trip to Lanai for the day. I've designed this itinerary assuming you'll stay in West Maui for 5 days. If you are staying elsewhere (like Wailea or Kihei), allow extra driving time.

Day 1: Arrival & Kapalua Beach ★★★

Check into your hotel, and then head for **Kapalua Beach** (p. 279). Don't overdo the sun on your first day. After an hour or two at the beach, drive to **Lahaina** (p. 265) and spend a couple of hours walking the historic old town. To really feel like you are in Hawaii, go to the **Old Lahaina Luau** (p. 302) at sunset to immerse yourself in Hawaiian culture.

Day 2: Up a 10,000-Foot Dormant Volcano & Down Again ★★★

You'll likely wake up early on your first day in Hawaii, so take advantage of it and head up to the 10,000-foot (dormant) volcano, **Haleakala.** You can **hike in the crater** (p. 290), **speed down the mountain on a bicycle** (p. 289), or just wander about **Haleakala National Park.** You don't have to be at the top for sunrise; in fact, it has gotten so crowded and congested at sunrise you may not have quite the awe-inspiring experience you were hoping for if you are fighting the crowds. I'd suggest wandering up any time during the day. On your way back down, stop and tour **Upcountry Maui** (p. 295), particularly the communities of **Kula, Makawao,** and **Paia.** Plan for a sunset dinner in **Paia** or **Kuau.**

Day 3: Hana Highway ★★★

Pack a lunch and spend the entire day driving the scenic **Hana Highway** (p. 274). Pull over often and get out to take photos, smell the flowers, and jump in the mountain-stream pools. Wave to everyone, move off the road for those speeding by, and breathe in Hawaii. Plan to spend at least 2 nights in Hana (hotel recommendations start on p. 249).

Day 4: A Day in Heavenly Hana ★★★

An entire day in paradise, so many things to do. Take an early-morning hike along the black sands of **Waianapanapa State Park** (p. 277); then explore the tiny town of **Hana** (coverage starts on p. 277). Be sure to see the **Hana Museum Cultural Center, Hasegawa General Store,** and **Hana Coast Gallery.** Get a picnic lunch and drive out to the Kipihulu end of Haleakala National Park at **Oheo Gulch** (p. 277). Hike to the waterfalls and swim in the pools. Splurge on dinner at the dining room at the **Hotel Hana-Maui.** Spend another night in Hana.

Day 5: Wine, Food & (Hawaiian) Song

Check to see if the road past Hana is open (it closed after the 2006 earthquake); if it is, continue driving around the island, past **Kaupo** and up to the **Ulupalakua Ranch** (p. 278) and the **Tedeschi Vineyards and Winery.** Stop at **Grandma's Coffee House** for a cup of java and head down the mountain, with a stop for lunch at **Haliimaile General Store** (p. 261). Spend the afternoon at the **Maui Ocean Center** in Maalaea (p. 268) checking out the marine life, especially the sharks. Plan a dinner in Lahaina and see the drama/dance/music show **Ulalena** (p. 301). If the road past Hana is closed, go back along the Hana

Maui in 1 Week

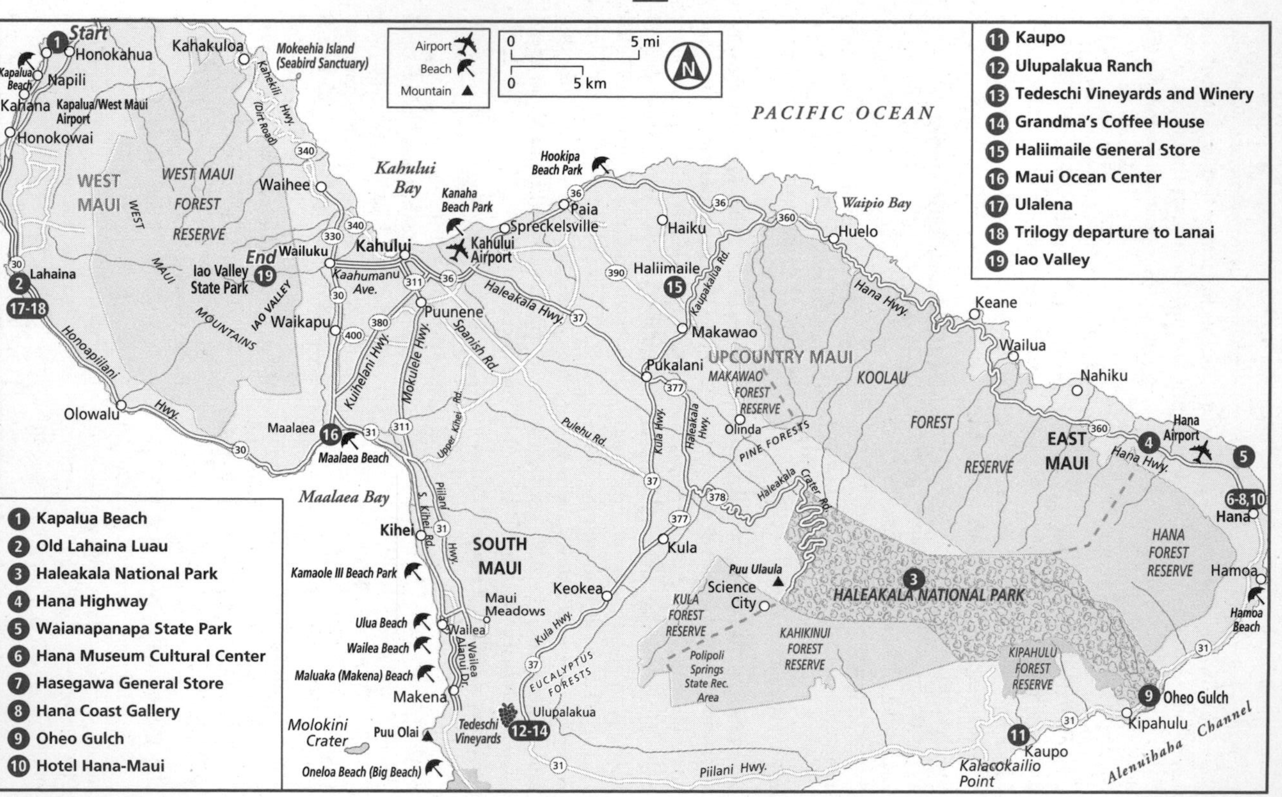

Highway the way you came, stopping for lunch at Haliimaile, and then follow the rest of the itinerary from there.

Day 6: Sailing to Lanai ★★★

Trilogy (p. 284) is the best sailing/snorkeling trip in Hawaii, so don't miss it. You'll spend the day (breakfast and lunch included) sailing to the island of Lanai, snorkeling, touring the island, and sailing back to Lahaina. Plus, you still have the afternoon to go shopping for souvenirs or take a nap.

Day 7: Relaxing & Shopping

Depending on how much time you have on your final day, you can choose from relaxing on the beach, being pampered in a spa, or shopping for souvenirs and bargains. Spa-goers have a range of terrific **spas,** and **shopping** aficionados should check out some of my favorite stores (recommendations start on p. 295). If you have a late flight, you might want to check out **Iao Valley** (p. 264).

4

Oahu

When people think of Oahu, they immediately visualize the sunny shores of Waikiki, where the white-sand beach and the calm azure waters are the stars. Families flock to this vacation wonder not only for the breathtaking beauty, but also for the wealth of activities. I love Waikiki for its abundance of ocean activities: swimming, snorkeling, sailing, surfing, and more. But there's also the Honolulu Zoo, the Waikiki Aquarium, and Kapiolani Park and all its fun-filled things to do and see.

Waikiki is just a tiny part of the island. Pile the kids in the rental car and drive around the small island. Your children will be gawking at the most beautiful beaches in the world; the rainbows in the mountain rainforests; the lush green tropical farms with bananas, papayas, and other exotic fruit; and the quaint oceanside small rural towns. Dotted around the island are great family outings such as Sea Life Park, the Polynesian Cultural Center, and even a water adventure park for those who haven't gotten enough water time from the great beaches.

The lifestyle on Oahu is geared toward the families who live here. Waikiki has movies on the beach, lush parks fill the landscape, and there's even a family hike to a waterfall just a 15-minute drive from downtown Honolulu.

Plus, the island is filled with history, from the USS *Arizona* Memorial at Pearl Harbor to a replica of an ancient sailing canoe to a real palace where royalty once lived. Take your young ones to the interactive exhibits of Bishop Museum, which houses not only Hawaii's history, but the histories of most of the Pacific islands as well.

And in terms of weather, no other Hawaiian island has it as fine as Oahu. The Big Island is hotter, Kauai is wetter, Maui has more wind, Molokai and Lanai are drier. Oahu enjoys a kind of perpetual late spring, with light trade winds and 82°F (28°C) days almost year-round. In fact, the climate is supposed to be the best on the planet.

Be careful: Once your family experiences Oahu, other islands will pale in comparison.

1 ORIENTATION

ARRIVING

Honolulu is your gateway to the Hawaiian Islands; even though more and more transpacific flights are going directly to the neighbor islands these days, chances are still good that you'll touch down on Oahu first. **Honolulu International Airport** (© **808/836-6413**) sits on the south shore of Oahu, west of downtown Honolulu and Waikiki, near Pearl Harbor. Many major American and international carriers fly to Honolulu from the mainland; see "Getting There" in chapter 2 for a list of carriers and their toll-free numbers.

Landing at Honolulu International Airport

The airport at Honolulu is probably the most cosmopolitan spot in the Pacific, with passengers from every corner of the globe. Although the airport is large and constantly expanding, the layout is quite simple and easy to grasp. You can walk or take the **Wiki-Wiki Bus,** a free airport shuttle, from your arrival gate to the main terminal and baggage claim, on the ground level. After collecting your bags, unless you're getting on an inter-island flight immediately, you'll exit to the palm-lined street, where uniformed attendants can either flag down a taxi or direct you to **TheBus** (for transportation information, see below). For Waikiki shuttles and car rental vans, cross the street to the center island and wait at the designated stop.

Getting To & From the Airport

BY CAR All major rental companies have cars available at the airport. (See "By Car" under "Getting Around Hawaii," in chapter 2.) Rental-agency vans will pick you up curbside at the center island outside baggage claim and take you to their off-site lot.

BY TAXI Taxis are abundant at the airport; an attendant will be happy to flag one down for you. Taxi fare is about $30 to $40 from Honolulu International to downtown Honolulu, about $35 to $45 to Waikiki. If you need to call a taxi, see "Getting Around," below, for a list of cab companies.

BY AIRPORT SHUTTLE Shuttle vans operate 24 hours a day, every day of the year, between the airport and all 350 hotels and condos in Waikiki. The shuttle service to Waikiki is **Airport Waikiki Express** (✆ **808/566-7333;** http://waikikitransport.com), with 24-hour service in air-conditioned vans for just $9 per person from the airport to Waikiki ($15 round-trip). You'll find the shuttle at street level outside baggage claim. You can board with two pieces of luggage and a carry-on at no extra charge. Tips are welcome. For advance purchase of group tickets, call the number above.

BY BUS **TheBus** nos. 19 and 20 (WAIKIKI BEACH AND HOTELS) run from the airport to downtown Honolulu and Waikiki. The first bus from Waikiki to the airport leaves at 4:50am Monday through Friday and 5:25am Saturday and Sunday; the last bus departs the airport for Waikiki at 11:45pm Monday through Friday, 11:25pm Saturday and Sunday. There are two bus stops on the main terminal's upper level; a third is on the second level of the interisland terminal. We don't recommend the bus for families because you are only allowed a carry-on or small suitcase that fits under the seat and doesn't disrupt other passengers. The approximate travel time to Waikiki is an hour. The one-way fare is $2 for adults and $1 for students ages 6 to 19 (exact change only). For more information on TheBus, see "Getting Around," below.

VISITOR INFORMATION

The **Hawaii Visitors and Convention Bureau,** 2270 Kalakaua Ave., 7th Floor, Honolulu, HI 96815 (✆ **800/GO-HAWAII** [464-29244] or 808/923-1811; www.gohawaii.com), supplies free brochures, maps, accommodations guides, and *Islands of Aloha,* the official HVCB magazine. The **Oahu Visitors Bureau,** 735 Bishop St., Suite 1872, Honolulu, HI 96813 (✆ **877/525-OAHU** [525-6248] or 808/524-0722; www.visit-oahu.com), distributes a free travel planner and map.

A number of free publications, such as ***This Week Oahu,*** are packed with money-saving coupons and good regional maps; look for them on racks at the airport and around town.

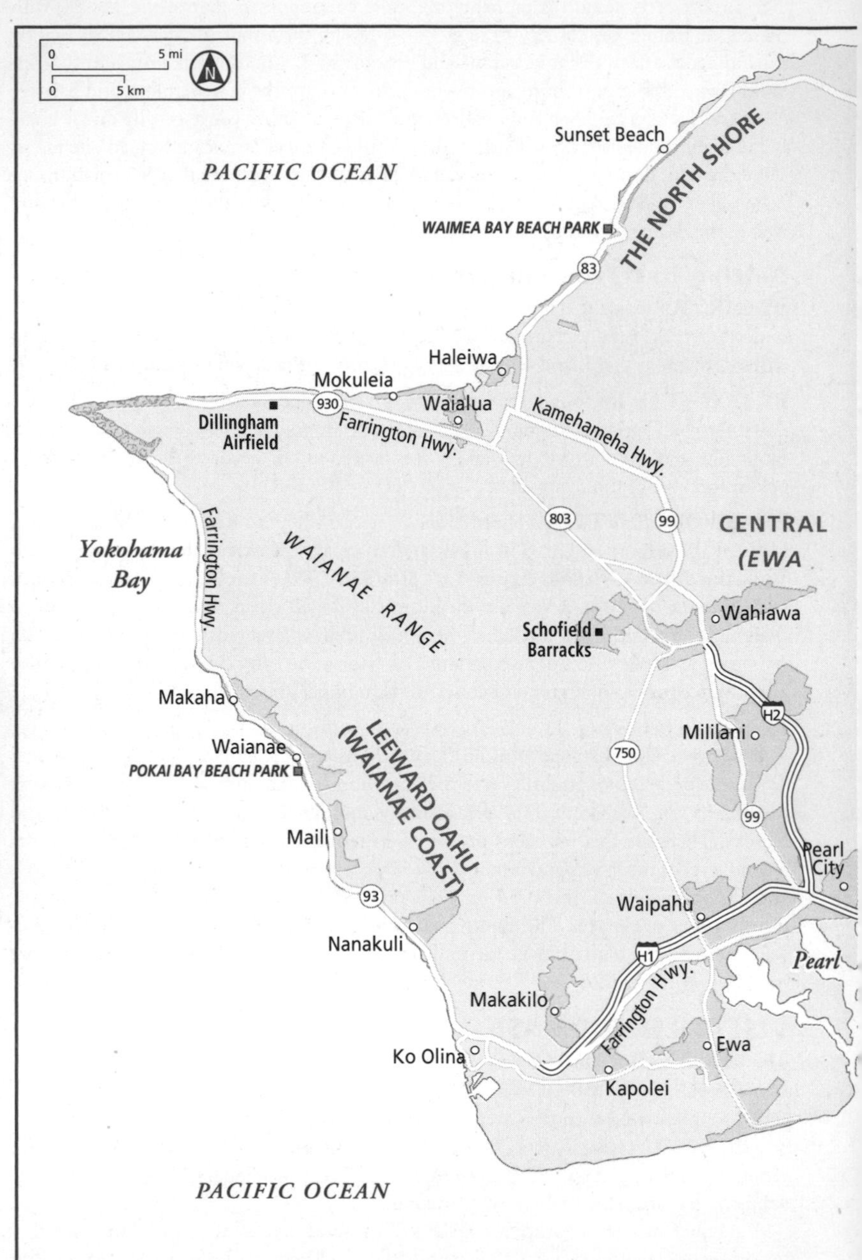
0
5 mi
0
5 km
N
PACIFIC OCEAN
Sunset Beach
THE NORTH SHORE
WAIMEA BAY BEACH PARK
83
Haleiwa
Mokuleia
Waialua
930
Dillingham Airfield
Farrington Hwy.
Kamehameha Hwy.
803
99
CENTRAL (EWA
Yokohama Bay
Farrington Hwy.
WAIANAE RANGE
Wahiawa
Schofield Barracks
Makaha
H2
Mililani
Waianae
POKAI BAY BEACH PARK
LEEWARD OAHU (WAIANAE COAST)
750
99
Maili
Pearl City
93
Waipahu
Nanakuli
H1
Pearl
Farrington Hwy.
Makakilo
Ewa
Ko Olina
Kapolei
PACIFIC OCEAN

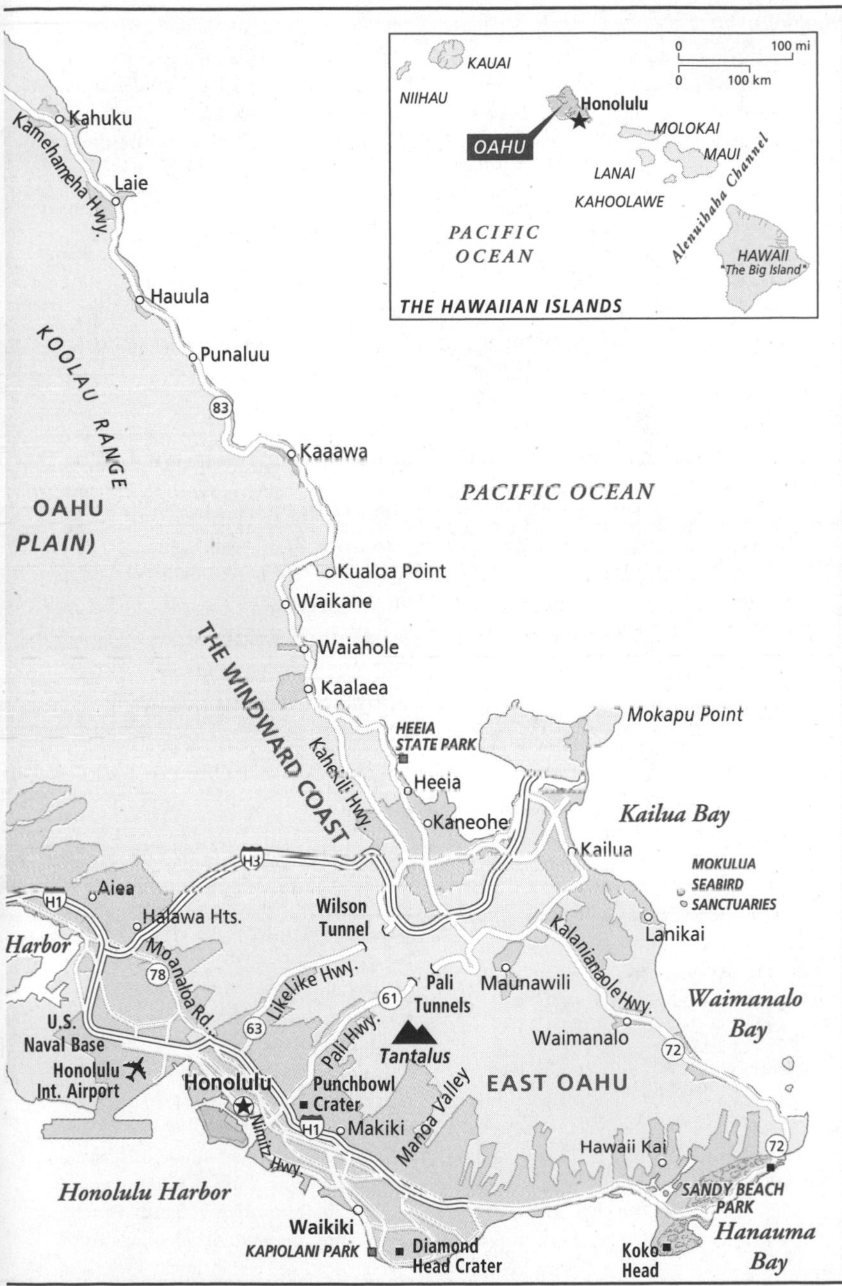

KAUAI
NIIHAU
Honolulu
OAHU
MOLOKAI
MAUI
LANAI
KAHOOLAWE
Alenuihaha Channel
PACIFIC OCEAN
HAWAII "The Big Island"
0 100 mi
0 100 km
THE HAWAIIAN ISLANDS
Kahuku
Kamehameha Hwy.
Laie
Hauula
Punaluu
KOOLAU RANGE
83
Kaaawa
PACIFIC OCEAN
OAHU
PLAIN)
Kualoa Point
Waikane
THE WINDWARD COAST
Waiahole
Kaalaea
Mokapu Point
HEEIA STATE PARK
Kahekili Hwy.
Heeia
Kaneohe
Kailua Bay
Kailua
H3
MOKULUA SEABIRD SANCTUARIES
H1
Aiea
Halawa Hts.
Wilson Tunnel
Lanikai
Harbor
Moanaloa Rd.
Kalanianaole Hwy.
78
Likelike Hwy.
Pali Tunnels
Maunawili
61
Waimanalo Bay
U.S. Naval Base
63
Pali Hwy.
Waimanalo
Tantalus
72
Honolulu Int. Airport
Honolulu
Punchbowl Crater
Manoa Valley
EAST OAHU
Nimitz Hwy.
H1
Makiki
Hawaii Kai
72
Honolulu Harbor
SANDY BEACH PARK
Waikiki
Hanauma Bay
KAPIOLANI PARK
Diamond Head Crater
Koko Head

OAHU IN BRIEF

Honolulu

Hawaii's largest city looks like any other big metropolitan center with tall buildings. But within Honolulu's boundaries, you and your family will find rainforests, deep canyons, valleys, waterfalls, a nearly mile-high mountain range, coral reefs, and gold-sand beaches. The city proper—where most of Honolulu's 850,000 residents live—is approximately 12 miles wide and 26 miles long, running east-west roughly between Diamond Head and Pearl Harbor. Within the city are seven hills laced by seven streams that run to Mamala Bay.

Waikiki ★★★ Hawaii's top resort destination is perfect for families. Some five million tourists visit Oahu every year, and 9 out of 10 of them stay in Waikiki. This urban beach is where all the action is; it's backed by 175 high-rise hotels with more than 33,000 guest rooms and hundreds of restaurants. There are dozens of different activities that kids will love, from diving under the waves in a real submarine to hiking to the top of an extinct volcano.

Ala Moana ★★ A great beach as well as a famous shopping mall, Ala Moana is the retail and transportation heart of Honolulu, a place where you can both shop and suntan in one afternoon. All bus routes lead to the open-air **Ala Moana Shopping Center,** across the street from **Ala Moana Beach Park.**

Downtown ★★ A tiny cluster of high-rises west of Waikiki, downtown Honolulu is the financial, business, and government center of Hawaii. On the waterfront stands the iconic 1926 Aloha Tower, now the centerpiece of a harborfront shopping and restaurant complex known as the **Aloha Tower Marketplace.** The whole history of Honolulu can be seen in just a few short blocks: Street vendors sell papayas from trucks on skyscraper-lined concrete canyons; joggers and BMWs rush by a lacy palace where U.S. Marines overthrew Hawaii's last queen and stole her kingdom; burly bus drivers sport fragrant white ginger flowers on their dashboards; Methodist churches look like Asian temples; and businessmen wear aloha shirts to billion-dollar meetings.

Manoa Valley ★ First inhabited by white settlers, the Manoa Valley above Waikiki still has vintage *kamaaina* (native-born) homes, one of Hawaii's premier botanical gardens in the Lyon Arboretum, the ever-gushing Manoa Falls, and the 320-acre campus of the University of Hawaii, where 50,000 students hit the books when they're not on the beach.

To the East: Kahala Except for the estates of millionaires and the luxurious Kahala Hotel (home of Hoku's, an outstanding beachfront restaurant), there's not much out this way that's of interest to visitors.

East Oahu

Beyond Kahala lies East Honolulu and suburban bedroom communities like Aina Haina, Niu Valley, and Hawaii Kai, among others, all linked by the Kalanianaole Highway and loaded with homes, condos, fast-food joints, and shopping malls. It looks like Southern California on a good day. There are only a few reasons to come here: to have dinner at **Roy's Restaurant,** the original and still outstanding Hawaiian Regional Cuisine restaurant in Hawaii Kai; to snorkel at **Hanauma Bay** or watch daredevil surfers at **Sandy Beach;** or to enjoy the natural splendor of the lovely coastline, which might include a hike to **Makapuu Lighthouse.**

The Windward Coast

Get out of Waikiki and take the family to the opposite side of the island from Waikiki, the windward coast. On this coast, trade winds blow cooling breezes over gorgeous beaches; rain squalls inspire lush, tropical vegetation; and miles of subdivisions dot the landscape. Vacations here are spent enjoying ocean activities and exploring the surrounding areas. Waikiki is just a 25-minute drive away.

Kailua ★ The biggest little beach town in Hawaii, Kailua sits at the foot of the sheer green Koolau Mountains, on a great bay with two of Hawaii's best beaches. The town itself is a funky low-rise cluster of timeworn shops, vacation homes, and B&Bs.

Kaneohe ★ Helter skelter suburbia sprawls around the edges of Kaneohe, one of the most scenic bays in the Pacific. A handful of B&Bs dots its edge. After you clear the trafficky maze of town, Oahu returns to its more natural state.

Kualoa/Laie ★★ Don't miss the upper northeast shore, one of Oahu's most sacred places, an early Hawaiian landing spot where kings dipped their sails, cliffs hold ancient burial sites, and ghosts still march in the night. Sheer cliffs stab the reef-fringed seacoast, while old fishponds are tucked along the two-lane coast road that winds past empty gold-sand beaches around beautiful Kahana Bay. Thousands "explore" the South Pacific at the **Polynesian Cultural Center,** in Laie, a Mormon settlement with its own Tabernacle Choir of sweet Samoan harmony.

The North Shore ★★★

Here's the Hawaii of Hollywood—giant waves, surfers galore, tropical jungles, waterfalls, and mysterious Hawaiian temples. If you're looking for a quieter family vacation, closer to nature and filled with swimming, snorkeling, diving, surfing, or just plain hanging out on some of the world's most beautiful beaches, the North Shore is your place. The artsy little beach town of **Haleiwa ★★** and the surrounding shoreline seem a world away from Waikiki. The North Shore boasts good restaurants, shopping, and cultural activities—but here they come with the quiet of country living. ***Be forewarned:*** It's a long trip—nearly an hour's drive—to Honolulu and Waikiki, and it's about twice as rainy on the North Shore as in Honolulu.

Central Oahu: The Ewa Plain

Flanked by the Koolau and Waianae mountain ranges, the hot, sun-baked Ewa Plain runs up and down the center of Oahu. Once covered with sandalwood forests (hacked down for the China trade), and later the sugar-cane

Tips — Finding Your Way Around, Oahu-Style

Mainlanders sometimes find the directions given by locals a bit confusing. Seldom will you hear the terms *east, west, north, and south;* instead, islanders refer to directions as either ***makai*** (ma-*kae*), meaning toward the sea, or ***mauka*** (*mow*-kah), toward the mountains. In Honolulu, people use **Diamond Head** as a direction meaning to the east (in the direction of the world-famous crater called Diamond Head), and **Ewa** as a direction meaning to the west (toward the town called Ewa, on the other side of Pearl Harbor).

So, if you ask a local for directions, this is what you're likely to hear: "Drive 2 blocks makai [toward the sea], then turn Diamond Head [east] at the stoplight. Go 1 block, and turn mauka [toward the mountains]. It's on the Ewa [western] side of the street."

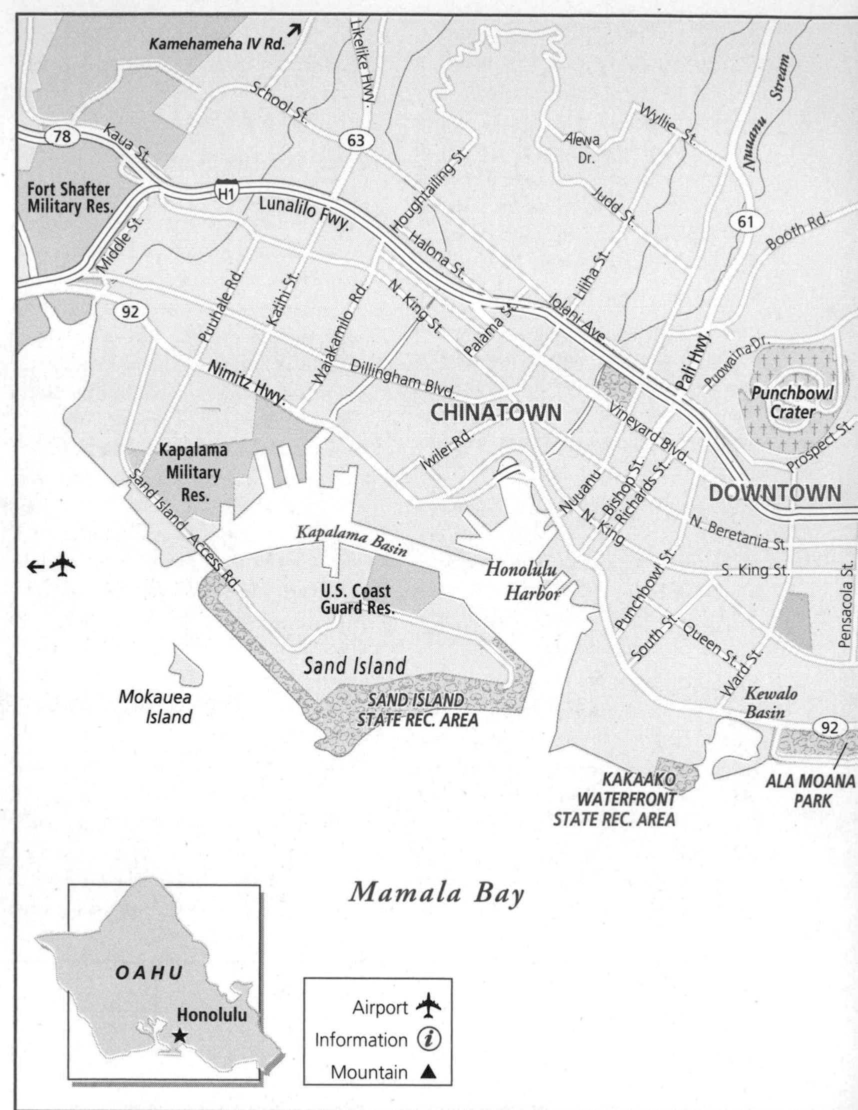

and pineapple backbone of Hawaii, Ewa today sports a new crop: suburban houses stretching to the sea. But let your eyes wander west to the Waianae Range and Mount Kaala, at 4,020 feet the highest summit on Oahu; up there in the misty rainforest, native birds thrive in the hummocky bog.

Leeward Oahu: The Waianae Coast

The west coast of Oahu is a hot and dry place of dramatic beauty: white-sand beaches bordering the deep blue ocean,

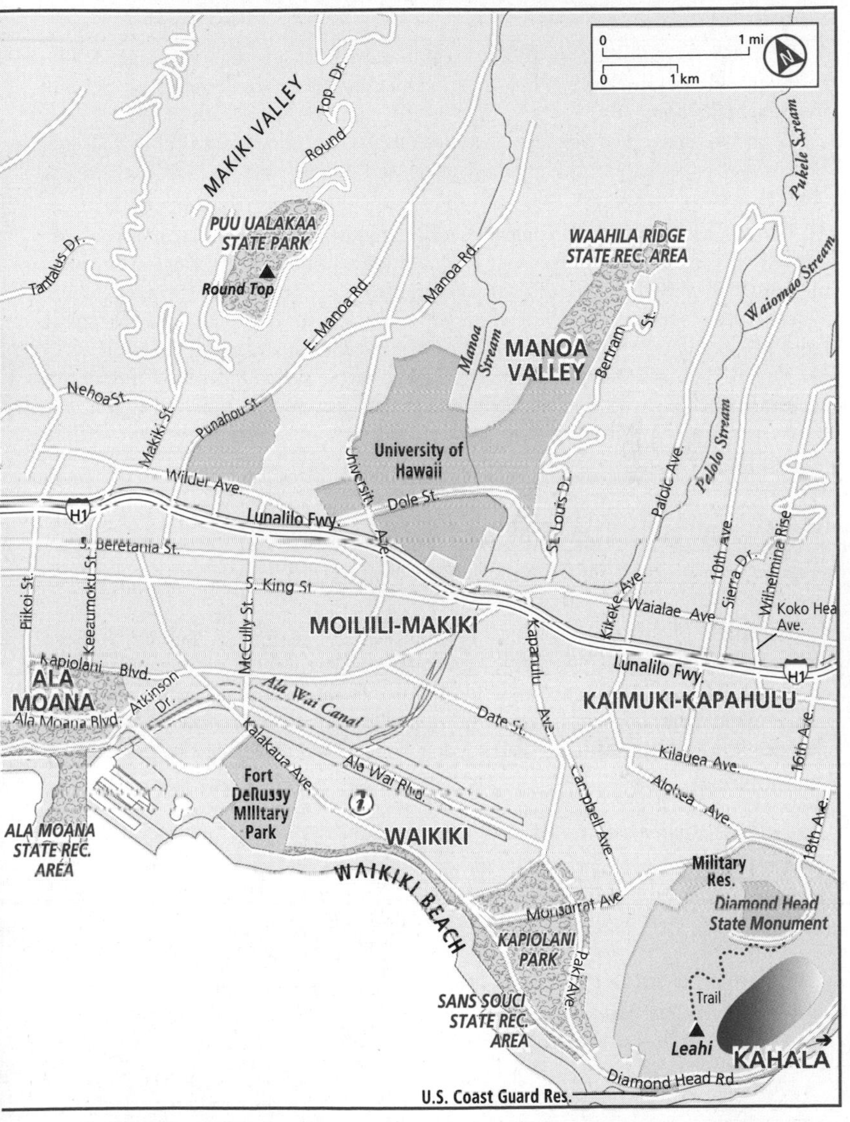

steep, verdant green cliffs, and miles of Mother Nature's wildness. Except for the luxurious JW Marriott Ihilani Resort & Spa at Ko Olina, you'll find virtually no tourist services out here. This side of Oahu is seldom visited, except by surfers and those coming to see needle-nosed **Kaena Point** (the island's westernmost outpost), which has a coastal wilderness park.

2 GETTING AROUND

BY CAR Oahu residents own 600,000 registered vehicles, but they have only 1,500 miles of mostly two-lane roads to use. You can avoid the gridlock by driving between 9am and 3pm or after 6pm.

All the major car rental firms have agencies on Oahu, at the airport, and in Waikiki. For a complete list, as well as tips on insurance and driving rules, see "By Car" under "Getting Around Hawaii," in chapter 2.

BY TAXI Oahu's major cab companies offer islandwide, 24-hour, radio-dispatched service, with multilingual drivers and air-conditioned cars, limos, vans, and vehicles equipped with wheelchair lifts. (There's no charge for wheelchairs.) Fares are standard for all taxi firms; from the airport, expect to pay about $35 to $45 (plus tip) to Waikiki, about $30 to $40 to downtown, about $55 to $65 to Kailua, about $55 to Hawaii Kai, and about $95 to $125 to the North Shore. For a flat fee of $30, **Star Taxi Hawaii** ★ (✆ **808/942-7827;** www.startaxihawaii.com) will take up to four passengers from the airport to Waikiki (with no extra charges for baggage); however, you must book in advance. After you have arrived and before you pick up your luggage, call Star again to make sure that they will be outside waiting for you when your luggage arrives.

For a metered cab, try **Charley's Taxi & Tours** (✆ 808/531-1333), **City Taxi** (✆ 808/524-2121), or **TheCab** (✆ 808/422-2222). **Coast Taxi** (✆ 808/261-3755) serves windward Oahu, and **Hawaii Kai Hui/Koko Head Taxi** (✆ 808/396-6633) serves east Honolulu/southeast Oahu.

BY TROLLEY It's fun to ride the 34-seat, open-air, motorized **Waikiki Trolley** (✆ **800/824-8804** or 808/593-2822; www.waikikitrolley.com), which looks like a San Francisco cable car (see "Sightseeing Tours," later in this chapter). The trolley loops around Waikiki and downtown Honolulu, stopping every 40 minutes at 12 key places like Iolani Palace, Chinatown, the State Capitol, King Kamehameha's Statue, the Mission House Museum, the Aloha Tower, the Honolulu Academy of Arts, the Hawaii Maritime Museum, Fisherman's Wharf, and Restaurant Row. The driver provides commentary along the way. Stops on the new 2-hour, fully narrated Ocean Coast Line (the blue line) of the southeast side of Oahu include Sea Life Park, Diamond Head, and Waikiki Beach. A 1-day trolley pass—which costs $27 for adults, $20 for adults over 62, and $13 for kids ages 4 to 11—allows you to jump on and off all day long (8:30am–11:35pm). Four-day passes cost $48 for adults, $28 for seniors, and $20 for kids 4 to 11.

WHEELCHAIR TRANSPORTATION **Handicabs of the Pacific** (✆ **808/946-6666**) offers wheelchair taxi services and tours in air-conditioned vehicles that are specially equipped with ramps and wheelchair lockdowns. Handicabs offers a range of taxi services as well as tours.

Fast Facts Oahu

Airport See "Orientation," earlier in this chapter.

American Express The Honolulu office is at 1440 Kapiolani Blvd., Suite 104 (✆ **808/946-7741**), and is open Monday through Friday from 8am to 5pm. There's also an office at **Hilton Hawaiian Village,** 2005 Kalia Rd. (✆ **808/947-2607** or

808/951-0644), and one at the **Hyatt Regency Waikiki,** 2424 Kalakaua Ave. (✆ **808/926-5441**); both offer financial services daily from 8am to 8pm.

Babysitters **PATCH** (✆ **808/839-1988**) or your hotel can refer you to qualified babysitters. Many hotels use the licensed and bonded sitters of **Sitters Unlimited** (www.sittershawaii.com); if you book their services directly, their rates begin at $16 an hour for the first child, $18 per hour for two children, and $20 an hour for three children (4-hr. minimum). If you book through the hotel, rates can start at $20 an hour for just one child, and go up.

Dentists If you need a dentist on Oahu, contact the **Hawaii Dental Association** (✆ **808/593-2135;** www.hawaiidentalassociation.net).

Doctors **Doctors on Call,** 2335 Kalakaua Ave., #207, Honolulu (✆ **808/971-6000**), can dispatch a van if you need help getting to the main clinic or to any of their additional clinics in Waikiki: **Outrigger Waikiki Hotel,** 2335 Kalakaua Ave. (✆ 808/971-6000), daily, 24 hours; **Hawaiian Regent Hotel,** 2552 Kalakaua Ave., Kuhio Tower, 2nd Floor (✆ 808/971-6000), Monday to Friday 8am to 4:30pm; **Hyatt Regency Waikiki,** 2424 Kalakaua Ave., Diamond Head Tower, 4th Floor (✆ 808/971-8001), Monday to Friday 8am to 4pm; **Royal Hawaiian Hotel,** 2259 Kalakaua Ave., Lower Arcade (✆ 808/923-4499), daily 8am to 5pm.

Emergencies Call ✆ **911** for police, fire, and ambulance.

Hospitals Hospitals offering 24-hour emergency care include **Queens Medical Center,** 1301 Punchbowl St. (✆ 808/538-9011); **Kuakini Medical Center,** 347 Kuakini St. (✆ 808/536-2236); **Straub Clinic and Hospital,** 888 S. King St. (✆ 808/522-4000); **Kapiolani Medical Center for Women and Children,** 1319 Punahou St. (✆ 808/973-8511); and **Kapiolani Medical Center** at Pali Momi, 98-1079 Moanalua Rd. (✆ 808/486-6000). Central Oahu has **Wahiawa General Hospital,** 128 Lehua St. (✆ 808/621-8411). On the windward side is **Castle Medical Center,** 640 Ulukahiki St., Kailua (✆ 808/263-5500).

Internet Access ShakaNet, www.shaka.net, Hawaii's largest wireless Internet service provider, has completed the first phase of its free Wireless Waikiki network. Phase I covers a significant portion of Waikiki and includes an estimated 1,000 hotel rooms, portions of the Honolulu Zoo, Kapi'olani Park, Queens Beach, Kuhio Beach, and the adjacent shoreline. The boundaries of Phase I are roughly Kalakaua Avenue from Liliuokalani Avenue to Queen's Beach in the Diamond Head direction, and Liliuokalani Avenue/Kuhio Avenue on the Ewa side, down Kuhio Avenue across Kapiolani Park to Monsarrat Avenue.

Newspapers The *Honolulu Advertiser* and *Honolulu Star-Bulletin* are Oahu's daily papers. *Pacific Business News* and *Honolulu Weekly* are weekly papers. *Honolulu Weekly,* available free at restaurants, clubs, shops, and newspaper racks around Oahu, is the best source for what's going on around town.

Post Office The downtown branch is in the old U.S. Post Office, Customs & Court House Building (referred to as the "old Federal Building") at 335 Merchant St., across from Iolani Palace and next to the Kamehameha Statue (bus: 2). Other branch offices include the Waikiki Post Office, 330 Saratoga Ave. (Diamond Head side of Fort DeRussy; bus: 19 or 20); and the Ala Moana Shopping Center (bus: 8, 19, or 20). For other locations, call ✆ **800/275-8777.**

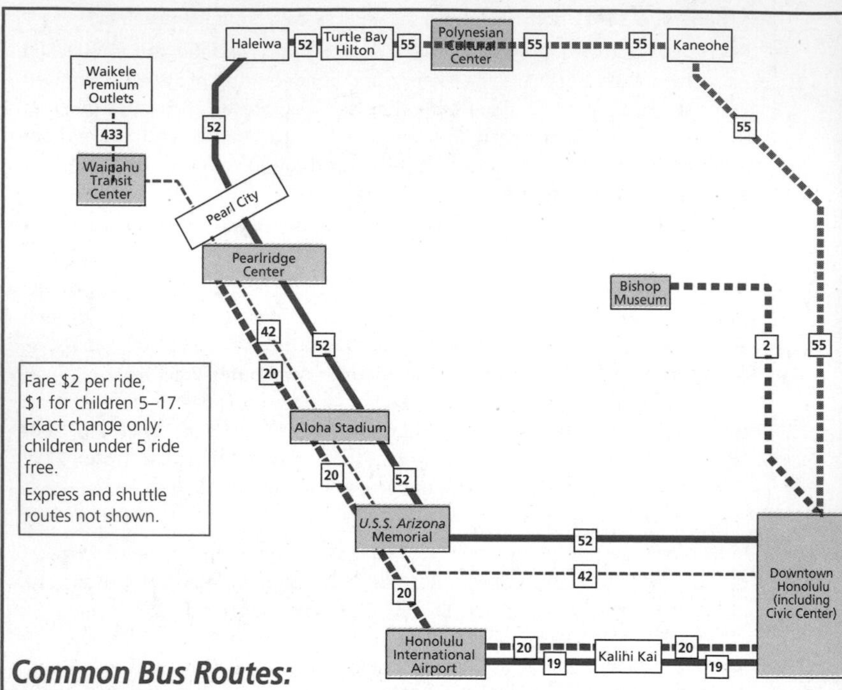

Common Bus Routes:

Ala Moana Shopping Center: Take bus #19 & #20 AIRPORT. Return via #19 WAIKIKI, or cross Ala Moana Blvd. for #20.

Bishop Museum: Take #2 SCHOOL STREET. Get off at Kapalama St., cross School St., walk down Bernice St. Return to School St. and take #2 WAIKIKI.

Circle Island: Take a bus to ALA MOANA CENTER (TRF) to #52 WAHIAWA CIRCLE ISLAND or #55 KANEOHE CIRCLE ISLAND. This is a 4-hour bus ride.

Chinatown or Downtown: Take any #2 bus going out of Waikiki to Hotel St. Return, take #2 WAIKIKI on Hotel St., or #19 or #20 on King St.

Diamond Head Crater: Take #22 HAWAII KAI-SEA LIFE PARK to the crater. Take a flashlight. Return to the same area and take #22 WAIKIKI.

Dole Pineapple Plantation: Take bus to ALA MOANA CENTER (TRF) to #52 WAHIAWA CIRCLE ISLAND.

Aloha Tower Marketplace & Hawaii Maritime Center: Take #19-#20 AIRPORT and get off at Alakea–Ala Moana. Cross the street to the Aloha Tower.

Honolulu Zoo: Take any bus on Kuhio Ave. going DIAMOND HEAD direction to Kapahulu Ave.

Radio Major stations include **KINE** 105 FM, which plays traditional and contemporary Hawaiian music; **KCCN** 100 FM, contemporary Hawaiian and reggae; **KQMG** 93.5 FM/57 AM, Hawaiian and Top 40; and **KRATER** 96 FM, Hawaiian, Top 40, and soft rock. For news and talk radio, tune to **KHNR** 650 AM; for sports, try **KKEA** 1420 AM. Children's radio is at **KORL** 690 AM, and **KHPR** public radio can be found at 88.1 FM or 90.7 FM.

Safety Honolulu is like any other big city—there is crime. Women should beware of purse snatching, in which thieves in slow-moving cars or on foot snatch

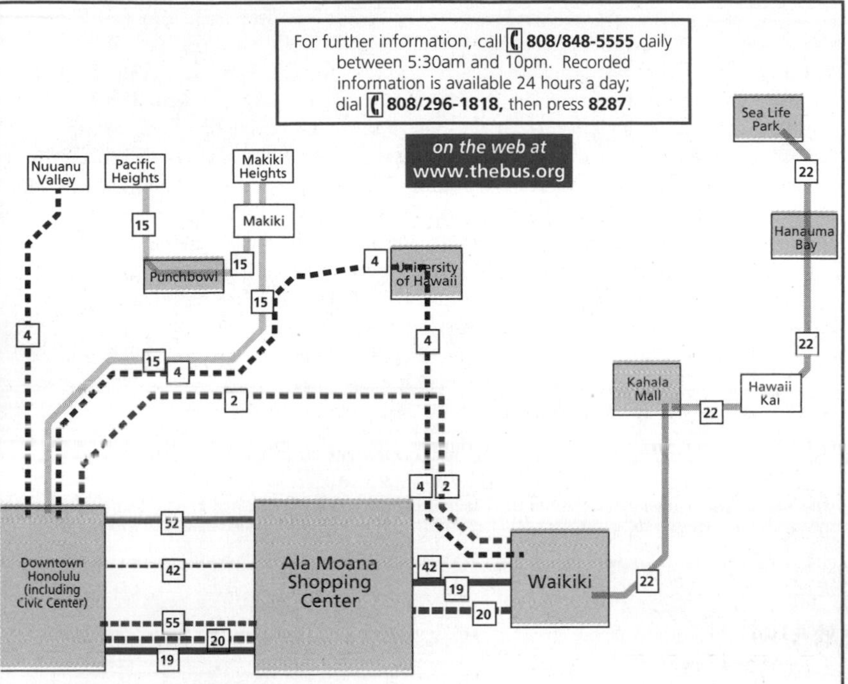

Iolani Palace (also **State Capitol and Kamehameha Statu**) Take any #2 bus and get off at Punchbowl and Beretania St. Walk to King St. Return #2 WAIKIKI on King St.

Kahala Mall: Take #22 HAWAII KAI–SEA LIFE PARK to Kilauea Ave. Return, #22 WAIKIKI.

Pearl Harbor (*Arizona* Memorial): Take #20 AIRPORT. Get off across from Memorial, or take a bus to ALA MOANA CENTER (TRF) to #52.

Polynesian Cultural Center: Take a bus to ALA MOANA CENTER (TRF) to #55 KANEOHE CIRCLE ISLAND. Bus ride takes 2 hours one-way.

Sea Life Park: Take #22 HAWAII KAI-SEA LIFE PARK. #22 will stop at Hanauma Bay en route to the park.

University of Hawaii: Take #4 NUUANU. The bus will go to the University en route to Nuuanu.

Waimea Valley & Adventure Park: Take a bus to ALA MOANA CENTER (TRF) to #52 WAHIAWA CIRCLE ISLAND or #55 KANEOHE CIRCLE ISLAND.

Waikele Premium Outlets: Take bus #42 from Waikiki to Wapahu Transit Center, then bus #433 to Waikele.

handbags from female pedestrians (in some instances, dragging women who refuse to let go of their pocketbooks down the street). The Honolulu police department advises women to carry their purses on the shoulder away from the street or, better yet, to wear the strap across the chest instead of on one shoulder. Women with clutch bags should hold them close to their chest.

Useful Telephone Numbers For National Weather Service recorded forecasts for Honolulu, call ✆ **808/973-4380;** for elsewhere on the island, call ✆ **808/973-4381.** For marine reports, call ✆ **808/973-4382.** For surf reports, call ✆ **808/973-4383.**

3 FAMILY-FRIENDLY ACCOMMODATIONS

Before you reach for the phone to book a place to stay, consider when you'll be visiting. The high season, when hotels are full and rates are at their highest, is mid-December to March, when the weather on the U.S. Mainland is cold and yucky. The secondary high season, when rates are high but rooms are somewhat easier to come by, is June to September, when kids get a summer break from school. The low seasons—when you can expect fewer tourists and better deals—are April to June and September to mid-December. (For more on Hawaii's travel seasons, see "When to Go," in chapter 2.) No matter when you travel, you can often get the best rate at many of Waikiki's hotels by booking a package; for details, see "Packages for the Independent Traveler," in chapter 2.

See "Oahu in Brief," earlier in this chapter, for a description of each neighborhood. It can help you decide where you'd like to base yourself.

Remember that **hotel and room taxes** of 11.962% will be added to your bill (Oahu has a .005% additional tax that the other islands do not have). And don't forget about parking charges—at up to $25 a day in Waikiki, they can add up quickly.

AIRPORT HOTELS If you're arriving late at night or leaving early in the morning, consider a hotel near the airport (just for a night—this is not the place to spend your whole vacation). **Best Western—The Plaza Hotel,** 3253 N. Nimitz Hwy., Honolulu (✆ **800/780-7234** or 808/836-3636; www.bestwestern.com), has rooms from $149 up; and the **Honolulu Airport Hotel** (✆ **800/462-6262** or 808/836-0661; www.ohanahotels.com) has rooms from $145. Both offer free airport shuttle service.

WAIKIKI

Ewa Waikiki

All the hotels listed below are located from the ocean to Kalakaua Avenue, and between Ala Wai Terrace in the Ewa direction (or western side of Waikiki), and Olohana Street and Fort DeRussy Park in the Diamond Head direction (or eastern side of Waikiki).

Very Expensive

Hawaii Prince Hotel Waikiki ★★ This ultramodern structure (twin 33-story high-tech towers), with a grand piano in the midst of a pink, Italian-marble lobby, may look intimidating, but it actually is very family-friendly. During the peak family vacation period (Apr–Sept), the hotel offers a "Kids Eat Free and Golf Free" program, which can save you a bundle. Kid-savvy concierges are armed and ready with everything from advice on where to take your tots to helping your youngsters send a coconut to a friend. They will even provide free strollers for use around town.

The kids will be fascinated with the glass-encased elevator with views of all of Honolulu. All guest rooms face the Ala Wai Yacht Harbor, with floor-to-ceiling sliding-glass windows that let you enjoy the view (sorry, no balconies, or as we call them in Hawaii, lanai). All of the comfortably appointed rooms are basically the same, but the higher the floor, the higher the price. Although the rooms can accommodate a rollaway or a crib, if the kids are older, I'd recommend a connecting room or a junior suite with a large separate bedroom and a living room with a daybed.

Following Japanese standards, the level of service is impeccable; no detail is ignored, and no request is too large. The location is perfect for shopping—Ala Moana Center is a 10-minute walk away—and Waikiki's beaches are just a 5-minute walk away. (Both are also accessible via the hotel's own shuttle bus.)

100 Holomoana St. (just across Ala Wai Canal Bridge, on the ocean side of Ala Moana Blvd.), Honolulu, HI 96815. ✆ **800/321-OAHU** (321-6248) or 808/956-1111. Fax 808/946-0811. www.princeresortshawaii.com. 521 units. $390–$520 double; from $610 suite. Extra person $60. Children 17 and under stay free in parent's room. Cribs free; rollaway beds $35 per day. AE, DC, MC, V. Valet parking $21; self-parking $15. Bus: 19 or 20. **Amenities:** 2 excellent restaurants; outdoor bar; outdoor pool; 27-hole golf club a 30-min. drive away in Ewa Beach (reached by hotel shuttle); small but newly renovated fitness room; Jacuzzi; concierge; car rental desk; business center; room service (6am–10pm); babysitting; laundry service; dry cleaning; executive-level rooms. *In room:* A/C, TV, dataport, fridge, coffeemaker, hair dryer, iron, safe.

Hilton Hawaiian Village Beach Resort & Spa ★★ Sprawling over 22 acres, this is Waikiki's biggest resort—a minicity unto itself, so big it even has its own post office. This is a great place to stay with the kids. You'll find tropical gardens dotted with exotic wildlife (pink flamingos, painted ducks, and even South African penguins), award-winning restaurants (kids eat free with a paying adult at the Tapa Café and The Rainbow Lani restaurants, which are set up to handle families), 100 different shops, a secluded lagoon, two minigolf courses, and a gorgeous stretch of Waikiki Beach.

There's a wide choice of accommodations. Rooms, which range from simply lovely to ultradeluxe, are housed in five towers. Despite the hotel's mega-Vegas size, this division into towers, each with its own restaurants and shopping, cuts down on the chaotic, impersonal feeling that might have resulted. Still, this is the place for a lively, activity-packed vacation; those seeking a more intimate experience might want to look elsewhere.

Cribs and rollaway beds can fit into any room, and a family with primary-school-age children will be comfortable with a single room. One room is fine if your kids are small, but if you have teenagers, the price of an extra room (and extra bathroom) is worth paying.

As with most Hiltons, the programs for kids ages 5 to 12 (the Rainbow Express Keiki Club) are open 7 days a week and offer a range of excursions and activities. Plus there are plenty of family activities like lei making, hula lessons, coconut weaving, and ukulele lessons. Every room has movies available, plus Nintendo games and MSNTV. The hotel also has a wide selection of children's board games and toddler toys your kids can borrow for a day and take back to their rooms. The Rainbow Express Keiki Club, the resort's children's program, is $50 for a half-day and $80 full day.

2005 Kalia Rd. (at Ala Moana Blvd.), Honolulu, HI 96815. ✆ **800/HILTONS** (445-8667) or 808/949-4321. Fax 808/947-7898. www.hawaiianvillage.hilton.com. 2,904 units. $279–$429 double; from $449 suite. Extra person (over 4 adults) $50. Children 18 and under stay free in parent's room. Package deals start as low as $189. Cribs and rollaway beds free. AE, DISC, MC, V. Valet parking $28; self-parking $20. Bus: 19 or 20. **Amenities:** 22 restaurants; 6 bars; 5 outdoor pools; health club w/high-tech equipment; superplush Mandara Spa; watersports equipment/rentals; year-round children's program (one of Waikiki's best); concierge; activities desk; car rental desk; 24-hr. business center; huge shopping arcade; salon; room service (6am–11pm); in-room massage; babysitting; same-day laundry service; dry cleaning; concierge-level rooms. *In room:* A/C, TV, dataport, fridge, coffeemaker, hair dryer, iron, safe.

Expensive

Doubletree Alana Hotel–Waikiki ★ This boutique hotel is a welcome oasis of beauty, comfort, and prompt service. It's an intimate choice, offering the amenities of a much larger, more luxurious hotel at more affordable prices. The guest rooms are comfortable and homey; some of the rooms can be small but make good use of the space and offer all the amenities you'd expect from a more expensive hotel. If you're with

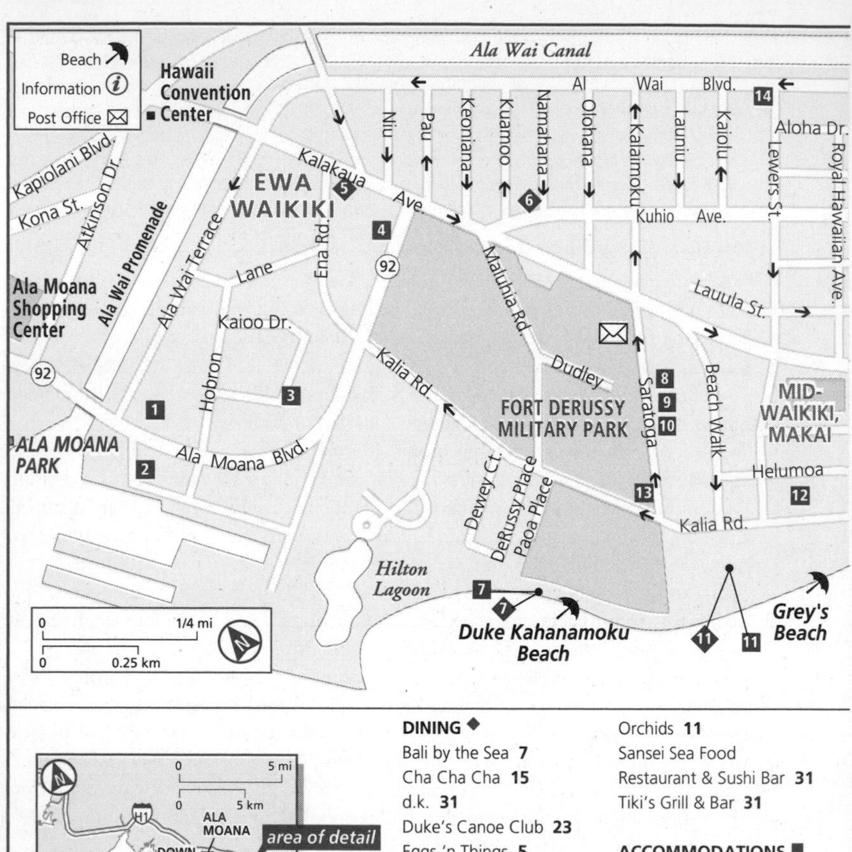

DINING ◆

Bali by the Sea **7**
Cha Cha Cha **15**
d.k. **31**
Duke's Canoe Club **23**
Eggs 'n Things **5**
Hau Tree lanai **33**
Hula Grill Waikiki **23**
Keo's in Waikiki **6**
La Mer **11**
MAC 24-7 **27**
Orchids **11**
Sansei Sea Food Restaurant & Sushi Bar **31**
Tiki's Grill & Bar **31**

ACCOMMODATIONS ■

Aloha Punawai **8**
Aqua Bamboo **19**
Aqua Coconut Plaza **14**
Aqua Waikiki Wave **16**
The Breakers **10**

small children, book a suite (which has a separate bedroom and a pullout sofa in the living room); for older children, two rooms would offer more space. Many guests are business travelers who expect top-drawer service—and the Alana Waikiki delivers. The staff is attentive to detail and willing to go to any lengths to make sure your family is happy. Waikiki Beach is a 10-minute walk away and the Convention Center is about a 7-minute walk.

1956 Ala Moana Blvd. (on the Ewa side, near Kalakaua Ave.), Honolulu, HI 96815. ✆ **800/222-TREE** (222-8733) or 808/941-7275. Fax 808/949-0996. www.doubletreealana.com. 317 units. $189–$279 double; from $229 suite. Extra person $40. Children 17 and under stay free in parent's room. Cribs and rollaway beds free. AE, DC, DISC, MC, V. Valet parking $22. Bus: 19 or 20. **Amenities:** Excellent restaurant; bar; outdoor heated pool; poolside health club w/sauna and massage services; concierge; activities desk; car

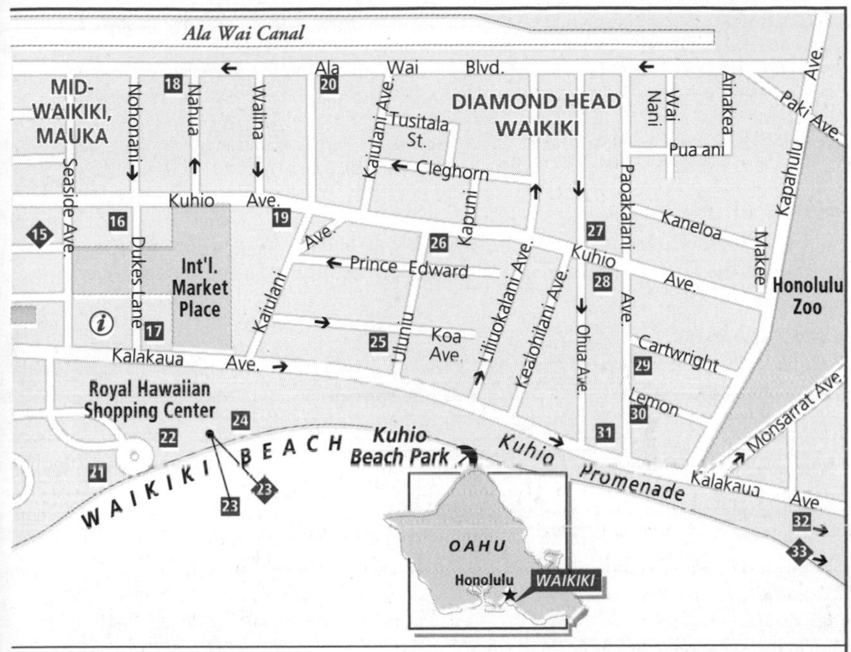

Doubletree Alana Hotel – Waikiki **4**
Embassy Suites Hotel – Waikiki Beach Walk **13**
Equus **1**
Halekulani **11**
Hawaii Prince Hotel Waikiki **2**
Hawaiiana Hotel **9**
Hilton Hawaiian Village Beach Resort & Spa **7**
Hilton Waikiki Prince Kuhio **27**
Holiday Inn Waikiki **3**
Hotel Renew **29**
Hyatt Regency Waikiki **25**
Ilima Hotel **18**
Moana Surfrider Resort, A Westin Resort **24**
New Otani Kaimana Beach Hotel **32**
Ohana Waikiki Beachcomber **17**
Outrigger Waikiki on the Beach **23**
ResortQuest at the Waikiki Banyan **28**
ResortQuest Waikiki Beach Hotel **30**
Royal Grove Hotel **26**
Royal Hawaiian **22**
Sheraton Waikiki **21**
W Honolulu **32**
Waikiki Beach Marriott **31**
Waikiki Parc **12**
Waikiki Sand Villa **20**

rental desk; well-equipped business center; room service (6am–10pm); in-room massage; babysitting; laundry service; dry cleaning. *In room:* A/C, TV, dataport, fridge, coffeemaker, hair dryer, iron, safe.

Inexpensive

The Equus Formerly the Hawaii Polo Inn, now under the management of the Aqua Hotels and Resorts, this small boutique hotel has been renovated and upgraded into a very comfortable inn within walking distance to the Ala Moana Shopping Center, Waikiki Beach, and the Hawaii Convention Center. The small suites have microwaves and hot plates. A few years ago, the management added additional studio units (with kitchenettes, two-burner stove, dishwasher, microwave, and such) next door at the condo-hotel, Aqua Marina Hotel). Individual hotel rooms may be too small for a family; I'd suggest going with the studio with kitchenettes located next door if you need more room. ***Warning:*** Ala Moana Boulevard is very noisy; ask for a room in the back or bring earplugs.

1696 Ala Moana Blvd. (btw Hobron Lane and Ala Wai Canal), Honolulu, HI 96815. ✆ **866/406-2782** or 808/949-0061. Fax 808/949-4906. www.aquaresorts.com/aqua-equus. Managed by Aqua Hotels and Resorts. 68 units, with shower only. $89–$149 double hotel rooms with complimentary continental breakfast; $89–$159 studios with kitchenettes next door. Extra person $25 per night both properties.. AE, DC, DISC, MC, V. Parking $18. Bus: 19 or 20. **Amenities:** Tiny outdoor wading pool; activities desk; car rental desk; coin-op washer/dryers. *In room:* A/C, TV, free wireless Internet access, fridge, microwave, coffeemaker, hair dryer and iron and safe all available at the front desk, daily newspaper.

Mid-Waikiki, Makai

All the hotels listed below are between Kalakaua Avenue and the ocean, and between Fort DeRussy in the Ewa (west) direction and Kaiulani Street in the Diamond Head (east) direction.

Very Expensive

Halekulani ★★★ Here's the ultimate heavenly Hawaii vacation. Halekulani translates as "House Befitting Heaven"—an apt description of this luxury resort, selected the number one hotel in the world by *Gourmet* magazine. It's spread over 5 acres of prime Waikiki beachfront in five buildings that are connected by open courtyards and lush, tropical gardens. Upon arrival, you're immediately greeted and escorted to your room, where registration is handled in comfort and privacy.

Many things set this luxury hotel apart from the others, the most important being the rooms: About 90% face the ocean, and they're big (averaging 620 sq. ft.), each with a separate sitting area and a large, furnished lanai. There's plenty of room for a crib or a rollaway; but the rooms are limited to a maximum of three people, so larger families should look at connecting rooms or a suite.

One of the best children's programs in Waikiki tops the list of amenities. For only $50 a day, the kids get lunch and excursions (via a chauffeur-driven stretch limo) to places like Bishop Museum or the Waikiki Aquarium. Unfortunately, it is offered only during the summer and at Christmastime. Teens can book into the SpaHalekulani Teen programs, which include a makeup lesson ($65), a minifacial ($75), and even "too cool tattoos" with temporary body art ($20). For parents, perks include complimentary tickets to any or all of the following: Ihilani Palace, Bishop Museum, Contemporary Art Museum, Honolulu Academy of Art, and the Honolulu Symphony (about $100 per person worth of art and culture). You can't find a better location on Waikiki Beach or a more luxurious hotel.

2199 Kalia Rd. (at the ocean end of Lewers St.), Honolulu, HI 96815. ✆ **800/367-2343** or 808/923-2311. Fax 808/926-8004. www.halekulani.com. 455 units. $445–$555 double; from $875 suite. Extra person $125. 1 child 16 or under stays free in parent's room using existing bedding. Rollaway beds $40. Maximum 3 people per room. AE, DC, MC, V. Self-parking $22; complimentary valet. Bus: 19 or 20. **Amenities:** 4 superb restaurants; 2 bars; gorgeous outdoor pool; fitness center; spa; watersports equipment/rentals; bike rentals; seasonal children's program; concierge; activities desk; complete business center; top-drawer shopping arcade; salon; 24-hr. room service; in-room massage; babysitting; same-day laundry service and dry cleaning. *In room:* A/C, TV/VCR, dataport, minibar, hair dryer, iron, safe.

Royal Hawaiian ★★ This flamingo-pink oasis, hidden away among blooming gardens within the concrete jungle of Waikiki, is a symbol of luxury. Entry into the hotel is past the lush gardens, with their spectacular banyan tree, into the black terrazzo-marble lobby, which features hand-woven pink carpets and giant floral arrangements. It's comfy beyond belief and very welcoming to families: Each one of your little darlings will get a candy lei and a pair of sunglasses when they check in. I'd recommend booking connecting rooms in the Historic Wing, straight out of the 1920s, when steamships sailed to Hawaii. The rooms feature carved wooden entry doors, four-poster canopy beds, flowered wallpaper, and period furniture. The older kids, say 12 and above, will really love it here. Check for special package rates, when at certain times of the year they offer as much as 35% off rack rates and meals. (In fact, you can get a deal in which kids 12 and younger eat free with a paying adult.)

In the culinary department, the Surf Room is the place to take the kids. Not only is it known for its elaborate seafood buffets, but it also has child-friendly amenities such as a kids' menu, highchairs, and booster seats. The hotel also offers the year-round Keiki Aloha Program, which features activities that families can do together (including excursions) and a complete child-care program with a range of activities for children ages 5 to 12.

If you have especially active kids and need to do laundry every other day, coin-operated washers and dryers are located next door at the mammoth Sheraton Waikiki. (See review below.)

2259 Kalakaua Ave. (at Royal Hawaiian Ave., on the ocean side of the Royal Hawaiian Shopping Center), Honolulu, HI 96815. ✆ **800/325-3535** or 808/923-7311. Fax 808/924-7098. www.royal-hawaiian.com. 527 units. $299–$745 double; from $570 suite (check for deals). Extra person $100. Cribs free; rollaway beds $100. AE, MC, V. Valet parking $25; self-parking at Sheraton Waikiki $15. Bus: 19 or 20. **Amenities:** 2 restaurants; landmark bar; good-size outdoor pool; preferential tee times at various golf courses; nearby health club (next door at the Sheraton Waikiki); excellent full-service spa (Abhasa), one of Waikiki's best; watersports equipment/rentals; bike rentals; excellent year-round children's program ($30 full day, $20 half-day); game room; multilingual concierge desk; activities desk; car rental desk; business center; elegant shopping arcade; 24-hr. room service; in-room massage; babysitting; 24-hr. laundry service and dry cleaning (except Sun). *In room:* A/C, TV, high-speed Internet $14/day, fridge, hair dryer, iron, safe.

Sheraton Waikiki ★ Occupying two 30-story towers, this is by far the biggest of the four Sheratons on the beach. It's hard to get a bad room here: A whopping 1,200 units have some sort of ocean view, and 650 rooms overlook Diamond Head. Accommodations are spacious, with big lanais to take in those magnificent views. You can easily fit a rollaway bed or a crib into the rooms, but if you're traveling with teens, look for connecting rooms. The lobby and the entire property are immense and filled with shops, travel desks, and people. Your kids could get lost just walking from the Ocean Terrace (the best restaurant on the property for kids) back to your room. Not surprisingly, this hotel hosts numerous conventions; if you're not comfortable with crowds and conventioneers, book elsewhere. However, size has its advantages: The Sheraton has everything from a fabulous children's program (and a swimming pool just for kids) to historical walks and cooking demonstrations for Mom and Dad. Plus, the concierges are great at recommending activities for families.

2255 Kalakaua Ave. (at Royal Hawaiian Ave., on the ocean side of the Royal Hawaiian Shopping Center and west of the Royal Hawaiian), Honolulu, HI 96815. ✆ **800/325-3535** or 808/922-4422. Fax 808/923-8785. www.sheraton-waikiki.com. 1,852 units; $285–$605 double; from $735 suite. Extra person $75. Children 17 and under stay free in parent's room. Cribs free; rollaway beds $80. AE, DC, DISC, MC, V. Valet parking $26; self-parking $20. Bus: 19 or 20. **Amenities:** 4 restaurants; 3 bars; nightclub; 2 large outdoor pools, including one of the biggest and sunniest along the Waikiki beachfront; access to Makaha Golf Club's golf and tennis facilities (about 1 hr. away); health club; watersports equipment/rentals; bike rentals; children's program w/activities ranging from catamaran sailing to nightly movies; game room; concierge; activities desk; car rental desk; business center; shopping arcade; room service (6am–midnight); in-room massage; babysitting; coin-op laundry; same-day laundry service and dry cleaning (except holidays). *In room:* A/C, TV, dataport, kitchenette, minibar, fridge, coffeemaker, hair dryer, iron, safe.

Expensive

Moana Surfrider Resort, A Westin Resort ★★ Step back in time at Waikiki's first hotel, which dates from 1901 and is listed on the National Register of Historic Places. Yesteryear lives on at this grand hotel: Entry is through the original colonial porte-cochere, past the highly polished front porch dotted with rocking chairs, and into the perfectly restored lobby with detailed millwork and intricate plasterwork. The aloha spirit that pervades this classy and charming place is infectious.

The hotel consists of three wings: the original (and totally restored) Banyan Wing, the Diamond Wing, and the Tower Wing. It's hard to get a bad room here; most have ocean views, and all come with pampering amenities such as bedside controls and plush robes. But I'm especially taken with the Banyan Wing rooms: What they lack in size (they're on the smallish side and don't have lanais), they make up for in style. If you are a family of three, a crib or rollaway will fit nicely, but if you are four or more, look to the other wings or consider two rooms for maximum comfort.

You get the feel for Old Hawaii here, with daily activities such as Hawaiian arts and crafts, coconut-palm weaving, and Hawaiian quilting; be sure to visit the Historical Room, where a variety of memorabilia is on display. Like all Sheratons, they provide a year-round children's program with activities ranging from excursions to playing on the beach.

One of the best reasons to stay here is the hotel's prime stretch of beach, with lifeguard, beach chairs, towels, and any other service you desire. The Beach Bar and a poolside snack bar are located in the oceanfront courtyard that's centered on a 100-year-old banyan tree, where there's live music in the evenings. The Beach Side Café is the perfect place for kids; they have their own menu and the waitstaff is trained to cater to their every whim.

2365 Kalakaua Ave. (ocean side of the street, across from Kaiulani St.), Honolulu, HI 96815. ✆ **800/325-3535** or 808/922-3111. Fax 808/923-0308. www.moana-surfrider.com. 793 units. $299–$675 double; from $1,300 suite. Extra person $65. Children 17 and under stay free in parent's room. Cribs free; rollaway beds $65. Ask about special package rates, which could save you as much as 35%. AE, DC, MC, V. Valet parking $26; self-parking at sister property $20. Bus: 19 or 20. **Amenities:** 3 restaurants; bar; outdoor pool; nearby health club (about a 2-min. walk down the beach at the Sheraton Waikiki); watersports equipment/rentals; children's program (featuring both on-site activities and excursions to the Honolulu Zoo and the Waikiki Aquarium—$50 half-day with lunch, $80 full day with lunch); nearby game room (a stroll down the beach at the Sheraton Waikiki); concierge; activities desk; car rental desk; nearby business center (a few min. away at the Royal Hawaiian); very upscale shopping arcade; salon; room service; massage; babysitting; coin-op laundry; same-day laundry service and dry cleaning. *In room:* A/C, TV, dataport, fridge, coffeemaker, hair dryer, iron, safe.

Outrigger Waikiki on the Beach ★ If you want to stay on the beach but don't want to borrow against the kids' college funds to do it, this family-oriented hotel could be perfect for you. Even the standard rooms in this 16-story oceanfront hotel are large and comfortable. All guest rooms have medium-sized closets, upgraded bathrooms, and plenty of amenities, plus a lanai; the price is entirely dependent on the view. When booking, ask if you and the kids would be more comfortable in a suite (with separate bedroom and pullout sofa); also ask about package deals, as sometimes you can get a suite cheaper than two connecting rooms.

2335 Kalakaua Ave. (on the ocean, btw the Royal Hawaiian Shopping Center and the Sheraton Moana Surfrider), Honolulu, HI 96815. ✆ **800/OUTRIGGER** (688-7444) or 808/923-0711. Fax 800/622-4852. www.outriggerwaikiki.com. 530 units. $239–$649 double; from $639 suite. Extra person $50. Children 17 and under stay free in parent's room. Cribs and rollaway beds $20 each. Ask about other package deals. AE, DC, DISC, MC, V. Valet-only parking $25. Bus: 19 or 20. **Amenities:** 3 restaurants (including Hula Grill

Waikiki, p. 97, and Duke's Canoe Club, p. 97); 3 bars; showroom w/nightly entertainment; giant outdoor pool; fitness center; new Waikiki Plantation Spa; Jacuzzi; watersports equipment rentals; concierge; activities desk; car rental desk; business center; large shopping arcade; salon; room service (7am–2pm and 5–9:45pm); babysitting; coin-op laundry; laundry service; dry cleaning; concierge-level rooms. *In room:* A/C, TV, dataport, some kitchenettes, fridge, coffeemaker, hair dryer, iron, safe.

Waikiki Parc Hotel ★ Terrifically located just 100 yards from the beach, this hotel is for people who want a taste of the Halekulani's elegance, grace, and style but at a more reasonable price. It's tucked just behind the Halekulani and is owned and operated by the same company. The compact, beautifully appointed rooms all have lanais with ocean, mountain, or city views; ceramic-tile floors with plush carpeting; and conversation areas with a writing desk and rattan couch and chair. From July to September, kids 12 and younger eat free breakfast with every paying adult.

2233 Helumoa Rd. (at Lewers St.), Honolulu, HI 96815. ✆ **800/422-0450** or 808/921-7272. Fax 808/923-1336. www.waikikiparc.com. 298 units. $275–$415 double. Extra person $65. Children 17 and under stay free in parent's room. Cribs and rollaway beds free for children 17 and under. Ask about room/car, bed-and-breakfast, and family packages. AE, DC, MC, V. Valet or self-parking $20. Bus: 19 or 20. **Amenities:** 2 restaurants; concierge; activities desk; business center; limited room service; babysitting; coin-op laundry; same-day laundry and dry cleaning. *In room:* A/C, TV, dataport (in some rooms), fridge, hair dryer, safe.

Inexpensive

Aloha Punawai *Value* Here's one of Waikiki's best-kept secrets: a low-profile, family-operated (since 1959) apartment hotel just 2 blocks from the beach and within walking distance of most Waikiki attractions. The Aloha Punawai offers some of the lowest prices in Waikiki; if you stay a week, prices drop even more. And the location is great, just across the street from Fort DeRussy Park and 2 blocks to Grey's Beach—the same great beach facing the luxury Halekulani and Sheraton Waikiki hotels. The staff is very welcoming to families and will happily direct you to all the activities in the neighborhood. Don't expect the Ritz (or any interior decoration, for that matter)—just sparkling-clean accommodations in a great location. The apartments contain a mishmash of furniture and come with full kitchens and lanais. Towels and linens are provided, but there are no phones (bring your cell) and no pool (hey, the beach is just a couple of blocks away). Families should book the deluxe one-bedroom with a queen bed, a twin bed, and a double pullout sofa, all for the low price of $150.

305 Saratoga Rd. (across from Fort DeRussy and the Waikiki Post Office, btw Kalia Rd. and Kalakaua Ave.), Honolulu, HI 96815. ✆ **808/923-5211.** Fax 808/622-4688. www.alternative-hawaii.com/alohapunawai. 19 units (studios have shower only). $110–$120 studio double; $125–$135 1-bedroom double (sleeps up to 4). Extra person $12. Children 16 and under stay free in parent's room with existing bedding. Cribs and rollaway beds free. Discounts for weeklong (or longer) stays. MC, V. Self-parking $10. Bus: 19 or 20. **Amenities:** Coin-op laundry. *In room:* A/C, TV, kitchen, fridge, coffeemaker.

The Breakers ★ *Value* The Breakers is full of old-fashioned Hawaiian aloha—and it's only steps from the sands of Waikiki. This two-story hotel has a friendly staff and a loyal following. Its six buildings are set around a pool and a tropical garden blooming with brilliant red and yellow hibiscus; wooden jalousies and shoji doors further the tropical ambience. Each of the tastefully decorated, slightly oversize rooms comes with a lanai and a kitchenette. Smaller families will fit comfortably into the double rooms, but if you need more room, book a larger garden studio. One of the best things about the Breakers is the location, just a 2-minute walk to numerous restaurants, shopping, and Waikiki beach.

250 Beach Walk (btw Kalakaua Ave. and Kalia Rd.), Honolulu, HI 96815. ✆ **800/426-0494** or 808/923-3181. Fax 808/923-7174. www.breakers-hawaii.com. 63 units (shower only). $125 double; $135 garden studio double ($205 for 3, $225 for 4, and $245 for 5). AE, DC, DISC, MC, V. Limited parking across the street $11. Bus: 19 or 20. **Amenities:** Restaurant; outdoor pool; babysitting; coin-op laundry; dry cleaning. *In room:* A/C, TV, kitchenette, fridge, coffeemaker, iron on request, safe.

Hawaiiana Hotel ★ Finds The hotel's slogan—"The spirit of old Hawaii"—says it all. The staff here will treat your family like their own: holding the babies; offering puzzles, books, and games to the youngsters; and kidding the teenagers until they start laughing. The lush tropical flowers and carved tiki at the entrance on tiny Beach Walk set the tone for this intimate low-rise hotel. From the moment you arrive, you'll be embraced by the aloha spirit: At check-in, you're given a pineapple, and every morning, complimentary Kona coffee and tropical juice are served poolside. All the concrete, hollow-tiled guest rooms feature kitchenettes, two beds (a double and a single or a queen plus a sofa bed)—perfect for a family of three—and a view of the gardens and two swimming pools. Larger families should book the one-bedroom unit. Hawaiian entertainment is featured every week. ***Note:*** Bring the grandparents; seniors 62 and older get 25% off rack rates. The hotel is about a block from the beach and within walking distance of Waikiki shopping and nightlife.

260 Beach Walk (near Kalakaua Ave.), Honolulu, HI 96815. ✆ **800/367-5122** or 808/923-3811. Fax 808/926-5728. www.hawaiianahotelatwaikiki.com. 93 units (some with shower only). $125–$215 double; $235 1-bedroom with kitchenette (sleeps up to 4). Extra person $25. Children 5 and under stay free in parent's room with existing bedding. Cribs $20; rollaway beds $25. AE, DC, DISC, MC, V. Self-parking $15. Bus: 19 or 20. **Amenities:** 2 good-size outdoor pools; coin-op laundry. *In room:* A/C, TV, kitchenette, fridge, coffeemaker, iron, safe.

Mid-Waikiki, Mauka

These mid-Waikiki hotels, on the mountain side of Kalakaua Avenue, are a little farther away from the beach than those listed above. All are between Kalakaua Avenue and Ala Wai Canal, and between Niu Street in the Ewa direction and Kaiulani Street in the Diamond Head direction.

Expensive

Ohana Waikiki Beachcomber One of the main pluses of this high-rise hotel is the great location—a block from Waikiki Beach, across the street from the upscale Royal Hawaiian Shopping Center, and next door to bargain shopping at the International Market Place. The spacious rooms can easily handle a family of four and feature Berber carpets, big TV armoires, contemporary furniture, hand-held showers, and convenient hot pots for making coffee or tea or hot chocolate. If you need more room, one-bedroom suites are available. This property also has great entertainment: *The Magic of Polynesia,* a show with illusionist John Hirokana, is great for the entire family.

2300 Kalakaua Ave. (at Duke's Lane), Honolulu, HI 96815. ✆ **800/622-4646** or 808/922-4646. Fax 808/926-9973. www.waikikibeachcomber.com. 495 units (shower only). $179–$369 double; from $439 suite. Check the website for special rates. Extra person from $30. Children 17 and under stay free in parent's room. Cribs and rollaway beds $30 each. AE, DC, MC, V. Self-parking $18. Bus: 19 or 20. **Amenities:** Poolside coffee shop; Hawaiian entertainment show; outdoor pool; children's program (July–Aug); activities desk; car rental desk; small shopping arcade; room service (6am–11am); coin-op laundry; laundry service; dry cleaning. *In room:* A/C, TV, fridge, coffeemaker, hair dryer, iron on request, safe.

Moderate

Aqua Waikiki Wave ★ Finds It is hard to believe that from the wreck of a hotel, the old Coral Reef, this sleek, modern oasis could emerge. After spending $7,630,000 in practically gutting the old hotel, Aqua has renovated the rooms and the result is a clean, hip decor with bright white walls, offset by the burnt-orange fabric on the bed headboard, which extends up to the ceiling. Potted plants and real, live orchids liven up the rooms. The 21st century has arrived at this older hotel with flatscreen TVs, free Wi-Fi Internet, and high-speed Internet access. About a 10-minute walk to the beach and located next door to the International Market Place, the rooms at the Wave have either two queen beds or a king (with the very sleepable Serta mattress). The decades-old bathrooms have new plumbing, modern fixtures, resurfaced tiles and tubs. Other pluses for this moderately priced hotel include complimentary daily continental breakfast, fitness center, spa, and small swimming pool.

2299 Kuhio Ave. (at Duke's Lane), Honolulu, HI 96817. ✆ **866/406-2782** or 808/922-1262. Fax 808/922-5048. www.aquaresorts.com. 247 units. $147–$179 double; $175–$225 suite. Extra person $25. AE, DISC, MC, V. Parking $20. Bus: 19 or 20. **Amenities:** 2 restaurants; outdoor pool; fitness room; spa; activities desk; babysitting; laundry service; dry cleaning. *In room:* A/C, flatscreen TV, DVD, complimentary Wi-Fi and high-speed Internet, fridge, coffeemaker, hair dryer, iron, safe.

Ilima Hotel ★ The Teruya brothers, former owners of Hawaii's Times Supermarket, wanted to offer comfortable accommodations that families could afford, and they've succeeded. One of Hawaii's small, well-located condo-style hotels, the 17-story, pale pink Ilima (named for the native orange flower used in royal leis) offers value for your money. A variety of rooms accommodate families of two to eight. Rooms are huge, the location (near the International Market Place and the Royal Hawaiian Shopping Center, 2 blocks to Waikiki Beach) is great, and prices are affordable. Every unit, from the studio to the three bedrooms, has a full kitchen and a couch that folds out into a bed, making this a particularly good deal for families. A family of four can fit easily into the studio, but if you need more room, a one-bedroom unit costs just 30% more. The staff, most of whom have young children of their own, will happily give you hints on how to get the most out of your family vacation on Oahu. In fact, the front desk has a great selection of children's books on Hawaiian subjects (from fish to flowers) that your kids can borrow, and they also have the Disney Channel and Nintendo (with a fee) in every room.

445 Nohonani St. (near Ala Wai Blvd.), Honolulu, HI 96815. ✆ **800/801-9366** or 808/923-1877. Fax 888/864-5462. www.ilima.com. 98 units. $178–$268 double; $245–$289 1-bedroom (4-person rate); $356–$386 2-bedroom (4-person rate; sleeps up to 6); $560–$600 3-bedroom (6-person rate; sleeps up to 8). Extra person $10. Children 17 and under stay free in parent's room. Cribs and rollaway beds $10 each. Discounts available for seniors and business travelers. AE, DC, DISC, MC, V. Limited free parking, $18 across the street. Bus: 19 or 20. **Amenities:** Outdoor pool w/sauna; health club; tour desk; coin-op laundry. *In room:* A/C, TV, kitchen, fridge, coffeemaker, hair dryer, iron, safe, Jacuzzi (in 1-bedroom units).

Diamond Head Waikiki

You'll find all these hotels between Ala Wai Boulevard and the ocean, and between Kaiulani Street (1 block east of the International Market Place) and world-famous Diamond Head itself.

Very Expensive

Hyatt Regency Waikiki Resort and Spa ★ This is one of Waikiki's biggest hotels, a $100-million project sporting two 40-story towers and covering nearly an entire city block, just across the street from the Diamond Head end of Waikiki Beach. Some may love the location, but others will find this behemoth too big and impersonal—you can get lost just trying to find the registration desk.

The guest rooms are spacious and luxuriously furnished, with plenty of room for a rollaway or a crib. A family of four with young children should have plenty of space, but if you need more, you can get 50% off the rack rate for a connecting room. My only complaint is when room rates start at $280 a night, do they have to charge you extra for the coffee in the "free coffeemaker" in your room? (Not only that, but if you would like a fridge for kids, the cost is $12 per day!)

The children's program, Camp Hyatt (for ages 5–12), has a wide array of activities, from excursions to the Waikiki Aquarium to scientific experiments. Several on-site restaurants offer *keiki* (children's) menus with smaller portions and food that kids would prefer to eat.

2424 Kalakaua Ave. (at Kaiulani St., across the street from the beach), Honolulu, HI 96815. ✆ **800/233-1234** or 808/923-1234. Fax 808/923-7839. ttp://waikiki.hyatt.com. 1,230 units. $280–$635 double; $480–$755 Regency Club double; from $885 suite. Extra person $50 ($75 Regency Club). Children 17 and under stay free in parent's room. Cribs and rollaway beds free for children 18 and under. AE, DC, DISC, MC, V. Valet parking $29; self-parking $20. Bus: 19 or 20. **Amenities:** 7 restaurants; 4 bars; outdoor pool w/ view of Waikiki; health club; elegant spa; Jacuzzi; children's program (Fri–Sat year-round and daily in June–Sept; $85 full day or $15 per child per hour); game room; concierge; activities desk; car rental desk; business center; large shopping arcade; salon; room service (6am–11pm); in-room massage; babysitting; coin-op laundry; same-day laundry service and dry cleaning; concierge-level rooms. *In room:* A/C, TV, dataport, kitchenette (in some units), minibar, coffeemaker, hair dryer, iron, safe.

W Honolulu ★★★ It's ultra-expensive but this luxury hotel located on the outskirts of Waikiki, in a quieter, more residential neighborhood, will make your stay in Waikiki a memorable one. If you're craving peace and quiet away from the crowds of Waikiki, but want to be close enough (about a 15-min. walk) to shops and restaurants, this is a perfect location. The hotel lobby looks like an elegant living room, and check-in occurs in the privacy of the guest rooms, which are decorated with handmade teak furniture from Bali. In addition to the large balconies with great views of Diamond Head, there are numerous excellent touches: from Hawaiian-music CDs to dual-line cordless phones, plush robes, top-drawer bathroom amenities, twice-daily maid service, and various business equipment available on request. Although the W is not on the beach, guests have access to the small, private beach in front of the Colony Surf (great swimming here), less than a 60-second walk away; Kapiolani Park is across the street, and the Waikiki Aquarium is just a few steps away. The famous "W" pledge (whatever, whenever) still lives up to its reputation. I asked for the best place to get a manicure and pedicure late at night; not only did they make an immediate appointment but they Googled a map and directions for me, and within 10 minutes of making my request, I was soaking my feet in warm bubbling water.

2885 Kalakaua Ave. (on the ocean side btw the Waikiki Aquarium and Outrigger Canoe Club), Honolulu, HI 96815. ✆ **888/528-9465** or 808/922-1700. Fax 808/923-2249. www.starwood.com/hawaii. 51 units. $275–$355 double; from $1,600 2-bedroom ocean penthouse suite. Extra person $75. Children 17 and under stay free in parent's room. AE, DC, DISC, MC, V. Valet parking $18 (no self-parking available). Bus: 19 or 20. **Amenities:** Restaurant (Diamond Head Grill); elegant bar (entertainment nightly); concierge service; laundry service; dry cleaning. *In room:* A/C, TV/DVD, dataport, high-speed Internet (fee), minibar, coffeemaker, hair dryer, iron, safe.

Moderate

Hilton Waikiki Prince Kuhio Hilton took over this 37-floor hotel, several long blocks from the beach and a couple of blocks from the zoo, in 2007 and spent $50 million in renovations to take this former midpriced, moderate Radisson hotel into a high-tech, 21st-century luxury hotel. This hotel is a 5-minute walk to the beach; if you have small children and want to take them to the beach, it could be a bit much for them (especially coming back to the hotel after a day at the beach). The sleek, modern rooms all have high-speed Internet (for a fee), a flatscreen 42-inch plasma high-def TV with multimedia monitor that you can use with a laptop computer, game station consoles, video/camera, or MP3 player. The contemporary-designed rooms feature Hilton's comfy beds and the bathrooms feature marble and natural stone and top-end amenities. All of the rooms are the same; the floor and the view determine the price (from the 18th floor and up, the mountain views overlooking the Ala Wai Canal are spectacular and not as pricey as the oceanview rooms). Hilton has added a 24-hour eatery, MAC 24-7 (see p. 98), which comes in handy if you arrive late at night.

2500 Kuhio Ave. (Liliuokalani Ave.), Honolulu, HI 96815. ✆ **800-HILTONS** (445-8667 or 808/922-0811. Fax 808/921-5511. www.waikikiprincekuhio.hilton.com. 601 units. $229–$500 double; from $450 suite for 4. Extra person $40. AE, DC, DISC, MC, V. Valet-only parking $20. Bus: 19 or 20. **Amenities:** Restaurant; bar; outdoor pool; small fitness room; Jacuzzi; concierge; activities desk; small business center; shopping arcade; limited room service; coin-op washer/dryers; laundry service; dry cleaning; concierge-level rooms. *In room:* A/C, TV, dataport, fridge, coffeemaker, hair dryer, iron, safe.

Hotel Renew ★★ Finds Once upon a time this now-70-room boutique hotel was one of the towers to the ResortQuest Waikiki Beach Hotel (see below); that was the "before." The "after" is an oasis of tranquillity, excellent taste, high-speed electronic equipment in a sea of schlock of aging Waikiki hotels. After several millions in renovations (in which every single surface was redone), the new Hotel Renew offers a quiet, relaxing vacation, just a block from the beach. Guests are seated at the front desks to check in, while their luggage is whisked to their rooms. The new rooms are designed with a clean, Zen-like decor with black-and-white walls, discreet lighting with the slight scent of candles in the air (similar to the W Hotel chain, but for only a fraction of the price). But its the high-tech electronics that won us over—a DVD system that projects out to a 6×4-foot screen (and can work with your computer), a 42-inch high-definition flatscreen TV, complimentary high-speed Internet, a host of 500-plus movies, and even an iPod docking station. Daily complimentary gourmet breakfast, free fitness center and yoga classes, and, when you depart (vs. arrive), a fresh flower lei to remember your sweet time here.

129 Paoakalani Ave. (at Lemon Rd.), Honolulu, HI 96815. ✆ **866/406-2782** or 808/687-7700. Fax 808/687-7701. www.aquaresorts.com. 72 units. $225–$370 double. Extra person $50. AE, DC, MC, V. Valet-only parking $20. Bus: 19 or 20. **Amenities:** Cafe and lounge; complimentary gourmet breakfast; spa; concierge; business services; laundry service; dry cleaning. *In room:* A/C, flatscreen high-definition TV, DVD, CD player, complimentary high-speed Internet, refrigerator, coffeemaker, hair dryer, iron, safe.

New Otani Kaimana Beach Hotel ★ Finds This is one of Waikiki's best-kept secrets: a boutique hotel nestled right on a lovely stretch of beach at the foot of Diamond Head, with Kapiolani Park just across the street. The Waikiki-side guest rooms are too tiny for families. (In fact, two people are a crowd in these rooms.) But there's such a terrific selection of rooms that you can find one to fit your family and budget. If you get a unit with a kitchenette, you can stock up on provisions from the on-site Mini-Mart, open until 11pm.

Because the hotel overlooks Kapiolani Park, guests have easy access to activities such as golf, tennis, jogging, and bicycling; kayaking and snorkeling are available at the beach. The hotel also arranges for visitors to climb to the top of Diamond Head. The airy lobby opens onto the alfresco Hau Tree Lanai restaurant, a delightfully romantic but family-friendly beachfront restaurant set under a banyan tree.

2863 Kalakaua Ave. (ocean side of the street just east of the Waikiki Aquarium, across from Kapiolani Park), Honolulu, HI 96815. ✆ **800/356-8264** or 808/923-1555. Fax 808/922-9404. www.kaimana.com. 124 units. $160–$280 double; from $300 junior suites; from $480–$1,240 regular suites. Extra person $50. Children 12 and under stay free in parent's room. Cribs free; rollaway beds $50. AE, DC, DISC, MC, V. Valet parking $18. Bus: 2 or 14. **Amenities:** 2 restaurants; beachside bar; health club; watersports equipment/rentals; concierge; activities desk; small shopping arcade; salon; room service (7am–8:45pm); in-room massage; babysitting; coin-op laundry; laundry service; dry cleaning. *In room:* A/C, TV/VCR, dataport, some kitchenettes, minibar (on request), fridge, coffeemaker (on request), hair dryer, iron (on request), safe.

ResortQuest Waikiki Beach Hotel After a $30-million renovation on a very old and tired hotel, this former Aston resort opened the 717-room property in late 2002. The location, directly across the street from the beach, couldn't be better, but the rooms couldn't be smaller—averaging 225 to 266 square feet (though 85% of them have ocean views). When ResortQuest took over in 2006 they immediately got rid of the Hawaiian "kitschy nostalgia" theme and repainted (the horrible garish colors are gone, replaced with wooden baseboards and bamboo trim over a floral carpet), installed a 32-inch flatscreen TV, a bamboo dresser and kept the bright floral headboards and accents in the room without it being over done. One of the good ideas ResortQuest kept was the "Breakfast on the Beach" deal—you get a free breakfast, which you can pack up in an insulated carrying bag and walk across the street to eat. This is a full, hot breakfast, too, with several food stations offering everything from burritos (veggie, ham, or cheese), pastries, fruit, and cereals to a Japanese breakfast of miso, rice, and fish. There are a couple of great places to eat here: Tiki's Grill and Wolfgang Puck Express. ***Hot tip:*** For the best rate, check the website, under "e-specials," or choose one of their package deals.

2570 Kalakaua Ave. (at Paoakalani St.), Honolulu, HI 96815. ✆ **877/997-6667** or 808/922-2511. Fax 808/923-3656. www.ResortQuestHawaii.com. 717 units. $295–$425 double; $475 suite double. Extra person $45. AE, DC, DISC, MC, V. Valet parking $25. Bus: 19 or 20. **Amenities:** Restaurant/bar (Tiki's Grill, Wolfgang Puck Express; and Cold Stone Creamery); outdoor pool; activities desk; coin-op washer/dryers; dry cleaning. *In room:* A/C, TV, dataport, high-speed Internet access ($10), fridge, coffeemaker, hair dryer, iron, safe (fee).

Waikiki Beach Marriott Resort & Spa Terrifically located, just across the street from Waikiki Beach, this 1,310-room hotel, which was completely renovated in 2002 (to the tune of $60 million), has a lot to offer families. The 5.2-acre property has two towers (one 33 stories, the other 25 stories). The rooms are large and can easily handle a crib or rollaway, but if you have a couple of kids, ask for the "family" room. Starting at $419, the family room is larger than the normal hotel room and has four beds. The hotel also has board games at the front desk that you can take back to your rooms to entertain the little ones, and the kid-savvy concierges offer plenty of help in deciding what to do.

2552 Kalakaua Ave. (entrance on Ohua Ave.), Honolulu, HI 96815. ✆ **800/367-5370** or 808/922-6611. Fax 808/921-5255. www.marriottwaikiki.com. 1,310 units. $249–$319 double; $419–$489 family rooms. Extra person $40. Children 17 and under stay free in parent's room. Cribs free; rollaway beds $40. AE, DC, DISC, MC, V. Valet parking $29; self-parking $24. Bus: 19 or 20. **Amenities:** 5 restaurants; 2 bars; outdoor pool w/view of Waikiki; health club; brand-new elegant spa; Jacuzzi; concierge; activities desk; car rental desk; business center; shopping arcade; salon; room service (5am–10pm); in-room massage; babysitting; coin-op laundry; same-day laundry service and dry cleaning. *In room:* A/C, TV, dataport, coffeemaker, hair dryer, iron, safe.

Inexpensive

Aqua Bamboo ★ *Value* Formerly a very neglected budget hotel, just a block from Waikiki Beach, Bamboo has been transformed into a contemporary condotel (a condominium/hotel), decorated with an Asian flair. The rooms are stylish and functional with modern furniture, marble bathrooms, and with kitchenettes or kitchens. The location is good, too—it's within walking distance to numerous restaurants, shopping, and the Honolulu Zoo, and just 3 minutes to the beach. Because it's small, the staff gives guests personalized attention. Like all the Aqua Resort properties, there's a complimentary continental breakfast every morning, but this hotel has its own spa on property. When booking, be sure to "reserve" a parking space, because the parking lot has a limited number of spaces.

2425 Kuhio Ave. (Kaiulani Ave.), Honolulu, HI 96815. ✆ **800/367-5004** or 808/922-7777. Fax 808/922-9473. www.aquaresorts.com. 94 units. $200–$215 double; $225–$255 studio double; $285–$325 1-bedroom; from $350–$850 luxury suites. Extra person $25. AE, DISC, MC, V. Parking $20. Bus: 19 or 20. **Amenities:** Complimentary continental breakfast; outdoor pool; fitness center; spa; Jacuzzi; sauna; concierge; coin washer and dryers; laundry service; dry cleaning. *In room:* A/C, flatscreen TV, complimentary high-speed Internet access, kitchenette or kitchen, fridge, coffeemaker, hair dryer, iron, safe, free local and toll calls.

Waikiki Sand Villa Budget travelers, take note: This very affordable condo-hotel is located on the quieter side of Waikiki, across the street from the Ala Wai Canal. The 10-story tower has medium-size rooms, most with a double bed plus a single bed (convenient for families) and a lanai with great views of the green mountains. The adjacent three-story building features studio apartments with kitchenettes (fridge, stove, and microwave). Another plus for families is the Nintendo system in every room (available for $8 an hour). For guests arriving early or catching a late flight, there's a hospitality room (complete with shower) for late checkout and a luggage-storage area.

2375 Ala Wai Blvd. (entrance on Kanekapolei Ave.), Honolulu, HI 96815. ✆ **800/247-1903** or 808/922-4744. Fax 808/923-2541. www.waikikisandvillahotel.com. 214 units. $139–$205 double; $261–$347 studio with kitchenette; suites from $405. Rates include continental breakfast served poolside every morning. Extra person $25. Children 16 and under stay free in parent's room using existing bedding. Internet specials (available at the website) start as low as $81. AE, DC, DISC, MC, V. Valet-only parking $15. Bus: 19 or 20. **Amenities:** 70-ft. outdoor pool w/adjoining whirlpool spa; activities desk; coin-op washer/dryers; laundry service; dry cleaning. *In room:* A/C, TV w/Nintendo, complimentary high-speed Internet, kitchenette (in some rooms), fridge (in some rooms), microwave (in some rooms), coffeemaker (in some rooms), safe.

HONOLULU BEYOND WAIKIKI

Ala Moana

Ala Moana Hotel A multimillion-dollar transformation converted this former 1,152-room hotel (on 36 floors) into a hotel-condominium (sometimes called a condotel), where the units are individually owned, but are put back into the rental pool for guests. Since the renovations—which include redone rooms, new pool, sundeck, and fitness center/spa—the prices for the rooms have almost doubled, yet the small size of the rooms has stayed the same. The main advantage of staying here is its proximity to Waikiki, the downtown financial and business district, the new convention center, and Hawaii's largest mall, Ala Moana Shopping Center. If you are headed for a convention at the convention center, this hotel is the closest. The rooms vary in price according to size: The cheaper rooms are petite, but all come with two double beds. If the kids are small, you can squeeze them into the second bed, but some rooms are even too small to add a crib (they do not have rollaway beds). Kids 12 and older really need a second room.

410 Atkinson Dr. (at Kona St., next to Ala Moana Center), Honolulu, HI 96814. ✆ **800/367-6025** or 808/955-4811. Fax 808/944-6839. www.thealamoana.com. 1,152 units. $229–$329 double; from $429 suite. Extra person $40. Children 17 and under stay free in parent's room. Cribs free; no rollaway beds. AE, DC, DISC, MC, V. Valet parking $20; self-parking $15. Bus: 19 or 20. **Amenities:** 5 restaurants (from coffee shop to Japanese food); 2 bars; large outdoor pool; small health club; game room; concierge; activities desk; business center; shopping arcade; salon; coin-op laundry; laundry service; dry cleaning. *In room:* A/C, TV, dataport, fridge, coffeemaker, hair dryer, iron, safe.

Pagoda Hotel This is where local residents from neighbor islands stay when they come to Honolulu. Not in Waikiki, although it is close to shopping areas and downtown, this budget hotel has very plain motel-ish rooms: clean and utilitarian with no frills. For a quieter stay, ask for a mountain view where you'll be away from the street noise. There's easy access to Waikiki via TheBus—the nearest stop is just a half-block away. Studios and one- and two-bedroom units have kitchenettes. ***Tip:*** Sunday through Thursday rates are cheaper than weekend rates.

1525 Rycroft St. (btw Keeaumoku and Kaheka sts.), Honolulu, HI 96814. ✆ **800/367-6060** or 808/941-6611. Fax 808/922-8061. www.pagodahotel.com. 361 units. $126–$160 double hotel room; $126–$148 studio with kitchenette; $154–$215 1-bedroom double; $192–$226 2-bedroom double (sleeps up to 5) lowest rates Sun–Thurs. Extra person $25. Free cribs available. Ask about car/room deals. AE, DC, DISC, MC, V. Parking $15. Bus: 5 or 6. **Amenities:** Restaurant; bar; 2 outdoor pools; activities desk; salon; babysitting; coin-op washer/dryers; laundry service; dry cleaning. *In room:* A/C, TV, dataport, kitchenette (some units), fridge, coffeemaker, hair dryer, iron, safe.

To the East: Kahala

The Kahala Hotel & Resort ★★★ This is *the* place to relax in luxury, far from the crowds of Waikiki. A veritable who's who of celebrities have stayed here, including several U.S. presidents. The Kahala offers the peace and serenity of a neighbor-island vacation, but with the conveniences of Waikiki just a 10-minute drive away. The lush, tropical grounds include an 800-foot crescent-shaped beach and a 26,000-square-foot lagoon (home to two bottle-nosed dolphins, sea turtles, and tropical fish).

As soon as you check in, your kids (ages 5–12) get a "Keiki Passport," where they can collect Hawaiian-themed stamps throughout the resort. When they check out, they "redeem" their stamps for prizes.

Families will be quite happy in the guest rooms, which feature 19th-century mahogany reproductions, teak parquet floors with hand-loomed Tibetan rugs, overstuffed chairs, canopy beds covered with soft throw pillows, and works by local artists adorning the grass-cloth–covered walls. Views from the floor-to-ceiling sliding-glass doors are of the ocean, Diamond Head, and Koko Head. The resort offers a "keiki club" for kids, with activities ranging from lei-making to snorkeling. Cost for the full day (9am—4pm) program is $65 ($40 for each additional child) or $45 for a half day with lunch and $35 without lunch. Plus there's an educational program which allows kids (and adults) to feed and swim with the resident dolphins. All of the restaurants feature keiki menus and go out of the way to make sure the little ones are happy at every meal. Other extras that make this property outstanding: Hawaiian cultural programs, shuttle service to Waikiki and major shopping centers, a kids-only swimming pool, and a staff that goes above and beyond the call of duty to help families during their Hawaii vacation. Babysitting service is $12 an hour for one child, $15 for two.

5000 Kahala Ave. (next to the Waialae Country Club), Honolulu, HI 96816. ✆ **800/367-2525** or 808/739-8888. Fax 808/739-8800. www.kahalaresort.com. 343 units. $395–$820 double; rates vary depending on views. From $1,600–$4,000 suites. Extra person $140. Children 17 and under stay free in parent's room. Cribs free; rollaway beds $40. AE, DC, DISC, MC, V. Valet parking $22. **Amenities:** 4 restaurants (see Hoku's on p. 109); bar; large outdoor pool; nearby golf course; tennis courts; great health club w/steam rooms, Jacuzzis, and dry sauna; watersports equipment/rentals; bike rentals; children's program; game room; concierge; activities desk; car rental desk; multilingual business center; shopping arcade; salon; 24-hr. room service; in-room massage; babysitting; laundry service; dry cleaning. *In room:* A/C, TV, dataport, high-speed Internet access ($15/day), minibar, hair dryer, iron, safe.

Kailua

Pat O'Malley of **Pat's Kailua Beach Properties,** 204 S. Kalaheo Ave., Kailua, HI 96734 (✆ **808/261-1653** or 808/262-4128; www.patskailua.com), books a wide range of houses and cottages on or near Kailua Beach. Rates start at $100 a day for a studio cottage near the beach and go up to $600 per day for a multimillion-dollar home right on the sand with room to sleep eight. All units are fully furnished, with everything from cooking utensils to telephone and TV, even laundry machines.

Sheffield House Unlike many other B&Bs, Sheffield House welcomes children. The owners, Paul Sheffield and his wife, Rachel, have three kids, so they can help you with where to go, what to do, and the best family restaurants in Kailua. There are two units here, a one-bedroom and a studio (which is fully wheelchair accessible), each with a private entry (through elaborately landscaped tropical gardens), with full kitchen. The two units can be combined and rented as a two-bedroom/two-bathroom unit.

131 Kuulei Rd. (at Kalaheo Dr.), Kailua, HI 96734. ✆/fax **808/262-0721.** www.hawaiisheffieldhouse.com 2 units. $95–$105 double studio (shower only); $105–$125 double apt (some lower rates depending on the season). $200–$225 2-bedroom for 6. Rates include 1st day's continental breakfast. Extra person $15. DISC, MC, V. Free parking. Bus: 56 or 57. *In room:* TV, Wi-Fi available, kitchen, fridge, coffeemaker.

Kaneohe

Schrader's Windward Country Inn Despite the name, the ambience here is more motel than resort, but Schrader's offers a good alternative for families. The property is nestled in a tranquil, tropical setting on Kaneohe Bay, only a 40-minute drive from Waikiki. The complex is made up of well-worn, cottage-style motels and a collection of well-used, older homes. Cottages contain either a kitchenette with refrigerator and microwave or a full kitchen. The furniture may have seen better days, but the units are all scrubbed clean. There's also a picnic area with barbecue grills. Prices are based on the views; depending on how much you're willing to pay, you can look out over a Kahaluu fish pond, the Koolau Mountains, or Kaneohe Bay. Lots of watersports are available at an additional cost; don't miss the complimentary 2-hour boat cruise with snorkeling and kayaking. Evening activities include Hawaiian music night and karaoke night, both with free *pupu* (Hawaii-style appetizers). ***Tip:*** When booking, ask for a unit with a lanai; that way, you'll end up with at least a partial view of the bay.

47-039 Lihikai Dr. (off Kamehameha Hwy.), Kaneohe, HI 96744. ✆ **800/735-5071** or 808/239-5711. Fax 808/239-6658. www.hawaiiscene.com/schrader. 20 units. $72–$143 1-bedroom double; $127–$215 2-bedroom for 4; $226–$358 3-bedroom for 6; $446–$501 4-bedroom for 8. Rates include continental breakfast. Extra person $7.50. 2-night minimum. AE, DC, DISC, MC, V. Free parking. Bus: 52, 55, or 56. **Amenities:** Outdoor pool; watersports equipment rentals. *In room:* TV, kitchenette, fridge, coffeemaker.

THE NORTH SHORE

The North Shore doesn't have many accommodations or an abundance of tourist facilities—some say that is its charm. **Team Real Estate,** 66-250 Kamehameha Hwy., Suite D–103, Haleiwa, HI 96712 (✆ **800/982-8602** or 808/637-3507; www.teamrealestate.com), manages vacation rentals on the North Shore. Its units range from affordable cottages to condos to oceanfront homes, at rates ranging from $65 for a condo unit and $120 for a one-bedroom apartment to $1,035/night for an 11-bedroom oceanfront luxury home. A minimum stay of 1 week is required for some properties, but shorter stays are available as well.

Ke Iki Beach Bungalows This collection of rustic studio, one-, and two-bedroom duplex cottages (with three- and four-bedroom cottages scheduled to be added) has a divine location. It's snuggled on a large lot with its own 200-foot stretch of white-sand beach between two legendary surf spots: Waimea Bay and Banzai Pipeline. The winter waves are rough stuff; families and especially kids can only venture in to swim in the flat summer seas. But there's a large lava reef nearby with tide pools to explore and, on the other side, Shark's Cove, a relatively protected snorkeling area. Nearby are tennis courts and a jogging path. Ke Iki is not for everyone, though. The well-worn furnishings range from modest to garage sale decor, though all the units are clean and comfortable; kitchens, barbecues, and hammocks provide some of the comforts of home. The one-bedrooms have one or two single beds in the living room, a double in the separate bedroom, and a full kitchen. The attraction here is that great beach just steps from your front door. Other pluses are the complimentary beach equipment and coin-operated washer and dryers on-site. ***Tip:*** Stay on the beach side, where the views are well worth the extra bucks.

59-579 Ke Iki Rd. (off Kamehameha Hwy.), Haleiwa, HI 96712. ✆ **866/638-8229** or 808/638-8829. Fax 808/637-6100. www.keikibeach.com. 11 units. $135–$160 1-bedroom double garden-view; $185–$215 1-bedroom double beachfront; $155–$185 2-bedroom double garden-view; $210–$230 2-bedroom double beachfront. Cribs and rollaway beds free. AE, MC, V. Free parking. Bus: 52. **Amenities:** Complimentary watersports equipment and bicycles; in-room massage; coin-op laundry. *In room:* TV, kitchen, fridge, coffeemaker.

Turtle Bay Resort ★★★ If you are looking for a relaxing luxury resort, away from the urban pace of Waikiki, this is the place for your family. This property has recently undergone a management change (for years it was a Hilton) and a $35-million massive renovation of all the rooms. The lobby is now open and airy with floor-to-ceiling windows to the dramatic ocean shoreline view. The resort is spectacular: an hour's drive from Waikiki, but eons away in its country feeling. Sitting on 808 acres, this place is loaded with activities and 5 miles of shoreline with secluded white-sand coves. It's located on Kalaeokaunu Point ("point of the altar"), where ancient Hawaiians built a small altar to the fish gods.

All the rooms are of a good size and have ocean views and balconies. You can request two double beds or a king bed and still have room for a complimentary crib or futon. They also offer a Keiki Club for kids ages 5 to 12, with swimming, reef walks, pole fishing, and Hawaiian arts and crafts, for $65 per child during the day, 9am to 3pm, or evening, 5 to 9pm (including a meal).

If you can afford it, book the separate beach cottages. Positioned right on the ocean (the views alone are worth the price), the 42 bungalows have been renovated and feature hardwood floors, poster beds with feather comforters, they even offer butler service and as well as separate check-in and private concierge (like a hotel within a hotel).

For rainy days, there's video on demand in each room. Dining is no problem at the Palm Terrace, Sand Bar, and Hang Ten Bar (pool side); all have keiki menus. For a special adults' night out, don't miss the romantic **21 Degrees North** (p. 110).

P.O. Box 187 (Kuilima Dr., off Kamehameha Hwy. [Hwy. 83]), Kahuku, HI 96731. ✆ **800/203-3650** or 808/293-6000. Fax 808/293-9147. www.turtlebayresort.com. 460 units. $340–$432 double; $703–$774 cottage; from $500 suite and $888 villa. Daily resort fee of $20 includes self-parking, Internet access unlimited local phone calls, long-distance access and toll-free number; self-service coffee and tea in room; newspaper; 1-hr. snorkel rental for 2 per day; access to fitness club; 1 hr. of tennis court time per day; indoor safe; and incoming faxes. Extra person $50. Children 17 and under stay free in parent's room. Cribs and rollaway beds $50 each. AE, DC, DISC, MC, V. Bus: 52 or 55. **Amenities:** 4 restaurants; 2 bars (live entertainment Thurs–Sat at the Bay Club Lounge, plus a poolside bar for sunset cocktails); 2 outdoor heated pools (w/80-ft. water slide); 36 holes of golf; 10 Plexipave tennis courts; health club; spa; 2 Jacuzzis; watersports equipment/rentals; concierge; activity desk; business center; shopping arcade; salon; room service; babysitting; coin-op laundry; laundry service; dry cleaning. *In room:* A/C, TV, wireless Wi-Fi, fridge, coffeemaker, hair dryer, iron.

LEEWARD OAHU: THE WAIANAE COAST

JW Marriott Ihilani Resort & Spa at Ko Olina ★★★ It's definitely not Waikiki, but it is on a 640-acre resort, some 17 miles and 25 minutes west of Honolulu Airport (and worlds away from the tourist scene of Waikiki). Ihilani ("heavenly splendor") is nestled in a quiet location between the Pacific Ocean and the first of four man-made beach lagoons. Featuring a luxury spa and fitness center, plus tennis and one of Hawaii's premier golf courses, it's a haven of relaxation and well-being. Plus the resort is extremely family-friendly, from the huge rooms to the interactive marine life program.

It's hard to get a bad room in the 15-story building—some 85% of the units enjoy lagoon or ocean views. Accommodations are luxuriously appointed and spacious (680 sq. ft.), and come with huge lanais outfitted with very comfortable, cushioned teak furniture. The staff will supply you with a complimentary crib or rollaway bed if needed. Although the rooms are not interconnecting, they are grouped in sets of two, where the main outer door can be closed and you can enter the two separate bedrooms through a foyer.

The Ihilani's children's program puts all others to shame, offering year-round outdoor adventures and indoor learning activities for toddlers and teens alike. There's a computer learning center, a 125-gallon fish tank, an evening lounge for teen-themed parties, and more.

All of the hotel's restaurants welcome families with kids' menus, highchairs, and booster seats. And the spa is no longer just for adults, with special teen facials, teen yoga, and even a fitness-equipment and weight-training orientation for 11- to 13-year-olds.

92-1001 Olani St., Kapolei, HI 96707. ✆ **800/626-4446** or 808/679-0079. Fax 808/679-0080. www.ihilani.com. 387 units. $405–$750 double, from $850–$4,500 suite. Extra person $50. Children 17 and under stay free in parent's room. Cribs and rollaway beds free. AE, DC, MC, V. Valet parking $29. No bus service. Take H-1 west toward Pearl City/Ewa Beach; stay on H-1 until it becomes Hwy. 93 (Farrington Hwy.); look for the exit sign for Ko Olina Resort; turn right on Olani St. **Amenities:** 3 restaurants; 2 bars (w/nightly entertainment poolside); 2 outdoor pools; championship 18-hole Ko Olina golf course (designed by Ted Robinson); tennis club w/pro shop; world-class spa; watersports equipment/rentals; excellent children's program $58 full day w/lunch, additional child $15, half-day $40 w/lunch and half-day $35 without lunch; game room; concierge; activities desk; 24-hr. business center; shopping arcade; salon; room service; in-room massage; babysitting; same-day laundry service and dry cleaning. *In room:* A/C, TV, dataport, minibar, hair dryer, iron, safe.

4 FAMILY-FRIENDLY DINING

On Oahu, family dining doesn't have to mean fast-food joints—the full range of choices includes chef-owned glamour restaurants, neighborhood eateries, ethnic spots, and restaurants and food courts in shopping malls. I've listed places that will welcome your little ones and make both you and them comfortable. I did stick in a few romantic spots where you and your honey can spend some time by yourselves if you've ordered up a sitter for the night.

WAIKIKI

See the "Waikiki" map on p. 80 to locate the restaurants below.

Very Expensive

La Mer ★★★ NEOCLASSIC FRENCH This is the splurge restaurant of Hawaii, the oceanfront bastion of haute cuisine where the state's finest chefs quietly redefined fine dining in Hawaii. Get a sitter for the night—this is the place for romance. La Mer is elegant, and expensive; dress up not to be seen but to match the ambience and food (jackets or long-sleeved shirts required for men). It's the only AAA Five-Diamond restaurant in the state, with a second-floor, open-sided room with views of Diamond Head and the sound of trade winds rustling the nearby coconut fronds. Michelin-award–winning Chef Yves Garnier melds classical French influences with fresh island ingredients to create an elegant soup with saffron, chanterelles, and savory fresh fish filets; *moano* (a delicate goatfish) in strudel with basil and niçoise olives; ruby snapper—skin crisped—in sublime sauces napped with truffle and herbs. The wine list, desserts, and service—formal without being stiff—complete the dining experience. Not appropriate for kids.

In the Halekulani, 2199 Kalia Rd. ✆ **808/923-2311.** Reservations recommended. Long-sleeve collared dress shirts for men; jackets provided if necessary. Prix-fixe dinners with wine pairings $90 3-course, $150 9-course. AE, MC, V. Daily 6–10pm.

Expensive

Bali by the Sea ★★ CONTINENTAL/PACIFIC RIM This is another "adults-only" dining experience in a memorable oceanfront room—pale and full of light, with a white grand piano at the entrance and sweeping views of the ocean (ask for a table by the window). The menu merges island cooking styles and ingredients with the chef's Alsatian roots: an excellent herb-infused rack of lamb coated with orange hoisin glaze; sake-steamed Kona lobster; and fresh seafood in sauces hinting of plum wine, kaffir lime, black bean, ginger, and lemon grass. Save room for dessert—a replica of Diamond Head (the one you see out the window) created with chocolate truffles. If you cannot or don't want to leave the kids behind, it's really best for children 12 and older.

In the Hilton Hawaiian Village, 2005 Kalia Rd. ✆ **808/941-2254.** Highchairs, boosters, and crayons. Reservations recommended. Main courses $26–$60. AE, DC, DISC, MC, V. Mon–Sat 6–9pm.

Orchids ★★ INTERNATIONAL/SEAFOOD Orchids features fresh local produce and seafood in elegant presentations and in a fantasy setting with consummate service. It's an extraordinary setting, the food is good to excellent, and they will treat your young ones like kings and queens. Blinding-white linens and a view of Diamond Head from the open oceanfront dining room will start you off with a smile. At lunch, the

Room Service

You are no longer limited by the room service menu in your hotel room. **Room Service in Paradise** (✆ **808/941-DINE** [941-3463]; www.rsiponline.com) delivers almost a dozen different cuisines (from American/Pacific Rim to Italian to sandwiches and burgers) from 50 restaurants to your hotel room. All you do is select a restaurant and order what you want. (See their online menu or pick up one of their magazines in various Waikiki locations.) You are charged for the food, a $6.75 delivery fee in Waikiki (more in outlying areas), and a tip for the driver. Best of all, you can pay with your credit card. Both lunch and dinner are available; you can even call in advance, and they'll deliver whenever you want.

seafood and vegetable curries, though pricey, are winners, and the steamed *ehu* (short-tail red snapper) is an Orchids signature. Kids may be more interested in the hamburgers and hot dogs. For dinner, *onaga* (ruby snapper) is steamed with ginger, Chinese parsley, shiitake mushrooms, and soy sauce, and then drizzled with hot sesame oil—delightful. Sunday brunch, with its outstanding selection of dishes, is one of the best in Hawaii.

In the Halekulani, 2199 Kalia Rd. ✆ **808/923-2311.** Kids' menu, highchairs, boosters, crayons. Reservations recommended. Dinner main courses $25–$58; kids' menu $5–$11. AE, DC, MC, V. Mon–Sat 7:30–11am and 11:30am–2pm; Sun brunch 9:30am–2:30pm; dinner daily 6–10pm.

Moderate

Duke's Canoe Club ★ Value SEAFOOD/STEAK Hip, busy, and oceanfront, this is what dining in Waikiki should be. There's hardly a time when the open-air dining room isn't filled with good Hawaiian music. It's crowded at sunset, though. Named after fabled surfer Duke Kahanamoku, this casual, upbeat hot spot buzzes with diners and Hawaiian-music lovers throughout the day. Lunch and the Barefoot Bar menu include pizza, sandwiches, burgers, salads, and appetizers such as mac-nut and crab wontons and the ever-popular grilled chicken quesadillas. Dinner fare is steak and seafood, with decent marks for the fresh catch, prepared in your choice of five styles. There's live entertainment nightly from 4pm to midnight, with no cover. Although there's a kids' menu, your little ones can also opt for the keiki buffet, an all-you-can-eat array of kids' favorites.

In the Outrigger Waikiki on the Beach, 2335 Kalakaua Ave. ✆ **808/922-2268.** www.dukeswaikiki.com. Kids' menu, highchairs, boosters, crayons. Reservations recommended for dinner. Main courses $20–$30; breakfast buffet $15 adults, $8 kids; kids' menu $5.95–$6.95. AE, DC, MC, V. Daily 7am–midnight.

Hau Tree Lanai ★ PACIFIC RIM Informal and delightful, this Honolulu institution scores higher on ambience than on food. The outdoor setting makes it a popular informal dining spot; an ancient hau tree provides shade and charm for diners. Breakfast here is a must: Choices include salmon Florentine, served with a fresh-baked scone; poi pancakes; Belgian waffles; eggs Benedict; and the Hawaiian platter of miniature poi pancakes, eggs, and a medley of island sausages. Lunchtime offerings include house-cured Atlantic salmon and an assortment of burgers, sandwiches, salads, and fresh fish and pasta specialties. Dinner selections are more ambitious and less reliable: fresh moonfish, red snapper, *opakapaka* (pink snapper), ahi, and chef's specials, in preparations ranging from plain grilled to stuffed and over-the-top rich. Although there isn't a kids' menu, they welcome families and will happily whip up a grilled cheese or a small bowl of spaghetti for your little ones.

In the New Otani Kaimana Beach Hotel, 2863 Kalakaua Ave. ✆ **808/921-7066.** Highchairs, boosters. Reservations recommended. Main courses $19–$33. AE, DC, DISC, MC, V. Daily 7–11am; 11:45 am–2pm (from noon on Sun); and 5:30–9pm. Late lunch in the open-air bar daily 2–4pm.

Hula Grill Waikiki ★★ Value HAWAIIAN REGIONAL This is the best place for breakfast in Waikiki. Not only does it have a terrific view of all of Waikiki (clear to Diamond Head), but the food is fabulous and a great value. Breakfast is a generous selection of pancakes (banana, mac nut, pineapple, even coconut) and eggs (from crab-cake eggs Benedict to a ham, bacon, and Portuguese sausage omelet with cheddar). Come back for a romantic dinner—the restaurant is decorated in a 1930s Hawaii waterfront home theme, with touches like the ohia log bar, a hula doll collection, slate flooring, and lauhala pine–soffited ceilings. Signature dinner dishes at this beachside bistro include

Dining in Waikiki 24-7

If your flight to Honolulu arrives late and you are starving, there now is help in Waikiki with the newly opened **MAC 24-7** (which stands for Modern American Cooking, 24 hours a day, 7 days a week), at the **Hilton Waikiki Prince Kuhio Hotel,** 2500 Kuhio Ave., at Liliuokalani Ave. (✆ **808/921-5564**). All day, every day, the menu has everything from breakfast, lunch, and dinner to snacks and desserts (though the bar stops pouring drinks between 4 and 6am for some reason). It's not just for late-night dining (although it comes in handy, as Waikiki eateries shut down by 10 or 11pm), but it's also a great place to get picnic lunches during the day. The view from the floor-to-ceiling windows is of the landscaped gardens in the lobby, the interior design is the new "in" decor—sophisticated but sparse in a Zen-like way, with splashes of bright color—and the waitstaff is friendly and helpful.

The cuisine is hotel coffee shop/diner "comfort" food, reasonably priced for Waikiki ($4–$28, with most entrees in the $11–$16 range), and plenty of it. The portion sizes can feed two and, in some cases, three people (even three hungry people). My pick for best meal of the day is breakfast, where the six-pack of buttery cinnamon rolls ($6) will feed three and the yummy wild blueberry pancakes ($11) are supersized (3 pancakes, each one 14 inches in diameter), plenty for two hungry people. Another "must-try" from the menu: the delicious meatloaf with garlic mashed potatoes and mushroom gravy ($17).

Hawaiian seviche, fire-grilled ono (wahoo), oven-roasted sesame opah (moonfish), and a nightly collection of specials.

In the Outrigger Waikiki on the Beach, 2335 Kalakaua Ave. ✆ **808/923-HULA** (923-4852). www.hulagrillwaikiki.com. Reservations recommended for dinner. Breakfast $5–$14; main courses $17–$29. AE, DC, MC, V. Daily breakfast 6:30–10:30am; happy hour 4–6pm with light menu; dinner 5–10pm.

Keo's in Waikiki ★ THAI With freshly spiced and spirited dishes and a familiar menu of Thai delights, Keo's arrived in Waikiki with a splashy tropical ambience and a menu that islanders and visitors love. Owner Keo Sananikone grows his own herbs, fruits, and vegetables without pesticides on his North Shore farm. Satay shrimp; basil-infused eggplant with tofu; evil jungle prince (shrimp, chicken, or vegetables in a basil-coconut-chile sauce); Thai garlic shrimp with mushrooms; pad Thai noodles; and the ever-delectable panang, green, and yellow curries are among his abiding delights. There's no kids' menu, but waitstaff will point out the faves among the under-8 crowd: crispy noodles and fried rice.

2028 Kuhio Ave. ✆ **808/951-9355.** www.keosthaicuisine.com. Highchairs, boosters. Reservations recommended. Main courses $13–$60. AE, DC, DISC, MC, V. Daily 7:30am–2pm and 5–10:30pm.

Sansei Seafood Restaurant and Sushi Bar ★★ ASIAN/PACIFIC RIM/SUSHI Perpetual award winner D. K. Kodama, who built Kapalua's Sansei into one of Maui's most popular eateries, has become something of a local legend with his exuberant brand of sushi and fusion cooking. Although some of the flavors (sweet Thai chile sauce with cilantro, for example) may be too fussy for sushi purists, there are ample choices for a full range of palates. Kids have their own menu, on which old standbys such as Southern-fried chicken strips and french fries are the most popular items. On the extensive main menu appear Sansei's trademark, award-winning Asian rock shrimp cake; Sansei special sushi (crab, cilantro, cucumber, and avocado with a sweet chile sauce); and miso scallops. In the traditional selections, you can choose from a wide range of selections, from very fresh yellowtail sushi to Japanese miso eggplant. If you are out for the evening sans kids, Kodama has added karaoke and late-night programs beginning at 10pm.

Waikiki Beach Marriott, 2552 Kalakaua Ave. ✆ **808/931-6286.** www.sanseihawaii.com. Kids' menu, highchairs, boosters, crayons. Reservations recommended. Main courses $19–$43; kids' menu $9–$11. AE, DISC, MC, V. Daily 5:30–10pm.

Inexpensive

Cha Cha Cha CARIBBEAN/MEXICAN Its heroic margaritas, cheap happy-hour beer, pupu, excellent homemade chips, and all-around lovable menu make this a Waikiki treasure. If your family is partial to salsa and to Mexican and Caribbean cuisine, you will be in heaven. A reasonably priced kids' menu (from which the quesadilla is the number-one pick) and friendly staff make this a terrific family treat. Ask about the specials because they're likely to be wonderful. Blackened swordfish, curried fresh grilled vegetables, and homemade desserts (including a creamy toasted coconut custard you won't want to miss) are some of the highlights.

342 Seaside Ave. ✆ **808/923-7797.** Kids' menu, highchairs. Complete dinners $8–$16; kids' menu $5.75. MC, V. Daily 11:30am–midnight; happy hour 4–6pm and 9–11pm.

Eggs 'n Things ★★ BREAKFAST This popular place is famous not only for its great food but also for its all-night hours. (At 3am, the clientele is scarfing down the humongous breakfasts.) Go when you are hungry; you'll find the fluffiest omelets (which come with pancakes, potatoes, and toast), melt-in-your-mouth waffles (piled high with fruit and whipped cream), and hot coffee constantly being poured into your cup. Prices are surprisingly reasonable, making this place worth standing in line for. Although there is no kids' menu, there is a "kids' plate" breakfast. Most kids will find everything they want on the regular menu.

1911-B Kalakaua Ave. (at Ala Moana Blvd.). ✆ **808/949-0820.** www.eggsnthings.com. Highchairs, boosters, crayons. Breakfast entrees $8–$12; kids' plate $4. AE, MC, V. Mon–Wed 6pm–2am (the next day) and Thurs–Sun 11pm–2am (the next day).

HONOLULU BEYOND WAIKIKI

Ala Moana & Kakaako

Expensive

Mariposa ★★ PACIFIC RIM/SOUTHWESTERN Once you get past the gourmet food department of Neiman Marcus, you'll be in Mariposa, a popular lunch spot in town. High ceilings for indoor diners, plus tables on the deck with views of Ala Moana Park and its Art Deco bridges, add up to a pleasing ambience, with or without the shopping. The waitstaff will welcome your family cordially with both a keiki menu and an adult menu of Pacific and American (called "heritage cuisine") specialties that include everything from opakapaka with a three-pepper vinaigrette to an excellent seared salmon salad. But the lunchtime favorite is invariably the starter of chicken broth—such as the towering, eggy popover with *poha* (cape gooseberry) butter you receive at the start of your

Honolulu Dining Beyond Waikiki

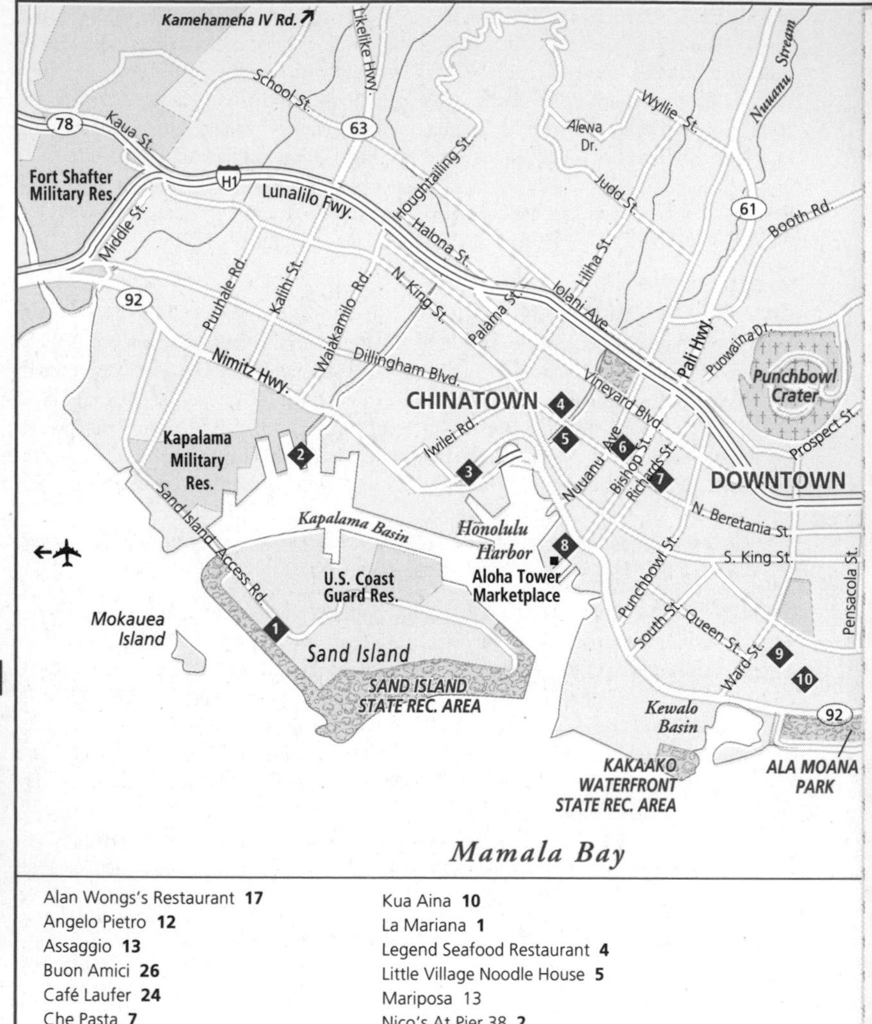

Alan Wongs's Restaurant **17**
Angelo Pietro **12**
Assaggio **13**
Buon Amici **26**
Café Laufer **24**
Che Pasta **7**
Chef Mavro Restaurant **18**
Chiang Mai Thai Cuisine **19**
Contemporary Museum Café **15**
Don Ho's Island Grill **8**
Genki Sushi **21**
Hoku's **28**
I♥ Country Café **11**
Indigo Eurasian Cuisine **6**
Jimbo's Restaurant **16**
Kaka'ako Kitchen **9**
Kua Aina **10**
La Mariana **1**
Legend Seafood Restaurant **4**
Little Village Noodle House **5**
Mariposa 13
Nico's At Pier 38 **2**
Ninniku-Ya Garlic Restaurant **22**
Olive Tree Café **28**
Panda Cuisine **14**
The Pineapple Room by Alan Wong **13**
Roy's Restaurant **28**
Sam Choy's Breakfast, Lunch, Crab & Big Aloha Brewery **3**
3660 On the Rise **27**
Town **23**
12th Avenue Grill **25**
Well Bento **20**

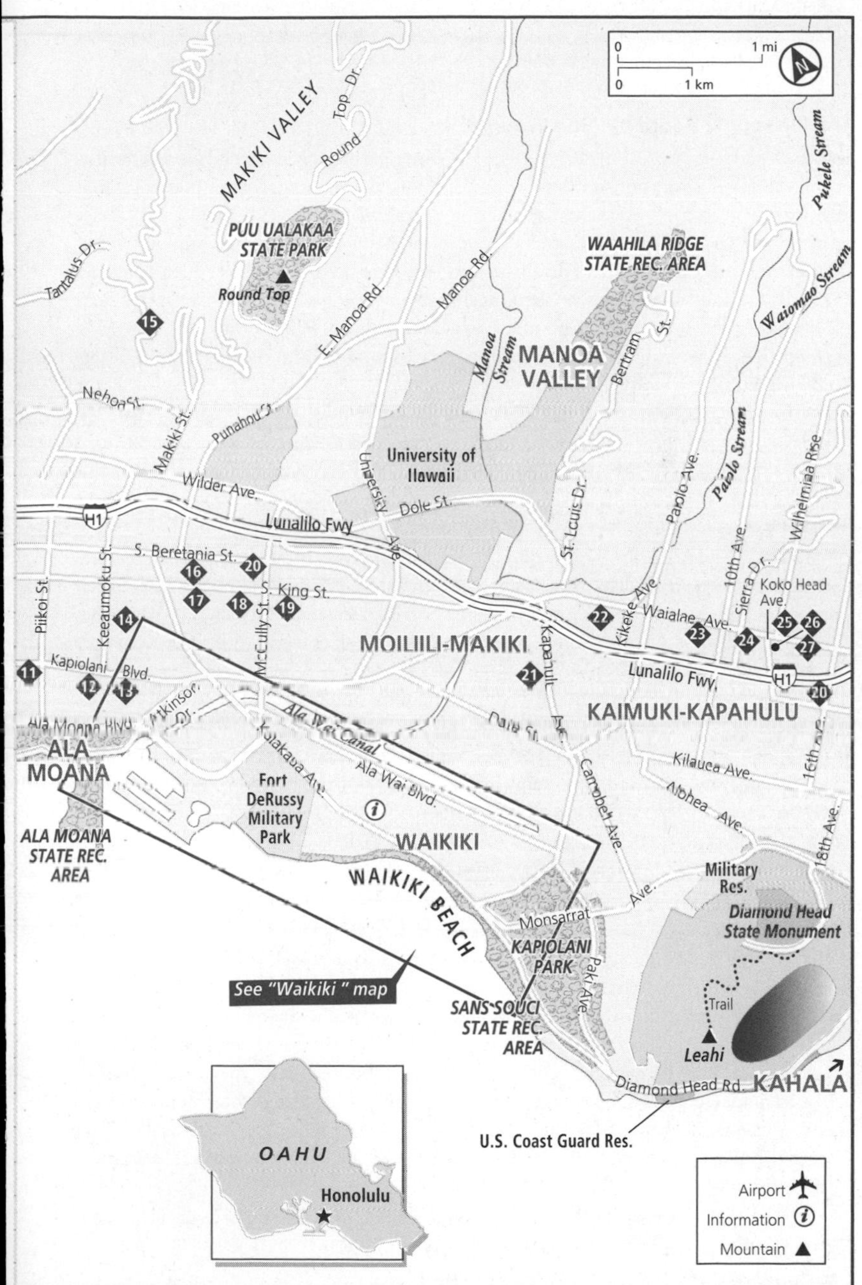

0
1 mi
0
1 km
MAKIKI VALLEY
Round Top Dr.
PUU UALAKAA STATE PARK
Round Top
Tantalus Dr.
15
E. Manoa Rd.
Manoa Rd.
WAAHILA RIDGE STATE REC. AREA
Manoa Stream
MANOA VALLEY
Bertram St.
Pukele Stream
Waiomao Stream
Nehoa St.
Makiki St.
Punahou St.
University of Hawaii
University Ave.
Wilder Ave.
Dole St.
St. Louis Dr.
Palolo Ave.
Palolo Stream
Wilhelmina Rise
H1
Lunalilo Fwy
S. Beretania St.
Keeaumoku St.
16
20
Piikoi St.
S. King St.
McCully St.
17
18
19
Kikeke Ave.
10th Ave.
Sierra Dr.
Koko Head Ave.
14
22
Waialae Ave.
23
24
25
26
27
MOILIILI-MAKIKI
Kapahulu Ave.
11
Kapiolani Blvd.
12
13
21
Lunalilo Fwy.
H1
20
Ala Moana Blvd.
Atkinson Dr.
Ala Wai Canal
Date St.
KAIMUKI-KAPAHULU
ALA MOANA
Kalakaua Ave.
Ala Wai Blvd.
Campbell Ave.
Kilauea Ave.
16th Ave.
Fort DeRussy Military Park
Alohea Ave.
ALA MOANA STATE REC. AREA
WAIKIKI
18th Ave.
WAIKIKI BEACH
Military Res.
Monsarrat Ave.
Diamond Head State Monument
KAPIOLANI PARK
Paki Ave.
See "Waikiki" map
SANS SOUCI STATE REC. AREA
Trail
Leahi
Diamond Head Rd.
KAHALA
U.S. Coast Guard Res.
OAHU
Honolulu
Airport
Information
Mountain

meal; it's the perfect welcome. The kids' menu has a choice of entrees (cheese pizza, grilled garlic fish kabobs, barbecue chicken) and a choice of desserts for $16.

In Neiman Marcus, Ala Moana Center, 1450 Ala Moana Blvd. ✆ **808/951-3420.** Kids' menu, highchairs, boosters. Reservations recommended. Main courses $14–$24 lunch, $14–$39 dinner; kids' menu $16. AE, DC, MC, V. Sun–Wed 11am–9pm; Thurs–Sat 11am–10pm.

The Pineapple Room by Alan Wong ★★ HAWAIIAN REGIONAL Yes, it's in a Macy's department store, but the chef is Alan Wong, a culinary icon. The food is terrific, and the kids will come out smiling. Wong conjures culinary masterpieces that will probably leave you wanting to come back and try breakfast, lunch, and dinner, just to see what he will serve. The room features an open kitchen with a lava-rock wall and abundant natural light, but these are details in a room where food is king. The menu changes regularly, but keep an eye out for the ginger scallion shrimp scampi, nori-wrapped tempura salmon, and superb gazpacho made of yellow and red Waimea tomatoes. The kids' menu includes cheese pizza, a keiki hamburger, Caesar salad, and the old standby PB&J sandwich with the Pineapple Room's crispy fries.

Macy's, 1450 Ala Moana Blvd. ✆ **808/945-6573.** www.alanwongs.com. Kids' menu, highchairs, boosters. Reservations recommended for lunch and dinner. Main courses $16–$20 lunch; prix-fixe lunch $29; main courses $28–$38 dinner; sampling dinner $75; kids' menu $4–$6.50. AE, DC, DISC, MC, V. Mon–Fri 11am–8:30pm; Sat 8am–8:30pm; Sun 9am–3pm.

Moderate

Assaggio ★ ITALIAN This wildly popular chain (also located in Kailua) features extensive, high-quality Italian offerings at good prices. There's no kids' menu, just smaller portions of the adults' menu (at lower prices). The lighter lunch menu features pasta dishes and house specialties such as shrimp scampi and rigatoni alla ricotta. At dinner, a panoply of pastas and specialties streams out of the kitchen: at least nine chicken entrees, pasta dishes ranging from mushroom and clam to linguine primavera, and eight veal choices. The number one kids' favorite pick is pasta with meatballs. One of Assaggio's best features is its prodigious seafood selection: shrimp, scallops, mussels, calamari, and fresh fish in many preparations, ranging from plain garlic and olive oil to spicy tomato and wine sauces. Assaggio's excellent service paired with entrees priced under $20 deserves applause.

In the Ala Moana Center, 1450 Ala Moana Blvd. ✆ **808/942-3446.** Highchairs, boosters. Reservations recommended. Main courses $10–$20 lunch, $16–$35 dinner. AE, DC, DISC, MC, V. Daily 11am–3pm; Sun–Thurs 4:30–9:30pm; Fri–Sat 4:30–10pm.

Inexpensive

Angelo Pietro PIZZA/SPAGHETTI Two motifs go over well here: the create-your-own pasta and the quirky take on Italian food that could come only from Japan. At this Italian-Japanese pasta house, you can order raw potato salad with any of four dressings—shoyu, ginger, *ume* (plum), and sesame-miso—and chase it with more than four dozen spaghetti choices, with sauces and toppings ranging from several types each of mushroom, shrimp, chicken, spinach, and sausage to squid ink and eggplant. There's no kids' menu (most kids are happy with the regular menu), but they do offer a kids' meal of pizza or ragout Bolognese. Garlic lovers adore the crisp garlic chips that are heaped atop some of the selections.

1585 Kapiolani Blvd. ✆ **808/941-0555.** Highchairs, boosters. Reservations accepted for groups of 5 or more. Main courses $7–$14; kids' meal $5. AE, DC, DISC, MC, V. Sun–Thurs 11am–10pm; Fri–Sat 11am–11pm.

I ❤ Country Cafe INTERNATIONAL Give yourself time to peruse the lengthy list of specials posted on the menu board, as well as the prodigious printed menu. Stand in line at the counter, place your order and pay, find a Formica-topped table, and wait for your order to appear on a plate heaped with salad and other accompaniments. The mind-boggling selection includes nine types of cheese steaks (including vegetarian tofu), Cajun meatloaf, Thai curries, various stir-fries, shoyu chicken, vegetarian or eggplant lasagna, chicken Dijon, Cajun-style ahi, and other choices spanning many cultures and tastes. Surely there is something here for everyone in the family. Take a good look at the diners, and you'll see that the menu appeals equally to bodybuilders and hedonists.

In Ala Moana Plaza, 451 Piikoi St. ✆ **808/596-8108.** Kids' menu, highchairs, boosters. Main courses $5–$9.75; kids' menu $5. AE, DC, DISC, MC, V. Daily 8am–9pm.

Kaka'ako Kitchen ★★ Finds GOURMET PLATE LUNCHES This is an excellent place for families; it's owned by Chef Russell Siu, of **3660 on the Rise** (p. 108). You'll get excellent home-style cooking served on Styrofoam plates in a warehouse ambience at budget prices. The menu, which changes every 3 to 4 months, includes a keiki menu, on which the chicken nuggets are the most popular dish. For adults, you can choose from seared ahi sandwich with *tobiko* (flying-fish roe) aioli; the signature charbroiled ahi steak; sandwiches; beef stew; five-spice shoyu chicken; the very popular meatloaf; and other multi-ethnic entrees.

In the Ward Centre, 1200 Ala Moana Blvd. ✆ **808/596-7400.** Kids' menu, highchairs. Breakfast $6–$9; lunch and dinner main courses $8–$14; kids' menu $5. AE, DC, MC, V. Mon–Thurs 8am–9pm; Fri–Sat 8am–10pm; Sun 8am–5pm.

Kua Aina ★ Value AMERICAN The ultimate sandwich shop, for years a North Shore fixture, expanded to the Ward Centre area (near Borders and Starbucks), and the result is dizzying. Phone in your order if you can. During lunch and dinner hours, people wait patiently in long lines for the famous burgers and sandwiches: the beef burgers with heroic toppings; mahimahi with Ortega Mexican seasoning and cheese (a legend); grilled eggplant and peppers; roast turkey; tuna and avocado; roast beef and avocado; and about a dozen other selections on a kaiser roll or multigrain wheat or rye breads. The sandwiches and fries are excellent, and the outdoor section with tables, thankfully, has grown—but there still may be a wait during lunch hour. The takeout business is brisk. No kids' menu, but there is a smaller, very yummy "kiddie burger."

In Ward Village, 1116 Auahi St. ✆ **808/591-9133.** Highchairs. Sandwiches $6.50–$8.50; kiddie burger $4.20. No credit cards. Mon–Sat 10:30am–9pm; Sun 10:30am–8pm.

Panda Cuisine ★ DIM SUM/HONG KONG–STYLE CHINESE/SEAFOOD This is dim sum heaven, not only for the selection, but also for the late-night dim sum service, a rare thing for what is a morning and lunchtime tradition in Hong Kong. Panda's dim sum selection—spinach-scallop, chive, taro, shrimp dumplings, pork hash, and some 50-plus others—is a real pleaser. (***Tip:*** The spinach-scallop and taro puff varieties are a cut above.) The reckless can spring for the live Maine lobster and Dungeness crab in season, or the king clam and steamed fresh fish, but the steaming bamboo carts yielding toothsome surprises are hard to resist. Noodles and sizzling platters are good accompaniments to the dim sum. There's plenty for kids to choose from, especially the fried rice, noodles, and soups.

641 Keeaumoku St. ✆ **808/947-1688.** Highchairs, boosters, crayons on request. Main courses $8–$29. MC, V. Mon–Sat 10:30am–2:30pm and 5pm–1am; Sun 5:30–10pm.

Aloha Tower Marketplace

Don Ho's Island Grill CONTEMPORARY ISLAND/HAWAIIAN Don Ho's Island Grill's shrine to Don Ho is a mix of nostalgic interior elements: koa paneling, thatched roof, split-bamboo ceilings, old pictures of Ho with celebrities, faux palm trees, and open sides looking out onto the harbor. It's kitschy and charming, down to the vinyl pareu-printed tablecloths and the flower behind the server's ear. The kids have their own menu (pizza seems to be the most popular item) and will be fascinated with the decor. If you want to sneak back later in the evening after the kids are tucked away, Don Ho's has become one of the significant late-night musical venues of Honolulu, packing in sold-out crowds for special concerts by local musical icons like Amy Gilliom and Willie K.

Aloha Tower Marketplace, 1 Aloha Tower Dr. ✆ **808/528-0807.** Kids' menu, highchairs, boosters, crayons. Reservations recommended. Main courses $11–$26; kids' menu $5.25 including drink. AE, DC, DISC, MC, V. Daily 10am–9pm; nightclub (days vary) open until 2am.

Downtown

Downtowners love the informal walk-in cafes lining one side of attractive **Bishop Square,** at 1001 Bishop St. (at King St.), in the middle of the business district, where free entertainment is offered every Friday during lunch hour. The popular **Che Pasta** is a stalwart here, chic enough for business meetings and not too formal (or expensive) for a family meal of pasta and minestrone. Some places in Bishop Square open for breakfast and lunch, others just for lunch, but most close when business offices empty.

Note: Keep in mind that **Restaurant Row** (Ala Moana Blvd., between Punchbowl and South sts.), which features several hot new establishments, offers free validated parking in the evening.

Indigo Eurasian Cuisine ★★ EURASIAN Hardwood floors, red brick, wicker, high ceilings, and an overall feeling of Indochine luxury give Indigo a stylish edge. You can dine indoors or in a garden setting on menu offerings such as pot stickers, Buddhist bao buns, savory brochettes, tandoori chicken breast, vegetable tarts, Asian-style noodles and dumplings, lilikoi-glazed baby back ribs, and cleverly named offerings from East and West. No kids' menu, but there are lots of kid-friendly items to choose from such as dim sum, noodles, and chicken dishes.

1121 Nuuanu Ave. ✆ **808/521-2900.** Highchairs, boosters. Reservations recommended. Lunch $17–$24; dinner main dishes $23–$37. DC, DISC, MC, V. Tues–Fri 11:30am–2pm; Tues–Sat 6–9:30pm; martini time in the Green Room Tues–Fri 4–8pm.

Legend Seafood Restaurant ★ DIM SUM/SEAFOOD It's like dining in Hong Kong here, with a Chinese-speaking clientele poring over Chinese newspapers and the clatter of chopsticks punctuating conversations. Excellent dim sum comes in bamboo steamers that beckon seductively from carts. Although dining here is a form of assertiveness training (you must wave madly to catch the server's eye and then point to what you want), the system doesn't deter fans from returning. Among our favorites: deep-fried taro puffs and prawn dumplings, shrimp dim sum, vegetable dumplings, and the open-faced seafood with shiitake, scallops, and a tofu product called *aburage.* Dim sum is served only at lunch, but dinnertime seafood dishes comfort sufficiently. Not a very elegant restaurant, but the food is serious and great. Kids usually love picking their own dim sum off the rolling carts, but be prepared to finish the ones they sample and decide against.

In the Chinese Cultural Plaza, 100 N. Beretania St. ✆ **808/532-1868.** Highchairs. Reservations recommended. Most items under $16. AE, DC, MC, V. Mon–Fri 10:30am–2pm and 5:30–9pm; Sat–Sun 8am–2pm and 5:30–9pm.

Little Village Noodle House CHINESE Ignore the decor, which reminds me of the back porch of a small French bistro with overhanging roof in Provence. The food here is "simple and healthy" (their motto), and authentic Chinese (Northern, Canton, and

Hong Kong–style). My picks are the Shanghai noodles with stir-fried veggies, the walnut shrimp, and the butterfish in black bean sauce. The menu is eclectic and offers some interesting selections you don't often see such as congree and pig knuckles; kids share dishes with the rest of the family (if your kids turn up their noses at Chinese cuisine, then order grilled chicken wings or french fries). Not only is the service friendly (a rarity in Chinatown), but the waitstaff are quite knowledgeable about the dishes. Yes, there is takeout, but even more unique (for Chinatown): They have parking in the back!

1113 Smith St. ✆ **808/545-3008.** Highchairs. Most items under $13. AE, DISC, MC, V. Sun–Thurs 10:30am–10:30pm; Fri–Sat 10am–midnight.

Kalihi/Sand Island

La Mariana AMERICAN Just try to find a spot more evocative or nostalgic than this South Seas oasis at lagoon's edge in the bowels of industrial Honolulu, with carved tikis, glass balls suspended in fishing nets, shell chandeliers, and old tables made from koa trees. In the back section, the entire ceiling is made of tree limbs. This unique, nearly 50-year-old restaurant is popular for lunch, sunset appetizers, and impromptu Friday- and Saturday-night singalongs at the piano bar, where a colorful crowd (including some Don Ho look-alikes) gathers to sing Hawaiian classics like a 1950s high-school glee club. It is delightful; your kid will think they are on a movie set. The seared Cajun-style ahi is your best bet as an appetizer or entree; La Mariana is more about spirit and ambience than food.

50 Sand Island Rd. ✆ **808/848-2800.** Reservations recommended, especially on weekends. Main courses $6–$12 lunch, $10–$22 dinner. AE, MC, V. Daily 11am–3pm, 3–5pm (pupu), and 5–9pm. Turn makai (toward the ocean) on Sand Island Rd. from Nimitz Hwy.; immediately after the first stoplight on Sand Island, take a right and drive toward the ocean; it's not far from the airport.

Sam Choy's Breakfast, Lunch, Crab & Big Aloha Brewery ISLAND CUISINE/ SEAFOOD This is a happy, carefree eatery—elegance and cholesterol be damned. Chef/ restaurateur Sam Choy's crab house features great fun and gigantic meals (a Choy trademark). Imagine dining in an all-wood sampan (the centerpiece of the 11,000-sq.-ft. restaurant) and washing your hands in an oversize wok in the center of the room. A 2,000-gallon live-crab tank lines the open kitchen with an assortment of crabs in season. Clam chowder, seafood gumbos, oysters from the oyster bar, and assorted *poke* (pronounced "po-*kay*"; chopped raw fish mixed with seaweed and spices) are also offered at dinner, which, in Choy fashion, comes complete with soup, salad, and entree. Little ones who aren't fond of seafood can opt for the burger and fries or the spaghetti and meatballs from the kids' menu.

580 Nimitz Hwy., Iwilei. ✆ **808/545-7979.** www.samchoy.com. Kids' menu, highchairs, boosters, crayons. Reservations recommended for lunch and dinner. Main courses $5–$13 breakfast, $9–$40 lunch, $19–$45 dinner; kids' menu $4–$6.25. AE, DC, DISC, MC, V. Daily 7–10pm. Located in the Iwilei industrial area near Honolulu Harbor, across the street from Gentry Pacific Center.

Manoa Valley/Moiliili/Makiki

Very Expensive

Chef Mavro Restaurant ★★★ HAWAIIAN REGIONAL/PROVENÇAL This is another romantic pick for an adults-only night out. Chef/owner George Mavrothalassitis, a native of Provence, has fans all over the world who have admired his creativity. He also has the only independently operated AAA Four Diamond restaurant in Hawaii. Located in a conveniently accessible, nontouristy neighborhood in McCully, you can order prix fixe or a la carte, with or without wine pairings. And they are dazzling pairings. To his list of signature items—filet of *moi* (Hawaiian fish) with crisp scales, sautéed mushrooms, and saffron coulis; and award-winning *onaga* (Hawaiian fish) baked in Hawaiian salt crust—he's

Local Chains & Familiar Names

Todai, 1910 Ala Moana Blvd. (✆ **808/947-1000**), a string of Japanese seafood buffet restaurants with locations ranging from Dallas to Portland to Beverly Center, is packing 'em in at the gateway to Waikiki with bountiful tables of sushi (40 kinds), hot seafood entrees (tempura, calamari, fresh fish, gyoza, king crab legs, teppanyaki), and delectable desserts. There's not much ambience, but no one cares; the food is terrific, the selection impressive, and the operation as smooth as the green tea cheesecake. Lunch is $15 weekdays and $18 on weekends; dinner is $28 weekdays and $29 on weekends.

Ala Moana Center's third floor is a mecca for dining and schmoozing. Here you'll find the family-friendly **Bubba Gump Shrimp Company** (✆ **808/949-4867**) and **California Pizza Kitchen** (✆ **808/941-7715**), which also maintains branches in Kahala Mall, 4211 Waialae Ave. (✆ **808/737-9446**), and at Pearlridge, 98-1005 Moanalua Rd. (✆ **808/487-7741**).

L&L Drive-Inn remains a plate-lunch bonanza islandwide, with 45 locations in Hawaii (36 on Oahu alone). Local island families flock to **Zippy's Restaurants** ★ (at last count 21 of them on Oahu; www.zippys.com), the maestro of quick meals, with a surprisingly good selection of fresh seafood, saimin, chili, and local fare, plus the wholesome new low-fat, vegetarian "Shintani Cuisine," sold in selected branches and deli counters.

It's hard to spend more than $10 for the French and Vietnamese specials at the **Ba-le Sandwich Shops:** *pho* (Vietnamese noodle soup), croissants as

added new favorites, including a you-can-cut-it-with-a-fork filet of beef tenderloin crusted with red wine confit onion. Hints of Tahitian vanilla, lemon grass, *ogo* (seaweed), rosemary, and Madras curry add exotic flavors to the French-inspired cooking and fresh island ingredients. The desserts are extraordinary, especially the all-American apple tart with Hawaiian vanilla yogurt ice cream. The split-level room is quietly cordial, and the menu changes monthly to highlight seasonal ingredients. Not really appropriate for children; if you bring your kids, they will have to live with the menu and, depending on how well-behaved your kids are in an adult restaurant, the other patrons may give you the "stink eye."

1969 S. King St. ✆ **808/944-4714.** Highchairs. Reservations recommended. Prix-fixe dinners 3-course $65, 4-course $71, 6-course $104, 11-course $150 ($98–$154 with wine pairings). AE, DC, DISC, MC, V. Tues–Sun 6–9:30pm.

Expensive

Alan Wong's Restaurant ★★★ HAWAIIAN REGIONAL Alan Wong is one of Hawaii's most popular chefs, and it's definitely worth the sometimes long waits at this bustling eatery to sample his culinary wizardry. Worshipful foodies come from all over the state, drawn by the food—which is brilliant—and a menu that is irresistible. The daily changing menu includes cutting-edge offerings sizzling with the Asian flavors of lemon grass, sweet-and-sour, garlic, and wasabi, deftly melded with the fresh seafood and produce of the islands. Although there's no dedicated kids' menu, Wong dishes out pasta and specially made hamburgers just for the keiki. The 90-seat room has a glassed-in terrace and an open kitchen.

good as the espresso, and wonderful taro/tapioca desserts. Among Ba-le's 20 locations are those at Ala Moana Center (✆ **808/944-4752**) and at 333 Ward Ave. (✆ **808/591-0935**). A Ba-le location at Manoa Marketplace, 2855 E. Manoa Rd. (✆ **808/988-1407**), serves a terrific selection of Thai dishes in an enlarged dining area, making it as much a restaurant as a place for takeout food. For smoothies, head to **Jamba Juice,** with 11 locations at last count, from Kahala Mall to Ward Village, Kapahulu, Pearlridge, Kailua, the DFS Galleria on Kalakaua Avenue, the Royal Hawaiian Shopping Center, the Aiea Shopping Center, the Ewa Town Center, the Financial Plaza, and the Waikiki Trade Center (✆ **808/926-4944**). The ubiquitous **Boston's North End Pizza Bakery** chain claims an enthusiastic following with its reasonable prices and generous toppings. Boston's can be found in Kaimuki, Kailua, Kaneohe, Pearlridge, and Makakilo.

For Italian food, the American chain **Buca di Beppo** is in the Ward Entertainment Center, 1030 Auahi St. (✆ **808/591-0880**). Heaping plates of Italian food—enough to feed a very hungry family—along with the reasonable prices, make this place quite popular. Reservations are a must.

In Waikiki, the local **Hard Rock Cafe** is at 1837 Kapiolani Blvd. (✆ **808/955-7383**), while at the Ala Moana end of Waikiki, **Outback Steakhouse,** 1765 Ala Moana Blvd. (✆ **808/951-6274**), serves great steaks and is always full. In downtown's Restaurant Row, beef eaters can also chow down at **Ruth's Chris Steak House,** 500 Ala Moana Blvd. (✆ **808/599-3860**).

1857 S. King St., 3rd Floor. ✆ **808/949-2526.** www.alanwongs.com. Highchairs, boosters, paper, crayons. Reservations recommended. Main courses $35–$52; 5-course sampling menu $75 ($105 with wine); chef's 7-course tasting menu $95 ($135 with wine). AE, DC, MC, V. Daily 5–10pm.

Moderate

Contemporary Museum Cafe ★ *Finds* HEALTHFUL GOURMET The surroundings are an integral part of the dining experience at this tiny lunchtime cafe, part of an art museum nestled on the slopes of Tantalus amid carefully cultivated Asian gardens, with a breathtaking view of Diamond Head and priceless contemporary artwork displayed indoors and out. The menu is limited to sandwiches, soups, salads, and appetizers; the staff will happily make a grilled cheese sandwich if there is nothing else on the menu to please your little eater. The lunchtime fare consists of grilled vegetable bruschetta, Gorgonzola-walnut spread, tofu burger, black-bean pita wrap, or fresh-fish specials, and desserts such as flourless chocolate cake and fresh-baked chocolate chip cookies.

In The Contemporary Museum, 2411 Makiki Heights Dr. ✆ **808/523-3362.** www.tcmhi.org. Highchairs, boosters. Reservations recommended. Main courses $10–$12. MC, V. Tues–Sat 11:30am–2:30pm; Sun noon–2:30pm.

Inexpensive

Chiang Mai Thai Cuisine THAI Chiang Mai made sticky rice famous in Honolulu, serving it in bamboo steamers with fish and exotic curries that have a dedicated following. Menu items include toothsome red, green, and yellow curries; the signature Cornish game hen in lemon grass and spices; and a garlic-infused green papaya salad marinated in tamarind sauce. Spicy shrimp soup, eggplant with basil and tofu, and the vegetarian green curry are favorites. Since the dining is family-style, there is no kids' menu, but they will add extra plates so your family can share dishes.

2239 S. King St. ✆ **808/941-1151.** Highchairs, boosters. Reservations recommended for dinner. Main courses $9–$16. AE, DC, DISC, MC, V. Mon–Fri 11am–2pm; daily 5:30–9:30pm.

Jimbo's Restaurant ★ Value JAPANESE Jimbo's is the quintessential neighborhood restaurant—small, a line of regulars outside, fantastic house-made noodles and broths, everything good and affordable. A must for any noodle lover, Jimbo's serves homemade udon in a flawless broth with a subtle, smoky flavor, then tops the works with shrimp tempura, chicken, eggs, vegetables, seaweed, roasted mochi, and a variety of accompaniments of your choice. But our fave is the *nabeyaki* (an earthenware pot of udon with tempura on top). Owner Jimbo Motojima, a perfectionist, uses only the finest ingredients from Japan. Although he doesn't have a kids' menu, Jimbo will whip up plain noodles for picky eaters.

1936 S. King St. ✆ **808/947-2211.** Highchairs, boosters. No reservations. Main courses $7–$20. MC, V. Daily 11am–2:50pm; Sun–Thurs 5–9:50pm; Fri–Sat 5–10:30pm.

Well Bento Finds HEALTHFUL/GOURMET We wondered whether such healthy organic food—without the use of eggs, refined sugar, or dairy products—would be satisfying. Countless plate lunches later, we can report that Well Bento will make a guiltless gourmet out of even the fussiest palate. Each plate is aesthetically pleasing, wholesome, and tasty. Louisiana tempeh, salmon grilled over lava rocks or poached with shiitake mushrooms, Cajun-style chicken, and creative vegetarian selections ("plant-based plates") make this a place worth trying. Bean salad, cabbage and seaweed salads, and organic brown rice accompany each plate and are as decorative as they are delicious. This is a good picnic choice, as it's mostly takeout, and only a few seats are provided.

2570 S. Beretania St., 2nd Floor. ✆ **808/941-5261.** www.wellbento.com. Plate lunches $8–$13. AE, MC, V. Daily 10:30am–9pm.

Kaimuki/Kapahulu

Expensive

3660 on the Rise ★★ FUSION Since the *Wine Spectator* gave this restaurant its "Award of Excellence," this place has been packed, and with good reason. In his 200-seat restaurant, Chef Russell Siu adds an Asian or local touch to the basics: rack of lamb with macadamia nuts, filets of catfish in ponzu sauce, and seared ahi salad with grilled shiitake mushrooms, a local favorite. The ahi katsu, wrapped in nori and fried medium-rare, is a main attraction in the appetizer department, and for dessert, Lisa Siu's warm chocolate cake garners raves. If your kids are gourmets, they may enjoy it here (there actually is a kids' menu), but if they are finicky eaters, get a sitter and go and enjoy this wonderful cuisine by yourself.

3660 Waialae Ave. ✆ **808/737-1177.** www.3660.com. Kids' menu, highchairs, boosters. Reservations suggested. Main courses $21–$45; prix-fixe dinner $40; kids' menu $5.75–$15. AE, DC, DISC, MC, V. Tues–Sun 5:30–9pm.

Moderate

Buon Amici ★★ Finds ITALIAN The former C&C Pasta was sold, renovated, and reopened in 2007 with much of the same great Italian dishes, a new chef (Alfredo Lee, formerly of Spada), and the same charming waiter (Marc Andres from Switzerland); and the result is that the homey, neighborhood restaurant remains. Buon Amici (which means "good sense") specializes in homemade pastas with big servings (from $19); the night we dined there they did allow us to order half portions to try as many as possible. Other good bets on the menu: fresh, creative salads (especially the spinach with organic leaves, applewood smoked bacon, ricotta cheese, and sautéed mushrooms and walnuts); great appetizers (the beef carpaccio is divine); and excellent meat dishes. As we went to press they still were BYOB, with a $5 corkage fee per table.

3605 Waialae Ave. ✆ **808/732-5999.** Reservations required for dinner. Main courses $17–$34. MC, V. Tues–Fri and Sun 5–9pm; Sat–Sun 5–9:30pm.

Genki Sushi ★ SUSHI If your kids like sushi, this is one of the most inexpensive places to go. Take your place in line for a seat at one of the U-shaped counters. Conveyor belts parade by with freshly made sushi, usually two pieces per color-coded plate, priced inexpensively. The possibilities are dizzying: spicy tuna topped with scallions, ahi, scallops with mayonnaise, Canadian roll (like California roll, except with salmon), sea urchin, flavored octopus, sweet shrimp, surf clam, corn, tuna salad, and so on. Genki starts with a Japanese culinary tradition and takes liberties with it, so don't be a purist. By the end of the meal, the piled-high plates are tallied up by color, and presto, your bill appears. Combination platters are available for takeout.

900 Kapahulu Ave. ✆ **808/735-7700.** Highchairs, boosters. No reservations. A la carte sushi $1.40–$4.60 for 2 pieces; combination platters $5–$41. AE, DC, DISC, MC, V. Sun–Thurs 11am–9pm; Fri–Sat 11am–10pm; takeout available daily 11am–9pm.

Inexpensive

Cafe Laufer ★ BAKERY/SANDWICH SHOP This small, cheerful cafe features frilly decor and sublime pastries—from apple scones and linzer tortes to fruit flan, decadent chocolate mousse, and carrot cake—to accompany the lattes and espressos. Fans drop in for simple soups and deli sandwiches on fresh-baked breads; biscotti during coffee break; or a hearty loaf of seven-grain, rye, pumpernickel, or French bread. The place is a solid hit for lunch; the small but satisfying menu includes soup/salad/sandwich specials for a song, a fabulous spinach salad with dried cranberries and Gorgonzola, and gourmet greens with mango-infused, honey-mustard dressing. The orange-seared shrimp salad and the Chinese chicken salad are great for the light eater, and the smoked Atlantic salmon with fresh pumpernickel bread and cream cheese, Maui onions, and capers is excellent. They will always make a plain cheese sandwich for your little ones. The special Saturday-night desserts draw a brisk post-movie business.

3565 Waialae Ave. ✆ **808/735-7717.** No reservations. Most items $5–$23. AE, DC, DISC, MC, V. Wed–Thurs and Sun 10am–9pm; Fri–Sat 10am–10pm; Mon 10am–3pm.

EAST OF WAIKIKI: KAHALA

Hoku's ★★★ EUROPEAN/PACIFIC Elegant without being stuffy, and creative without being overwrought, the fine-dining room of the Kahala Hotel offers elegant lunches and dinners combining European finesse with an island touch and is a wonderful place to bring the kids. The ocean view, open kitchen, and astonishing bamboo floor are stellar features. Reflecting the restaurant's cross-cultural influences, the kitchen is equipped with a *kiawe* grill (the kiawe cold smoked pork chops are divine); the pancetta crusted onaga, lobster, and lemon risotto melts in your mouth; and the Szechuan wok-fried lobster and Asian vegetables rounds out the varieties of ethnic specialties in this must-try dining room. Your kids may not be as curious, and they can order off the kids' menu, on which hot dogs and pizza are king.

In the Kahala Mandarin Oriental Hotel, 5000 Kahala Ave. ✆ **808/739-8780.** Kids' menu, highchairs, boosters, crayons. Reservations recommended. Main courses $32–$90; kids' menu $7.50–$13. AE, DC, DISC, MC, V. Daily 5:30–10pm; Sun brunch 10:30am–2pm.

Olive Tree Cafe ★★ Finds EASTERN MEDITERRANEAN/GREEK Delectables at bargain prices stream out of the tiny open kitchen here. Recently voted "Best Restaurant in Hawaii under $20" in a local survey, Olive Tree is every neighborhood's dream—a totally hip restaurant with divine Greek fare and friendly prices. There are umbrella tables outside and a few seats indoors, and you order and pay at the counter. Larger parties now have an awning over the sturdy wooden tables on the Koko Head side. The mussel ceviche is fabulous, and the creamy, tender chicken saffron, a frequent special, always elicits groans of pleasure, as does the robust and generous Greek salad, another Olive Tree attraction. We also love the souvlakia, ranging from fresh fish to lamb, spruced up with the chef's homemade yogurt-dill sauce. A family can dine here like sultans without breaking the bank, and take in a movie next door, too. Kids will find plenty to eat on the regular menu, especially the popular chicken souvlakia. Adults can BYOB.

4614 Kilauea Ave., next to Kahala Mall. ✆ **808/737-0303.** No reservations. Main courses $8–$11. No credit cards; checks accepted. Daily 5–10pm.

EAST OAHU

Hawaii Kai

Roy's Restaurant ★★★ ASIAN/EUROPEAN This is the first of Roy Yamaguchi's six signature restaurants in Hawaii (he has two dozen all over the world). It is still the flagship and many people's favorite, true to its Euro-Asian roots and Yamaguchi's winning formula: open kitchen, fresh ingredients, ethnic touches, and a good dose of nostalgia mingled with European techniques. The menu changes nightly, but you can generally count on individual pizzas, a varied appetizer menu (summer rolls, blackened ahi, hibachi-style salmon), a small pasta selection, and entrees such as lemon grass–roasted chicken, garlic-mustard short ribs, hibachi-style salmon in ponzu sauce, and several types of fresh catch. The separate kids' menu mainly features pasta. One of Hawaii's most popular restaurants, Roy's is lit up at night with tiki torches outside; the view from within is of scenic Maunalua Bay. Roy's is also renowned for its high-decibel style of dining—it's always full and noisy. Other Roy's restaurants in Hawaii appear on Oahu at Ko Olina, in Poipu, Kauai; Waikoloa, Big Island; and two on Maui in Kihei and Napili. There's also live music every other weekend; if you bring your preteens or teens along, they'll most likely roll their eyes at "your music."

6600 Kalanianaole Hwy. ✆ **808/396-7697.** www.roysrestaurant.com. Kids' menu, highchairs, boosters, crayons. Reservations recommended. Main courses $20–$45; kids' menu $13. AE, DC, DISC, MC, V. Mon–Thurs 5:30–9:30pm; Fri 5:30–10pm; Sat 5–10pm; Sun 5–9:30pm.

THE WINDWARD COAST

Lucy's Grill 'n Bar ★★ HAWAIIAN REGIONAL This is one of Kailua's most popular restaurants, not just because of the open-air bar and the outdoor lanai seating, but because the food is terrific. The menu is eclectic Hawaiian cuisine with lots of choices and giant-size portions. Be sure to order the spicy ahi tower with sushi rice, avocado, wasabi cream, and roasted nori to get you started. Any of the fresh fish and seafood is wonderful, especially the Szechuan spiced jumbo tiger prawns with black-bean cream and penne pasta or the lemon grass–crusted scallops with yellow Thai curry. The little tykes will love the pizza, pasta, and lip-smacking ribs (all found on the regular menu). Save room for desserts: crème brûleé with Tahitian vanilla bean, dark chocolate soufflé cake, or their "damn fine" apple pie—a la mode, of course. The dress is casual, and the clientele is from the neighborhood.

33 Aulike St., Kailua. ✆ **808/230-8188.** Highchairs, boosters, crayons. Reservations recommended. Main courses $15–$28. MC, V. Daily 5–10pm.

Expensive

21 Degrees North ★★★ PACIFIC RIM ***Foodies alert:*** It is well worth the drive from Waikiki (45–60 min.) to the North Shore to enjoy this signature restaurant at Turtle Bay Resort. This is dining for grown-ups; although they will prepare a few items for the kids, we suggest you get a sitter and enjoy a night out. Under the impressive hand of Chef Andrew Anion-Copley, not only is the restaurant visually inspiring, but the food is outstanding. The dishes emerging from the kitchen take Hawaii dining to a new level. The chef has taken contemporary island cuisine and made it fresh and interesting. The ever-changing menu has such unusual combinations as pineapple-guava glazed baby back ribs with sweet-and-sour cabbage and Thai chile braised island fish in a cucumber gazpacho with grilled baby bok choy and mango salsa. Save room for the signature dessert, "The 21 Phyllo," a dreamy ganache brownie wrapped in phyllo studded with toasted macadamia nuts and served in a raspberry sauce. We highly recommend the four-course, $76 tasting menu ($95 with wine pairings).

57-091 Kamehameha Hwy., Kahuku. ✆ **808/293-8811.** www.turtlebayresort.com. Highchairs, boosters. Reservations required. Main courses $28–$50; 5-course tasting menu $76 without wine, $95 with wine. AE, DC, DISC, MC, V. Tues–Sat 6–10pm.

Moderate

Jameson's by the Sea SEAFOOD Bring the kids to this roadside watering hole across the street from the ocean for cocktails, sashimi, and its celebrated salmon pâté, or for other hot and cold appetizers, salads, and sandwiches. The kids will most likely order the cheeseburger off the keiki menu, but you'll be tempted by the grilled crab and shrimp sandwich on sourdough bread or the fresh-fish sandwich of the day, grilled plain and simple. Upstairs, the much pricier dining room opens its doors 5 nights a week for the usual surf and turf choices: fresh opakapaka, *ulua* (Hawaiian jackfish), and mahimahi; scallops in lemon butter and capers; and lobster tail, New York steak, and filet mignon.

62-540 Kamehameha Hwy., Haleiwa. ✆ **808/637-4336.** Kids' menu, highchairs, boosters, crayons. Reservations recommended. Main courses $13–$39, downstairs lunch menu $9–$21; kids' menu $4.50–$7.50. AE, DC, DISC, MC, V. Mon–Fri 11am–9pm; Sat–Sun 9am–9pm.

Ola at Turtle Bay Resort ★★ Finds HAWAIIAN/SEAFOOD Even if you are staying in Waikiki, plan a day at the beach on the North Shore and eat here for lunch or dinner. You will not regret it. First, there's the location—literally on the sand on the beach next door to the Turtle Bay Resort. Second, the restaurant is an open-air ("open" as in no walls) beach pavilion, made from ironwood trees harvested from the surrounding area. The view is the lapping waves of the Pacific onto the sand. The atmosphere when they light the tiki torches at sunset is very, very romantic. Third, and best of all, is the food! Chef Fred DeAngelo named his restaurant Ola, which means "alive" or "healthy" in Hawaii, and he insists on only the freshest of ingredients. The menu is filled with creative selections (the ahi and lobster poke served with a wonton spoon) and some of the best food you will eat in Hawaii. My favorites are the incredible slow-poached togarashi salmon with a sweet, sugar cane crust served with Okinawan sweet potato and locally grown corn; the Lawai'a fishermen's stew with lobster, shrimp, scallops and fresh fish; and an unforgettable kiawe smoked beef tenderloin.

Turtle Bay Resort, 57-091 Kamehameha Hwy., Kahuku. ✆ **808/293-0801.** www.turtlebayresort.com/Dining/Ola.asp. Reservations recommended for dinner. Lunch entrees $16–$22; dinner entrees $18–$38; kids' menu $6–$10. AE, DC, DISC, MC, V. Daily 8–10:30am, 11am–3pm, and 5:30–9:30pm.

Inexpensive

Cafe Haleiwa BREAKFAST/LUNCH/MEXICAN Haleiwa's legendary breakfast joint is a big hit with surfers, urban gentry with weekend country homes, reclusive artists, and hungry families looking for breakfast or lunch. No kids' menu, but it's not needed as kids can pick the fruit pancakes for breakfast and the grilled cheese for lunch. This is a wake-up-and-hit-the-beach kind of place, serving generous omelets with names like "Off the Wall," "Off the Lip," and "Breakfast in a Barrel." Surf pictures line the walls, and the ambience is Formica casual. And, for the grown-ups, what could be better than an espresso to start the day?

66-460 Kamehameha Hwy., Haleiwa. ✆ **808/637-5516.** Highchairs. No reservations. Main courses $6–$11. AE, MC, V. Sun–Fri 7am–2pm; Sat 7am–12:30pm.

Kua Aina ★ Value AMERICAN "What's the name of that sandwich shop on the North Shore?" I hear that often. Although this North Shore staple has expanded to the Ward Centre area in Kakaako, you'd never know it by the lines here. After nearly 3 decades at the same spot, they moved some 150 yards down the street and opened a new 75-seat eatery. It's as busy as ever; many diners get their burgers to go and head for the beach. Kua Aina's thin and spindly french fries are renowned islandwide and are the perfect accompaniment to its legendary burgers. (They offer "kiddie burgers" for young diners.) The tuna/avocado, roast turkey, and mahimahi sandwiches are excellent alternatives to the burgers. Kua Aina is unparalleled on the island and is a North Shore must, eclipsing its fancier competitors at lunch.

66-160 Kamehameha Hwy., Haleiwa. ✆ **808/637-6067.** Highchairs. No reservations. Most items less than $8. No credit cards. Daily 11am–8pm.

Paradise Found Cafe VEGETARIAN A tiny cafe behind Celestial Natural Foods, Paradise Found is a bit of a hunt, but stick with it. For more than a few townies, the North Shore sojourn begins at Paradise, the only pure vegetarian restaurant in these parts. Their smoothies (especially the Waimea Shorebreak) are legendary, and their organic soups, fresh-pressed vegetable juices, sandwiches, and healthy plate lunches are a great launch to a Haleiwa day. Vegan substitutes are willingly made in place of dairy products and to accommodate dietary needs. Kids will love the nan 'nut, a tortilla with peanut butter, honey, and bananas.

66-443 Kamehameha Hwy., Haleiwa. ✆ **808/637-4540.** No reservations. All items less than $10. AE, DC, DISC, MC, V. Mon–Sat 9am–5pm; Sun 10am–4pm.

5 EXPLORING OAHU WITH YOUR KIDS

Note: Very few attractions have strollers available for use; unless noted below, assume that you will have to bring your own stroller.

KIDS' TOP 10 ATTRACTIONS

Battleship USS Missouri Memorial ★ **Ages 5 and up.** On the deck of this 58,000-ton battleship (the last one the Navy built), World War II came to an end with the signing of the Japanese surrender on September 2, 1945. The *Missouri* was part of the force that carried out bombing raids over Tokyo and provided firepower in the battles of Iwo Jima and Okinawa. In 1955, the navy decommissioned the ship and placed it in mothballs at the Puget Sound Naval Shipyard, in Washington State. But the *Missouri* was modernized and called back into action in 1986, eventually being deployed in the Persian Gulf War, before retiring once again in 1992. Here it sat until another battle ensued, this time over who would have the privilege of keeping this living legend. Hawaii won that battle and brought the ship to Pearl Harbor in 1998. The next year, the 887-foot ship, like a phoenix, rose again into the public spotlight; it's now open to visitors as a museum memorial.

If you have the time, take the tour, which begins at the visitor center. Guests are shuttled on military-style buses to Ford Island while listening to a 1940s-style radio program (complete with news clips, wartime commercials, and music). Once on the ship, guests watch an informational film and are then free to explore on their own or take a guided tour. Highlights of this massive (more than 200-ft.-tall) battleship include the forecastle (or *foc's'le,* in navy talk), where the 30,000-pound anchors are "dropped" on 1,080 feet of anchor chain; the 16-inch guns (each 65 ft. long and weighing 116 tons), which can accurately fire a 2,700-pound shell some 23 miles in 50 seconds; and the spot where the Instrument of Surrender was signed as Douglas MacArthur, Chester Nimitz, and "Bull" Halsey looked on.

Battleship Row, Pearl Harbor. ✆ **808/423-2263.** www.ussmissouri.com. Admission $16 adults, $8 children 4–12. Battleship Guided Tour $7 additional (60 min.); Explorer's Tour (90 min.) $29 additional. Daily 9am–5pm; guided tours 9:30am–4:30pm. Check in at the *USS Bowfin Submarine* Museum, next to the *USS Arizona* Memorial Visitors Center. Drive west on H-1 past the airport, take the USS Arizona Memorial exit, and follow the brown-and-white signs; there's ample free parking. Bus: 20 or 47.

Bishop Museum ★★ All ages. Founded in 1889 by Charles Reed Bishop as a living memorial to his wife, Princess Bernice Pauahi Bishop (the last direct descendant of King Kamehameha I, who united the Hawaiian islands), the Bishop Museum campus holds the world's greatest collection of natural and cultural artifacts from Hawaii and the Pacific. It's a great rainy-day diversion; plan to spend at least half a day here. The museum has something for everyone. Ola Nā Mo'olelo—"Living Stories"—is a daily storytelling presentation of Hawaiian stories and culture. For preschoolers and kindergartners, there's "Here Comes the Lava Flow," a 30-minute hands-on demonstration of how a volcano works; a 1-hour program called "Ali'i," including a guided tour of the Hawaiian royalty exhibits; and "The Science of Pōhaku," an hour-long interactive demonstration of the art of adz making. There are numerous activities for older kids, including cultural demonstrations, interactive exhibits and games about Hawaii culture, canoe building, and kapa making. A visit here will give you a good understanding of Hawaiian life and culture. You'll see the great feathered capes of kings, the last grass shack in Hawaii, preindustrial Polynesian art, even the skeleton of a 50-foot sperm whale.

Don't miss the terrific new Science Adventure Center, which specializes in volcanology, oceanography, and biodiversity. You'll become a kid again in this fun interactive environment where you walk down a "Hawaiian origins" tunnel into the deep ocean zone, stopping along the way to play with all the cool, high-tech toys, then explore the interior of a volcano and climb to the top to get a bird's-eye view of an erupting caldera (it looks like the real thing!).

Hula performances ★ take place weekdays at 11am and 2pm, and various Hawaiian crafts such as lei making, feather working, and quilting are demonstrated. This cultural event is worth making time for. Also, for a look at spectacular artifacts such as the ancient feather cloak of King Kamehameha and other items not shown to the general public, take the "Behind the Scenes Tour" offered weekdays at 1:30pm for an additional fee of $15.

1525 Bernice St., just off Kalihi St. (also known as Likelike Hwy.). ✆ **808/847-3511.** www.bishopmuseum.org. Admission $16 adults, $13 children 4–12 and seniors, free for children 3 and under. Daily 9am–5pm. Bus: 2.

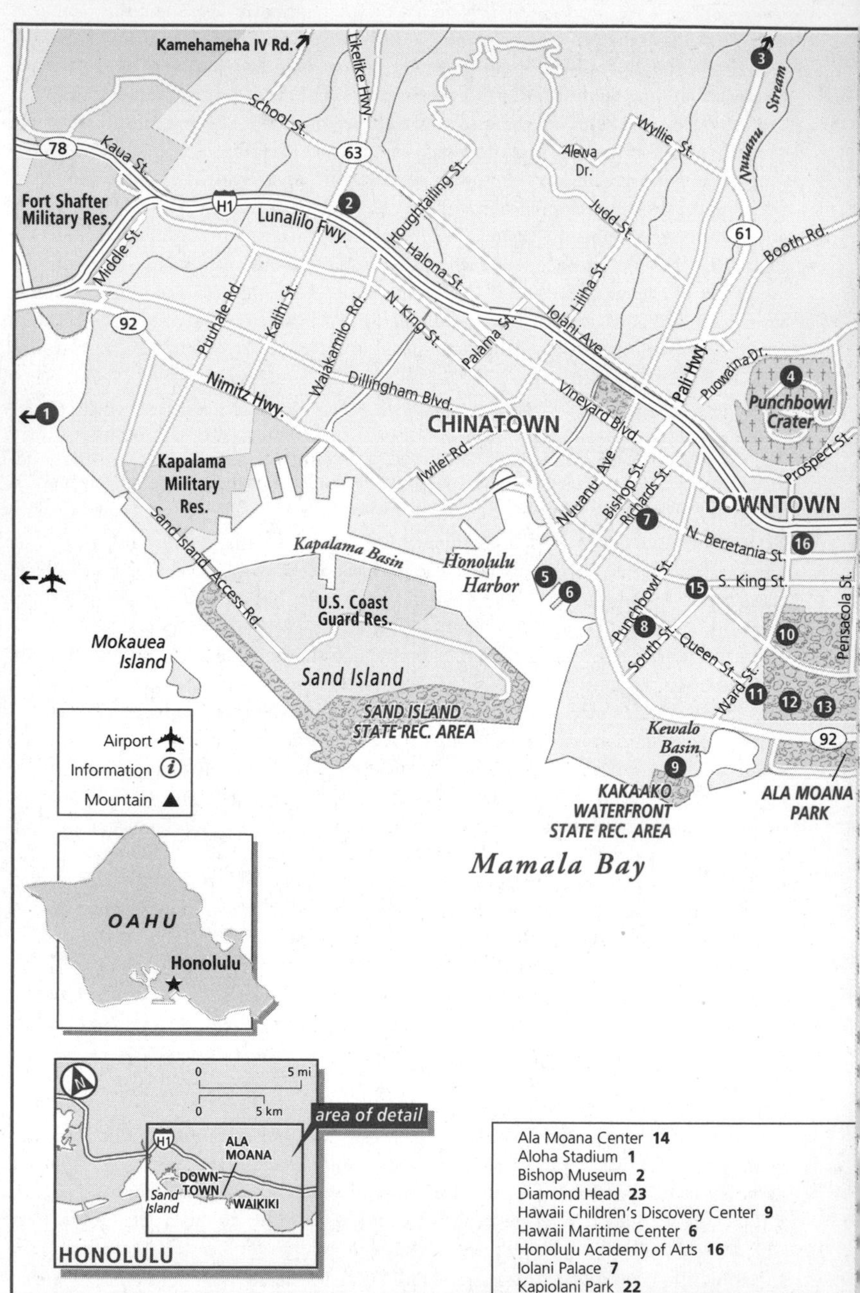

Kamehameha IV Rd.
Likelike Hwy.
School St.
78
Kaua St.
63
Fort Shafter Military Res.
H1
Lunalilo Fwy.
Houghtailing St.
Halona St.
Middle St.
Puuhale Rd.
Kalihi St.
Waiakamilo Rd.
N. King St.
Palama St.
92
Nimitz Hwy.
Dillingham Blvd.
CHINATOWN
Iwilei Rd.
Kapalama Military Res.
Sand Island Access Rd.
Kapalama Basin
Honolulu Harbor
U.S. Coast Guard Res.
Mokauea Island
Sand Island
SAND ISLAND STATE REC. AREA
Alewa Dr.
Wyllie St.
Nuuanu Stream
Judd St.
61
Booth Rd.
Liliha St.
Iolani Ave.
Pali Hwy.
Puowaina Dr.
Punchbowl Crater
Vineyard Blvd.
Prospect St.
Nuuanu Ave
Bishop St.
Richards St.
DOWNTOWN
N. Beretania St.
S. King St.
Punchbowl St.
South St.
Queen St.
Ward St.
Pensacola St.
Kewalo Basin
KAKAAKO WATERFRONT STATE REC. AREA
ALA MOANA PARK
Mamala Bay
Airport
Information
Mountain
OAHU
Honolulu
0 5 mi
0 5 km
area of detail
ALA MOANA
DOWN-TOWN
Sand Island
WAIKIKI
HONOLULU
Ala Moana Center 14
Aloha Stadium 1
Bishop Museum 2
Diamond Head 23
Hawaii Children's Discovery Center 9
Hawaii Maritime Center 6
Honolulu Academy of Arts 16
Iolani Palace 7
Kapiolani Park 22

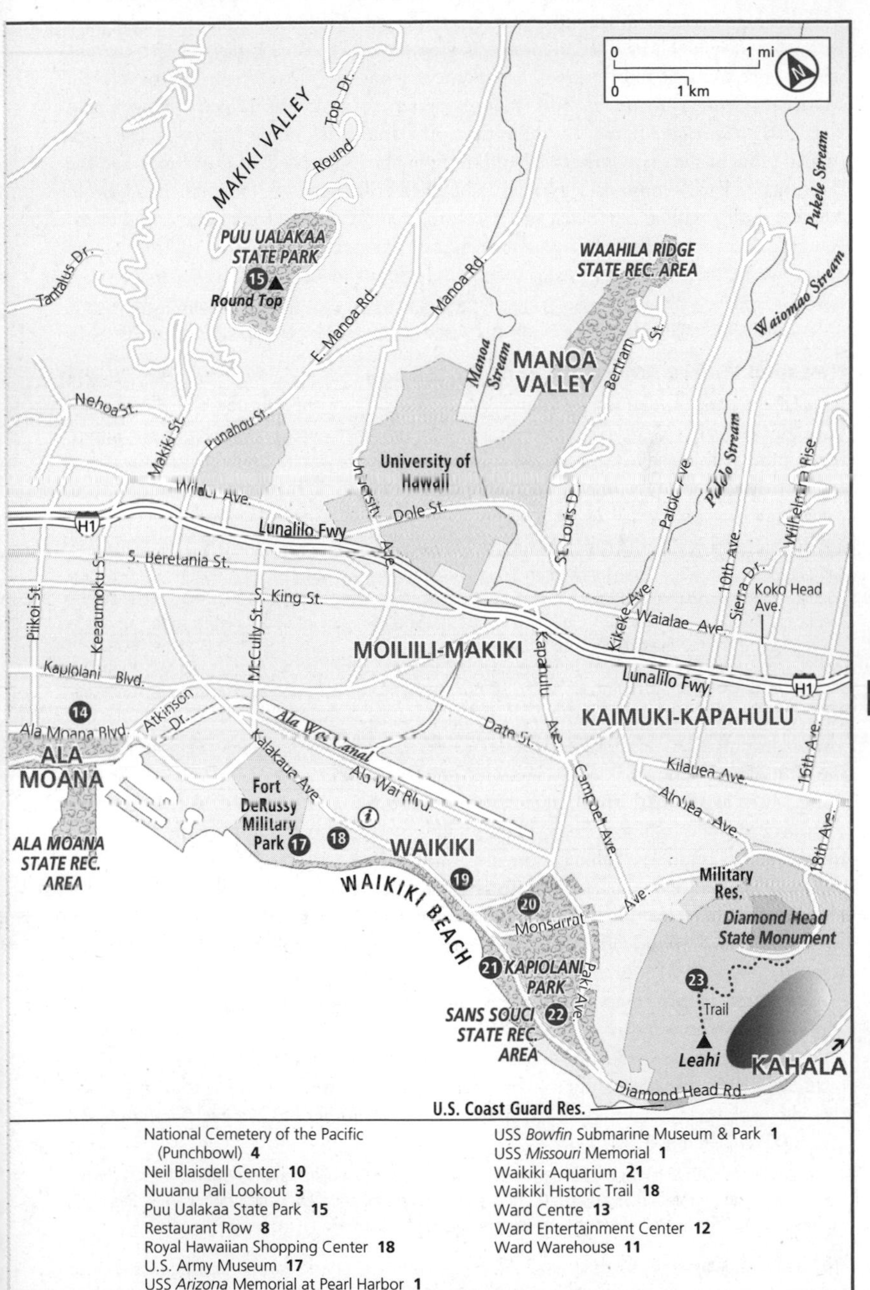

National Cemetery of the Pacific (Punchbowl) **4**
Neil Blaisdell Center **10**
Nuuanu Pali Lookout **3**
Puu Ualakaa State Park **15**
Restaurant Row **8**
Royal Hawaiian Shopping Center **18**
U.S. Army Museum **17**
USS *Arizona* Memorial at Pearl Harbor **1**
USS *Bowfin* Submarine Museum & Park **1**
USS *Missouri* Memorial **1**
Waikiki Aquarium **21**
Waikiki Historic Trail **18**
Ward Centre **13**
Ward Entertainment Center **12**
Ward Warehouse **11**

Hawaii Maritime Center ★ Finds Ages 3 and up. You can easily spend a couple of hours here, wandering around and learning the story of Hawaii's rich maritime past, from the ancient journey of Polynesian voyagers to the nostalgic days of the *Lurline,* which once brought tourists from San Francisco on 4-day cruises. Inside the Hawaii Maritime Center's Kalakaua Boat House, patterned after His Majesty King David Kalakaua's own canoe house, are more than 30 exhibits, including Matson cruise ships (which brought the first tourists to Waikiki), flying boats that delivered the mail, and the skeleton of a Pacific humpback whale that beached on Kahoolawe. Outside, the *Hokulea,* a double-hulled sailing canoe that in 1976 reenacted the Polynesian voyage of discovery, is moored next to the *Falls of Clyde,* a four-masted schooner that once ran tea from China to the West Coast. There are lots of interactive exhibits to keep the kids occupied.

Pier 7 (next to Aloha Tower), Honolulu Harbor. ✆ **808/536-6373.** www.bishopmuseum.org. Admission $7.50 adults, $4.50 children 4–12, free for children 3 and under. Daily 8:30am–5pm. Bus: 19 or 20.

Hawaiian Waters Adventure Park ★ All ages. Your kids will love this 29-acre amusement park, so plan to spend a day here. Highlights are a football field–size wave pool for bodysurfing, two 65-foot-high free-fall slides, two water-toboggan bullet slides, inner tube slides, body flume slides, a continuous river for floating inner tubes, and separate pools for adults, teens, and children. In addition, there are restaurants, food carts, Hawaiian performances, and shops.

400 Farrington Hwy., Kapolei. ✆ **808/674-9283.** www.hawaiianwaters.com. Admission $36 adults, $15 seniors, $26 children 3–11, free for children 2 and under. Hours vary, but generally the park is open daily 10:30am–4 or 5pm in peak season (summer); during off-peak season 10:30am–3:30 or 4pm; closed some weekdays. Take H-1 west to exit 1 (Campbell Industrial Park). Make an immediate left turn to Farrington Hwy., and you will see the park on your left.

Honolulu Zoo ★ All ages. Nobody comes to Hawaii to see an Indian elephant, or African lions and zebras. Right? Wrong. This 43-acre municipal zoo in Waikiki attracts visitors in droves. Allot at least half a day to explore all the attractions. The highlight is the new African Savannah, a 10-acre wild preserve exhibit with more than 40 African critters roaming around in the open. The zoo also has a rare Hawaiian nene goose, a Hawaiian pig, and mouflon sheep. There's a kids' petting zoo and, during the summer, a heap of things to do (see "Hot Fun in the Summertime," on p. 140).

For a real treat, take the **Twilight Tours,** geared toward families with kids ages 5 and older. Learn what sort of monkey business takes place at twilight at Honolulu Zoo, Saturdays from 5:30 to 7:30pm. It's a fun evening of education never experienced by day visitors; the cost is $12 for adults and $8 for children ages 4 to 12.

Other great family programs include **Snooze in the Zoo,** in which you discover "who is roaring and who is snoring" during the night with pizza, tours, and campfire time with s'mores, plus breakfast and a morning stroll (check website for dates), 5:30pm to 9am the next day, $50 for ages 4 and up; and **Star Gazing at the Zoo,** an evening tour of the zoo that also explores the night sky above Hawaii with astronomer Dr. Michael Chauvin ($12 adults, $8 children 4–12).

151 Kapahulu Ave. (btw Paki and Kalakaua aves.), at entrance to Kapiolani Park. ✆ **808/971-7171.** www.honoluluzoo.org. Admission $8 adults, $1 children 6–12, free for children 5 and under. Family Pass $25. Stroller rental $7 for single. Daily 9am–4:30pm. Bus: 2, 8, 19, 20, or 47.

Polynesian Cultural Center ★ All ages. You can experience the natural beauty and culture of the vast Pacific in a single day at the Polynesian Cultural Center, a kind of living museum of Polynesia. Here, you can see firsthand the lifestyles, songs, dance, costumes, and architecture of seven Pacific islands—Fiji, New Zealand, Marquesas, Samoa, Tahiti, Tonga, and Hawaii—in the re-created villages scattered throughout the 42-acre lagoon park. A recent $1.1-million renovation project remodeled the front entrance and added an exhibit on the story of the Polynesian immigration.

Your family will "travel" through this museum by foot or in a canoe on a man-made freshwater lagoon. Each village is "inhabited" by native students from Polynesia who attend Hawaii's Brigham Young University. There are plenty of activities at each village for the kids to do, from pounding a drum in a Fijian Village to face painting to Hawaiian bowling. The park, which is operated by the Mormon Church, also features a variety of stage shows celebrating the music, dance, history, and culture of Polynesia. There's a luau every evening. Because a visit can take up to 8 hours, it's a good idea to arrive before 2pm. Just beyond the center is the **Hawaii Temple** of the Church of Jesus Christ of Latter-day Saints, which is built of volcanic rock and concrete in the form of a Greek cross and includes reflecting pools, formal gardens, and royal palms. Completed in 1919, it was the first Mormon temple built outside the continental United States. An optional tour of the Temple Visitors Center, as well as neighboring Brigham Young University, Hawaii, is included in the package admission prices.

55-370 Kamehameha Hwy., Laie. ✆ **800/367-7060,** 808/293-3333, or 808/923-2911. www.polynesia.com. Admission packages $58–$215 adults and $47–$165 children 3–11. Mon–Sat 12:30–9:30pm. Take H-1 to Pali Hwy. (Hwy. 61) and turn left on Kamehameha Hwy. (Hwy. 83). Bus: 55. Polynesian Cultural Center coaches $15 round-trip; call numbers above to book.

Sea Life Park ★ All ages. This 62-acre ocean theme park, located in East Oahu, is one of the island's top attractions. It features whales from Puget Sound, Atlantic bottle-nosed dolphins, California sea lions, and penguins going through their hoops to the delight of kids of all ages. Allow all day to take in the sights. There's also a Hawaiian reef tank full of tropical fish; a "touch" pool, where you can touch a real sea cucumber (commonly found in tide pools); and a bird sanctuary, where you can see birds such as the red-footed booby and the frigate bird. The chief curiosity, though, is the world's only "wholphin"—a cross between a false killer whale and an Atlantic bottle-nosed dolphin. On-site, marine biologists operate a recovery center for endangered marine life; during your visit, you'll be able to see rehabilitated Hawaiian monk seals and seabirds. I feel it is very pricey (two adults and two kids will cost more than $100—very expensive, and frankly not worth $100).

41-202 Kalanianaole Hwy. (at Makapuu Point), Honolulu. ✆ **808/259-7933.** www.sealifeparkhawaii.com. Admission $31 adults, $25 children 4–12. Daily 9:30am–5pm. Parking $3. Shuttle buses from Waikiki $5. Bus: 22 or 58.

USS Arizona National Memorial ★★★ Ages 7 and up. On December 7, 1941, the USS *Arizona,* while moored here in Pearl Harbor, was bombed in a Japanese air raid. The 608-foot battleship sank in 9 minutes without firing a shot, taking 1,177 sailors and Marines to their deaths—and catapulting the United States into World War II.

Nobody who visits the memorial will ever forget it. The deck of the ship lies 6 feet below the surface of the sea. Oil still oozes slowly up from the Arizona's engine room to stain the harbor's calm, blue water; some say the ship still weeps for its lost crew. The memorial is a stark, white, 184-foot rectangle that spans the sunken hull of the ship; it was designed by Alfred Pries, a German architect interned on Sand Island during the war. It contains the ship's bell, recovered from the wreckage, and a shrine room with the names of the dead carved in stone.

Today, free U.S. Navy launches take visitors to the *Arizona.* Try to arrive at the visitor center, operated jointly by the National Park Service and the U.S. Navy, no later than

1:30pm to avoid the huge crowds; waits of 1 to 3 hours are common, and they don't take reservations. While you're waiting for the shuttle to take you out to the ship—you'll be issued a number and time of departure—you can explore the interesting museum's personal mementos, photographs, and historic documents. A moving 20-minute film precedes your trip to the ship. Allow a total of at least 4 hours for your visit.

While you're waiting for the free shuttle (operated by the U.S. Navy) to take you out to the ship, get the ★★★ **Audio Tour.** This is will make the trip even more meaningful. The tour (on an MP3 player) is about 2½ hours long and is like having your own personal park ranger as your guide. It costs $5 and is worth every nickel. The tape is narrated by Ernest Borgnine and features stories told by actual Pearl Harbor survivors—both American and Japanese. Plus, while you are waiting for the launch, the tour will take you step by step through the museum's personal mementos, photographs, and historic documents. You can pause the tour for the moving 20-minute film that precedes your trip to the ship. The tour continues on the launch, describing the shoreline and letting you know what's in store at the Memorial itself. At the Memorial, the tour gives you a mental picture of that fateful day, and the narration continues on your boat ride back. Allow a total of at least 4 hours for your visit.

Due to increased security measures, visitors cannot carry purses, handbags, fanny packs, backpacks, camera bags, diaper bags, or other items that offer concealment on the boat. However, there is a container to store carry-on–size items (no bigger than 30×30×18 in.), with a small fee of $2 (per item). Note that baby strollers, baby carriages, and baby backpacks are not allowed in the theater, on the boat, or on the USS *Arizona* Memorial. All babies must be carried. (This attraction isn't a great idea with toddlers or tots as it's almost impossible to take a small child out for 4 hours without at least a diaper bag.) ***One last note:*** Most unfortunately, the USS *Arizona* Memorial is a high-theft area—leave your valuables at the hotel.

Also, you must wear **closed-toe shoes;** no sandals allowed.

Pearl Harbor. ✆ **808/422-0561** (recorded info) or 422-2771. www.nps.gov/usar. Free admission. Daily 7:30am–5pm (programs run 7:45am–3pm). Children 11 and under should be accompanied by an adult. Shirts and closed-toe shoes required; no swimsuits or flip-flops allowed (shorts are okay). Wheelchairs gladly accommodated. Drive west on H-1 past the airport; take the USS *Arizona* Memorial exit and follow the green-and-white signs; there's ample free parking. Bus: 20; or *Arizona* Memorial Shuttle Bus VIP (✆ **808/839-0911**), which picks up at Waikiki hotels 6:50am–1pm ($11/person round-trip; babies sitting on parent's lap are free).

USS Bowfin Submarine Museum & Park ★ **Ages 5 and up.** The USS *Bowfin* is one of only 15 World War II submarines still in existence today. You can go below deck of this famous submarine—nicknamed the "Pearl Harbor Avenger" for its successful attacks on the Japanese—and see how the 80-man crew lived during wartime. The *Bowfin* Museum has an impressive collection of submarine-related artifacts. The Waterfront Memorial honors submariners lost during World War II.

11 Arizona Memorial Dr. (next to the USS *Arizona* Memorial Visitor Center). ✆ **808/423-1341.** www.bowfin.org. Admission $10 adults, $7 active-duty military personnel and seniors, $4 children 4–12 (children 3 and under are not permitted for safety reasons). Daily 8am–5pm. See USS *Arizona* Memorial, above, for driving, bus, and shuttle directions.

Waikiki Aquarium ★★★ **All ages.** Do not miss this! Half of Hawaii is its underwater world; plan to spend at least 2 hours discovering it. Behold the chambered nautilus, nature's submarine and inspiration for Jules Verne's *20,000 Leagues Under the Sea.* You may see this tropical spiral-shelled cephalopod mollusk—the only living one born in captivity—any day of the week here. Its natural habitat is the deep waters of Micronesia, but aquarium director Bruce Carlson not only succeeded in trapping the pearly-shelled creature in 1,500 feet of water (by dangling chunks of raw tuna), but also managed to breed this ancient relative of the octopus. There are also plenty of other fish in this small but first-class aquarium, located on a live coral reef. The Hawaiian reef habitat features sharks, eels, a touch tank, and habitats for the endangered Hawaiian monk seal and green sea turtle. Recently added: a rotating biodiversity exhibit and interactive displays focusing on corals and coral reefs.

2777 Kalakaua Ave. (across from Kapiolani Park). ✆ **808/923-9741.** www.waquarium.org. Admission $9 adults; $6 active military, seniors, and college students; $4 children 13–17; $2 children 5–12; free for children 4 and under. Daily 9am–5pm. Bus: 2.

HISTORIC HONOLULU & OTHER CULTURAL ATTRACTIONS

The Waikiki you see today bears no resemblance to the Waikiki of yesteryear, a place of vast taro fields extending from the ocean deep into Manoa Valley, dotted with numerous fishponds and gardens tended by thousands of people. This picture of old Waikiki can be recaptured by following the emerging **Waikiki Historic Trail ★**, a meandering 2-mile walk with 20 bronze surfboard markers (standing 6 ft., 5 in. tall—you can't miss 'em), complete with descriptions and archive photos of the historic sites. It's an easy stroll through Waikiki that all ages will enjoy. Let the kids hunt for each surfboard marker, which notes everything from the ancient fishponds to the history of the Ala Wai Canal. The trail begins at Kuhio Beach and ends at the King Kalakaua statue, at the intersection of Kuhio and Kalakaua avenues. Free 90-minute walking tours are given Monday through Friday at 9am and on Saturday at 4:30pm; meet at the beachside surfboard marker (THE BEACHES OF WAIKIKI) at the entrance to Kapiolani Park, on Kalakaua Avenue, across from the Honolulu Zoo.

A hula performance is a popular way for visitors to get a taste of traditional Hawaiian culture. Unfortunately, the **Kodak Hula Show** at the Waikiki Band Shell at Kapiolani Park closed in 2002. For a more genuine Hawaiian hula experience, catch the hula *halau* performed at the **Bishop Museum** (p. 113).

Iolani Palace ★ Ages 5 and up. If you want to really understand Hawaii, this 45-minute tour is well worth the time. The kids will love seeing a royal palace and you'll love the history of the Iolani Palace, by King David Kalakaua, who spared no expense. The 4-year project, completed in 1882, cost $360,000—and nearly bankrupted the Hawaiian kingdom. This four-story Italian Renaissance palace was the first electrified building in Honolulu (it had electricity before the White House and Buckingham Palace). Royals lived here for 11 years, until Queen Liliuokalani was deposed and the Hawaiian monarchy fell forever, in a palace coup led by U.S. Marines on January 17, 1893, at the demand of sugar planters and missionary descendants. Allow at least an hour for a self-guided tour of the 10-room palace (reservations are a must!). Tours include a comprehensive **Guided Tour ★**, which offers visitors a brief video about the history of the palace, a docent-guided tour of the inside of the Palace, and a self-guided tour of the basement; an **Audio Tour,** which provides guests with an audio wand for a tour through the first and second floors and concludes with a self-guided tour of the Gallery; and the **Galleries Tour,** a self-guided tour of the Palace Galleries, complete with crown jewels, the ancient feathered cloaks, the royal china, and more.

At S. King and Richards sts. ✆ **800/532-1051** or 808/522-0832. www.iolanipalace.org. Grand Tour $20 adults, $5 children 5–12; Audio Tour $12 adults, $5 children ages 5–12; Self-Guided Galleries Tour $6 adults, $3 children 5–12. Tues–Sat 8:30am–2pm; call ahead to reserve the Guided Tour. Children 4 and under not permitted. Extremely limited parking on palace grounds; try metered parking on the street. Bus: 2.

Frommer's Favorite Oahu Family Experiences

Seeing an Erupting Volcano (p. 113) It looks like the real thing (only you are standing just a few feet away)—a real molten-spewing, roaring, rock-launching volcano—and it's in the **Bishop Museum.** It's the new 16,500-square-foot Science Adventure Center, specializing in volcanology, oceanography, and biodiversity. The kids will be spellbound wandering through the "Hawaiian origins" tunnel into the deep ocean, stopping along the way to play with all the cool, high-tech toys, then exploring the interior of a volcano and climbing to the top to get a bird's-eye view of an erupting caldera.

Flying a Kite at Kapiolani Park Great open expanses of green and constant trade winds make this urban park one of Hawaii's prime locations for kite flying. You can watch the pros fly dragon kites and stage kite-fighting contests, or join in the fun after checking out the convenient kite shop across the street in New Otani's arcade.

Visiting the Honolulu Zoo (p. 116) Visit Africa in Hawaii at the **Honolulu Zoo**. The lions, giraffes, zebras, and elephants delight youngsters and parents alike. But the great new thrill is the Zoo by Moonlight tour—so kids can see and hear what really goes bump in the night.

Beating Bamboo Drums in a Fijian Village (p. 116) The **Polynesian Cultural Center** introduces kids to the games played by Polynesian and Melanesian children. The activities, which range from face painting to Hawaiian bowling, go on every day from 12:30 to 5:30pm.

Seeing the World's Only Wholphin (p. 117) It's a freak of nature, a cross between a whale and a dolphin—and you can see it at **Sea Life Park**. Kids love this marine amusement park, where trained dolphins, whales, and seals do their thing.

Blowing Bubbles Bigger Than You Are (p. 123) The **Hawaii Children's Discovery Center** has a host of fun interactive exhibits for kids ages 2 to 13, from sitting in a giant tooth in a giant grin to finding out how our bodies and brains work.

Eating Shave Ice at Haleiwa (p. 126) No visit to Hawaii is complete without an authentic shave ice. You can find shave ice in all kinds of tropical flavors throughout the islands, but for some reason, it tastes better in this funky North Shore surf town. See "Beyond Honolulu: Exploring the Island by Car," below.

Spending a Day at the Parks at Waimea (p. 132) What many think is only a botanical garden tucked away on the North Shore is really a child's garden of delight. Hike through the tropical jungle to waterfalls and stop and look for the birds singing in the rainforest. See "For the Active Family," later in this chapter.

Shopping Aloha Flea Market (p. 149) Some kids hate to shop. But the Aloha Flea Market is more than shopping, it's an experience akin to a carnival, full of strange food, odd goods, and bold barkers.

Just Beyond Pearl Harbor

Hawaiian Railway **All ages.** All aboard! The kids will get a kick out of this train ride back into history. Between 1890 and 1947, the chief mode of transportation for Oahu's sugar mills was the Oahu Railway and Land Co.'s narrow-gauge trains. The line carried not only equipment, raw sugar, and supplies, but also passengers from one side of the island to the other. You can relive those days every Sunday with a 1½-hour narrated ride through Ko Olina Resort and out to Makaha. If you have older kids (13 and up), on the second Sunday of the month, you can ride on the nearly 100-year-old, custom-built, parlor–observation car belonging to Benjamin F. Dillingham, founder of the Oahu Railway and Land Co.; the fare is $15, and you must reserve in advance.

Ewa Station, Ewa Beach. ✆ **808/681-5461.** www.hawaiianrailway.com. Admission $10 adults, $7 seniors and children 2–12. Departures Sun at 1 and 3pm and weekdays by appointment. Take H-1 west to Exit 5A; take Hwy. 76 south for 2½ miles to Tesoro gas station; turn right on Renton Rd. and drive 1½ miles to end of paved section. The station is on the left. Bus: C-Express to Kapalei, then transfer to no. 41, which goes through Ewa and drops you off outside the gate.

Hawaii's Plantation Village **Ages 7 and up.** The hour-long tour of a restored 50-acre village offers a glimpse back in time to when sugar planters from America shaped the land, economy, and culture of territorial Hawaii. From 1852, when the first contract laborers arrived here from China, to 1947, when the plantation era ended, more than 400,000 men, women, and children from China, Japan, Portugal, Puerto Rico, Korea, and the Philippines came to work the sugar cane fields. The "talk story" tour brings the old village alive with 30 faithfully restored camp houses, Chinese and Japanese temples, the Plantation Store, and even a sumo-wrestling ring. Younger kids may get bored here, however.

Waipahu Cultural Garden Park, 94-695 Waipahu St. (at Waipahu Depot Rd.), Waipahu. ✆ **808/677-0110.** www.hawaiiplantationvillage.org. Admission (including escorted tour) $10 adults, $7 military personnel and seniors, $5 children 4–11, free for children 3 and under. Mon–Sat 10am–2pm. Take H-1 west to Waikele-Waipahu exit (Exit 7); get in the left lane on exit and turn left on Paiwa St.; at the 5th light, turn right onto Waipahu St.; after the 2nd light, turn left. Bus: 47.

OTHER NATURAL WONDERS & SPECTACULAR VIEWS

In addition to the attractions listed below, check out "Diamond Head Crater" under "For the Active Family," later in this chapter; almost everybody can handle this hike, and the 360-degree views from the top are fabulous.

Nuuanu Pali Lookout ★ **Moments** **All ages.** Gale-force winds sometimes howl through the mountain pass at this 1,186-foot-high perch guarded by 3,000-foot peaks, so hold on to your hat—and small children. But if you walk up from the parking lot to the precipice, you'll be rewarded with a view that'll blow you away. At the edge, the dizzying panorama of Oahu's windward side is breathtaking: Clouds low enough to pinch scoot by on trade winds; pinnacles of the *pali* (cliffs), green with ferns, often disappear in the mist. From on high, the tropical palette of green and blue runs down to the sea. Combine this 10-minute stop with a trip over the Pali to the windward side.

Near the summit of Pali Hwy. (Hwy. 61); take the Nuuanu Pali Lookout turnoff.

Nuuanu Valley Rain Forest **Finds** **All ages.** It's not the same as a peaceful nature walk, but if time is short and hiking isn't your thing, Honolulu has a rainforest you can drive through. It's only a few minutes from downtown Honolulu in verdant Nuuanu Valley, where it rains nearly 300 inches a year. And it's easy to reach in about 15 minutes.

As the Pali Highway leaves residential Nuuanu and begins its climb though the forest, the last stoplight is the Nuuanu Pali Road turnoff; turn right for a jungly detour of about 2 miles under a thick canopy strung with liana vines, past giant bamboo that creaks in the wind, Norfolk pines, and wild shell ginger. The road rises and the vegetation clears as you drive, blinking in the bright light of day, past a small mountain reservoir.

Soon the road rejoins the Pali Highway. Kailua is to the right and Honolulu to the left—but it can be a hair-raising turn. Instead, turn right, go a half-mile to the Nuuanu Pali Lookout (see above), stop for a panoramic view of Oahu's windward side, and return to the town-bound highway on the other side.

Take the Old Nuuanu Pali Rd. exit off Pali Hwy. (Hwy. 61).

Puu Ualakaa State Park ★ Moments **All ages.** The best sunset view of Honolulu is from a 1,048-foot-high hill named for sweet potatoes. Actually, the poetic Hawaiian name means "rolling sweet potato hill," because of how early planters used gravity to harvest their crop. The panorama is sweeping and majestic. On a clear day—which is almost always—you can see from Diamond Head to the Waianae Range, almost the length of Oahu. At night, several scenic overlooks provide romantic spots for young lovers who like to smooch under the stars with the city lights at their feet. It's a top-of-the-world experience—the view, that is. Plan to arrive about a half-hour before sunset and stay another 10 minutes after sunset to watch the stars come out.

At the end of Round Hill Dr. Daily 7am–6:45pm (to 7:45pm in summer). From Waikiki, take Ala Wai Blvd. to McCully St., turn right, and drive mauka (inland) beyond the H-1 on-ramps to Wilder St.; turn left and go to Makiki St.; turn right, and continue onward and upward about 3 miles.

TWO MORE MUSEUMS

Honolulu Academy of Arts **Ages 10 and above.** This is a great place to spend a rainy day. The Academy is the state's only general fine-arts museum; it boasts one of the top Asian art collections in the country and also on exhibit are American and European masters and prehistoric works of Mayan, Greek, and Hawaiian art. Considered Hawaii's premier example of kamaaina-style architecture, the museum features magnificent courtyards, lily ponds, and a cafe.

900 S. Beretania St. (✆ **808/532-8700,** or 808/532-8701 for recorded information. www.honoluluacademy.org. Admission $10 adults; $5 students, seniors, and military personnel; free for children 11 and under. Tues–Sat 10am–4:30pm; Sun 1–5pm. Tours Tues–Sat at 11am and Sun at 1:15pm. Bus: 2.

U.S. Army Museum of Hawaii **Ages 4 and above.** This museum, a former military fort built in 1909 and used in defense of Honolulu and Pearl Harbor, houses military memorabilia ranging from ancient Hawaiian warfare items to modern-day, high-tech munitions. (Kids will love the big guns.)

Fort DeRussy Park, Waikiki. ✆ **808/438-2822.** www.hiarmymuseumsoc.org/museum/index.html. Free admission. Tues–Sun 10am–4:15pm. Bus: 8.

BEYOND HONOLULU: EXPLORING THE ISLAND BY CAR

The moment always arrives—usually after a couple of days at the beach, snorkeling in the warm, blue-green waters of Hanauma Bay—when a certain curiosity kicks in about the rest of Oahu, largely unknown to most visitors. It's time to find the rental car in the hotel garage, load up the kids, and set out around the island. You can also explore Oahu using **TheBus** (see "Getting Around," earlier in this chapter).

More to Discover

It's a rainy day and the kids are bored. Or your little darlings are lobster red from being in the sun (even after you told them to put more sunscreen on). Take them directly to the **Hawaii Children's Discovery Center,** 111 Ohe St., Honolulu (✆ **808/524-5437;** www.discoverycenterhawaii.org). Perfect for children ages 2 to 13, this 38,000-square-foot hub of color, motion, and activities will entertain them for hours with hands-on exhibits and interactive stations. Where else can they play volleyball with a robot or put on sparkling costumes from India or dress up as a purple octopus or write their names with backward letters while looking in a mirror? Lots of summer classes and activities range from playing with clay to painting (most of them invite adults to participate, too). In 2008 the Center spent $5.4 million to add another 9,000 square feet of space for more fun activities for toddlers, a place for traveling exhibits, and a cafe so families won't have to leave for a bite to eat. Admission is $8 for adults, $6.75 for children ages 2 to 17, and free for children 1 and under. Open Tuesday to Friday 9am to 1pm, Saturday and Sunday 10am to 3pm. Take TheBus no. 19 or 20 from Waikiki and no. 55, 56, or 57 from Ala Moana Center.

Oahu's Southeast Coast

From the high-rises of Waikiki, venture down Kalakaua Avenue through tree-lined Kapiolani Park to take a look at a different side of Oahu, the arid south shore. The landscape here is more moonscape, with prickly cacti onshore and, in winter, spouting whales cavorting in the water. Some call it the South Shore, others Sandy's (after the mile-long beach here), but Hawaiians call it **Ka Iwi,** which means "the bone"—no doubt because of all the bone-cracking shore breaks along this popular bodyboarding coastline. The beaches here are long, wide, and popular with local daredevils.

To get to this coast, follow Kalakaua Avenue past the multitiered Dillingham Fountain and around the bend in the road, which now becomes Poni Moi Road. Make a right on Diamond Head Road and begin the climb up the side of the old crater. At the top are several lookout points, so if the official Diamond Head Lookout is jammed with cars, try one of the other lookouts just down the road. The view of the rolling waves is spectacular; take the time to pull over.

Diamond Head Road rolls downhill now into the ritzy community of **Kahala.** At the V in the road at the triangular Fort Ruger Park, veer to your right and continue on the palm-tree-lined Kahala Avenue. Make a left on Hunakai Street, then a right on Kilauea Avenue, and look for the sign: H-1 WEST—WAIMANALO. Turn right at the sign, although you won't get on the H-1 freeway; instead, get on Kalanianaole Highway, a four-lane highway interrupted every few blocks by a stoplight. This is the suburban bedroom community for Honolulu, marked by malls on the left and beach parks on the right.

One of these parks is **Hanauma Bay ★★** (p. 128); you'll see the turnoff on the right when you're about a half-hour from Waikiki. This marine preserve is a great place to stop for a swim; you'll find the friendliest fish on the island here. ***A reminder:*** The beach park is closed on Tuesday.

Around mile marker 11, the jagged lava coast itself spouts sea foam at the **Halona Blowhole.** Look out to sea from Halona over Sandy Beach and across the 26-mile gulf to neighboring Molokai and the faint triangular shadow of Lanai on the far horizon. **Sandy Beach** (p. 128) is Oahu's most dangerous beach; it's the only one with an ambulance always standing by to whisk injured wave catchers to the hospital. Bodyboarders just love this beach.

The coast looks raw and empty along this stretch, but the road weaves past old Hawaiian fishponds and the famous formation known as **Pele's Chair,** just off Kalanianaole Highway (Hwy. 72) above Queen's Beach. From a distance, the lava-rock outcropping looks like a mighty throne; it's believed to be the fire goddess's last resting place on Oahu before she flew off to continue her work on other islands.

Ahead lies 647-foot-high **Makapuu Point,** with a lighthouse that once signaled safe passage for steamship passengers arriving from San Francisco. The automated light now brightens Oahu's south coast for passing tankers, fishing boats, and sailors. You can take a short hike up here for a spectacular vista (p. 142). You could also spend the rest of the day at **Sea Life Park ★**, a marine amusement park described on p. 117.

Turn the corner at Makapuu, and you're on Oahu's windward side, where cooling trade winds propel windsurfers across turquoise bays; the waves at **Makapuu Beach Park** (p. 128) are perfect for bodysurfing.

Ahead, the coastal vista is a profusion of fluted green mountains and strange peaks, edged by golden beaches and the blue, blue Pacific. The 3,000-foot-high sheer green Koolau Mountains plunge almost straight down, presenting an irresistible jumping-off spot for hang glider pilots, who catch the thermals on hours-long rides.

Winding up the coast, Kalanianaole Highway (Hwy. 72) leads through rural **Waimanalo,** a country beach town of nurseries and stables, fresh-fruit stands, and some of the island's best conch and triton shell specimens at roadside stands. Nearly 4 miles long, **Waimanalo Beach** is Oahu's longest beach and the most popular for bodysurfing. Take a swim here or head on to **Kailua Beach ★★**, one of Hawaii's best (p. 129).

The Windward Coast

From the **Nuuanu Pali Lookout ★**, near the summit of the Pali Highway (Hwy. 61), you get the first hint of the other side of Oahu, a region so green and lovely that it could be an island sibling of Tahiti. With its many beaches and bays, the scenic 30-mile windward coast parallels the corduroy-ridged, nearly perpendicular cliffs of the Koolau Range, which separates the windward side of the island from Honolulu and the rest of Oahu. As you descend on the serpentine Pali Highway beneath often gushing waterfalls, you'll see the nearly 1,000-foot spike of **Olomana,** the bold pinnacle that always reminds us of Devil's Tower National Monument in Wyoming. Beyond it lies the Hawaiian village of **Waimanalo.**

From the Pali Highway, to the right is Kailua, Hawaii's biggest beach town, with more than 50,000 residents and two special beaches, Kailua and Lanikai, begging for visitors. (See "Beaches," below, for more details.) Funky little Kailua is lined with million-dollar houses next to tar-paper shacks, antiques shops, and bed-and-breakfasts. Although the Pali Highway (Hwy. 61) proceeds directly to the coast, it undergoes two name changes, becoming first Kalanianaole Highway—from the intersection of Kamehameha Highway (Hwy. 83)—and then Kailua Road as it heads into Kailua town; but the road remains Highway 61 the whole way. Kailua Road ends at the T intersection at Kalaheo Drive, which follows the coast in a northerly and southerly direction. Turn right on South Kalaheo Drive to get to Kailua Beach Park and Lanikai Beach. No signs point the way, but you can't miss them.

If you spend a day at the beach here, stick around for sunset, when the sun sinks behind the Koolau Range and tints the clouds pink and orange. After a hard day at the beach, you'll work up an appetite, and Kailua has several great, inexpensive restaurants. (See "Family-Friendly Dining," earlier in this chapter.)

If you want to skip the beaches this time, turn left on North Kalaheo Drive, which becomes Kaneohe Bay Drive as it skirts Kaneohe Bay and leads back to Kamehameha Highway (Hwy. 83), which then passes through Kaneohe. The suburban maze of Kaneohe is one giant strip mall of retail excess that mars one of the Pacific's most picturesque bays. After you clear this obstacle, the place begins to look like Hawaii again.

Incredibly scenic Kaneohe Bay is spiked with islets and lined with gold-sand beach parks like **Kualoa** (p. 129), a favorite picnic spot. The bay has a barrier reef and four tiny islets, one of which is known as Moku o loe, or Coconut Island. Don't be surprised if it looks familiar—it appeared in *Gilligan's Island.*

At Heeia State Park is **Heeia Fish Pond,** which ancient Hawaiians built by enclosing natural bays with rocks to trap fish on the incoming tide. The 88-acre fishpond, which is made of lava rock and had four watchtowers to observe fish movement and several sluice gates along the 5,000-foot-long wall, is now in the process of being restored.

Stop by the **Heeia Pier,** which juts onto Kaneohe Bay. You can take a snorkel cruise here, or sail out to a sandbar in the middle of the bay for an incredible view of Oahu that most people, even those who live here, never see. If it's Tuesday through Sunday between 7am and 5pm, stop in at the **Deli on Heeia Kea Pier** (**© 808/235-2192**), serving fishermen, sailors, and kayakers the town's best omelets and plate lunches at reasonable prices since 1979.

Everyone calls it Chinaman's Hat, but the tiny island off the eastern shore of Kualoa Regional Park is really named **Mokolii.** It's a sacred *puu honua,* or place of refuge, such as the restored Puu Honua Honaunau on the Big Island of Hawaii. Excavations have unearthed evidence that this area was the home of ancient *alii* (royalty). Early Hawaiians believed that Mokolii ("fin of the lizard") is all that remains of a *mo'o,* or lizard, slain by Pele's sister, Hiiaka, and hurled into the sea. At low tide, you can swim out to the island, but keep watch on the changing tide, which can sweep you out to sea. The islet has a small, sandy beach and is a bird preserve, so don't spook the red-footed boobies.

Little poly-voweled beach towns such as **Kaaawa, Hauula, Punaluu,** and **Kahaluu** pop up along the coast, offering passersby shell shops and art galleries to explore. You'll also see working cattle ranches, fishermen's wharves, and roadside fruit and flower stands vending ice-cold coconuts (to drink) and tree-ripened mangoes, papayas, and apple bananas. From here, continue along Kamehameha Highway (Hwy. 83) to the North Shore.

Central Oahu & the North Shore

If you can afford the splurge, rent a convertible—the perfect car for Oahu, because you can tan as you go—and head for the North Shore and Hawaii's surf city: **Haleiwa ★**, a quaint turn-of-the-20th-century sugar-plantation town designated a historic site. A collection of faded clapboard stores with a picturesque harbor, Haleiwa has evolved into a surfer outpost and major roadside attraction with art galleries, restaurants, and shops.

Getting here is half the fun. You have two choices: The first is to meander north along the lush windward coast, through country hamlets with roadside stands selling mangoes, bright tropical pareus, fresh corn, and pond-raised prawns. Attractions along that route are discussed in the previous section.

The second choice is to cruise up the H-2 through Oahu's broad and fertile central valley, past Pearl Harbor and the Schofield Barracks of *From Here to Eternity* fame, and on through the red-earthed heart of the island, where pineapple and sugar cane fields stretch from the Koolau to the Waianae mountains, until the sea reappears on the horizon. If you take this route, the tough part is getting on and off the H-1 freeway from Waikiki, which is done by way of convoluted routing on neighborhood streets. Try McCully Street off Ala Wai Boulevard, which is always crowded but usually the most direct route.

Once you're on H-1, stay to the right side; the freeway tends to divide abruptly. Keep following the signs for the H-1 (it separates off to Hwy. 78 at the airport and reunites later on; either way will get you there), then the H-1/H-2. Leave the H-1 where the two "interstates" divide; take the H-2 up the middle of the island, heading north toward the town of Wahiawa. That's what the sign will say—not North Shore or Haleiwa, but Wahiawa.

The H-2 runs out and becomes a two-lane country road about 18 miles outside downtown Honolulu, near Schofield Barracks. The highway becomes Kamehameha Highway (Hwy. 99 and later Hwy. 83) at Wahiawa. Just past Wahiawa, about a half-hour out of Honolulu, the **Dole Plantation Hawaii,** 64-1550 Kamehameha Hwy. (✆ **808/621-8408;** www.dole-plantation.com; bus: 52), offers a rest stop and activities for all ages, not to mention lots of pineapples, pineapple history, pineapple trinkets, and pineapple juice. It's open daily from 9am to 6pm; plan to spend at least an hour (and maybe more) here, not only to see this agricultural exhibit/retail area but also to let the kids loose. Admission is $6 for adults and $4 for children 4 to 12 (free for ages 3 and under). The latest attraction is the Pineapple Express, a single-engine diesel locomotive with four cars that takes a 22-minute tour around 2¼ miles of the plantation's grounds, with an educational spiel on the legacy of the pineapple and agriculture in Hawaii. The first tour departs at 9:30am, and the last tour gets back to the station at 5:20pm. Cost is $8 for adults, $6 for children 4 to 12 (free for ages 3 and under). The latest attraction is the Plantation Garden tour, a self-guided tour through the various crops that have been grown on Oahu's North Shore. The tour costs $4 for adults and $3.50 for children. "Kam" Highway, as everyone calls it, will be your road for most of the rest of the trip to Haleiwa.

Surf City: Haleiwa

Only 28 miles from Waikiki is Haleiwa, the funky ex-sugar-plantation town that's the world capital of big-wave surfing. This beach town really comes alive in winter, when waves rise, light rain falls, and temperatures dip into the 70s; then, it seems, every surfer in the world is here to see and be seen.

Officially designated a historic cultural and scenic district, Haleiwa thrives in a time warp recalling the turn of the 20th century, when it was founded by sugar baron Benjamin Dillingham. He built a 30-mile railroad to link his Honolulu and North Shore plantations in 1899. He opened a Victorian hotel overlooking Kaiaka Bay and named it Haleiwa, or "house of the Iwa," the tropical seabird often seen here. The hotel and railroad are gone, but Haleiwa, which was rediscovered in the late 1960s by hippies, resonates with rare rustic charm. Tofu, not taro, is a staple in the local diet. Arts and crafts, boutiques, and burger stands line both sides of the town. There's also a busy fishing harbor full of charter boats and captains who hunt the Kauai Channel daily for tuna, mahimahi, and marlin.

Once in Haleiwa, the hot and thirsty family should report directly to the nearest shave-ice stand, like **Matsumoto Shave Ice ★★**, 66-087 Kamehameha Hwy. (✆ **808/**

637-4827**). For 40 years, this small, humble shop operated by the Matsumoto family has served a popular rendition of the Hawaii-style snow cone flavored with tropical tastes. The cooling treat is also available at neighboring stores, some of which still shave the ice with a hand-cranked device.

Just down the road are some of the fabled shrines of surfing—**Waimea Beach, Banzai Pipeline, Sunset Beach**—where some of the world's largest waves, reaching 20 feet and more, rise between November and January. They draw professional surfers as well as reckless daredevils and hordes of onlookers, who jump into their cars and head north when word goes out that "surf's up." Don't forget your binoculars. For more details on North Shore beaches, see "Beaches," below.

If there are surfers in your tribe, don't miss the **North Shore Surf & Cultural Museum,** North Shore Marketplace, 66-250 Kamehameha Hwy., behind KFC (© **808/637-8888**). Even if you've never set foot on a surfboard, you'll want to visit Oahu's only surf museum to learn the history of this Hawaiian sport of kings. And it's free.

6 BEACHES

THE WAIKIKI COAST

Ala Moana Beach Park ★★

Quite possibly America's best urban beach, gold-sand Ala Moana ("by the sea"), on sunny Mamala Bay, is a great family beach. It's big, stretching more than a mile along Honolulu's coast between downtown and Waikiki and encompassing 76 acres in midtown, with spreading lawns shaded by banyans and palms. The water is calm almost year-round, protected by black lava rocks set offshore. Other facilities include a yacht harbor, tennis courts, music pavilion, bathhouses, picnic tables, and enough wide-open green spaces to accommodate four million visitors a year. There's a large parking lot as well as metered street parking.

Waikiki Beach ★★★

No beach anywhere is so widely known or so universally sought after as this narrow, 1½-mile-long crescent of imported sand (from Molokai) at the foot of a string of high-rise hotels. Home to the world's longest-running beach party, Waikiki attracts nearly five million visitors a year from every corner of the planet. First-timers are always amazed to discover how small Waikiki Beach actually is, but there's always a place for them under the tropical sun here.

Waikiki is actually a string of beaches that extends between **Sans Souci State Recreational Area,** near Diamond Head to the east, and **Duke Kahanamoku Beach,** in front of the Hilton Hawaiian Village, to the west. Great stretches along Waikiki include **Kuhio Beach,** next to the Sheraton Moana Surfrider, which provides the quickest access to the Waikiki shoreline; the stretch in front of the Royal Hawaiian Hotel known as **Grey's Beach,** which is canted so it catches the rays perfectly; and **Sans Souci,** the small, popular beach in front of the New Otani Kaimana Beach Hotel that's locally known as "Dig Me" Beach because of all the gorgeous bods who strut their stuff here.

Your family will find plenty to do here: swimming, board- and bodysurfing, outrigger canoeing, diving, sailing, snorkeling, and pole fishing. Every imaginable type of marine equipment is available for rent. Facilities include showers, lifeguards, restrooms, grills, picnic tables, and pavilions at the **Queen's Surf** end of the beach (at Kapiolani Park, between the zoo and the aquarium). The best place to park is at Kapiolani Park, near Sans Souci. You can take TheBus no. 19 or 20 to all beaches in Waikiki.

EAST OAHU

Hanauma Bay ★★

Do not miss Oahu's most popular snorkeling spot, this volcanic crater with a broken sea wall. The curved, 2,000-foot gold-sand beach is packed elbow-to-elbow with people year-round because of the bay's shallow shoreline water and abundant marine life. Your kids can snorkel in the safe, shallow (10-ft.) inner bay. Because Hanauma Bay is a conservation district, you may look at but not touch or take any marine life here. Feeding the fish is also prohibited.

The first stop is a mandatory visit to the $13-million Marine Education Center, with exhibits and a 7-minute video orienting visitors on this Marine Life Sanctuary. The 10,000-square-foot center includes a training room, gift shop, public restrooms, snack bar, and staging area for the motorized tram, which, for a fee (50¢ for one ride, or $2 for an all-day pass), will take you down the steep road to the beach. Facilities include parking, restrooms, a pavilion, a grass volleyball court, lifeguards, barbecues, picnic tables, and food concessions. Alcohol is prohibited in the park; there is no smoking past the visitor center. Expect to pay $1 per vehicle to park and a $5-per-person entrance fee. (Children 12 and younger are free.) If you're driving, take Kalanianaole Highway to Koko Head Regional Park. Avoid the crowds by going early, about 8am, on a weekday morning; once the parking lot's full, you're out of luck. Alternatively, take TheBus to escape the parking problem: The Hanauma Bay Shuttle runs from Waikiki to Hanauma Bay every half-hour from 8:45am to 1pm; you can catch it at the Ala Moana Hotel, the Ilikai Hotel, or any city bus stop. It returns every hour from noon to 4:30pm. Hanauma Bay is closed on Tuesday, so the fish can have a day off.

Makapuu Beach Park ★

Makapuu Beach, the most famous bodysurfing beach in Hawaii, is a beautiful 1,000-foot-long gold-sand beach cupped in the stark black Koolau cliffs on Oahu's easternmost point. Even if your kids never venture into the water, it's worth a visit just to enjoy the great natural beauty of this classic Hawaiian beach.

In summer, the ocean here is as gentle as a Jacuzzi, and swimming and diving are perfect; come winter, however, Makapuu is hit with expert bodysurfers, who come for big, pounding waves that are too dangerous for regular swimmers. Small boards—3 feet or less with no skeg (bottom fin)—are permitted; regular board surfing is banned by state law.

Facilities include restrooms, lifeguards, barbecue grills, picnic tables, and parking. To get here, follow Kalanianaole Highway toward Waimanalo, or take TheBus no. 57 or 58.

Sandy Beach ★

This is a great beach to take the kids to in order to watch the best bodysurfers on Oahu; it's also one of the most dangerous. It's better to just stand and watch the daredevils literally risk their necks at this 1,200-foot-long gold-sand beach that's pounded by wild waves and haunted by a dangerous shore break and strong backwash. Weak swimmers and children should definitely stay out of the water here; Sandy Beach's heroic lifeguards make more rescues in a year than those at any other beach. Visitors, easily fooled by experienced bodysurfers who make wave-riding look easy, often fall victim to the bone-crunching waves. Lifeguards post flags to alert beachgoers to the day's surf: Green means safe, yellow caution, and red indicates very dangerous water conditions; always check the flags before you dive in.

Facilities include restrooms and parking. Go on weekdays to avoid the crowds, and go on weekends to catch the bodysurfers in action. From Waikiki, drive east on the H-1, which becomes Kalanianaole Highway; proceed past Hawaii Kai, up the hill to Hanauma Bay, past the Halona Blow Hole, and along the coast. The next big, gold, sandy beach you see ahead on the right is Sandy Beach. TheBus no. 22 will also get you here.

THE WINDWARD COAST

Kailua Beach ★★★

Looking for a day at the beach with lots of water activities? Windward Oahu's premier beach is a 2-mile-long, wide golden strand with dunes, palm trees, panoramic views, and offshore islets that are home to seabirds. The swimming is excellent, and the azure waters are usually decorated with bright sails; this is Oahu's premier windsurfing beach as well. It's also a favorite spot to sail catamarans, bodysurf the gentle waves, or paddle a kayak. Water conditions are quite safe, especially at the mouth of Kaelepulu Stream, where toddlers play in the freshwater shallows at the middle of the beach park. The water's usually about 78°F (26°C), the views are spectacular, and the setting, at the foot of the sheer, green Koolaus, is idyllic. Go on weekdays; weekends can be extremely crowded.

The 35-acre beach park is intersected by a freshwater stream and watched over by lifeguards. Facilities include picnic tables, barbecues, restrooms, a volleyball court, a public boat ramp, free parking, and an open-air cafe. Kailua's new bike path weaves through the park, and windsurfer and kayak rentals are available as well. To get here, take the Pali Highway (Hwy. 61) to Kailua, drive through town, turn right on Kalaheo Avenue, and go a mile until you see the beach on your left. Or take TheBus no. 56 or 57 into Kailua, then the no. 70 shuttle.

Kualoa Regional Park ★★

For a family beach picnic, this 150-acre coco palm–fringed peninsula is the biggest beach park on the windward side and one of Hawaii's most scenic. It's located on Kaneohe Bay's north shore, at the foot of the spiky Koolau Ridge. The park has a broad, grassy lawn and a long, narrow, white-sand beach ideal for swimming, walking, beachcombing, kite flying, or just enjoying the natural beauty of this once-sacred Hawaiian shore, listed on the National Register of Historic Places. The waters are shallow and safe for swimming year-round. Offshore is Mokolii, the picturesque islet otherwise known as Chinaman's Hat. At low tide, you can swim or wade out to the island, which has a small sandy beach and is a bird preserve—so don't spook the red-footed boobies. Lifeguards are on duty.

The park is located on Kamehameha Highway (Hwy. 83) in Kualoa; you can get here via TheBus no. 55.

Lanikai Beach ★★

If you are looking for a less crowded swimming beach for the kids, this is one of Hawaii's best. Lanikai's crystal-clear lagoon is like a giant saltwater swimming pool that you and your kids get to share with the resident tropical fish and sea turtles. Seemingly too gorgeous to be real, this is one of Hawaii's postcard-perfect beaches: It's a mile long and thin in places, but the sand's as soft as talcum powder. Prevailing onshore trade winds make this an excellent place for sailing and windsurfing. Kayakers often paddle out to the two

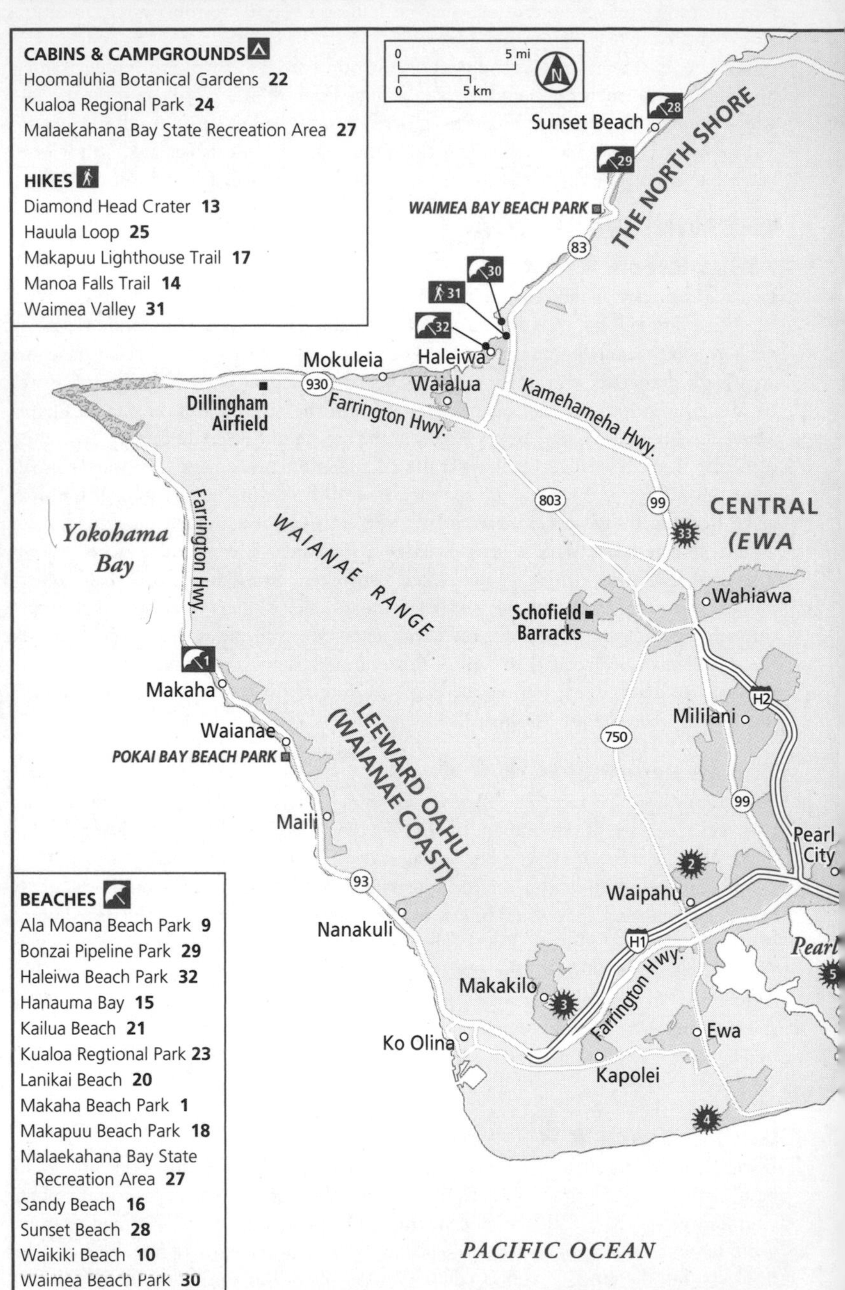
CABINS & CAMPGROUNDS
Hoomaluhia Botanical Gardens 22
Kualoa Regional Park 24
Malaekahana Bay State Recreation Area 27
HIKES
Diamond Head Crater 13
Hauula Loop 25
Makapuu Lighthouse Trail 17
Manoa Falls Trail 14
Waimea Valley 31
0
5 mi
0
5 km
N
Sunset Beach
THE NORTH SHORE
WAIMEA BAY BEACH PARK
83
Mokuleia
Haleiwa
Waialua
930
Dillingham Airfield
Farrington Hwy.
Kamehameha Hwy.
803
99
CENTRAL (EWA
Yokohama Bay
Farrington Hwy.
WAIANAE RANGE
Wahiawa
Schofield Barracks
Makaha
Waianae
POKAI BAY BEACH PARK
LEEWARD OAHU (WAIANAE COAST)
H2
Mililani
750
99
Maili
Pearl City
93
Waipahu
Nanakuli
H1
Pearl
Farrington Hwy.
Makakilo
Ko Olina
Ewa
Kapolei
BEACHES
Ala Moana Beach Park 9
Bonzai Pipeline Park 29
Haleiwa Beach Park 32
Hanauma Bay 15
Kailua Beach 21
Kualoa Regtional Park 23
Lanikai Beach 20
Makaha Beach Park 1
Makapuu Beach Park 18
Malaekahana Bay State Recreation Area 27
Sandy Beach 16
Sunset Beach 28
Waikiki Beach 10
Waimea Beach Park 30
PACIFIC OCEAN

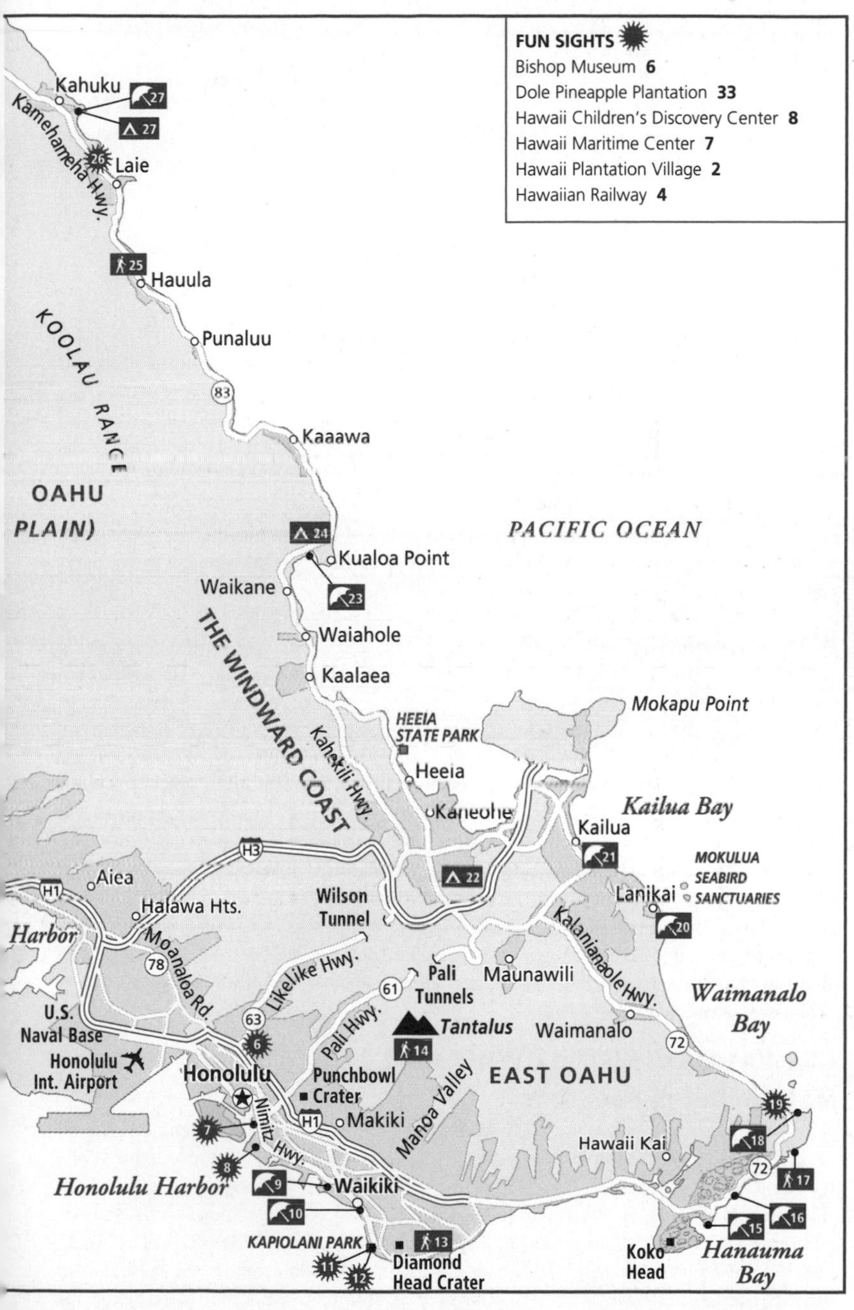
FUN SIGHTS
Bishop Museum 6
Dole Pineapple Plantation 33
Hawaii Children's Discovery Center 8
Hawaii Maritime Center 7
Hawaii Plantation Village 2
Hawaiian Railway 4
Kahuku
Kamehameha Hwy.
Laie
Hauula
Punaluu
KOOLAU RANGE
Kaaawa
OAHU
PLAIN)
PACIFIC OCEAN
Kualoa Point
Waikane
THE WINDWARD COAST
Waiahole
Kaalaea
Mokapu Point
HEEIA STATE PARK
Kahekili Hwy.
Heeia
Kaneohe
Kailua Bay
Kailua
MOKULUA SEABIRD SANCTUARIES
Aiea
Wilson Tunnel
Lanikai
Halawa Hts.
Harbor
Moanaloa Rd.
Likelike Hwy.
Pali Tunnels
Maunawili
Kalanianaole Hwy.
Waimanalo Bay
U.S. Naval Base
Pali Hwy.
Tantalus
Waimanalo
Honolulu Int. Airport
Honolulu
Punchbowl Crater
EAST OAHU
Manoa Valley
Nimitz Hwy.
Makiki
Hawaii Kai
Honolulu Harbor
Waikiki
KAPIOLANI PARK
Diamond Head Crater
Koko Head
Hanauma Bay

tiny offshore Mokulua islands, which are seabird sanctuaries. Because Lanikai is in a residential neighborhood, it's less crowded than other Oahu beaches; the perfect place to enjoy a quiet day. Sun worshipers should arrive in the morning, though, as the Koolau Range blocks the afternoon rays.

There are no facilities here, just off-street parking. From Waikiki, take the H-1 to the Pali Highway (Hwy. 61) through the Nuuanu Pali Tunnel to Kailua, where the Pali Highway becomes Kailua Road as it proceeds through town. At Kalaheo Avenue, turn right and follow the coast about 2 miles to Kailua Beach Park; just past it, turn left at the T intersection and drive uphill on Aalapapa Drive, a one-way street that loops back as Mokulua Drive. Park on Mokulua Drive and walk down any of the eight public-access lanes to the shore. Or take TheBus no. 56 or 57 (Kailua) and then transfer to the shuttle bus.

THE NORTH SHORE

Malaekahana Bay State Recreation Area ★★

This white-sand crescent, almost a mile long, lives up to just about everyone's image of the perfect Hawaii beach. It's excellent for swimming. On a weekday, you may be the only ones here; you can also swim out to Goat Island (or wade across at low tide) and play Robinson Crusoe. (The islet is a sanctuary for seabirds and turtles, so don't let the kids chase 'em.) Facilities include restrooms, barbecue grills, picnic tables, outdoor showers, and parking.

To get here, take Kamehameha Highway (Hwy. 83) 2 miles north of the Polynesian Cultural Center; as you enter the main gate, you'll come upon the wooded beach park. Or you can take TheBus no. 52.

Waimea Beach Park ★★

In the summer, this deep, sandy bowl has gentle waves that are excellent for swimming, snorkeling, and bodysurfing. To one side of the bay is a huge rock that local kids like to climb and dive from. In this placid scene, the only clues of what's to come in winter are those evacuation whistles on poles beside the road. But what a difference a season makes: Winter waves pound the narrow bay, sometimes rising to 50 feet high. When the surf's really up, very strong currents and shore breaks sweep the bay—and it seems like everyone on Oahu drives out to Waimea to get a look at the monster waves and those who ride them. Weekends are great for watching the surfers; to avoid the crowds, go on weekdays. ***A safety tip:*** Don't get too distracted by the waves and forget to pay attention when parking or crossing the road.

Facilities include lifeguards, restrooms, showers, parking, and nearby restaurants and shops in Haleiwa town. The beach is located on Kamehameha Highway (Hwy. 83); from Waikiki, you can take TheBus no. 52.

LEEWARD OAHU/THE WAIANAE COAST

Makaha Beach Park ★★

When surf's up here, it's spectacular: Monstrous waves pound the beach. This is the original home of Hawaii's big-wave surfing championship; surfers today know it as the home of Buffalo's Big Board Surf Classic, where surfers ride the waves on 10-foot-long wooden boards in the old Hawaiian style of surfing. Nearly a mile long, this half-moon, gold-sand beach is tucked between 231-foot Lahilahi Point, which locals call Black Rock, and Kepuhi Point, a toe of the Waianae mountain range. Summer is the best time to hit this beach—the waves are small, the sand is abundant, and the water is safe for

Moments Rolling through Waikiki on a Segway

One of my favorite ways to tour Waikiki is on a Segway Personal Transporter, the silly-looking two-wheeled machine that looks like an old push lawn mower (big wheels and a long handle). But amazingly enough, within just a few minutes, you get the hang of this contraption, which works through a series of high-tech stabilization mechanisms that read the motion of your body to turn or go forward or backward, and is propelled forward through twisting of the hand throttle. It's lots of fun—think back to the first time you rode your bicycle, and the incredible freedom of zipping through space without walking. **Glide Ride Tours and Rentals,** located in the Hawaii Tapa Tower of the Hilton Hawaiian Village Beach Resort & Spa, 2005 Kalia Rd. (✆ **808/941-3151;** www.segwayofhawaii.com), will instruct you on the Segway (they make sure that you are fully competent before you leave their training area) and then take you on a series of tours ranging from a 40-minute introduction tour for $89 per person to a 2½-hour tour of Waikiki, Kapiolani Park, and Diamond Head for $135 per person.

swimming. Children hug the shore on the north side of the beach, near the lifeguard stand, while surfers dodge the rocks and divers seek an offshore channel full of big fish. ***A caveat:*** Recently this beach has become a major "tent city" for the homeless. City officials have made some promises about cleaning this park up, but if the squatters are still there, I'd recommend going elsewhere.

Facilities include restrooms, lifeguards, and parking. To get here, take the H-1 freeway to the end of the line, where it becomes Farrington Highway (Hwy. 93), and follow it to the beach; or you can take TheBus no. 51.

7 KID-FRIENDLY TOURS

If your time is limited, you might want to consider a guided tour. These tours are informative, can give you a good overview of Honolulu or Oahu in a limited amount of time, and are surprisingly entertaining. But if you have young kids, don't plan an all-day tour—it's a bit much for children 6 and under.

If you'd rather go touring independently, **TourTalk Oahu** (✆ **877/585-7499;** www.tourtalkhawaii.com) offers a complete package of 2½-hour narrated compact disks (or cassettes), driving instructions, and a 72-page booklet containing color maps, photos, site information, and Hawaiian facts, for $25. The self-guided driving tour not only guides you around the island to see the most popular sites, but has cultural and historical information as well.

SIGHTSEEING TOURS

E Noa Tours, 1141 Waimanu St., Suite 105, Honolulu (✆ **800/824-8804** or 808/591-2561; www.enoa.com), offers a range of tours, from island loops to explorations of historic Honolulu. These narrated tours are on air-conditioned, 27-passenger minibuses.

The Royal Circle Island tour ($62 for adults, $50 for children 6–11, $44 for children 5 and under) stops at Diamond Head Crater, Hanauma Bay, Byodo-In Temple, Sunset Beach, Waimea Valley (admission included), and various beach sites along the way. Other tours go to Pearl Harbor/USS *Arizona* Memorial and the Polynesian Cultural Center.

Waikiki Trolley Tours ★, 1141 Waimanu St., Suite 105, Honolulu (✆ **800/824-8804** or 808/596-2199; www.waikikitrolley.com), offers three fun tours of sightseeing, entertainment, dining, and shopping. These tours are a great way to get the lay of the land. You can get on and off the trolley as needed (trolleys come along every 2–20 min.). An all-day pass (8:30am–11:35pm) is $25 for adults, $18 for seniors, and $12 for children (4–11); a 4-day pass is $45 for adults, $27 for seniors, and $18 for children. For the same price, you can experience the 2-hour narrated Ocean Coastline tour of the southeast side of Oahu, an easy way to see the stunning views.

ECO-TOURS

Oahu isn't just high-rises in Waikiki or urban sprawl in Honolulu, but extinct craters, hidden waterfalls, lush rainforests, forgotten coastlines, and rainbow-filled valleys. To experience the other side of Oahu, contact **Oahu Nature Tours** (✆ **808/924-2473;** www.oahunaturetours.com). They have a range of eco-tours, best for kids ages 6 and older, which start at $24 a person. They provide everything: experts in geology, history, Hawaiian mythology, and archaeology; round-trip transportation; entrance fees; bottled water and snacks; and use of day packs, binoculars, flashlights, and rain gear.

If you want to explore a hidden, ancient Hawaii that most lifelong residents have never seen, book a tour with **Mauka Makai Excursions** ★, 350 Ward Ave., Honolulu (✆ **808/593-3525;** www.hawaiianecotours.net), a Hawaiian-owned and -operated eco-tour company specializing in field trips (best for ages 6 and older) to off-the-beaten-path (and sometimes hidden in the jungle) ancient temples, sea caves, sacred stones, petroglyphs, and other cultural treasures. Tours range from a half-day ($50 adults, $40 children 6–17) to a full day ($80 adults, $60 children). They provide bottled water, insect repellent, rain gear, beach gear, fishing tackle, and hotel pickup; you bring your imagination.

8 FOR THE ACTIVE FAMILY

For general advice on the activities listed below, see "Special-Interest Trips," in chapter 2.

IN THE WATER

If you want to rent beach toys (such as a mask, snorkel, and fins; boogie boards; surfboards; kayaks; and more), check out the following Waikiki rental shops: **Snorkel Bob's,** on the way to Hanauma Bay at 700 Kapahulu Ave. (at Date St.), Honolulu (✆ **808/735-7944;** www.snorkelbob.com); and **Aloha Beach Service,** in the Moana Surfrider Resort, A Westin Resort, 2365 Kalakaua Ave. (✆ **808/922-3111,** ext. 2341), in Waikiki. On Oahu's windward side, try **Kailua Sailboards & Kayaks,** 130 Kailua Rd., a block from the Kailua Beach Park (✆ **808/262-2555;** www.kailuasailboards.com). On the North Shore, get equipment from **Surf-N-Sea,** 62-595 Kamehameha Hwy., Haleiwa (✆ **808/637-9887;** www.surfnsea.com).

Boating

A funny thing happens to families when they come to Hawaii: Maybe it's the salt air, the warm tropical nights, or the blue Hawaiian moonlight, but otherwise-rational people who have never set foot on a boat in their life suddenly want to go out to sea. All of the special yachts discussed below will take you **whale-watching** in season (roughly Dec–Apr).

Captain Bob's Adventure Cruises ★ All ages. See the majestic windward coast the way it should be seen—from a boat. Captain Bob takes families on a 4-hour, lazy day sail of Kaneohe Bay aboard his 42-foot catamaran, which skims across the almost-always calm water above the shallow coral reef, lands at the disappearing sandbar Ahu o Laka, and takes you past two small islands to snorkel spots full of tropical fish and, sometimes, turtles. The color of the water alone is worth the price. This is an all-day affair, but hey, getting out on the water is the reason you came to Hawaii, right? A shuttle will pick you up at your Waikiki hotel between 9 and 9:30am and bring you back at about 4pm—it's a lot quicker than taking TheBus.

Kaneohe Bay. ✆ **808/942-5077.** $79 adults, $60 children 3–17, free for children under 3. Rates include all-you-can-eat barbecue lunch and transportation from Waikiki hotels. No cruises Sun and holidays. Bus: 55 or 56.

Navatek I ★★ Ages 2 & up. This is for families who are afraid to go on a boat for fear of *mal de mar* (seasickness). This boat guarantees that you'll be "seasick free"—that's enough reason to book. The 140-foot-long *Navatek I* isn't even called a boat; it's actually a SWATH (Small Waterplane Area Twin Hull) vessel. That means the ship's superstructure—the part you ride on—rests on twin torpedo-like hulls that cut through the water so you don't bob like a cork. It's the smoothest ride on Mamala Bay. In fact, *Navatek I* is the only dinner-cruise ship to receive U.S. Coast Guard certification to travel beyond Diamond Head.

The boat trips range from 2 to 3 hours. **Sunset dinner cruises** leave Pier 6 (across from the Hawaii Maritime Museum) nightly. If you have your heart set on seeing the city lights, take the Royal Sunset Dinner Cruise, which runs from 5:15 to 7:15pm. The best deal is the **lunch cruise,** with a full buffet lunch and a great view of Oahu offshore. The lunch cruise lasts from 11:30am to 2pm. Both cruises include live Hawaiian music.

Aloha Tower Marketplace, Pier 6, c/o Hawaiian Cruises Ltd. ✆ **808/973-1311.** www.atlantisadventures.com/oahu.cfm. Dinner cruises $86–$118 adults, $57–$74 children 2–12; lunch cruises $67 adults, $34 children 2–11. Validated parking before 4:30pm $3, after 4:30pm flat parking fee of $2. Bus: 8, 19, 20, 55, 56, or 57.

Bodyboarding (Boogie Boarding) & Bodysurfing

Good places to learn to bodyboard are in the small waves of **Waikiki Beach** and **Kailua Beach,** and **Bellows Field Beach Park,** off Kalanianaole Highway (Hwy. 72) in Waimanalo, which is open to the public on weekends (from noon Fri to midnight on Sun and holidays). To get here, turn toward the ocean on Hughs Road, then right on Tinker Road, which takes you right to the park. Waikiki Beach has vendors to teach you and your kids how to learn to surf for $25 an hour per person. (The kids must be strong swimmers to take the surfing lessons.)

Ocean Kayaking

For a wonderful family adventure, rent a kayak, arrive at Lanikai Beach just as the sun is appearing, and paddle across the emerald lagoon to the pyramid-shaped islands off the beach called Mokulua—it's an experience no one in the family will forget. If the kids are small, rent a double kayak and just let them sit and enjoy the view; the older kids should get in on the paddling action. Kayak equipment rental starts at $10 an hour for a single kayak, and $16 an hour for a double kayak. In Waikiki, try **Prime Time Sports,** Fort DeRussy Beach (✆ **808/949-8952**). On the windward side, check out **Kailua**

Sailboards & Kayaks, 130 Kailua Rd., a block from Kailua Beach Park (✆ **808/262-2555;** www.kailuasailboards.com), where single kayaks rent for $39 half-day and double kayaks $49 half-day. On the North Shore, **Surf-N-Sea,** 62-595 Kamehameha Hwy., Haleiwa (✆ **808/637-9887;** www.surfnsea.com), kayak rentals start at $7 an hour or $35 a day.

First-timers should go to **Kailua Sailboards & Kayaks,** 130 Kailua Rd., in Kailua (✆ **808/262-2555;** www.kailuasailboards.com), where single kayaks rent for $39 for a half-day and double kayaks rent for $49 for a half-day. The company offers a guided tour (from $89 adults, $62 kids ages 3–12) with the novice in mind in a safe, protected environment. Lunch, all equipment, and transportation from Waikiki hotels are included. Kayak lessons and self-guided trips are also available.

Snorkeling

If the kids can swim (or float with a floating device), snorkeling is a great family outing. Some of the best snorkeling in Oahu is at **Hanauma Bay ★★**. It's crowded—sometimes it seems there are more people than fish—but Hanauma has clear, warm, protected waters and an abundance of friendly reef fish, including Moorish idols, scores of butterfly fish, damselfish, and wrasses. Hanauma Bay has two reefs, an inner and an outer—the first for novices, the other for experts. The inner reef is calm and shallow (less than 10 ft.); in some places, you can just wade and put your face in the water. Go early: It's packed by 10am and closed on Tuesday. For details, see "Beaches," earlier in this chapter.

Braver snorkelers may want to head to **Shark's Cove,** on the North Shore just off Kamehameha Highway, between Haleiwa and Pupukea. Sounds risky, we know, but we've never seen or heard of any sharks in this cove, and in summer, this big, lava-edged pool is one of Oahu's best snorkel spots. Waves splash over the natural lava grotto and cascade like waterfalls into the pool full of tropical fish. To the right of the cove are deep-sea caves to explore.

Submarine Dives

Here's your chance to play Jules Verne and experience the underwater world from the comfort of a submarine, which will take your family on an adventure below the surface in high-tech comfort. The entire trip is narrated as you watch tropical fish and sunken ships just outside the sub; if swimming's not your thing, this is a great way to see Hawaii's spectacular sea life. Shuttle boats to the sub leave from Hilton Hawaiian Village Pier. The cost is $95 to $113 for adults, $80 to $98 for kids 12 and under (children must be at least 36 in. tall). ***Budget tip:*** Book online for discount rates of $95 for adults and $48 for kids age 12 and under at **Atlantis Adventures ★** (✆ **800/548-6262** or 808/973-9811; www.atlantisadventures.com). Allow a couple of hours for the trip. ***Warning:*** The ride is safe for everyone, but skip it if you suffer from claustrophobia.

Surfing

In summer, when the water's warm and there's a soft breeze in the air, the south swell comes up. It's surf season in Waikiki, Oahu's best place to learn how to surf. Kids must know how to swim, but even 6-year-olds can learn to surf. For lessons, go early to **Aloha Beach Service,** next to the Sheraton Moana Surfrider, 2365 Kalakaua Ave., Waikiki (✆ **808/922-3111**). The beach boys offer surfing lessons for $30 an hour; board rentals are $10 for the first hour and $5 every hour after that.

On the North Shore, there's no excuse not to learn to surf in Hawaii: Hans Hedemann, a champion surfer for some 34 years, has opened the **Hans Hedemann Surf**

Moments Experiencing Jaws: Up Close & Personal

You're 4 miles out from land, which is just a speck on the horizon, with hundreds of feet of open ocean. Suddenly from out of the blue depths a shape emerges: the sleek, pale shadow of a 6-foot-long gray reef shark, followed quickly by a couple of 10-foot-long Galápagos sharks. Within a couple of heartbeats, you are surrounded by sharks on all sides. Do you panic? No, you paid $120 to be in the midst of these jaws of the deep. Of course, there is a 6×6×10-foot aluminum shark cage separating you from all those teeth.

It happens every day on the **North Shore Shark Adventure** (**© 808/256-2769;** www.hawaiisharkadventures.com). They will take the entire family on their cruises, but use your judgment on allowing kids to go into the shark cage. Generally, kids 13 and older are mature enough to enjoy the experience. The adventure is a dream of Capt. Joe Pavsek, who decided after some 30 years of surfing and diving to share the experience of seeing a shark with visitors. To make sure that the predators of the deep will show up for the viewing, Captain Pavsek heaves "chum," a not very appetizing concoction of fish trimmings and entrails, over the side of his 26-foot boat, *Kailolo.* It's sort of like ringing the dinner bell—after a few minutes the sharks (generally gray reef, Galápagos, and sandbars, ranging 5–15 ft.) show up—sometimes just a few, sometimes a couple dozen. Depending on the sea conditions and the weather, snorkelers can stay in the cage as long as they wish, with the sharks just inches away. The shark cage, connected to the boat with wire line, floats several feet back and holds up to four snorkelers. (It's comfortable for two but pretty snug at full capacity.) You can stay on the boat and view the sharks from a more respectable distance for just $60. The more adventurous, down in the cage with just thin aluminum separating them from the sharks, are sure to have an unforgettable experience.

School at the Turtle Bay Resort (**© 808/924-7778;** www.hhsurf.com). His classes range from one-on-one private sessions to group lessons (four students to one teacher) and begin at $115 an hour. If the expenditure is beyond your budget, go for a $50 1-hour group lesson (maximum four people). If you aren't staying at the Turtle Bay, he will provide complimentary hotel transportation from Waikiki hotels to one of his six locations: North Shore, Waikiki, and the Kohala Hotel.

Surfboards are also available for rent on the North Shore at **Surf-N-Sea,** 62-595 Kamehameha Hwy., Haleiwa (**© 808/637-9887;** www.surfnsea.com), for $5 to $7 an hour. They also offer lessons for $85 for 2 hours. For the best surf shops, where you can soak in the culture as well as pick up gear, also see "Shopping with Your Kids," later in this chapter.

More experienced surfers should drop by any surf shop around Oahu, or call the **Surf News Network Surfline** (**© 808/596-SURF** [596-7873]) to get the latest surf conditions. **The Cliffs,** at the base of Diamond Head, is a good spot for advanced surfers; 4- to 6-foot waves churn here, allowing high-performance surfing.

If you're in Hawaii in winter and want to see the serious surfers catch the really big waves, bring your binoculars and grab a front-row seat on the beach near **Kalalua Point.** To get here from Waikiki, take the H-1 toward the North Shore, veering off at H-2, which becomes Kamehameha Highway (Hwy. 83). Keep going to the funky surf town of Haleiwa and Waimea Bay; the big waves will be on your left, just past Pupukea Beach Park.

ON THE LAND

People think Oahu is just one big urban island, so they're always surprised to discover that the great outdoors is less than 15 minutes away from downtown Honolulu.

Bicycling

Bicycling is a great way to see Oahu. Most streets here have bike lanes. For information on biking trails, races, and tours, check out **Bike Hawaii** at www.bikehawaii.com (✆ **877/682-7433** or 808/734-4214 in Oahu). For information on bikeways and maps, contact the **Honolulu City and County Bike Coordinator** (✆ **808/527-5044**).

If you're in Waikiki, you can rent a bike for as little as $10 for a half-day and $20 for 24 hours at **Big Kuhuna Motorcycle Tours & Rentals,** 407 Seaside Ave. (✆ **808/924-2736;** www.bigkahunarentals.com/sntmainbikes.htm). On the North Shore, for a full-suspension mountain bike, try **Barnfield's Raging Isle Surf & Cycle,** 66-250 Kamehameha Hwy., Haleiwa (✆ **808/637-7707;** www.ragingisle.com), which rents bikes for $40 for 24 hours.

For a bike-and-hike adventure, call **Bike Hawaii** (✆ **877/682-7433** or 808/734-4214; www.bikehawaii.com). They have a variety of group tours, such as their Downhill Coasting Ride, which gives you a bird's-eye view of Oahu from 1,800 feet above Waikiki. The tour includes coasting down 5 miles on a paved mountain road with scenic views above Waikiki, Honolulu, and Manoa Valley. Listen to the songs of birds and the wind through the trees, and learn about the culture, plants, and geology of the Hawaiian Islands. After that, you leave your bike for a 2-mile round-trip hike to a 200-foot waterfall. The 9am-to-2pm trip—which includes van transportation from your hotel, continental breakfast, bike, helmet, snacks, water bottle, and guide—is $96 for adults and $72 for children 13 and under. There's no minimum age for kids, but to fit the bikes, your youngsters should be around 4 feet and 8 inches tall, depending on how long their legs are.

Camping

Hawaii is not very camping-friendly. Permits are not easy to get if you are a nonresident. If you plan to camp, you must bring your own gear, as no one on Oahu rents gear.

The best places to camp on Oahu are listed below. TheBus's Circle Island route can get you to or near all these sites, but remember: On TheBus, you're allowed only one bag, which has to fit under the seat. If you have more gear, you're going to have to rent a car or take a cab.

Windward Oahu

HOOMALUHIA BOTANICAL GARDENS ★ Finds This windward campground outside Kaneohe is an almost secret place and a real treasure. It's hard to believe that you're just a half-hour from downtown Honolulu. Facilities for this tent-camp area include restrooms, cold showers, dishwashing stations, picnic tables, and water. A public phone is available at the visitor center. Shopping and gas are available in Kaneohe, 2 miles away. Permits are free, but stays are limited to 3 nights (Fri–Sun only); the office is closed on Sunday. The gate is locked at 4pm and doesn't open again until 9am, so you're locked in for the night. Hoomaluhia Botanical Gardens is at 45-680 Luluku Rd. (at Kamehameha Hwy.), Kaneohe (✆ **808/233-7323;** www.co.honolulu.hi.us/parks/hbg/hmbg.htm). From Waikiki, take H-1 to the Pali Highway (Hwy. 61); turn left on Kamehameha Highway (Hwy. 83); and at the fourth light, turn left on Luluku Road. TheBus nos. 55 and 56 stop nearby on Kamehameha Highway; from here, you have to walk 2 miles to the visitor center.

KUALOA REGIONAL PARK★★ This park has a spectacular setting on a peninsula on Kaneohe Bay. The gold-sand beach is excellent for snorkeling, and fishing can be rewarding as well. (See "Beaches," earlier in this chapter.) Facilities include restrooms, showers, picnic tables, drinking fountains, and a public phone. Campground A also has sinks for dishwashing, a volleyball court, and a kitchen building. Gas and groceries are available in Kaaawa, 2½ miles away. The gate hours at Kualoa Regional Park are 7am to 8pm; if you're not back at the park by 8pm, you're locked out for the night. Permits are free but limited to 5 days (no camping Wed–Thurs). Contact the **Honolulu Department of Parks and Recreation,** 650 S. King St., Honolulu, HI 96713 (✆ **808/523-4525;** www.co.honolulu.hi.us), for information and permits. Kualoa Regional Park is located in the 49-600 area of Kamehameha Highway, across from Mokolii Island. Take the Likelike Highway (Hwy. 63); after the Wilson Tunnel, get in the right lane and turn off on Kahakili Highway (Hwy. 83). Or take TheBus no. 55.

The North Shore

MALAEKAHANA BAY STATE RECREATION AREA★★ This is one of the most beautiful beach-camping areas in the state, with a mile-long, gold-sand beach on Oahu's windward coast. (See "Beaches," earlier in this chapter, for details.) There are two areas for tent camping. Facilities include picnic tables, restrooms, showers, sinks, drinking water, and a phone. For your safety, the park gate is closed between 6:45pm and 7am; vehicles cannot enter or exit during those hours. Groceries and gas are available in Laie and Kahuku, each less than a mile away.

Permits are $5 and limited to 5 nights; they may be obtained at any state park office, including the **Hawaii Department of Land and Natural Resources,** Division of State Parks, P.O. Box 621, Honolulu, HI 96809 (✆ **808/587-0300;** www.state.hi.us/dlnr). The recreation area is located on Kamehameha Highway (Hwy. 83) between Laie and Kahuku. Take the H-2 to Highway 99 to Highway 83 (both roads are called Kamehameha Hwy.); continue on Highway 83 just past Kahuku. You can also get here via TheBus no. 55.

Hiking

Highlights of the island's 33 major hiking trails include razor-thin ridgebacks and deep waterfall valleys. Hiking is a great family outing, and you can pick the trails that will allow the whole gang to wander through a rainforest or walk to a waterfall. Check out Stuart Ball's *The Hikers Guide to Oahu* (University of Hawaii Press, 1993) before you go. Another good source of hiking information on Oahu is the state's **Na Ala Hele (Trails to Go On) Program** (✆ **808/973-9782** or 808/587-0058).

For a free Oahu recreation map listing all 33 trails in the program, contact the **Department of Land and Natural Resources,** 1151 Punchbowl St., Room 131, Honolulu, HI 96813 (✆ **808/587-0300**). The department will also send free topographic trail maps on request and issue camping permits.

Another good source of information is the *Hiking/Camping Information Packet,* which costs $7 (postage included); to order, contact **Hawaii Geographic Maps and Books,** 49

Hot Fun in the Summertime

It's always fun on Oahu for kids, but during the summer, it's double fun with the following great activities:

- **Vacation Adventures Day Camp:** At the Honolulu Zoo, kids ages 5 to 11 can experience behind-the-scenes encounters at the zoo, hang out with the zookeepers and hear their tales, and participate in animal arts and games. Other great programs for families include **Junior Zookeeper,** in which kids ages 11 to 18 see what it is like to be a zookeeper for a day and actually feed the animals (the fee is $25), and their younger siblings, ages 6 to 10, can participate in the **Keiki Zookeeper** program ($35); **Twilight Tours,** a way for families to discover the zoo after the sun goes down (fees $12 adults, $8 kids ages 4–12); and **Snooze in the Zoo,** in which families spend the night at the zoo with storytelling, pizza eating, tours, campfires with songs, and breakfast ($50 per person ages 4 and up). For more information, contact the Honolulu Zoo (✆ **808/926-3191;** www.honoluluzoo.org).
- **Waikiki Aquarium:** The aquarium has an amazing number of children's programs, including **Small Fry,** for kids ages 1 to 3 (with an adult) to discover the wonders of the underwater world; **Aquarium After Dark,** in which kids ages 5 and older see how the reef changes from day to night and tour the Aquarium by flashlight; **Fish School,** where kids 6 and older learn what makes a fish a fish; and **Exploring the Reef by Day,** for kids ages 5 and older (with parents) to explore the shoreline, reef flat, and tidal pool with naturalists from the aquarium. For more information, call ✆ **808/923-9741** or visit www.waquarium.org.
- **Bishop Museum:** The museum has lots of summertime events, from monthly **Moonlight Mele** concerts featuring top Hawaiian entertainers to high-energy interactive exhibits designed for families. Call ✆ **808/847-3511** or visit www.bishopmuseum.org for complete details.

S. Hotel St., Honolulu, HI 96813 (✆ **800/538-3950** or 808/538-3952). This store also carries a full line of United States Geographic Survey topographic maps, very handy for hikers.

Also be sure to get a copy of *Hiking on Oahu: The Official Guide,* a hiking safety brochure that includes instructions on hiking preparation, safety procedures, emergency phone numbers, and necessary equipment; for a copy, contact Erin Lau, Trails and Access Manager, **City and County of Honolulu** (✆ **808/973-9782**); the **Hawaii Nature Center,** 2131 Makiki Heights Dr. (✆ **808/955-0100**); or **The Bike Shop,** 1149 S. King St. (✆ **808/596-0588**).

The **Hawaiian Trail and Mountain Club,** P.O. Box 2238, Honolulu, HI 96804, offers regular hikes on Oahu. You bring your own lunch and drinking water and meet up with the club at the Iolani Palace to join them on a hike. The club also has an information packet on hiking and camping in Hawaii, as well as a schedule of all upcoming hikes; send $2 plus a legal-size, self-addressed, stamped envelope to the address above.

Other organizations that offer regularly scheduled hikes are the **Sierra Club,** P.O. Box 2577, Honolulu, HI 96803 (www.hi.sierraclub.org); the **Nature Conservancy,** 1116 Smith St., Suite 201, Honolulu, HI 96817 (✆ **808/537-4508,** ext. 220); and the **Hawaii Nature Center,** 2131 Makiki Heights Dr. (✆ **808/955-0100**).

HONOLULU-AREA HIKES

DIAMOND HEAD CRATER ★★★ This is a moderate but steep (with an emphasis on steep) walk to the summit of Hawaii's most famous landmark. Kids love to look out from the top of the 760-foot volcanic cone, where they have 360-degree views of Oahu up the leeward coast from Waikiki. Small kids may have to be carried, so be prepared. Strollers will not make it up the zillions of steps. The 1.5-mile round-trip journey takes about 1½ hours and the entry fee is $1.

Diamond Head was created by a volcanic explosion about half a million years ago. The Hawaiians called the crater *Leahi* (meaning the brow of the ahi, or tuna, referring to the shape of the crater). Diamond Head was considered a sacred spot; King Kamehameha offered human sacrifices at a *heiau* (temple) on the western slope. It wasn't until the 19th century that Mount Leahi got its current name: A group of sailors found what they thought were diamonds in the crater; it turned out they were just worthless calcite crystals, but the Diamond Head moniker stuck.

Before you begin your journey to the top of the crater, put on some decent shoes (rubber-soled tennies are fine) and gather a flashlight (you'll walk through several dark tunnels), binoculars (for better viewing at the top), water (very important), a hat to protect you from the sun, and a camera. You might want to put all your gear in a pack to leave your hands free for the climb. If you don't have a flashlight or if your hotel can't lend you one, you can buy a small one for a few dollars as part of a Diamond Head climbers' "kit" at the gift shop at the **New Otani Kaimana Beach Hotel,** on the Diamond Head end of Kalakaua Avenue, just past the Waikiki Aquarium and across from Kapiolani Park.

Go early, preferably just after the 6:30am opening, before the midday sun starts beating down. The hike to the summit of Diamond Head starts at Monsarrat and 18th avenues on the crater's inland (or mauka) side. To get here, take TheBus no. 58 from the Ala Moana Shopping Center or drive to the intersection of Diamond Head Road and 18th Avenue. Follow the road through the tunnel (which is closed 6pm–6am) and park in the lot. The trailhead starts in the parking lot and proceeds along a paved walkway (with handrails) as it climbs the slope. You'll pass old World War I and II pillboxes, gun emplacements, and tunnels built as part of the Pacific defense network. Several steps take you up to the top observation post on Point Leahi. The views are incredible.

If you want to go with a guide, the Clean Air Team leads a guided hike to the top of Diamond Head every Saturday. The group gathers at 9am, near the front entrance to the Honolulu Zoo. (Look for the rainbow windsock.) Hikers should bring a flashlight and a $5 fee. Each person will be given a bag and asked to help keep the trail clean by picking up litter. For more information, call ✆ **808/948-3299.**

MANOA FALLS TRAIL ★★ This easy, .75-mile (one-way) hike is terrific for families; it takes less than an hour to reach idyllic Manoa Falls. The trailhead, marked by a footbridge, is at the end of Manoa Road, past Lyon Arboretum. The staff at the arboretum prefers that hikers do not park in their lot, so the best place to park is in the residential area below Paradise Park; you can also get to the arboretum via TheBus no. 5. The often-muddy trail follows Waihi Stream and meanders through the forest reserve past guavas, mountain apples, and wild ginger. The forest is moist and humid and is inhabited by giant bloodthirsty mosquitoes, so bring repellent and wear appropriate shoes (like running shoes, tennis shoes, or hiking shoes). If it has rained recently, stay on the trail and step carefully, as it can be very slippery (and it's a long way down if you slide off the side). Before you venture out, call ✆ **808/587-0300** to check if the trail is open.

East Oahu Hikes

MAKAPUU LIGHTHOUSE TRAIL ★ For kids 12 and older, this is a great coastal trail hike, but a little too dangerous for youngsters. Your goal at the end of this precipitous cliff trail is the old lighthouse where the views are down the windward coast, and out to sea—Manana (Rabbit) Island and the azure Pacific. It's about a 45-minute, mile-long hike from Kalanianaole Highway (Hwy. 72), along a paved road that begins across from Hawaii Kai Executive Golf Course and winds around the 646-foot-high sea bluff to the lighthouse lookout.

To get to the trailhead from Waikiki, take Kalanianaole Highway (Hwy. 72) past Hanauma Bay and Sandy Beach to Makapuu Head, the southeastern tip of the island; you can also take TheBus no. 57 or 58. Look for a sign that says NO VEHICLES ALLOWED on a gate to the right, a few hundred yards past the entrance to the golf course. The trail isn't marked, but it's fairly obvious: Just follow the abandoned road that leads gradually uphill to a trail that wraps around Makapuu Point. It's a little precarious, but anyone in reasonably good shape can handle it.

Blowhole alert: When the south swell is running, usually in summer, a couple of blowholes on the south side of Makapuu Head put the famous Halona blowhole to shame.

Windward Oahu Hikes

HAUULA LOOP ★ If your clan is in fairly good shape and used to hiking, follow the Hauula Loop Trail on the windward side of the island for one of the best views of the coast and the ocean. It's an easy, 2.5-mile loop on a well-maintained path that passes through a whispering ironwood forest and a grove of tall Norfolk pines. The trip takes about 3 hours and gains some 600 feet in elevation.

To get to the trail, take TheBus no. 55 or follow Highway 83 to Hauula Beach Park. Turn toward the mountains on Hauula Homestead Road; when it forks to the left at Maakua Road, park on the side of the road. Walk along Maakua Road to the wide, grassy trail that begins the hike into the mountains. The climb is fairly steep for about 300 yards but turns into easier-on-the-calves switchbacks as you go up the ridge. Look down as you climb: You'll spot wildflowers and mushrooms among the matted needles. The trail continues up, crossing Waipilopilo Gulch, where you'll see several forms of native plant life. Eventually, you reach the top of the ridge, where the views are spectacular.

Camping is permitted along the trail, but it's difficult to find a place to pitch a tent on the steep slopes and in the dense forest growth. There are a few places along the ridge, however, that are wide enough for a tent. Contact the **Division of Forestry and Wildlife,** 1151 Punchbowl St., Honolulu, HI 96813 (✆ **808/587-0166**), for information on camping permits.

North Shore Hikes

For nearly 3 decades, 1,875-acre **Waimea Valley** (59-864 Kamehameha Hwy., Haleiwa; ✆ **808/638-7766;** www.waimeavalley.org) has lured visitors with activities from cliff diving and hula performances to kayaking and ATV tours. In 2008 the Office of Hawaiian Affairs took over and formed a new nonprofit corporation, Hi'ipaka, to run the park, with the emphasis on perpetuating and sharing the "living Hawaiian culture." As we went to press, the new corporation was just taking over and had plans to have authentic hula performances and demonstrations of native Hawaiian crafts. It offers a lush walk into the past. The valley is packed with archaeological sites, including the 600-year-old Hale O Lono, a heiau dedicated to the Hawaiian god Lono. The botanical collection has 35 different gardens, including super-rare Hawaiian species such as the endangered Kokia cookie hibiscus. The valley is also home to fauna such as the endangered Hawaiian moorhen; look for a black bird with a red face cruising in the ponds. Walk through the gardens (take the paved paths or dirt trails) and you wind up at 30-foot-high Waimea Falls—bring your bathing suit and you can dive into the cold, murky water. The public is invited to hike the trails and spend a day in this quiet oasis. Admission price: $10 for adults, $5 for children 4 to 12, and $5 for seniors (and parking now is free).

Horseback Riding

You can gallop on the beach at the **Turtle Bay Resort,** 57-091 Kamehameha Hwy., Kahuku (✆ **808/293-8811;** www.turtlebayresort.com; bus: 52 or 55), where 45-minute rides along sandy beaches with spectacular ocean views and through a forest of ironwood trees cost $50 for adults and $30 for children 7 to 12. (They must be at least 54 in. tall.) Romantic evening rides are $80 per person. Advanced riders can sign up for a 60-minute trot-and-canter ride along Kawela Bay ($100).

9 SHOPPING WITH YOUR KIDS

Shopping with kids can be a great escapade. Hawaiian malls are outdoors with plenty of entertainment, and among the brand names are shops unique to Hawaii; so just browsing through the merchandise can be an adventure.

Most stores are happy to ship, but be aware that shipping from Hawaii is either inexpensive with a 3-month lag time or so expensive that sometimes the cost of shipping is more than the product you are buying. Sales tax in Hawaii is 4.16% on everything (even food).

THE SHOPPING SCENE

Shopping competes with golf, surfing, and sightseeing as a bona fide Hawaiian activity. And why not? The proliferation of top-notch made-in-Hawaii products, the vitality of the local crafts scene, and the unquenchable thirst for mementos of the islands lend respectability to shopping here.

The section that follows is not about finding cheap souvenirs or tony items from designer fashion chains; you can find these on your own. Rather, I'm offering a guide to finding those special treasures that lie somewhere in between.

Great Shopping Areas

WAIKIKI Nestled amid the Louis Vuitton, Chanel, and Tiffany boutiques on Waikiki's Kalakaua Avenue are plenty of tacky booths hawking air-brushed T-shirts, gold by the inch, and tasteless aloha shirts. The International Marketplace is scheduled for a massive (much-needed) makeover; until it is transformed, I suggest shopping at a couple of Waikiki malls: the **Royal Hawaiian Shopping Center** (see "Mall Rats," below) and the **DFS Galleria,** Kalakaua and Royal Hawaiian avenues (✆ **808/931-2655**). At the entrance to the Galleria, your kids will probably be the first to spot "The Tube," a walk-through aquarium complete with spotted sting rays. "Boat Days" is the theme of this three-floor extravaganza of shops ranging from the top dollar (Givenchy, Coach, and many more) to the very touristy. Great Hawaii food products include the incomparable Big Island Candies. There are multitudes of aloha shirts and T-shirts, a virtual golf course, surf and skate equipment, and a labyrinth of fashionable stores once you get past the Waikiki Walk. On the fringe of Waikiki is Hawaii's best-known shopping center, **Ala Moana.** (See "Mall Rats," below.)

HONOLULU At the base of the Aloha Tower lies a harborfront shopping and restaurant complex known as the **Aloha Tower Marketplace,** 1 Aloha Tower Dr., on the waterfront between piers 8 and 11, Honolulu Harbor (© **808/528-5700**). There are lots of unique Hawaii shops here—from **Martin & MacArthur,** a gift shop with finely crafted furniture, to **Hawaiian Ukulele Company,** featuring everyone's favorite Hawaiian instrument—plus entertainment from hula shows to contemporary Hawaiian musicians to old-fashioned rock 'n' roll.

WINDWARD Windward Oahu's largest shopping complex is the **Windward Mall,** 46-056 Kamehameha Hwy., in Kaneohe (© **808/235-1143**). The 100 stores and services at this standard suburban mall include **Macy's** and **Sears,** health stores, airline counters, surf shops, and **LensCrafters.** A small food court serves pizza, Chinese fare, tacos, and other morsels. In Kailua, the shopping nexus is formed by **Longs Drugs** and **Macy's** department store, located side by side on Kailua Road, where several unique Hawaii shops feature everything from clothes to antiques.

NORTH SHORE The main town of **Haleiwa** means serious shopping for those who know that the unhurried pace of rural life can conceal vast material treasures. Ask the legions of townies who drive an hour each way just to stock up on wine and clothes at Haleiwa stores. (Of course, a cooler is de rigueur for perishables.) Here you'll find excellent crafts and art galleries, such as **Haleiwa Art Gallery,** next door to the North Shore Marketplace (© **808/637-3368**); surf shops such as **Northshore Boardriders Club,** North Shore Marketplace, 66-250 Kamehameha Hwy. (© **808/637-5026**); and shops such as **Silver Moon Emporium,** North Shore Marketplace (© **808/637-7710**), which stocks an eclectic mix of everything from great T-shirts to unique jewelry.

THE GOODS A TO Z

Aloha Wear

One of Hawaii's lasting afflictions is the penchant tourists have for wearing loud, matching aloha shirts and muumuus. We applaud such visitors' good intentions (to act local), but no local resident would be caught dead in such a get-up (especially matching his-and-hers outfits). Muumuus and aloha shirts are wonderful, but the real thing is what island folks wear on Aloha Friday (every Fri), to the Brothers Cazimero Lei Day Concert (every May 1), or to work (where allowed). It's what they wear at home and to special parties where the invitation reads "aloha attire."

For the best prices in children's aloha wear, I recommend **Hilo Hattie,** at 700 Nimitz Hwy. (© **808/535-6500**) or at the Ala Moana Shopping Center (© **808/973-3266**). Hilo Hattie has everything for infants to teens, including shirts, T-shirts, dresses, footwear, and even toys. In business since 1965, Hilo Hattie has become very fashionable in recent years and offers contemporary clothing for adults, too.

Aside from the vintage Hawaiian wear (1930s–1950s) found in collectibles shops and at swap meets, our favorite contemporary aloha-wear designer is Hawaii's **Tori Richards.** The best aloha shirts are pricey these days, going for $80 to $125. For the vintage look, **Avanti** has a corner on the market with its stunning line of silk shirts and dresses in authentic 1930s to 1950s patterns. These shirts ($60–$105) boast all the qualities of a

Waikiki Beach Walk

One of the biggest projects to take place in Waikiki in decades is the total renovation of an 8-acre area (bound by Saratoga Rd., Kalakaua Ave., Lewers St., and Kalia Rd.) called the Waikiki Beach Walk. The project, by Outrigger Hotels & Resorts, cost some $460 million.

Phase 1, completed in 2007, reconfigured the formerly very congested area (narrow streets, with lots of delivery trucks double-parked, crowded sidewalks, and no vegetation) into an oasis of broad sidewalks, tropical foliage, water features, open space, and new, totally renovated hotels. Eleven hotels were razed, upgraded, or changed to suites or condos. Five hotels and one timeshare condominium remain. The bad news is that the near-oceanfront budget hotels, neighborhood eateries, and small independent shops have been replaced with luxury (higher-priced) properties and 90,000 square feet of swank shops and trendy restaurants to match, all linked through pedestrian bridges and connecting walkways.

vintage silk, but without the high price or the web-thin fragility of an authentic antique. The dresses and other styles are the epitome of comfort and nostalgic good looks. The line is distributed in better boutiques and department stores throughout Hawaii or at www.avantishirts.com.

Also popular is **Kahala Sportswear,** a well-known local company established in 1936. Kahala has faithfully reproduced, with astounding success, the linoleum-block prints of noted Maui artist Avi Kiriaty and the designs of other contemporary artists. Kahala is sold in department stores (from Macy's to Nordstrom), surf shops, and stylish boutiques; for a list of retail outlets, check www.kahala.com.

Baby & Preschooler Clothes

Apart from aloha wear (see above), Hawaii is a very expensive place for clothes. Most island families shop at department stores like Macy's. For reasonable prices and a wide selection, try **Gymboree** (www.gymboree.com), which has something for newborns to 9-year-olds. There are three stores on Oahu: at Ala Moana Center (© **808/955-2110**), Kahala Mall (© **808/735-1038**), and Pearlridge Center, 98-1005 Moanalua Rd., Pearl City (© **808/484-1846**). The **Children's Place,** in the Ala Moana Shopping Center (© **808/947-0003;** www.childrensplace.com) or their outlet at the Waikele Premium Outlets (see below) (© **808/671-9566**), has clothes for kids from newborn to size 14.

Books

Hawaii loves to read; you can tell by the sheer number of bookstores. You'll never be far from a great book to take to the beach, but take the time to wander through the Hawaiiana sections, where you'll find books on everything from the art of lei making to how to identify those colorful fish in the ocean. **Borders,** with its main branch at Ward Centre, 1200 Ala Moana Blvd. (© **808/591-8995**), is a great place for kids to hang out and read (they even have kid-size chairs); check out special weekend events for children. **Barnes & Noble,** Kahala Mall, 4211 Waialae Ave. (© **808/737-3323;** www.barnesandnoble.com), with

Mall Rats

Oahu is also a haven for mall mavens. More than 1,000 stores occupy the 11 major shopping centers on this island. From T-shirts to high fashion, chain stores to down-home local, avant-garde to unspeakably tacky, Oahu's offerings are wide-ranging indeed. But you must sometimes wade through oceans of schlock to arrive at the mother lode.

Ala Moana Center, 1450 Ala Moana Blvd. (✆ **808/955-9517**), Hawaii's largest and most prestigious shopping mall, features mainland chain stories such as Neiman Marcus, DKNY, Old Navy, Gap, Banana Republic, and Macy's. Great kids' wear here includes the Disney Store, Gap Kids, Gymboree, Splash! Girls, The Children's Place, and Up & Riding. And there are lots of toy stores: Build-A-Bear Workshop, K•B Toys, and Thinker Toys. Your teens will be thrilled by all the other teens hanging out here (and it is generally a safe place for them to wander off by themselves). There are practical touches in the center, too, such as banks, a foreign-exchange service (Travelex Foreign Exchange), a post office, several optical companies (including 1-hr. service by LensCrafters), Foodland Supermarket, Longs Drugs, and a handful of photo-processing services. Nearly 400 shops and restaurants sprawl over several blocks (and 1.8 million sq. ft. of store space), catering to every imaginable need, from over-the-top upscale (Tiffany, Chanel, Louis Vuitton) to local stores such as **Islands' Best. Splash! Hawaii** is a good source for women's swimwear; and **Reyn's** is great for men's aloha shirts. The food court is abuzz with dozens of stalls purveying Cajun food, ramen, pizza, plate lunches, vegetarian fare, green tea, fruit freezes (like frozen yogurt), panini, and countless other treats.

Chic, manageable, and unfrenzied, **Kahala Mall,** 4211 Waialae Ave., Kahala (✆ **808/732-7736**), is home to some of Honolulu's best shops. Teens will be in heaven as this is a great hangout, and safe for them. Located east of Waikiki in the posh neighborhood of Kahala, the mall has everything from a small Macy's

more than 150,000 titles, has a respectable kids' selection and strong Hawaiiana and fiction departments, as well as a popular coffee bar. A likely favorite for your teenagers is **Rainbow Books and Records,** 1010 University Ave. (✆ **808/955-7994**). A little weird but totally lovable, especially among students, eccentrics, and insatiable readers, the store is known for its selection of popular fiction, records, and Hawaii-themed books, secondhand and at reduced prices.

Discount Shopping

Just say the word "Waikele" and my eyes glaze over. So many shops, so little time! And so much money to be saved while shopping for what you don't need. There are two sections to this sprawling discount shopping mecca: the **Waikele Premium Outlets,** some 51 retailers offering designer and name-brand merchandise; and the **Waikele Value Center** across the street, with another 25 stores more practical than fashion-oriented (Eagle Hardware, Sports Authority). The 64-acre complex has made discount shopping a major activity and a travel pursuit in itself, with shopping tours for visitor groups and to chain stores such as Banana Republic and Gap—nearly 100 specialty shops (including dozens of eateries and eight movie theaters) in an enclosed, air-conditioned area. You can take the younger kids to a movie and meet up with the teens later.

In Waikiki, after 2 years and $84 million in remodeling and renovations, a new, larger, upscale **Royal Hawaiian Shopping Center,** 2201 Kalakaua Ave. (✆ **808/922-0961;** www.shopwaikiki.com), opened in 2008 with new shops, restaurants, a nightclub and theater, entry porte-cochere, and even a garden grove of 70 coconut trees with entertainment area. The result is a 293,000-square-foot open-air mall (17,000 sq. ft. larger than before) with 110 stores, restaurants, and entertainment on four levels. One of the flagship stores is **Hilo Hattie,** with some 30,000 square feet. The center also has a garden grove in the center of the mall with a pond, artesian fountain, stream running through, and performance area. The most exciting addition is the $15-million, 760-seat theater, with moving stages and acrobatic rigging. Then after the show, half of the theater's seating will retract to create a nightclub that can hold up to 1,000 people. *Upscale* is the operative word here. Although there are drugstores, lei stands, restaurants, and food kiosks, the most conspicuous stores are the European designer boutiques (**Chanel, Cartier, Hermès, L'Occitane, Fendi, Kate Spade, Bvlgari, Salvatore Ferragamo,** and more) that cater largely to visitors from Japan.

Ward Centre, 1200 Ala Moana Blvd. (✆ **808/591-8411**), is a standout for its concentration of restaurants and shops. **Ryan's** and **Kakaako Kitchen** are as popular as ever, the former overlooking Ala Moana Park and the latter with lanai views of the sprawling Pier 1 Imports across the street. The megaplex cinema here is so popular with teens that you will be hard pressed to find anyone over 25 here on a Friday night.

carloads of neighbor islanders and Oahu residents making pilgrimages from all corners of the state. They come to hunt down bargains on everything from perfumes, luggage, and hardware to sporting goods, fashions, vitamins, and china. Examples: Banana Republic, Anne Klein, Bebe, Brooks Brothers, Calvin Klein, Adidas, Sketchers, Polo Ralph Lauren, and dozens of other name brands at a fraction of retail. Kids will love Big Dog Sportswear, Blue Hawaii Surf, Crazy Shirt, Hawaiian Moon, and Local Motion. (You'll probably want to check out the deals at The Children's Place and OshKosh.) The ultrachic Barneys has added new cachet to this shopping haven. Open Monday through Friday from 9am to 9pm and Sunday from 10am to 6pm, the complex is located about 20 miles from Waikiki at 94-790 Lumiaina St., Waikele (✆ **808/676-5656;** www.premiumoutlets.com). Take H-1 west toward Waianae and turn off at Exit 7. Or take bus no. 42 from Waikiki to Waipahu Transit Center, then no. 433 from the Transit Center to Waikele. To find out which companies offer shopping tours with Waikiki pickups, call the **Information Center** at ✆ **808/678-0786.**

Flowers & Leis

At most lei shops, simple leis sell for $4 and up, deluxe leis for $10 and up. For a special-occasion designer bouquet or lei, you can't do better than Michael Miyashiro of **Rainforest Plantes et Fleurs** (✆ **808/591-9999**). He's an ecologically aware, highly gifted lei maker—his leis are pricey (in the $20 range), but worth it. He custom-designs the lei for the person, occasion, and even destination. Order by phone or stop by the Ward Warehouse, where his tiny shop is an oasis of green and beauty. Upon request, Miyashiro's leis will come in ti-leaf bundles, called *pu`olo.* He also offers custom gift baskets (in woven green coconut baskets) and special arrangements. You can even request the card sentiments in Hawaiian, with English translations.

The other primary sources of flowers and leis are the shops lining the streets of Moiliili and Chinatown. Moiliili favorites include **Rudy's Flowers,** 2722 S. King St. (✆ **808/944-8844**), a local institution with the best prices on roses, Micronesian ginger leis, and a variety of cut blooms. Across the street, **Flowers for a Friend,** 2739 S. King St. (✆ **808/955-4227**), has good prices on leis, floral arrangements, and cut flowers. Nearby, **Flowers by Jr. and Lou,** 2652 S. King St. (✆ **808/941-2022**), offers calla lilies, Gerber daisies, a riot of potted orchids, and the full range of cut flowers along with its lei selection.

In Chinatown, lei vendors line Beretania and Maunakea streets, and the fragrances of their wares mix with the earthy scents of incense and ethnic foods. Our top picks are **Lita's Leis,** 59 N. Beretania St. (✆ **808/521-9065**), which has fresh puakenikeni, gardenias that last, and a supply of fresh and reasonable leis; **Po'ohala Lei & Flowers,** 69 N. Beretania St. (✆ **808/537-3011**), with a worthy selection of the classics at fair prices; **Lin's Lei Shop,** 1017-A Maunakea St. (✆ **808/537-4112**), with creatively fashioned, unusual leis; and **Cindy's Lei Shoppe,** 1034 Maunakea St. (✆ **808/536-6538**), with terrific sources for unusual leis such as feather dendrobiums, firecracker combinations, and everyday favorites such as ginger, tuberose, orchid, and pikake. Ask Cindy's about its unique "curb service," available with phone orders. Give them your car's color and model, and you can pick up your lei curbside—a great convenience on this busy street.

Food

For a food experience that you probably won't get at home, take the kids to the **Mauna Kea Marketplace Food Court,** 1120 Maunakea St., Chinatown (✆ **808/524-3409**). Hungry patrons line up in front of these no-nonsense food booths that sell everything from pizza and plate lunches to quick, authentic, and inexpensive Vietnamese, Thai, Italian, Chinese, Japanese, and Filipino dishes. The best seafood fried rice comes from the woks of **Malee Thai/Vietnamese Cuisine,** at the mauka (inland) end of the marketplace—perfectly flavored with morsels of fish, squid, and shrimp. Right next to it is **Tandoori Chicken Cafe,** a fount of Indian culinary pleasures, from curries and jasmine-chicken rice balls to spiced rounds of curried potatoes and a wonderful lentil dal. On the other side of Malee, **Masa's** serves bento and Japanese dishes, such as miso eggplant, that are locally famous. A few stalls makai (toward the ocean) you'll find the best dessert around at **Pho Lau,** which serves *haupia* (coconut pudding), tapioca, and taro in individual baskets made of pandanus. Walk the few steps down to the produce stalls (pungent odors, fish heads, and chicken feet on counters—not for the squeamish) and join the spirit of discovery. Vendors sell everything from fresh ahi and whole snapper to yams and taro, seaweed, and fresh fruits and vegetables of every shape and size. Wander around Chinatown, where the island's best produce is at **Paradise Produce Co.,** 83 N. King St. (✆ 808/533-2125); its neat rows of mangoes, top-quality papayas, and reasonably priced and very fresh produce make this a paradise for food lovers.

Hawaiiana & Gift Items

The perfect gift from Hawaii? Bring back something from the islands. Here's where I shop: **Native Books & Beautiful Things,** Ward Warehouse, 1050 Ala Moana Blvd. (✆ **808/596-8885**), a cooperative of artists and craftspeople creating "things Hawaiian," from musical instruments to calabashes, jewelry, leis, and books, including contemporary Hawaiian clothing, handmade koa journals, Hawaii-themed home accessories, lauhala handbags and accessories, jams, jellies, food products, etched glass, hand-painted fabrics and clothing, stone poi pounders, and other high-quality gift items. Also in the Ward Warehouse is **Nohea Gallery** (✆ **808/596-0074**), a fine showcase for contemporary Hawaii art, from pit-fired raku and finely turned wood vessels to jewelry, hand-blown glass, paintings, prints, fabrics (including Hawaiian-quilt cushions), and furniture; and **Shop Pacifica,** in the Bishop Museum, 1525 Bernice St. (✆ **808/848-4158**), offering local crafts, lauhala and Cook Island woven coconut, Hawaiian music tapes and CDs, pareus, and a vast selection of Hawaii-themed books.

Markets

Truck farmers bring their produce to 25 market sites in Oahu's neighborhoods for regularly scheduled, city-sponsored **People's Open Markets** at various locations all over the island (✆ **808/552-7088;** www.honolulu.gov/parks/programs/pom/sked.htm). This can be a fun outing for you and your kids as you wander among the vendors and see the tables of unusual and exotic tropical vegetables and fruits such as ong choy, choi sum, Okinawan spinach, opal basil, papayas, mangoes, and seaweed. Talk to the vendors, who'll be happy to explain the produce, vegetables, and unusual fish—some will even offer free samples.

Some kids hate to shop, but the **Aloha Flea Market,** a giant outdoor bazaar at Aloha Stadium every Wednesday, Saturday, and Sunday from 7:30am to 3pm, is more than shopping. It's an experience akin to a carnival, full of strange food, odd goods, and bold barkers. Nobody ever leaves this place empty-handed—or without having had lots of fun.

Museum Stores

My top recommendations are the **Academy Shop,** at the Honolulu Academy of Arts, 900 S. Beretania St. (✆ **808/523-8703**), and the **Contemporary Museum Gift Shop,** 2411 Makiki Heights Rd. (✆ **808/523-3447**), two of the finest shopping stops on Oahu and worth a special trip whether or not you want to see the museums themselves. (And you will want to see the museums, especially the recently expanded Honolulu Academy of Arts.) The Academy Shop offers art books, jewelry, basketry, ethnic fabrics, native crafts from all over the world, posters and books, and fiber vessels and accessories. The Contemporary Museum shop focuses on arts and crafts such as avant-garde jewelry, cards and stationery, books, home accessories, and gift items made by artists from Hawaii and across the country. We love the glammy selection of jewelry and novelties, such as the twisted-wire wall hangings.

Music

For a variety of music, the two best sources are **Rainbow Books and Records Hawaii,** 1010 University Ave. (✆ **808/955-7994**), and **Borders Books & Music Café,** Ward Centre, 1200 Ala Moana Blvd. (✆ **808/591-8995**). If you are looking for authentic, traditional Hawaiian music, check out **Hawaiian Paradise Music,** in the International Marketplace, Waikiki (✆ **800/252-7731;** www.hawaiianparadisemusic.com), for a terrific selection of contemporary island music, traditional falsetto, hula music, ancient

Health-Food Stores

If you have raised your kids on fresh, organic produce, Honolulu will be a paradise for you. In the University district, **Down to Earth,** 2525 S. King St., Moiliili (✆ **808/947-7678**), is a respectable source of organic vegetables and vegetarian bulk foods, with good prices, a strong selection of supplements and herbs, and a vegetarian juice-and-sandwich bar. But our favorite is nearby **Kokua Market,** 2643 S. King St. (✆ **808/941-1922**), a health food cooperative and Honolulu's best source for organic vegetables. It also has an excellent variety of cheeses; pastas and bulk grains; sandwiches, salads, and prepared foods; organic wines; and an expanded vitamin section.

In Nuuanu Valley, mauka (inland) of downtown Honolulu, **Huckleberry Farms,** 1613 Nuuanu Ave. (✆ **808/524-7960**), has a wide range of produce, vitamins, cosmetics, books, and prepared vegetarian foods. A few doors down, the beauty and vitamin retail outlet is stocked with cosmetics, nutritional supplements, and nonperishable, nongrocery health products.

Hawaiian chants, Tahitian music, Hawaiian Christmas music, island reggae, and Hawaiian slack-key guitar. DVDs and videos are available here, too.

Shoes

Oahu (and, really, all of Hawaii) is not a haven for shoe fans. Most local families buy kids' shoes at discount stores such as Payless, since the kids will just grow out of the shoes and don't want to wear anything but slippers anyway. The cheapest source for slippers (go-aheads or rubber sandals) is **Longs Drugs,** where for $2.50 you can get a pair of slippers that will last just about as long as your vacation. For the closest Longs, call ✆ **800/547-7943** or check www.longs.com.

Surf & Sports

The surf-and-sports shops scattered throughout Honolulu are a highly competitive lot, each trying to capture your interest (and dollars). The top sources for sports gear and accessories in town are **McCully Bicycle & Sporting Goods,** 2124 S. King St. (✆ **808/955-6329**), with everything from bicycles and fishing gear to athletic shoes and accessories, along with a stunning selection of sunglasses; and **The Bike Shop,** 1149 S. King St., near Piikoi Street (✆ **808/596-0588**), excellent for cycling and backpacking equipment for all levels, with major camping lines such as North Face, MSR, and Kelty. Avid cyclists coming to Oahu should make this a definite stop, as it's the hub of cycling news on the island, offering night tours of downtown Honolulu by bicycle and other cycling activities island-wide. The **Sports Authority,** at 333 Ward Ave. (✆ **808/596-0166**) and at Waikele Center (✆ **808/677-9933**), is a discount megaoutlet offering clothing, cycles, and equipment.

Surf shops, centers of fashion as well as definers of daring, include **Local Motion,** at Waikiki Shopping Mall (✆ **808/924-4406**), Windward Mall (✆ **808/263-7873**), Waikele Premium Outlets (✆ **808/668-7873**), and Pearlridge Center (✆ **808/234-7873**); **Town and Country Surf Stores** at Ala Moana Center and Ward Warehouse (✆ **808/973-5199** and 808/592-5299); and **Hawaiian Island Creations** at Ala Moana Center (✆ **808/941-4491**). Local Motion is the icon of surfers and skateboarders, both professionals and wannabes; the shop offers surfboards, T-shirts, aloha and casual wear, boogie boards, and countless accessories for life in the sun. Hawaiian Island Creations is another supercool surf shop offering sunglasses, sun lotions, surf wear, and accessories galore.

Sweets for the Sweet

Life's greatest pleasures are dispensed with abandon at the **Honolulu Chocolate Co.,** Ward Centre, 1200 Ala Moana Blvd. (✆ **808/591-2997**). Okay, it's expensive, but it's worth every penny. The gourmet chocolates made in Honolulu include Italian and Hawaiian biscotti, boulder-size turtles (caramel and pecans covered with chocolate), truffles, chocolate-covered coffee beans, and jumbo apricots in white and dark chocolate, to name a few. There are also tinned biscuits, European candies, and sweets in a million disguises. ***Hint:*** You pay dearly for them, but the dark-chocolate-dipped macadamia nut clusters are beyond comparison.

The reigning queen of bakers is **Cafe Laufer,** 3565 Waialae Ave. (✆ **808/735-7717;** p. 109), where you can sample Russian tea cookies, macadamia nut shortbread, dark rye bread, and spaetzle (a yummy noodle dumpling). Nearby, old-timers still line up at **Sconees,** 1117 12th Ave. (✆ **808/734-4024**), formerly Bea's Pies. Sconees has fantastic scones, pumpkin-custard pies, and Danishes. One more unforgettable bakery is **Mary Catherine's,** 2820 S. King St. (✆ **808/946-4333**), across from the Hawaiian Humane Society. It's a great place for quality cakes and European pastries.

Toys

Oahu has plenty of the same chain toy stores (K•B Toys, Toy-Rific, Toys 'N Toys, and Toys "R" Us) that you can find at home (most likely at cheaper prices!). For cute Hawaii-themed stuffed animals, look for Nani Stufs, such as a Hawaii Nani Bear or Hawaii Parrot, at the **Nani Makana,** Iwalei Business Center, 501 Sumner St. off Nimitz Highway, Honolulu (✆ **808/537-6937;** www.nanistufs.com/NaniStufs/specials.html).

For educational toys, check out **Thinker Toys,** which carries educational and Hawaiian toys, arts and crafts, and puzzles for kids of all ages. The store has three locations: Ala Moana Center, 1450 Ala Moana Blvd. (✆ **808/946-3378**); Kahala Mall, 4211 Waialae Ave. (✆ **808/735-5442**); and Pearlridge Center, 98-1005 Moanalua Rd., in Aiea (✆ **808/485-5442**).

10 ENTERTAINMENT FOR THE WHOLE FAMILY

Most of Hawaii's entertainment occurs when the sun is shining—playing in the ocean, hiking to waterfalls, pedaling down mountain trails. In fact, the sunset itself is part of Hawaii's entertainment. It's a time to stop and celebrate the end of the day and watch the sun slowly sink into the Pacific. On Friday and Saturday at 6:30pm, as the sun casts its golden glow on the beach and surfers and beach boys paddle in for the day, **Kuhio Beach,** where Kalakaua Avenue intersects with Kaiulani, eases into evening with hula dancing and a torch-lighting ceremony. Take the kids to this free and thoroughly delightful weekend offering. Start off earlier with a picnic basket and walk along the oceanside path fronting Queen's Surf, near the Waikiki Aquarium. (You can park alongside Kapiolani Park or near the zoo.) There are few more pleasing spots in Waikiki than the benches at water's edge at this Diamond Head end of Kalakaua Avenue. A short walk across the intersection of Kalakaua and Kapahulu avenues, where the seawall and daring boogie boarders attract hordes of spectators, takes you to the Duke Kahanamoku statue on Kuhio Beach and the nearby Wizard Stones. Here, you can view the torch-lighting and hula and gear up for the strolling musicians who amble down Kalakaua Avenue every Friday from 8 to 10pm. The musicians begin at Beachwalk Avenue at the Ewa (western) end of Waikiki and end up at the statue.

For other nighttime entertainment, check out the two local daily newspapers or *Honolulu Weekly* (www.honoluluweekly.com) for the latest listings. Unfortunately, there are no discount ticket outlets for Hawaii productions. With the exception of "hot" rock concerts and very successful Broadway shows on tour, most tickets can be purchased once you arrive on island.

THE BIG VENUES

The largest big venue is the **Neal S. Blaisdell Center,** 777 Ward Ave., Honolulu (✆ **808/527-5400;** www.blaisdellcenter.com). This catchall venue hosts a variety of events, from major rock concerts to Hawaii Lion Dance Competition to opera and symphony performances. The other major venue on Oahu is smaller but so much nicer: **Waikiki Shell,** 2805 Monsarrat Ave., in Kapiolani Park (✆ **808/527-5400;** www.blaisdellcenter.com). The best way to see a concert in Hawaii is under the stars at this outdoor amphitheater. Walking distance from most Waikiki hotels, with Diamond Head for a backdrop, and with Waikiki Beach just across the street, the Waikiki Shell is a unique venue for outdoor concerts, from Hawaiian music and dance performances to rock and reggae.

THEATER

Audiences have stomped to the big off-Broadway percussion hit *Stomp,* and have enjoyed the talent of *Tap Dogs,* Forever Tango, Urban Beat, the Jim Nabors Christmas show, the Hawaii International Jazz Festival, the American Repertory Dance Company, barbershop quartets, and John Kaimikaua's halau—all at the **Hawaii Theatre,** 1130 Bethel St., downtown (✆ **808/528-0506**), still basking in its renaissance following a 4-year, $22-million renovation. The neoclassical Beaux Arts landmark features a 1922 dome, 1,400 plush seats, a hydraulically elevated organ, a mezzanine lobby with two full bars, Corinthian columns, and gilt galore. Breathtaking murals, including a restored proscenium centerpiece lauded as Lionel Walden's "greatest creation," create an atmosphere that's making the theater a leading multipurpose center for the performing arts.

Every year **Honolulu Theater for Youth,** 2846 Ualena St., Honolulu (✆ **808/839-9885;** www.htyweb.org), presents a full season of plays for children (preschool to high school) across the state. HTY produces plays based on children's literature, adaptations of classics, and work that draws from or reflects on the cultures that make up modern Hawaii—including history, folklore, or issues that impact the children in Hawaii. Plays scheduled for the 2008–09 season include a unique performance of *Aladdin's Luck, A Midsummer Night's Dream, A Christmas Carol, Goodnight, Moon,* and a local favorite, *Musubi Man.* Tickets are $8 for children and $16 for adults; call for a schedule of current attractions and location of the performances.

HAWAIIAN MUSIC

Oahu has several key spots for Hawaiian music. Most of them are in lounges, restaurants, and bars; children generally are okay for afternoon music (4–6pm) and in restaurants during dinner hours, but later evening performances (say, after 10pm) generally are reserved for adults.

Sunset on the Beach

The City and County of Honolulu presents **"Sunset on the Beach"** throughout the year with free Hawaiian entertainment and a free family movie, shown on a 30-foot screen, at Queen's Surf, located across the street from the Honolulu Zoo, at Monsarrat and Kapahulu avenues, right on Waikiki Beach. You sit next to the rolling surf and listen to live Hawaii music (which begins about 2 hr. before sunset), and after the sun goes down, (7pm in the summer and 6:30pm in the winter) and the stars come out, you enjoy a free family movie. Generally there are food vendors with snacks and dinner available for sale (or you can bring your own picnic dinner). For a schedule of movies, go to www.sunsetonthebeach.net.

Brothers Cazimero remains one of Hawaii's most gifted duos (Robert on bass, Roland on 12-string guitar), appearing every Wednesday at 7pm at **Chai's Island Bistro** (✆ **808/585-0011**) in the Aloha Tower Marketplace. Also at Chai's: Robert Cazimero plays by himself on the piano, and **Jerry Santos** and **Olomana** perform. In the past couple of years, Chai's has emerged as the leading venue for Hawaiian entertainment. But if you're here on May 1 (Lei Day), try to make it to the special concert the Brothers Caz give every year at the Waikiki Shell—it's one of the loveliest events in Hawaii. Locals dress up in their leis and best aloha shirts, the air smells like pikake and pakalana, and if you're lucky, you'll see the moon rise over Diamond Head.

Impromptu hula and spirited music from the family and friends of the performers are an island tradition at places such as the Hilton Hawaiian Village's **Paradise Lounge** (✆ **808/949-4321**), which, despite its pillars, serves as a large living room for the full-bodied music of **Olomana.** The group plays Friday and Saturday from 8pm to midnight (no cover, one-drink minimum). At **Duke's Canoe Club** at the Outrigger Waikiki (✆ **808/922-2268**), it's always three deep at the beachside bar when the sun is setting; extraspecial entertainment is a given here—usually from 4 to 6pm on Friday, Saturday, and Sunday, and nightly from 10pm to midnight.

Nearby, the Sheraton Moana Surfrider offers a regular nightly program of live Hawaiian music and piano at its **Banyan Veranda** (✆ **808/922-3111**), which surrounds an islet-size canopy of banyan tree and roots where Robert Louis Stevenson loved to linger. The Veranda serves afternoon tea, a sunset buffet, and cocktails.

Showroom acts that have maintained a following include the **Society of Seven,** which performs at **Outrigger Waikiki on the Beach** (✆ **808/923-0711**) and features a blend of skits, Broadway hits, popular music, and costumed musical acts. The group has been performing in Waikiki for more than 3 decades—no small feat for performers.

DINNER CRUISES

A great way for the entire family to watch the sunset is via a dinner cruise. **Navatek Dinner Cruise** (✆ **808/441-4500**) offers nightly dinner cruises off the coast of Waikiki. This means that the 140-foot-long, ultrastable vessel not only promises spill-proof mai tais and a seasick-less ride, but also is now in the gourmet dinner arena. The ride (and now the food, too) is worth a splurge. Prices vary and Navatek offers discounts if you book in advance online.

Luau!

The sun is setting, the tiki torches are lit, the pig is taken from the *imu* (an oven in the earth), the drums begin pounding—it's luau time. Recently three new luau have started from across the island in Waikiki, on the North Shore and in windward Oahu at Sea Life Park.

On the North Shore, the **Turtle Bay Resort** presents **"Voyages of Polynesia Luau,"** on the lawn overlooking the ocean with a "Taste of the Islands" luau buffet and a Polynesian revue featuring the songs and dances of the Tuamotu Islands, Samoa, Tahiti, Fiji, and Hawaii. Tickets for the Friday-night dinner and show are $85 adults and $55 children ages 4 to 11. To book, call ✆ **808/293-6000.**

On the Windward side, by Makapuu Point, **Sea Life Park** has the **"Sea Life Park Luau,"** Wednesday, Friday, and Sunday nights, which offers a dolphin show, Hawaiian food, and a Polynesian revue. Prices are $89 for adults and $55 for kids ages 4 to 12. For information, call ✆ **808/259-7933.**

MOVIES

Your kids will love the 16-theater megaplex in the **Ward Centers'** entertainment center, at the corner of Auahi and Kamakee streets; and the **Windward Mall**'s 10-screen megaplex, which has the current celluloid favorites. This makes Honolulu's movie scene a galloping sprawl of more screens, more seats, and more multiplexes than ever before. You can expect to spend $6.75 for children ages 2 to 12, and $9.50 for everyone 13 and older.

A quick check in both dailies and the *Honolulu Weekly* will tell you what's playing where in the world of feature films. For film buffs and esoteric movie lovers, **The Movie Museum,** 3566 Harding Ave. (✆ **808/735-8771**), has special screenings of vintage films and rents a collection of hard-to-find, obscure, and classic films. Tickets are in the $5 range. The **Honolulu Academy of Arts Theatre,** 900 S. Beretania St. (✆ **808/532-8768**), is the film-as-art center of Honolulu, offering special screenings, guest appearances, and cultural performances, as well as noteworthy programs in the visual arts.

Kahala Mall's **Kahala 8-Plex** (✆ **808/593-3000**) and **Kapolei Megaplex,** a 16-theater complex (✆ **808/593-3000**), once the biggest movie theater complexes on the island, are eclipsed by the 18-screen **Dole Cannery,** Nimitz Highway and Pacific Street (✆ **808/526-FILM** [526-3456]), the pineapple king of celluloid.

At the nine **Wallace Theatres,** on Restaurant Row near downtown Honolulu (✆ **808/263-4171**), free parking in the evenings, discount matinees, and special discounted midnight shows take a big step toward making movies friendlier and more affordable.

STORY HOURS

A range of free storytelling and read-aloud programs are offered by the public library. One of the more popular programs is presented by professional storytellers, retirees, and even professional actors who tour the libraries with their 45- to 60-minute stories entertaining kids from preschool to even a few seniors who bring their grandkids. For additional information on these and other storytelling programs, contact the **Hawaii State Public Library** (✆ **808/586-3500;** www.librarieshawaii.org).

5

The Big Island of Hawaii

The Big Island of Hawaii—the island that lends its name to the entire 1,500-mile-long Hawaiian archipelago—is where Mother Nature pulled out all the stops. Simply put, it's spectacular. Because it's so big and so diverse, you will most likely enjoy the family vacation of your dreams here.

The Big Island has it all: fiery volcanoes and sparkling waterfalls, black-lava deserts and snowcapped mountain peaks, tropical rainforests and alpine meadows, a glacial lake and miles of golden-, black-, and green- (!) sand beaches. A 50-mile drive will take you from snowy winter to sultry summer, passing through spring or fall along the way.

The Big Island is the largest island in the Hawaiian chain (4,038 sq. miles about the size of Connecticut), the youngest (800,000 years), and the least populated (with 30 people per sq. mile). It contains the nation's wettest city, the southernmost point in the United States, the world's biggest telescope, the ocean's biggest trophy marlin, and America's greatest collection of tropical luxury resorts. It also has the highest peaks in the Pacific, the most volcanoes of any Hawaiian island, and the newest land on earth.

Five volcanoes—one still erupting—have created this continental island, which is growing bigger daily. At its heart is snowcapped Mauna Kea, the world's tallest sea mountain (measured from the ocean floor), complete with its own glacial lake. Mauna Kea's nearest neighbor is Mauna Loa (or "Long Mountain"), creator of one-sixth of the island; it's the largest volcano on earth, rising 30,000 feet out of the ocean floor. (Of course, you can see only the 13,796 ft. that are above sea level.) Erupting Kilauea makes the Big Island bigger every day—and, if you're lucky and your timing is good, you can stand just a few feet away and watch it do its work. (In just a week, Kilauea volcano can produce enough lava to fill the Astrodome.)

The things to keep in mind when planning a trip is just how big the island is (lots of driving) and how young it is (there are some but not a lot of white-sand beaches). On the other hand, if your family loves watersports, this is paradise. The two tall volcanoes mean 350 days of calm water on the leeward (or Kona) side. The underwater landscape of caves, cliffs, and tunnels attracts a stunning array of colorful marine life. The island's west coast is one of the best destinations in the world for big-game fishing. And its miles of remote coastline are a kayaker's dream of caves, secluded coves, and crescent-shaped beaches reachable only by sea.

On land, hikers, bikers, and horseback riders can head up and down a volcano, across black-sand beaches, into remote valleys, and through rainforests without seeing another soul. Where else can you witness fiery creation and swim with dolphins; ponder the stars from the world's tallest mountain and catch a blue marlin; downhill ski and surf the waves in a single day? You can do all this, and more, on only one island in the world: the Big Island of Hawaii.

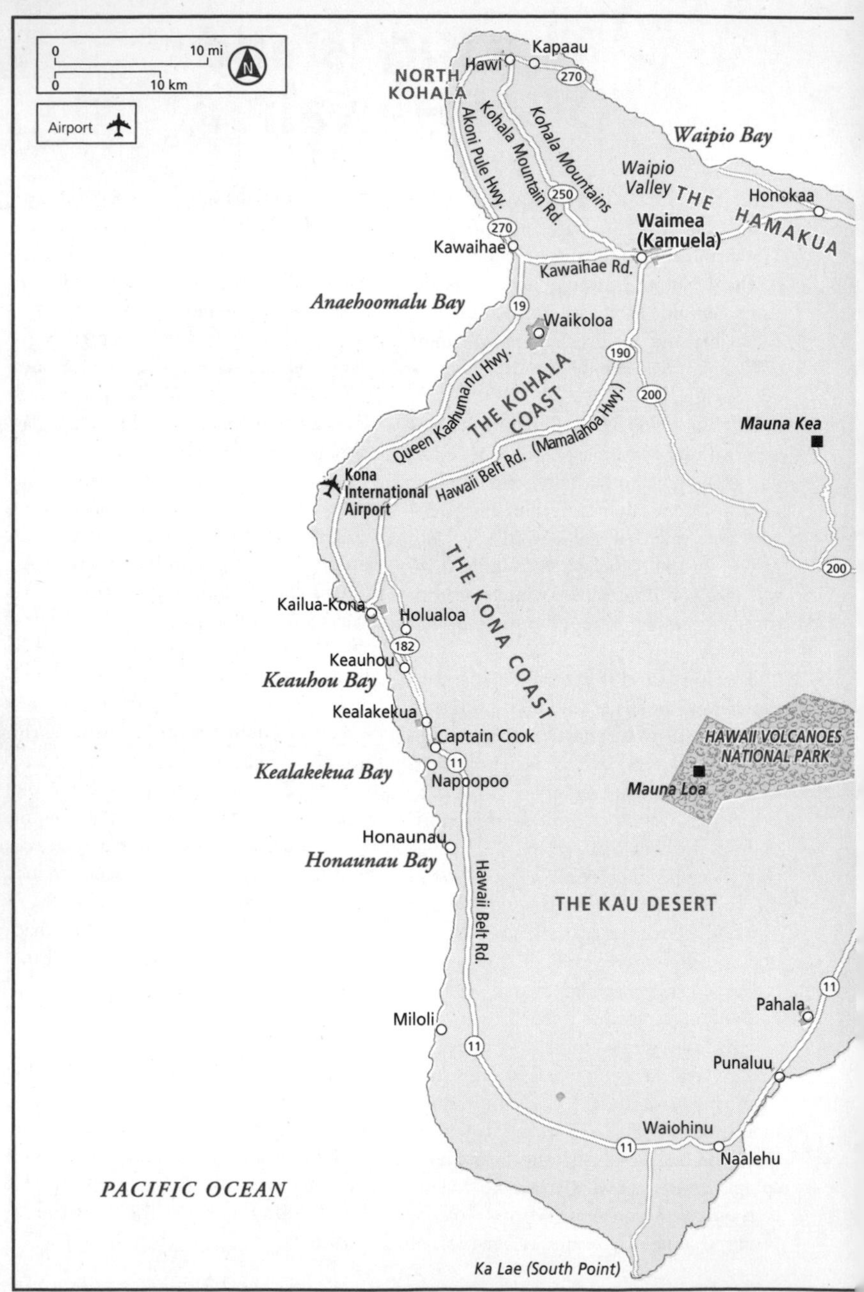
0
10 mi
0
10 km
N
Airport
Kapaau
Hawi
NORTH KOHALA
270
Akoni Pule Hwy.
Kohala Mountain Rd.
Kohala Mountains
Waipio Bay
Waipio Valley
THE HAMAKUA
Honokaa
250
270
Waimea (Kamuela)
Kawaihae
Kawaihae Rd.
Anaehoomalu Bay
19
Waikoloa
190
Queen Kaahumanu Hwy.
THE KOHALA COAST
200
Hawaii Belt Rd. (Mamalahoa Hwy.)
Mauna Kea
Kona International Airport
THE KONA COAST
200
Kailua-Kona
Holualoa
182
Keauhou
Keauhou Bay
Kealakekua
Captain Cook
11
Kealakekua Bay
Napoopoo
HAWAII VOLCANOES NATIONAL PARK
Mauna Loa
Honaunau
Honaunau Bay
Hawaii Belt Rd.
THE KAU DESERT
11
Pahala
Miloli
11
Punaluu
Waiohinu
11
Naalehu
PACIFIC OCEAN
Ka Lae (South Point)

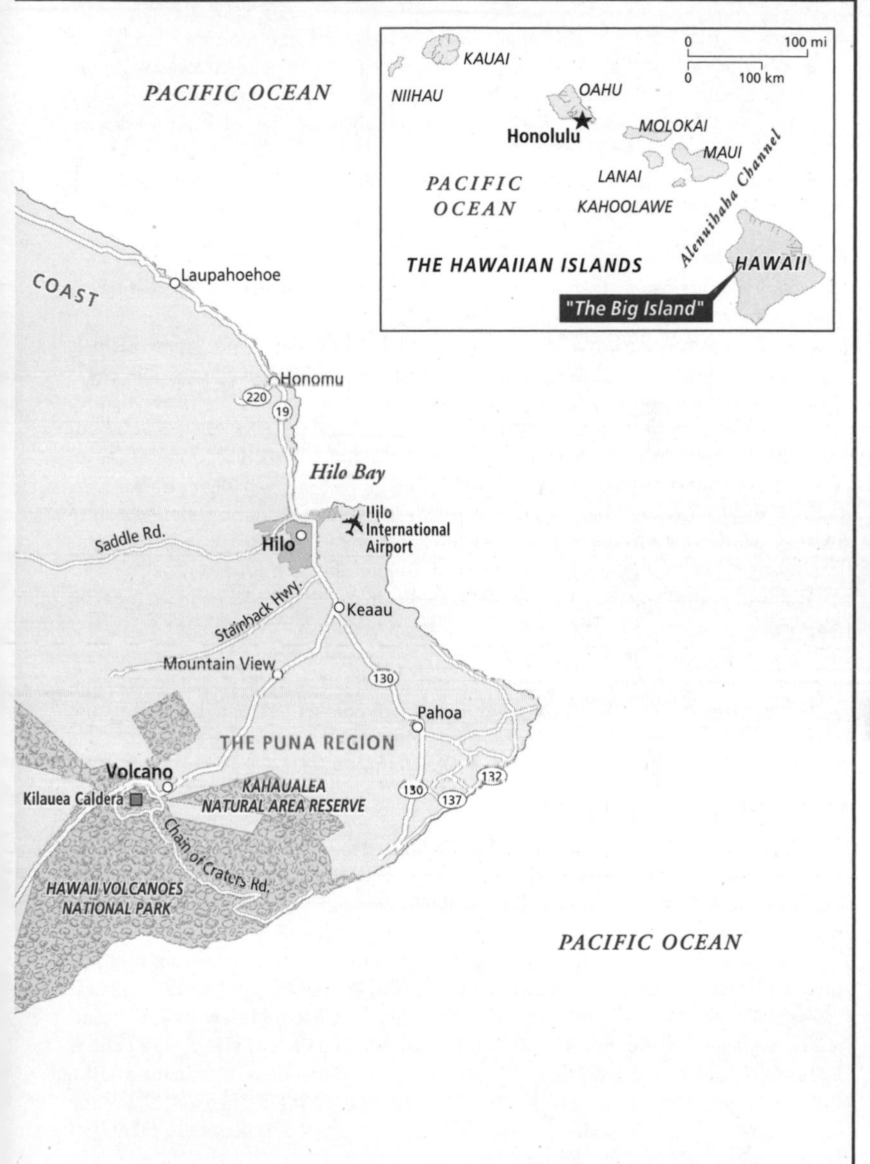
PACIFIC OCEAN
KAUAI
NIIHAU
OAHU
Honolulu
MOLOKAI
MAUI
LANAI
KAHOOLAWE
PACIFIC OCEAN
Alenuihaha Channel
THE HAWAIIAN ISLANDS
HAWAII
"The Big Island"
0 100 mi
0 100 km
COAST
Laupahoehoe
Honomu
220
19
Hilo Bay
Hilo
Hilo International Airport
Saddle Rd.
Stainback Hwy.
Keaau
Mountain View
130
Pahoa
THE PUNA REGION
Volcano
Kilauea Caldera
KAHAUALEA NATURAL AREA RESERVE
132
130
137
Chain of Craters Rd.
HAWAII VOLCANOES NATIONAL PARK
PACIFIC OCEAN

1 ORIENTATION

Most people arrive on the Big Island at Kona International Airport, on the island's west coast, and discover there are only two ways to go: clockwise or counterclockwise. From the airport, Kilauea volcano is to the right or counterclockwise, and the ritzy Kohala coast is to the left or clockwise. (If you land in Hilo, of course, the volcano is clockwise, and Kohala is counterclockwise.)

If you think you can "do" the Big Island in a day, forget it. You need about 3 days to really see Hawaii Volcanoes National Park alone. It's best to spend at least a week here.

ARRIVING

The Big Island has two major airports for jet traffic between the islands: **Kona International Airport** and **Hilo International Airport.**

The **Kona Airport** receives direct overseas flights from Japan on **Japan Airlines** (© **800/525-3663;** www.jal.co.jp/en) and Vancouver on **Air Canada** (© **888/247-2262;** www.aircanada.com). Carriers from the mainland include **American Airlines** (© **800/433-7300;** www.aa.com), with flights to Los Angeles; **Delta Airlines** (© **800/221-1212;** www.delta.com), with nonstop flights from Salt Lake City (originating in Atlanta); **Northwest Airlines** (© **800/225-2525;** www.nwa.com), with flights from Seattle; **U.S. Airways/American West** (© **800/428-4322;** www.usairways.com), with flights from Phoenix; and **United Airlines** (© **800/241-6522;** www.united.com), with nonstop flights from Denver, Los Angeles, and San Francisco, and a direct flight to Chicago.

At the time of writing there were no direct flights from the U.S. mainland to the **Hilo Airport.**

If you cannot get a direct flight to the Big Island, you'll have to pick up an interisland flight in Honolulu: **Hawaiian Airlines** (© **800/367-5320;** www.hawaiianair.com) and **go!** (© **888/IFLYGO2** [435-9462]**;** www.iflygo.com) offer jet service to both Big Island airports. All major rental companies have cars available at both airports. See "Getting Around Hawaii," in chapter 2, for more details on interisland travel and car rentals.

VISITOR INFORMATION

The **Big Island Visitors Bureau** has two offices on the Big Island: one at 250 Keawe St., Hilo, HI 96720 (© **808/961-5797;** fax 808/961-2126); and one on the other side of the island at 250 Waikoloa Beach Dr., Waikoloa, HI 96738 (© **808/886-1652**). Its website is www.bigisland.org.

On the west side of the island, there are two additional sources to contact for information: the **Kona–Kohala Resort Association,** 69-275 Waikoloa Beach Dr., Kamuela, HI 96743 (© **800/318-3637** or 808/886-4915; fax 808/886-1044; www.kohalacoastresorts.com); and **Destination Kona,** P.O. Box 2850, Kailua-Kona, HI 96745 (© **808/322-6809;** fax 808/322-8899). On the east side, you can contact **Destination Hilo,** P.O. Box 1391, Hilo, HI 96721 (© **808/935-5294;** fax 808/969-1984). At the center of the island, contact the **Waimea Visitor Center,** P.O. Box 6570, Kamuela, HI 96743 (© **808/885-6707;** fax 808/885-0885).

The Big Island's best free tourist publications are *This Week,* the *Beach and Activity Guide,* and *101 Things to Do on Hawaii the Big Island.* All three offer lots of useful information, as well as discount coupons on a variety of island adventures. Copies are easy to find all around the island.

The *Beach and Activity Guide* is affiliated with the **Activity Connection,** Bougainvillea Plaza, Suite 102, 75-5656 Kuakini Hwy., Kailua-Kona (✆ **800/459-7156** or 808/329-1038), a discount activities desk offering real savings (no fees, no timeshares) of up to 15% on activities including island tours, snorkel and dive trips, submarine and horseback rides, luau, and more. The office is open daily from 7:30am to 5:30pm.

THE BIG ISLAND IN BRIEF

THE KONA COAST

One Hawaiian word everyone seems to know is *Kona,* probably because it's synonymous with great coffee and big fish—both of which are found in abundance along this 70-mile-long stretch of black lava–covered coast.

A collection of tiny communities devoted to farming and fishing along the sunbaked leeward side of the island, the Kona coast has an amazingly diverse geography and climate for such a compact area. The oceanfront town of **Kailua-Kona,** a quaint fishing village that now caters more to tourists than boat captains, is its commercial center.

Kona means "leeward side" in Hawaiian—and that means full on summer sun every day of the year. This is an affordable vacation spot for a family; an ample selection of midpriced condo units, peppered with a few older hotels and B&Bs, lines the shore, which is mostly rocky lava reef, interrupted by an occasional pocket beach. Just north of the Kona Airport is one of Hawaii's luxury retreats, the Four Seasons at Hualalai.

Away from the bright lights of the town of Kailua lies the rural **south Kona coast,** home to coffee farmers, macadamia nut growers, and people escaping to the country. There aren't a lot of accommodations options for families here, but there are lots of day excursions, such as to **Kealakekua Bay,** a marine-life preserve that's the island's best snorkeling spot (and the place where Capt. James Cook met his demise), or to **Honaunau,** where a national historic park recalls the days of Ancient Hawaii.

THE KOHALA COAST

This is where the Lear jet–set escapes to play in world-class beachfront hotels set like jewels in the golden sand. You don't have to be a billionaire, however, to visit the Waikoloa, Mauna Lani, and Mauna Kea resorts: The fabulous beaches and abundant historic sites are open to the public, with parking and other facilities provided by the resorts, including restaurants, golf courses, and shopping.

NORTH KOHALA

Once, sugar cane was king in this knobby peninsula jutting out to the north. Today, **Hawi**'s quaint, 3-block-long strip of sun-faded, false-fronted buildings and 1920s vintage shops lives on as a minor tourist stop in one of Hawaii's most scenic rural regions.

WAIMEA (KAMUELA)

This old upcountry cow town on the northern road between the coasts is set in lovely country: rolling green pastures, wide-open spaces dotted by *puu* (hills), and real cowpokes who ride at mammoth **Parker Ranch,** Hawaii's biggest working ranch. The town is also headquarters for the **Keck Telescope,** the largest and most powerful in the world, bringing world-class, starry-eyed astronomers to town. Waimea is home to several affordable restaurants and terrific shops.

The Hamakua Coast

This emerald coast, a 52-mile stretch from Honokaa to Hilo on the island's windward northeast side, was once planted with sugar cane; it now blooms with flowers, macadamia nuts, papayas, and eucalyptus trees. Resort-free and virtually without beaches, the Hamakua coast still has a few special destinations, such as spectacular **Waipio Valley,** a picture-perfect valley with impossibly steep sides, taro patches, a green riot of wild plants, and a winding stream leading to a broad, black-sand beach; and the historic plantation town of **Honokaa.**

Hilo

When the sun shines in Hilo, it's one of the most beautiful tropical cities in the Pacific. Being here is an entirely different kind of island experience: Hawaii's largest metropolis after Honolulu is a quaint, misty, flower-filled city of Victorian houses overlooking a half-moon bay, with a restored historic downtown and a clear view of Mauna Loa's often snowcapped peak. Hilo catches everyone's eye until it rains—it rains a lot in Hilo—and when it rains, it pours.

Hilo is America's wettest town, with 128 inches of rain annually. It's ideal for growing ferns, orchids, and anthuriums, but not for catching a few rays. But there's lots to see and do in Hilo, so grab your umbrella. The rain is warm (the temperature seldom dips below 70°F/21°C), and there's usually a rainbow afterward.

Hilo is also the gateway to Hawaii Volcanoes National Park; it's just an hour's up-slope drive away.

Hawaii Volcanoes National Park

This is the location of America's most exciting national park, where the live Kilauea volcano erupts daily. (If you're lucky, it will be a spectacular sight. At other times, you may not be able to see the molten lava at all, but there's still a lot to see and learn.) Ideally, you should plan to spend 3 days at the park exploring the trails, watching the volcano, visiting the rainforest, and just enjoying this most unusual, spectacular place. But even if you have only a day, get here—it's worth the trip. Bring your sweats or jacket (honest!); it's cool up here, especially at night.

If you plan to dally in the park—and you should—you can find a great place to stay in the sleepy hamlet of Volcano Village (located in a rainforest just outside the National Park entrance, at 4,000 ft.). Several terrifically cozy B&Bs, some with fireplaces, hide under tree ferns in this cool mountain hideaway.

Ka Lae: South Point

This is the Plymouth Rock of Hawaii, where the first Polynesians arrived in seagoing canoes, probably from the Marquesas Islands or Tahiti, around A.D. 500. You'll feel like you're at the end of the world on this lonely, windswept place, the southernmost point of the United States (a geographic claim that belonged to Key West, Florida, until 1959, when Hawaii became the 50th state). Hawaii ends in a sharp, black-lava point. Bold 500-foot cliffs stand against the blue sea to the west and shelter the old fishing village of Waiahukini, which was born in A.D. 750 and lasted until the 1860s.

2 GETTING AROUND

BY CAR

You'll need a rental car on the Big Island; not having one will really limit what you'll be able to see and do. All the major car rental firms have agencies at the airports and at the Kohala coast resorts; for a complete list, as well as tips on insurance and driving rules, see "Getting Around Hawaii," in chapter 2.

There are more than 480 miles of paved road on the Big Island. The highway that circles the island is called the **Hawaii Belt Road.** On the Kona side of the island, you have two choices: the scenic "upper" road, **Mamalahoa Highway** (Hwy. 190), or the speedier "lower" road, **Queen Kaahumanu Highway** (Hwy. 19). The road that links east to west is called the **Saddle Road** (Hwy. 200), because it crosses the "saddle" between Mauna Kea and Mauna Loa. Saddle Road looks like a shortcut from Kona to Hilo, but it usually doesn't make for a shorter trip. It's rough, narrow, and plagued by bad weather; as a result, most car rental agencies forbid you from taking their cars on it.

BY TAXI

Taxis are readily available at both Keahole and Hilo airports. In Hilo, call **Ace-1** (© **808/935-8303**). In Kailua-Kona, call **Kona Airport Taxi** (© **808/329-7779**). Taxis will take you wherever you want to go on the Big Island, but it's prohibitively expensive to use them for long distances.

BY BUS & SHUTTLE

For transportation from the Kona Airport, there are three options: two shuttle services that will come when you call them, and a discount shuttle that leaves the airport every hour on the hour and drops you at your hotel. Door-to-door service is provided by **SpeediShuttle** (© **808/329-5433;** www.speedishuttle.com). Some sample one-way rates: From the airport to Kailua-Kona, the fare is $25 per person, to the Four Seasons, $25; to the Sheraton Keauhou, $37; and to Mauna Lani Resort, $65.

The islandwide bus system is the **Hele-On Bus** (© **808/961-8744;** www.co.hawaii.hi.us/mass_transit/heleonbus.html). The Hele-On Bus has the best deal on the island—ride free—but unfortunately it does not go to either the Kona or the Hilo airports. The recently created Kokua Zone allows riders in West Hawaii to travel from as far south as Ocean View to as far north as Kawaihae for free; in East Hawaii, riders can ride free from Pahoa to Hilo. Visitors to Hawaii can pick up the free, air-conditioned bus from the Kohala hotels and ride the bus south to shopping centers like Costco, Lanihau Center, Kmart, Wal-Mart, and Keauhou Shopping Center. The Hele-On Bus also stops at the Kona Community Hospital and provides wheelchair access.

In the Keauhou Resort area, there's a free, open-air, 44-seat **Keauhou Resort Trolley,** with stops at the Keauhou Bay, Sheraton Keauhou Bay Resort & Spa, Kona Country Club, Keauhou Shopping Center, Outrigger Keauhou Beach Resort, and Kahaluu Beach Park. In addition, three times a day the Trolley travels round-trip, via Alii Drive to Kailua Village, stopping at White Sands Beach on the way. For information, contact concierges at either the Sheraton Keauhou Bay Resort & Spa (© **808/930-4900**) or the Outrigger Keauhou Beach Hotel (© **808/322-3411**).

Fast Facts The Big Island

American Express There are offices on the Kohala coast at the **Hilton Waikoloa Village** (✆ **808/886-7958**) and at the **Fairmont Orchid** in Mauna Lani Resort (✆ **808/885-2000**). To report lost or stolen traveler's checks, call ✆ **800/221-7282.**

Babysitters Call **PATCH** (✆ **808/839-1988**); or your hotel can refer you to qualified babysitters. Many hotels use the licensed and bonded sitters of **Sitters Unlimited** (www.sittershawaii.com); if you book their services directly, their rates begin at $16 per hour for the first child, $18 per hour for two children, and $20 an hour for three children (4-hr. minimum). If you book through the hotel, rates can start at $25 an hour for just one child, and go up.

Dentists In an emergency, contact **Dr. Craig C. Kimura** at Kamuela Office Center (✆ **808/885-5947**); in Kona, call **Dr. Frank Sayre,** Frame 10 Center, behind Lanihau Shopping Center on Palani Road (✆ **808/329-8067**); in Hilo, call **Hawaii Smile Center,** Hilo Lagoon Center, 101 Aupuni St. (✆ **808/961-9181**).

Doctors In Hilo, the **Hilo Medical Center** is at 1190 Waianuenue Ave. (✆ **808/974-4700**); on the Kona side, call **Hualalai Urgent Care,** 75-1028 Henry St., across the street from Safeway (✆ **808/327-HELP** [327-4357]).

Drugstores There are no 24-hour pharmacies on the Big Island. I recommend **Longs,** located in Kona in the Lanihau Shopping Center, 75-5595 Palani Rd. (✆ **808/329-1380**); in Keauhou, in the Keauhou Shopping Center (✆ **808/322-5122**); and in Hilo at 555 Kilaeau St. (✆ **808/935-3357**), Prince Kuhio Plaza (✆ **808/959-5881**), and 2100 Kanoelehua Ave. (✆ **808/959-5871**).

Emergencies For ambulance, fire, and rescue services, dial ✆ **911** or call ✆ **808/961-6022.** The **Poison Control Center** hot line is ✆ **800/362-3585.**

Hospitals Hospitals offering 24-hour urgent-care facilities include the **Hilo Medical Center,** 1190 Waianuenue Ave., Hilo (✆ **808/974-4700**); **North Hawaii Community Hospital,** Waimea (✆ **808/885-4444**); and **Kona Community Hospital,** on the Kona coast in Kealakekua (✆ **808/322-9311**).

Internet Access If your hotel doesn't have Web access, head to the nearest library (see below).

Newspapers The two dailies on the Big Island are *West Hawaii Today* and the *Hawaii Tribune Herald.*

Police Dial ✆ **911** in case of emergency; otherwise, call the **Hawaii Police Department** at ✆ **808/326-4646** in Kona or ✆ **808/961-2213** in Hilo.

Post Office There are local branches in Hilo, at 1299 Kekuanaoa Ave.; in Kailua-Kona, at 74-5577 Palani Rd.; and in Waimea, on Lindsey Road.

Radio Music stations on the Big Island include **KLUA** 93.9 FM, contemporary hits; **KKBG** 97.9 FM, Hawaii's hits; **KAPA** 100.3 FM, Hawaiian music; **KAOY** 101.5 FM, island contemporary; **KRTR** 105.5 FM, adult contemporary; and **KHLO** 850 AM, oldies.

Safety Generally, the Big Island is very safe, but never (ever) leave anything in your trunk; car thieves can get in and out of your trunk faster than you can with keys.

Weather For conditions in and around Hilo, call ✆ **808/935-8555;** for the rest of the Big Island, call ✆ **808/961-5582.** For marine forecasts, call ✆ **808/935-9883.**

3 FAMILY-FRIENDLY ACCOMMODATIONS

Before you book your dream-vacation accommodations, refer to "Tips on Accommodations," in chapter 2, to make sure you book the kind of place you want. Also remember that the Big Island is really big; see "The Big Island in Brief," earlier in this chapter, to make sure you choose the best area in which to base yourself.

If you're interested in additional information on bed-and-breakfasts, contact the **Hawaii Island B&B Association,** P.O. Box 1890, Honokaa, HI 96727 (no phone; www.stayhawaii.com).

In the listings below, all rooms come with a full private bathroom (with tub or shower) and free parking unless otherwise noted. Remember to add Hawaii's 11.42% in taxes to your final bill.

If you would like to take the kids on the road, **Island RV Hawaii** (✆ **800/406-4555** or 808/334-0464; www.islandrv.com) offers weekly rentals of a 22-foot class-C motor home, which sleeps up to four for $2,200. Included in the package are airport pickup, linens, barbecue grill, all park registration fees and permits, your last night in a hotel (Royal Kona Resort), and help on planning your itinerary and booking activities.

THE KONA COAST

In & Around Kailua-Kona

Very Expensive

Four Seasons Resort Hualalai at Historic Kaupulehu ★★★ If you're looking for a relaxing vacation in the lap of luxury, one that will pamper not only you but your kids as well, look no further—you can't get any better than this. As soon as you make a reservation, the Four Seasons goes into gear to make your family's experience memorable.

When you arrive at these clusters of low-rise oceanfront villas, nestled between the sea and the greens of the golf course, your kids (3–12 years) will get complimentary milk and cookies, along with a plush toy souvenir, and teens (13–17) receive a welcome gift such as mac-nut, pineapple, and coconut popcorn and a Fuze banana cola drink. When you arrive at your unit (the Four Seasons has no concrete corridors and no massive central building—it looks like a two-story town house complex, clustered around three seaside swimming pools), send the kids into the bathroom, where their names will be spelled out in colorful sponges on the side of the tub. Hanging in the closet will be kid-sized robes. Whatever you need, the Four Seasons will see to it that it is done. Need a jogger stroller, car seat, or bottle warmer? No problem, it'll be waiting for you in your room. Want a crib set up with bumper pads and quilt, or age-appropriate diapers? They'll supply it. They'll even baby-proof the room, including netting along the lanai's railing, bumper pads for glass coffee tables, outlet protectors, and nightlights.

Throughout the property are free laundry facilities with free detergent. Another thoughtful touch: kids' menus in all the restaurants (including a separate buffet for children—with lower tables and kid-pleasing items such as chocolate chip pancakes—during certain peak family periods). There's a complimentary children's program (ages 5–12) filled with activities; and for teens, there's the "Hale Kula," an activities center open daily from 8am to 9pm, with a state-of-the-art entertainment center (54-in. TV), two Sega game centers, pool, Ping-Pong, foosball, and zillions of board games and puzzles (plus you can take DVDs and games back to your room if you like).

P.O. Box 1269, Kailua-Kona, HI 96745. ✆ **888/340-5662** or 808/325-8000. Fax 808/325-8100. www.fourseasons.com/hualalai. 243 units. $725–$1,115 double; from $1,450 suite. Extra person $170. Cribs and rollaway beds free. AE, DC, MC, V. **Amenities:** 3 restaurants (see Pahu i'a on p. 175 and Beach Tree Bar & Grill on p. 175); 3 bars (w/nightly entertainment); 5 exquisite outdoor pools (including a giant infinity pool and a gorgeous lap pool); 18-hole Jack Nicklaus signature golf course; 8 tennis courts (4 lit for night play); complete health club; award-winning spa; 6 Jacuzzis; watersports equipment/rentals; bike rentals; children's program; game room; attentive concierge; activities desk; car rental desk; business center; top-drawer shopping arcade; salon; 24-hr. room service; massage; babysitting; free use of laundry machines; same-day laundry service and dry cleaning. *In room:* A/C, TV, dataport, fridge, coffeemaker, hair dryer, iron, safe.

Kona Village Resort Once my favorite Kona resort, this one-time luxury resort, which resembles an eclectic Polynesian village with historic sites and beaches on a secluded cove, has lost its magic. New owners have been slow to do maintenance work, employees have lost their friendly smiles, and longtime clients (who have returned to the "village" for decades) have sent us letters complaining that "the village is just not the same." Too bad because it still offers a great program for families with kids (except during May and Sept, when the resort is reserved for couples only) to relax and play on 82 acres by the sea, behind a lava barrier that keeps the world at bay. Thatched-roof, island-style bungalows with no air-conditioning and no TVs, a central dining house, and phones only at the office mean you can really leave the everyday world behind. The all-inclusive policy means you won't be reaching for your wallet for everything your kids want to do: all meals, the children's program, beach activities (kayaking, sailboats, snorkeling), the fitness center, and the fabulous Friday-night luau are covered in the price.

All bungalows have a bedroom, bathroom, and lanai, and the maids replenish the fridge daily with free sodas and bottled water. Some units have an outdoor hot tub and an extra anteroom with a single bed. The units range in size from comfortable for three to housing nine. The lack of televisions in the rooms means that your family will have a vacation during which they discover one another and Hawaii.

P.O. Box 1299, Kailua-Kona, HI 96745. ✆ **800/367-5290** or 808/325-5555. Fax 808/325-5124. www.konavillage.com. 125 units. $660–$1,475 double. Extra person $245 adults (13 and older), $135 children 5–9, $180 children 10–12 (no extra charge for children 4 and under). Rates include all meals, tennis, watersports, walking tours, airport transfers, and a Fri-night luau. Packages available. Cribs $25 per stay; rollaway beds free. AE, DC, MC, V. **Amenities:** 2 restaurants; 2 bars (w/live entertainment most nights); 2 outdoor pools; tennis courts; fitness room; 2 Jacuzzis; complimentary watersports; extensive children's program (especially during the summer, when it extends past dinner); concierge; activities desk; Polynesian general store; babysitting; complimentary washer/dryers; laundry service; dry cleaning. *In room:* Fridge, coffeemaker, hair dryer, iron, safe, no phone.

Expensive

Outrigger Royal Sea Cliff Resort Families will love these luxuriously appointed apartments and the affordable rates. The architecturally striking, five-story white buildings that make up this resort/condo complex, 2 miles from Kailua-Kona, are stepped back from the ocean for maximum views and privacy. (The downside is that there's no ocean swimming here, but the waves are near enough to lull you to sleep; if you really want to take a dip, there are two swimming pools on the property.) All units have a full kitchen and a washer/dryer, plus the property has several barbecue and picnic facilities for oceanfront dining. The one-bedroom units have a rollaway bed and can sleep four; the two-bedroom units can sleep up to six. Kids ages 5 to 12 (staying 5 nights or more) will get an Island Explorers backpack when they check in. If it rains, ask the front desk for games you can take back to your unit.

75-6040 Alii Dr., Kailua-Kona, HI 96740. ✆ **800/688-7444** or 808/329-8021. Fax 808/326-1887. www.outriggerroyalseacliff.com. 148 units. $219–$259 studio double; $249–$419 1-bedroom apt for 4; $289–$459 2-bedroom apt for 6. Cribs free. AE, DC, DISC, MC, V. **Amenities:** 2 outdoor pools; tennis courts; Jacuzzi; activities desk; business center. *In room:* A/C, TV, kitchen, fridge, coffeemaker, hair dryer, iron, safe.

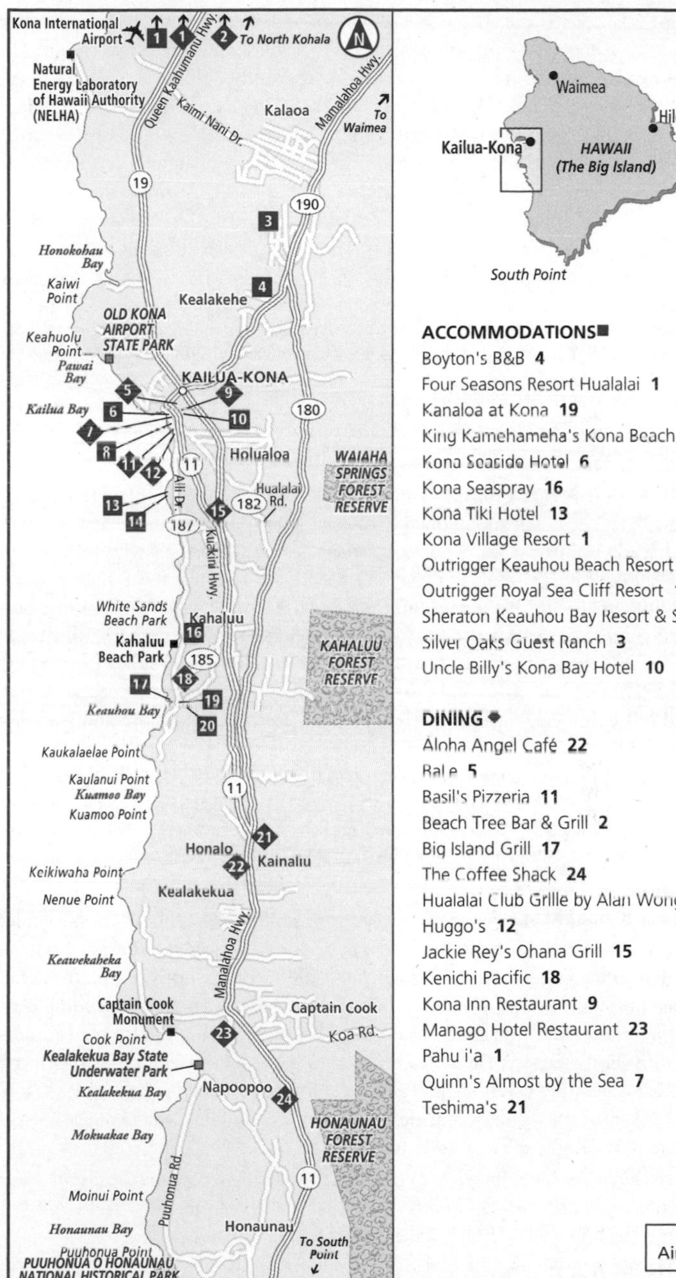
Kona International Airport
To North Kohala
Natural Energy Laboratory of Hawaii Authority (NELHA)
Queen Kaahumanu Hwy.
Kaimi Nani Dr.
Kalaoa
Mamalahoa Hwy.
To Waimea
19
190
Honokohau Bay
Kaiwi Point
Kealakehe
OLD KONA AIRPORT STATE PARK
Keahuolu Point
Pawai Bay
KAILUA-KONA
Kailua Bay
180
Holualoa
WAIAHA SPRINGS FOREST RESERVE
11
Hualalai Rd.
182
Alii Dr.
187
Kuakini Hwy.
White Sands Beach Park
Kahaluu
Kahaluu Beach Park
185
KAHALUU FOREST RESERVE
Keauhou Bay
Kaukalaelae Point
Kaulanui Point
Kuamoo Bay
Kuamoo Point
Honalo
Kainaliu
Keikiwaha Point
Nenue Point
Kealakekua
Keawekaheka Bay
Captain Cook Monument
Captain Cook
Koa Rd.
Cook Point
Kealakekua Bay State Underwater Park
Kealakekua Bay
Napoopoo
HONAUNAU FOREST RESERVE
Mokuakae Bay
Puuhonua Rd.
Moinui Point
Honaunau Bay
Honaunau
Puuhonua Point
PUUHONUA O HONAUNAU NATIONAL HISTORICAL PARK
To South Point
Waimea
Hilo
Kailua-Kona
HAWAII (The Big Island)
South Point
ACCOMMODATIONS
Boyton's B&B 4
Four Seasons Resort Hualalai 1
Kanaloa at Kona 19
King Kamehameha's Kona Beach Hotel 8
Kona Seaside Hotel 6
Kona Seaspray 16
Kona Tiki Hotel 13
Kona Village Resort 1
Outrigger Keauhou Beach Resort 17
Outrigger Royal Sea Cliff Resort 14
Sheraton Keauhou Bay Resort & Spa 20
Silver Oaks Guest Ranch 3
Uncle Billy's Kona Bay Hotel 10
DINING
Aloha Angel Café 22
Bale 5
Basil's Pizzeria 11
Beach Tree Bar & Grill 2
Big Island Grill 17
The Coffee Shack 24
Hualalai Club Grille by Alan Wong 1
Huggo's 12
Jackie Rey's Ohana Grill 15
Kenichi Pacific 18
Kona Inn Restaurant 9
Manago Hotel Restaurant 23
Pahu i'a 1
Quinn's Almost by the Sea 7
Teshima's 21
Airport

Moderate

King Kamehameha's Kona Beach Hotel The best deal at this convenient downtown Kailua-Kona hotel is the Aloha Special—room and breakfast, which comes with a double room (large enough to accommodate a kid or two in addition to two adults), and breakfast for two, starting at just $120—a price that makes the "King Kam" (as locals call it) attractive to travelers on a budget. This place isn't anything fancy—just a standard hotel in need of a little TLC—but it's well located, right in the heart of town, across the street from the pier, where record Pacific blue marlin are weighed in every afternoon. The rooms show their age, but they are clean and can have views of an ancient banyan tree, the Kona Pier, or sparkling Kailua Bay. There are lots of connecting rooms if your family needs the extra space. The hotel's own small, gold-sand beach is right out the front door.

75-5660 Palani Rd., Kailua-Kona, HI 96740. ✆ **800/367-6060** or 808/329-2911. Fax 808/922-8061. www.konabeachhotel.com. 460 units. $190–$290 double. Room and breakfast packages $130–$200 (subject to availability); Paradise on Wheels includes breakfast, car, partial ocean view $230–$290 (subject to availability). Extra person $35. Children 17 and under stay free in parent's room. Cribs free; rollaway beds $35. AE, DC, DISC, MC, V. Parking $10. **Amenities:** 3 restaurants; outdoor bar w/Hawaiian entertainment; outdoor pool; 4 tennis courts; Jacuzzi; watersports equipment/rentals; activities desk; shopping arcade; salon; limited room service; coin-op laundry; laundry service; dry cleaning. *In room:* A/C, TV, dataport, fridge, coffeemaker, iron, safe.

Silver Oaks Ranch ★★★ Finds If a hotel doesn't fit your picture of a Hawaii vacation, this "guest ranch" is a great alternative: two cottages spread over a 10-acre working ranch with friendly miniature dairy goats, chickens, show horses, and wild turkeys that come to get fed once a day—kids can watch or even help. Located at 1,300 feet, where the temperatures are in the 70s year-round, the ranch has units ranging from one-bedroom to family-size. The views are spectacular, some 40 miles of coastline from the ocean to Mauna Loa, yet the ranch is just 5 miles from the airport and 5 miles from all the activities in downtown Kailua-Kona. Hosts Amy and Rick Decker have impeccable taste, and both units are uniquely decorated. Each unit has a private bathroom and complete kitchen.

Off Palani Rd. (about a mile up the hill from the town of Kailua Kona). Reservations: 75-1027 Henry St., Suite 310, Kailua-Kona, HI 96740. ✆ **877/325-2300** or 808/325-2000. Fax 808/325-2200. www.silveroaksranch.com. 2 units. $200, includes welcome basket with breakfast items. Extra person $20. MC, V. **Amenities:** Outdoor pool; Jacuzzi; laundry. *In room:* TV/VCR, dataport, kitchen, fridge, coffeemaker.

Inexpensive

Boyton's Bed & Breakfast ★ Just 3 miles from Kailua-Kona, but up in the cooler, rolling hills, is this quaint two-bedroom B&B, perfect for a family vacation. The outside lanai has a view of the coastline from this perch at 1,000 feet. The private entrance leads you into the complete kitchen, which is stocked with breakfast fixings (including eggs, cereals, muffins, juice, and just about everything else you can think of). One bedroom looks out on tropical greenery; the other bedroom has an ocean view. Hosts contractor Peter Boyton and his wife, psychologist Tracy, have lovingly created a little bit of heaven here. There's a Jacuzzi on the deck outside, and lots of privacy in a quiet country neighborhood. The beach is just a 5-minute drive away.

74-4920-A Palani Rd., Kailua-Kona, HI 96740 ✆/fax **808/329-4178.** www.boyntonsbandb.com. 1 unit. $120 2-bedroom double. Extra person $15. 3-night minimum. No credit cards. **Amenities:** Jacuzzi. *In room:* TV/VCR, Wi-Fi, kitchen, fridge, coffeemaker, hair dryer, iron.

Kona Tiki Hotel ★★★ Finds It's hard to believe that places like this still exist. The Kona Tiki, located right on the ocean, away from the hustle and bustle of downtown

Kailua-Kona, is one of the best budget deals in Hawaii. All of the rooms are tastefully decorated and feature queen beds, ceiling fans, minifridges, and private lanais overlooking the ocean. Although it's called a hotel, this small, family-run operation is more like a large B&B, with lots of aloha and plenty of friendly conversation at the morning breakfast buffet around the pool. The staff is helpful in planning activities. There are no TVs or phones in the rooms, but there's a pay phone in the lobby. If a double with a kitchenette is available, grab it—the few bucks will save you a bundle in food costs. Book way, way, way in advance.

75-5968 Alii Dr. (about a mile from downtown Kailua-Kona), Kailua-Kona, HI 96740. ✆ **808/329-1425.** Fax 808/327-9402. www.konatiki.com. 15 units. $69–$82 double; $92 double with kitchenette; rates include continental breakfast. Extra person $10 ages 13 and over, $7 children ages 2–12. No credit cards. **Amenities:** Outdoor pool. *In room:* Kitchenette in some units, minifridge, no phone.

Uncle Billy's Kona Bay Hotel An institution in Kona, Uncle Billy's is where visitors from the other islands stay when they come to this coast. A thatched roof hangs over the lobby area, and a Polynesian longhouse restaurant is next door. The hotel rooms are old but comfortable and come with large lanais; but they're too small for a family, so instead ask for one of the 16 condo-style units with kitchens. This budget hotel is a good place to sleep, but don't expect new furniture, new carpets, or fancy soap in the bathroom. It can be noisy at night when big groups book in. Avoid Labor Day weekend, when all the canoe paddlers in the state want to stay here and rehash the race into the wee morning hours.

75-5739 Alii Dr., Kailua-Kona, HI 96740. ✆ **800/367-5102** or 808/961-5818. Fax 808/935-7903. www.unclebilly.com. 139 units. $119–$144 double. Check Internet for specials starting at $94 and car/room deals for just $30 more a night. Extra person $20. Children 12 and under stay free in parent's room. Cribs and rollaway beds $15 per night. AE, DC, DISC, MC, V. **Amenities:** Restaurant (buffet); bar (w/Hawaiian entertainment); 2 outdoor pools (1 for children); watersports equipment/rentals; activities desk; coin-op laundry. *In room:* A/C, TV, dataport, kitchenette in some units, fridge upon request.

Keauhou

Kanaloa at Kona ★★★ These big, comfortable, well-managed, and spacious vacation condos border the rocky coast beside Keauhou Bay, 6 miles south of Kailua-Kona. They're exceptional units, ideal for families, with comforts such as huge bathrooms with whirlpool bathtubs, dressing rooms, and bidets. In addition, the spacious lanais, tropical decor, and many appliances (washers and dryers) make for free and easy living. The units range from one-bedroom (sleeps up to four) to two-bedroom with loft (sleeps up to eight). When you book, they will help you choose the largest unit available at the best prices. (Some two-bedroom units are only $30 more than a one-bedroom.) It's easy to stock up on supplies at the supermarket at the mall just up the hill, but the oceanfront restaurant (with a kids' menu) offers an alternative to your own cooking.

78-261 Manukai St., Kailua-Kona, HI 96740. ✆ **800/688-7444** or 808/322-9625 Outrigger Resorts. Fax 800/622-4852. www.kanaloaatkona.com. 76 units. $249–$365 1-bedroom apt (sleeps up to 4); $279–$499 2-bedroom apt (up to 6). Children 18 and under stay free in parent's room with existing bedding. Cribs and rollaway beds $10 each per day. AE, DC, DISC, MC, V. **Amenities:** Restaurant; oceanside bar; 3 outdoor pools (1 for adults only); 2 (lighted) tennis courts; 3 Jacuzzis; concierge; activities desk; babysitting. *In room:* TV, kitchen, fridge, coffeemaker, hair dryer, iron, safe.

Kona Seaspray ★ Value The Kona Seaspray has a couple of great things going for it: location and price. It's just across from the Kahaluu Beach Park, possibly the best snorkeling area in Kona. The rates are a great deal when you consider that the one-bedroom apartments easily sleep four and the two-bedroom/one-bathroom unit can sleep six. All apartments have a full kitchen, complete with all the amenities of home. Plus every unit has a lanai and fabulous ocean view. Golf and tennis are nearby. This is the place to book if you are going to spend a lot of time lounging around.

78-6671 Alii Dr. (reservations: c/o Johnson Resort Properties, 78-6665 Alii Dr.), Kailua-Kona, HI 96740. ✆ **808/322-2403.** Fax 808/322-0105. www.konaseaspray.com. 12 units. $150–$175 1-bedroom double; $175–$200 2-bedroom/2-bathroom for 4. Cleaning fees $55 for 1-bedroom; $75 for 2-bedroom. Extra person $20. 3-night minimum. AE, DISC, MC, V. **Amenities:** Gorgeous outdoor pool w/waterfall; coin-op laundry. *In room:* TV, kitchen, fridge, coffeemaker, hair dryer, iron.

Outrigger Keauhou Beach Resort (Value) Located on 10 acres, this former OHANA Keauhou Beach Hotel, has been upgraded to the more upscale Outrigger brand. The kids will love the location: a large reef system (where sea turtles come ashore for a brief nap), and next door to one of Kona's best white-sand beaches, Kahaluu, with recently restored *heiau* (temples) lining the southern shoreline. Lush tropical gardens of native plants and flowers surround the hotel, and it's just a mile from the Kona Country Club's 36 holes of golf. The rooms are small (you could fit a crib in there, but a family of four should get two rooms); the oceanview rooms are well worth the extra money. The main dining room has vastly improved its cuisine (don't miss the locally grown, organic salad bar), and you're just minutes from other restaurants and shopping at the nearby Keauhou Shopping Center. Rates are much cheaper than those at the nearby Sheraton Keauhou (see below).

78-6740 Alii Dr., Kailua-Kona, HI 96740. ✆ **800/OUTRIGGER** or 808/322-3441. Fax 808/322-3117. www.outriggerkeauhoubeachhotel.com. 309 units. $249–$409 double; from $509 suites. Extra person $50. AE, DC, DISC, MC, V. Valet parking $10 all day; self-parking $10. **Amenities:** 2 restaurants; 4 bars; outdoor pool; 36-hole golf course nearby; 6 tennis courts (2 lighted); health club; spa; Jacuzzi; year-round children's program; concierge; activities desk; business center; room service; coin-op washer/dryers; laundry service, dry cleaning; shuttle to shopping center. *In room:* A/C, TV, fridge, coffeemaker, hair dryer, iron, safe.

Sheraton Keauhou Bay Resort & Spa ★★★ In 2005, nearly 6 years after the old Kona Surf Resort closed, and after $70 million in renovations, the Sheraton Keauhou Bay Resort had a formal opening. The complete overhaul of this 1970s resort is remarkable: Walls were torn out in the lobby and the main dining room to allow access to the incredible view of Keauhou Bay, and the 420-square-foot rooms were completely redone to bring them into the 21st century. Your kids may never want to leave once they see the mammoth pool: Tucked in around the tropical gardens and splashing waterfalls, this enormous freshwater pool includes its own small man-made beach, the island's largest water slide, bubbling whirlpool spas, and a children's play area. Speaking of kids, there's a children's center and program on property and plenty of activities to keep the little ones occupied (water activities, cultural games and arts and crafts, play stations, and so on). Fee for children's program is $50 half-day with lunch ($40 each additional child) and $70 full day with lunch ($50 for each additional child). Plus, the Sheraton has a golf course next door and tennis courts on the property, and there's a shopping center (with restaurants) close by.

78-128 Ehukai St., Kailua-Kona, HI 96740. ✆ **888/488-3535** or 808/930-4900. Fax 808/930-4800. www.sheratonkeauhou.com. 522 units. $350–$460 double. Extra person $60. Children 18 and under stay free in parent's room with existing bedding. AE, DC, DISC, MC, V. Valet parking $16; self-parking $9. **Amenities:** 2 restaurants (luau twice a week); bar; multilevel pool w/200-ft. water slide; 36-hole golf course nearby w/preferred guest rate; 2 tennis courts; sand volleyball court; basketball court; health club; spa; Jacuzzi; year-round children's program; concierge; activities desk; business center; room service; babysitting; coin-op washer/dryers; laundry service; dry cleaning. *In room:* A/C, TV, dataport, high-speed Internet access (additional fee), fridge, coffeemaker, hair dryer, iron, safe.

THE KOHALA COAST

You'll find Kohala Coast accommodations on the "North Kohala & Waimea" map on p. 195.

Very Expensive

Hapuna Beach Prince Hotel ★★★ This hotel enjoys one of the best locations on the Kohala coast, adjacent to the magnificent white sands of Hapuna Beach. The staff here goes out of their way to make sure your families are comfortable. The units are all attuned to the fabulous ocean view and the sea breezes. Although the rooms are small for a luxury hotel, the sprawling grounds make up for it. The best family deal is the Ohana Package, where the first room is rack rate and the second room is free. Ohana packages start at $390. During the summer (May 1–Sept 30), kids ages 12 and younger eat free.

At check-in, kids get treats such as a beach ball, sand pail, and shovel (kids 2 and younger); crayons, coloring books, and a foam ball (kids 3–7); and a water bottle, plastic key keeper, and art supplies (kids 8–12). During the day there's the Keiki Club for kids ages 5 to 12, filled with great things to do and games to play; it's half-price during the summer ($30 for a half-day or $60 for a full day with lunch).

At Mauna Kea Resort, 62-100 Kaunaoa Dr., Kohala Coast, HI 96743. ✆ **800/882-6060** or 808/880-1111. Fax 808/880-3112. www.princeresortshawaii.com. 350 units. $395–$690 double; from $1,300 suite. Extra person $60. Children 17 and under stay free in parent's room using existing bedding. Cribs free; rollaway beds $60. AE, DC, MC, V. **Amenities:** 5 restaurants (including the Coast Grille, p. 180); 2 bars (1 is an open-air beachfront bar w/live evening entertainment); huge outdoor pool; golf course; 13 tennis courts; fitness center; salon and spa; Jacuzzi; watersports equipment rentals; year-round Keiki Kamp children's program; concierge; activities desk; car rental desk; business center; shopping arcade; room service; massage; babysitting; same-day laundry service and dry cleaning. *In room:* A/C, TV, high-speed Internet access, fridge, coffeemaker, hair dryer, iron, safe.

Mauna Kea Beach Hotel ★★★ As we were going to press, this grande dame of hotel resorts in Hawaii was closed for extensive renovations due to the 2006 earthquake. The construction was estimated to be complete by the end of 2008.

This resort dates back to the early 1960s. Laurance S. Rockefeller was sailing around Hawaii when he spotted a perfect crescent of gold sand and dropped anchor. In 1965 he built the Mauna Kea on the spot. Over the years, new luxury hotels have eclipsed the Mauna Kea in architectural style and amenities, but the beach out front is divine, the landscaped grounds have a maturity seen nowhere else on this coast, and its loyal old-money guests keep returning to savor the relaxed clubby ambience, remote setting, world-class golf course, and old Hawaii ways.

The two championship golf courses—Robert Trent Jones, Sr.'s famous Mauna Kea course and the Arnold Palmer–designed Hapuna course—are both award winners.

The rooms are huge by today's standards. The hotel is positioned to catch the cooling trade winds, and the views from the large lanais are breathtaking.

62-100 Mauna Kea Beach Dr., Kohala Coast, HI 96743. ✆ **800/882-6060** or 808/882-7222. Fax 808/880-3112. www.princeresortshawaii.com. 310 units. AE, DC, MC, V. **Amenities:** 6 restaurants; 3 bars w/live music; large outdoor pool; 2 championship golf courses; 13-court oceanside tennis complex; excellent fitness center; Jacuzzi; watersports equipment rentals; children's program; concierge; activities desk; car rental desk; shopping arcade; salon; room service; massage; babysitting; coin-op washer/dryers; laundry service; dry cleaning. *In room:* A/C, TV, high-speed Internet access, minibar, hair dryer, iron, safe.

Mauna Lani Hotel & Bungalows ★★★ Burned out? In need of tranquillity and gorgeous surroundings? Look no further. Sandy beaches and lava tide pools are the focus of this serene seaside resort, where gracious hospitality is dispensed in a setting that's exceptional for its historic features. From the lounge chairs on the pristine beach to the turndown service at night, everything here is done impeccably. Even the plush guest rooms are arranged to capture maximum ocean views.

The Ohana Package includes two rooms and starts at $315 a night (3-night minimum, maximum three people per room). Plus, when the kids check in, they get a bag of cookies.

In addition to their very complete children's programs (9am–3:30pm daily for $50 for the first child, $50 for the second) and kid-friendly restaurants, this is a great place for kids to explore. The saltwater stream that meanders through the hotel and onto the property outside is filled with reef fish and even a shark. The fishponds on the property are a great educational experience for *keiki* (children), and the beach has plenty of room for the youngsters to run and play. Next door to the resort are ancient Hawaiian petroglyph fields, where older kids can learn about Hawaii's past.

68-1400 Mauna Lani Dr., Kohala Coast, HI 96743. ✆ **800/327-8585** or 808/885-6622. Fax 808/885-1484. www.maunalani.com. 350 units. $445–$820 double; $985 suite; $1,800 villa (3-night minimum); $6,050–$6,850 bungalow (sleeps up to 4). Extra person $75. Children 16 and under stay free in parent's room. Cribs and rollaway beds free. AE, DC, DISC, MC, V. **Amenities:** 5 excellent restaurants; bar; large outdoor pool; 2 celebrated 18-hole championship golf courses; 10 Plexipave tennis courts; full-service health club; spa; Jacuzzi; watersports equipment/rentals; bike rentals; year-round children's program; game room; concierge; activities desk; car rental desk; business center; shopping arcade; salon; room service; massage; babysitting; coin-op laundry; laundry service; dry cleaning. *In room:* A/C, TV, dataport, minibar, coffeemaker, hair dryer, iron, safe.

Waikoloa Beach Marriott Resort & Spa ★ This resort has always had one outstanding attribute: an excellent location on Anaehoomalu Bay (or A-Bay, as the locals call it), one of the best ocean sports bays on the Kohala coast. The gentle sloping beach has everything: swimming, snorkeling, diving, kayaking, windsurfing, and even old royal fishponds. The resort isn't as posh as other luxury hotels along the Kohala coast, but it also isn't nearly as expensive. The size and layout of the guest rooms are perfectly nice, but not in the luxurious category of some of the other Kohala hotels. Even in the units with two double beds, however, there's room for a rollaway bed or a crib. The resort offers child-friendly amenities such as a kids' sandy-bottom swimming pool.

69-275 Waikoloa Beach Dr., Waikoloa, HI 96738. ✆ **888/924-5656** or 808/886-6789. Fax 808/886-7852. www.waikoloabeachmarriott.com. 555 units. $425–$565 double; $850–$2,500 suite. Extra person $40. Children 17 and under stay free in parent's room. Cribs and rollaway beds free. AE, DC, DISC, MC, V. Valet parking $15. **Amenities:** 2 restaurants; bar w/nightly live entertainment; 2 outdoor pools (a huge pool w/water slide and separate children's pool); 6 tennis courts; small health club; spa; Jacuzzi; watersports equipment/rentals; year-round children's program; game room; concierge; activities desk; small shopping arcade; salon; limited room service; massage; babysitting; coin-op laundry; laundry service; dry cleaning; concierge-level rooms. *In room:* A/C, TV, dataport, fridge, coffeemaker, hair dryer, iron, safe.

Expensive

The Fairmont Orchid, Hawaii ★★★ Located on 32 acres of oceanfront property, the Orchid is the place for watersports nuts, cultural explorers, or those who just want to lie back and soak up the sun. This elegant beach resort takes full advantage of the spectacular ocean views and historical sites on its grounds. The sports facilities here are extensive, and there's an excellent Hawaiiana program (terrific for kids): The "beach boys" demonstrate how to do everything from creating drums from the trunks of coconut trees to paddling a Hawaiian canoe or strumming a ukulele.

The best deal for families is the "Twice as Nice" package, which allows you to book a second room at 50% off rack rates, and which includes a breakfast buffet for two and two full-day Keiki Aloha programs per stay. The Orchid Court and Brown's Beach House offer kids' menus and a relaxed family atmosphere. They also have recently installed barbecue areas, called Mesa Grills, which are available for families to barbecue their meals by the ocean.

The Keiki Aloha program, for kids ages 5 to 12, features supervised activities such as watersports and Hawaiian cultural activities. The resort has added an evening program on Tuesday, Thursday, and Saturday from 6 to 9pm ($50 fee) that offers the kids arts and crafts plus a dinner and a movie (so parents can be alone for a few hours).

1 N. Kaniku Dr., Kohala Coast, HI 96743. ✆ **800/845-9905** or 808/885-2000. Fax 808/885-1064. www.fairmont.com. 539 units. $399–$849 double; from $1,399 suite. Extra person $75. Children 17 and under stay free in parent's room. Cribs and rollaway beds free. AE, DC, DISC, MC, V. Valet parking $21; self-parking $15. **Amenities:** 4 restaurants; 5 bars (w/evening entertainment in the Paniolo Lounge); large outdoor pool; 2 lava rock whirlpools; 2 championship golf courses; award-winning tennis w/10 Plexipave courts (7 lighted); well-equipped health club; outstanding spa; watersports equipment/rentals; bike rentals; year-round children's program ($65 for a half-day and $85 for a full day, which includes lunch); concierge; activities desk; car rental desk; business center; shopping arcade; salon; 24-hr. room service; babysitting; same-day laundry service and dry cleaning. *In room:* A/C, TV, dataport, minibar, hair dryer, iron, safe.

Hilton Waikoloa Village ★ This is not just another beach hotel (it actually has no real beach)—it's a fantasy world all its own, perfect for those who love Vegas and Disneyland. Its high-rise towers are connected by silver-bullet trams, boats, and museum-like walkways lined with $7 million in Asian/Pacific reproductions. The kids will love it, but you may get a little weary waiting for the tram or boat to take you to breakfast (sometimes a 20-min. ordeal or a mile-long walk). The 62 acres feature tropical gardens, cascading waterfalls, exotic wildlife, exaggerated architecture, a 175-foot water slide twisting into a 1-acre pool, hidden grottos, a river pool with a current, a sandy-bottom children's pool, and man-made lagoons. The biggest hit of all (for some) is the dolphin lagoon, where you can pay to swim with dolphins.

The contemporary guest rooms are spacious (530 sq. ft.) and luxurious, with built-in platform beds, lanais, and loads of amenities, from spacious dressing areas with comfy bathrobes to a second phone and second line in all units. There are nine—yes, nine!—restaurants to choose from, serving everything from Japanese food to family-style buffets, and all with kids' menus.

There are plenty of complimentary family activities: a stargazing program, petroglyph trail tours, fish feeding, resort tours, and pickup basketball and volleyball games. There's also Camp Menehune, for kids ages 5 to 12, featuring activities from ocean sports to a night camp during the dinner hours. Laundry facilities are in the Lagoon and Ocean Towers. (Book these towers if you need a washer or dryer, or it will be a long, long walk with your laundry.) Children's programs are available on the TV-screen menu.

425 Waikoloa Beach Dr., Waikoloa, HI 96738. ✆ **800/HILTONS** (445-8667) or 808/886-1234. Fax 808/886-2900. www.hiltonwaikoloavillage.com. 1,240 units. $229–$534 double; $314–$649 double on Executive Club floor; from $529 suite; $329–$599 double cabanas. Daily resort fee $15 for complimentary round of golf for 2 people at the seaside putting course; daily fitness access for 2 at the Kohala Sports Club & Spa; $25 daily credit for Lagoon Beach Equipment (not including any motorized equipment); 1 hr. of court time per day at the Kohala Tennis Garden. Extra person $45. Children 18 and under stay free in parent's room. Cribs free; rollaway beds $45. AE, DC, DISC, MC, V. Valet parking $19. **Amenities:** 9 restaurants; 8 bars, many w/entertainment; 3 huge outdoor pools (w/waterfalls, slides, and even a quiet adults-only pool); 2 18-hole golf courses; 8 tennis courts; 25,000-sq.-ft. health club/spa w/cardio machines, weights, and a multitude of massages and body treatments; Jacuzzi; watersports equipment/rentals; bike rentals; fabulous children's program; game room; concierge; activities desk; car rental desk; business center;

shopping arcade; salon; room service; in-room massage; babysitting; coin-op laundry; same-day laundry service and dry cleaning; concierge-level rooms. *In room:* A/C, TV, dataport, high-speed Internet access ($14/day), minibar, coffeemaker, hair dryer, iron, safe.

THE HAMAKUA COAST

You'll find the following hotels on the "North Kohala & Waimea" map on p. 195.

Cliff House Hawaii ★★★ Finds Perched on the cliffs above the ocean is this charming two-bedroom getaway, surrounded by horse pastures and million-dollar views. A large deck takes in that ocean vista, where whales frolic offshore in winter. Impeccably decorated (the owner also owns Waipio Valley Artworks), the unit features a full kitchen (stocked with everything you could possibly want—even a salad spinner), two large bedrooms, and a full bathroom. Lots of little touches make this property stand out from the others: an answering machine for the phone, a pair of binoculars, a chess set, and even an umbrella for the rain squalls. A family of four could comfortably share this unit.

P.O. Box 5070, Kukuihaele, HI 96727. ✆ **800/492-4746** or 808/775-0005. Fax 808/775-0058. www.cliffhousehawaii.com. 1 unit. $199 double. Extra person $35 (maximum 4 people). 2-night minimum. MC, V. *In room:* TV, dataport, high-speed Internet access, kitchen, fridge, coffeemaker, hair dryer, iron.

HILO

You'll find the following accommodations on the "Hilo" map on p. 201.

Dolphin Bay Hotel ★ Value This two-story motel-like building, 4 blocks from downtown, is a clean, family-run property that offers good value in a quiet garden setting. Ripe star fruit hang from the trees, flowers abound, and there's a jungle-like trail by a stream. The tidy concrete-block apartments are small and often breezeless, but they're equipped with ceiling fans and louvered windows. All units have fully equipped kitchens, and are brightly painted and outfitted with rattan furniture and Hawaiian prints. The one-bedroom apartments will easily sleep four, with a queen bed in the bedroom and two twin beds in the living room. (You can sleep more with a rollaway bed.) There are no phones in the rooms, but there's one in the lobby. You're welcome to all the papayas and bananas you can eat.

333 Iliahi St., Hilo, HI 96720. ✆ **808/935-1466.** Fax 808/935-1523. www.dolphinbayhilo.com. 18 units. $99–$109 studio double; $139 1-bedroom apt double; $159 2-bedroom apt double. Extra person $10. Playpens and rollaway beds $10 each. MC, V. From Hwy. 19, turn mauka (toward the mountains) on Hwy. 200 (Waianuenue St.), then right on Puueo St.; go over the bridge and turn left on Iliahi St. **Amenities:** Concierge; car rental desk; coin-op laundry. *In room:* TV, kitchenette, fridge, coffeemaker, hair dryer, iron.

Hawaii Naniloa Resort Hilo's biggest hotel offers nice rooms with lanais and enjoys a quiet, leafy Banyan Drive setting on the ocean. The hotel is a little old and tired, but so are all the other hotels on Banyan Drive; in terms of comfort and amenities, this is one of the best that Hilo has to offer. Although it needs work (new carpet, a paint job, and overall remodeling), the rooms are clean and the oceanfront views are spectacular. A single room with two double beds has room for a crib or a rollaway, so you most likely can fit a family of four (even four and an infant) into the room. Not only can you see the ocean from the rooms, but on a cloudless day, you can see to the top of Mauna Kea. Check out deals on their website for the best prices.

93 Banyan Dr. (off Hwy. 19), Hilo, HI 96720. ✆ **800/367-5360** or 808/969-3333. Fax 808/969-6622. www.naniloa.com. 325 units. $100–$160 double; from $190 suite. Internet rates from $109. Children 12 and under stay free in parent's room. Cribs free; rollaway beds $25. AE, DC, DISC, MC, V. **Amenities:** 2 restaurants; bar; 2 outdoor pools; 18-hole golf course nearby w/special rates for guests; coin-op laundry. *In room:* A/C, TV, fridge, coffeemaker, hair dryer, iron.

Uncle Billy's Hilo Bay Hotel Uncle Billy's is the least expensive place to stay along Hilo's hotel row on Banyan Drive. This oceanfront budget hotel boasts a dynamite location, and the car/room package offers extra incentive to stay here. You enter via a tiny lobby, gussied up Polynesian style; it's slightly overdone, with sagging fishnets and tapa-covered walls. The guest rooms are simple: bed, TV, phone, closet, and soap and clean towels in the bathroom—that's about it. When booking, ask for a room with two double beds and a twin bed (or a pullout sofa) to fit your family. Keep in mind that this is a budget hotel, and as such, the walls seem paper-thin. It can get very noisy at night (you may want to bring earplugs)—but at rates like these, you're still getting your money's worth.

87 Banyan Dr. (off Hwy. 19), Hilo, HI 96720. ✆ **800/367-5102** or 808/961-5818. Fax 808/935-7903. www.unclebilly.com. 144 units. $104–$134 double. Car/room packages and special senior rates available. Extra person $20. Children 12 and under stay free in parent's room. Cribs and rollaway beds $20 each. AE, DC, DISC, MC, V. **Amenities:** Restaurant; bar w/nightly hula show; oceanfront outdoor pool; activities desk; coin-op laundry. *In room:* A/C, TV, kitchenette in some units, fridge.

HAWAII VOLCANOES NATIONAL PARK

Since Hawaii Volcanoes was officially designated a national park in 1916, a village has popped up at its front door. Volcano Village isn't so much a town as a wide spot in Old Volcano Road: a 10-block area with two general stores, a handful of restaurants, a post office, a coffee shop, a new firehouse, and even an ATM. Volcano has no stoplights or jail—not even a church or a cemetery—though it does have a winery.

It gets cool here at night—Volcano Village is located at 3,700 feet above sea level—so while air-conditioning is not an issue, a fireplace or space heater might be an attractive amenity. It also rains a lot in Volcano—100 inches a year—which makes everything grow Jack-and-the-Beanstalk–style.

I recommend spending at least 3 days here to really see and enjoy the park. For a family, the best way to do this is to rent a cottage or house, and the best rental agency is **Hawaii Volcano Vacations ★★★**, P.O. Box 913, Volcano, HI 96785 (✆ **800/709-0907** or 808/967-7271; www.hawaiivolcanovacations.com). Manager Aurelia Gutierrez selects only the top cottages, cabins, and houses in Volcano and makes sure that they are perfect for you. Extremely reasonably priced, her units range from $109 to $200, and each one is outfitted with full kitchen, outdoor grill, cooler, flashlight, umbrella, and fresh flower arrangement for your arrival.

The **Volcano Guest House ★** (✆ **808/967-7775;** www.volcanoguesthouse.com) is a terrific cottage that rents rooms in the main house from $115 to $135 double. It's an ideal place to stay with the kids: completely childproofed and complete with toys (even a basketball hoop). It has two twin beds and a queen in the upstairs bedroom, a sofa bed in the living room, a full kitchen, and a backyard forest trail that goes all the way through 2 miles of tropical rainforest to the Thurston Lava Tube in Hawaii Volcanoes National Park.

The **Log Cabin** (✆ **808/262-7249;** www.crubinstein.com) is a century-old ohia log cabin for the young at heart, for just $125 for four and $150 for six.

Inexpensive

Hale Ohia Cottages ★ Finds Take a step back in time to the 1930s. Here you'll have a choice of suites, each with private entrance, located in the main residence or a cottage. There are also four guest cottages, ranging from one bedroom to three. The surrounding botanical gardens contribute to the overall tranquil ambience of the estate. They were groomed in the 1930s by a resident Japanese gardener, who worked with the natural volcanic terrain but gently tamed the flora into soothing shapes and designs. The lush grounds are just a mile from Hawaii Volcanoes National Park.

P.O. Box 758 (Hale Ohia Rd., off Hwy. 11), Volcano, HI 96785. ✆ **800/455-3803** or 808/967-7986. Fax 808/967-8610. www.haleohia.com. 8 units. $105–$299 double. Rates include continental breakfast. Extra person $25. No cribs or rollaway beds available. MC, V. *In room:* Fridge, coffeemaker, hair dryer, no phone.

SOUTH POINT

Macadamia Meadows Farm Bed & Breakfast ★ Near the southernmost point in the United States and just 45 minutes from Volcanoes National Park lies one of the Big Island's most welcoming B&Bs. It's located on an 8-acre working macadamia nut farm, in a great place for stargazing. The warmth and hospitality of host Charlene Cowan is unsurpassed: Each guest is treated like a favorite relative. This is an excellent place for children because the owner has children herself, and the entire property is very kid-friendly. In addition to exploring the groves of mac-nut trees, kids can swim in the pool or play tennis. Owner Charlene also has puzzles, games, and other rainy-day items to entertain the kids. Accommodations include a two-bedroom suite, a private room, and a honeymoon suite, which has an antique claw-foot tub on a private lanai. All rooms have private entrances and are immaculately clean.

94-6263 Kamaoa Rd., Waiohinu. Reservations: P.O. Box 756, Naalehu, HI 96772. ✆ **888/929-8118** or 808/929-8097. Fax 808/929-8097. www.macadamiameadows.com. 5 units. $99–$129 double. Rates include continental breakfast. Extra person $10–$15. Children 4 and under stay free in parent's room. AE, DISC, MC, V. **Amenities:** Resort-size outdoor pool; tennis courts; activities desk; coin-op laundry. *In room:* TV, fridge, no phone.

4 FAMILY-FRIENDLY DINING

Rather than an afterthought, dining is an authentic attraction here. The Big Island's volcanic soil produces fine tomatoes, lettuces, beets, beans, fruit, and basic herbs and vegetables that were once difficult to find locally. Along with the lamb and beef from Big Island ranches and seafood from local fishermen, the freshness of the produce forms the backbone of ethnic cookery and Hawaiian Regional Cuisine.

So many restaurants, so little time. What's a traveling family to do? Load the kids in the car and drive the Big Island, sampling the cuisine as you travel from one end of the island to the other. Kailua-Kona is teeming with restaurants for all pocketbooks and taste. The haute cuisine of the island is concentrated in the Kohala coast resorts, where the tony resorts claim their share of the action for deep pockets and special-occasion tastes.

Waimea, also known as Kamuela, is a thriving upcountry community, a haven for yuppies, techies, and retirees who know a good place when they see one. In Hawi, North Kohala, expect bakeries, neighborhood diners, and one tropical-chic restaurant that's worth a special trip. In Hilo, in eastern Hawaii, you'll find pockets of trendiness among the precious old Japanese and ethnic restaurants that provide honest, tasty, and affordable meals in unpretentious surroundings.

In the listings below, reservations are not necessary unless otherwise noted.

THE KONA COAST

In & Around Kailua-Kona

Note: Hualalai Club Grille, Pahu i'a, and Beach Tree Bar & Grill are located north of Kailua-Kona, 6 miles north of the airport and just south of the Kohala coast.

Very Expensive

Pahu i'a ★ CONTEMPORARY PACIFIC You can't find a better oceanfront location on the Big Island (maybe in the entire state). Just feet from the lapping waves is this icon of culinary masterpieces. A small bridge of natural logs leads to the oceanfront dining room, where views on three sides expand on the aquatic theme. (*Pahu i'a* is Hawaiian for "aquarium," and there's a large one at the entrance.) Dining here is a completely enchanting experience. The food features fresh produce and seafood from the island—and even from the resort's own aquaculture ponds, teeming with shrimp and *moi* (threadfish), a rich-tasting island fish. The day begins with the excellent breakfast buffet. At dinner, part of the menu changes daily and always includes several fresh seafood preparations, such as ahi chateaubriand with grilled foie gras or a black truffle-yaki sauce, and Hawaiian lobster Thermidor with pineapple fried rice. The kids may be more interested in the chicken nuggets or burgers. From ambience to execution to presentation, Pahu i'a is top-drawer.

In the Four Seasons Resort Hualalai, Queen Kaahumanu Hwy., Kaupulehu-Kona. ✆ **808/325-8000.** Kids' menu, highchairs, boosters, crayons. Reservations recommended. Breakfast $15–$30; buffets $30–$40; dinner main courses $40–$75; kids' menu $4.50–$15. AE, DC, DISC, MC, V. Daily 6–11:30am (buffet 7–11:30am) and 5:30–9:30pm.

Expensive

Beach Tree Bar & Grill ★ CASUAL GOURMET Here's an example of outstanding cuisine in a perfect setting, without being fancy, fussy, or prohibitively expensive. The bar on the sand is a sunset paradise, and the sandwiches, seafood, and grilled items at the casual outdoor restaurant (a few feet from the bar) are in a class of their own—simple, excellent, and imaginatively prepared. The menu, which varies, includes items like grilled fresh fish sandwiches, steaks, alternative healthy cuisine, and vegetarian specialties. The kids' menu features old standbys such as mac and cheese or a quesadilla. On Saturday the "Surf, Sand and Stars" feast offers an array of buffet-style items from fresh fish to grilled New York sirloin, and on Wednesday there's a special "Viva Italia" menu. The kids not only have their own buffet bar, but it is located close to the ground at "kid's level," with their favorites: very few vegetables, lots of pasta, and plenty of dessert. An added attraction is entertainment from 5 to 8pm nightly.

In the Four Seasons Resort Hualalai, Queen Kaahumanu Hwy., Kaupulehu-Kona. ✆ **808/325-8000.** Kids' menu, highchairs, crayons. Reservations recommended for dinner. Main courses $18–$22 lunch, $23–$50 dinner; kids' menu $4.50–$15. Sat buffet "Surf, Sand and Stars" $78 adults, $37 children 5–12; Wed "Viva Italia" menu entrees $17–$35. AE, DC, DISC, MC, V. Daily 11am–8:30pm.

Hualalai Club Grille by Alan Wong ★★★ CONTEMPORARY PACIFIC This open-air oasis of koa, marble, and island artwork just got better. Chef Alan Wong, who put the Canoe House Restaurant on the map and was one of the founders of Hawaiian Regional Cuisine, has taken the helm at this popular golf course–club restaurant. Wong's distinctive cooking is the star in this already star-studded location (overlooking the golf course and the Pacific). Your kids will love the indoor-outdoor feel to the restaurant. Lunch features soups, sandwiches, and daily specials such as seared peppered ahi over crispy Asian slaw. Dinner entrees include ginger-crusted onaga, steamed moi (raised on the property at Hualalai Resort), mac-nut–crusted lamb chops, and a host of other mouthwatering items. Kids get their own menu, where burgers, pizza, and chicken fingers rule. Save room for dessert: chocolate crunch bars, *lilikoi* (passion fruit) cheesecake, or homemade ginger-ale floats with house-made sorbets. Don't pass up the opportunity to enjoy one of the Big Island's best restaurants.

 In the Hualalai Resort, Queen Kaahumanu Hwy., Kaupulehu-Kona. ✆ **808/325-8525.** www.hualalai resort.com. Kids' menu, highchairs, boosters, crayons. Reservations recommended. Main courses $12–$21 lunch, $37–$54 dinner; kids' menu $11–$17. AE, DC, DISC, MC, V. Daily 5:30–9pm.

Huggo's ★ PACIFIC RIM/SEAFOOD You can't get closer to the water than this or you'd be swimming. But the food still is the star here. Fresh fish rules lunch and dinner, but Huggo's also has a well-deserved reputation for its barbecued ribs. Your kids will love watching the tide pools in front (ask for an oceanside table) and may not even be interested in the keiki menu. (Order the teriyaki steak for them; it's the most popular item.) Next door, **Huggo's on the Rocks ★**, a mound of thatch, rock, and grassy-sandy ground, is a sunset lover's nirvana. At sundown, it's choked with people either on chaises or at the 50-seat thatched bar, sipping mai tais and noshing on salads, poke, sandwiches, plate lunches, sashimi, and fish and chips. From 6 to 11am, this same location turns into **Java on the Rocks ★★★**, an espresso bar *not* to be missed—it's your chance to sip Kona coffee, enjoy your eggs, and watch the waves roll onto the shore. Island-style pupu (appetizers) are offered here from 11:30am to 11pm. From 5:30pm to 1am there's dancing at the water's edge.

75-5828 Kahakai Rd. ✆ **808/329-1493.** www.huggos.com. Kids' menu, highchairs, boosters, crayons. Reservations requested. Main courses $9–$23 lunch, $20–$50 dinner; kids' menu $9.95–$16. AE, DC, DISC, MC, V. Daily 11:30am–2:30pm and 5:30–10pm.

Kona Inn Restaurant ★ AMERICAN/SEAFOOD This is touristy, but it can be a very pleasant experience if the sun is setting or you've just arrived from the airport and don't want your hotel's offerings. The wide-ranging menu and fresh seafood in the open-air oceanfront setting tell you why you have come to Kailua-Kona. Kids will love the large, open room and panoramic view of the Kailua shoreline. Adults will probably be more interested in the huge menu, with choices ranging from nachos and chicken Caesar salad to sandwiches, pasta, stir-fried dishes, and the highlight: the fresh fish served Cajun-style or broiled and basted in lemon butter. The restaurant also has a section called the Cafe Grill, which serves casual food. Kids get their own menu, where cheeseburgers are the number one choice.

In Kona Inn Shopping Village, 75-5744 Alii Dr. ✆ **808/329-4455.** Kids' menu, highchairs, boosters, crayons. Reservations recommended at dinner. Main courses $20–$36; kids' menu $4.95; Cafe Grill $7–$15. AE, MC, V. Oct–Apr daily 5–9pm; May–Sept daily 5:30–9:30pm; Cafe Grill daily 11:30am–9:30pm.

Moderate

Jackie Rey's Ohana Grill ★★★ Finds ECLECTIC This off-the-beaten-path eatery is hard to categorize: part sports bar, part family restaurant, part music/dancing (salsa, country western), part neighborhood cafe. No matter what you call it, you'll get great food at wallet-pleasing prices. Locals pile in at lunch for burgers, roasted turkey sandwiches, seared ahi poke, and crispy chicken-finger sandwiches (with spicy hoisin sauce). On weekdays, a happy hour crowd downs a few brews and pupu. Starting at 5pm, families with kids in tow show up for the delicious curry-crusted ahi (over organic greens), grilled fresh catch over soba noodles and stir-fried veggies, pan-seared pork chops, filet mignon and shrimp (with crumbled blue cheese), and beef short ribs (with a ko-chu-jang glazed sauce). When you order a cocktail, order your wee ones a keiki (nonalcoholic) frozen piña colada.

75-5995 Kuakini Hwy., Kailua-Koha. ✆ **808/327-0209.** Kids' menu, highchairs, boosters, crayons. Reservations recommended for dinner. Main courses $7–$14 lunch, $11–$29 dinner; pupu menu $8–$14; kids' menu $4.95–$9.95. Mon–Fri 11am–5pm; Sat 5–9pm.

Kenichi Pacific ★★★ (Finds PACIFIC RIM FUSION/SUSHI BAR This gem of a restaurant is hidden in the Keauhou Shopping Center. Decorated in muted tones and understated furnishings, the food is fantastic, the service is efficient, and the experience leaves you smiling. Although they have no kids' menu, they will be happy to whip up whatever your youngsters want. (The chicken teriyaki appetizer is a very popular choice.) The menu is so tempting that you might want to graze from one dish to the next of ginger marinated squid, blackened tuna, Dungeness crab cakes, and fresh lobster summer rolls. The entrees range from pan-seared mahimahi with eggplant mousse to macadamia-crusted lamb accompanied by taro risotto. Whatever you order, leave room for the molten chocolate cake, a warm, flourless cake covered with espresso crème anglaise and served with Kona coffee-chip ice cream.

Keauhou Shopping Center, Keauhou. ✆ **808/322-6400.** Highchairs, boosters. Reservations recommended for dinner. Main courses $19–$36. AE, MC, V. Tues–Fri 11:30am–1:30pm; daily 5–9:30pm.

Inexpensive

Big Island Grill (Finds AMERICAN One of the best-kept secrets among local residents is the Big Island Grill, where you get huge servings of home cooking at reasonable prices. The place is always packed from the first cup of coffee at breakfast to the last bite of dessert at night. Chef Bruce Goold has been cooking in Kona for decades and has a loyal following for his "localized" American cuisine. This is a place to take the family for dinner (excellent fresh salmon, generous-size salads, and the world's tastiest mashed potatoes) without having to go into debt. Since there is no kids' menu and the portions are so large, just order an extra plate and share dinners with the kids. The service the past couple of times we visited was s-l-o-w, with no apology. Be prepared to wait to be seated, and remember that getting a table doesn't promise service.

75-5702 Kuakini Hwy. ✆ **808/326-1153.** Highchairs, boosters. Main courses $8.75–$22. AE, MC, V. Mon–Fri 6–10am; Mon–Sat 11:15am–9pm.

Boston Basil's Pizzeria PIZZA/ITALIAN Long time pizzeria Basil's became Boston Basil's in 2007 and grew up. Yes, they still have delicious pizzas but their Italian food now shines. Two dining rooms seat 100 in a garlic-infused atmosphere; its location is across the street from the ocean on Alii Drive. Shrimp pesto and the original barbecue-chicken pizzas are long-standing favorites, as is the artichoke-olive-caper version, a Greek-Italian hybrid. Recently they have expanded the menu to include sandwiches and burgers. Very popular with the 20-something crowd and hungry visitors drawn in by the wonderful aroma wafting out into the street. No kids' menu, but great pizza.

75-5707 Alii Dr. ✆ **808/326-7836.** Highchairs, boosters. Individual pizzas $9.95–$12; main courses $9–$15. MC, V. Daily 11am–9:30pm.

Quinn's Almost by the Sea ★ SEAFOOD/STEAK Late-night noshers take note: This is one of the few places you can grab a bite to eat in Kona after 9pm. Quinn's, located at the northern gateway to town, has a nautical/sports-bar atmosphere and offers casual alfresco dining on a garden lanai, with an air-conditioned, nonsmoking area also available. Kids are welcome and the prices are perfect for not breaking the family's budget. The menu is surf and turf basic: burgers, sandwiches, and a limited dinner menu of dependably good fresh fish, filet mignon, and a few shrimp dishes. There are six burger selections, and, when available, fresh ahi or ono sandwiches.

75-5655-A Palani Rd. ✆ **808/329-3822.** Kids' menu, highchairs. Main courses $10–$25; kids' menu $5.95. MC, V. Daily 11am–11pm.

South Kona

Moderate

Aloha Angel Cafe ★★★ ISLAND CUISINE On your way to visit Puukohola Heiau National Historic Site (Place of Refuge) or to Hawaii Volcanoes National Park, stop here for huge breakfasts, yummy lunches, or very creative dinners. This great family restaurant not only welcomes kids, but caters to them. Breakfast and lunch are served on the veranda that wraps around the old Aloha Theatre, with sweeping views down from the coffee fields to the shoreline. Dinner is in the tiny dining room (which unfortunately has no view); space is limited, so phone ahead to assure that you get a table. The cheaper daytime staples include omelets, burritos, tostadas, quesadillas, and home-baked goods. Most of the produce is organic, and fresh-squeezed orange juice and fresh-fruit smoothies are served daily. Sandwiches, from turkey to tofu-avocado and a wonderful fresh ahi, are heaped with vegetables on tasty whole-wheat buns, still generous after all these years. The dinner entrees cover the basics, from fresh catch to grilled New York steak and Cajun chicken with tropical salsa. The kids' menu features burgers and chips.

Hwy. 11, Kainaliu. ✆ **808/322-3383.** www.alohatheatre.com. Kids' menu, highchairs, boosters, crayons. Reservations recommended for dinner and large parties. Dinner main courses $8–$25; kids' menu $6.95. AE, DC, MC, V. Thurs–Mon 7:30am–8pm; Tues–Wed 7:30am–2:30pm.

Inexpensive

The Coffee Shack ★★★ COFFEEHOUSE/DELI Great food, crisp air, and a sweeping ocean view make the Coffee Shack one of South Kona's great finds. Kids are welcome at this informal cafe with a charming wooden deck offering one of the best views of Kealakekua Bay. Breakfasts are best: French toast made with homemade poi bread or eggs Benedict with a delectable hollandaise. At lunch, you'll find excellent sandwiches on home-baked breads and fresh, hearty salads made with organic lettuces. Let the kids order peanut-butter-and-jelly or grilled cheese sandwiches while you try the smoked Alaskan salmon sandwich or the hot, authentic Reuben (complete with sauerkraut and tangy Russian dressing).

Hwy. 11, 1 mile south of Captain Cook. ✆ **808/328-9555.** Highchairs. Breakfast $9–$14; lunch $7–$15; pizzas $11–$14. DISC, MC, V. Daily 7:30am–3pm.

Manago Hotel Restaurant (Value) AMERICAN This is old-style family dining. The dining room of the decades-old H. Manago Hotel is a local legend, greatly loved for its unpretentious, tasty food at bargain prices. At breakfast, $5.50 buys you eggs, bacon, papaya, rice, and coffee. At lunch or dinner, you can dine handsomely on local favorites: a 12-ounce T-bone, fried ahi, opelu, or the house specialty, pork chops (Manago's T-shirts announce THE BEST PORK CHOPS IN TOWN, and the restaurant serves nearly 1,500 pounds monthly). There's no kids' menu, but they'll find plenty of items to choose from. This place is nothing fancy, and there's a lot of frying going on in the big kitchen; but the local folks would riot if anything were to change after so many years.

In the Manago Hotel, Hwy. 11, Captain Cook. ✆ **808/323-2642.** Highchairs, boosters. Reservations recommended for dinner. Main courses $8–$14. DISC, MC, V. Tues–Sun 7–9am, 11am–2pm, and 5–7:30pm.

Teshima's AMERICAN/JAPANESE This is the Japanese restaurant where local families go. Shizuko Teshima has a strong following among those who have made her miso soup and sukiyaki an integral part of their lives. The early-morning crowd starts gathering while it's still dark for omelets or Japanese breakfasts (soup, rice, and fish). As the day progresses, the orders pour in for shrimp tempura and sukiyaki. By dinner, Number 3 teishoku trays—miso soup, sashimi, sukiyaki, shrimp, pickles, and other delights—are streaming out of the kitchen. Other combinations include steak and shrimp tempura; beef teriyaki and shrimp tempura; and the deep-sea trio of shrimp tempura, fried fish, and sashimi. Kids can order from the American side of the menu (grilled cheese sandwiches) if Japanese fare is not their favorite.

Hwy. 11, Honalo. ✆ **808/322-9140.** Highchairs, boosters. Reservations recommended for large parties. Complete dinners $13–$22. No credit cards. Daily 6:30am–1:45pm and 5–9pm.

THE KOHALA COAST

You'll find the following restaurants on the "North Kohala & Waimea" map on p. 195.

Very Expensive

Batik ★★★ EURASIAN As we went to press, this wonderful restaurant, a room of hushed tones and great restraint, with high, dark-wood ceilings, sedate (and loyal) guests, and sensitive lighting—a shrine to fine dining—was still under reconstruction due to the 2006 earthquake, but was scheduled to open in late 2008. Leave the kids with a sitter and come for a romantic dinner. Although they do have a kids' menu (pizza is the most popular item), this is definitely a grown-ups' restaurant. Items like the artichoke salad—its leaves spread out flamboyantly, like flower petals—is one of several standouts on the appetizer menu. Fresh snapper in various exotic preparations (with Kona mushrooms and lobster), grilled fresh fish with seaweed-herb sauces, and Keahole lobster Provençale are among the elegant entrees blending local ingredients and Asian preparations with Continental techniques. The drawback is that the restaurant is open only seasonally. (It's generally closed in Sept, open 3–4 nights a week Oct–Dec 25, and open 5 nights a week Dec 25–Apr and during the summer months.)

In the Mauna Kea Beach Hotel, 62-100 Mauna Kea Beach Dr. ✆ **808/882-7222.** www.maunakeabeachhotel.com. Kids' menu, highchairs, boosters, crayons. Reservations recommended. Collared, button-down shirts and dress slacks requested for men. Main courses $32–$45; prix fixe from $65; kids' menu $7.50–$10. AE, DC, MC, V. Seasonally 6:30–9pm.

Brown's Beach House ★★★ HAWAIIAN REGIONAL The nearby lagoon takes on the pink orange glow of sunset, while torches flicker among the coconut trees. This is a spectacular setting white tablecloths, candles, and seating near the lagoon—complemented by a menu that keeps getting better by the year. The open exhibition kitchen sets the stage with new and unusual dishes such as sizzling ahi tataki with local exotic mushrooms, or twice-cooked *ama ebi* (prawns) and scallop tempura. If the kids don't fancy the food on the kids' menu (PB&J to cheeseburger and waffle fries), they can order off the main menu for half-price.

Another option for families is **Brown's Deli,** where there's an assortment of items for breakfast (freshly made breads, pastries, and espresso), lunch, and dinner (pizza, salad, panini, and sandwiches). There are even grill tables along the oceanfront where you can grill your own uncooked items and have a sunset picnic.

At the Fairmont Orchid, Hawaii, 1 N. Kaniku Dr. ✆ **808/885-2000.** Kids' menu, highchairs, boosters, crayons. Reservations recommended for dinner. Main courses $18–$28 lunch, $30–$68 dinner; kids' menu $8–$15. AE, DC, DISC, MC, V. Daily11:30am–2:30pm and 5:30–9:30pm.

CanoeHouse ★★★ HAWAIIAN REGIONAL Take the kids and go at sunset, ask for an outside table (although the tables in the open-air dining room of the "canoe house," with a koa canoe hanging from the ceiling, aren't too shabby, either), and enjoy the culinary creations. The menu features nori-wrapped tempura ahi and wasabi lobster tempura on a stick, in addition to an array of seafood, from seared and peppered ono to mahimahi wrapped in pancetta and grilled salmon misoyaki. The kids' menu has more comfort-type food, from fish and chips to burgers. Save room for dessert, especially the chocolate pillar, a rich chocolate torte with vanilla sauce and fresh berries, or white chocolate *li hing mui* mousse, a classic white-chocolate mousse with a local Asian flavoring, served in a phyllo cup.

At Mauna Lani Bay Hotel and Bungalows, 68-1400 Mauna Lani Dr. ✆ **808/885-6622.** Kids' menu, highchairs, boosters, crayons. Reservations recommended. Main courses $29–$49; kids' menu $11–$13. AE, DC, DISC, MC, V. Summer daily 5:30–9pm; winter daily 6–9:30pm.

Coast Grille ★★★ HAWAIIAN REGIONAL/SEAFOOD/STEAK It's a 3-minute walk from the main lobby to the open-air Grille, but the view along the way is nothing to complain about and will help you work up an appetite. The split-level dining room has banquettes and wicker furniture, open-air seating, and a renowned oyster bar. The extensive seafood selection includes poke, clams, and fresh oysters from all over the world, as well as fresh seafood from island waters, served in multicultural preparations. Kona lobster–tempura sushi and an excellent clam chowder are among the finer pleasures. Kids are welcome and are given their own menu (chicken is the usual choice). Come early to enjoy the sunset.

In the Hapuna Beach Prince Hotel. ✆ **808/880-1111.** www.hapunabeachprincehotel.com. Kids' menu, highchairs, boosters, crayons. Reservations recommended. Main courses $24–$55; kids' menu $5–$11. AE, DC, MC, V. Daily 6–9:30pm.

Expensive

Hawaii Calls ★ PACIFIC RIM Families staying in this oceanside resort are the main clientele in this replica of the Hawaii of the '30s and '40s: John Kelly prints, Pan Am Clipper posters, old RCA record covers, and mementos of Hawaii's boat days. Hawaii Calls is one of the most pleasing features of the resort. Kids will love the open-air dining room with views of Anaehoomalu Bay and the surrounding ponds. At night, tablecloths and lighting at indoor tables are added. Every meal features a keiki's menu, but your kids may be more interested in the great offerings on the adult menu. Take the family to the Hula Sunsets, 1½ hours of Hawaiian song and dance on the nearby poolside lawn, from 5:30 to 7pm Friday. Also on Friday night is a seafood buffet with an array of appetizers (such as clams; and the "hukilau sampler" of Keahole lobster claw, seared ahi, and poke on a bed of greens) and the signature Kamuela lamb. There's live entertainment nightly in the adjoining Clipper Lounge, where you can order from a special bistro menu from 5:30 to 11pm.

In the Marriott Waikoloa Beach Resort, 69-275 Waikoloa Beach Dr. ✆ **808/886-6789.** Kids' menu, highchairs, boosters, crayons. Reservations recommended. Main courses $10–$18 lunch, $19–$49 dinner; kids' menu $9.95–$15. AE, DC, DISC, MC, V. Daily 6am–2pm and 5:30–9:30pm. Clipper Lounge 5–11:30pm.

Roy's Waikoloa Bar & Grill ★★★ EURASIAN/PACIFIC RIM Families will love the great food at Roy's. Don't let the strip mall location fool you. Roy's Waikoloa has several distinctive and inviting features: a golf-course view, large windows overlooking part of a 10-acre lake, and the East-West cuisine and upbeat service that are Roy Yamaguchi signatures. This is a clone of his Oahu restaurant, offering dishes we've come to love: Szechuan baby back ribs, blackened island ahi, and six other types of fresh fish prepared charred, steamed, or seared, and topped with exotic sauces such as shiitake miso and gingered lime-chile butter. Kids have their own menu to choose from, with items ranging from pasta to grilled chicken. Yamaguchi's tireless exploration of local ingredients and world traditions produces food that keeps him at Hawaii's culinary cutting edge.

In the Waikoloa Beach Resort, Kings' Shops, 250 Waikoloa Beach Dr. ✆ **808/886-4321.** www.roysrestaurant.com. Kids' menu, highchairs, cushions, crayons. Reservations recommended. Main courses $25–$35 dinner; kids' menu $12. AE, DC, DISC, MC, V. Daily 5–9:30pm.

Moderate

Cafe Pesto ★★★ ITALIAN/MEDITERRANEAN Fans drive long miles for these gourmet pizzas, calzones, and fresh organic greens grown from Kealakekua to Kamuela. The menu is pricey but worth it. The herb-infused Italian pies are adorned with lobster from the aquaculture farms on Keahole Point, shiitake mushrooms from a few miles *mauka* (inland), and fresh fish, shrimp, and crab. Honey-miso crab cakes, Santa Fe chicken pasta, sweet roasted peppers, and herb-garlic Gorgonzola dressing are other favorites. Kids have their own menu (but pizza still reigns).

In Kawaihae Shopping Center, at Kawaihae Harbor (Pule Hwy. and Kawaihae Rd.). ✆ **808/882-1071.** Also in Hilo, in the S. Hata Building, 308 Kamehameha Ave. ✆ **808/969-6640.** Kids' menu, highchairs, boosters, crayons. Main courses $10–$26; kids' menu $5.95–$7.95. AE, DC, DISC, MC, V. Sun–Thurs 11am–9pm; Fri–Sat 11am–10pm.

Merriman's Market Café ★ DELI/MEDITERRANEAN Peter Merriman, who has long reigned as king of Hawaiian Regional Cuisine with Merriman's in Waimea, has opened this tiny "market cafe" featuring cuisines of the Mediterranean, made with fresh local produce, house-made sausages, artisan-style breads, and great cheese and wines for a fun place for lunch or a light dinner. The 3,000-square-foot restaurant and deli features full-service indoor and outdoor dining in a casual atmosphere and a gourmet deli with daily specials. Lunch ranges from salads to sandwiches. Dinner consists of small plate dishes, small pizzas, and entrees from grilled fish to large salads. The kids' menu completes the picture (spaghetti with meatballs is a fave) of this family-friendly cafe.

Kings' Shops at Waikoloa Beach Resort, 250 Waikoloa Beach Dr., Waikoloa. ✆ **808/886-1700.** www.merrimanshawaii.com. Kids' menu, highchairs, boosters. Main courses $9.95–$28 lunch, $30–$45 dinner; kids' menu $7.95. Daily 11am–9pm.

Sansei Seafood Restaurant & Sushi Bar ★★★ SUSHI BAR/CONTEMPORARY JAPANESE Perpetual award winner Chef D. K. Kodama opened a branch of his popular Sansei (Maui and Oahu) in 2008 on the Big Island. The very classy restaurant offers an extensive menu of Japanese and East-West delicacies. Part fusion, part Hawaii Regional Cuisine, Sansei is tirelessly creative, with a menu that scores higher with adventurous palates than with purists (although there are endless traditional choices as well). Choices include panko-crusted ahi sashimi, sashimi trio, ahi carpaccio, noodle dishes, traditional Japanese tempura, and sauces that surprise, in creative combinations such as ginger-lime chile butter and cilantro pesto. But there's simpler fare as well, such as shrimp tempura, noodles, and wok-tossed upcountry vegetables. Desserts are not to be missed. If it's autumn, don't pass up the Granny Smith apple tart with vanilla ice cream and homemade caramel sauce. In other seasons, opt for tempura-fried ice cream with chocolate sauce. There's karaoke on Friday nights from 10pm to 1am. ***Money-saving tip:*** Eat early when specials like 25% off are offered between 5:30 and 6pm Monday to Thursday.

Queen's Market Place, Waikoloa Beach Resort. ✆ **808/886-2686.** www.sanseihawaii.com. Reservations recommended. Main courses $19–$23; sushi $3.50–$17. AE, DISC, MC, V. Daily 5:30–10pm.

NORTH KOHALA

Note: You'll find the following restaurants on the "North Kohala & Waimea" map on p. 195.

Tropical Dreams of Ice Cream

Tropical Dreams ice creams have spread out over the island, and North Kohala is where the line began. Across the street from Bamboo, **Kohala Coffee Mill and Tropical Dreams Ice Cream,** Highway 270, Hawi (✆ **808/889-5577**), serves their upscale ice creams along with sandwiches, pastries, and a selection of island coffees, including 100% Kona. The Tahitian vanilla and lychee ice creams are local legends, but we also love the macadamia nut torte and the lilikoi bars, made by a Kohala Coast pastry chef. Jams, jellies, herb vinegars, Hawaiian honey, herbal salts, and macadamia nut oils are among the gift items for sale. Residents meet here to start the day, in the afternoon for an espresso pick-me-up, and at all times in between. They are open Monday through Friday from 6:30am to 6pm, Saturday and Sunday from 7am to 5:30pm.

Bamboo ★★★ Finds PACIFIC RIM Serving fresh fish and Asian specialties in a turn-of-the-20th-century building, Hawi's self-professed "tropical saloon" is a major attraction on the island's northern coastline. The exotic interior is a nod to nostalgia, with high wicker chairs from Waikiki's historic Moana Hotel, works by local artists, and old Matson liner menus accenting the bamboo-lined walls. The fare, island favorites in sophisticated presentations, is a match for all this style: smoked pork quesadillas, fish prepared several ways, sesame nori-crusted or tequila-lime shrimp, and selections of pork, beef, and chicken. The great kids' menu features everything from buttered noodles to cheeseburgers. Produce from nearby gardens and fish fresh off the chef's own hook are among the highlights. Don't miss the Sunday brunch, when diners gather for eggs Bamboo (eggs Benedict with a lilikoi-hollandaise sauce) and the famous passion fruit margaritas. Hawaiian music wafts through the Bamboo from 7pm to closing time on weekends.

Hwy. 270, Hawi. ✆ **808/889-5555.** Kids' menu, highchairs, boosters. Reservations recommended. Main courses $10–$24 (full- and half-size portions available); kids' menu $4.95–$9.95. MC, V. Tues–Sat 11:30am–2:30pm and 6:30–9:30pm; Sun brunch 11:30am–2:30pm.

Kohala Rainbow Cafe Value GOURMET DELI This place, known for its healthful fare and made-with-care wraps, is a great stop for a picnic lunch or a quick midmorning or late-afternoon pick-me-up. Choose from fresh soups and salads, homemade sandwiches and burgers, and giant salads, but most in demand are the wraps, herb-garlic flatbread filled with local organic baby greens and vine-ripened organic tomatoes, cheese, and various fillings. If none of these items inspires your kids, there's a keiki menu (for grilled cheese fans). There are about 30 seats indoors and a few outdoors next to an art gallery with a striking mural.

Hwy. 270, Kapaau, in front of the King Kamehameha Statue. ✆ **808/889-0099.** Kids' menu, boosters, crayons. Main courses under $10; kids' menu $4. MC, V. Mon–Fri 11am–5pm.

WAIMEA

Note: You'll find the following restaurants on the "North Kohala & Waimea" map on p. 195.

Expensive

Daniel Thiebaut Restaurant ★ ASIAN/FRENCH This wonderful (but expensive) restaurant is a great family trip, but be warned: the portions are small and the bill is high. The building, the 100-year-old Chock Inn Store, is fun to wander through to see all the items from the old general store. Chef Daniel Thiebaut's menu highlights Big Island products (Kamuela Pride beef, Kahua Ranch lettuces, Hirabara Farms field greens, herbs and greens from Adaptations in South Kona) interpreted by the French-trained chef. Highlights include a greaseless, perfect duck *lumpia* (a Philippine egg roll); vegetarian spring rolls; wok-fried scallops; and fresh mahimahi in kaffir lime reduction. The kids' menu includes chicken nuggets with curly fries, fresh fish, and hamburgers. The restaurant, with a gaily lit plantation-style veranda, is full of intimate enclaves allowing all kinds of demographics, from an intimate tête-à-tête to groups of 40 or more. In the past couple of years, I've become increasingly disappointed at the alarming rise in prices and the corresponding decrease in the amount of food on my plate.

65-1259 Kawaihae Rd. (the Historic Yellow Building). ✆ **808/887-2200.** www.danielthiebaut.com. Kids' menu, highchairs, boosters. Reservations recommended. Kids' menu. Main courses $15–$49; desserts $6.95. AE, DISC, MC, V. Mon–Fri 11:30am–1:30pm; daily 3:30–9:30pm; happy hour 3:30–5:30pm. Kama'aina Sunday brunch 10am–1:30pm.

Inexpensive

Tako Taco Taqueria HEALTHY MEXICAN Once a tiny "hole in the wall," with the most delicious (and healthy) Mexican food, Tako Taco recently moved to the other side of Waimea into bigger quarters. Alas, the food is not what it once was. There is plenty of room to eat in or you can take out. Most items fall in the $6.50 to $10 range, so you can feed a family of hungry kids fairly cheaply. The fresh-fish burrito (with beans, rice, cheese, guacamole, sour cream, slaw, and salsa) is a hot deal at $8.50. There are plenty of vegetarian selections. If the Mexican chocolate chip wedding cookies are available, grab one (they're huge, and only $1 each).

64-1066 Mamalahoa Hwy., Waimea. ✆ **808/887-1717.** All items $15 and under. MC, V. Mon–Sat 11am–8:30pm. Sunday noon–8pm.

THE HAMAKUA COAST

Cafe Il Mondo ★ ESPRESSO BAR/PIZZA A tiny cafe with a big spirit has taken over the Andrade Building in the heart of Honokaa. Tropical watercolors and local art, the irresistible aromas of garlic sauces and pizzas, and a 1924 koa bar meld gracefully in Sergio and Dena Ramirez's tribute to the Old World. A classical and flamenco guitarist, Sergio occasionally plays solo guitar in his restaurant while contented drinkers tuck into the stone oven–baked pizzas. I recommend the Waipio vegetable pizza or the Sergio (pesto with marinated artichokes and mushroom). Sandwiches come cradled in fresh French, onion, or rosemary buns, all made by local bakeries. There's fresh soup daily, roasted chicken, and other specials; all greens are fresh, local, and organic.

Mamane St., Honokaa. ✆ **808/775-7711.** Boosters, crayons. Pizzas $12–$21; sandwiches $6.75–$7.50; pasta $12. No credit cards. Mon–Sat 11am–8pm.

Simply Natural ★ Value HEALTH FOOD/SANDWICH SHOP Simply Natural is a superb find on Honokaa's main street. I love this charming deli with its friendly staff, wholesome food, and vintage interior. It offers a counter and a few small tables with bright tablecloths and fresh anthuriums. The menu is wholesome, with no sacrifice in flavor: sautéed mushroom-onion sandwich, tempeh burger, and breakfast delights that include taro-banana pancakes. Even a simple vegetable-mushroom sandwich is special, made to order with grilled mushrooms and onions, luscious fresh tomato, and your choice of squaw, onion, or rosemary bread. It's a great place to get a picnic lunch.

 Mamane St., Honokaa. ✆ **808/775-0119.** Deli items $3.50–$11. No credit cards. Mon–Sat 9am–4pm. Sun 9am–1pm.

Tex Drive In & Restaurant AMERICAN/LOCAL ETHNIC Warning: Your kids will fall in love with their *malassadas*! When Ada Lamme bought the old Tex Drive In, she made significant changes, such as improving upon an ages-old recipe for Portuguese *malassadas,* cakelike doughnuts without a hole. Tex sells tens of thousands of these sugar-rolled morsels a month, including malassadas filled with pineapple/papaya preserves, pepper jelly, or Bavarian cream. The kids get their own meal (chicken nuggets, fries, and a drink for $3.75) and you can choose from ethnic specialties such as Korean chicken, teriyaki, kalua pork with cabbage, and Filipino specials. New on the menu are wraps served with homemade sweet-potato chips. With its gift shop and visitor center, Tex is a roadside attraction and a local hangout; residents have been gathering here for decades over early-morning coffee.

Hwy. 19, Honokaa. ✆ **808/775-0598.** Kids' menu, highchairs, boosters. Main courses $8–$12; kids' menu $3.75. DC, DISC, MC, V. Daily 6:30am–8pm.

HILO

Note: You'll find the following restaurants on the "Hilo" map on p. 201.

Expensive

Harrington's ★ SEAFOOD/STEAK Take the kids here for the location: on a clear rocky pool teeming with koi (carp) at Reeds Bay, which is close to the waterfront but not on it. The house specialty, thinly sliced Slavic steak swimming in butter and garlic, is part of the old-fashioned steak-and-seafood formula that makes the Harrington's experience a predictable one. The strongest feature of Harrington's is the tranquil beauty of Reeds Pond (also known as Ice Pond), one of Hilo's visual wonders. The open-air restaurant perches on the pond's shores, creating a sublime ambience. No kids' menu, but you can order smaller portions for your keiki.

135 Kalanianaole Ave. ✆ **808/961-4966.** Highchairs, boosters. Reservations recommended. Main courses $8.25–$15 lunch, from $16 to market price dinner. MC, V. Daily 11am–2pm and 5:30–9pm.

Pescatore ★ SOUTHERN ITALIAN For a special occasion, this is a good place to take the family. It's ornate, especially for Hilo, with gilded frames on antique paintings, chairs of vintage velvet, koa walls, and a tile floor. The fresh catch is offered in several preparations, including cream and Parmesan or capers and wine. Chicken, veal, fish Marsala, a rich and garlicky scampi Alfredo, and the Fra Diavolo (a spicy seafood marinara) are among the dinner offerings, which come with soup and salad. Kids get their own menu, where pizza is a star. Lighter fare, such as simple pasta marinara and chicken Parmesan, prevails at lunch.

235 Keawe St. ✆ **808/969-9090.** Kids' menu, highchairs, boosters, crayons. Reservations recommended for dinner. Main courses $5–$8 breakfast, $5–$12 lunch, $16–$29 dinner; kids' menu $4.95–$6.95. AE, DC, DISC, MC, V. Daily 11am–2pm and 5:30–9pm; Sat–Sun buffet 7:30–11am.

Moderate

Hilo Bay Café ★★★ (Finds PACIFIC RIM Foodie alert: In the midst of a suburban shopping mall is this upscale, elegant eatery, like something out of New York's SoHo. Only it's on the outskirts of Hilo and created by the people from the Island Naturals Market and Deli, located on the other side of the shopping center. The creative (and healthy) menu ranges from house-made ravioli (stuffed with Gorgonzola cheese and portobello mushrooms and topped with red pepper sauce) to potato-crusted fresh catch to grilled New York pepper steak with garlic Yukon potato purée. Lunch is made up of salads (such as blackened ahi over romaine greens), sandwiches (pastrami with Swiss), and entrees (flaky-crusted chicken or vegetarian potpies, slow-cooked pork barbecue ribs, or crispy spanakopita). Kids are welcome and given their own menu; the mac and cheese is very popular. Don't miss eating here.

Waiakea Center, 315 Makaala St. ✆ **808/935-4939.** Kids' menu, highchairs, crayons. Reservations recommended for dinner. Main courses $8–$15 lunch, $9–$30 dinner; kids' menu $5. AE, DC, DISC, MC, V. Mon–Sat 11am–9pm.

Nihon Restaurant & Cultural Center ★ JAPANESE The room offers a beautiful view of Hilo Bay on one side and the soothing green sprawl of Liliuokalani Gardens on the other. This is a magnificent part of Hilo that's often overlooked because of its location away from the central business district. The reasonably priced menu features steak-and-seafood combination dinners and selections from the sushi bar, including the innovative poke and lomi salmon hand rolls. The "Businessman's Lunch," a terrific deal, comes with sushi, potato salad, soup, vegetables, and two choices from the following: butterfish, shrimp tempura, sashimi, chicken, and other morsels. This isn't inexpensive dining, but the value is sky-high, with a presentation that matches the serenity of the room and its stunning view of the bay. Plus they are very family-friendly and their kids' menu is very low-priced.

123 Lihiwai St. (overlooking Liliuokalani Gardens and Hilo Bay). ✆ **808/969-1133.** Kids' menu, highchairs. Reservations recommended. Main courses $11–$25; combination dinner $21; kids' menu $4.50. AE, DC, DISC, MC, V. Mon–Sat 11am–1:30pm and 5–8pm.

Inexpensive

Ken's House of Pancakes AMERICAN/LOCAL This is Hilo's favorite family restaurant. The only 24-hour coffee shop on the Big Island, Ken's fulfills basic dining needs simply and efficiently, with a good dose of local color. It's sort of a Hawaii version of Denny's. Lighter servings and a concession toward health-conscious meals and salads have been added to the menu, a clever antidote to the more than a dozen pies available. Omelets, pancakes, French toast made with Portuguese sweet bread, saimin, sandwiches, and soup—what they call a "poi dog menu"—stream out of the busy kitchen. The waitresses will treat your little ones like their favorite nieces and nephews. Wednesday is prime rib night, and Sunday is the "All You Can Eat Spaghetti Night."

1730 Kamehameha Ave. ✆ **808/935-8711.** Kids' menu, boosters, sassy seats, Most items less than $8; kids' menu $2.85–$5.95. DC, DISC, MC, V. Daily 24 hr.

Miyo's JAPANESE Often cited by local publications as the island's "best Japanese restaurant," Miyo's offers home-cooked, healthy food, served in an open-air room on Wailoa Pond, where an idyll of curving footpaths and greenery fills the horizon. Kids will get a kick out of the open sliding shoji doors bordering the dining area, which are left open so you can take in the view and gaze at Mauna Kea on a clear day. There's no kids' menu, but they will do child's portions (at reduced prices) of anything on the menu, which ranges from sesame chicken and vegetable tempura to vegetarian shabu-shabu (cooked in a chafing dish at your table, then dipped in a special sauce) and noodle and seaweed dishes. Special diets (low-sodium, sugarless) are cheerfully accommodated, and no MSG is used.

In Waiakea Villas, 400 Hualani St. ✆ **808/935-2273.** Highchairs, boosters. Lunch $6.50–$11; dinner $8.50–$17; child's portions $2 off. MC, V. Mon–Sat 11am–2pm and 5:30–8:30pm.

Moments Bet You Can't Eat Just One

Hawaii Island Gourmet Products, which, under the brand Atebara Chips, has been making potato and taro- and shrimp-flavored chips in Hilo for 70 years, recently added a couple of new products that you just cannot miss: purple sweet-potato chips and the delicious sweet-potato, taro, and regular potato chips covered in chocolate (the first-place winner at the Taste of Hilo). You can find them at most stores on the Big Island (or at the major resorts on the Big Island) or contact them directly (✆ **808/969-9600;** www.hawaii chips.com). ***Warning:*** As we say in Hawaii, these chips are so *ono* (delicious) that you will be mail-ordering more when you get home.

HAWAII VOLCANOES NATIONAL PARK

Expensive

Kiawe Kitchen MEDITERANEAN/PIZZA Although it has a somewhat limited menu, this small eatery is a great place to stop for hot soup or fresh salad after viewing the volcano. The pizza is excellent (all fresh ingredients) but pricey; I recommend the insalata caprese and a bowl of soup for lunch. Dinners include lamb, pasta, a vegetarian item, and usually beef. The menu changes daily (depending on whatever they can get fresh that day). You can eat on the lanai or inside the restaurant.

19-4005 Haunani Rd., Volcano. ✆ **808/967-7711.** Main courses $9–$13 lunch, $16–$20 dinner. MC, V. Thurs–Tues noon–2:30pm. Dinner daily 5:30–9pm.

Kilauea Lodge & Restaurant ★ CONTINENTAL Diners travel long distances to escape from the crisp upland air into the warmth of this high-ceilinged lodge. The decor is a cross between chalet-cozy and volcano-rugged; the sofa in front of the 1938 fireplace is especially inviting when a fire is roaring. The European cooking is a fine culinary act on the big volcano. Favorites include the fresh catch, hasenpfeffer (rabbit stew), potato-leek soup (all flavor and no cream), and Alsatian soup. Dinners come with soup, a loaf of freshly baked bread, and salad. Kids are welcome at this family-friendly restaurant and have their own menu (not quite as European, more buttered-noodle American selections).

Hwy. 11 (Volcano Village exit). ✆ **808/967-7366.** Kids' menu, highchairs, boosters, crayons. Reservations recommended. Main courses $20–$45; kids' menu $7–$9.95. MC, V. Daily 5:30–9pm.

Moderate

Lava Rock Café ★ ECLECTIC/LOCAL This cheerful, airy oasis in knotty pine, with tables and booths indoors and semi-outdoors, under a clear corrugated-plastic ceiling, is a great place to bring the kids for breakfast, lunch, or dinner. The cross-cultural menu includes everything from chow fun to fajitas. The choices include three-egg omelets and pancakes with wonderful house-made lilikoi butter, teriyaki beef and chicken, serious desserts (lilikoi or mango cheesecake), fresh catch, T-bone steak, and steak-and-shrimp combos. The lunchtime winners are the "seismic sandwiches" (which the cafe will pack for hikers), chili, quarter-pound burgers, and a host of salads, plate lunches, and "volcanic" heavies such as Southern fried chicken and grilled meats. Pizza and chicken nuggets are the most popular items on the kids' menu.

Hwy. 11 (Volcano Village exit, next to Kilauea Kreations). ✆ **808/967-8526.** Kids' menu, highchairs, boosters, crayons. Main courses $5.50–$10 lunch, $10–$22 dinner; kids' menu $5–$7. MC, V. Sun 7:30am–4pm; Mon 7:30am–5pm; Tues–Sat 7:30am–9pm.

Inexpensive

Thai Thai Restaurant THAI Volcano's only Thai restaurant adds warming curries to the chill of upcountry life. The menu features spicy curries and rich satays; coconut-rich soups; noodles and rice; and sweet-and-sour stir-fries of fish, vegetables, beef, cashew chicken, and garlic shrimp. A big hit is the green papaya salad made with tomatoes, crunchy green beans, green onions, and a heap of raw and roasted peanuts—heat and texture and a full symphony of color, aroma, and flavor. There are five types of curries, each with its own array of choices and each quite rich with coconut milk and spices. If this is a bit too exotic for your keiki, they will whip up more comfort-food items such as chicken or noodles. As we went to press, the owners said they have plans to open for lunch.

19-4084 Old Volcano Rd. ✆ **808/967-7969.** Highchairs, boosters, crayons. Main courses $10–$26. AE, DISC, MC, V. Daily 5–9pm.

5 EXPLORING THE BIG ISLAND WITH YOUR KIDS

THE KONA COAST

GUIDED WALKING TOURS Older kids (10 and up) or kids very interested in history will be enthralled with the **Kona Historical Society**'s (✆ **808/323-2005;** www.kona historical.org) two historic walking tours. All walks must be booked in advance; call for reservations and departure locations. The 75-minute **Historic Kailua Village Walking Tour** ★ is the most comprehensive tour of the Kona coast. It takes you all around Kailua-Kona, from King Kamehameha's last seat of government to the summer palace of the Hawaiian royal family and beyond, with lots of Hawaiian history and colorful lore along the way. Tours depart from the King Kamehameha Hotel lobby Monday through Friday at 9 and 11am. Tickets are $15 for adults, $10 for children ages 5 to 12. For reservations, call ✆ **808/323-3222.**

The 1-hour **Living History Tour** takes you through the everyday life of a Japanese family on the historic Uchida Coffee Farm during the 1900s. Younger kids will love interacting with costumed interpreters as they enact life on a coffee farm. The tour is offered Monday through Friday on the hour from 10am to 2pm, at a cost of $20 for adults and $7.50 for kids ages 5 to 12. Meet at the Kona Historical Society office, 81-6551 Mamalahoa Hwy. (next to Kona Specialty Meats), Kealakekua, or call for transportation. For reservations, call ✆ **808/323-2006.**

A SELF-GUIDED DRIVING TOUR A self-guided audio tour on CD, **Big Island Audio Tour** (✆ **808/879-8800;** www.bigislandaudiotour.com), features 36 tracks of information on seeing the Big Island. Not only does it give directions to well-known sites, but it has tracks on various beaches, short hikes, and side trips, as well as information on pronouncing Hawaiian words and on Hawaiian history and culture. The cost is $20 plus $2 for shipping.

If you're interested in seeing how your morning cup of joe goes from beans to brew, get a copy of the **Coffee Country Driving Tour.** This self-guided drive will take you farm by farm through Kona's famous coffee country; it also features a fascinating history of the area, the lowdown on coffee making lingo, some insider tips on how to make a great cup, and even a recipe for Kona coffee macadamia nut chocolate-chunk pie (goes great with a cup of java). The free brochure is available at the **Big Island Visitors Bureau,** 250 Waikoloa Beach Dr., Waikoloa, HI 96738 (© **808/886-1652**).

In & Around Kailua-Kona ★★★

Ellison S. Onizuka Space Center **All ages.** If you've checked in early for your flight back home, walk the kids over to this small museum at the airport to kill an hour. There's a real moon rock and memorabilia in honor of Big Island–born astronaut Ellison Onizuka, who died in the 1986 *Challenger* space shuttle disaster. Fun displays in the museum include a gravity well, which illustrates orbital motion, and an interactive rocket-propulsion exhibit, where you can launch your own miniature space shuttle.

At Kona International Airport, Kailua-Kona. © **808/329-3441.** www.onizukaspacecenter.org. Admission $3 adults, $1 children 12 and under. Daily 8:30am–4:30pm. Parking in airport lot $2 per hour.

Hulihee Palace ★★★ **Ages 7 and up.** This two-story New England–style mansion of lava rock and coral mortar, erected in 1838 by the governor of the island of Hawaii, John Adams Kuakini, overlooks the harbor at Kailua-Kona. Plan to spend an hour touring the gracious summer home of Hawaii's royalty, making it the other royal palace in the United States (the most famous being Oahu's Iolani Palace). Now run by Daughters of Hawaii, it features many 19th-century mementos and gorgeous koa furniture. You'll get lots of background and royal lore on the guided tour. No photography is allowed.

The Palace hosts 12 **Hawaiian music and hula concerts** a year, each dedicated to a Hawaiian monarch, at 4pm on the last Sunday of the month (except June and Dec, when the performances are held in conjunction with King Kamehameha Day and Christmas).

Across the street is **Mokuaikaua Church** (© **808/329-1589**), the oldest Christian church in Hawaii. It's constructed of lava stones, but its architecture is New England–style all the way. The 112-foot steeple is still the tallest man-made structure in Kailua-Kona.

75-5718 Alii Dr., Kailua-Kona. © **808/329-1877.** www.huliheepalace.org. Admission $6 adults, $4 seniors, $1 children. Daily 9am–4pm. Daily tours held throughout the day (arrive at least 1 hr. before closing).

Kamehameha's Compound at Kamakahonu Bay ★★★ **All ages.** On the ocean side of the Kona Beach Hotel is a restored area of deep spiritual meaning to Hawaiians. This was the spot that King Kamehameha the Great chose to retreat to in 1812 after conquering the Hawaiian Islands. He stayed until his death in 1819. The king built a temple, Ahuena Heiau, and used it as a gathering place for his *kahuna* (priests) to counsel him on governing his people in times of peace. In 1820, it was on this sacred ground that Kamehameha's son Liholiho, as king, sat down to eat with his mother, Keopuolani, and Kamehameha's principal queen, Kaahumanu, thus breaking the ancient *kapu* (taboo) against eating with women; this act established a new order in the Hawaiian kingdom. Although the temple grounds are now just a third of their original size, they're still impressive. You're free to come and wander the grounds. Allow at least a half-hour to envision the days when King Kamehameha appealed to the gods to help him rule with the spirit of humanity's highest nature.

On the grounds of King Kamehameha's Kona Beach Hotel, 75-5660 Palani Rd., Kailua-Kona. © **808/329-2911.** www.konabeachhotel.com. Free admission. Daily 9am–4pm; guided tours Mon–Fri at 1:30pm.

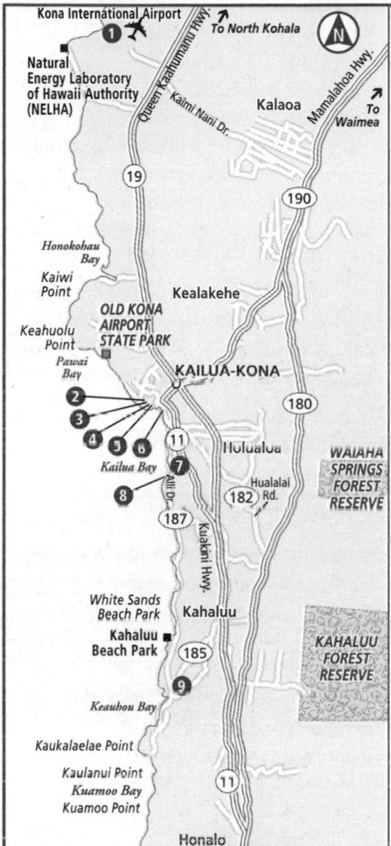

Kona International Airport
To North Kohala
Natural Energy Laboratory of Hawaii Authority (NELHA)
Queen Kaahumanu Hwy.
Kaimi Nani Dr.
Kalaoa
Mamalahoa Hwy.
To Waimea
19
190
Honokohau Bay
Kaiwi Point
Kealakehe
OLD KONA AIRPORT STATE PARK
Keahuolu Point
Pawai Bay
KAILUA-KONA
180
11
Holualoa
WAIAHA SPRINGS FOREST RESERVE
Kailua Bay
Alii Dr.
Hualalai Rd.
182
187
Kuakini Hwy.
White Sands Beach Park
Kahaluu
Kahaluu Beach Park
185
KAHALUU FOREST RESERVE
Keauhou Bay
Kaukalaelae Point
Kaulanui Point
Kuamoo Bay
Kuamoo Point
Honalo
Kainaliu
Keikiwaha Point
Nenue Point
Kealakekua
Manalahoa Hwy.
Keawekaheka Bay
Captain Cook Monument
Captain Cook
Koa Rd.
Cook Point
Kealakekua Bay State Underwater Park
Napoopoo
Kealakekua Bay
HONAUNAU FOREST RESERVE
Mokuakae Bay
Puuhonua Rd.
Moinui Point
Honaunau Bay
Honaunau
Puuhonua Point
To South Point
PUUHONUA O HONAUNAU NATIONAL HISTORICAL PARK

Waimea
Hilo
Kailua-Kona
HAWAII (The Big Island)
South Point

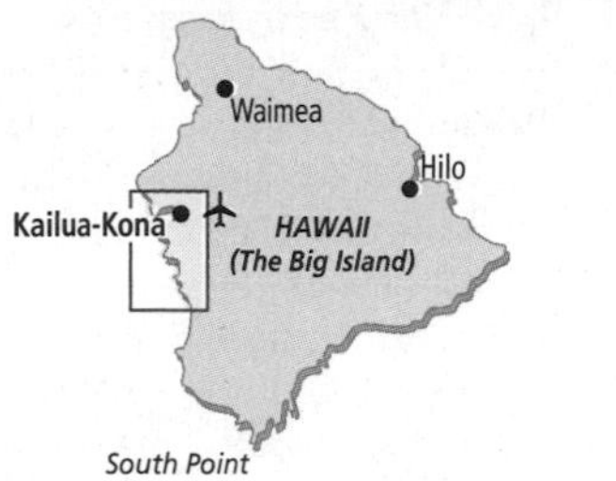

Ahuena Heaiu **2**
Aloha Theatre **10**
Coconut Grove Market Place **7**
Ellison S. Onizuka Space Center **1**
Hulihee Palace **5**
Keauhou Shopping Center **9**
Kailua Pier **4**
Kamehameha's Compound at Kamakahonou Bay **3**
Kona Historical Society Museum **11**
Mokuaikaua Church **6**
The Painted Church **12**
Puuhonua O Honaunau National Historical Park **13**
Snorkel Bob's **8**

Airport

Frommer's Favorite Big Island Family Experiences

Walking Through Thurston Lava Tube at Hawaii Volcanoes National Park (p. 207) It's scary, it's spooky, and most kids love it. You hike downhill through a rainforest full of little chittering native birds to enter this huge, silent black hole full of drips, cobwebs, and tree roots that stretch underground for almost half a mile. At the end, there's a fork in the tunnel, which leads either up a stairway to our world or—here's the best part—down an unexplored hole that probably goes all the way to China.

Going Underwater at Kealakekua Bay (p. 215) The islands have lots of extraordinary snorkel and dive sites, but none is so easily accessible or has as much to offer as mile-wide Kealakekua Bay, an uncrowded marine preserve on the south Kona coast. Here, even your little ones (as young as 3 years with a life preserver) can float through the calm waters with dolphins, sea turtles, octopuses, and every species of tropical fish that calls Hawaii's waters home.

Riding a Submarine into the Underwater World (p. 216) The huge viewing windows will have the kids enthralled as the high-tech sub leaves the surface and plunges 120 feet down through the mysterious Neptunian waters. The trip isn't too long—just an hour—and there are plenty of reef fish and prehistoric-looking corals to hold the young ones' attention.

Launching Your Own Space Shuttle (p. 188) Okay, it's a model of a space shuttle, but it's close enough to the real thing to be a real blast. The Ellison S. Onizuka Space Center has dozens of interactive displays to thrill budding young astronauts, such as a hands-on experience with gyroscopic stabilization. Great video clips of astronauts working and living in space are inspiring as well.

Hunting for Petroglyphs (p. 194) There's plenty of space to run around and discover ancient stone carvings at either the Puako Petroglyph Archaeological District at Mauna Lani Resort, or the King's Trail by the Outrigger Waikoloan. And finding the petroglyphs is only part of the game—once you find them, you have to guess what the designs mean.

Watching the Volcano (p. 208) Any kid who doesn't get a kick out of watching a live volcano set the night on fire has been watching too much television.

Upcountry Kona: Holualoa ★★★

On the slope of Hualalai volcano above Kailua-Kona sits the small village of Holualoa, which attracts travelers weary of super-resorts. Here you'll find a little art and culture—and shade.

This funky upcountry town, centered on two-lane Mamalaloa Highway, is nestled amid a lush, tropical landscape where avocados grow as big as footballs. Little more than a wide spot in the road, Holualoa is a cluster of brightly painted, tin-roofed plantation shacks, art galleries, and quaint shops. In 2 blocks, it manages to pack in two first-rate galleries, a frame shop, a potter, a glassworks, a goldsmith, an old-fashioned general store,

Take bottled water, flashlights, and sturdy shoes, and follow the ranger's instructions on where to view the lava safely. You might want to make the trip during daylight first so the kids can see the Technicolor difference in experiencing a lava flow in the dark.

Discovering Old Hawaii at Puuhonua O Honaunau National Historical Park (p. 192) Protected by a huge rock wall, this sacred Honaunau site was once a refuge for ancient Hawaiian warriors. Today, you can walk the consecrated grounds and glimpse a former way of life in a partially restored 16th-century village, complete with thatched huts, canoes, forbidding idols, and a temple that holds the bones of 23 Hawaiian chiefs.

Stargazing from Mauna Kea (p. 198) A jacket, beach mat, and binoculars are all you need to see every star and planet in this ultraclean atmosphere, where the visibility is so keen that 11 nations have set up telescopes (two of them the biggest in the world) to probe deep space.

Watching for Whales Humpback whales pass through waters off the Kona coast every December through April. To spot them from shore, head down to the Keahole National Energy Lab, just south of the Kona airport, and keep your eyes peeled as you walk the shoreline. To get here, follow Queen Kaahumanu Highway (Hwy. 19) toward the Keahole airport; 6 miles outside of town, look for the sign NATURAL ENERGY LAB, and turn left. Just after the road takes a sharp turn to the right, there's a small paved parking area with restrooms; a beach trail is on the ocean side of the lot.

Hanging Out in Waipio Valley Pack a picnic and head for this gorgeously lush valley that time forgot. Delve deep into the jungle on foot, comb the black-sand beach, or just laze the day away by a babbling stream, the tail end of a 1,000-foot waterfall.

Chasing Rainbows at Akaka Falls (p. 199) When the light is right, a perfect prism is formed and a rainbow leaps out of this spectacular 442-foot waterfall, about 11 miles north of Hilo. Take time to roam through the surrounding rainforest, where you're sure to have close encounters with exotic birds, aromatic plumeria trees, and shocking red-torch ginger.

a vintage 1930s gas station, a tiny post office, a Catholic church, and the **Kona Hotel,** a hot-pink clapboard structure that looks like a Western movie set—you're welcome to peek in, and you should.

The cool upslope village is the best place in Hawaii for a coffee break. That's because Holualoa is in the heart of the coffee belt, a 20-mile-long strip at an elevation between 1,000 and 1,400 feet, where all the Kona coffee in the world is grown in the rich volcanic soil of the cool uplands. (See "Kona Coffee Craze!" on p. 223.) Everyone's backyard seems to teem with glossy green leaves and ruby-red cherries (which contain the seeds, or beans, used to make coffee), and the air smells like a San Francisco espresso bar. The

Holuakoa Cafe, on Mamalahoa Highway (Hwy. 180) in Holualoa (© **808/322-2233**), is a great place to get a freshly brewed cup.

To reach Holualoa, follow narrow, winding Hualalai Road up the hill from Highway 19; it's about a 15-minute drive.

South Kona ★★★

Kona Historical Society Museum ★★★ Ages 10 and up. This well-organized museum is housed in the historic Greenwell Store, built in 1875 by Henry Nicholas Greenwell out of native stone and lime mortar made from burnt coral. Antiques, artifacts, and photos tell the story of this fabled coast. In less than an hour, you can tour the museum, filled with items common to everyday life here in the last century, when coffee growing and cattle raising were the main industries. Serious history buffs should sign up for one of the museum's walking tours; see "Guided Walking Tours," above.

Hwy. 11 (MM 111 and 112), Kealakekua. © **808/323-3222** or 323-2006. www.konahistorical.org. $7 adults and $3 children 5–12. Mon–Fri 10am–2pm. Parking on grassy area next to Kona Specialty Meats parking lot.

Kula Kai Caverns ★★★ Finds Ages 5 and up. Before you trudge up to Pele's volcanic eruption, take a look at her underground handiwork. Ric Elhard and Rose Herrera have explored and mapped out the labyrinth of lava tubes and caves, carved out over the past 1,000 years or so, that crisscross their property on the southwest rift zone on the slopes of Mauna Loa near South Point. As soon as you enter their thatched yurt field office (which resembles something out of an Indiana Jones movie), you know you're in for an amazing tour. Choices range from an easy half-hour walk on a well-lit underground route ($15 adults, $8 children 5–12) to a more adventuresome 2-hour caving trip ($45 adults) to a deluxe half-day exploration ($65, minimum age 12). Helmets, lights, gloves, and kneepads are all included. Sturdy shoes are recommended for caving.

Off Hwy. 11 (btw MM 79 and 78), Ocean View. © **808/929-7539.** www.kulakaicaverns.com. Tours by appointment. Half-hour tour $15 adults, $8 children 5–12; 2-hr. tour $65 adults.

The Painted Church ★ Finds All ages. The kids will get a kick out of this church filled with murals. At the turn of the century, Father John Berchman Velghe borrowed a page from Michelangelo and painted biblical scenes inside St. Benedict's Catholic Church, so the illiterate Hawaiians could visualize the white man's version of creation. Stop by for a 10-minute look-see.

Toward the ocean off Hwy. 19, on Middle Ke'ei Rd., Honaunau. © **808/328-2227.** Church always open; donations accepted.

Puuhonua O Honaunau National Historical Park ★★★ All ages. With its fierce, haunting idols, this sacred site on the black-lava Kona coast certainly looks forbidding. To ancient Hawaiians, however, it must have been a welcome sight, for Puuhonua O Honaunau served as a 16th-century place of refuge, providing sanctuary for defeated warriors and kapu violators. A great rock wall—1,000 feet long, 10 feet high, and 17 feet thick—defines the refuge where Hawaiians found safety. On the wall's north end is Hale O Keawe Heiau, which holds the bones of 23 Hawaiian chiefs. Other archaeological finds include burial sites, old trails, and a portion of an ancient village. On a self-guided tour of the 180-acre site—which has been restored to its precontact state—you can see and learn about reconstructed thatched huts, canoes, and idols, and feel the *mana* (power) of Old Hawaii. Bring a picnic lunch and swimsuits and spend the day.

A cultural festival, usually held in June, allows you to join games, learn crafts, sample Hawaiian food, see traditional hula, and experience life in the islands before outsiders

Land's End

The history of Hawaii is condensed here, at the end of 11 miles of bad road that peters out at Kaulana Bay, in the lee of a jagged, black-lava point—the **southernmost point** ★★★ of the United States. No historic marker marks the spot or gives any clue as to the geographical significance of the place. If you walk out to the very tip, beware of the big waves that lash the shore.

The nearest continental landfall is Antarctica, 7,500 miles away.

arrived in the late 1700s. Every Labor Day weekend, one of Hawaii's major outrigger canoe races starts here and ends in Kailua-Kona. Call for details on both events.

Hwy. 160 (off Hwy. 11 at MM 104), Honaunau. ✆ **808/328-2288.** www.nps.gov/puho. Admission $5 per vehicle. Visitor center daily 8am–4:30pm; park Mon–Thurs 6am–8pm, Fri–Sun 6am–11pm. From Hwy. 11, it's 3½ miles to the park entrance.

THE KOHALA COAST ★★★

Puukohola Heiau National Historic Site ★★★ **All ages.** This seacoast temple, called "the hill of the whale," is the single most imposing and dramatic structure of the ancient Hawaiians. It was built by Kamehameha I from 1790 to 1791. The temple stands 224 feet long by 100 feet wide, with three narrow terraces on the seaside and an amphitheater to view canoes. Kamehameha built this temple of sacrifice with mortarless stone after a prophet told him he would conquer and unite the islands if he did so; 4 years later, he fulfilled his kingly goal. The site also includes the house of John Young, a trusted advisor of Kamehameha, and, offshore, the submerged ruins of Hale O Ka Puni, a shrine dedicated to the shark gods. Plan on at least an hour to tour.

Hwy. 270, near Kawaihae Harbor. ✆ **808/882-7218.** www.nps.gov/puhe. Free admission, tours $2. Daily 7:30am–4pm. The visitor center is on Hwy 270; the heiau is a short walk away. The trail is closed when it's too windy, so call ahead.

Ancient Hawaiian Fishponds

Like their Polynesian forebears, Hawaiians were among the first aquaculturists on the planet. Scientists still marvel at the ways they used the brackish ponds along the shoreline to stock and harvest fish. There are actually two different types of ancient fishponds (or *loko i'a*). Closed ponds, inshore and closed off from the ocean, were used to raise mullet and milkfish, while other ponds were open to the sea, with rock walls as a barrier to the ocean and sluice gates that connected the ponds to the ocean. The gates were woven vines, with just enough room for juvenile fish to swim in at high tide while keeping the bigger, fatter fish from swimming out. Generally, the Hawaiians kept and raised mullet, milkfish, and shrimp in these open ponds; juvenile manini, papio, eels, and barracuda occasionally found their way in, too.

The **Kalahuipuaa Fish Ponds,** at Mauna Lani Resort (✆ **808/885-6622**), are great examples of both types of ponds in a lush tropical setting. South of the Mauna Lani Resort are **Kuualii** and **Kahapapa Fish Ponds,** at the Marriott Waikoloa Beach Resort (✆ **808/885-6789**). Both resorts have taken great pains to restore the ponds to their original state and to preserve them for future generations; call ahead to arrange a free guided tour.

Kohala Coast Petroglyphs

The Hawaiian petroglyph is a great enigma of the Pacific. No one knows who made them or why, only that they're here. The petroglyphs appear at 135 different sites on six inhabited islands, but most of them are found on the Big Island.

At first glance, the huge slate of pahoehoe looks like any other smooth black slate of lava on the seacoast of the Big Island—until gradually, in slanting rays of the sun, a wonderful cast of characters leaps to life before your eyes. You might see dancers and paddlers, fishermen and chiefs, hundreds of marchers all in a row. Pictures of the tools of daily life are everywhere: fish hooks, spears, poi pounders, canoes. The most common representations are family groups: father, mother, and child. There are also post–European contact petroglyphs of ships, anchors, goats, horses, and guns.

The largest concentration of these stone symbols in the Pacific lies within the 233-acre **Puako Petroglyph Archaeological District** ★, near Mauna Lani Resort. Once hard to find, the enigmatic graffiti is now easily reachable. The 1.5-mile **Malama Trail** starts north of Mauna Lani Resort; take Highway 19 to the resort turnoff and drive toward the coast on North Kaniku Drive, which ends at a parking lot; the trailhead is marked by a sign and an interpretive kiosk. Go in the early morning or late afternoon, when it's cool. Plan to stay an hour. A total of 3,000 designs have been identified, including paddlers, sails, marchers, dancers, and family groups, as well as dog, chicken, turtle, and deity symbols.

The **Kings' Shops** (✆ **808/886-8811**), at the Waikoloa Beach Resort, offers a free half-hour tour of the surrounding petroglyphs Tuesday through Friday at 10:30am and Saturday at 8:30am; it meets in front of the Food Pavilion. For the best viewing, go Saturday morning.

Visitors with disabilities, as well as others, can explore petroglyphs at **Kaupulehu Petroglyphs** ★ in the Kona Village Resort, Queen Kaahumanu Highway (✆ **808/325-5555**). Free guided tours are offered three times a week, but reservations are required (or you won't get past the gatehouse). Here you can see some of the finest images in the Hawaiian Islands. There are many petroglyphs of sails, canoes, fish, and chiefs in headdresses, plus a burial scene with three stick figures. Kite motifs—rare in rock art—similar to those found in New Zealand are also here. This is Hawaii's only ADA-accessible petroglyph trail.

Warning: The petroglyphs are thousands of years old and easily destroyed. Do not walk on them or attempt to take a "rubbing." (There's a special area in the Puako Preserve for doing so.) The best way to capture a petroglyph is with a photo in the late afternoon, when the shadows are long.

NORTH KOHALA ★★★

Lapakahi State Historical Park ★ **All ages.** This 14th-century fishing village, on a hot, dry, dusty stretch of coast, offers a glimpse into the lifestyle of the ancients. Lapakahi is the best-preserved fishing village in Hawaii. Take the self-guided, 1-mile loop trail past stone platforms, fish shrines, rock shelters, salt pans, and restored *hale* (houses) to a coral-sand beach and the deep blue sea (good snorkeling). Wear good hiking shoes or tennies; it's a hearty 45-minute walk. Go early or later in the afternoon; during most of the day the sun is hot and shade is at a premium.

Hwy. 270, Mahukona. ✆ **808/889-5566.** Free admission. Daily 8am–4pm. Guided tours by appointment.

Mo'okini Luakini Heiau ★★★ Moments **All ages.** On the coast where King Kamehameha the Great was born stands Hawaii's oldest, largest, and most sacred religious site, now a National Historic Landmark—the 1,500-year-old Mo'okini Heiau, used by kings

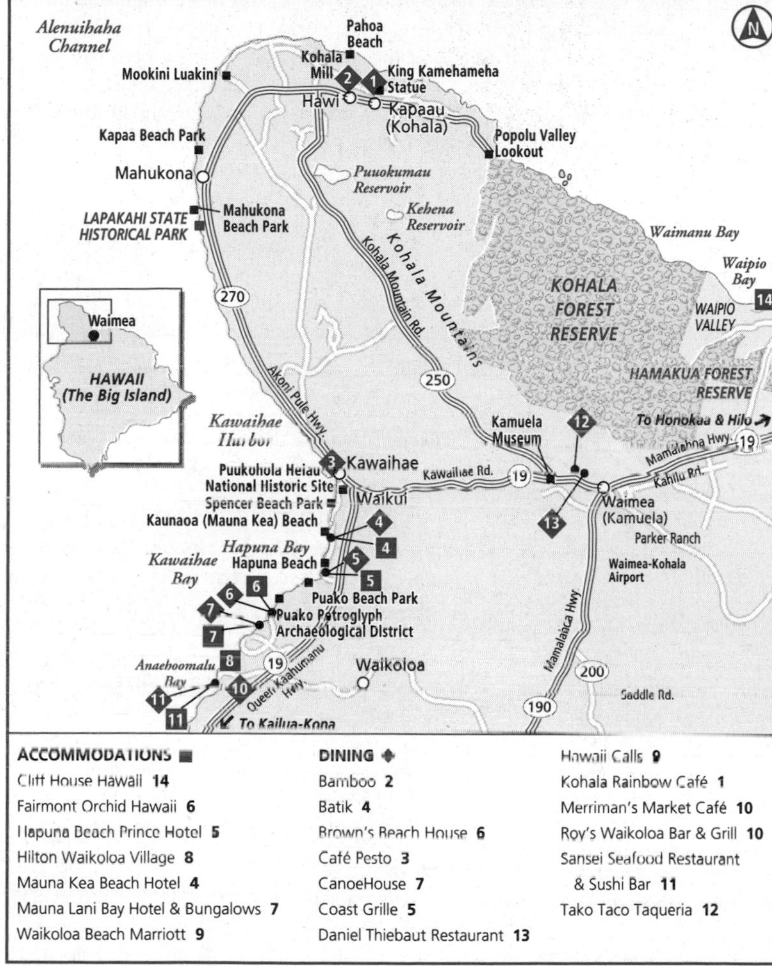

to pray and offer human sacrifices. The massive three-story stone temple, dedicated to Ku, the Hawaiian god of war, was erected in A.D. 480; each stone is said to have been passed hand to hand from Pololu Valley, 14 miles away, by 18,000 men who worked from sunset to sunrise. Kamehameha, born nearby under Halley's Comet, sought spiritual guidance here before embarking on his campaign to unite Hawaii. The temple is not open to the public, but you can see it on the third Saturday of the month, when a group of volunteers meets at the site to pull weeds and clean up property surrounding the temple. If you are interested, call the Mo'okini Preservation Foundation Oahu at ✆ **808/373-8000;** be prepared to do some work.

On the north shore, near Upolu Point Airport.

The Original King Kamehameha Statue ★★★ All ages. It's worth a 5-minute stop to see the statue of the leader who united the Hawaiian Islands. There's one just like it in Honolulu, across the street from Iolani Palace, but this is the original: an 8-foot, 6-inch bronze by Thomas R. Gould, a Boston sculptor. It was cast in Europe in 1880 but was lost at sea on its way to Hawaii. A sea captain eventually recovered and returned the statue, which was finally placed here, near Kamehameha's Kohala birthplace, in 1912.

Kamehameha was born in 1750, became ruler of Hawaii in 1810, and died in Kailua-Kona in 1819. His burial site remains a mystery.

Hwy. 270, Kapaau.

Pololu Valley Lookout ★★★ All ages. At this end-of-the-road scenic lookout, you can gaze at the vertical jade-green cliffs of the Hamakua coast and two islets offshore. The view may look familiar once you get here—it often appears on travel posters. Most people race up, jump out, take a snapshot, and turn around and drive off; but it's a beautiful scene, so linger if you can. For the more adventurous, a switchback trail leads to a secluded black-sand beach at the mouth of a wild valley once planted in taro; bring water and bug spray.

At the end of Hwy. 270, Makapala.

Pua Mau Place Kids Perched on the sun-kissed western slopes of the Kohala Mountains and dotted with deep, craggy ravines, lies one of Hawaii's most unusual botanical gardens: Pua Mau Place, a 45-acre oasis with breathtaking views of both the ocean and the majestic mountains. It's dedicated to plants that are "ever blooming," an expansive collection of continuously flowering tropical flowers, trees, and shrubs. The gardens also have an aviary of exotic birds and a unique hibiscus maze planted with some 200 varieties of hibiscus. This is a great place for families (children are invited to feed the birds in the aviary). Visitors can take the self-guided tour (along with a booklet filled with the names and descriptions of all the plants) along mulched pathways meandering through the gardens, where every plant is clearly marked.

10 Ala Kahua, Kawaihae. ✆ **808/882-0888.** www.puamau.com. Admission $10 adults, $8 seniors and students, free for children 12 and under. Daily 9am–4pm. Located off Hwy. 270 on Ala Kahua Dr. (in Kohala Estates) just north of Kawaihae. Turn at the 6-mile marker, 1/2 mile up the hill to the gate at a lava rock wall.

WAIMEA (KAMUELA) ★★★

Parker Ranch ★ All ages. The *paniolo* (cowboy) tradition began here in 1809, when John Parker, a 19-year-old New England sailor, jumped ship and rounded up wild cows for King Kamehameha. There's some evidence that Hawaiian cowboys were the first to be taught by the great Spanish horsemen, the *vaqueros;* they were cowboying 40 years before their counterparts in California, Texas, and the Pacific Northwest. The Parker Ranch, after six generations of cowboys, is smaller today than in its glory, but it still is a working ranch. Some 12 cowboys work 250 horses and 30,000 to 35,000 head of cattle on 200,000 acres.

The **Visitor Center,** located at the Parker Ranch Shopping Center on Highway 190 (✆ **808/885-7655**), is open daily from 9am to 5pm and houses the **Parker Ranch Museum,** which displays items that have been used throughout the ranch's history, dating from 1847, and illustrates six generations of Parker family history. An interesting video takes you inside the ranch and captures the essence of day-to-day life when it was a working ranch. Allow an hour or so to really see the museum.

You can also tour two historic homes on the ranch. In 1989, the late Richard Smart—the sixth-generation heir who sought a career on Broadway—opened his 8,000-square-foot yellow Victorian home, **Puuopelu,** to art lovers. The French Regency gallery here includes original works by Renoir, Degas, Dufy, Corot, Utrillo, and Pissarro. Next door is **Mana Hale,** a little New England saltbox built from koa wood 140 years ago.

If you want to get out and see the ranch itself, a 45-minute narrated **Kohala Carriage Tour** (Tues–Sat) takes place in an old-fashioned wagon—pulled by two large Belgian draft horses—with seating for 20, roll-down protection from the elements, and warm blankets for the upcountry temperatures. The tour rolls past ancient Hawaiian artifacts, 19th-century stone corrals (still in use), and miles of vast rolling hills; it stops at a working cowboy station, where visitors can get out, take photos, and stretch their legs.

Parker Ranch Center, Waimea. ✆ **808/885-7655** for visitor center. www.parkerranch.com. Admission to museum $7 adults, $4.50 children 11 and under; tour of ranch homes $8.50 adults, $6 children; Kohala Carriage Tour $15 adults, $12 children. Visitor center and museum Mon–Sat 9am–5pm. If you're seeing the museum only, you can arrive as late as 4pm; the last museum/ranch homes tickets are sold at 4pm; the final museum/carriage tour tickets are sold at 2pm.

MAUNA KEA ★★★

If you have a teenager, plan to tour Mauna Kea's summit, the tallest mountain (when measured from its base) in the world and also the best place on earth for astronomical observations. (The skies are clear and pollution free, and nights are pitch-black with no urban light to interfere.) That's why Mauna Kea is home to the world's largest telescope. Needless to say, the stargazing from here is fantastic, even with the naked eye. Allow about 6 hours to drive to the summit and time to get out and see the stars.

SETTING OUT You'll need a four-wheel-drive vehicle to climb to the peak, **Observatory Hill.** A standard car will get you as far as the visitor center, but check your rental agreement before you go; some agencies prohibit you from taking your car on the Saddle Road, which is narrow and rutted, and has a soft shoulder.

SAFETY TIPS Always check the weather and Mauna Kea road conditions before you head out (✆ **808/969-3218**). Dress warmly; the temperatures drop into the 30s after dark. To avoid dehydration, drink as much liquid as possible, avoiding alcohol and coffee, in the 36 hours surrounding your trip. Don't go within 24 hours of scuba diving—you could get the bends. The day before you go, avoid gas-producing foods, such as beans, cabbage, onions, soft drinks, or starches. If you smoke, take a break for 48 hours to allow the carbon monoxide in your bloodstream to dissipate—you need all the oxygen you can get. Wear dark sunglasses to avoid snow blindness, and use lots of sunscreen and lip balm. Pregnant women and anyone 12 and under or with a heart condition or lung ailment are advised to stay below. Once you're at the top, don't overexert yourself; it's bad for your heart. Take it easy up here.

ACCESS POINTS & VISITOR CENTERS Before you climb the mountain, you've got to find it. It's about an hour from Hilo or Waimea to the visitor center and another 30 to 45 minutes from here to the summit. Take the Saddle Road (Hwy. 200) from Highway 190; it's about 19 miles to Mauna Kea State Recreation Area, a good place to stop and stretch your legs. Go another 9 miles to the unmarked Summit Road turnoff, at mile marker 28 (about 9,300 ft.), across from the Hunter's Check-in Station. The higher you go, the more lightheaded you get, sometimes even dizzy; this usually sets in after the 9,600-foot marker (about 6¼ miles up Summit Rd.), the site of the last comfort zone and the **Onizuka Center for International Astronomy Visitor Information Station**

Moments Experiencing Where the Gods Live

"The ancient Hawaiians thought of the top of Mauna Kea as heaven, or at least where the gods and goddess lived," according to Monte "Pat" Wright, owner and chief guide of **Mauna Kea Summit Adventures.** Wright, the first guide to take people up to the top of the Mauna Kea, the world's tallest mountain when measured from the base and an astonishing 13,796 feet when measured from the sea, says he fell in love with this often-snowcapped peak the first time he saw it.

Mauna Kea Summit Adventures offers a luxurious trip to the top of the world. The 7- to 8-hour adventure actually begins mid-afternoon with pickup along the Kona-Kohala coast in a custom Ford four-wheel-drive, turbo-diesel van. After a dinner of gourmet sandwiches, vegetarian onion soup, and hot chocolate, coffee, or tea, everyone climbs back into the van for the half-hour ride to the summit.

Arriving in time to catch the sun sinking into the Pacific nearly 14,000 feet below, the guide points out the various world-renowned telescopes as the observatories open and the high-tech, multimirrored telescopes rotate into position for night viewing. After the last trace of sunset color has disappeared from the sky, the tour again descends to midmountain, where the climate is more agreeable, for stargazing.

Pregnant woman, children 12 and under, and obese people should not travel to the summit due to the decreased oxygen. Because the roads to the summit are bumpy, anyone with a bad back might want to reconsider the trip.

The cost for this celestial adventure is $197 (15% discounted if you book online at www.maunakea.com 2 weeks in advance). For more information, call ✆ **888/322-2366** or 808/322-2366.

(✆ **808/961-2180;** www.ifa.hawaii.edu/info/vis). Named in memory of Hawaii's fallen astronaut, a native of the Big Island and a victim of the *Challenger* explosion, the center is open daily from 9am to 10pm.

Every night from 6 to 10pm, you can do some serious **stargazing** from the Onizuka Visitor Center. There's a free lecture at 6pm, followed by a video, a question-and-answer session, and your chance to peer through 11-inch, 14-inch, and 16-inch telescopes. Bring a snack and, if you've got them, your own telescope or binoculars, along with a flashlight (with a red filter). Dress for 30° to 40°F (–1° to 4°C) temperatures, but call for the weather report first (✆ **808/961-5582**).

THE HAMAKUA COAST ★★★

The rich history of 117 years of the sugar industry, along the scenic 45-mile coastline from Hilo to Hamakua, comes alive in the interpretive *Hilo-Hamakua Heritage Coast* drive guide, produced by the **Hawaii Island Economic Development Board,** 200 Kanoelehua Ave., Suite 103, Hilo, HI 96720 (✆ **808/966-5416**).

The free guide not only points out the historic sites and museums, scenic photo opportunities, restaurants and stores, and even restrooms along the Hawaii Belt Road (Hwy. 19), but has corresponding brown-and-white points-of-interest signs on the highway. Visitor information centers anchored at either end in Hilo and in Hamakua offer additional information on the area.

Natural Wonders Along the Coast

Akaka Falls ★★★ All ages. In about a half-hour you can see one of Hawaii's most scenic waterfalls via an easy, 1-mile paved loop through a rainforest, past bamboo and ginger, and down to an observation point. You'll have a perfect view of 442-foot Akaka Falls and nearby Kahuna Falls (a mere 100 ft.). Keep your eyes peeled for rainbows.

On Hwy. 19, Honomu (8 miles north of Hilo). Turn left at Honomu and head 3½ miles inland on Akaka Falls Rd. (Hwy. 220).

Hawaii Tropical Botanical Garden ★★★ All ages. Spend a couple of hours among more than 1,800 species of tropical plants in this little-known Eden by the sea. The 40-acre garden, nestled between the crashing surf and a thundering waterfall, has the world's largest selection of tropical plants growing in a natural environment, including a torch ginger forest, a banyan canyon, an orchid garden, a banana grove, a bromeliad hill, and a golden bamboo grove, which rattles like a jungle drum in the trade winds. The torch gingers tower on 12-foot stalks. Each spectacular specimen is named by genus and species, and caretakers point out new or rare buds in bloom. Some endangered Hawaiian specimens, such as the rare *Gardenia remyi,* are flourishing in this habitat. The gardens are seldom crowded; you can wander around by yourself all day.

Off Hwy. 19 on the 4-mile Scenic Route, Onomea Bay (8 miles north of Hilo). ✆ **808/964-5233.** www.htbg.com. Admission $15 adults, $5 children 6–16. Daily 9am–5pm.

World Botanical Gardens ★★★ All ages. Just north of Hilo is Hawaii's largest botanical garden in the state, on 300 acres of former sugar cane land, with some 5,000 species and still growing. When the fruit are in season, they hand out free chilled juices. One of the most spectacular sites is the .25-mile rainforest walk, which is also wheelchair accessible, along a stream on a path lined with flowers, to the viewing area of the three-tiered, 300-foot Umauma Falls. Parents will appreciate the children's maze, nearly the size of a football field, where the "prize" is a playing field near the exit. The mock orange hedge, which defines the various paths in the maze, is only 5 feet tall, so most parents can peer over the edge to keep an eye on their keiki. There's also a Hawaii wellness garden with medicinal Hawaiian plants, an ethno-botanical garden, an arboretum, and a phylogenetic garden with various plants and trees arranged in roughly the same sequence they first appeared on earth. You could spend a day here but it's more likely that after a couple of hours, your kids will be ready to leave. If your kids are old enough and interested, there's a tour with lunch (dessert is a sampling of the Garden's fresh fruit).

Off Hwy. 19 (near MM 16) in Umauma. ✆ **808/963-5427.** www.worldbotanicalgardens.com. Admission $13 adults, $6 teens 13–17, $3 children 5–12, free for children 4 and under; guided tours $40 adults, $30 teens, $20 children. Mon–Sat 9am–5:30pm.

The End of the Road: Waipio Valley ★★★

Long ago, this lush, tropical place was the valley of kings, who called it the valley of "curving water" (which is what *Waipio* means). From the black-sand bay at its mouth, Waipio sweeps back 6 miles between sheer, cathedral-like walls that reach almost a mile high. Here, 40,000 Hawaiians lived amid taro, red bananas, and wild guavas in an area etched by streams and waterfalls. Only about 50 Hawaiians live in the valley today, tending taro, fishing, and soaking up the ambience of this old Hawaiian place.

Many of the ancient royals are buried in Waipio's hidden crevices; some believe they rise up to become Marchers of the Night, whose chants reverberate through the valley. It's here that the caskets of Hawaiian chiefs Liloa and Lono Ika Makahiki, recently stolen from Bishop Museum, are believed to have been returned by Hawaiians. The sacred valley is steeped in myth and legend, some of which you may hear—usually after dark in the company of Hawaiian elders.

To get to Waipio Valley, take Highway 19 from Hilo to Honokaa, then Highway 240 to **Waipio Valley Lookout ★★★**, a grassy park on the edge of Waipio Valley's sheer cliffs with splendid views of the wild oasis below. This is a great place for a picnic; you can sit at old redwood picnic tables and watch the white combers race on the black-sand beach at the mouth of Waipio Valley.

From the lookout, you can hike down into the valley. Do not, I repeat, ***do not*** attempt to drive your rental car down into the valley (even if you see someone else doing it). The problem is not so much going down as coming back up. Every day, rental cars have to be "rescued" and towed back up to the top, at great expense to the driver. Instead, take the **Waipio Valley Shuttle** (**✆ 808/775-7121**) on a 90-minute guided tour. The shuttle runs Monday through Saturday from 9am to 4pm; tickets are $45 for adults, $20 for children 11 and under. Get your tickets at **Waipio Valley Art Works,** on Highway 240, 2 miles from the lookout (**✆ 808/775-0958**).

You can also explore the valley on a narrated, 90-minute **Waipio Valley Wagon Tour** (**✆ 808/775-9518;** www.waipiovalleywagontours.com), a historical ride by mule-drawn surrey. Tours are offered Monday through Saturday at 9:30am, 11:30am, 1:30pm, and 3:30pm. It costs $55 for adults, $50 for seniors, $25 for children ages 4 to 12; call for reservations.

HILO ★★★

Contact or stop by the **Downtown Hilo Improvement Association,** 252 Kamehameha Ave., Hilo, HI 96720 (**✆ 808/935-8850;** www.downtownhilo.com), for a copy of its very informative self-guided walking tour of 18 historic sites in Hilo, focusing on various sites from the 1870s to the present.

On the Waterfront

Old banyan trees shade **Banyan Drive ★★★**, the lane that curves along the waterfront to the Hilo Bay hotels. Most of the trees were planted in the mid-1930s by memorable visitors such as Cecil B. DeMille (who was here in 1933 filming *Four Frightened People*), Babe Ruth (his tree is in front of Hilo Hawaiian Hotel), King George V, and Amelia Earhart, but many were planted by celebrities whose fleeting fame didn't last as long as the trees themselves.

It's worth a stop along Banyan Drive—especially if the coast is clear and the summit of Mauna Kea is free of clouds—to make the short walk across the concrete-arch bridge in front of the Naniloa Hotel to **Coconut Island ★**, if only to gain a panoramic sense of the place.

Also along Banyan Drive is **Liliuokalani Gardens ★★★**, the largest formal Japanese garden this side of Tokyo. This 30-acre park, named for Hawaii's last monarch, Queen Liliuokalani, is as pretty as a postcard from the East, with bonsai, carp ponds, pagodas, and a moon-gate bridge. Admission is free; it's open 24 hours.

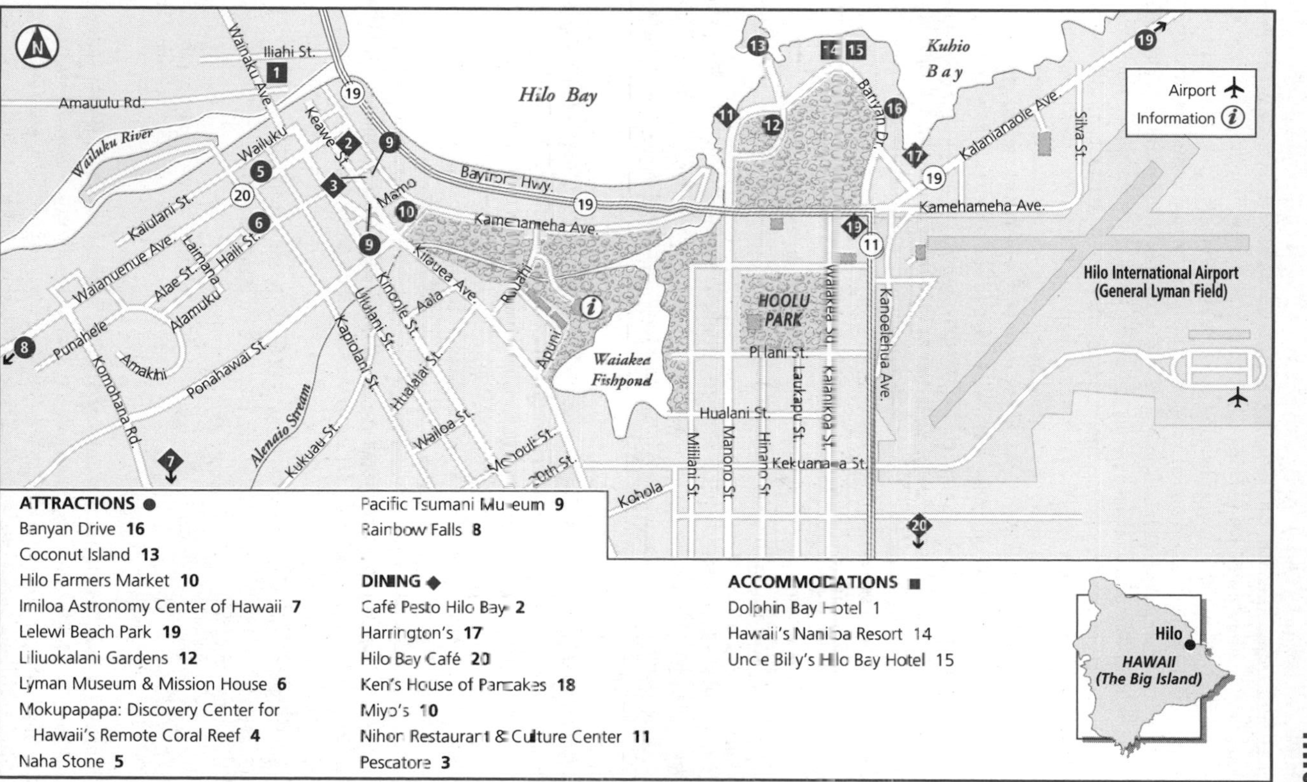
Hilo Bay
Kuhio Bay
Airport
Information
Hilo International Airport (General Lyman Field)
HOOLU PARK
Waiakea Fishpond
Wailuku River
Alenaio Stream
Amauulu Rd.
Iliahi St.
Wainaku Ave.
Keawe St.
Wailuku
Kaiulani St.
Waianuenue Ave.
Laimana
Haili St.
Alae St.
Alamuku
Punahele
Amakihi
Komohana Rd.
Ponahawai St.
Kukuau St.
Kapiolani St.
Ululani St.
Kinoole St.
Aala
Kilauea Ave.
Hualalai St.
Waikoa St.
Mamo
Bayfront Hwy.
Kamehameha Ave.
Pauahi
Apuni
Manono St.
Mililani St.
Hinano St.
Laukapu St.
Kalanikoa St.
Waiakea St.
Pilani St.
Hualani St.
Kekuanaoa St.
Kohola
20th St.
Kanoelehua Ave.
Banyan Dr.
Kalanianaole Ave.
Silva St.
Hilo
HAWAII (The Big Island)
ATTRACTIONS
Banyan Drive 16
Coconut Island 13
Hilo Farmers Market 10
Imiloa Astronomy Center of Hawaii 7
Lelewi Beach Park 19
Liliuokalani Gardens 12
Lyman Museum & Mission House 6
Mokupapapa: Discovery Center for Hawaii's Remote Coral Reef 4
Naha Stone 5
Pacific Tsunami Museum 9
Rainbow Falls 8
DINING
Café Pesto Hilo Bay 2
Harrington's 17
Hilo Bay Café 20
Ken's House of Pancakes 18
Miyo's 10
Nihon Restaurant & Culture Center 11
Pescatore 3
ACCOMMODATIONS
Dolphin Bay Hotel 1
Hawaii's Naniloa Resort 14
Uncle Billy's Hilo Bay Hotel 15

Other Hilo Sights

Imiloa Astronomy Center of Hawaii★★★ **All ages.** Do not miss this incredible planetarium/museum; it will be the highlight of Hilo. Perched high on a hill, overlooking Hilo Bay, titanium cones, representing the volcanoes of the Big Island, rise majestically, just outside of the University of Hawaii's Science and Technology Park. Even the landscaping of the 9-acre property is spectacular, featuring the largest and most diverse collections of native and Hawaiian "canoe" plants (plants the Polynesians brought with them on their canoes). Everything means something, even this landscaping: mimicking the vegetation of the different elevations as you travel from the ocean to the top of Mauna Kea. Inside of the 12,000-square-foot gallery, the 300 interactive exhibits weave the science of astronomy with the Hawaiian culture and describe the story of human exploration of the skies and the ocean. The name of the center, *imiloa* means explorer or seeker of the truth. Make sure you schedule your trip to correspond to one of the shows at the planetarium, which has a state-of-the-art digital projection and sound system. Your kids will want to stay here for hours; allow at least a half-day to really explore and play with all the exhibits. There's a cafe on-site so you can plan to eat lunch here.

600 Imiloa Place, Hilo. ✆ **808/969-9700.** www.imiloahawaii.org. Admission $18 adults, $9.50 children 4–12. Tues–Sat 9am–4pm.

Lyman Museum ★ **Ages 6 and up.** The oldest wood-frame house on the island was built in 1839 by David and Sarah Lyman, a missionary couple who arrived from New England in 1832. This hybrid combined New England– and Hawaiian-style architecture and is built of hand-hewn koa planks and native timbers. Here, the Lymans received such guests as Mark Twain and Hawaii's monarchs. The well-preserved house is the best example of missionary life and times in Hawaii. You'll find lots of artifacts from the last century, including furniture and clothing from the Lymans and one of the first mirrors in Hawaii.

Allow a couple of hours to visit not only the Museum, but also the **Earth Heritage Gallery** in the complex next door. Here the story of the islands continues with geology and volcanology exhibits, a mineral rock collection that's rated one of the best in the country, and a section on local flora and fauna. The **Island Heritage Gallery** features displays on Hawaiian culture, including a replica of a grass hale, as well as on other cultures transplanted to Hawaii's shores. A special exhibit gallery features changing exhibits on the history, art, and culture of Hawaii.

276 Haili St. (at Kapiolani St.), Hilo. ✆ **808/935-5021.** www.lymanmuseum.org. Admission $10 adults, $8 seniors 61 and over, $3 children 6–17, $21 family. Mon–Sat 9:30am–4:30pm; guided tours 11am, 1pm, and 3pm.

Maunaloa Macadamia Nut Factory **All ages.** Spend a half-hour exploring this unique factory and learn how Hawaii's favorite nut is grown and processed. And, of course, you'll want to sample the tasty mac nuts, too.

Macadamia Nut Rd. (8 miles from Hilo, off Hwy. 11), Hilo. ✆ **808/966-8618.** www.maunaloa.com. Free admission; self-guided factory tours. Daily 8:30am–5pm. From Hwy. 11, turn on Macadamia Nut Rd.; go 3 miles down the road to the factory.

Mokupapapa: Discovery Center for Hawaii's Remote Coral Reef **Ages 6 and up.** This 4,000-square-foot center is perfect for kids, who can explore the Northwest Hawaiian Islands coral reef ecosystem. Through interactive displays, engaging three-dimensional models, and an immersion theater, the kids can learn natural science, culture, and history while having a great time. A 2,500-gallon saltwater aquarium provides a habitat for a collection of fish from the Northwest Hawaiian Islands reefs. Lots of fun at a terrific price: free.

308 Kamehameha Ave., Suite 109, Hilo. ✆ **808/933-8198.** www.hawaiireef.noaa.gov/center/welcome.html. Free admission. Tues–Sat 9am–4pm.

Naha Stone **All ages.** Make a quick 10-minute stop at this 2¹/₂-ton stone, which was used as a test of royal strength: Ancient legend said that whoever could move the stone would conquer and unite the islands. As a 14-year-old boy, King Kamehameha the Great moved the stone—and later fulfilled his destiny. The Pinao stone, next to it, once guarded an ancient temple.

In front of Hilo Public Library, 300 Waianuenue Ave.

Pacific Tsunami Museum ★ **Ages 7 and above.** Oddly enough, preteen boys love this museum. Volunteers who survived Hawaii's most deadly "walls of water" in 1946 and 1960, both of which reshaped the town of Hilo, tell their stories of terror as they walk you through a range of exhibits, from interactive computers to a children's section to a display on what happens when a local earthquake triggers a seismic wave, as it did in 1975 during the Big Island's last tsunami. Plan at least an hour here.

130 Kamehameha Ave., Hilo. ✆ **808/935-0926.** www.tsunami.org. Admission $7 adults, $6 seniors, $2 students and children. Mon–Sat 9am–4pm.

Panaewa Rainforest Zoo ★ **All ages.** This 12-acre zoo, nestled in the heart of the Panaewa Forest Reserve south of Hilo, is the only outdoor rainforest zoo in the United States. Some 50 species of animals from rainforests around the globe call Panaewa home—including several endangered Hawaiian birds. All of them are exhibited in a natural setting. This is one of the few zoos where you can observe Sumatran tigers, Brazilian tapirs, and the rare pygmy hippopotamus, an endangered "minihippo" found in Western Africa. Plan to spend a couple of hours and bring a picnic lunch.

Stainback Hwy. (off Hwy. 11), Hilo. ✆ **808/959-7224.** www.hilozoo.com. Free admission. Daily 9am–4pm; petting zoo Sat 1:30–2:30pm; tiger feeding daily 3:30pm.

Rainbow Falls ★ Moments **All ages.** Go in the morning, around 9 or 10am, just as the sun comes up over the mango trees, to see Rainbow Falls at its best. If it's not raining, within 10 minutes the 80-foot falls, spilling into a big round natural pool surrounded by wild ginger, should spawn a vivid rainbow. According to legend, Hina, the mother of Maui, lives in the cave behind the falls. In the old days, before liability suits and lawyers, people swam in the pool, but that's now prohibited.

West on Waianuenue Ave., past Kaumana Dr.

HAWAII VOLCANOES NATIONAL PARK ★★★

Yellowstone, Yosemite, and other national parks are spectacular, no doubt about it. But in my opinion, they're all ho-hum compared to this one: Here, nothing less than the miracle of creation is the daily attraction.

In the 19th century, before tourism became Hawaii's middle name, the islands' singular attraction for world travelers wasn't the beach, but the volcano. From the world over, curious spectators gathered on the rim of Kilauea's Halemaumau crater to see one of the greatest wonders of the globe. Nearly a century after it was named a national park (in 1916), Hawaii Volcanoes remains the state's premier natural attraction.

Hawaii Volcanoes has the only rainforest in the U.S. National Park system—and it's the only park that's home to an active volcano. Most people drive through the park (it has 50 miles of good roads, some of them often covered by lava flows) and call it a day. But it takes at least 3 days to explore the whole park, including such not-to-be missed oddities as **Halemaumau Crater,** a still-fuming pit of steam and sulfur; the intestinal-looking **Thurston Lava Tube; Devastation Trail,** a short hike through a desolated area destroyed by lava; and, finally, the end of **Chain of Craters Road,** where lava regularly spills across the man-made two-lane blacktop to create its own red-hot freeway to the sea. In addition to some of the world's weirdest landscapes, the park also has hiking trails, rainforests, campgrounds, a historic old hotel on the crater's rim, and that spectacular, still-erupting volcano.

NOTES ON THE ERUPTING VOLCANO In Hawaii, volcanoes aren't violent killers like Mount Pinatubo in the Philippines or even Mount St. Helens in Washington State. Volcanologists refer to Hawaii's volcanic eruptions as "quiet" eruptions, because gases escape slowly instead of building up and exploding violently all at once. Hawaii's eruptions produce slow-moving, oozing lava that provides excellent, safe viewing most of the time. In Hawaii, people run to volcanoes instead of fleeing from them.

Since the current eruption of Kilauea began on January 3, 1983, lava has covered some 16,000 acres of lowland and rainforest, threatening rare hawks, honeycreeper birds, spiders, and bats, while destroying power and telephone lines and eliminating water service possibly forever. Some areas have been mantled repeatedly and are now buried underneath 80 feet of lava.

The most prominent vent of the eruption has been Puu Oo, a 760-foot-high cinder-and-spatter cone. The most recent flow—the one you'll be able to see, if you're lucky—follows a 7-mile-long tube from the Puu Oo vent area to the sea. This lava flow has extended the Big Island's shoreline seaward and added hundreds of acres of new land along the steep southern slopes. Periodically, the new land proves unstable, falls under its own weight, and slides into the ocean. (These areas of ground gained and lost are not included in the tally of new acreage—only the land that sticks counts.)

In addition to the nearly continuous eruption of Kilauea, in 2008, Pele again erupted but in a different spot—inside the main Halema'uma'u Crater in the Hawaii Volcanoes National Park. This was a very different **volcano eruption** from the past, which generally have been curtains of fire with lava shooting several hundred feet into the air and then slowly rolling down the side of the volcano, into the ocean. The 2008 eruption from Halema'uma'u was different: the earth shook; rocks, some the size of Volkswagens, were thrown into the air; and a pink ash was spit into the sky and rained back to earth, covering nearby communities. The March 2008 episode also raised the level of hazardous sulfur dioxide to the point that the County of Hawaii's Civil Defense Department put out a **brochure** (available online, http://co.hawaii.hi.us/cd/emissions_brochure.pdf) on the color-coded warning system on how safe it is to venture into the park to view the volcano. The county also put out a lava viewing safety card (www.lavainfo.us/Kalapana SafetyInsert.pdf), which should be read before you decide to take in this once-in-a-lifetime opportunity to see the earth being created.

Scientists are also keeping an eye on Mauna Loa, which has been swelling since its last eruption in 1983. If there's a new eruption, there could be a fast-moving flow down the southwest side of the island, possibly into South Kona or Kau.

WHAT YOU'RE LIKELY TO SEE With luck, the volcano will still be streaming rivers of red lava when you visit the park, but a continuous eruption of this length (more than 2 decades) is setting new ground, so to speak. Kilauea continues to perplex volcanologists, because most major eruptions in the past have ended abruptly after only several months.

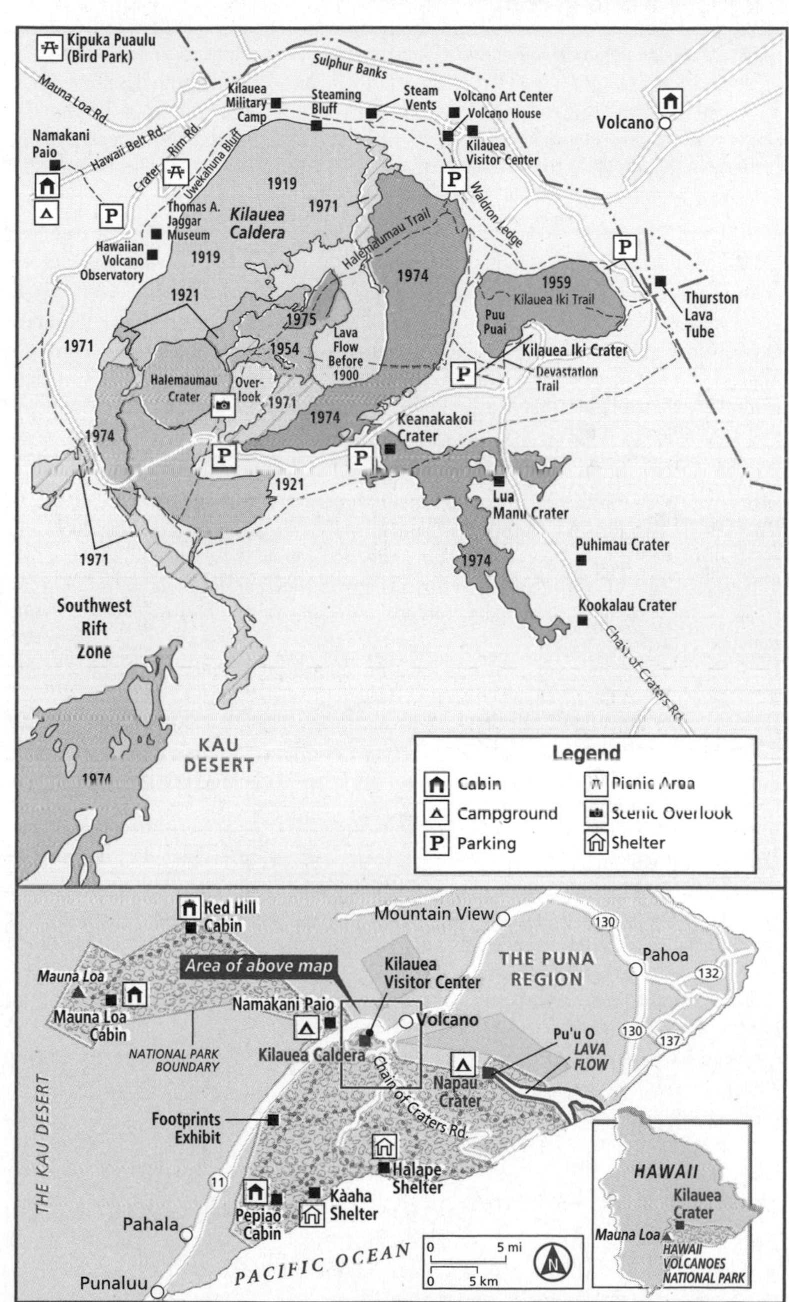
Kipuka Puaulu (Bird Park)
Sulphur Banks
Mauna Loa Rd.
Kilauea Military Camp
Steaming Bluff
Steam Vents
Volcano Art Center
Volcano House
Kilauea Visitor Center
Volcano
Namakani Paio
Hawaii Belt Rd.
Crater Rim Rd.
Uwekahuna Bluff
Thomas A. Jaggar Museum
Hawaiian Volcano Observatory
Kilauea Caldera
Halemaumau Trail
Waldron Ledge
Kilauea Iki Trail
Puu Puai
Kilauea Iki Crater
Thurston Lava Tube
Devastation Trail
Halemaumau Crater
Over-look
Lava Flow Before 1900
Keanakakoi Crater
Lua Manu Crater
Puhimau Crater
Kookalau Crater
Chain of Craters Rd.
Southwest Rift Zone
KAU DESERT
1919
1971
1974
1959
1921
1975
1954
Legend
Cabin
Campground
Parking
Picnic Area
Scenic Overlook
Shelter
Red Hill Cabin
Mountain View
Area of above map
Kilauea Visitor Center
THE PUNA REGION
Pahoa
Mauna Loa
Mauna Loa Cabin
Namakani Paio
Volcano
NATIONAL PARK BOUNDARY
Kilauea Caldera
Pu'u O LAVA FLOW
Napau Crater
THE KAU DESERT
Footprints Exhibit
Halape Shelter
Kàaha Shelter
Pepiao Cabin
Pahala
Punaluu
PACIFIC OCEAN
0 5 mi
0 5 km
HAWAII
Kilauea Crater
HAWAII VOLCANOES NATIONAL PARK
130
132
137
11

Tips Volcano-Visiting

Thanks to its higher elevation and windward (rainier) location, this neck of the woods is always colder than it is at the beach. If you're coming from the Kona side of the island in summer, expect it to be at least 10° to 20° cooler at the volcano; bring a sweater or light jacket. In the winter months, expect temperatures to be in the 40s (4° and up Celsius) or 50s (teens Celsius), and dress accordingly. Always have rain gear on hand, especially in winter.

But neither Mother Nature nor Madame Pele (the volcano goddess) runs on a schedule. The volcano could be shooting fountains of lava hundreds of feet into the air on the day you arrive, or it could be completely quiet—there are no guarantees with nature. On many days, the lava flows right by accessible roads, and you can get as close as the heat will allow; sometimes, however, the flow is miles away from the nearest access point, visible only in the distance or in underground tubes where you can't see it. Always ask the park rangers before you set out on any lava-viewing expeditions.

VOLCANO VOCABULARY The volcano has its own unique, poetic vocabulary that describes in Hawaiian what cannot be said so well in English. The lava that looks like swirls of chocolate cake frosting is called **pahoehoe** (pa-*hoy*-hoy); it results from a fast-moving flow that curls artistically as it flows. The big, blocky, jumbled lava that looks like a chopped-up parking lot is called **aa** (ah-ah); it's caused by lava that moves slowly, pulling apart as it overruns itself.

Newer words include **vog,** which is volcanic smog made of volcanic gases and smoke from forests set on fire by aa and pahoehoe. **Laze** results when sulfuric acid hits the water and vaporizes and mixes with chlorine to become, as any chemistry student knows, hydrochloric acid. Both vog and laze sting your eyes and can cause respiratory illness; don't expose yourself to either for too long. Pregnant women and anyone with heart or breathing trouble should avoid both vog and laze.

Just the Facts

WHEN TO GO The best time to go is when Kilauea is really pumping. If you're lucky, you'll be in the park when the volcano is active and there's a fountain of lava; mostly, the lava runs like a red river downslope into the sea. If you're on another island and hear a TV news bulletin that the volcano is acting up, catch the next flight to Hilo to see the spectacle. You won't be sorry—and your favorite beach will still be there when you get back.

ACCESS POINTS Hawaii Volcanoes National Park is 29 miles from Hilo, on Hawaii Belt Road (Hwy. 11). If you're staying in Kailua-Kona, it's 100 miles, or about a 2½-hour drive, to the park. Admission is $10 per vehicle; you can come and go as often as you want for 7 days. Hikers and bicyclists pay $5; bikes are allowed only on roads and paved trails.

VISITOR CENTERS & INFORMATION Contact **Hawaii Volcanoes National Park,** P.O. Box 52, Hawaii Volcanoes National Park, HI 96718 (✆ **808/985-6000;** www.nps.gov/havo). **Kilauea Visitor Center** is at the entrance to the park, just off Highway 11; it's open daily from 7:45am to 5pm.

ERUPTION UPDATES Everything you wanted to know about Hawaii's volcanoes, from what's going on with the current eruptions to where the next eruption is likely to be, is now available on the **Hawaiian Volcano Observatory**'s new website, at http://volcano.wr.usgs.gov/kilaueastatus.php. The site is divided into areas on Kilauea (the currently erupting volcano), Mauna Loa (which last erupted in 1984), and Hawaii's other volcanoes (including Lo'ihi, the submerged volcano off the coast of the Big Island). Each section provides photos, maps, eruption summaries, and historical information.

You can also get the latest on volcanic activity in the park by calling the park's **24-hour hot line** (✆ **808/985-6000**). Updates on volcanic activity are also posted daily on the bulletin board at the visitor center.

HIKING & CAMPING IN THE PARK Hawaii Volcanoes National Park offers a wealth of hiking and camping possibilities. See "For the Active Family," later in this chapter, for details.

ACCOMMODATIONS IN & AROUND THE PARK If camping isn't your thing, don't worry. There's a hotel, **Volcano House,** within the park boundary, on the rim of Halemaumau Crater. **Volcano Village,** just outside the park, has plenty of comfortable and convenient hotels and restaurants. (See "Family-Friendly Accommodations" and "Family-Friendly Dining," earlier in this chapter.)

Seeing the Highlights

Your first stop should be **Kilauea Visitor Center** ★★★, a rustic structure in a shady grove of trees just inside the entrance to the park. Here, you can get up-to-the-minute reports on the volcano's activity, learn how volcanoes work, see a film showing blasts from the past, get information on hiking and camping, and pick up the obligatory postcards.

Filled with a new understanding of volcanology and the volcano goddess, Pele, you should then walk across the street to **Volcano House;** go through the lobby and out the other side, where you can get a look at **Kilauea Caldera** ★★★, a 2½-mile-wide, 500-foot-deep pit. The caldera used to be a bubbling pit of fountaining lava; today, you can still see wisps of steam that might, while you're standing there, turn into something more.

Now get out on the road and drive by the **Sulphur Banks** ★, which smell like rotten eggs, and the **Steam Vents** ★★★, where trails of smoke, once molten lava, rise from the inner reaches of the earth. This is one of the few places where you feel that the volcano is really alive. Stop at the **Thomas A. Jaggar Museum** ★★★ (daily 8:30am–5pm; free admission) for a good look at Halemaumau Crater, which is a half-mile across and 1,000 feet deep. On a clear day, you might also see Mauna Loa, 20 miles to the west. The museum shows video from days when the volcano is really spewing, explains the Pele legend in murals, and monitors earthquakes (a precursor of eruptions) on a seismograph, recording every twitch in the earth.

Once you've seen the museum, drive around the caldera to the south side, park, and take the short walk to Halemaumau Crater's edge, past stinky sulfur banks and steam vents, to stand at the overlook and stare in awe at this once-fuming old fire pit, which still generates ferocious heat out of vestigial vents.

If you feel the need to cool off now, go to the **Thurston Lava Tube** ★★★, the coolest place in the park. You'll hike down into a natural bowl in the earth, a forest preserve the lava didn't touch—full of native bird songs and giant tree ferns. Then you'll see a black hole in the earth; step in. It's all drippy and cool here, with bare roots hanging down. You can either resurface into the bright daylight or, if you have a flashlight, poke on deeper into the tube, which goes for another half-mile or so.

Moments Driving up to an Erupting Volcano

When the hot tropical sun quits for the day, don't miss seeing the eruption—after dark. At night, it's the greatest show on earth: Red rivers of fire flow just below the surface, visible through the fissures between your feet, and Jell-O–like globs of molten lava inch down the mountain and pour into the steaming Pacific, creating the newest land on earth. The ongoing eruption has been pouring out lava for more than 20 years, with no sign of stopping. Visitors wanting to see the lava flow have had difficulties in the past, as Madame Pele would roll her lava across the very roads leading to the eruption. Be sure to call ahead (✆ **808/985-6000**) to check where the current eruption is and how to get there.

Every time you go, the eruption will be different. The best plan is to go about an hour or two before sunset. Before you jump into your car, be sure to bring a flashlight, plenty of water, sturdy closed-toe shoes, and a jacket for after the sun has set. Pack a piece of fruit or some juice (for later, to rid your mouth of the lingering sulfur taste), plus an extra jug of water because it's hot out there on the lava, even after dark. Keep in mind that you often have to walk a mile or two at night to see the eruption (depending on where the lava flow is, which changes weekly). If you are tough and can carry a 2- or 3-year-old in a pack on your back, then I'd consider taking a toddler. Otherwise, 5-year-olds and up generally are thrilled at the experience (so long as they are okay walking a couple of miles, with a flashlight, in the dark). Bring lots of water and some fruit (such as bananas) to make sure their energy stays high.

By the time you can see the telltale plume of smog that rises 1,000 feet in the sky, like a giant exclamation point, you will be near the end of Highway 130. Follow the signs to the newly constructed road, where you will be directed to the park. From there you usually can see ruby rivers of lava running to the sea. Close to the parking area is a pile of steaming black pillowy-looking stuff with a silvery sheen—it's actually rock-hard pahoehoe lava, like swirls of chocolate frosting.

The first step onto the hardened lava is scary. It crunches like crushed glass under your heels. (You'll be happy you have closed-toe shoes or hiking boots.) In the distance, you can see a red road map of molten lava glowing in the cracks and flowing in fiery rivulets about a foot below the surface. Depending on where the eruption is, you will have to walk a quarter-mile to a mile, in pitch-black darkness (except for your flashlight), to the intersection of lava and sea—but it's a walk that is well worth the trouble.

Silhouetted against the fire, visitors stand at the edge of the earth witnessing the double act of creation and destruction. The lava hisses and spits and crackles as it moves, snakelike, in its perpetual flow to the sea, dripping like candle wax into the wavy surf—fire and water, the very stuff of the islands. The lava still burns underwater until the vast Pacific Ocean finally douses the fire and transforms the flow into yet more black-sand beach.

It's a sight you will never forget.

If you're still game for a good hike, try **Kilauea Iki Crater** ★, a 4-mile, 2-hour hike across the floor of the crater, which became a bubbling pool of lava in 1959 and sent fountains of lava 1,900 feet in the air, completely devastating a nearby ohia forest and leaving another popular hike ominously known as **Devastation Trail** ★★★. This .5-mile walk is a startling look at the powers of a volcanic eruption on the environment. (See "For the Active Family," below, for details on these and other park hikes.)

Check out ancient Hawaiian art at the **Puu Loa Petroglyphs** ★, around the 15-mile marker down Chain of Craters Road. Look for the stack of rocks on the road. A brief, .5-mile walk will bring you to a circular boardwalk where you can see thousands of mysterious Hawaiian petroglyphs carved in stone. ***Warning:*** It's very easy to destroy these ancient works of art. Do not leave the boardwalk, and do not walk on or around the petroglyphs. Rubbings of petroglyphs will destroy them; the best way to capture them is by taking a photo.

This area, Puu Loa, was a sacred place for generations. Fathers came here to bury their newborns' umbilical cords in the numerous small holes in the lava, thus ensuring a long life for the child.

A BIRD'S-EYE VIEW The best way to see Kilauea's bubbling caldera is from on high, in a helicopter. This bird's-eye view puts the enormity of it all into perspective. I recommend **Blue Hawaiian Helicopters** ★★★ (**© 800/745-BLUE** [745-2583] or 808/886-1768; www.bluehawaiian.com), a professionally run, locally based company with an excellent safety record; comfortable, top-of-the-line copters; and pilots who are extremely knowledgeable about everything from volcanology to Hawaii lore. The company flies out of both Hilo and Waikoloa. (Hilo is cheaper because it's closer.) From Hilo, the 45-minute **Circle of Fire tour** ★★★ takes you over the boiling volcano and then on to a bird's-eye view of the destruction the lava has caused and remote beaches ($210 per person; $169 if you book online in advance). From Waikoloa, the 2-hour **Big Island Spectacular** ★★★ stars the volcano, tropical valleys, Hamakua coast waterfalls, and Kohala Mountains (from $424, or $364 online), worth every penny.

6 BEACHES

Too young geologically to have many great beaches, the Big Island instead has an odd collection of unusual ones that your family will find fascinating: brand-new black-sand beaches, green-sand beaches, salt-and-pepper beaches, and even a rare (for this island) white-sand beach.

All beaches in Hawaii belong to the public, and resorts are mandated by law to provide public access and parking. Even if you are not staying at a resort, you can go to the beach through these public access areas.

THE KONA COAST

Kahaluu Beach Park ★★★

This family-friendly beach is the most popular on the Kona coast; the reef-protected lagoons attract 1,000 people a day almost year-round. Kahaluu is the best all-around beach on Alii Drive, with coconut trees lining a narrow salt-and-pepper sand shore that gently slopes to turquoise pools. The schools of brilliantly colored tropical fish that weave in and out of the well-established reef make this an ideal spot for children and beginning snorkelers to get their fins wet; the water is so shallow that you can stand up if you feel

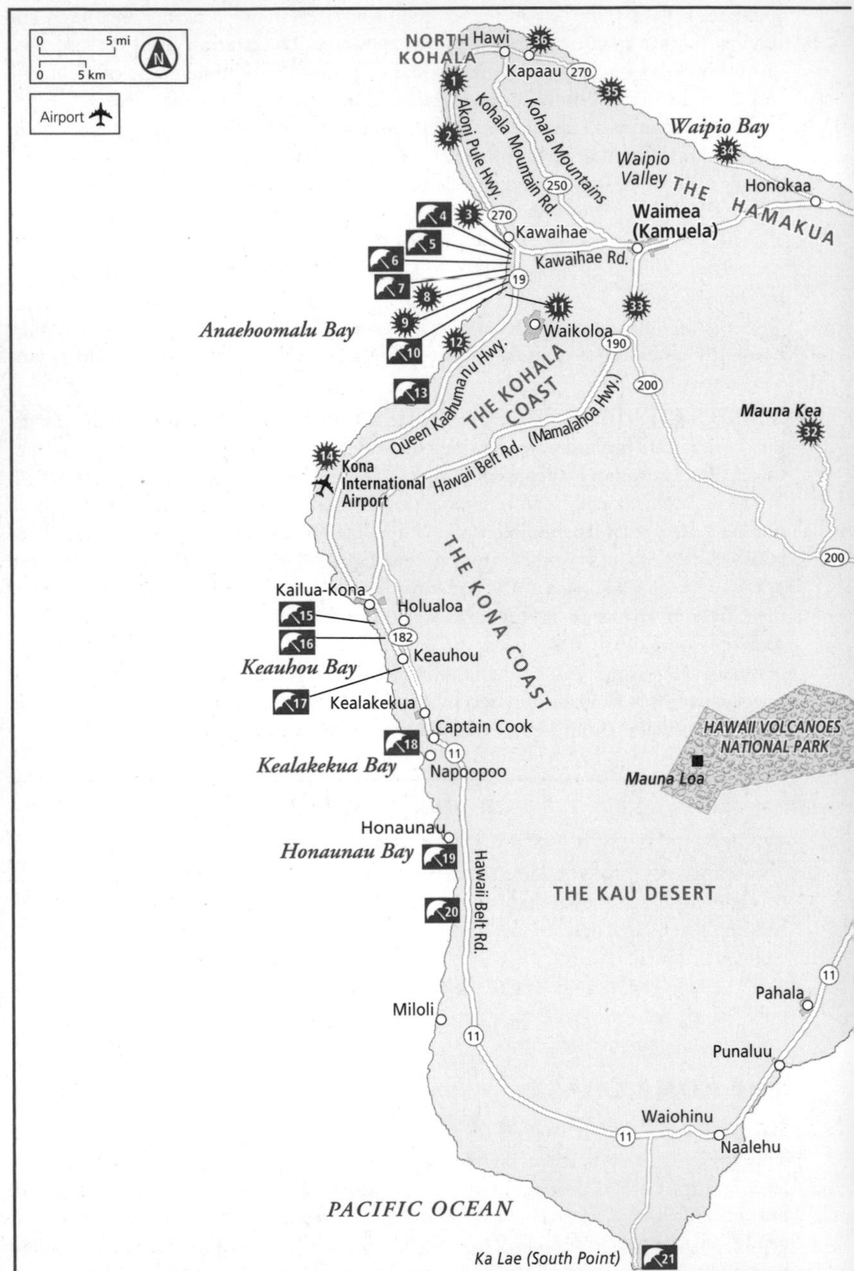

0 5 mi
0 5 km
N
Airport
NORTH KOHALA
Hawi
Kapaau
Akoni Pule Hwy.
Kohala Mountain Rd.
Kohala Mountains
Waipio Bay
Waipio Valley
THE HAMAKUA
Honokaa
Waimea (Kamuela)
Kawaihae
Kawaihae Rd.
Anaehoomalu Bay
Waikoloa
Queen Kaahumanu Hwy.
THE KOHALA COAST
Hawaii Belt Rd. (Mamalahoa Hwy.)
Mauna Kea
Kona International Airport
THE KONA COAST
Kailua-Kona
Holualoa
Keauhou
Keauhou Bay
Kealakekua
Captain Cook
Kealakekua Bay
Napoopoo
HAWAII VOLCANOES NATIONAL PARK
Mauna Loa
Honaunau
Honaunau Bay
Hawaii Belt Rd.
THE KAU DESERT
Pahala
Punaluu
Miloli
Waiohinu
Naalehu
PACIFIC OCEAN
Ka Lae (South Point)

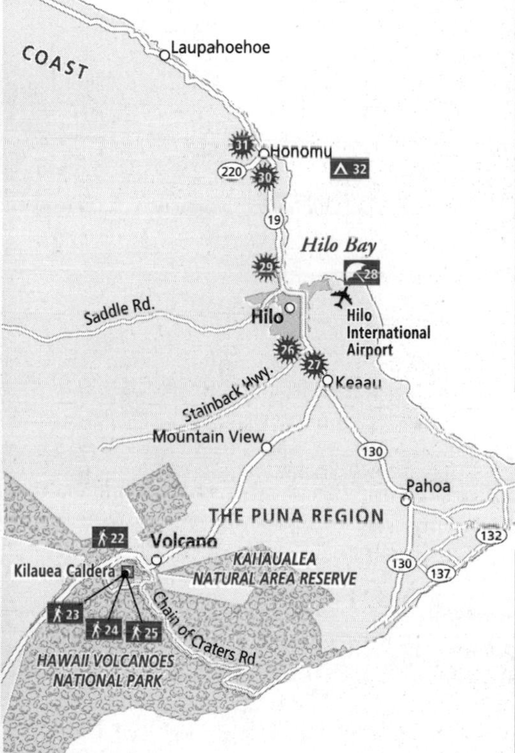

A CAMPGROUND
Namakani Paio Campground **22**

HIKES
Devastation Trail **24**
Halemaumau Trail **23**
Kilauea Iki Trail **25**
Kipuka Puaulu (Bird Park) Trail **22**

BEACHES
Anaehoomalu Beach (A-Bay) **10**
Green Sand (Papakolea) Beach **21**
Hapuna Beach **6**
Honaunau Beach Park **19**
Hookena Beach Park **20**
Kahuluu Beach Park **16**
Kaunaoa (Mauna Kea) Beach **5**
Keauhou Bay **17**
Kealakekua Bay **18**
Kekaha Kai (Kona Coast) State Park **13**
Lelewi Beach Park **28**
Spencer Beach Park **4**
Puako Beach Park **7**
White Sands Beach **15**

FUN SIGHTS
Akaka Falls **31**
Hawaii Tropical Botanical Garden **29**
Kalahuipuaa Fish Ponds **9**
Kaupulehu Petroglyphs **12**
King Kamehameha Statue **36**
Kuualii and Kahapapa Fish Ponds **11**
Lapakahi State Historical Park **2**
Mauna Kea **32**
Maunaloa Macademia Nut Factory **27**
Mo'okini Luakini Heiau **1**
Onizuka Visitor Center **14**
Panaewa Rainforest Zoo **26**
Parker Ranch **33**
Pololu Valley Lookout **35**
Puako Petroglyph Archeological District **8**
Puukohala Heiau National Historic Site **3**
Waipio Valley Lookout **34**
World Botanical Garden **30**

uncomfortable. Be careful in winter, though: The placid waters become turbulent, and there's a rip current when high surf rolls in; look for the lifeguard warnings.

Kahaluu isn't the biggest beach on the island, but it's one of the best equipped, with off-road parking, beach-gear rentals, a covered pavilion, and a food concession. It gets crowded, so come early to stake out a spot.

Kekaha Kai State ParK (Kona Coast State Park) ★

You'll glimpse this beach as your plane makes its final approach to Kona Airport. It's about 2 miles north of the airport on Queen Kaahumanu Highway; turn left at a sign pointing improbably down a bumpy road. Pack a picnic lunch before you head out. You won't need a four-wheel-drive vehicle to make it down here—just drive slowly and watch out for potholes. What you'll find at the end is 5 miles of shoreline with a half-dozen long, curving beaches and a big cove on Mahaiula Bay, as well as archaeological and historical sites. The series of well-protected coves is excellent for swimming, and there's great snorkeling and diving offshore; the big winter waves attract surfers.

Facilities include restrooms, picnic tables, and barbecue pits; you'll have to bring your own drinking water. Because it's a state park, the beach is open daily from 8am to 8pm. (The closing is strictly enforced, and there's no overnight camping.)

White Sands Beach ★

Don't blink as you cruise Alii Drive, or you'll miss White Sands Beach. This small, white-sand pocket beach about 4½ miles south of Kailua-Kona—very unusual on this lava-rock coast—is sometimes called Disappearing Beach because it does just that, especially at high tide or during storms. It vanished completely when Hurricane Iniki hit in 1991, but it's now back in place. (At least it was the last time we looked.) On calm days, the water is perfect for swimming and snorkeling. Locals use the elementary waves to teach their children how to surf and boogie board. In winter, the waves swell to expert levels, attracting both surfers and spectators. Facilities include restrooms, showers, lifeguards, and a small parking lot.

THE KOHALA COAST

Hapuna Beach ★★★

Just off Queen Kaahumanu Highway, south of the Hapuna Beach Prince Hotel, lies this crescent of gold sand—big, wide, and a half-mile long. In summer, when the beach is widest, the ocean calmest, and the crowds biggest, this is the island's best beach for swimming, snorkeling, and bodysurfing. But beware of Hapuna in winter, when its thundering waves, strong rip currents, and lack of lifeguards can be dangerous. Facilities include A-frame cabins for camping, pavilions, restrooms, showers, and plenty of parking.

Kaunaoa Beach (Mauna Kea Beach) ★★★

For nearly 40 years, this gold-sand beach at the foot of Mauna Kea Beach Hotel has been the top vacation spot among America's corporate chiefs. Everyone calls it Mauna Kea Beach, but its real name is Hawaiian for "native dodder," a lacy, yellow-orange vine that once thrived on the shore. A coconut grove sweeps around this golden crescent, where the water is calm and protected by two black-lava points. The sandy bottom slopes gently into the bay, which often fills with schools of tropical fish, green sea turtles, and manta rays, especially at night, when the hotel lights flood the shore. Swimming is excellent year-round, except in rare winter storms. Snorkelers prefer the rocky points, where fish thrive in the surge. Facilities include restrooms, showers, and ample parking, but there are no lifeguards.

Anaehoomalu Bay (A-Bay) ★★★

The Big Island makes up for its dearth of beaches with a few spectacular ones, like Anaehoomalu, or A-Bay, as the locals call it. This popular gold-sand beach, fringed by a grove of palms and backed by royal fishponds still full of mullet, is one of Hawaii's most beautiful. It fronts the Marriott Waikoloa Beach Resort and is enjoyed by guests and locals alike. (It's a little busier in summer, but it doesn't ever get truly crowded.) The beach slopes gently from shallow to deep water; swimming, snorkeling, diving, kayaking, and windsurfing are all excellent here. Equipment rental and snorkeling, scuba, and windsurfing instruction are available at the north end of the beach. At the far edge of the bay is a rare turtle-cleaning station, where snorkelers and divers can watch endangered green sea turtles line up, waiting their turn to have small fish clean them. Facilities include restrooms, showers, picnic tables, and plenty of parking.

HILO

Leleiwi Beach Park ★

Hilo's beaches may be few, but Leleiwi is one of Hawaii's most beautiful. This unusual cove of palm-fringed black-lava tide pools fed by freshwater springs and rippled by gentle waves is a photographer's delight—and the perfect place to take a plunge. In winter, big waves can splash these ponds, but the shallow pools are generally free of currents and ideal for children, especially in the protected inlets at the center of the park. Leleiwi often attracts endangered sea turtles, making this one of Hawaii's most popular snorkeling spots. The beach is 4 miles out of town on Kalanianaole Avenue. Facilities include restrooms, showers, lifeguards, picnic pavilions, and paved walkways. There's also a marine-life facility here.

7 FOR THE ACTIVE FAMILY

IN THE WATER

If you want to rent beach toys, such as snorkel gear or boogie boards, the beach concessions at all the big resorts, as well as tour desks and dive shops, offer equipment rentals and sometimes lessons for beginners. The cheapest place to get great rental equipment is **Snorkel Bob's,** in the parking lot of Huggo's Restaurant at 75-5831 Kahakai Rd., at Alii Drive, Kailua-Kona (✆ **808/329-0770;** www.snorkelbob.com).

Boating

Body Glove Hawaii Cruises ★ **Ages 5 and up.** The *Body Glove,* a 55-foot trimaran that carries up to 100 passengers, runs an adventurous sail-snorkel-dive cruise at a reasonable price. You'll be greeted with fresh Kona coffee (and the kids will get fruit juice), breakfast pastries, and fresh fruit; you'll then sail north of Kailua to Pawai Bay, a marine preserve where you can snorkel, scuba dive, swim, or just hang out on the deck for a couple of hours. After a buffet deli lunch spread, you might want to take the plunge off the boat's water slide or diving board before heading back to Kailua Pier. The boat departs daily from the pier at 9am and returns at 1:30pm. The only thing you need to bring is a towel; snorkeling equipment (and scuba equipment, if you choose to dive) is provided. ***Money-saving tip:*** The afternoon trip is cheaper.

Kailua Pier. ✆ **800/551-8911** or 808/326-7122. www.bodyglovehawaii.com. Morning cruise $112 adults, $72 children 6–12, free for children 5 and under; afternoon cruise $73 adults, $53 children 6–12, free for children 5 and under; additional $59 for certified scuba divers with own equipment ($69 without own equipment) and $79 additional for introductory scuba; whale-watching (Dec–Apr) $73 adults, $53 children 6–12, free for children 5 and under.

Captain Dan McSweeney's Whale Watch Learning Adventures ★★★ All ages. Your kids will love this 3-hour cruise to see Hawaii's most impressive visitors—45-foot humpback whales—when they return to the waters off Kona every winter. Captain Dan McSweeney, a whale researcher for more than 30 years, is always here to greet them, as well as other whales who spend the warmer months in Hawaiian waters. Because Captain Dan works daily with the whales, he has no problem finding them. Frequently, he drops an underwater microphone into the water so you can listen to their songs. If the whales aren't singing, he may use his underwater video camera to show you what's going on. In humpback season—roughly December to April—Dan makes two 3-hour trips daily. From July 1 to December 20, he schedules one morning trip on Tuesday, Thursday, and Saturday to look for pilot, sperm, false killer, melon-headed, pygmy killer, and beaked whales. Captain Dan guarantees a sighting, or he'll take you out again for free. There are no cruises in May and June; that's when he goes whale-watching in Alaska.

Honokohau Harbor. ✆ **888/WHALE-76** (942-5376) or 808/322-0028. www.ilovewhales.com. $80 adults, $70 children 10 and under.

Captain Zodiac Ages 7 and up. If you'd prefer to take a snorkel cruise to Kealakekua Bay in a small boat, go in Captain Zodiac's 16-passenger, 24-foot inflatable rubber life raft. The boat takes you on a wild ride 14 miles down the Kona coast to Kealakekua, where you'll spend about an hour snorkeling in the bay and then enjoy snacks and beverages at a picnic site. Trips are twice daily, from 8am to 12:15pm and from 12:45 to 5pm. ***Warning:*** Pregnant women and those with bad backs should avoid this often-bumpy ride. It's a bit rough for young children, too.

Gentry's Marina, Honokohau Harbor. ✆ **808/329-3199.** www.captainzodiac.com. $90 adults, $75 children (3–12) for 4-hr. tour; $59 adults, $45 children (4–12) for 3-hr. whale-watching (book on the Internet for better rates).

Fair Wind Snorkeling and Diving Adventures ★★★ Kids One of the best ways to snorkel Kealakekua Bay, the marine-life preserve that's one of the best snorkel spots in Hawaii, is on Fair Wind's half-day **sail-and-snorkel cruise to Kealakekua.** Recently the company has added the latest (state-of-the-art) luxury 55-foot foil-assist catamaran (the first on the Big Island) for an upscale experience that promises a faster and smoother ride on a boat full of luxury. We recommend the ***Hula Kai*** cruise, a 5-hour morning snorkel and dive cruise that includes a light breakfast, a gourmet barbecue lunch, two snorkeling sites, a guided tour, and optional scuba diving for $155 adults (minimum age 18). Hula Kai also has an afternoon snorkeling and sunset barbecue for $125 (minimum age 18). ***Fair Wind II*** has a 60-foot catamaran that holds up to 100 passengers. The morning cruise leaves from Keauhou Bay at 9am and returns at 1:30pm, and includes a light breakfast, lunch, snorkel gear, and lessons; it goes for $119 for adults, $75 for kids 4 to 12, and $29 for toddlers. The afternoon deluxe cruise runs from 2 to 6:30pm and includes BBQ lunch, sailing, snorkeling, and equipment, at a cost of $109 for adults, $69 for 4- to 12-year olds, and free for kids 3 and under. Also on the *Fair*

Wind II is a shorter (and cheaper) snack, sailing, and snorkeling cruise for $75 adults and $45 children (no lunch, just fruit and snack plus snorkeling equipment). During whale season, the *Hula Kai* has a 3-hour whale-watching trip for $75, minimum age 8.

78-7130 Kaleiopapa St., Kailua-Kona. ✆ **800/677-9461** or 808/322-2788. www.fair-wind.com. Snorkel cruises $75–$155 adults, $45–$75 children 4–12 (prices vary depending on cruise).

Bodyboarding & Bodysurfing

On the Kona side of the island, the best beaches for bodyboarding and bodysurfing are **Hapuna Beach, White Sands Beach,** and **Kekaha Kai State Park.** On the east side, try **Leleiwi Beach.**

Kayaking

OCEAN KAYAKING Imagine sitting at sea level, eye to eye with a turtle, a dolphin, even a whale—it's possible in an oceangoing kayak. Anyone can kayak: Get in, find your balance, and paddle. After a few minutes of instruction and a little practice in a calm area (such as the lagoon in front of **King Kamehameha's Kona Beach Hotel**), you'll be ready to explore. Beginners can practice their skills in **Kailua** and **Kealakekua bays;** intermediates might try paddling from **Honokohau Harbor** to **Kekaha Kai Beach Park;** the **Hamakua coast** is a challenge for experienced kayakers. Kids will be happier if they can paddle the kayak; use your judgment, but by the time they are 7 years old, they are usually tall enough to maneuver the paddles.

You can rent one- and two-person kayaks (and other ocean toys) from **Aloha Kayak ★★★** (✆ **877/322-1441** or 808/322-2868; www.alohakayak.com) for $25 for a half-day single and $35 for a half-day double ($45 for a full-day single and $60 for a full-day double). They also have a unique tour from Keauhou Bay and the Captain Cook Monument, with Hawaiian guides showing you sea caves and snorkeling areas full of fish and turtles. The tours are either 4 hours ($79 adults, $59 for children ages 11 and under) or 2½ hours ($59 adults, $30 children 11 and under) and include all equipment, beverages, snorkeling gear, and snacks.

Snorkeling

If you come to Hawaii and don't snorkel, you'll miss half the fun. The year-round calm waters along the Kona and Kohala coasts are home to spectacular marine life. Some of the best snorkeling areas on the Kona-Kohala coast include **Hapuna Beach Cove,** at the foot of the Hapuna Beach Prince Hotel, a secluded little cove where you can snorkel not only with schools of yellow tangs, needlefish, and green sea turtles, but also, once in a while, with somebody rich and famous. If you've never snorkeled in your life, **Kahaluu Beach Park** is the best place to start. Wade in and look down at the schools of fish in the bay's black-lava tide pools. Another "hidden" snorkeling spot is off the rocks north of the boat-launch ramp at **Honaunau Bay.** Other great snorkel sites include **White Sands Beach,** as well as **Kekaha Kai State Park, Hookena, Honaunau, Puako,** and **Spencer** beach parks.

In addition to **Snorkel Bob's,** mentioned in the intro to this section, you can rent gear from **Kona Coast Divers ★**, Honokohau Marina, Kailua-Kona (✆ **808/329-8802;** www.konacoastdivers.com).

SNORKELING CRUISES TO KEALAKEKUA BAY ★★★ Probably the best snorkeling for all levels can be found in **Kealakekua Bay.** The calm waters of this underwater preserve teem with a wealth of marine life. Coral heads, lava tubes, and underwater caves all provide an excellent habitat for Hawaii's vast array of tropical fish, making mile-wide

 Kealakekua the Big Island's best accessible spot for snorkeling and diving. Without looking very hard, you can see octopuses, free-swimming moray eels, parrotfish, and goatfish; once in a while, a pod of spinner dolphins streaks across the bay. Kealakekua is reachable only by boat; in addition to **Fair Wind** (p. 214) and **Captain Zodiac** (p. 214), check out **Sea Quest Snorkeling and Rafting Adventures** (© **808/329-RAFT** [329-7238]; www.seaquesthawaii.com), which offers unique coastal adventures through sea caves and lava tubes on the Kona Coast, as well as snorkeling plunges into the ocean at the Historic Place of Refuge in Honaunau and at the Captain Cook Monument at Kealakekua. The six-passenger, rigid-hull, inflatable rafts can go where larger boats can't. The 4-hour morning tour is $85 adults and $72 children, while the 3-hour afternoon tour goes for $64 adults and $54 children. During whale season, they have a 3-hour whale-watching cruise for $53 adults and children. They do not allow children 5 and under, pregnant women, or people with bad backs.

Snuba

If you're not quite ready to make the commitment to scuba but you want more time underwater than snorkeling allows, **Big Island Snuba Tours** (© **808/326-7446;** www.snubabigisland.com) may be the answer. Just like in scuba, the diver wears a regulator and mask; however, the tank floats on the surface on a raft and is connected to the diver's regulator by a hose that allows the diver to go 20 to 25 feet down. You need only 15 minutes of instruction before you're ready to go. Snuba can actually be easier than snorkeling, as the water is calmer beneath the surface. It costs $89 for a 1½-hour dive from the beach, $145 for one dive from a boat, and $170 for two dives from a boat; children must be at least 8 years old.

Submarine Dives

This is the stuff movies are made of: venturing 100 feet below the sea in a high-tech, 65-foot submarine. On a 1-hour trip, you'll be able to explore a 25-acre coral reef teeming with schools of colorful tropical fish. Look closely, and you may catch glimpses of moray eels—or even a shark—in and around the reef. On selected trips, you'll watch as divers swim among these aquatic creatures, luring them to the view ports for face-to-face observation. Call **Atlantis Adventures** ★, 75-5669 Alii Dr. (across the street from Kailua Pier), Kailua-Kona (© **800/548-6262;** www.atlantisadventures.com). Trips leave daily between 10am and 3pm. The cost is $80 for adults and $41 for children 11 and under, or book on their website. ***Note:*** The ride is safe for everyone, but skip it if you suffer from claustrophobia.

Surfing

Most surfing off the Big Island is for the experienced only. As a general rule, the beaches on the north and west shores of the island get northern swells in winter, whereas those on the south and east shores get southern swells in summer. Experienced surfers should check out the waves at **Pine Trees** (north of Kailua-Kona), **Lyman's** (off Alii Dr. in Kailua-Kona), and **Banyan's** (also off Alii Dr.); reliable spots on the east side of the island include **Honolii Point** (outside Hilo), **Hilo Bay Front Park,** and **Keaukaha Beach Park.** But there are a few sites where beginners can catch a wave, too: You might want to try **Kahaluu Beach,** where the waves are manageable most of the year; other surfers are around to give you pointers, and there's a lifeguard onshore.

Ocean Eco Tours (© **808/324-SURF** [324-7873]; www.oceanecotours.com), owned and operated by veteran surfers, is one of the few companies on the Big Island that teaches surfing. Private lessons cost $150 per person (including all equipment) and usually last a minimum of 2 hours; 2- to 3-hour group lessons go for $95 (also including all equipment), with a maximum of four students. Both teachers love this ancient Hawaiian sport, and their enthusiasm is contagious. The minimum age is 8, and you must be a fairly good swimmer.

Your only Big Island choice for surfboard rentals is **Pacific Vibrations,** 75-5702 Likana Lane (just off Alii Dr., across from the pier), Kailua-Kona (✆ **808/329-4140;** www.laguerdobros.com/pacvib/pacificv.html), where they have short boards at $15 for 24 hours and long boards for $20 a day.

ON THE LAND

Camping & Hiking

For information on camping and hiking, contact **Hawaii Volcanoes National Park,** P.O. Box 52, Hawaii National Park, HI 96718 (✆ 808/985-6000; www.nps.gov/havo); **Puuhonua O Honaunau National Historic Park,** Honaunau, HI 96726 (✆ 808/328-2288; www.nps.gov/puho); the **Hawaii Division of Forestry and Wildlife,** 19 E. Kawili St., Hilo, HI 96720 (✆ 808/974-4221; www.dofaw.net); the **Division of State Parks,** P.O. Box 936, Hilo, HI 96721 (✆ 808/974-6200; www.hawaii.gov); the **County Department of Parks and Recreation,** 25 Aupuni St., Hilo, HI 96720 (✆ 808/961-8311; www.hawaii-county.com); or the **Sierra Club, Hawaii Chapter** (✆ 808/959-0452; www.hi.sierraclub.org). For other resources and general tips on hiking and camping in Hawaii, see "Special-Interest Trips," in chapter 2.

Camping equipment is *not* available for rent on the Big Island. Plan to bring your own or buy it at **Hilo Surplus Store** (✆ **808/935-6398**).

GUIDED DAY HIKES If you'd like to discover natural Hawaii off the beaten path but don't necessarily want to sleep under a tree to do it, a day hike is your ticket. Call the following outfitters ahead of time (even before you arrive) for a schedule of trips; they fill up quickly.

A longtime resident of Hawaii, Dr. Hugh Montgomery of **Hawaiian Walkways ★,** Honokaa (✆ **800/457-7759** or 808/775-0372; www.hawaiianwalkways.com), former "Tour Operator of the Year" by the Hawaii Ecotourism Association of Hawaii, offers a variety of options, ranging from excursions that skirt the rim of immense valleys to hikes through the clouds on the volcano. Hikes are $95 for adults, $75 for kids, to $150 for adults and $95 for kids. Custom hikes are available for $95 each for six hikers. Prices include food, beverages, and equipment.

Naturalist and educator Rob Pacheco of **Hawaii Forest & Trail ★★★,** 74-5035-B Queen Kaahumanu Hwy. (behind the Chevron station), Kailua-Kona (✆ **800/464-1993** or 808/331-8505; www.hawaii-forest.com), will take you on day trips to some of the island's most remote, pristine, natural areas, some of which he has exclusive access to. Rob's fully trained staff narrates the entire trip, offering extensive natural, geological, and cultural history interpretation (and more than a little humor). Because the tours are limited to a maximum of 10 people, they are highly personalized to meet the group's interests and abilities. A day with Hawaii Forest & Trail may just be the highlight of your Big Island experience. Options include waterfall adventures, rainforest discovery hikes, birding tours, a caving adventure, and a trip up to the summit of Mauna Kea. Each tour involves 2 to 4 hours of easy-to-moderate walking, over terrain manageable by anyone in average physical condition. Half-day trips, including snacks, beverages, water, and gear, range from $105 to $169 for adults, $85 to $125 for children ages 8 to 12.

Hawaii Volcanoes National Park ★★★

This national park is a wilderness wonderland. Miles of trails not only lace the lava but also cross deserts, rainforests, beaches, and, in winter, snow at 13,650 feet. Trail maps are sold at park headquarters and are highly recommended. Check conditions before you head out. Come prepared for hot sun, cold rain, and hard wind any time of year. Always wear sunscreen and bring plenty of drinking water.

Warning: If you have heart or respiratory problems or if you're pregnant, don't attempt any hike in the park; the fumes will bother you.

KILAUEA IKI TRAIL You'll experience the work of the volcano goddess, Pele, firsthand on this hike. The 4-mile trail begins at the visitor center, descends through a forest of ferns into still-fuming Kilauea Iki Crater, and then crosses the crater floor past the vent where a 1959 lava blast shot a fountain of fire 1,900 feet into the air for 36 days. Allow 2 hours for this fair-to-moderate hike.

HALEMAUMAU TRAIL This moderate 3.5-mile hike starts at the visitor center, goes down 500 feet to the floor of Kilauea Crater, crosses the crater, and ends at Halemaumau Overlook.

DEVASTATION TRAIL Up on the rim of Kilauea Iki Crater, you can see what an erupting volcano did to a once-flourishing ohia forest. The scorched earth with its ghostly tree skeletons stands in sharp contrast to the rest of the nearby lush forest that escaped the rain of hot molten lava, cinder, and debris. Everyone can—and should—take this .5-mile hike on a paved path across the eerie bed of black cinders. The trailhead is on Crater Rim Road at Puu Puai Overlook.

KIPUKA PUAULU (BIRD PARK) TRAIL This easy, 1.5-mile, hour-long hike lets you see native Hawaiian flora and fauna in a little oasis of living nature in a field of lava. For some reason (gravity or rate of flow or protection from the volcano goddess, Pele, perhaps), the once red-hot lava skirted this miniforest and let it survive. At the trailhead on Mauna Loa Road is a display of plants and birds you'll see on the walk. Go early in the morning or in the evening (or even better, just after a rain) to see native birds like the *apapane* (a small, bright-red bird with black wings and tail that sips the nectar of the red-blossomed ohia lehua trees) and the *iiwi* (larger and orange-vermilion, with a curved orange bill). Native trees along the trail include giant ohia, koa, soapberry, kolea, and mamani.

NAMAKANI PAIO CAMPGROUNDS & CABINS Just 5 miles west of the park entrance is a tall eucalyptus forest where you can pitch a tent in an open, grassy field. The trail to Kilauea Crater is just a half-mile away. No permit is needed, but stays are limited to 7 days. Facilities include pavilions with barbecues and a fireplace, picnic tables, outdoor dish-washing areas, restrooms, and drinking water. There are also 10 cabins that accommodate up to four people each. Each cabin has a covered picnic table at the entrance and a fireplace with a grill. Toilets, sinks, and hot showers are available in a separate building. You can get groceries and gas in the town of Volcano, 4 miles away. Make cabin reservations through **Volcano House,** P.O. Box 53, Hawaii National Park, HI 96718 (✆ **808/967-7321**). The cost is $40 per night for two adults and two children, $48 for three adults, and $56 for four adults.

Bicycling & Mountain Biking

For mountain bike and bike rentals in Kona, see **Hawaiian Pedals ★**, Kona Inn Shopping Village, Alii Drive, Kailua-Kona (✆ **808/329-2294**); and **Hawaiian Pedals Bike**

Works, 75-5599 Lihua St., Kailua-Kona (✆ **808/326-2453;** www.hawaiianpedals.com). Both have a huge selection of bikes, from mountain bikes and hybrids ($20 a day, $70 a week) to racing bikes to front-suspension and full-suspension mountain bikes ($45 a day, $105–$140 a week, respectively). Bike racks go for $5 a day, and you pay only for the days you actually use it (the honor system): If you have the rack for a week but use it for only 2 days, you'll be charged just $10. The folks at the shops are friendly and knowledgeable about cycling routes all over the Big Island.

Contact the **Big Island Mountain Biking Association,** P.O. Box 6819, Hilo, HI 96720 (✆ **808/961-4452**), for its free brochure, *Big Island Mountain Biking,* which has useful safety tips on biking as well as great off-road trails for both beginner and advanced riders. Check out www.bikehawaii.com for information on trails and access. Another good contact for biking information and maps is **PATH** (✆ **808/326-9495**).

Horseback Riding

Kohala Na'alapa ★, on Kohala Mountain Road (Hwy. 250) at mile marker 11 (ask for directions to the **Naalapa Stables** at the security-guard station; ✆ **808/889-0022;** www.naalapastables.com), offers unforgettable journeys into the rolling hills of Kahua and Kohala ranches, past ancient Hawaiian ruins, through lush pastures with grazing sheep and cows, and along mountaintops with panoramic coastal views. The horses and various riding areas are suited for everyone from first-timers to experienced equestrians. There are two trips a day: a 2½-hour tour at 9am for $89 and a 1½-hour tour at 1:30pm for $68. No riders over 230 pounds, no pregnant riders, and no children 7 and under.

To see Waipio Valley on horseback, call **Waipio Na'alapa Trail Rides ★** (✆ **808/775-0419;** www.naalapastables.com). The 2-hour tours of this gorgeous tropical valley depart Monday through Saturday at 9:30am and 1pm. (Don't forget your camera.) The guides are well versed in Hawaiian history and provide running commentary as you move through this historic place. The cost is $89 for adults. No kids 7 and under, no pregnant riders, and no riders over 230 pounds.

Skateboarding

The Big Island's first concrete skateboard park was dedicated in 2004. Located in the Waimea Community Park, on Kawaihae Road (Hwy. 19) near the intersection of Lindsey Road, the park is open from 7am to 7pm daily. The 7,500-square-foot park is divided into two sections: one for vertical skating with a peanut-shaped bowl with 10- and 7-foot-deep ends, and the other for street skating with ramps, curbs, and rails. Helmets are required at all times. Bring your own skateboard—there are no rentals on the Big Island.

Swimming

Most likely the hotel or condo where you are staying will have a pool. If it doesn't, Hawaii County has nine swimming pools located around the island. For information on the one closest to where you are staying, contact **Hawaii County Department of Parks and Recreation,** 25 Apuni St., Hilo, HI 96720 (✆ **808/961-8694;** www.hawaii-county.com/parks/aquatics_program_guide.htm).

8 SHOPPING WITH YOUR KIDS

The Big Island will give you plenty of opportunity to spend, spend, spend. There's not a lot of megamall shopping centers on Hawaii's largest island, but there are plenty of unique boutique shops to browse. The visual arts are flourishing on this island, but beware: The line between shop and gallery can often be too fine to determine. Too many self-proclaimed "galleries" sell schlock or a mixture of arts, crafts, and tacky souvenirs. T-shirts and Kona coffee mugs are souvenir staples in many so-called galleries.

Shops in resort areas generally open around 9 to 10am and close around 9pm. Shops in nonresort areas open around 9am and close about 5pm.

THE SHOPPING SCENE

Kailua-Kona

Kailua-Kona's shopping prospects pour into the streets in a festival atmosphere of T-shirts, trinkets, and dime-a-dozen souvenirs, with Alii Drive at the center of this activity. But the **Coconut Grove Market Place,** 75-5801 Alii Dr., across the street from the seawall, has a host of various shops (Sunglass Hut) and eateries (Hard Rock Café, Outback Steakhouse), all centered on a sand volleyball court.

Shopping stalwarts in Kona are the **Kona Square,** across from **King Kamehameha's Kona Beach Hotel;** the hotel's shopping mall, with close to two dozen shops; and the **Kona Inn Shopping Village,** on Alii Drive. All include the usual assortment of T-shirt shops. One highlight is **Alii Gardens Marketplace** at the southern end of Kailua-Kona, a pleasant, tented outdoor marketplace with fresh fruit, flowers, imports, local crafts, and a wonderful selection of orchid plants. There's cheesy stuff there, too, but somehow it's less noticeable outdoors.

The newly opened **Kona International Market,** 74-5533 Luhia St. (near Kaiwi St.), in the Old Industrial Area, is a great idea, a series of small open-air shops in a large pavilion with food vendors, similar to Waikiki's International Market. Unfortunately, with just a few exceptions, I am very disappointed in this "market." I searched all the vendors looking for something made in Hawaii, and with very few exceptions (some jewelry), most of the trinkets sold here were not from the Big Island, and not even from Hawaii, and prices were not that attractive. However, a major exception is **Emma's Flowers** (**✆ 808/329-7746**), a great place for leis and just-cut tropical flowers, at reasonable prices.

Holualoa

Charming Holualoa, 1,400 feet and 10 minutes above Kailua-Kona at the top of Hualalai Road, is a place for strong espresso, leisurely gallery hopping, and nostalgic explorations across several cultural and time zones. One narrow road takes you across generations and cultures. Prominent Holualoa artists include Setsuko and Hiroki Morinoue of **Studio 7** (**✆ 808/324-1335**), who exhibit their work in a serene, beautiful setting; Matthew and Mary Lovein, who show their own work at **Holualoa Gallery** (**✆ 808/322-8484**), as well as the work of selected Hawaii artists in this roadside gallery; and Gerald Ben, who not only is a skilled ceramist but also a custom woodworker who displays his work at **Dovetail Gallery and Design** (**✆ 808/322-4046**).

The Kohala Coast

Shops on the Kohala coast are concentrated in and around the resorts; among the pricey hotel shops, my favorites include **Sandal Tree,** in the Hilton Waikoloa Village (**✆ 808/886-7884**), which carries footwear with style and kick: Italian sandals at non-Italian prices, designer pumps, and other footwear to carry you from dockside to dance floor. **Ka'upulehu Store,** in the Four Seasons Resort Hualalai (**✆ 808/325-8000**), is a perfect blend of high quality and cultural integrity, with items made in Hawaii like handmade paper, hand-painted silks, seed leis, greeting cards, koa bowls, wreaths, John Kelly prints, and a selection of Hawaii-themed books. **Collectors Fine Art,** in the **Fairmont Orchid** in the Mauna Lani Resort (✆ **808/885-0950**), resembles an art museum of unique Hawaii art pieces.

North Kohala

You and your kids can make a day out of wandering into and out of the tiny towns of Hawi and Kapaau looking at the one-of-a-kind stores ranging from crafts and fine arts (**Ackerman Gallery,** Hawi; ✆ **808/889-5971**) to whimsical clothes and accessories (**As Hawi Turns;** ✆ **808/889-5023**).

Waimea

Nestled in the rolling hills between the Kohala and Mauna Kea mountains is this upcountry community of cowboys, retirees, and upscale yuppies. It has great farmers' markets (see markets below), beautiful flowers, and terrific galleries. Among my favorites are **Silk Road,** Parker Square (✆ **808/885-7474**), where you'll find the best Asian antiques outside of Tokyo; **Bentley's Home and Garden Collection,** Parker Square (✆ **808/885-5565**), which would be Martha Stewart's store if she lived in Hawaii; and **Waimea General Store,** Parker Square (✆ **808/885-4479**), where even your kids will be charmed by this old-fashioned country store with everything from dolls to cookies.

Hamakua Coast

This one-lane country town actually has great shopping for everyone, from New Age merchandise (**Starseed;** ✆ **808/775-9344**), to Hawaiian gifts and toys (**Taro Patch Gift;** ✆ **808/775-7228**), to everything a treasure hunter could desire (or, as Grace Walker, owner of **Honokaa Trading Company** [✆ **808/775-0808**] puts it: "Rustic, tacky, rare—there's something for everyone").

Hilo

Shopping in Hilo is centered on **Kaiko'o Hilo Mall**, 777 Kilauea Ave., near the state and county buildings, **Prince Kuhio Shopping Plaza,** 111 E. Puainako, just off Highway 11 on the road north to Volcano, where you'll find a supermarket, drugstore, Macy's, and other standards; the **Bayfront area** downtown, where the hippest new businesses have taken up residence in the historic buildings lining Kamehameha Avenue; and the new **Waiakea Plaza,** where the big-box retailers (Ross, Office Max, Borders, Wal-Mart) have moved in. For practical needs, there's a **KTA Super Store** at 323 Keawe St. and another at 50 E. Puainako St.

Volcano

Although there are not a lot of shopping opportunities in this quaint mountain village, what's there is unsurpassed. Some of the best artists on the Big Island live here and display their works at **Volcano Art Center,** in Hawaii Volcanoes National Park (✆ **808/967-8222**), which also has lots of workshops, lectures, and other activities; and at **Kilauea Kreations,** on Old Volcano Road (✆ **808/967-8090**), a co-op of artists and crafters who make quilts, jewelry, feather leis, ceramics, and other art forms. Don't miss the village's general store, **Volcano Store,** Huanani and Old Volcano Highway (✆ **808/967-7210**), where your kids will love the huge selection of flowers (they'll ship to the mainland), stone cookies (as in hard-as-stone but delicious), taro chips (yummy), and local *poha* (gooseberry) jam.

Mall Rats

The Big Island is not big on shopping centers; the series of tiny towns that dot the island generally have small boutique shops. However, the resort areas of Keauhou and Waikoloa and the capital city, Hilo, do have malls that offer many shopping opportunities.

In Hilo, **Prince Kuhio Plaza,** 111 E. Puainako, just off Highway 11 (✆ **808/959-3555;** www.princekuhioplaza.com), has something for everyone, with nearly 100 shops from Cold Stone Creamery to Macy's, plus a multiplex cinema. South of Kona in the resort area, the **Keauhou Shopping Center,** 78-6831 Alii Dr. (✆ **808/322-3000**), has some three dozen different stores, plus the seemingly required multiplex cinema. The **Kings' Shops,** 250 Waikoloa Beach Dr., Waikoloa Beach Resort, located near the Marriott (✆ **808/886-8811;** www.waikoloaresort.com/shops), features 50 different shops ranging from Crazy Shirts to Dairy Queen.

THE GOODS A TO Z

Aloha Wear

The best place for aloha wear is **Sig Zane Designs,** 122 Kamehameha Ave., Hilo (✆ **808/935-7077**). The store is awash in aloha shirts, pareus, muumuu, and T-shirts. High-quality, made-in-Hawaii crafts and works of art, such as gleaming woods, lauhala mats, and accessories (handmade house slippers), are also available. They all center on the Sig Zane fabric designs. Sig and his staff take time to talk story and explain the significance of the images, or to simply chat about Hilo, hula, and Hawaiian culture.

For great prices on aloha wear and a wide range of souvenirs and gifts from Hawaii, check out the two locations of **Hilo Hattie—The Store of Hawaii** at 75-5597-A Pualani Rd. (off of Pualani next door to Burger King; ✆ **808/329-7200**), in Kona, and 111 E. Puainako St., Hilo (✆ **808/961-3077**); or check out their fashion, gifts, books, and the like online at www.hilohattie.com. There's a great selection of kids' toys and books, too.

Baby & Preschooler Clothes

Probably the best clothing store for kids is **Giggles,** with two locations: in the Kings' Shops in Waikoloa Beach Resort (✆ **808/886-0014**) and the Parker Ranch Shopping Center, Wailea (✆ **808/885-2151**). Giggles is a clothing boutique just for kids with not only clothes but also Hawaiian gifts, toys, books, puppets, kites, and much more.

Books

You could spend a week browsing through Hawaii's bookstores. There's everything here from the big chains, **Borders Books & Music,** with two locations at 75-1000 Henry St., Kailua-Kona (✆ **808/331-1668**), and 310 Makaala St., Hilo (✆ **808/933-1410**); to the amazing **Kohala Book Shop,** Highway 270 (Akoni Pule Hwy.), a block from the Kamehameha statue, Kapaau (✆ **808/889-6732**). The largest new- and used-book store on the Big Island is worth the drive to North Kohala to see a priceless collection that includes out-of-print first editions, the $22,500 set of *Captain Cook's Journals,* and a copy of *The Morals of Confucius* (dated 1691 and priced at $350). Popular fiction is available as well, along with titles on Hawaii and Oceania. At last count, the inventory was 20,000 and climbing.

Flowers & Leis

In addition to the farmers' markets (see below), the best place for great leis and flowers is **Emma's Flowers,** New International Market Place, on Luhia Street, in the Old Industrial Area in Kona (✆ **808/329-7746**), with creative leis at bargain prices.

Food

For everyday grocery needs, **KTA Stores** (in the Kona Coast Shopping Center, at Palani Rd. and Queen Kaahumanu Hwy.; in the Keauhou Shopping Village on Alii Dr.; in Waimea, at 65-1158 Mamalahoa Hwy.; and in Hilo, at 50 E. Puainako St. and 321 Keawe St.) are always our first choice. Through its Mountain Apple brand, KTA sells hundreds of top-notch local products—from Kona smoked marlin and Hilo-grown

Kona Coffee Craze!

Coffeehouses are booming on the Big Island. Why not? This is, after all, the home of Kona coffee, and it's a wide-open field for the dozens of vendors competing for your loyalty and dollars.

Most of the farms are concentrated in the North and South Kona districts, where coffee remains a viable industry. Notable among them is the **Kona Blue Sky Coffee Company,** in Holualoa (✆ **877/322-1700** or 808/322-1700). You can also find Blue Sky at the Marriott Waikoloa Beach Resort and at the cheerful outdoor market, Alii Marketplace Gardens in Kailua-Kona, open Wednesday through Sunday.

Also in Holualoa, 10 minutes above Kailua-Kona, **Holualoa Kona Coffee Company** (✆ **800/334-0348** or 808/322-9937) purveys organic Kona from its own farm and other growers: unsprayed, hand-picked, sun-dried, and carefully roasted. Not only can you buy premium, unadulterated Kona coffee here, but you also can witness the hulling, sorting, roasting, and packaging of beans on a farm tour, Monday through Friday from 8am to 4pm.

The **Bad Ass Coffee Company** has franchises in Kainaliu, Kawaihae, Honokaa, Keauhou, and Kailua-Kona, all selling its 100% Kona as well as coffees from Molokai, Kauai, and other tropical regions.

In Waimea, the **Waimea Coffee Company,** Parker Square, Highway 19 (✆ **808/885-4472**), a deli/coffeehouse/retail operation, features the top of the line: organic pure Kona from Sakamoto Estate, organic Hamakua coast coffee from Carter's Coffee Farm, pure water-processed decaf—an impressive selection of the island's best estate-grown coffees—plus signature blends and coffee from Molokai Plantation.

A good bet in Hilo is **Bears' Coffee,** 106 Keawe St. (✆ **808/935-0708**), the quintessential sidewalk coffeehouse and a Hilo stalwart. Regulars love to start their day here, with coffee and specialties such as souffléed eggs, cooked light and fluffy in the espresso machine and served in a croissant. It's a great lunch spot as well.

rainbow trout to cookies, breads, jams and jellies, taro chips, and *kulolo,* the decadently dense taro-coconut steamed pudding—by dozens of local vendors. Our other favorite is **Kona Natural Foods,** in the Crossroads Center (✆ **808/329-2296**). It's been upgraded from a health food store to a full-on healthful supermarket. In Hilo, stop by **Abundant Life Natural Foods,** 292 Kamehameha Ave. (✆ **808/935-7411**), and **Island Natural Market and Deli,** 303 Makaala St. (✆ **808/935-5533**).

Hawaiiana & Gift Items

The best gift to take back to someone or a souvenir for yourself is something Hawaiian. Our selection of the best stores to find that certain something that will forever remind you and your kids about your fabulous trip to Hawaii begins with **The Grass Shack,** Highway 11, Kealakekua (✆ **808/323-2877**), which offers a large selection of local woodcrafts, Niihau shell and wiliwili-seed leis, packaged coffee, pahu drums, nose flutes, and lauhala (woven pandanus leaves) in every form. In Hulualoa, the **Kimura Lauhala Shop,** at Mamalahoa Highway and Hualalai Road (✆ **808/324-0053**), specializes in everything lauhala—from rolled-up mats and wide-brimmed hats to tote bags, coasters, and coin purses.

For a great selection of Hawaiian wood art (in the forms of bowls, rocking chairs, and jewelry boxes), books on Hawaii, and other Hawaiiana items, go to **Waipio Valley Artworks,** on the way to Waipio Valley in Kukuihaele (✆ 808/775-0958).

Markets

The best farmers' market on the Big Island—perhaps in all of Hawaii—is the **Hilo Farmers' Market,** Kamehameha Avenue at Mamo Street (✆ **808/933-1000**), where more than 120 vendors from around the island bring their flowers, produce, and baked goods to this teeming corner of Hilo every Wednesday and Saturday from sunrise to 4pm. Because many of the vendors sell out early, go as early as you can. The selection changes by the week, but it's always reasonable, fresh, and appealing, with a good cross section of the island's specialties. Although it's open daily, Wednesday and Saturday are the days when all the vendors are there.

For produce and flowers straight from the farm, go to the **Kona Farmers' Market,** New International Market Place, on Luhia Street, in the Old Industrial Area in Kona, open Monday to Saturday. You'll find taro, organic vine-ripened tomatoes, Kamuela string beans, lettuces, potatoes, and whatever is in season. Small and sublime, the **Waimea Farmers' Market,** Highway 19, at mile marker 55 on the Hamakua side of Waimea town (on the lawn in front of the Department of Hawaiian Home Lands, West Hawaii office), draws a loyal crowd from 7am to noon on Saturday.

Music

For a great selection of all kinds of music, but especially the sweet Hawaiian music you hear while you're in the islands, head for **Mele Kai Music,** 74-5467 Kaiwi St., Kailua-Kona (✆ **808/329-1454**).

Shoes

The cheapest source of slippers (go-aheads or rubber sandals) is **Longs Drugs,** where for $2.50 you can get a pair of slippers that will last just about as long as your vacation. Longs is located in Kona in the Launihou Shopping Center, 75-5595 Palani Rd. (✆ **808/329-1380**); in Keauhou in the Keauhou Shopping Center (✆ **808/322-5122**); and in Hilo at 555 Kileau St. (✆ **808/935-3357**), Prince Kuhio Plaza (✆ **808/959-5881**), and 2100 Kanoelehua Ave. (✆ **808/959-5871**).

Surf & Sports

The surf-and-sun enthusiast will find anything to do with the ocean, from bodyboards to sunglasses, plus swimwear, T-shirts, hats, bags, dresses, sweatshirts, even aloha shirts, at **Honolua Surf Company,** Kona Inn Shopping Village, Alii Drive (✆ **808/329-1001**).

Sweets for the Sweet

While you're on the Big Island, be sure to try the chocolates at the top two candy makers. **Kailua Candy Company,** 75-5612 Kauhola St., in the New Industrial Area (✆ **800/622-2462** or 808/329-2522; www.kailua-candy.com), was selected by *Bon Appétit* as one of the top-10 chocolate shops in the U.S.—try the legendary macadamia nut *honu* (turtle), or "Cathy's Favorite Dessert," a rich dark-chocolate Kona-coffee mousse on a dark-chocolate cookie crust with dark ganache frosting (yum!). On the Hilo side is **Big Island Candies,** 585 Hinano St. (✆ **800/935-5510** or 808/935-8890; www.bigisland candies.com), where owner Alan Ikawa has turned cookie making into an art and spectator sport. Large viewing windows allow you to watch the hand-dipping from huge vats of chocolate while the aroma of butter fills the room. Everything is wonderful, but the best are the shortbread cookies, dipped in chocolate, peanut butter, and white chocolate.

Toys

Roots and Wings, 81-6372 Mamalahoa Hwy., Kealakekua (✆ **808/323-2229**), has a wonderful selection of natural and educational toys, plus organic products for babies and small children. For the cowboy or cowgirl in your family, saddle up to the **Parker Ranch Store,** in the Parker Ranch Shopping Center, 67-1185 Mamalahoa Hwy. (Hwy. 190), Waimea (✆ **808/885-5669;** www.parkerranch.com), where they have toys, games, and clothes for your cowpoke to remember his or her trip to Hawaii. In Hilo, **Imiloa, Astronomy Center of Hawaii,** 600 Imiloa Place (✆ **808/969-9728**), has an excellent Museum Store with a great collection for kids of books, toys, and gifts that are not only educational but fun.

9 ENTERTAINMENT FOR THE WHOLE FAMILY

Jokes abound about island nightlife being an oxymoron, but there are a few pockets of entertainment here, largely in the Kailua-Kona and Kohala coast resorts. Your best bet is to check the local newspapers—*Honolulu Advertiser* and *West Hawaii Today*—for special shows, such as fundraisers, that are held at local venues. Other than that, regular entertainment in the local clubs usually consists of mellow Hawaiian music at sunset, small hula groups, or jazz trios.

THEATER

Some of the island's best events are held at **Kahilu Theatre,** in Waimea (✆ **808/885-6017;** www.kahilutheatre.org), so be on the lookout for any mention of it during your stay. Hula, the top Hawaiian music groups from all over Hawaii, drama, and all aspects of the performing arts use Kahilu as a venue.

Like most rural communities, the Big Island also has community theater, which ranges from kids' productions to surprisingly good musicals, dramas, and comedies. Check the schedule of events at **Aloha Theatre,** 79-7384 Mamalahoa Hwy., Kainaliu (✆ 808/322-2122; www.alohatheatre.com); **Hilo Theatre,** 291 Keawe St. (✆ 808/969-3939); **Hilo Community Players,** 141 Kalakaua St. (✆ 808/935-9155); **Honokaa Peoples Theatre,**

 Honokaa (© 808/775-0000); and **Palace Theatre,** 38 Haili St., Hilo (© 808/934-7010; www.palacehilo.org).

HAWAIIAN MUSIC

The Kohala Coast Resorts

Hawaiian entertainment for families can generally be found at a luau or in the lounge music at scenic terrace bars with scintillating sunset views. But newcomer **Marriott Waikoloa's Hawaii Calls** restaurant and adjoining **Clipper Lounge** are bright new venues for local musicians, with live music nightly from 8:30 to 11:30pm. The **Hilton Waikolo Beach**'s newly opened **Malolo Lounge** (© **808/886-1234;** www.hiltonwaikoloavillage.com) has nightly live entertainment of Hawaiian music (5–8pm) and jazz (9pm–midnight).

If you get a chance to see the **Lim Family,** don't miss them. Immensely talented in hula and song, members of the family perform in the intimate setting of the Mauna Lani Bay Hotel's **Atrium Bar** (© **808/885-6622**), and at the Hapuna Beach Prince Hotel's open-air **Reef Lounge** (© **808/880-1111**).

Hilo

Hilo's most notable events are special or annual occasions such as the **Merrie Monarch Hula Festival,** the state's largest, which continues for a week after Easter Sunday. The festivities include hula competitions from all over the world, demonstrations, and crafts fairs. A staggering spirit of pageantry takes over the entire town. Tickets are always hard to come by; call © **808/935-9168** well ahead of time.

Special concerts are also held at the **Hawaii Naniloa Hotel's Crown Room** (© **808/969-3333**), the Hilo venue for big-name performers from Oahu and the outer islands. You can always count on a great act here, whether it's the Brothers Cazimero or Willie K.

The Big Island's Best Luau

The longest continuously running luau on the island, **Kona Village Luau,** in Kona Village Resort (© **808/325-5555;** www.konavillage.com), is still the best—a combination of an authentic Polynesian venue with a menu that works, impressive entertainment, and the spirit of Old Hawaii. The feast begins with a ceremony in a sandy kiawe grove, where the pig is unearthed after a full day of cooking in a rock-heated underground oven. In the open-air dining room, next to prehistoric lagoons and tropical gardens, you'll sample a Polynesian buffet: poisson cru, poi, *laulau* (butterfish, seasoned pork, and taro leaves cooked in ti leaves), lomi salmon, squid luau (cooked taro leaves with steamed octopus and coconut milk), ahi poke, *opihi* (fresh limpets), coconut pudding, taro chips, sweet potatoes, chicken long rice, steamed breadfruit, and the shredded kalua pig. The generosity is striking. The Polynesian revue, a fast-moving, mesmerizing tour of South Pacific cultures, manages—miraculously—to avoid being clichéd or corny.

The luau begins Friday at 5:30pm; reservations are required. Admission is included in the full American plan for Kona Village guests; for nonguests, admission is $95 for adults, $56 for children 6 to 12, and $30 for children 2 to 5. American Express, Discover, MasterCard, and Visa are accepted.

Moments Old-Style Hawaiian Entertainment

The plaintive drone of the conch shell pierces the air, calling all to assemble. A sizzling orange sun sinks slowly toward the cobalt waters of the Pacific. In the distance the majestic mountain, Mauna Kea, reflects the waning sun's light with a fiery red that fades to a hazy purple and finally to an inky black as a voluptuous full moon dramatically rises over her shoulder.

It's **"Twilight at Kalahuipua'a,"** a monthly Hawaiian cultural celebration, which includes storytelling, singing, and dancing on the oceanside, grassy lawn that fronts a turn-of-the-20th-century–style wooden cottage at Mauna Lani Bay Resort (✆ **808/885-6622**). These full-moon events, created by Daniel Akaka, Jr., who is Mauna Lani Resort's director of cultural affairs, hearken back to another time in Hawaii, when family and neighbors would gather on back porches, in carports, and in yards to sing, dance, and "talk story."

Each month, guests, ranging from the ultra-well-known in the world of Hawaiian entertainment to the virtually unknown local *kupuna* (elder), gather to perpetuate the traditional folk art of storytelling, with plenty of music and dance thrown in.

For more than half a decade, Twilight at Kalahuipua'a, always set on a Saturday closest to the full moon, really gets underway at least an hour before the 5:30pm start. People from across the island, and guests staying at the hotel, arrive carrying picnic baskets, mats, coolers, babies, and cameras. A sort of oceanside, premusic, tailgate party takes place with *kamaaina* (local resident) families sharing their plate lunches, sushi, and beverages with visitors, who have catered lunches, packaged sandwiches, and taro chips, in a truly old-fashioned demonstration of aloha.

MOVIES

For mainstream movies in Kona, call **Makalapua Stadium Cinemas** in Kona (✆ **808/327-0444;** www.wallacetheaters.com); and **Keauhou 7 Cinemas** in Keauhou Shopping Center (✆ **808/324-7200;** www.signaturetheatres.com). In Hilo, call **Kress Cinemas** (✆ **808/961-3456;** www.wallacetheaters.com); **Prince Kuhio Stadium Cinemas** (✆ **808/959-4595;** www.wallacetheaters.com); and **Waikea Theatres,** Waikea Shopping Plaza (✆ **808/934-9747**).

There are three venues for "art" films that don't make it to the mainstream theaters: **Aloha Theatre,** 79-7384 Mamalahoa Hwy., Kainaliu (✆ **808/322-2122;** www.aloha theatre.com); **Kahilu Theatre,** in Waimea (✆ **808/885-6017;** www.kahilutheatre.org); and **Palace Theater,** 38 Haili St., Hilo (✆ **808/934-7010**).

STORY HOURS

A range of storytelling and read-aloud programs are offered by the public library branches, from magic shows for the preschoolers to storytelling for older children. For information on these and other storytelling programs, contact the **Hawaii State Public Library** (✆ **808/327-4327;** www.librarieshawaii.org).

6

Maui

Maui meets all the criteria for family fun in tropical paradise: beautiful scenery (swaying palm trees bordering perfect white-sand coves), plenty to do (from snorkeling in a sea of rainbow-hued fish to hiking to viewing thundering waterfalls), and a traditional luau where you can chow down on an earthen-baked pig.

And everybody, it seems, knows it. Next to Waikiki, Maui is Hawaii's most popular destination, welcoming 2.5 million people each year to its sunny shores. As soon as you arrive at Kahului Airport, a huge banner will tell you that readers of *Condé Nast Traveler* voted Maui the best island *in the world*—and they've done so for 14 years running.

On a map, Maui doesn't look like much, but it's bigger than you might think. The 727-square-mile island has three peaks more than a mile high, thousands of waterfalls, 120 miles of shoreline, and more than 80 golden-sand beaches (including two that are more than a mile long). The island is the result of a marriage of two shield volcanoes, 10,023-foot-high Haleakala and 5,788-foot-high Puu Kukui, that spilled enough lava between them to create a valley—and inspire the island's nickname, "The Valley Isle." Thanks to this unusual makeup, Maui packs a lot of nature in and around its landscape, and its microclimates offer distinct variations on the tropical-island theme: The island's as lush as an equatorial rainforest in Hana, as dry as the Arizona desert in Makena, as hot as Mexico in Lahaina, and as cool and misty as Oregon up in Kula.

Maui has become *the* Hawaiian destination for families. Indeed, sometimes it feels a little too well-known—especially when you're stuck in bumper-to-bumper traffic or the wall-to-wall boat jam at Maui's popular snorkeling/diving atoll, Molokini Crater. However, the congestion here pales in comparison to that in big-city Honolulu; Maui is really a casual collection of small towns. Once you move beyond the resort areas, you'll find a slower, more peaceful way of life, where car horns are used only to greet friends, posted store hours mean nothing if the surf's up, and taking time to watch the sunset is part of the daily routine.

Maui also has an underlying energy that can nudge even your most sluggish child right off his or her beach blanket. Kids (and even adults) get inspired to do things they might not do otherwise, such as rise before dawn to catch the sunrise over Haleakala Crater, then mount a bicycle to coast 37 switchbacked miles down to sea level; head out to sea to look for wintering humpback whales; swim in the clear pool of a waterfall; or discover a whole new world of exotic flowers and tropical fish.

1 ORIENTATION

ARRIVING

If you think of the island of Maui as the shape of a person's head and shoulders, you'll probably arrive on its neck, at **Kahului Airport.**

Try to fly directly to Maui—otherwise, you will be stuck with flying into Honolulu, with the likelihood of a 2-hour layover between flights. As of press time, these airlines fly directly from the mainland to Maui: **United Airlines** (✆ **800/241-6522;** www.united.com) has nonstop service from Chicago, Los Angeles, and San Francisco; **Hawaiian Airlines** (✆ **800/367-5320;** www.hawaiianair.com) offers direct flights from Portland and Seattle; **American Airlines** (✆ **800/433-7300;** www.aa.com) has direct service from Los Angeles and Dallas; **Delta Airlines** (✆ **800/221-1212;** www.delta.com) flies direct from Los Angeles and Salt Lake City; **Northwest Airlines** (✆ **800/221-1212;** www.nwa.com) travels from Seattle; and **U.S. Airways/American West** (✆ **800/428-4322;** www.usairways.com) flies from Phoenix.

Direct flights from Canada include **Air Canada** (✆ **888/247-2262;** www.aircanada.com), with flights from Vancouver, and **West Jet** (✆ **888/937-8538;** www.westjet.com), with flights from Vancouver.

The other major carriers fly to Honolulu, where you'll have to pick up an interisland flight to Maui. **Hawaiian Airlines** (✆ **800/367-5320** or 808/838-1555; www.hawaiianair.com) and **go!** (✆ **888/IFLYGO2** [435-9462]**;** www.iflygo.com) offer jet service from Honolulu and the other neighbor islands.

LANDING AT KAHULUI If there's a long wait at baggage claim, and the kids, already cranky from the long airplane ride, are getting even crankier, step over to the state-operated **Visitor Information Center** and pick up brochures and the latest issue of *Maui Visitor Magazine* or *This Week Maui;* both feature great regional maps of the islands.

If you're not renting a car (and you should, because there's no public transportation on Maui), the cheapest way to get to your hotel is via **SpeediShuttle** (✆ **800/977-2605** or 808/661-6667; www.speedishuttle.com). It can take you between Kahului Airport and all the major resorts between 6am and 11pm daily. Rates vary, but for one person, figure on $39 one-way to Wailea, $54 one-way to Kaanapali, and $74 one-way to Kapalua. Be sure to call ahead of time to arrange pickup.

VISITOR INFORMATION

The **Maui Visitors Bureau** is at 1727 Wili Pa Loop, Wailuku, Maui, HI 96793 (✆ **800/525-MAUI** [525-6284] or 808/244-3530; www.visitmaui.com). Contact them in advance and they'll send you heaps of information on things to do with your family.

MAUI IN BRIEF

Central Maui

Maui's main airport lies in this flat, often windy corridor between Maui's two volcanoes, where most of the island's population lives. You'll find good shopping and dining bargains here, as well as the heart of the business community and the local government.

West Maui

This is the fabled Maui you see on postcards: jagged peaks, green velvet valleys, a wilderness full of native species, and the majestic West Maui Mountains, the epitome of earthly paradise. The beaches here are some of the islands' best. And it's no secret: This stretch of coastline along Maui's "forehead," from Kapalua to the historic port of Lahaina, is the island's most bustling resort area (with south Maui close behind). Expect a few mainland-style traffic jams.

If you want to book into a resort or condo on this coast, first consider what community your family will be comfortable in. Starting at the southern end of west Maui and moving northward, the coastal communities look like this:

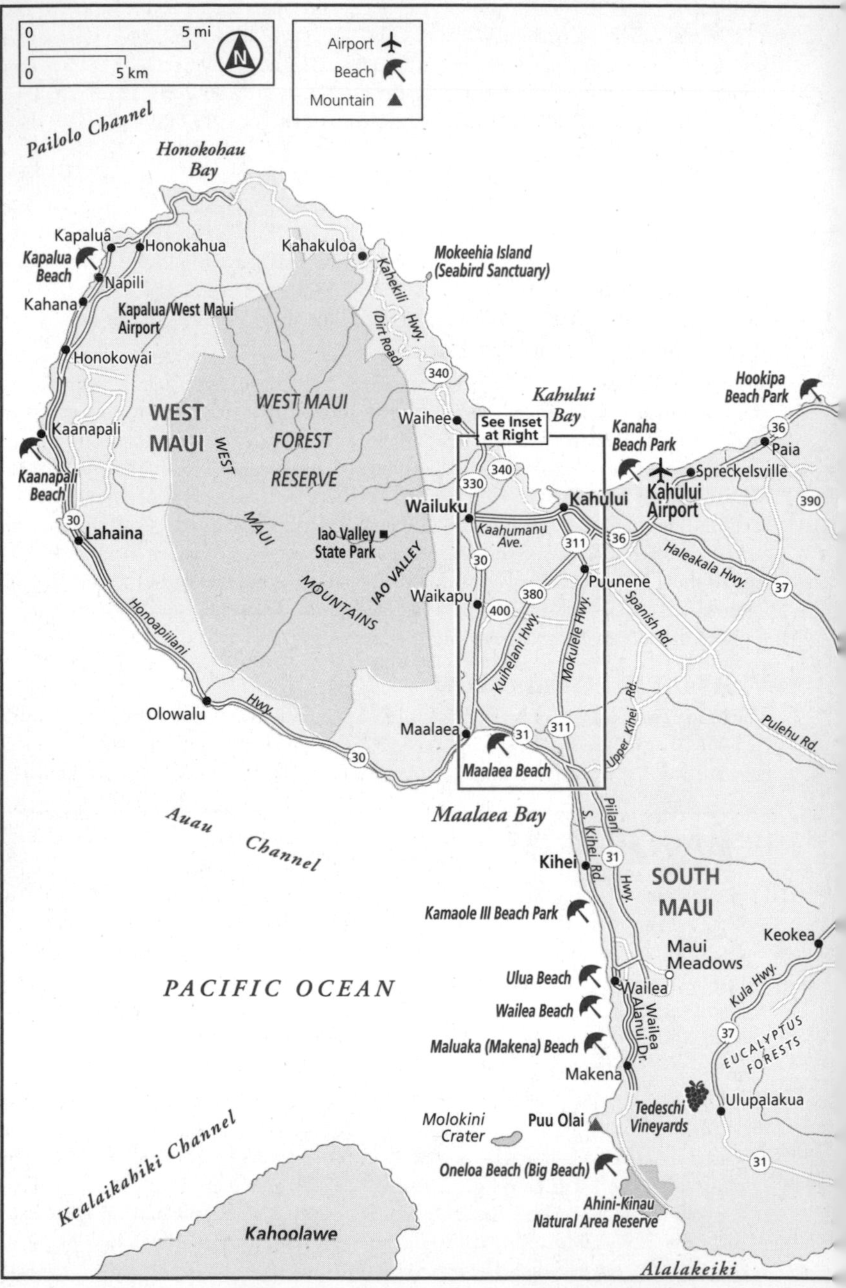

0
5 mi
0
5 km
N
Airport
Beach
Mountain
Pailolo Channel
Honokohau Bay
Kapalua
Kapalua Beach
Honokahua
Napili
Kahana
Kapalua/West Maui Airport
Honokowai
Kahakuloa
Kahekili Hwy. (Dirt Road)
Mokeehia Island (Seabird Sanctuary)
340
WEST MAUI
WEST MAUI FOREST RESERVE
WEST MAUI MOUNTAINS
Kaanapali
Kaanapali Beach
30
Lahaina
Waihee
See Inset at Right
Kahului Bay
340
330
Wailuku
Kahului
Kaahumanu Ave.
Iao Valley State Park
IAO VALLEY
311
30
Puunene
Waikapu
380
400
Kuihelani Hwy.
Mokulele Hwy.
Honoapiilani Hwy.
Olowalu
Maalaea
31
311
Maalaea Beach
30
Hookipa Beach Park
Kanaha Beach Park
36
Paia
Spreckelsville
Kahului Airport
390
36
Haleakala Hwy.
37
Spanish Rd.
Upper Kihei Rd.
Pulehu Rd.
Auau Channel
Maalaea Bay
Piilani Hwy.
S. Kihei Rd.
31
Kihei
SOUTH MAUI
Kamaole III Beach Park
Keokea
Maui Meadows
PACIFIC OCEAN
Ulua Beach
Wailea
Wailea Beach
Wailea Alanui Dr.
Kula Hwy.
37
EUCALYPTUS FORESTS
Maluaka (Makena) Beach
Makena
Tedeschi Vineyards
Ulupalakua
Molokini Crater
Puu Olai
Oneloa Beach (Big Beach)
31
Kealaikahiki Channel
Ahini-Kinau Natural Area Reserve
Kahoolawe
Alalakeiki

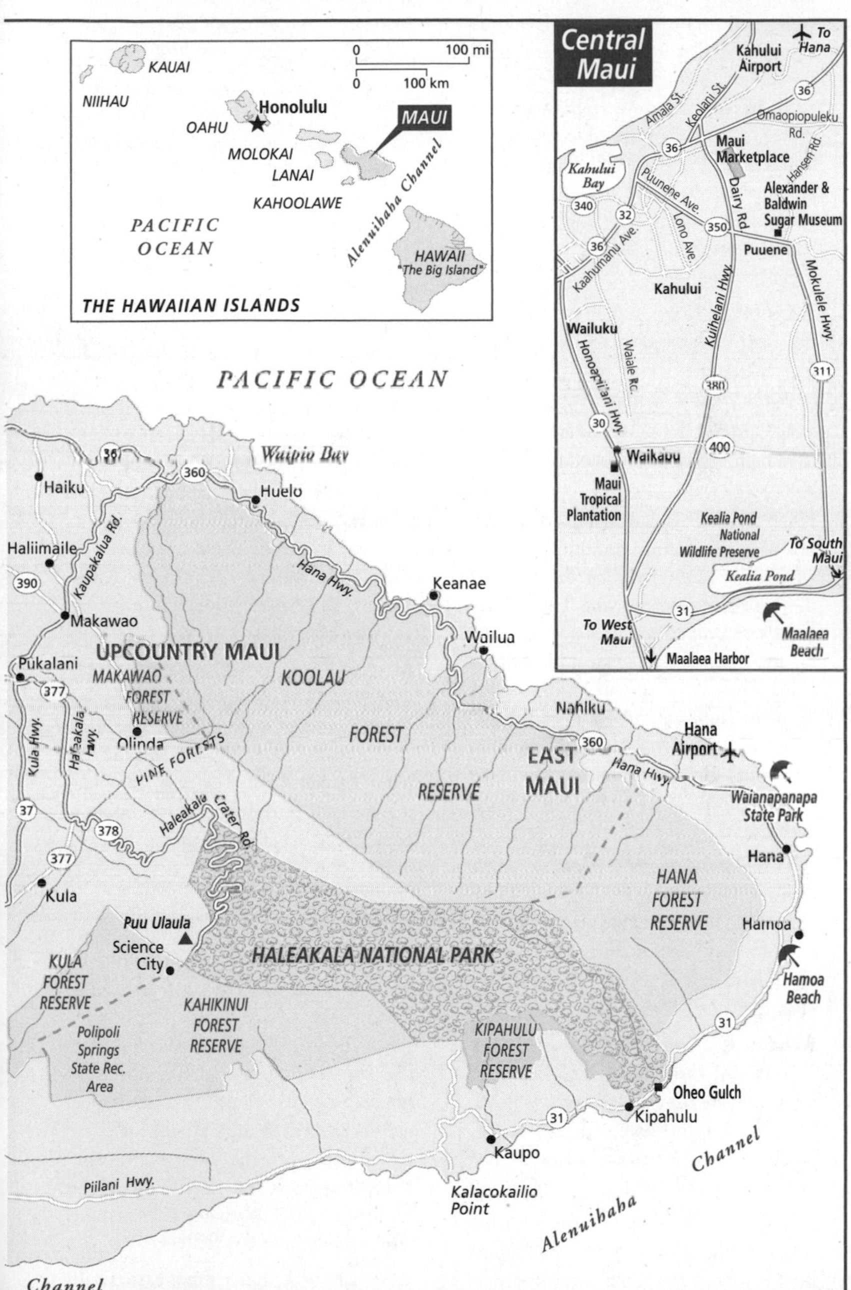
Central Maui
Kahului Airport
To Hana
Amala St.
Keolani St.
Omaopiopuleku Rd.
Maui Marketplace
Hansen Rd.
Kahului Bay
Puunene Ave.
Dairy Rd.
Alexander & Baldwin Sugar Museum
Lono Ave.
Puuene
Kaahumanu Ave.
Mokulele Hwy.
Kahului
Wailuku
Kuihelani Hwy.
Waiale Rd.
Maui Tropical Plantation
Kealia Pond National Wildlife Preserve
To South Maui
Kealia Pond
To West Maui
Maalaea Harbor
Maalaea Beach
KAUAI
NIIHAU
OAHU
Honolulu
MAUI
MOLOKAI
LANAI
KAHOOLAWE
Alenuihaha Channel
PACIFIC OCEAN
HAWAII "The Big Island"
THE HAWAIIAN ISLANDS
0 100 mi
0 100 km
PACIFIC OCEAN
Haiku
Huelo
Haliimaile
Kaupakalua Rd.
Hana Hwy.
Keanae
Makawao
Wailua
UPCOUNTRY MAUI
Pukalani
MAKAWAO FOREST RESERVE
KOOLAU
FOREST
RESERVE
Olinda
PINE FORESTS
Kula Hwy.
EAST MAUI
Hana Airport
Waianapanapa State Park
Haleakala Crater Rd.
Hana
Kula
HANA FOREST RESERVE
Hamoa
Puu Ulaula
Science City
HALEAKALA NATIONAL PARK
KULA FOREST RESERVE
KAHIKINUI FOREST RESERVE
Hamoa Beach
Polipoli Springs State Rec. Area
KIPAHULU FOREST RESERVE
Oheo Gulch
Kipahulu
Kaupo
Piilani Hwy.
Kalacokailio Point
Alenuihaha Channel
Channel

LAHAINA This old seaport is a tame version of its former self, when whalers swaggered ashore in search of women and grog. Today, the village teems with restaurants, T-shirt shops, and galleries, and parts of it are downright tacky; but there's still lots of real history to be found amid the gimcracks. Lahaina is a great place to stay; accommodation choices include a few hotels, quaint bed-and-breakfasts, and a handful of oceanfront condos.

KAANAPALI ★ Farther north along the west Maui coast is Hawaii's first master-planned family resort. Kids will love the nearly 3 miles of gold-sand beach here, but the hotels can be pricey (although the amenities may be worth it).

HONOKOWAI, KAHANA & NAPILI If a condominium unit is really what your family will be comfortable in, this is the place for you. These older oceanside units offer excellent bargains for astute travelers. The great location—along sandy beaches, within minutes of both the Kapalua and Kaanapali resort areas, and close enough to the goings-on in Lahaina town—makes this area an accommodations haven for the budget-minded.

In **Honokowai** and **Mahinahina,** you'll find mostly older units that tend to be cheaper. There's not much shopping here (mostly convenience stores), but you'll have easy access to the shops and restaurants of Kaanapali.

Kahana is a little more upscale than Honokowai and Mahinahina. Most of its condos are big high-rise types, newer than those immediately to the south. You'll find a nice selection of shops and restaurants in the area.

Napili is a much-sought-after area for condo seekers: It's quiet; has great beaches, restaurants, and shops; and is close to Kapalua. Units are generally more expensive here (although I've found a few hidden gems at affordable prices).

KAPALUA ★★★ This is the very exclusive domain of the expensive Ritz-Carlton Kapalua, surrounded by white-sand beaches, and next to two bays that are marine-life preserves (with fabulous surfing in winter). A host of condos and vacation homes are located here, but be aware that the astronomical prices match the incredible views.

South Maui

This is the hottest, sunniest, driest, most popular coastline on Maui for sun lovers—Arizona by the sea. Rain rarely falls here, and temperatures stick to around 85°F (29°C) year-round. On this former scrubland from Maalaea to Makena, where cactuses once grew wild and cows grazed, there are now four distinctive areas—Maalaea, Kihei, Wailea, and Makena—and a surprising amount of traffic.

MAALAEA This windy oceanfront village centers on the small boat harbor (with a general store, a few restaurants, and a small shopping arcade) and the **Maui Ocean Center** ★★★, an aquarium/ocean complex. Before booking your family here, be aware that it's often—about 350 days a year—very windy.

KIHEI Kihei is less a proper town than a nearly continuous series of condos and minimalls lining South Kihei Road. This is Maui's best family vacation bargain. Budget travelers swarm like sun-seeking geckos over the eight sandy beaches along this scalloped, condo-packed, 7-mile stretch of coast. Kihei is neither charming nor quaint; what it lacks in aesthetics, though, it more than makes up for in sunshine, affordability, and convenience.

WAILEA ★★★ This manicured oasis of multimillion-dollar resort hotels lines

2 miles of palm-fringed gold coast—sort of Beverly Hills by the sea, except California never had it so good: warm, clear water full of tropical fish; year-round golden sunshine and clear blue skies; and hedonistic pleasure palaces on 1,500 acres of black-lava shore indented by five beautiful beaches.

MAKENA ★★★ Suddenly, the road enters raw wilderness. After Wailea's overdone density, the thorny landscape is a welcome relief. It's a long drive from Makena to anywhere on Maui. If you're looking for an activity-filled family vacation, you might want to try somewhere else, or you'll spend most of your vacation in the car. But if you want a quiet, relaxing respite, where the biggest trip of the day is from your bed to the beach, Makena is the place.

UPCOUNTRY MAUI

After a few days at the beach, you'll probably take notice of the 10,000-foot mountain in the middle of Maui. The slopes of Haleakala ("House of the Sun") are home to cowboys, growers, and other country people who wave back as you drive by. You can see a thousand tropical sunsets reflected in the windows of houses old and new, strung along a road that runs like a loose hound from Makawao to Kula, where the road leads up to the crater and **Haleakala National Park ★★★**.

MAKAWAO ★★★ Until recently, this small, two-street upcountry town was little more than a post office, a gas station, a feed store, a bakery, and a restaurant/bar serving the cowboys and farmers living in the surrounding community; the hitching posts outside storefronts really were used to tie up horses. As the population of Maui started expanding in the 1970s, a health-food store sprang up, followed by boutiques, a chiropractic clinic, and a host of health-conscious restaurants. The result is an eclectic amalgam of old *paniolo* (cowboy) Hawaii and the baby boomer trends of transplanted mainlanders. **Hui No'Eau Visual Arts Center ★**, Hawaii's premier arts collective, is definitely worth a peek.

KULA A feeling of pastoral remoteness prevails in this upcountry community of old flower farms, humble cottages, and new suburban ranch houses with million-dollar views that take in the ocean, the isthmus, the West Maui Mountains, and, at night, the lights that run along the gold coast like a string of pearls, from Maalaea to Puu Olai.

EAST MAUI

THE ROAD TO HANA ★★★ When old sugar towns die, they usually fade away in rust and red dirt. Not **Paia ★★★**. The tangled spaghetti of electrical, phone, and cable wires hanging overhead symbolizes the town's ability to adapt to the times—it may look messy, but it works. Here, trendy restaurants, eclectic boutiques, and high-tech windsurf shops stand next door to a ma-and-pa grocery, a fish market, and stores that have been serving customers since plantation days. Hippies took over in the 1970s; although their macrobiotic restaurants and old-style artists' co-op have made way for Hawaiian Regional Cuisine and galleries featuring the works of renowned international artists, Paia still manages to maintain a pleasantly granola vibe. The town's main attraction, though, is **Hookipa Beach Park ★★★**, where the wind that roars through the isthmus of Maui brings windsurfers from around the world.

HANA ★★★ Set between an emerald rainforest and the blue Pacific is a village probably best defined by what it lacks: golf courses, shopping malls, and McDonald's. Except for a gas station and a bank with an ATM, you'll find little of what passes for progress here. Instead, you'll discover the simple joys of fragrant tropical flowers, the sweet taste of backyard bananas and papayas, and the easy calm and unabashed small-town aloha spirit of Old Hawaii. What saved "heavenly" Hana from the inevitable march of progress? The 52-mile **Hana Highway,** which winds around 600 curves and crosses more than 50 one-lane bridges on its way from Kahului. You can go to Hana for the day—it's a 3-hour drive from Kihei and Lahaina (and a half-century away)—but 3 days are better.

2 GETTING AROUND

BY CAR

The only way to really see Maui is by rental car; there's no islandwide public transit. All of the major car rental firms have agencies on Maui.

If you get into trouble on Maui's highways, look for the flashing blue strobe lights on 12-foot poles; at the base are emergency solar-powered call boxes (programmed to dial 911 as soon as you pick up the handset). There are 29 emergency call boxes on the island's busiest highways and remote areas, including along the Hana and Haleakala highways and on the north end of the island in the remote community of Kahakuloa.

BY TAXI

Alii Taxi (© 808/661-3688) offers 24-hour service islandwide. You can also call **Kihei Taxi** (© 808/879-3000), **Islandwide Taxi & Tours** (© 808/874-TAXI [874-8294]), or **Sunshine Cabs of Maui** (© 808/879-2220) if you need a ride.

BY SHUTTLE

Holo Ka'a Public Transit is a public/private partnership that has convenient, economical, and air-conditioned shuttle buses. **Maui Public Transit** consists of seven public bus routes, all operated by Roberts Hawaii (© **808/871-4838;** www.mauicounty.gov/bus). These routes are funded by the County of Maui and provide service in and between various central, south, and west Maui communities. All of the routes are operated Monday through Saturday only. There is no service on Sunday. The routes go from as far south as Wailea up to as far north as Kapalua. Fares are $1 to $2.

Fast Facts Maui

American Express Offices are located in south Maui, at the **Grand Wailea Resort & Spa** (© **808/875-4526**); and in west Maui, at the **Westin Maui** at Kaanapali Beach (© **808/661-7155**).

Babysitters Call **PATCH** (© **808/242-9232**), or your hotel can refer you to qualified babysitters.

Dentists Emergency dental care is available at **Kihei Dental Center,** 1847 S. Kihei Rd., Kihei (© **808/874-8401**); or in Lahaina at the **Aloha Lahaina Dentists,** 134 Luakini St. (in the Maui Medical Group Building), Lahaina (© **808/661-4005**).

Doctors **West Maui Healthcare Center,** Whalers Village, 2435 Kaanapali Pkwy., Suite H-7 (near Leilani's On the Beach), Kaanapali (✆ **808/667-9721;** fax 808/661-1584), is open 365 days a year until 8pm nightly; no appointment is necessary. In Kihei, call **Urgent Care Maui,** 1325 S. Kihei Rd., Suite 103 (at Lipoa St., across from Star Market), Kihei (✆ **808/879-7781**), which is open daily from 7am to 10pm.

Drugstores Unfortunately, there are no 24-hour pharmacies on Maui. In south Maui (Kihei, Wailea, and Maalaea), go to **Safeway Pharmacy,** 277 Pi'ikea Ave. (✆ **808/891-9130**). In west Maui (Lahaina to Kapalua), try the **Lahaina Pharmacy,** Lahaina Shopping Center (✆ **808/661-3119**).

Emergencies Call ✆ **911** for police, fire, and ambulance service. District stations are located in Lahaina (✆ **808/661-4441**) and in Hana (✆ **808/248-8311**).

Hospitals In central Maui, **Maui Memorial Hospital** is at 221 Mahalani, Wailuku (✆ **808/244-9056**). East Maui's **Hana Medical Center** is on Hana Highway (✆ **808/248-8924**). In upcountry Maui, **Kula Hospital** is at 204 Kula Hwy., Kula (✆ **808/878-1221**).

Internet Access Any public library offers Internet access to the public; for a nearby branch, call (✆ **808/243-5766**).

Libraries Maui has a half-dozen libraries. For the one closest to where you're staying, call ✆ **808/243-5766** or check www.librarieshawaii.org.

Post Office To find the nearest post office, call ✆ **800/ASK-USPS** (275-8777). In Lahaina, there are branches at the Lahaina Civic Center, 1760 Honoapiilani Hwy.; and at the Lahaina Shopping Center, 132 Papalaua St. In Kahului, there's a branch at 138 S. Puunene Ave.; and in Kihei, there's one at 1254 S. Kihei Rd.

Radio The most popular stations are **KHPR** 88.1/90.7 FM, the National Public Radio station; **KPOA** 93.5 FM for Hawaiian music; **KAOI** 95.1 FM for contemporary music; **KLHI** 99 FM for oldies music; and **KMVI** 550 AM for pop music and the top morning-drive DJs.

Safety Although Maui is generally a safe tourist destination, visitors have been crime victims, so stay alert. The most common crime against travelers is rental-car break-ins. Never leave any valuables in your car, not even in your trunk. Thieves can be in and out of your trunk faster than you can open it with your own key. Be especially careful at high-risk areas such as beaches and resorts. Never carry large amounts of cash with you. Stay in well-lighted areas after dark. Don't hike on deserted trails alone.

Useful Telephone Numbers For the current weather, call ✆ **808/871-5054;** for Haleakala National Park weather, call ✆ **808/572-9306;** for marine weather and surf and wave conditions, call ✆ **808/877-3477.**

3 FAMILY-FRIENDLY ACCOMMODATIONS

Maui has accommodations to fit every kind of family vacation, from deluxe oceanfront resorts to reasonably priced condos to historic bed-and-breakfasts. I'd suggest getting accommodations close to the activities you want to do on Maui; otherwise, your vacation could turn into long daily car rides with restless children.

Remember that Hawaii's 11.42% accommodations tax will be added to your final bill. Parking is free unless otherwise noted. Also, if you're booking a stay at an upscale hotel, be sure to ask if there is a "resort fee" ($10–$15 a day) tacked onto your bill.

CENTRAL MAUI

If you're arriving late at night or you have an early-morning flight out, the best choice near Kahului Airport is the **Maui Beach Hotel,** 170 Kaahumanu Ave. (✆ **800/367-5004;** 808/877-0051; www.castleresorts.com). The nondescript, motel-like rooms start at $130 ($117 if you book on the Internet) and include free airport shuttle service. It's okay for a night, but not a place to spend your vacation.

WEST MAUI

Lahaina

Expensive

Outrigger Aina Nalu ★ Set on 9 acres in the middle of Lahaina, this property was totally rebuilt, renovated, and remodeled in 2005. Then the units were sold off to private owners and put into a rental pool. The result is a first-class property which is brand-new, with all the latest appliances, new furniture, and 21st-century conveniences. The property isn't on the beach, but on a quiet side street (a rarity in Lahaina) and within walking distance of restaurants, shops, attractions, and the ocean (just 3 blocks away). All of the good-size rooms, decorated in tropical-island style, are comfortable and quiet. A family of four can fit into the one-bedroom suite with complete kitchen; if you want more space, a two-bedroom suite is also available. The entire complex includes a sun deck and swimming pool, a barbecue, and a picnic area. The aloha-friendly staff will take the time to answer all of your questions.

660 Wainee St. (btw Dickenson and Prison sts.), Lahaina, HI 96761. ✆ **866/253-9743** or 808/667-9766. Fax 808/661-3733. www.outriggerainanalucondo.com. 197 units. $185–$205 studio with kitchenette; $209–$239 1-bedroom with kitchen (sleeps up to 4); $289-$309 2-bedroom, 1-bathroom with kitchen (sleeps 6); $299–$375 2-bedroom, 2-bathroom with kitchen (sleeps 6). Children stay free in parent's room. Cribs $12 per stay; rollaway beds $20 per day. AE, DC, DISC, MC, V. Parking $15. **Amenities:** Outdoor pool; Jacuzzi; activities desk; laundry service; dry cleaning. *In room:* A/C, TV, full kitchen in 1- and 2-bedrooms, kitchenettes in studios, fridge, coffeemaker, hair dryer, iron, safe, washer/dryer in 1- and 2-bedrooms.

Moderate

Lahaina Shores Beach Resort ★ First, there's the location, right on the beach; second, there's the location, away from the hustle and bustle of downtown Lahaina; and third, there's the location, next door to 505 Front Street restaurants (with charging privileges) and shops. This recently upgraded condominium project (of studios and one-bedroom units) resembles an old plantation home with arched colonnades at the entry and an open-air, beachfront lobby. From the moment you step into the airy units (ranging in size from 550 sq. ft. to 1430 sq. ft.), your family will feel at home. The units all have full kitchens, large lanais, and ocean or mountain views. Ask for an oceanfront unit for that terrific ocean view and the island of Lanai in the background. In addition to the ocean right out front, the resort has a large swimming pool and a whirlpool spa.

475 Front St., Lahaina, HI 96761. ✆ **800/628-6699** or 808/661-4835. www.lahainashores.com. 145 units. $225–$295 studio double; $305–$355 1-bedroom double (sleeps 2); $355–$385 1-bedroom penthouse double (sleeps 4). Extra person $20. Cribs $20; rollaway beds available $15. AE, MC, V. Parking $7. **Amenities:**

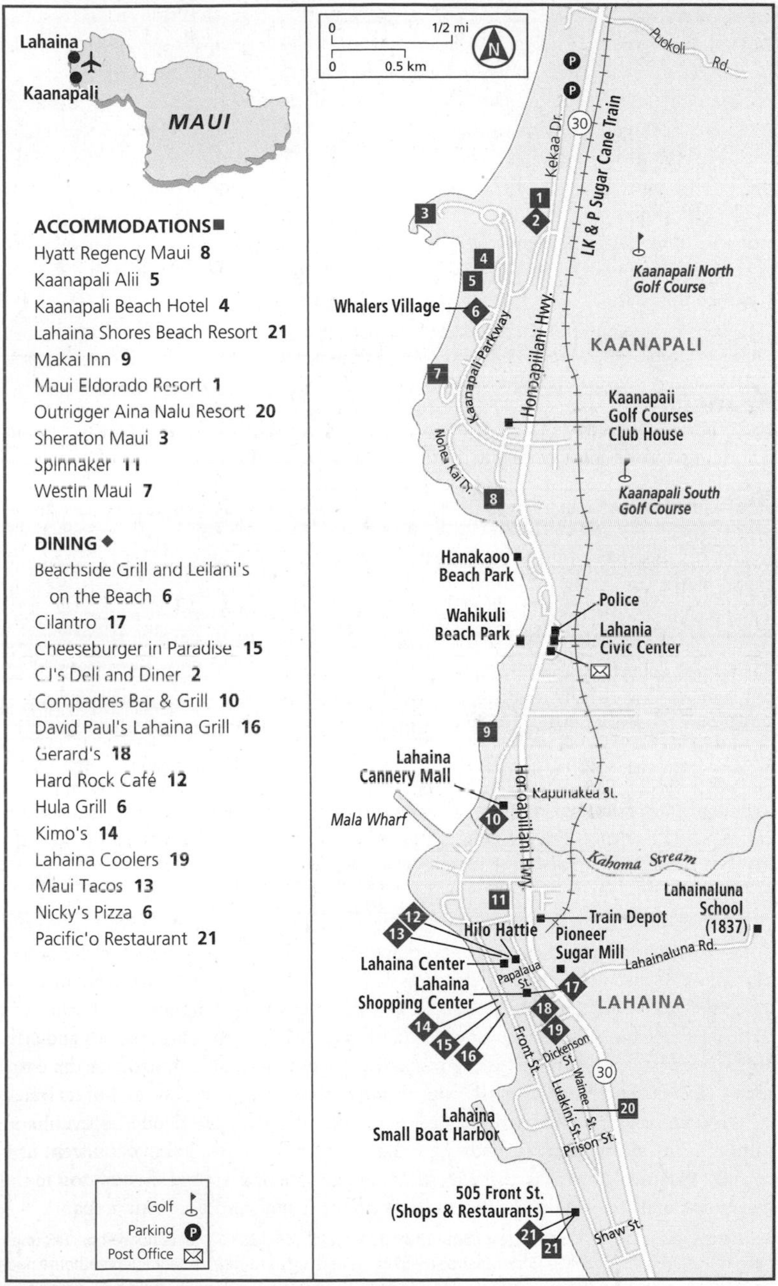

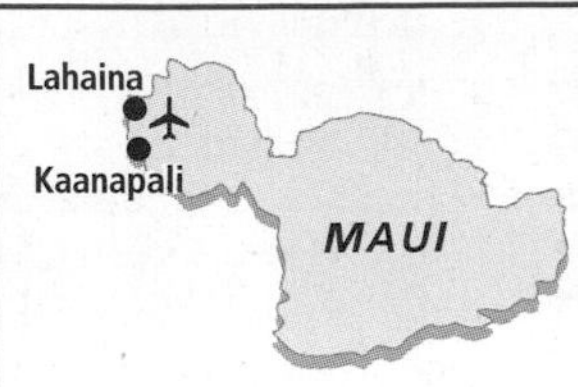

ACCOMMODATIONS ■

Hyatt Regency Maui **8**
Kaanapali Alii **5**
Kaanapali Beach Hotel **4**
Lahaina Shores Beach Resort **21**
Makai Inn **9**
Maui Eldorado Resort **1**
Outrigger Aina Nalu Resort **20**
Sheraton Maui **3**
Spinnaker **11**
Westin Maui **7**

DINING ◆

Beachside Grill and Leilani's on the Beach **6**
Cilantro **17**
Cheeseburger in Paradise **15**
CJ's Deli and Diner **2**
Compadres Bar & Grill **10**
David Paul's Lahaina Grill **16**
Gerard's **18**
Hard Rock Café **12**
Hula Grill **6**
Kimo's **14**
Lahaina Coolers **19**
Maui Tacos **13**
Nicky's Pizza **6**
Pacific'o Restaurant **21**

Golf
Parking
Post Office

0 1/2 mi
0 0.5 km
N
Puukolii Rd.
Kekaa Dr.
30
LK & P Sugar Cane Train
Kaanapali North Golf Course
Whalers Village
Kaanapali Parkway
Honoapiilani Hwy.
KAANAPALI
Kaanapaii Golf Courses Club House
Nohea Kai Dr.
Kaanapali South Golf Course
Hanakaoo Beach Park
Wahikuli Beach Park
Police
Lahania Civic Center
Lahaina Cannery Mall
Kapunakea St.
Mala Wharf
Honoapiilani Hwy.
Kahoma Stream
Lahainaluna School (1837)
Train Depot
Hilo Hattie
Pioneer Sugar Mill
Lahainaluna Rd.
Lahaina Center
Papalaua St.
Lahaina Shopping Center
LAHAINA
Front St.
Dickenson St.
30
Wainee St.
Luakini St.
Lahaina Small Boat Harbor
Prison St.
505 Front St. (Shops & Restaurants)
Shaw St.

Outdoor pool; beach activities; tennis courts across the street; Jacuzzi; concierge; coin-op laundry; dry cleaning; barbecue grill. *In room:* A/C, TV, kitchen, fridge, coffeemaker, hair dryer, iron.

Inexpensive

Makai Inn (Value) Budget travelers take note: Here's a small apartment complex located right on the water (no white-sand beach out front, but what do you want at these eye-popping prices?). You can take a 10-minute stroll to the closest beach or a 20-minute walk to the center of Lahaina town. The units are small (400 sq. ft.) but clean and filled with everything you should need for your vacation: full kitchens, views of the ocean (in most units), and separate bedrooms, all in a quiet neighborhood. There's a public phone by the office (none in the rooms, and no TVs either). In the middle of the complex is a tropical garden. I recommend the Ginger Hideaway unit with windows on two sides overlooking the ocean for just $180. Larger families will like the Pineapple Suite, the only two-bedroom unit (800 sq. ft.), for just $180.

1415 Front St., Lahaina, HI 96761. ✆ **808/662-3200.** Fax 808/661-9027. www.makaiinn.net. 18 units. $105–$180 double. Extra person $15. AE, MC, V. **Amenities:** Coin-op laundry. *In room:* Kitchen, no phone.

Kaanapali

You'll find Kaanapali hotels on the "Lahaina & Kaanapali Accommodations & Dining" map on p. 237.

Very Expensive

Hyatt Regency Maui Resort & Spa ★★★ Kids will love it here—it's Hawaii's version of Disneyland, with an assortment of imaginative touches including a collection of exotic species (including penguins) and nine waterfalls. This huge place covers some 40 acres; even if you don't stay here, you might want to walk through the expansive tree-filled atrium and the parklike grounds. The ½-acre outdoor pool has a 150-foot lava tube slide, a bar under the falls, a lava tube/cave, and a swinging rope bridge. There's even a children-only pool (and daily belly-flop contests) with its own beach, tide pools, and fountains.

Families appreciate the 50% discount on the price of a second room. (Request a Family Room Plan, in which you can get one room with a king bed connecting to a room with two double beds or a queen bed.) Hyatt's other family-friendly features include complimentary cribs and rollaway beds and hot-chocolate packets next to the in-room coffeemaker. If your kids are at that age at which everything they wear gets dirty immediately, then ask for a room in the Lahaina Tower, where there are washers and dryers on the bottom floor.

Parents also will like the activities of Camp Hyatt, a year-round program that accepts 5- to 12-year-olds. Every day, from 9am to 3pm, it offers a range of activities from "Olympic Games" to a scavenger hunt. The cost is $70 for a full day (includes lunch, snacks, and a Camp Hyatt T-shirt) and $35 for a half-day. There's also a game room for kids with video games, a pool table, Ping-Pong, and an air-hockey table. All of the on-site restaurants have special *keiki* (child) menus ($7 is the top price); or if they want to order from the "big" menu, children ages 4 to 12 get 50% off on some items. Kids ages 3 and under eat free.

Spa lovers will be thrilled with the oceanfront spa, the Spa Moana, offering everything from a menu of massages, to body treatments, to yoga classes. They also feature kid-friendly treatments such as the M&M manicure, children's yoga classes, movie-star makeovers, and "Glow Girl" facials, for $40 without lunch and $45 with lunch.

200 Nohea Kai Dr., Lahaina, HI 96761. ✆ **800/233-1234** or 808/661-1234. Fax 808/667-4714. www.maui.hyatt.com. 806 units. $485–$535 double; $613–$705 Deluxe Ocean Front; $755 Regency Club; $690–$820 Ocean; from $950 suite. Resort fee $15 for access to Moana Athletic Club, daily local newspaper,

local and toll-free phone calls, in-room coffee and tea, in-room safe, and 1-hr. tennis court time per day. Packages available. Extra person $50 ($75 in Regency Club rooms). Children 18 and under stay free in parent's room. Cribs and rollaway beds free. AE, DC, DISC, MC, V. Valet parking $20; self-parking free. **Amenities:** 5 restaurants; 2 bars; 1/2-acre outdoor pool; 36-hole golf course; 6 tennis courts; health club w/weight room; state-of-the-art spa; Jacuzzi; watersports equipment/rentals; bike rentals; Camp Hyatt kids' program offering supervised activities for kids ages 3–12; game room; concierge; activities desk; car rental desk; business center; big shopping arcade; salon; 24-hr. room service; massage; babysitting; coin-op laundry; laundry service; dry cleaning; concierge-level rooms. *In room:* A/C, TV, dataport, minibar, fridge (on request), coffeemaker, hair dryer, iron, safe, 2-line phone.

Kaanapali Alii ★★★ The Kaanapali Alii combines all the amenities of a luxury hotel (including a 24-hr. front desk and room service from the Marriott next door) with the convenience of a condominium. Kids 11 and younger get free membership in the Ali'i Kids Club, where they can join in activities such as tennis, lei making, lauhala weaving, and visits to the Maui Ocean Center. Adults will be happy in these luxurious, full-sized, oceanfront condominium units, sitting on 8 landscaped acres right on Kaanapali Beach. It's just steps to the ocean, restaurants, shops, and other activities. Each of the one-bedroom (1,500-sq.-ft.) and two-bedroom (1,900-sq.-ft.) units is impeccably decorated and comes with all the comforts of home (fully equipped kitchen, washer/dryer, lanai, two full bathrooms) and then some (room service, daily maid service). The beachside recreation area has a swimming pool and a separate children's pool, a whirlpool, gas barbecue grills and picnic areas, exercise rooms, saunas, and tennis courts.

50 Nohea Kai Dr., Lahaina, HI 96761. ✆ **800/642-6284** or 808/661-3339. Fax 808/667-1145. www.kaanapali-alii.com. 264 units. $395–$675 1-bedroom for 4; $590–$975 2-bedroom for 6. Cribs $20; rollaway beds $20. AE, DC, DISC, MC, V. Free parking. **Amenities:** 2 outdoor pools; 36-hole golf course; 3 lighted tennis courts; health club; Jacuzzi; watersports equipment/rentals; children's program; game room; concierge; activities desk; room service; in-room massage; babysitting; same-day dry cleaning. *In room:* A/C, TV, dataport, kitchen, fridge, coffeemaker, hair dryer, iron, safe.

Sheraton Maui Resort ★★★ The new emphasis here is on family appeal, with a class of rooms dedicated to those traveling with kids: Called Ohana family suites, they are huge (665 sq. ft.), with two double beds *and* a pull-down double Murphy bed. The bathrooms have separate shower and tub and two sinks. There's a sliding door to separate the living area from the bedroom, and each side has its own TV (with movies and a PlayStation), which may eliminate some fights. Plus (someone at Sheraton must have kids) they have placed the Ohana suites close to the keiki wading pool and on the same floor as the restaurants and lobby. The rack rate for the Ohana suite is $790 for up to two adults and three children in a suite. All that and an ocean view to boot!

This grande dame of Kaanapali Beach is built into the side of a cliff on the curving, white-sand cove next to Black Rock (a lava formation that rises 80 ft. above the beach), where there's excellent snorkeling just outside your room. The kids will be entertained by the nightly cliff divers swan-diving off the torch-lit lava-rock headland in a traditional sunset ceremony—a sight to see. And the views of Kaanapali Beach, with Lanai and Molokai in the distance, are some of the best around. Plus there are daily activities for kids at the Keiki Kamp. For the preteen and teen set there are water basketball games and lawn croquet.

2605 Kaanapali Pkwy., Lahaina, HI 96761. ✆ **800/782-9488** or 808/661-0031. Fax 808/661-0458. www.sheraton-maui.com. 510 units. $560–$700 double; from $790 Ohana suite (sleeps 2 adults, 3 children); from $1,000 suite. Resort fee of $25 for self-parking, local calls and credit card calls, in-room safe, daily coffee and newspaper, and use of health club. Extra person $60. Children 17 and under stay free in parent's room. Cribs free; rollaway beds $75. AE, DC, DISC, MC, V. Valet parking $15. **Amenities:** 3 restaurants; 2 bars (1 poolside); lagoon-style pool; 36-hole golf course; 3 tennis courts; health club; Jacuzzi; watersports equipment/rentals; children's program; concierge; activities desk; car rental desk; business center; shopping arcade; salon; limited room service (breakfast and dinner); babysitting; coin-op laundry; same-day laundry service and dry cleaning. *In room:* A/C, TV, dataport, fridge, coffeemaker, hair dryer, iron, safe.

Westin Maui Resort & Spa ★ What sets this resort apart from its peers along lovely Kaanapali Beach? The kid-pleasing "aquatic playground," an 87,000-square-foot pool area with five free-form heated pools joined by swim-through grottoes, waterfalls, and a 128-foot-long water slide. They even have a baby water slide for children ages 5 and younger. The fantasy theme extends from the estate-like grounds into the interior's public spaces, which are filled with the shrieks of tropical birds and the splash of waterfalls. Most of the rooms in the two 11-story towers overlook the aquatic playground, the ocean, and the island of Lanai in the distance.

Most rooms here will accommodate a family of four. The Ocean Tower rooms have two double beds, but if you need more space, get a second room, as you'd be hard-pressed to squeeze in a rollaway bed. When it comes to meals, kids 12 and younger eat free with a paying adult at the resort's two signature restaurants, OnO's Bar & Grill and Colonnade Café.

If you are looking for a package deal, check out the Family Splash Rate, with a lei for each kid plus milk and cookies as a welcome, and daily buffet breakfast for two kids and two adults.

2365 Kaanapali Pkwy., Lahaina, HI 96761. ✆ **888/625-4949** or 808/667-2525. Fax 808/661-5764. www.westinmaui.com. 758 units. $445–$795 double; $1,100–$1,900 suite. Resort fee of $20 for local calls, use of health club, coffee and tea, parking, and local paper. Extra person $75. Children 17 and under stay free in parent's room. Cribs and rollaway beds free. AE, DC, DISC, MC, V. Valet parking $10. **Amenities:** 5 restaurants; 3 bars; 5 free-form outdoor pools; 36-hole golf course; tennis courts; health club w/aerobics; spa w/steam baths, sauna, massage, and body treatments; Jacuzzi; watersports equipment/rentals; bike rentals; children's program (full day $70, $60 for 2nd child w/lunch and half-day $45 w/lunch); game room; concierge; activities desk; car rental desk; business center; shopping arcade; salon; limited room service; in-room massage; babysitting; coin-op laundry; same-day laundry service and dry cleaning; concierge-level rooms. *In room:* A/C, TV, dataport, minibar, fridge, coffeemaker, hair dryer, iron, safe.

Expensive

Kaanapali Beach Hotel ★ Value It's older and less high-tech than its upscale neighbors, but the Kaanapali has an irresistible local style and a real Hawaiian warmth that's missing from many other Maui hotels. The spacious, spotless, motel-like rooms (connecting rooms are available with either a king and single daybed or two double beds per room) each have a lanai that looks toward the courtyard and the beach. The beachfront rooms are separated from the water only by Kaanapali's landscaped walking trail.

Old Hawaii values and customs are always close at hand, and the service is some of the friendliest around. Children ages 5 and younger eat free, and kids ages 6 to 12 can order from the special discounted kids' menu when dining with parents. As part of the hotel's extensive Hawaiiana program, you can learn to cut pineapple, weave lauhala, or even dance the *real* hula. There's also an arts-and-crafts fair 4 days a week, a morning welcome reception on weekdays (with free coffee and tea), and a Hawaiian library. Take your family to see Kupanaha, a gourmet dinner show with world-renowned illusionists Jody and Kathleen Baran, combined with traditional hula and chants of the award-winning Kano'eau Dance Academy.

When you make your reservations, don't forget to give them your kids' names and ages, because at check-in, all children ages 12 and younger get the free "Aloha Passport for Kids." It allows them to visit various "destinations" on the resort property; they'll receive a free gift at each one.

2525 Kaanapali Pkwy., Lahaina, HI 96761. ✆ **800/262-8450** or 808/661-0011. Fax 808/667-5978. www.kbhmaui.com. 430 units. $199–$345 double; from $295–$475 suite. Car, golf, bed-and-breakfast, and romance packages available, as well as senior discounts. Extra person $30. Children 17 and under stay free in parent's room. Cribs free; rollaway beds $25. AE, DC, DISC, MC, V. Valet parking $11; self-parking $9. **Amenities:** 3 restaurants (w/special kids' menus and free meals for children 5 and under); poolside bar (that makes a mean piña colada); outdoor pool; 36-hole golf course; access to tennis courts; watersports equipment/rentals; children's program; concierge; activities desk; business center; convenience store; salon; coin-op laundry. *In room:* A/C, TV, dataport ($10-per-day charge) fridge, coffeemaker, iron, safe.

Maui Eldorado Resort ★ These spacious condominium units (1,200 sq. ft. in the one-bedrooms and 1,800 sq. ft. in the two-bedrooms)—each with full kitchen, washer/dryer, and daily maid service—were built at a time when land in Kaanapali was cheap, contractors took pride in their work, and visitors expected large, spacious units with views from every window. This is a great choice for families, with its big units, grassy areas that are perfect for running off excess energy, and a beachfront (with beach cabanas and a barbecue area) that's usually safe for swimming. Kids ages 5 to 12 get a free "Island Explorer" kit at check in with a backpack, binoculars, sunglasses, and an island activity book. The on-property market (a real convenience) has kids-rated videos for rent at just $4 a day. Tennis courts are nearby.

2661 Keka'a Dr., Lahaina, HI 96761. ✆ **800/688-7444** or 808/661-0021. Fax 808/667-7039. www.mauieldorado.com. 98 units. $275–$309 studio double; $290–$320 1-bedroom (up to 4); $435–$465 2-bedroom (up to 6). Numerous packages available, including 5th night free, car rental packages, senior rates, and more. Children 18 and under stay free in parent's room. Cribs free; rollaway beds $20. AE, DC, DISC, MC, V. Self-parking $7. **Amenities:** 3 outdoor pools; 36-hole golf course; concierge; activities desk. *In room:* A/C, TV, Wi-Fi, kitchen, fridge, coffeemaker, hair dryer, iron, safe, washer/dryer (in all units).

Honokowai, Kahana & Napili

Expensive

Napili Kai Beach Resort ★★★ Finds If you are looking for a family vacation in a comfortable location where you can spend most of your time, this is the place. Nestled in a small silky-sand cove, this comfortable oceanfront complex faces a gold-sand beach, safe for swimming. Many units have a view of the Pacific, with Molokai and Lanai in the distance. Every unit (except eight hotel rooms) has a fully stocked kitchen and washer/dryer. I'd recommend the special Family Studio units, which have extra space for families with young children. On-site pluses include daily maid service, even in the condo units; two shuffleboard courts; barbecue areas; complimentary coffee at the beach pagoda every morning; free tea in the lobby every afternoon; weekly lei making, hula lessons, and horticultural tours; and a free weekly mai tai party. For kids ages 6 to 10 years, during Easter vacation, mid-June to late August, and Christmas, the complimentary "Keiki Club" is in session with special activities including Hawaiian games, hula lessons, lei making, parent/child golf putting, and nature/ecology walks. There's even a free Wednesday night movie for kids so that their parents can have a little time to themselves.

5900 Honoapiilani Rd. (at the extreme north end of Napili, next to Kapalua), Lahaina, HI 96761. ✆ **800/367-5030** or 808/669-6271. Fax 808/669-0086. www.napilikai.com. 163 units. $230–$285 hotel room double; $275–$385 studio double (sleeps 3–4); $430–$475 1-bedroom suite (sleeps up to 5); $625–$810 2-bedroom suite (sleeps up to 7). Packages available. Cribs and rollaway beds free. AE, MC, V. Free parking. **Amenities:** 1 restaurant; bar; 4 outdoor pools; 2 18-hole putting greens (w/free golf putters for guest use); complimentary use of tennis racquets (no courts on property); good-size health club, the latest equipment; Jacuzzi; complimentary watersports equipment; free children's activities at Easter, June 15–Aug 31, and at Christmas; concierge; activities desk; babysitting; coin-op laundry; laundry service; dry cleaning. *In room:* A/C (in most units), TV, kitchenette, fridge, coffeemaker, hair dryer, iron, safe.

Moderate

Kahana Sunset ★★★ Lying in the crook of a sharp horseshoe curve on Lower Honoapiilani Road is this series of wooden condo units, stair-stepping down the side of a hill to a postcard-perfect white-sand beach. The unique location, nestled between the coastline and the road above, makes this a very private place to stay. In the midst of the buildings sits a grassy lawn with a small pool and Jacuzzi; down by the sandy beach are gazebos and picnic areas. The units feature full kitchens (complete with dishwashers), washer/dryers, large lanais with terrific views, and sleeper sofas. This is a great complex for families: The beach is safe for swimming, the grassy area is away from traffic, and the units are roomy. The two-bedroom units have parking just outside, making carrying luggage and groceries that much easier.

4909 Lower Honoapiilani Hwy. (at the northern end of Kahana, almost in Napili). Reservations: Premier Properties, c/o P.O. Box 10219, Lahaina, HI 96761. ✆ **800/669-1488** or 808/669-8011. Fax 808/669-9170. www.kahanasunset.com. 79 units. $165–$290 1-bedroom (sleeps up to 4); $225–$465 2-bedroom (sleeps up to 6). Cribs $10; rollaway beds $15. AE, MC, V. From Hwy. 30, turn *makai* (toward the ocean) at the Napili Plaza (Napilihau St.), and then left on Lower Honoapiilani Rd. **Amenities:** 2 outdoor pools (1 just for children); concierge. *In room:* TV/VCR/DVD, kitchen, coffeemaker, iron, safe (in some units), washer/dryer.

Inexpensive

Napili Sunset (Value) These clean, older, well-maintained units offer good value for families. Imagine an old beach home that's been in the family for years. At first glance, the plain two-story structures don't look like much, but the location, the bargain prices, and the friendly staff are the real treasures here. In addition to daily maid service, the units all have full kitchens (with dishwashers), ceiling fans, sofa beds, small dining rooms, and small bedrooms. The beach—one of Maui's best—can get a little crowded, because the public beach access is through this property (and everyone on Maui seems to want to come here). The one- and two-bedroom units are all on the beach (the downstairs units have lanais that lead right to the sand)—which means you won't have to schlep chairs, coolers, or gear very far. The staff makes sure each unit has the basics—paper towels, dishwasher soap, coffee filters, condiments—to get your stay off to a good start. There are restaurants within walking distance.

46 Hui Rd. (in Napili), Lahaina, HI 96761. ✆ **800/447-9229** or 808/669-8083. Fax 808/669-2730. www.napilisunset.com. 42 units. High season $160 studio double, $310 1-bedroom double, $465 2-bedroom (sleeps up to 4); low season $140 studio, $295 1-bedroom, $450 2-bedroom. Extra person $15. Children 2 and under stay free in parent's room. Cribs and rollaway beds $2.50 per day. MC, V. Free parking. **Amenities:** Small outdoor pool; coin-op laundry (detergent supplied). *In room:* TV, kitchen, fridge, coffeemaker.

Kapalua

If you're interested in a luxurious condo or town house, consider **Kapalua Villas** (✆ **800/545-0018** or 808/669-8088; http://villas.kapalua.com). The palatial units dotting the oceanfront cliffs and fairways of this idyllic coast are a (relative) bargain. The one- and two-bedroom condos go for $279 to $579, two-bedrooms for $389 to $809, three-bedrooms for $549 to $799; and there are numerous package deals that save you even more money.

Very Expensive

Ritz-Carlton Kapalua ★★★ The Ritz is a complete universe, one of those resorts where you can happily stay for 2 whole weeks and never leave the grounds. The kids will have plenty to do with the daily Ritz Kids program (half-days for $40, full day $70, additional siblings 20% discount), which is more than a child-care service: It's like a young explorers' program for kids who want to experience something different every day, from building a sand volcano and watching it erupt to delving into Hawaiian art, culture, ecology, and nature. Plus, parents love the "Kids Night Out," a weekly program from 5 to 9pm, in which the kids get a movie, popcorn, dinner, and activities ($50 per child) and mom and dad get the night off.

Rooms are up to the usual Ritz standard. Families of four can fit into the giant rooms but might prefer two connecting rooms. If you can afford it, stay on the Club Floor—it offers the best amenities in the state, from French roast coffee in the morning to a buffet at lunch to cookies in the afternoon to pupu and drinks at sunset. (Children 12 and under stay free, but there's a $50 charge for kids 13 and over.) Unfortunately, there are no coin-operated laundry machines here—you have to send laundry out. Yes, the rates are high (hey, it's a Ritz!) but the location at the very western end of the island is supreme isolation, the beaches are never crowded, and the views are panoramic. This is the place to come for a relaxing vacation with your family where you don't have to leave the property at all: There's everything you and your kids could possibly want here.

1 Ritz-Carlton Dr., Kapalua, HI 96761. ✆ **800/262-8440** or 808/669-6200. Fax 808/665-0026. www.ritzcarlton.com. 548 units. $499–$719 double; $599–$879 suite; from $599 Club Floor suites. Resort fee of $20 for use of health club, preferred tee times, Aloha Friday festivities, cultural history tours, self-parking, toll-free phone calls, resort shuttle service, tennis, morning coffee at the Lobby Lounge, use of the 9-hole putting green, and games of boccie ball on the lawn. Wedding/honeymoon, golf, and other packages available. Extra person $50 ($150 in Club Floor rooms). Children 17 and under stay free in parent's room except on the Club Level, where children 12 and under stay free and children 13 and up pay a $150 fee. Cribs and rollaway beds free. AE, DC, DISC, MC, V. Valet parking $18; free self-parking. **Amenities:** 4 restaurants; 4 bars (including 1 serving drinks and light fare on the sand); outdoor pool; access to the Kapalua Resort's 3 championship golf courses (each w/its own pro shop) and its deluxe tennis complex; health club; spa; Jacuzzi; watersports equipment/rentals; bike rentals; children's program; game room; concierge; activities desk; car rental desk; business center; shopping arcade; salon; room service; in-room and spa massage; babysitting; same-day laundry and dry cleaning; concierge-level rooms (some of Hawaii's best, w/top-drawer service and amenities). *In room:* A/C, TV, dataport, minibar, coffeemaker, hair dryer, iron, safe.

SOUTH MAUI

I recommend two booking agencies that rent a host of condominiums and unique vacation homes in the Kihei/Wailea/Maalaea area: **Kihei Maui Vacation** (✆ **800/541-6284** or 808/879-7581; www.kmvmaui.com) and **Condominium Rentals Hawaii** (✆ **800/367-5242** or 808/879-2778; www.crhmaui.com).

Kihei

In addition to the choices below, also consider the **ResortQuest at the Maui Banyan** (✆ **877/997-6667** or 808/875-0004; www.resortquesthawaii.com), a condo property across the street from Kamaole Beach Park II. The large one- to three-bedroom units are very nicely done and feature full kitchens, air-conditioning, and washer/dryers. Rates start at $175 (book online for $149) for hotel rooms, $215 for one-bedroom units ($173 online), and $275 ($231 online) for two-bedroom units; be sure to ask about packages.

Expensive

ResortQuest Maui Hill ★ If you can't decide between the privacy of a condo and the conveniences of a hotel, try this place, which gives you the best of both worlds, combining all the amenities and activities of a hotel—pool, hot tub, tennis courts, Hawaiiana classes, maid service, and more—with large luxury condos that have full kitchens and plenty of privacy. Nearly all units have ocean views, dishwashers, washer/dryers, queen sofa beds, and big lanais. Beaches, restaurants, and oceanside parks are nearby. (Walking up and down the hill, however, may be a bit more exercise than you had in mind.)

When you check in, your kids (12 and younger) get the "ResortQuest Kids Stay, Play & Eat FREE" card, which provides free activities (Maui Ocean Center), meals (Pizza Hut, KFC, and Sizzler), and merchandise (Hilo Hattie stores). The kids (and you) can chow down at the complimentary continental breakfast served daily. If it's raining, ask for games or family-friendly movies you can take back to your units.

2881 S. Kihei Rd. (across from Kamaole Park III, btw Keonekai St. and Kilohana Dr.), Kihei, HI 96753. ✆ **866/77-HAWAII** (774-2924) or 808/879-6321. Fax 808/879-8945. www.resortquesthawaii.com. 140 units. High season $295–$325 1-bedroom apt, $370–$410 2-bedroom, $535 3-bedroom; low season $220–$255 1-bedroom, $275–$315 2-bedroom, $405 3-bedroom. Children 17 and under stay free in parent's room. Cribs $12 each. AE, DC, DISC, MC, V. Free parking. **Amenities:** Outdoor pool; putting green; tennis courts; Jacuzzi; concierge; activities desk; car rental desk; coin-op laundry; laundry service; dry cleaning; barbecue grills. *In room:* A/C, TV/VCR, kitchen, fridge, coffeemaker, hair dryer, iron, safe, washer/dryer.

Moderate

Maui Coast Hotel ★★★ In this, one of the few actual hotels in Kihei, I recommend that a family of four go with either a one-bedroom suite (545 sq. ft. and starting at $345 a night) or a junior suite (a large studio with an alcove, 519 sq. ft., starting at $305). The standard rooms come with a king bed and a pullout sofa or two double beds (but you would be hard-pressed to squeeze in a crib, let alone a rollaway bed). The other chief advantage of this hotel is its location, about a block from Kamaole Beach Park I, with plenty of restaurants and shopping within walking distance and a golf course nearby.

2259 S. Kihei Rd. (1 block from Kamaole Beach Park I), Kihei, HI 96753. ✆ **800/895-6284** or 808/874-6284. Fax 808/875-4731. www.mauicoasthotel.com. 265 units. $265 double; $305 suite; $345 1-bedroom (sleeps up to 4). Room/car rental packages available. Children 17 and under stay free in parent's room. Cribs free; rollaway beds $20. AE, DC, DISC, MC, V. Free parking. **Amenities:** Restaurant; bar (poolside) w/ nightly entertainment; outdoor pool (plus children's wading pool); 2 lighted tennis courts; health club; concierge; activities desk; limited room service; complimentary self-serve laundry; laundry service; dry cleaning. *In room:* A/C, TV, fridge, coffeemaker, hair dryer, iron, safe.

Inexpensive

Koa Resort ★ If you didn't think you could afford a condominium on Maui, think again: These older but well-maintained one-, two-, and three-bedroom units offer real value for families. Located just across the street from the ocean, Koa Resort consists of five two-story wooden buildings on more than 5½ acres of landscaped grounds. The spacious, privately owned units are decorated with care and come fully equipped, right down to the dishwasher and disposal in the kitchens. The larger condos have both showers and tubs; the smaller units have showers only. (If your kids need a tub, be sure to inquire.) All feature large lanais, ceiling fans, and washer/dryers. For maximum peace and quiet, ask for a unit far from Kihei Road. Bars, restaurants, and beach parks with playgrounds are within a 5-minute drive.

811 S. Kihei Rd. (btw Kulanihakoi St. and Namau'u Place). Reservations: c/o Bello Realty, P.O. Box 1776, Kihei, HI 96753. ✆ **800/541-3060** or 808/879-3328. Fax 808/875-1483. www.bellomaui.com. 54 units (some with shower only). Low season $99 1-bedroom, $100–$125 2-bedroom, $160–$240 3-bedroom; high season $115 1-bedroom, $120–$145 2-bedroom, $180–$275 3-bedroom. MC, V. Free parking. **Amenities:** Outdoor pool; 2 tennis courts; Jacuzzi. *In room:* AC (some units), TV, kitchen, fridge, coffeemaker, hair dryer, iron, washer/dryer.

Punahoa Beach Apartments ★ Value Book this place! I can't put it any more simply than that. The location—off noisy, traffic-ridden Kihei Road, on a quiet side street with ocean frontage—is fabulous. A grassy lawn rolls about 50 feet down to the

ACCOMMODATIONS■

Fairmont Kea Lani Maui **15**
Four Seasons Resort Maui at Wailea **14**
Grand Wailea Resort Hotel & Spa **13**
Koa Resort **1**
Maui Coast Hotel **7**
Maui Prince Hotel **16**
Punahoa Beach Apartments **5**
ResortQuest at Maui Banyon **8**
ResortQuest Maui Hill **9**
Wailea Marriott **10**

DINING◆

Cheeseburger, Mai Tai's and Rock-n-Roll **11**
Honolulu Coffee Company **11**
Joe's Bar & Grill **12**
Longhi's **11**
Maui Taco **6**
Nick's Fishmarket Maui **15**
Peggy Sue's **3**
Ruth's Chris Steak House **11**
Shaka Sandwich & Pizza **4**
Spago **14**
Stella Blues Café **2**
Tommy Bahama's Tropical Grill **11**

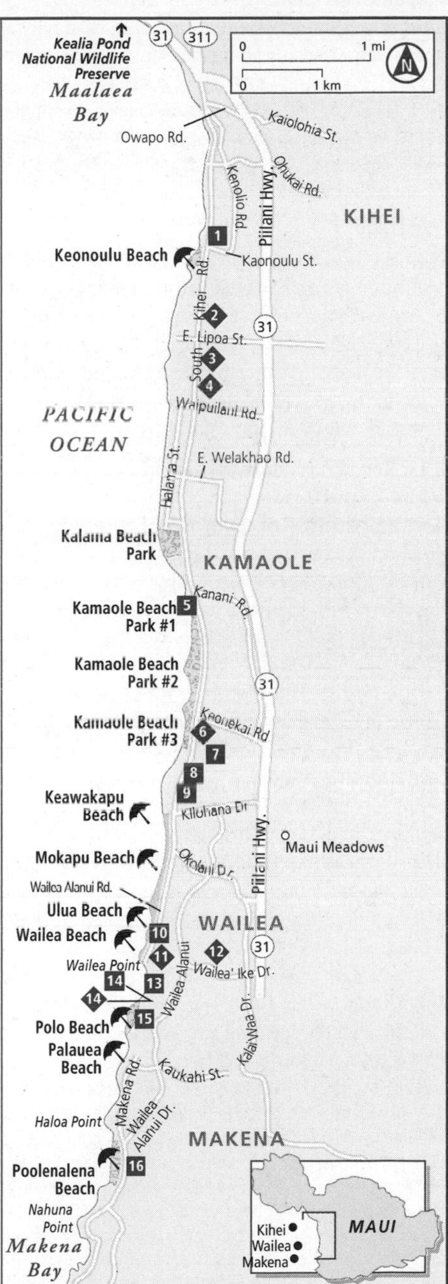

beach, where there's great snorkeling just offshore and a popular surfing spot next door; shopping and restaurants are all within walking distance. All of the beautifully decorated units in this small, four-story building have fully equipped kitchens and lanais with great ocean views. Rooms go quickly in winter, so reserve early.

2142 Iliili Rd. (off S. Kihei Rd., 300 ft. from Kamaole Beach I), Kihei, HI 96753. ✆ **800/564-4380** or 808/879-2720. Fax 808/875-9147. www.punahoabeach.com. 14 units. $116–$150 studio double, $160–$231 1-bedroom double, $198–$263 2-bedroom double; $188–$258 1-bedroom penthouse. 5-night minimum. Cribs and rollaway beds free. AE, DC, DISC, MC, V. Free parking. **Amenities:** Coin-op laundry. *In room:* TV, high-speed Internet, Wi-Fi, kitchen, fridge, coffeemaker, iron.

Wailea

Destination Resorts Hawaii (✆ **800/367-5246** or 808/879-1595; fax 808/874-3554; www.drhmaui.com) offers luxury units including studio doubles starting at $230; one-bedroom doubles from $255; two-bedrooms from $475; and three-bedrooms from $420 to $625. Other pluses about these luxury condos are free long-distance calls; high-speed Internet access, and free parking; one property, the Polo Beach Club, is completely non-smoking (not even on the lanai, in the common areas, in the pool or the Jacuzzi, and especially not in the units). Children 11 and younger stay free; minimum stays vary by property.

Very Expensive

The Fairmont Kea Lani Maui ★★★ Attention deal hunters: For the price of a hotel room elsewhere, you can get a suite here! These are terrific for families, as the suites contain a king bed or two double beds, along with a queen-sized pullout sofa in the living room, with plenty of room for a crib. Each unit in this all-suite luxury hotel has a kitchenette (ask for complimentary hot chocolate)—maybe not enough room to cook a Thanksgiving dinner, but you can keep hungry kids happy—plus a living room with entertainment center (with in-room video games) and a comfy sofa bed, a marble wet bar, an oversize marble bathroom with separate shower big enough for a party, a tub that can hold three preschoolers, a spacious bedroom, and a large lanai that overlooks the pools (one for kids only), lawns, and white-sand beach. You'll find coin-operated washers and dryers on every floor. All on-site restaurants welcome kids with a keiki menu and are equipped with highchairs and booster seats. The hotel is located on one of Wailea's most beautiful beaches; the kids will have a hard time deciding between the various swimming pools and the white sand out front. The resort's kids' program is $75 for a full day and $50 for a half-day (with lunch). The Fairmont is also walking distance to The Shops at Wailea, with lots of dining possibilities.

If you have the money to burn, the villas are definitely out of a fantasy. The rich and famous stay in these 2,000-square-foot, two- and three-bedroom beach bungalows, each with its own plunge pool and gourmet kitchen.

4100 Wailea Alanui Dr., Wailea, HI 96753. ✆ **800/659-4100** or 808/875-4100. Fax 808/875-1200. www.kealani.com. 450 units. $525–$1,200 double (sleeps up to 4); from $1,500 villa. Cribs free; rollaway beds $30. AE, DC, DISC, MC, V. Valet parking $18; free self-parking. **Amenities:** 4 restaurants; 3 bars (nightly entertainment at the Lobby Lounge); 2 large swimming "lagoons" connected by a 140-ft. water slide and swim-up bar, plus an adult lap pool; use of Wailea Golf Club's 3 18-hole championship golf courses, as well as the nearby Makena and Elleair golf courses; use of Wailea Tennis Center's 11 courts (3 lighted and a pro shop); fine 24-hr. health club; excellent full-service spa offering the latest in body treatments, facials, and massage; Jacuzzi; watersports equipment/rentals; bike rentals; children's program; game room; concierge; activities desk; car rental desk; business center; shopping arcade; salon; 24-hr. room service; in-room massage; babysitting; same-day laundry service and dry cleaning. *In room:* A/C, TV, dataport, kitchenette, minibar, fridge, coffeemaker, hair dryer, iron, safe.

Four Seasons Resort Maui at Wailea ★★★ If money's no object, this is the place to spend it. It's hard to beat this modern version of a Hawaiian palace by the sea, with a relaxing, casual atmosphere. Although it sits on a glorious beach between two other hotels, you won't feel like you're on chockablock resort row: The Four Seasons inhabits its own separate world, thanks to an open courtyard of pools and gardens. Amenities are first-rate here, including outstanding restaurants, an excellent spa, and one of Maui's most beautiful beaches in front. The spacious (about 600-sq.-ft.) rooms feature furnished lanais (a majority of the rooms have an ocean view) and they easily fit a family. If you want extra space, the junior suite gives you another 200 square feet (but still one bathroom). For two bathrooms (sometimes a necessity), get two connecting rooms.

This is the most kid-friendly hotel on Maui. The resort goes out of its way to make the keiki feel welcome. At check-in, kids 10 and younger get a stuffed animal and complimentary milk and cookies on the first day; kids ages 11 to 14 receive a baseball cap or a mini–duffel bag with a snack; and teens ages 15 to 17 also get an age-appropriate gift. The resort can prepurchase a range of necessities (such as diapers and baby food) for you before your arrival. There are free infant supplies (cribs, strollers, highchairs, playpens, and car seats), child-size bathrobes, child-safety features (such as toilet-seat locks and security gates), and kids' menus in all of the restaurants (including room service). The complimentary "Kids for All Seasons" program features activities from sand sculpting to kite flying. Teens have a huge list of diversions to choose from, including a game room, a scuba clinic, videos, and more. The concierge service, always top-notch, is a godsend to parents: They can do everything from helping you plan your activities to finding a babysitter with 4 hours' notice.

3900 Wailea Alanui Dr., Wailea, HI 96753. ✆ **800/334-MAUI** (334-6284) or 808/874-8000. Fax 808/874-2222. www.fourseasons.com/maui. 380 units. $475–$990 double; $1,065–$1,215 Club Floor; from $890 suite. Packages available. Extra person $100 ($300 in Club Floor rooms). Children 17 and under stay free in parent's room. Cribs and rollaway beds free. AE, DC, MC, V. Valet parking $12. **Amenities:** 3 restaurants; 3 bars (w/nightly entertainment), 3 fabulous outdoor pools; putting green; use of Wailea Golf Club's 3 18-hole championship golf courses, as well as the nearby Makena and Elleair golf courses; 2 lighted tennis courts and use of Wailea Tennis Center's 11 courts; health club featuring outdoor cardiovascular equipment (w/individual TV/video players); excellent spa (offering a variety of treatments in spa, in-room, or oceanside); 2 Jacuzzis (1 for adults only); beach pavilion w/watersports equipment/rentals and 1-hr. complimentary use of snorkel equipment; complimentary use of bikes; fabulous year-round kids' program, plus a teen recreation center and a children's video library and toys; game room (w/shuffleboard, pool tables, jukebox, big-screen TV, and video games); one of Maui's best concierge desks; activities desk; car rental desk; business center; shopping arcade; salon; 24-hr. room service; massage (in-room, spa, or oceanside); babysitting; same-day laundry service and dry cleaning; concierge-level rooms. *In room:* A/C, TV, dataport, minibar, fridge, coffeemaker, hair dryer, iron, safe.

Grand Wailea Resort Hotel & Spa ★★★ This "fantasy" hotel is beyond your wildest imagination. Just walking around is an adventure: There's Hawaii's most elaborate spa; a restaurant in a man-made tide pool; a Japanese restaurant decorated with real rocks hewn from the slopes of Mount Fuji; 10,000 tropical plants in the lobby; and nothing but oceanview rooms, outfitted with every amenity you could ask for. The rooms are a good size and have plenty of room for a crib or rollaway bed. (If there are more than four in your family, though, I recommend getting adjoining rooms.)

It's easy to see why kids love this resort. In fact, they will probably want to spend the entire vacation at the pool—or I should say pools. One of the most popular is the Wailea Canyon Activity Pool, a 2,000-foot river pool with valleys, water slides, waterfalls, caves, white-water rapids, and grottoes. The river pool is about five stories tall, and there's even a water elevator that lifts guests back up to the top.

Swimming in the pools (including Baby Beach for the very young) is just one of a host of activities. You can send the little nippers off to Camp Grande for hours of entertainment in arts and crafts and much more. Also check out the family workshops where you and the kids can take up hula and ukulele lessons, lei making, lauhala bracelet weaving, and T-shirt design. Programs for ultracool teenagers include Teen Spa Camp.

Though minimalists may be put off, there's no denying that the Grand Wailea is plush and professional, with all the diversions you could imagine. Oh, and did I mention the fantastic beach out back?

3850 Wailea Alanui Dr., Wailea, HI 96753. ✆ **800/888-6100** or 808/875-1234. Fax 808/874-2442. www.grandwailea.com. 780 units. $700–$1,180 double; from $2,030 suite; concierge (Na Pua) tower from $1,610. Resort fee $25 for lei greeting on arrival, welcome drink, local calls, coffee in room, use of spa (treatments extra), admission to scuba diving clinics and water aerobics, art and garden tours, nightly turndown service, self-parking, and shuttle service to Wailea area. Extra person $50 ($100 in concierge tower). Children 17 and under stay free in parent's room. Cribs free; rollaway beds $30. AE, DC, DISC, MC, V. **Amenities:** 6 restaurants; 12 bars (including a nightclub w/laser-light shows and a hydraulic dance floor); 2,000-ft.-long Action Pool, featuring a 10-min. swim/ride through mountains and grottoes; use of Wailea Golf Club's 3 18-hole championship golf courses, as well as the nearby Makena and Elleair golf courses; use of Wailea Tennis Center's 11 courts (3 lighted and a pro shop); complete health club; Hawaii's largest spa, the 50,000-sq.-ft. Spa Grande; Jacuzzi; watersports equipment/rentals; complimentary dive and windsurf lessons; bike rentals; children's program (including a computer center, video game room, arts and crafts, children's theater, outdoor playground, and infant-care center); game room; concierge; activities desk; car rental desk; business center; shopping arcade; salon; 24-hr. room service; in-room and spa massage; babysitting; same-day laundry service and dry cleaning; concierge-level rooms. *In room:* A/C, TV, dataport, kitchenette, minibar, fridge ($25 fee), coffeemaker, hair dryer, iron, safe.

Expensive

Wailea Beach Marriott Resort & Spa★★★ This classic open-air, 1970s-style hotel in a tropical garden by the sea gives you a sense of what Maui was like before the big resort boom. The rooms are big; even with two double beds there's still plenty of area to roam about with two kids in tow. You might want to consider a junior suite, which costs slightly less than two connecting rooms and comes with 1 1/2 bathrooms, a king bed, and two twin sofa beds.

What's truly special about this hotel is how it fits into its environment without overwhelming it. Eight buildings, all low-rise except for an eight-story tower, are spread along 22 gracious acres of lawns and gardens spiked by coco palms, with lots of open space and a half-mile of oceanfront on a point between Wailea and Ulua beaches. Five on-site pools will keep the kids entertained, including a 244,000-gallon pool and slide, a water park with a 32-foot drop slide, a spiral water slide, and a children's activity pool with its own sandy beach and a hydro spa.

3700 Wailea Alanui Dr., Wailea, HI 96753. ✆ **800/367-2960** or 808/879-1922. Fax 808/874-8331. www.waileamarriott.com. 545 units. $525–$825 single/double; from $514 suite. Resort fee $25 plus tax per night for self-parking, high-speed Internet access, local phone calls, daily sunset appetizer, luau and snorkel-gear-rental discounts, and free kids' meals with purchase of adult entree. Packages available. Extra person $40. Children 18 and under stay free in parent's room. Cribs and rollaway beds free. AE, DC, DISC, MC, V. Valet parking $13. **Amenities:** 2 restaurants; 2 bars; outdoor swimming pools; use of Wailea Golf Club's 3 18-hole championship golf courses; use of Wailea Tennis Center's 11 courts (3 lighted and a pro shop); fitness center; full-service Mandara Spa & Salon w/steam rooms and whirlpools; watersports equipment rentals; children's program (plus kids-only pool and recreation center); concierge; activities desk; business center; shopping arcade; salon; room service; in-room or outdoor massages; babysitting; same-day laundry service and dry cleaning. *In room:* A/C, flatscreen TV, coffeemaker, hair dryer, iron, safe, ergonomic desk and chair, 4-outlet technology console, wet bar.

Makena

Expensive

Maui Prince Hotel ★★★ If you're looking for a vacation in a beautiful, tranquil spot with a golden-sand beach, here's your place. But if you plan to tour Maui, you might want to try another hotel. The Maui Prince is at the end of the road, far, far away from anything else on the island, so sightseeing in other areas would require a lot of driving.

When you first see the stark-white hotel, it looks like a high-rise motel stuck in the woods—but only from the outside. Inside, you'll discover an atrium garden with a koi-filled waterfall stream, an ocean view from every room, and a simplicity to the furnishings that makes some people feel uncomfortable and others blissfully clutter free. Rooms are small; book two connecting rooms and you'll be a lot happier, or better yet, book a suite. Kids from around the world (there's a big Japanese clientele here) get together in the keiki program for activities such as net fishing, sandcastle building, swimming, Hawaiian arts and crafts, putting, Ping-Pong, shuffleboard, movies, and video games.

5400 Makena Alanui, Makena, HI 96753. ✆ **800/321-6284** or 808/874-1111. Fax 808/879-8763. www.mauiprincehotel.com. 310 units. $385–$555 double; from $700 suite. Packages available. Extra person $60. Children 17 and under stay free in parent's room. Cribs free; rollaway beds $40. AE, DC, MC, V. Free parking. **Amenities:** 4 restaurants; 2 bars w/local Hawaiian music nightly; 2 outdoor pools (adults' and children's); 36 holes of golf (designed by Robert Trent Jones); 6 Plexipave tennis courts (2 lighted); health club; Jacuzzi; watersports equipment/rentals; children's program; concierge; activities desk; business center; shopping arcade; salon; room service; in-room massage; babysitting; same-day laundry service and dry cleaning. *In room:* A/C, TV, dataport, fridge, hair dryer, iron, safe.

EAST MAUI: ON THE ROAD TO HANA

You'll find the accommodations in this section on the "Upcountry & East Maui" map on p. 250.

The Inn at Mama's Fish House ★★★ Here's a place that kids will love, right on a beach (though there's no swimming pool and sometimes the ocean is not very swimmable). The fabulous location, nestled in a coconut grove on secluded Kuau Beach; beautifully decorated interior with island-style rattan furniture and works by Hawaiian artists; full kitchen; and extras such as Weber gas barbecue grill, huge 27-in. TVs, and all the beach toys you can think of make this place a gem for those seeking a centrally located vacation rental. But, best of all, you are right next door to the award-winning (and mouthwatering) restaurant, Mama's Fish House (see p. 262). The one-bedrooms are nestled in tropical jungle (red ginger surrounds the garden patio), while the two-bedrooms face the beach. Both have terra-cotta floors, complete kitchens (even dishwashers), sofa beds, and free laundry facilities.

799 Poho Place (off the Hana Hwy. in Kuau), Paia, HI 96779. ✆ **800/860-HULA** (860-4852) or 808/579-9764. Fax 808/579-8594. www.mamasfishhouse.com. 6 units. $175 garden studio double; $225 1-bedroom (sleeps up to 4); $325–$575 2-bedroom (up to 6). 3-night minimum. AE, DISC, MC, V. **Amenities:** Restaurant. *In room:* A/C, TV/VCR, dataport ($10 per day Internet fee), kitchen, fridge, coffeemaker, hair dryer, iron, washer/dryer.

AT THE END OF THE ROAD IN EAST MAUI: HANA

Expensive

Hotel Hana-Maui and Honua Spa ★★★ I highly recommend this little slice of paradise. Picture Shangri-La, Hawaiian-style: 66 acres rolling down to the sea in a remote

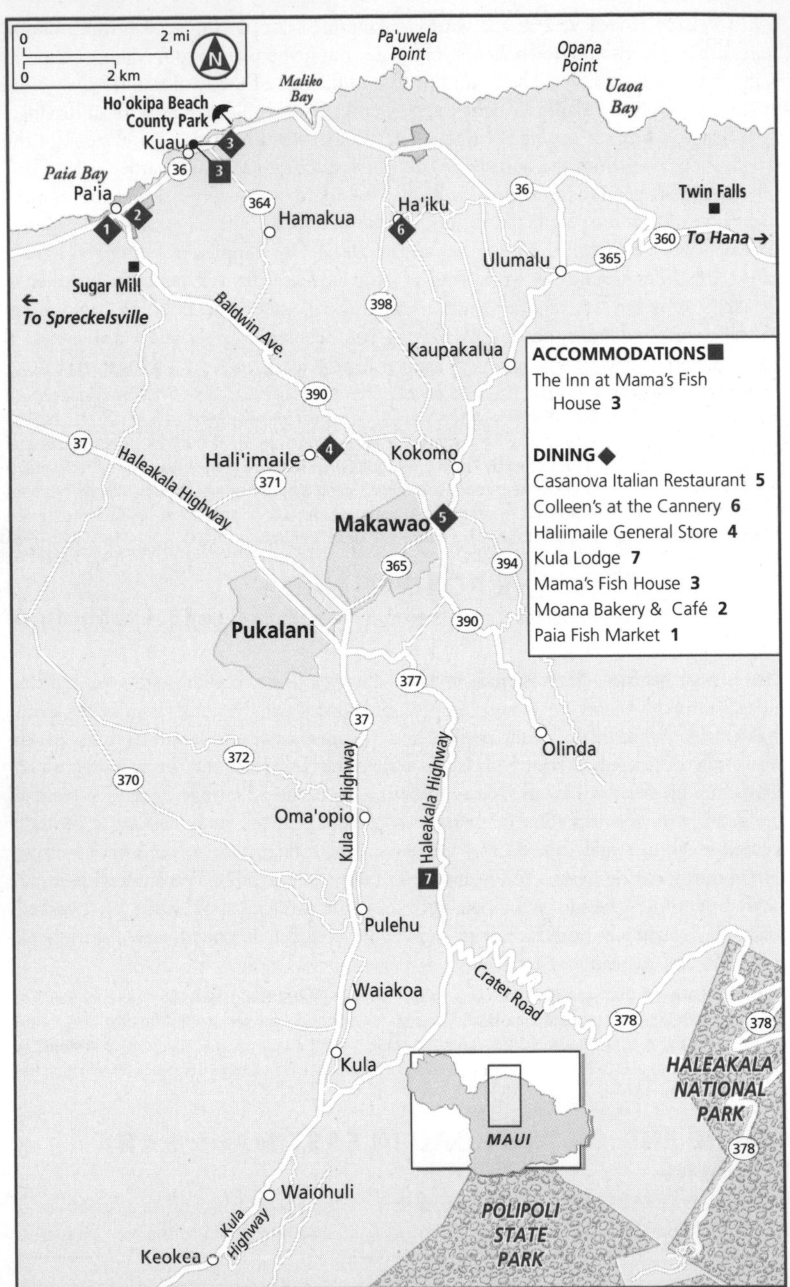
0
2 mi
0
2 km
N
Pa'uwela Point
Opana Point
Maliko Bay
Uaoa Bay
Ho'okipa Beach County Park
Kuau
Paia Bay
Pa'ia
Hamakua
Ha'iku
Twin Falls
To Hana →
Ulumalu
Sugar Mill
← To Spreckelsville
Baldwin Ave.
Kaupakalua
Hali'imaile
Kokomo
Haleakala Highway
Makawao
Pukalani
Olinda
Kula Highway
Haleakala Highway
Oma'opio
Pulehu
Crater Road
Waiakoa
Kula
MAUI
HALEAKALA NATIONAL PARK
Waiohuli
Kula Highway
Keokea
POLIPOLI STATE PARK
ACCOMMODATIONS
The Inn at Mama's Fish House 3
DINING
Casanova Italian Restaurant 5
Colleen's at the Cannery 6
Haliimaile General Store 4
Kula Lodge 7
Mama's Fish House 3
Moana Bakery & Café 2
Paia Fish Market 1

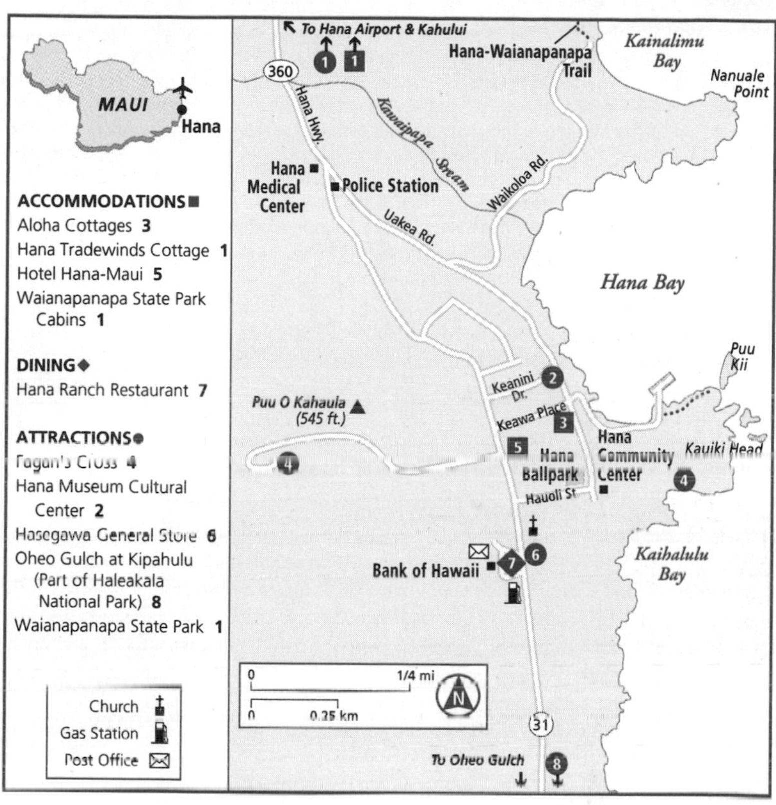

Hawaiian village, with a wellness center, two pools, and access to one of the best beaches in Hana. This is the atmosphere, the landscape, and the culture of Old Hawaii set in 21st-century accommodations. Every unit is excellent, but my favorites are the Sea Ranch Cottages (especially nos. 215–218 for the best views of turtles frolicking in the ocean), where individual duplex bungalows look out over the craggy shoreline to the rolling surf. You step out of the oversize, open, airy units (with floor-to-ceiling sliding doors) onto a huge lanai with views that will stay with you long after your tan has faded. These comfy units have been totally redecorated with every amenity you can think of, and you won't be nickel-and-dimed for things such as coffee and water—everything they give you, from the homemade banana bread to the bottled water, is complimentary. Cathedral ceilings, a plush feather bed, a giant-size soaking tub, Hawaiian artwork, bamboo hardwood floors—this is luxury.

Families most likely will fit best in the rooms with two queen beds. Cribs will fit in any room, but if you need a rollaway bed, look to the Bay Cottages for the best fit. The white-sand beach (just a 5-min. shuttle away), top-notch wellness center with some of the best massage therapists in Hawaii, and numerous activities (horseback riding, complimentary bicycles, tennis, pitch-and-putt golf) all add up to make this one of the top resorts in the state. There are no TVs in the rooms, but the Club Room has a giant-screen TV, plus DVD and Internet access. The staff will be happy to provide games you can take back to your room.

Hana, Maui 96713. ✆ **800/321-HANA** (321-4262) or 808/248-8211. Fax 808/248-7202. www.hotelhanamaui.com. 78 units. $495–$550 Bay Cottages double; $650–$1,125 Sea Ranch Cottages double; $1,675 2-bedroom suite (sleeps 4); from $4,000 2-bedroom Plantation Guest House (sleeps 4). Children 17 and under stay free in parent's room. Cribs free; rollaway beds $50 (available in garden and deluxe junior suites only). AE, DC, DISC, MC, V. **Amenities:** Restaurant (w/Hawaiian entertainment twice a week); bar (w/nightly entertainment); 2 outdoor pools; complimentary use of the 3-hole practice golf courses; tennis courts; health club; game room; concierge; activities desk; car rental desk; business center; small shopping arcade; salon; limited room service (7:30–9pm); massage; babysitting; laundry service. *In room:* Dataport, kitchenette, fridge, coffeemaker, hair dryer, iron, safe.

Inexpensive

Mrs. Nakamura has been renting her **Aloha Cottages** (✆ **808/248-8420**) since the 1970s. Located in residential areas near Hana Bay, these five budget rentals are simple but adequately furnished, varying in size from a roomy studio with kitchenette to a three-bedroom, two-bathroom unit. They're all fully equipped, clean, and fairly well kept. Rates run from $70 to $100 double ($15 for an extra person). Not all units have TVs, and none have phones; but Mrs. N. is happy to take messages.

Hana's Tradewinds Cottage ★ Value Nestled among the ginger and heliconias on a 5-acre flower farm are two separate cottages, each with full kitchen, carport, barbecue, private hot tub, TV, ceiling fans, and sofa bed. The studio cottage sleeps up to four; a bamboo shoji blind separates the sleeping area (with queen bed) from the sofa bed in the living room. The Tradewinds cottage has two bedrooms (with a queen bed in one room and two twins in the other), one bathroom (shower only), and a huge front porch. The atmosphere is quiet and relaxing. Hostess Rebecca Buckley, who has been in business for a decade, welcomes families. She has two children, a cat, and a very sweet golden retriever. You can use the laundry facilities at no extra charge. It's a 5-minute car ride to the nearest beach.

135 Alalele Place (the airport road), P.O. Box 385, Hana, HI 96713. ✆ **800/327-8097** or 808/248-8980. Fax 808/248-7735. www.hanamaui.net. 2 cottages. $175 studio double; $205 2-bedroom double. 2-night minimum. Extra person $15. AE, DISC, MC, V. **Amenities:** Private outdoor hot tubs. *In room:* TV, kitchen, fridge, coffeemaker, no phone.

Waianapanapa State Park Cabins Value These 12 rustic cabins are the best lodging deal on Maui. Everyone knows it, too—so make your reservations early (up to 6 months in advance). The cabins are warm and dry and come complete with kitchen, living room, bedroom, and bathroom with hot shower. Furnishings include bedding, linen, towels, dishes, and very basic cooking and eating utensils. Don't expect luxury—this is a step above camping, albeit in a beautiful tropical jungle setting. The key attraction at this 120-acre state beach park is the unusual horseshoe-shaped black-sand beach on Pailoa Bay, popular for shore fishing, snorkeling, and swimming. There's a caretaker on-site, along with restrooms, showers, picnic tables, shoreline hiking trails, and historic sites. But bring mosquito protection—this *is* the jungle, after all.

Off Hana Hwy. Reservations: c/o Hawaii Division of Forestry & Wildlife, 54 S. High St., Room 101, Wailuku, HI 96793. ✆ **808/984-8109.** 12 cabins. $45 for 4 (sleeps up to 6). 5-night maximum. Extra person $5. No credit cards. *In room:* Kitchen, fridge, coffeemaker, no phone.

4 FAMILY-FRIENDLY DINING

Dining on Maui ranges from glamorous swank restaurants with big-name chefs to old-fashioned, multigenerational mom-and-pop diners at budget prices. In this dizzying scenario, I'll steer you away from the open-air waterfront watering holes, where the view counts for 50% of the experience, and toward the truly creative cuisine, at prices that won't make you borrow against the kids' college fund to have a stellar dining experience for everyone in the family.

In the listings below, reservations are not necessary unless otherwise noted.

CENTRAL MAUI

The **Queen Kaahumanu Center,** the structure that looks like a white *Star Wars* umbrella in the center of Kahului, at 275 Kaahumanu Ave. (5 min. from Kahului Airport on Hwy. 32), has a very popular food court. Eateries include the following: **Edo Japan** teppanyaki is a real find, its flat Benihana-like grill dispensing marvelous, flavorful mounds of grilled fresh vegetables and chicken teriyaki for $6.50; **Panda Express** serves tasty Chinese food; and **Alexander's Fish and Chips** is a great place for fast takeout. Outside of the food court, but still in the shopping center, are **Ruby's,** dishing out hamburgers, fries, and shakes; and **Starbucks.** There's also a branch of **Maui Tacos**. When you leave Kaahumanu Center, take a moment to gaze at the West Maui Mountains to your left from the parking lot.

Moderate

Mañana Garage ★★★ Finds LATIN AMERICAN Kids will be enthralled with the industrial motif: table bases like hubcaps, a vertical garage door as a divider for private parties, blown-glass chandeliers, and gleaming chrome and cobalt walls with orange accents. And the entire family will be happy with the brilliantly conceived and executed menu. The "big person's" menu ranges from fried green tomatoes; to ceviche with lime, cilantro, chile, and coconut; to fresh fish; to *arepas* (cornmeal and cheese griddlecakes with smoked salmon and wasabi sour cream). The menu for *los niños* (10 and younger) is $5. If you are on this side of the island, don't miss this incredible experience.

33 Lono Ave., Kahului. ✆ **808/873-0220.** Kids' menu, highchairs, boosters, crayons. Reservations recommended. Main courses $8–$18 lunch, $18–$31 dinner; kids' menu $5. AE, DC, DISC, MC, V. Mon 11am–9pm; Tues and Fri 11am–10:30pm; Wed–Thurs 11am–9:30pm; Sat 5–10:30pm; Sun 5–9pm.

Inexpensive

AK's Cafe ★★★ Value HEALTHY PLATE LUNCHES Need to feed the kids in a hurry? Chef Elaine Rothermel has a winner with this tiny cafe in the industrial district of Wailuku. It may be slightly off the tourist path, but it's well worth the effort to find this delicious eatery, with healthy creative cuisine coming out of the kitchen. Prices are so eye-poppingly low, you might find yourself wandering back here during your vacation. Lunches feature everything from grilled chicken, garlic-crusted ono, and eggplant Parmesan to hamburger steak, beef stew, and spaghetti with meatballs. Dinner shines, with blackened ono with mango basil sauce, tofu napoleon with ginger pesto, crab cakes with papaya beurre blanc, cashew chicken, and baby back ribs. The keiki menu has the old standby, mac and cheese, as well as a turkey burger, and all the kids' dishes come with a side dish of vegetables or french fries.

1237 Lower Main St., Wailuku. ✆ **808/244-8774.** www.akscafe.com. Kids' menu, boosters, crayons. Plate lunches $7.50–$10; dinner $14–$18; kids' menu $4.50. MC, V. Tues–Sat 11am–2pm and 5–9pm. Sun and Mon closed.

Down to Earth *Value* ORGANIC HEALTH FOOD Here's the place for fast food (a buffet) with healthful organic ingredients (90% vegan) that's quicker than McDonald's. It offers scrumptious salads, vegetarian lasagna, chili, curries, and dozens of tasty dishes, presented at hot and cold serve-yourself stations. The younger crowd loves the mock (tofu) chicken and the teriyaki tofu. Eat in or take out, the food is great: Everything is organic and tasty, with herb-tamari marinades and pleasing condiments such as currants or raisins, apples, and cashews. Because the food is sold by the pound, you can buy a hearty, wholesome plate for $8. Check out the (healthy and tasty) bakery selections.

305 Dairy Rd., Kahului. ✆ **808/877-2661.** Highchairs. Average plate $7–$9. AE, MC, V. Mon–Sat 7am–9pm; Sun 8am–8pm.

WEST MAUI

Lahaina

There's a **Maui Tacos** in Lahaina Square (✆ **808/661-8883**). Maui's branch of the **Hard Rock Café** is in Lahaina at 900 Front St. (✆ **808/667-7400**).

Very Expensive

David Paul's Lahaina Grill ★ NEW AMERICAN Kids are not only welcome here, but treated like sophisticated young ladies and gentlemen. The chic stylish restaurant—black-and-white tile floors, pressed-tin ceilings, eclectic 1890s decor—is striking, and the bar, even without an ocean view, is the busiest spot in Lahaina. And surprisingly enough, this gourmet eatery offers a great kids' menu with kids' soup or salad of the day, fried chicken strips, corn dogs, or mahi and shrimp, as well as desserts such as ice cream and chocolate cake. The regular menu will have you salivating, especially the signature items: tequila shrimp and firecracker rice, Kona coffee–roasted rack of lamb, Maui onion–crusted seared ahi, and kalua duck quesadilla.

127 Lahainaluna Rd. ✆ **808/667-5117.** Kids' menu, highchairs, boosters, crayons. Reservations required. Main courses $33–$88; kids' menu $10–$15. AE, DC, DISC, MC, V. Daily 6–10pm; bar daily 6–10pm.

Expensive

Gerard's ★★★ *Finds* FRENCH When you need an adults' night out, head for this romantic restaurant. The charm of Gerard's—soft lighting, Edith Piaf on the sound system, excellent service—is matched by a menu of uncompromising standards. After nearly 3 decades in Lahaina, Gerard Reversade never runs out of creative offerings, yet stays true to his French roots. A frequent winner of the *Wine Spectator* Award of Excellence, Gerard's offers roasted opakapaka with star anise, fennel fondue, and hints of orange and ginger, a stellar entree on a menu of winners. If you're feeling extravagant, the Kona lobster ragout with pasta and morels promises ecstasy, and the spinach salad with scallops is among the finest I've tasted. Gerard's has an excellent appetizer menu, with shiitake and oyster mushrooms in puff pastry, fresh ahi and smoked salmon carpaccio, and a very rich, highly touted escargot ragout with burgundy butter and garlic cream. If you do bring the young ones, they have a kids' menu, on which the most popular item is pasta.

In the Plantation Inn, 174 Lahainaluna Rd. ✆ **808/661-8939.** www.gerardsmaui.com. Kids' menu, highchairs, boosters, crayons. Reservations recommended. Main courses $33–$54; kids' menu from $9.50. AE, DC, DISC, MC, V. Daily 6–9pm.

Pacific'o Restaurant ★ PACIFIC RIM/CONTEMPORARY PACIFIC You can't get any closer to the ocean than the tables here, which are literally on the beach. The split-level dining starts at the top, near the entrance, with a long bar (where you can also order lunch or dinner) and a few tables along the railing. Steps lead to the outdoor tables, where the succulent seafood dishes come to you with the backdrop of Lanai across the channel. This place is proof that parents can eat well and the kids will be happy too. The prawn and basil wontons, fresh fish over wilted arugula and bean sprouts, and ahi and ono tempura with miso and lime-basil sauce are among Pacific'o's memorable offerings. If you like seafood, sunsets, and touches of India and Indonesia in your fresh-from-the-sea dining choices, you should be happy here. The kids' menu ranges from hamburgers to the bestselling fish and chips, and includes a "drink" menu, with a lava flow (blended pineapple juice, coconut, banana, and strawberry) and a virgin piña colada.

505 Front St. ✆ **808/667-4341.** www.pacificomaui.com. Kids' menu, highchairs, crayons. Reservations recommended. Main courses $12–$16 lunch, $30–$40 dinner; kids' menu $10–$14. AE, DC, MC, V. Daily 11:30am–4pm and 5:30–10pm.

Moderate

Compadres Bar & Grill MEXICAN This place is so loud and full of laughter, no one will notice if your little darlings are acting up. You can sit inside with the industrial motif or outside in the open-air seating area. Beach fans can pick up lunch or dinner at the takeout taqueria window. The food is classic Tex-Mex, good any time of the day, beginning with huevos rancheros, egg burritos, hotcakes, and omelets, and progressing to enchiladas and appetizers for the margarita happy crowd. Stay spare (vegetable enchilada in fresh spinach tortilla) or get hefty (Texas T-bone and enchiladas). For kids 10 and younger, there are both American (corn dog, burger, chicken) and Mexican menus (nachos, quesadilla, minitacos, and chicken chingalinga), plus a great chocolate sundae for just $1.85: two scoops of ice cream covered with chocolate in a sugary tortilla. This is a carefree place with a large capacity for merrymaking.

Lahaina Cannery Mall, 1221 Honoapiilani Hwy. ✆ **808/661-7189.** Kids' menu, highchairs, boosters, crayons. Main courses $10–$20; kids' menu $2.95–$4.95. AE, DC, DISC, MC, V. Daily 8am–10pm.

Kimo's STEAK/SEAFOOD Kimo's has a loyal following that keeps it from falling into the faceless morass of waterfront restaurants serving surf and turf with great sunset views. It's a formula restaurant that works not only because of its oceanfront patio and upstairs dining room, but also because, for the price, there are some satisfying choices and a kids' menu with food that kids want to eat (grilled cheese, hamburger, chicken, and the very popular ribs). It's always crowded, buzzing with people on a deck offering views of Molokai, Lanai, and Kahoolawe. Burgers and sandwiches are affordable and consistent, and the fresh catch in a garlic-lemon or a sweet-basil glaze is a top seller. The waistline-defying hula pie—macadamia nut ice cream in a chocolate-wafer crust with fudge and whipped cream—originated here.

845 Front St. ✆ **808/661-4811.** www.kimosmaui.com. Kids' menu, highchairs, boosters, crayons. Reservations recommended for dinner. Main courses $7–$15 lunch, $18–$33 dinner; kids' menu $5.95–$6.95 lunch, $6.95–$13 dinner. AE, DC, DISC, MC, V. Daily 11am–3:30pm and 5–10:30pm; bar 11am–1am.

Inexpensive

Cheeseburger in Paradise AMERICAN Wildly successful, always crowded, highly visible, and very noisy with its live music in the evenings, Cheeseburger is a shrine to the American classic. The home of three-napkin cheeseburgers with attitude, this is burger country tropical style, with everything from tofu and garden burgers to the biggest, juiciest beef and chicken burgers, served on whole-wheat and sesame buns baked fresh daily. There are good reasons why the two-story green-and-white building next to the sea wall is always packed: good value, good eats, and a great ocean view. No kids' menu per se, but kids dig the cheese dog and grilled cheese sandwich.

 811 Front St. ✆ **808/661-4855.** www.cheeseburgerinparadise.com. Highchairs, crayons. Burgers $8.95–$13. AE, DISC, MC, V. Daily 8am–10pm.

Cilantro: Fresh Mexican Grill ★ Kids Finds MEXICAN This is Maui's best bet for fabulous Mexican food at frugal prices. And, believe it or not, this fast-food restaurant serves fresh, healthy food. The chef and owner, Pris Nabavi, creator of Nickey's Pizza (see review below), wanted a new challenge, so he took off to Mexico to explore the origins of the cuisine. He's back on Maui with this unbelievably delicious eatery where everything is made from scratch. Even the corn tortillas are handmade daily. Signature dishes include citrus-and-herb-marinated chipotle rotisserie chicken, veggie Mariposa salad, the popular Mother Clucker flautas, and the lip-smacking "al pastor"-style adobo pork. All this at budget-pleasing prices. It's a great place to take the kids; the Los Niños menu is $5.

170 Papalaua Ave. ✆ **808/667-5444.** www.cilantrogrill.com. Kids' menu, highchairs. Entrees $4–$14; kids' menu $5. MC, V. Mon–Sat 11am–9pm; Sun 11am–8pm.

Lahaina Coolers Restaurant & Bar ★ AMERICAN/INTERNATIONAL A huge marlin hangs above the bar, epic wave shots and wall sconces made of surfboard fins line the walls, and open windows on three sides of this ultracasual indoor/outdoor restaurant take advantage of the shade trees to create a laid-back, cheerful ambience. This is a great breakfast joint, with feta-cheese Mediterranean omelets, huevos rancheros, fried rice, and pancakes; they'll even downsize the breakfast portions for your keiki. At lunch, burgers rule. The sandwiches, from grilled portobello mushrooms to the classic tuna melt, are ideal for casual Lahaina. Made fresh daily, the pasta is prepared Asian style (chicken breast in a spicy Thai peanut sauce), with pesto, or vegetarian (in a spicy Creole sauce). Pizzas, pastas, fresh catch, steak, and enchiladas round out the entrees, and everything can be prepared vegetarian upon request. The menu is so extensive that there will be something for everyone in the family. The staff can whip up a grilled cheese sandwich or noodles and butter for picky eaters.

180 Dickenson St. ✆ **808/661-7082.** www.lahainacoolers.com. Highchairs, boosters, coloring books, crayons. Main courses $8.25–$10 breakfast, $8.50–$14 lunch, $10–$25 dinner. AE, DC, DISC, MC, V. Daily 8am–2am (full menu until midnight).

Kaanapali

Whalers Village has a food court where you can buy pizza, very good Japanese food (including tempura soba and other noodle dishes), Korean plates, and fast-food burgers at serve-yourself counters and courtyard tables. It's an inexpensive alternative and a quick, handy stop for shoppers and Kaanapali beachgoers.

CJ's Deli and Diner ★★★ Value AMERICAN/DELI Eat here! If you are staying in Kaanapali, it is walking distance from your resort (up to the highway), and if you're not staying in Kaanapali, it's worth the drive to sample the "comfort food" (as they call it) at this hip eatery with prices so low you can't believe you are on Maui. (There's nothing over $13 on the entire menu.) You can eat in or take out (hey, they even have "chefs to go" to come to your accommodations and cook for you), the atmosphere is friendly, and there's even high-speed Internet access. Huge, delicious breakfasts start at 7am (for those up that early, check out the $4.95 early-bird special of two eggs, bacon or sausage, rice, and coffee); for those who sleep in late, no worries—breakfast is served until 11am. Lunch ranges from deli sandwiches, burgers, and hot sandwiches to pot roast, ribs, and fish dishes. If you are on your way to Hana or to the top of Haleakala, stop by and get a box lunch.

Kaanapali Fairway Shops, 2580 Keka'a Dr. (just off Honoapiilani Hwy.), Kaanapali Resort. ✆ **808/667-0968.** Kids' menu, highchairs, boosters, crayons. Main courses $4–$10 breakfast, $5–$13 lunch; kids' menu under $7. AE, MC, V. Daily 7am–8pm.

Hula Grill Kaanapali ★ HAWAIIAN REGIONAL/SEAFOOD Here's your chance to stick your toes in the sand, admire the beach, and eat wonderful food at the same time. Hula Grill offers a wide range of prices and choices; it can be expensive but doesn't have to be. The menu includes firecracker mahimahi, seafood pot stickers, and several different fresh-fish preparations. At lunch the menu is more limited, with a choice of sandwiches, entrees, pizza, appetizers, and salads. There's happy-hour entertainment and Hawaiian music daily. If you want a more casual atmosphere, the Barefoot Bar, located on the beach, offers burgers, fish, pizza, and salads. Kids have their own menu ranging from grilled cheese and fries to fish and chips. Kids 3 and under can order the keiki pasta for free.

In Whalers Village, 2435 Kaanapali Pkwy. ✆ **808/667-6636.** www.hulagrill.com. Kids' menu, highchairs, boosters, crayons. Reservations recommended for dinner. Lunch and Barefoot Bar menus $8–$18; dinner main courses $17–$35; kids' menu $3.95–$8.95. AE, DC, DISC, MC, V. Daily 11am–11pm.

Leilani's Beachside Grill/On the Beach SEAFOOD/STEAK The Beachside Grill is the informal, less-expensive room downstairs on the beach, where folks wander in off the sand for a frothy beer and a beachside burger. Leilani's is the dinner-only room, with more expensive but still not outrageously priced steak and seafood offerings. At Leilani's, you can order everything from spinach, cheese, and mushroom ravioli to lobster and steak. Children can get a quarter-pound hamburger for under $5 or a broiled chicken breast for a couple of dollars more—a value, for sure. Pasta, rack of lamb, filet mignon, and Alaskan king crab at market price are among the choices in the upstairs room. Although the steak-and-lobster combinations can be pricey, the good thing about Leilani's is the strong middle range of entree prices, especially the fresh fish for around $24 to $32. All of this, of course, comes with an ocean view. There's live music every Friday, Saturday, and Sunday 3 to 5pm.

In Whalers Village, 2435 Kaanapali Pkwy. ✆ **808/661-4495.** www.leilanis.com. Kids' menu, highchairs, boosters, crayons. Reservations suggested for dinner. Lunch and dinner (Beachside Grill) $9.95–$17; dinner (Leilani's) $17–$32; kids' menu $5–$10. AE, DC, DISC, MC, V. Beachside Grill daily 11am–11pm (bar daily until 12:30am); Leilani's daily 5–9pm.

Nicky's Pizza PIZZA They've changed the name from Pizza Paradiso, but kept the menu of pastas, pizzas, and desserts, including smoothies, coffee, and ice cream. The pizza reflects a simple and effective formula that has won acclaim through the years: good crust, true-blue sauces, and toppings loyal to tradition but with just enough edge for those who want it. You and the kids can create your own pizza with roasted eggplant, mushrooms, anchovies, artichoke hearts, spicy sausages, cheeses, or a slew of other toppings.

In Whalers Village, 2435 Kaanapali Pkwy. ✆ **808/667-0333.** Gourmet whole pizzas $14–$27; pasta $7–$10. AE, MC, V. Daily 11am–9pm.

Honokowai, Kahana & Napili

Roy's Kahana Bar & Grill ★★★ PACIFIC RIM Long known for its Pacific Rim cuisine, this restaurant bustles with young, hip servers impeccably trained to deliver blackened ahi or perfectly seared lemon grass *shutome* (broadbill swordfish) hot to your table, in rooms that sizzle with cross-cultural tastings. Roy's chain of restaurants (across the state, as well as 20 different locations on the U.S. mainland) is known for the rack of lamb and fresh seafood (usually eight or nine choices), and for the large, open kitchens that turn out everything from pizza to sake-grilled New York steak. What is not well known is how carefully the waitstaff takes care of the kids. The four-course prix-fixe menu for kids starts with a quesadilla; is followed by apple, carrot, and celery sticks; gives kids a choice of butter Parmesan penne pasta, teriyaki grilled chicken, kiawe-fired steak, or hibachi salmon; and concludes with a sundae for dessert. Large picture windows open up Roy's Kahana but don't quell the noise, another enduring trait long ago established by Roy's Restaurant in Honolulu, the flagship of Yamaguchi's burgeoning empire.

There's another location at 303 Piikea Ave., Kihei (✆ **808/891-1120**).

In the Kahana Gateway Shopping Center, 4405 Honoapiilani Hwy. ✆ **808/669-6999.** www.roysrestaurant.com. Kids' menu, highchairs, boosters, crayons. Reservations strongly suggested. Main courses $27–$42; kids' prix-fixe menu $12. AE, DC, DISC, MC, V. Daily 5:30–10pm.

Kapalua

Sansei Seafood Restaurant & Sushi Bar ★★★ PACIFIC RIM Here's a restaurant that not only offers an extensive menu of highly regarded Japanese and East-West delicacies—furiously fusion, part Hawaiian Regional Cuisine, and all parts sushi—but also serves up fun. Be sure to ask to sit at the counter, where your kids will be entertained by the sushi chefs as they whip up incredibly imaginative dishes. Sansei is tirelessly creative, with a menu that scores higher with adventurous palates than with purists (although there are endless traditional choices as well). The kids' menu includes ramen noodles ($11), chicken and pasta ($9.95), and grilled fish ($9.95). Plus there are plenty of selections on the regular menu to choose from: panko-crusted ahi sashimi, ahi carpaccio, lobster, Asian rock-shrimp cakes, and sauces that surprise, in creative combinations such as ginger-lime chile butter and cilantro pesto. But there's simpler fare as well, such as shrimp tempura, noodles, and wok-tossed upcountry vegetables. Desserts are not to be missed. If it's autumn, don't pass up persimmon crème brûlée made with Kula persimmons. In other seasons, opt for tempura-fried ice cream with chocolate sauce. ***Tip:*** Eat early; all food is 25% off between 5:30 and 6pm weekdays.

There's another location at Kihei Town Center, Kihei (✆ **808/879-0004**).

600 Office Rd., Kapalua ✆ **808/669-6286.** www.sanseihawaii.com. Highchairs, boosters, crayons. Reservations recommended. Main courses $16–$43; kids' menu $9.95–$11. AE, DISC, MC, V. Daily 5:30–10pm.

Vino ★★★ (Finds) ITALIAN Overlooking the rolling hills of the Kapalua Golf Course, this creative Italian restaurant is run by D. K. Kodama, chef and owner of Sansei Seafood Restaurant & Sushi Bar (see above); and by master sommelier Chuck Furuya. The two teamed up to create a culinary adventure for foodies and children of foodies. The Bambini menu (for kids 11 and younger) starts with vegetables crudo (raw carrots, celery, and apple wedges) or warm, crispy mozzarella wedges and moves on to mac and cheese, spaghetti and meatballs, or fettuccine Alfredo with chicken.

On the big person's menu, dishes change constantly, but always feature homemade pastas, classic and contemporary preparations of poultry and meat, and fresh seafood dishes nightly. All entrees are offered with a perfect wine choice. The lunch menu is lighter fare: unusual salads, a "killer" chicken sandwich, a quarter-pounder hot dog, and fresh fish.

Kapalua Village Course Golf Club House, Kapalua Resort. ✆ **808/661-VINO** (661-8466). Kids' menu, highchairs, boosters. Reservations recommended. Tapas $6–$20; large plates $19–$38; kids' menu $4.95–$8.95. AE, DISC, MC, V. Daily 11am–2pm and 5–9:30pm.

SOUTH MAUI

Kihei/Maalaea

There's a **Maui Tacos** at Kamaole Beach Center in Kihei (✆ **808/879-5005**).

Moderate

Stella Blues Cafe ★ AMERICAN Stella Blues gets going at breakfast and continues through to dinner with something for everyone—vegetarians, kids, pasta and sandwich lovers, hefty steak eaters, and sensible diners who go for the inexpensive fresh Kula green salad. Grateful Dead posters line the walls, and a covey of gleaming motorcycles is invariably parked outside. It's loud and lively, irreverent, and unpretentious. Sandwiches are the highlight, ranging from Tofu Extraordinaire to Mom's egg salad on a croissant to garden burgers to grilled chicken. Tofu wraps and mountain-size Cobb salads are popular. For the reckless, large coffee shakes come with mounds of whipped cream. Daily specials include fresh seafood and other surprises—all home-style cooking, made from scratch, down to the pesto mayonnaise and herb bread. At dinner, selections are geared toward good-value family dining, from affordable full dinners to pastas and burgers. A kids' menu is available for all three meals, with buttered noodles and mac and cheese the favorites.

In Long's Center, 1215 S. Kihei Rd. ✆ **808/874-3779.** www.stellablues.com. Kids' menu, highchairs, boosters, crayons. Breakfast entrees $6–$12, lunch sandwiches $6–$11; lunch entrees $9–$14; dinner entrees $12–$28; pizza $13; kids' menu $3.95–$12. AE, DISC, MC, V. Daily 7:30am–10pm.

Inexpensive

Peggy Sue's AMERICAN Just for a moment, forget that diet and take a leap. It's Peggy Sue's to the rescue! This 1950s-style diner has oodles of charm and is a swell place to spring for the best chocolate malt on the island. You'll also find sodas, shakes, floats, egg creams, milkshakes, and scoops of made-on-Maui Roselani-brand gourmet ice cream—14 flavors. Old-fashioned soda-shop stools, an Elvis Presley Boulevard sign, and jukeboxes on every Formica table serve as a backdrop for the famous burgers (and garden burgers), brushed with teriyaki sauce and served with all the goodies. The fries are great, too. The kids' menu includes grilled cheese and PB&J sandwiches, hot dogs, and hamburgers, all served with fries.

In Azeka Place II, 1279 S. Kihei Rd. ✆ **808/875-8944.** Kids' menu, highchairs, boosters, crayons. Burgers $8.45–$11; plate lunches $6.95–$16; kids' menu $6. DC, MC, V. Sun–Thurs 11am–9pm; Fri–Sat 11am–10pm.

Shaka Sandwich & Pizza PIZZA Pizzas share the limelight with New York–style heroes and Philly cheese steaks, calzones, salads, homemade garlic bread, and homemade meatball sandwiches. Shaka uses fresh Maui produce, long-simmering sauces, and homemade Italian bread. Choose thin or Sicilian thick crust with gourmet toppings: Maui onions, spinach, anchovies, jalapeños, and a spate of other vegetables. No kids' menu, but with the pizza selection, your children will be in heaven.

1770 S. Kihei Rd. ✆ **808/874-0331.** Highchairs. Sandwiches $6.65–$15; pizzas $17–$29. MC, V. Sun–Thurs 10:30am–9pm; Fri–Sat 10:30am–10pm.

Wailea

The Shops at Wailea, in a sprawling location between the Grand Wailea Hotel and Wailea Marriott Resort, has added a spate of new shops and restaurants to this stretch of south Maui. Five restaurants and dozens of shops, most of them upscale, are among the new tenants of this complex. **Ruth's Chris Steak House** is here, as well as **Tommy Bahama's Tropical Cafe & Emporium, Honolulu Coffee Company Café Wailea, Cheeseburger, Mai Tai's and Rock-n-Roll,** and **Longhi's.** Next door at the Outrigger

Wailea, **Hula Moons,** the retro-Hawaiian-themed restaurant, has reopened after a $3-million renovation and moved to the upper level of the lobby building, where it serves midpriced steak and seafood with an ocean view.

Very Expensive

Nick's Fishmarket Maui ★★★ SEAFOOD Here's another romantic getaway option for an adults' night out. The ambience is spectacular, the fragrant stephanotis flowers send out gentle wafts of perfume in the air, and the seafood is fresh. This is a classic seafood restaurant that sticks to the tried and true (in other words, *not* an overwrought menu) but stays fresh with excellent ingredients and a high degree of professionalism in service and preparation. The Greek Maui Wowie salad gets my vote as one of the top salads in Hawaii. The blackened mahimahi has been a Nick's signature for eons, and why not—it's wonderful. There's a kids' menu if you want to bring them to this sophisticated restaurant, plus crayons to keep them happy.

In the Fairmont Kea Lani Hotel, 4100 Wailea Alanui Dr. ✆ **808/879-7224.** www.tri-star-restaurants.com. Reservations recommended. Main courses $30–$60; prix-fixe dinners $55–$85. AE, DC, DISC, MC, V. Daily 5:30–10pm; bar until 11pm.

Spago ★★★ CALIFORNIA/HAWAIIAN/PACIFIC REGIONAL California meets Hawaii in this contemporary-designed eatery featuring fresh, local Hawaii ingredients prepared under the culinary watch of Master Chef Wolfgang Puck. Although children are welcome, this is a sophisticated place where adults enjoy cutting-edge cuisine that lives up to Puck's reputation of adding his innovations to traditional Hawaiian dishes. Open for dinner only, the menu features an unbelievable coconut soup with local lobster, kaffir, chile, and galangal. For entrees, try the whole steamed fish served with chile and ginger, or Kona lobster with sweet-and-sour banana curry and coconut rice, or the grilled côte de boeuf with braised celery. The wine and beverage list is well thought out and extensive. Don't pass up the warm guanaja chocolate tart with Tahitian vanilla-bean ice cream for dessert. Make reservations as soon as you land on the island (if not before); this place is popular. And bring plenty of cash or your platinum card.

Four Seasons Resort Maui, 3900 Wailea Alanui Dr., ✆ **808/879-2999.** www.fourseasons.com/maui/dining/spago.html. Kids' menu, highchairs, boosters,. Reservations required. Main courses $37–$59; kids' prix-fixe menu $15. AE, DC, DISC, MC, V. Daily 5:30–9:30pm; bar with pupu daily 5–11pm.

Moderate

Joe's Bar & Grill ★★★ AMERICAN GRILL The 270-degree view at Joe's spans the golf course, tennis courts, ocean, and Haleakala—a worthy setting for Beverly Gannon's style of American home cooking with a regional twist. The kids' menu features staples from meatloaf and mashed potatoes to barbecued ribs. The regular menu also has that great meatloaf (except that big people get a whole loaf, like Mom used to make) and other hearty dishes such as excellent mashed potatoes, lobster, fresh fish, and filet mignon. Daily specials could be grilled ahi with white truffle–Yukon gold mashed potatoes, or sautéed mahimahi with shrimp bisque and sautéed spinach. If chocolate cake is on the menu, you should definitely spring for it.

In the Wailea Tennis Club, 131 Wailea Ike Place. ✆ **808/875-7767.** Kids' menu, highchairs, boosters, crayons. Reservations recommended. Main courses $20–$42; kids' menu $4–$8. AE, DC, DISC, MC, V. Daily 5:30–9pm.

UPCOUNTRY MAUI

You'll find the restaurants in this section on the "Upcountry & East Maui" map on p. 250.

Haliimaile (on the Way to Upcountry Maui)

Haliimaile General Store ★★★ AMERICAN Chef Bev Gannon, one of the 12 original Hawaiian Regional Cuisine chefs, is still going strong at her foodie haven in the pineapple fields. You'll dine at tables set on old wood floors under high ceilings (sound ricochets fiercely here), in a peach-colored room emblazoned with works by local artists. The food is a blend of eclectic American with ethnic Hawaiian touches. Sip the lilikoi lemonade and nibble the sashimi napoleon or the house salad—island greens with mandarin oranges, onions, toasted walnuts, and blue cheese crumble. All are notable items on a menu that bridges Hawaii with Gannon's Texas roots. Kids have their own meals such as cheesy cheese pizza, delicious macaroni, barbecue chicken, and cookies and ice cream.

Haliimaile Rd., Haliimaile. ✆ **808/572-2666.** www.haliimailegeneralstore.com. Kids' menu, highchairs, boosters, crayons. Reservations recommended. Main courses $8–$24 lunch, $24–$42 dinner; kids' menu $5–$14. DC, MC, V. Mon–Fri 11am–2:30pm; daily 5:30–9:30pm.

Makawao & Pukalani

Casanova Italian Restaurant and Deli ★ ITALIAN Look for the tiny veranda with a few stools, always full, in front of a deli at Makawao's busiest intersection—that's the most visible part of the Casanova restaurant and lounge. Makawao's nightlife center contains a stage, dance floor, restaurant, and bar—and food to love and remember. This is pasta heaven; try the spaghetti Fra Diavolo or the spinach gnocchi in a fresh tomato-Gorgonzola sauce. Other choices include a huge pizza selection, grilled lamb chops in an Italian mushroom marinade, every possible type of pasta, and luscious desserts. They don't have a kids' menu, but they will whip up spaghetti (plain, with butter, or with cheese) for just $5.

1188 Makawao Ave. ✆ **808/572-0220.** www.casanovamaui.com. Highchairs, boosters, crayons. Reservations recommended for dinner. Main courses $6–$18 lunch, $12–$34 dinner; 12-in. pizzas $12–$20; pasta $12–$18. AE, DC, DISC, MC, V. Mon–Sat 11:30am–2pm and 5:30–9:30pm; Sun 5:30–9pm. Dancing Wed–Sat 9:45pm–1am. Lounge daily 5:30pm–12:30am or 1am. Deli Mon–Sat 7:30am–6pm; Sun 8:30am–6pm.

Kula (at the Base of Haleakala National Park)

Kula Lodge ★ AMERICAN/HAWAIIAN REGIONAL Don't let the dinner prices scare you; the Kula Lodge is equally enjoyable, if not more so, at breakfast and lunch, when the prices are lower and the views through the picture windows have an eye-popping intensity. The million dollar vista spans the flanks of Haleakala, rolling 3,200 feet down to central Maui, the ocean, and the West Maui Mountains. The Kula Lodge has always been known for its breakfasts: fabulous eggs Benedict, including a vegetarian version with Kula onions, shiitake mushrooms, and scallions; legendary banana mac-nut pancakes; and a highly recommended tofu scramble with green onions, Kula vegetables, and garlic chives. Kids can order cinnamon-raisin French toast, keiki pancakes, or an egg, bacon, and cottage fries for just $6.50. If possible, go for sunset cocktails and watch the colors change into deep end-of-day hues. When darkness descends, a roaring fire and lodge atmosphere add to the coziness of the room. Sesame-seared ono, Cuban-style spicy swordfish with rum-soaked bananas, and miso salmon with wild mushrooms are seafood attractions on the dinner menu, and there's also pasta, rack of lamb, filet mignon, and free-range chicken breast. The kids' menu has more familiar items like mac and cheese, a grilled cheese sandwich (with potato spears), and grilled chicken breast.

Haleakala Hwy. (Hwy. 377). ✆ **808/878-2517.** Kids' menu, highchairs, boosters, crayons. Reservations recommended for dinner. Main courses $8–$17 breakfast, $10–$18 lunch, $14–$35 dinner; kids' menu $5.50–$12. AE, MC, V. Daily 6:30am–9pm.

You'll find the restaurants in this section on the "Upcountry & East Maui" map on p. 250.

Paia

Moana Bakery & Cafe ★★★ EUROPEAN/LOCAL This no-nonsense restaurant loves kids and has a menu to prove it: only $5 for anything on the list, from pancakes to burgers and PB&J sandwiches. The Moana also gets high marks for its stylish concrete floors, high ceilings, booths and cafe tables, and fabulous food. Don Ritchey, formerly a chef at Haliimaile General Store, has created the perfect Paia eatery, a casual bakery-cafe that highlights his stellar skills. All the bases are covered: saimin, omelets, wraps, pancakes, and fresh-baked goods in the morning; soups, sandwiches, pasta, and satisfying salads for lunch; and for dinner, varied selections with Asian and European influences and fresh island ingredients. I also vouch for his special gift with fish: The nori-sesame-crusted opakapaka with wasabi beurre blanc is cooked to perfection.

71 Baldwin Ave. ✆ **808/579-9999.** Kids' menu, highchairs, boosters, crayons. Reservations recommended for dinner. Main courses $7–$11 breakfast, $10–$17 lunch, $10–$39 dinner; kids' menu $5. MC, V. Daily 8am–9pm: breakfast and lunch 8am–3pm; dinner 3–8pm.

Paia Fish Market ★ SEAFOOD This really is a fish market, with fresh fish to take home, and cooked seafood, salads, pastas, fajitas, and quesadillas to take out or enjoy at the few picnic tables inside the restaurant. Great for families for their appealing and budget-friendly selection: Cajun-style fresh catch, fresh-fish specials (usually ahi or salmon), fresh-fish tacos, and seafood and chicken pastas. You can also order hamburgers, cheeseburgers, fish and chips (or shrimp and chips), and wonderful lunch and dinner plates, cheap and tasty. Peppering the walls are photos of the number one sport here, windsurfing. The quesadillas (just under $4) are popular with the younger set.

110 Hana Hwy. ✆ **808/579-8030.** Highchairs. Lunch and dinner plates $8–$22. DISC, MC, V. Daily 11am–9:30pm.

Haiku

Colleen's at the Cannery ★★★ *Finds* ECLECTIC Way, way, way off the beaten path lies this fabulous find in the rural Haiku Cannery Marketplace. Once through the doors, you'll swear you've dropped down in the middle of a hot, chic boutique restaurant in SoHo in Manhattan (only, when you look around at the patrons, they are pure Haiku upcountry residents). It's worth the drive to enjoy Colleen's fabulous culinary creations, like a wild mushroom ravioli with sautéed portobello mushrooms, tomatoes, herbs, and a roasted pepper coulis for $14 (not New York City prices); pan-seared ahi for $15; or filet mignon with a side salad for $16. Colleen also serves up smaller meals, such as burgers and fish and chips. Breakfast includes mouth-watering bakery products such as French toast ($7.75) with Colleen's own homemade bread or the wonderful omelets ($9). Lunch stars baguette sandwiches, wraps, salads, and burgers and fries. I only wish they would take reservations. No kids' menu, but the grilled cheese with fries ($5) is the hands-down favorite among the younger set.

Haiku Cannery Marketplace, 810 Haiku Rd. ✆ **808/575-9211.** www.colleensinhaiku.com. Reservations not accepted. Breakfast $5.75–$9; lunch $7–$15; dinner entrees $10–$33. MC, V. Daily 6am–10pm.

On the Road to Hana

Mama's Fish House ★★★ If you love fish, this is the place for you. The restaurant's entrance, a cove with windsurfers, tide pools, white sand, and a canoe resting under palm trees, is a South Seas fantasy worthy of Gauguin. With servers wearing Polynesian prints and flowers behind their ears, and the sun setting in Kuau Cove, Mama's mood is hard to beat. The fish is fresh (the fishermen are even credited by name on the menu) and prepared Hawaiian-style, with tropical fruit or baked in a macadamia nut and vanilla-bean crust, or in a number of preparations involving ferns, seaweed, Maui onions, and roasted kukui nuts. Menu items include mahimahi laulau with luau leaves (taro greens) and Maui onions, baked in ti leaves and served with kalua pig and Hanalei poi—the best. Other special touches include the use of Molokai sweet potato, Hana breadfruit, organic lettuces, Haiku bananas, and fresh coconut, which evoke the mood and tastes of Old Hawaii. The keiki menu (for children 8 and younger) features an entree (fish, chicken, or deep-fried shrimp) plus Mama's delicious banana pudding (yum-yum) for $15.

799 Poho Place, just off the Hana Hwy., Kuau. ✆ **808/579-8488.** Kids' menu, highchairs, boosters, crayons. Reservations recommended for lunch, required for dinner. Main courses $29–$54 lunch, $36–$115 dinner; kids' menu $15. AE, DC, DISC, MC, V. Daily 11am–3pm, light menu 3–4:45pm, and last seating 4:45–9pm.

Hana

Hotel Hana Maui ★★★ ECLECTIC Not even Executive Chef John Cox, who is in charge of developing the daily menu changes here, can put his finger on the delicious type of cuisine served for breakfast, lunch, and dinner in the open-aired, large window dining room. "I call it cuisine inspired by Eastern Maui," he said, pointing to the ingredients driven menu: the fresh fish caught by local fishermen, the produce brought in by nearby farmers, the fruits that are in season. The result is true "Hawaiian" food, grown right on the island. Breakfast features an omelet with local Maui onions and a Hana fern salad, almond-crusted French toast, or local papaya with yogurt and homemade granola. Lunch ranges from Maui Cattle Company burgers to just-caught fish sandwiches. Dinner, which changes daily and should be reserved for a special adult night out, can include just-picked lettuce for salads (Kula-grown baby romaine with Gruyère crostini and sherry-thyme vinaigrette or baby lettuces with Kula citrus, local radishes, and Kalamata olives), a range of soups (such as a chilled Kula cucumber soup), and a range of entrees (seared rare Hana caught ahi with smoked bacon, forest mushrooms, and wilted greens; or oven-roasted chicken breast with crispy polenta, Nihiku bush beans, and mole sauce).

Hana Hwy. ✆ **808/248-8211.** Reservations recommended for Fri–Sat dinner. Main courses $12–$20 breakfast, $10–$21 lunch, $20–$40 dinner; Friday buffet $50 adults, $35 kids. AE, DISC, MC, V. Daily 7:30–10:30am, 11:30am–2:30pm, and 6–9pm; Fri Hawaiian show 6–8:30pm.

5 EXPLORING MAUI WITH YOUR KIDS

None of the sights below offer stroller rentals on-site, so plan to bring your own.

CENTRAL MAUI

Central Maui isn't exactly tourist central; this is where real people live. Most likely, you'll land here and head directly to the beach. However, there are a few sights worth checking out if you feel like a respite from the sun 'n' surf.

Wailuku & Waikapu

About 3 miles south of Wailuku lies the tiny, one-street village of Waikapu, which has a great kids' attraction. Relive Maui's past by taking a 40-minute narrated tram ride around

Moments Flying High: Helicopter Rides

Okay, it's expensive, and maybe a little scary to the uninitiated. But you will kick yourself if you don't take the family on a helicopter ride to really "see" Maui. Only a helicopter can bring you face to face with volcanoes, waterfalls, and remote places such as Maui's little-known Wall of Tears, up near the summit of Puu Kukui in the West Maui Mountains. A helicopter trip on Maui isn't a wild ride; it's more like a gentle zip into a seldom-seen Eden. Today's pilots are part Hawaiian historian, part DJ, part amusement-ride operator, and part tour guide, telling you about Hawaii's flora and fauna, history, and culture. **Blue Hawaiian Helicopters ★★★** (✆ **800/745-BLUE** [745-2583] or 808/871-8844; www.bluehawaiian.com) is the Cadillac of helicopter-tour companies. They have the latest, high-tech, environmentally friendly (and quiet) Eco-Star helicopter, specially designed for air-tour operators. Flights vary from 30 to 100 minutes and range from $165 to $385 per person. Children 1 and under ride free on a parent's lap, but older kids are required by FAA rules to have their own seat. ***Budget tip:*** Book on the Internet for substantial savings!

fields of pineapple, sugar cane, and papaya trees at **Maui Tropical Plantation,** 1670 Honoapiilani Hwy. (✆ **800/451-6805** or 808/244-7643), a real working plantation, open daily from 9am to 5pm. A shop sells fresh and dried fruit, and a restaurant serves lunch. Allow at least a couple of hours to wander about. Admission is free; the tram tours, which start at 10am and leave about every 45 minutes, are $11 for adults, $4 for kids ages 3 to 12.

Iao Valley ★

If you are looking to get away from the "urban" Maui and maybe take a short walk with the kids, just a couple of miles north of Wailuku, where the little plantation houses stop and the road climbs ever higher, is where Maui's true nature begins to reveal itself. The transition from suburban sprawl to raw nature is so abrupt that most people who drive up into the valley don't realize they're suddenly in a rainforest. The moist, cool air and the shade are a welcome comfort after the hot tropic sun. This is Iao Valley, a 6¼-acre state park whose great nature, history, and beauty have been enjoyed by millions of people from around the world for more than a century. Iao ("Supreme Light") Valley, 10 miles long and encompassing 4,000 acres, is the eroded volcanic caldera of the West Maui Mountains. The head of the valley is a broad circular amphitheater where four major streams converge into Iao Stream. At the back of the amphitheater is rain-drenched Puu Kukui, the West Maui Mountains' highest point. No other Hawaiian valley lets you go from seacoast to rainforest so easily. This peaceful valley, full of tropical plants, rainbows, waterfalls, swimming holes, and hiking trails, is a place of solitude, reflection, and escape for residents and visitors alike.

To get here from Wailuku, take Main Street to Iao Valley Road to the entrance to the state park.

Two paved walkways loop into the massive green amphitheater, across the bridge of Iao Valley Stream, and along the stream itself. This paved, .3-mile loop is Maui's easiest hike—everyone can handle it. The leisurely walk will allow you to enjoy lovely views of the Iao Needle and the lush vegetation. Others often proceed beyond the state park border and take two trails deeper into the valley, but the trails enter private land, and NO TRESPASSING signs are posted.

Tiny tots and very cool teenagers alike are impressed with the **Iao Needle,** an erosional remnant consisting of basalt dikes that jut an impressive 2,250 feet above sea level. Youngsters play in **Iao Stream,** a peaceful brook that belies its bloody history. In 1790, King Kamehameha the Great and his men engaged in the bloody battle of Iao Valley to gain control of Maui. When the battle ended, so many bodies blocked Iao Stream that the battle site was named Kepaniwai, or "damming of the waters." An architectural heritage park of Hawaiian, Japanese, Chinese, Filipino, and New England–style houses stands in harmony by Iao Stream at **Kepaniwai Heritage Garden.** This is a good picnic spot, with plenty of tables and benches. You can see ferns, banana trees, and other native and exotic plants in the **Iao Valley Botanic Garden** along the stream.

WHEN TO GO The park is open daily from 7am to 7pm. Go early in the morning or late in the afternoon, when the sun's rays slant into the valley and create a mystical mood. You can bring a picnic and spend the day, but be prepared at any time for a tropical cloudburst, which often soaks the valley and swells both waterfalls and streams. Plan to spend at least 30 minutes, and maybe more if you picnic here.

INFORMATION & VISITOR CENTERS For information, contact **Iao Valley State Park,** State Parks and Recreation, 54 High St., Room 101, Wailuku, HI 96793 (✆ **808/984-8100**). The **Hawaii Nature Center,** 875 Iao Valley Rd. (✆ **808/244-6500;** www.hawaiinaturecenter.org), home to the Iao Valley Nature Center, features hands-on, interactive exhibits and displays relating the story of Hawaiian natural history; it's an important stop for all who want to explore Iao Valley. Hours are daily from 10am to 4pm; admission is $6 for adults and $4 for children ages 4 to 12. Rainforest Walks are something the entire family will enjoy; book in advance, for the Monday through Friday walks at 11:30am or 1:30pm or the Saturday and Sunday walks at 11am or 2pm. Children must be 5 years old or older. They advise all walkers to wear closed-toe shoes suitable for an uneven trail. Cost for the Rainforest Walk is $30 for adults and $20 for children. (The fee includes a visit to the museum.)

WEST MAUI

Historic Lahaina

Back when "there was no God west of the Horn," Lahaina was the capital of Hawaii and the Pacific's wildest port. Today, it's a milder version of its old self—mostly a hustle-bustle of whale art, timeshares, and JUST GOT LEI'D T-shirts. I'm not sure the rowdy whalers would be pleased. But if you look hard, you'll still find the historic port town they loved, filled with the kind of history that inspired James Michener to write his best-selling epic novel *Hawaii.*

Baldwin Home Museum ★ All ages. The oldest house in Lahaina, this coral-and-rock structure was built in 1834 by Rev. Dwight Baldwin, a doctor with the fourth company of American missionaries to sail around the Horn to Hawaii. Like many missionaries, he came to Hawaii to do good—and did very well for himself. After 17 years of service, Baldwin was granted 2,600 acres in Kapalua for farming and grazing. His ranch manager experimented with what Hawaiians called *hala-kahiki,* or pineapple, on a 4-acre plot; the rest is history. The house looks as if Baldwin has just stepped out for a minute to tend a sick neighbor down the street.

Next door is the **Master's Reading Room,** Maui's oldest building. This became the favorite hangout of visiting sea captains once the missionaries closed down all of Lahaina's grog shops and banned prostitution. By 1844, when hotels and bars started reopening, it lost its appeal. It's now the headquarters of the **Lahaina Restoration Foundation** (✆ **808/661-3262**), a plucky band of historians who try to keep this town alive and antique at the same time. Stop in and pick up a self-guided walking-tour map, which will take you to Lahaina's most historic sites. Plan at least 15 minutes for a quick look-see.

120 Dickenson St. (at Front St.). ✆ **808/661-3262.** Admission $3 adults, $2 seniors, $5 family. Daily 10am–4:30pm.

Maluuluolele Park **All ages.** At first glance, this Front Street park appears to be only a hot, dry, dusty softball field. But under home plate, buried beneath tons of red dirt and sand, is an edge of Mokuula, where a royal compound once stood more than 100 years ago. Here, Prince Kauikeaolui, who ascended the throne as King Kamehameha III when he was only 10, lived with the love of his life, his sister, Princess Nahienaena. Missionaries took a dim view of incest, which was acceptable to Hawaiian nobles in order to preserve the royal bloodline. Torn between love for her brother and the new Christian morality, Nahienaena grew despondent and died at the age of 21. King Kamehameha III, who reigned for 29 years—longer than any other Hawaiian monarch—presided over Hawaii as it went from kingdom to constitutional monarchy, and as power over the islands began to shift from island nobles to missionaries, merchants, and sugar planters. Kamehameha died in 1854; he was 39. In 1918, his royal compound, containing a mausoleum and artifacts of the kingdom, was demolished and covered with dirt to create a public park. The baseball team from Lahainaluna School, the first American school founded by missionaries west of the Rockies, now plays games on the site of this royal place, still considered sacred to many Hawaiians. If you are just looking, you can see this site in 5 minutes.

Front and Shaw sts.

Riding the Sugarcane Train **All ages.** Small kids love this ride, as do train buffs of all ages. A steam engine pulls open-passenger cars of the Lahaina/Kaanapali and Pacific Railroad on a 30-minute, 12-mile round-trip through sugar cane fields between Lahaina and Kaanapali while the conductor sings and calls out the landmarks. Along the way, you can see the hidden parts of Kaanapali, and the islands of Molokai and Lanai beyond. Tickets are available at the station; call for details.

975 Limahana Place. ✆ **808/667-6851.** www.sugarcanetrain.com. Admission $22 adults, $15 children 3–12, free for children 2 and under. Daily 10:15am–4pm.

Seeing Stars at a Whale of a Place in Kaanapali

After sunset, the stars over Kaanapali shine big and bright, because the tropical sky is almost pollutant free and no big-city lights interfere with the cosmic view. Amateur astronomers can probe the Milky Way, see the rings of Saturn and Jupiter's moons, and scan the Sea of Tranquility in a 60-minute **"Tour of the stars"** on the resort's computer-driven telescope. This cosmic adventure takes place nightly at the **Hyatt Regency Maui,** 200 Nohea Kai Dr. (✆ **808/661-1234**), at 8, 9, and 10pm, and should thrill your kids from ages 4 and up. (Even bored teenagers love this.) If you are staying at the hotel, it's $26 for adults and $16 for children 6 to 12, free for ages 5 and younger; nonguests pay $31 for adults and $21 for children 6 to 12, and ages 5 and younger are free.

While you are in Kaanapali, if you haven't seen a real whale yet, go to **Whalers Village,** 2435 Kaanapali Pkwy., an oceanfront shopping center that has adopted the whale

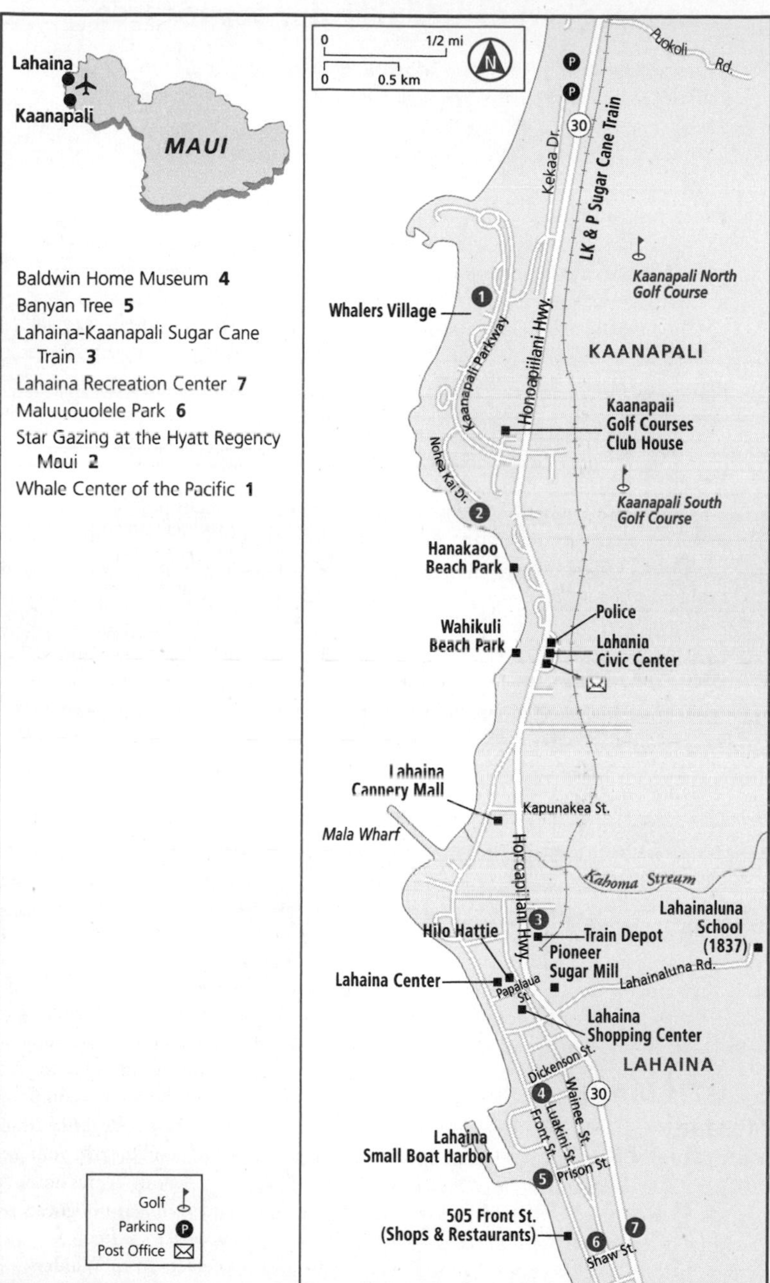

Lahaina
Kaanapali
MAUI
Baldwin Home Museum 4
Banyan Tree 5
Lahaina-Kaanapali Sugar Cane Train 3
Lahaina Recreation Center 7
Maluuouolele Park 6
Star Gazing at the Hyatt Regency Maui 2
Whale Center of the Pacific 1
Golf
Parking
Post Office
0 1/2 mi
0 0.5 km
N
Puokoli Rd.
30
Kekaa Dr.
LK & P Sugar Cane Train
Kaanapali North Golf Course
Whalers Village
Kaanapali Parkway
Honoapiilani Hwy.
KAANAPALI
Kaanapaii Golf Courses Club House
Nohea Kai Dr.
Kaanapali South Golf Course
Hanakaoo Beach Park
Wahikuli Beach Park
Police
Lahania Civic Center
Lahaina Cannery Mall
Kapunakea St.
Mala Wharf
Kahoma Stream
Lahainaluna School (1837)
Hilo Hattie
Train Depot
Pioneer Sugar Mill
Lahainaluna Rd.
Lahaina Center
Papalaua St.
Lahaina Shopping Center
Dickenson St.
LAHAINA
Wainee St.
Luakini St.
Front St.
Lahaina Small Boat Harbor
Prison St.
505 Front St. (Shops & Restaurants)
Shaw St.

Frommer's Favorite Maui Family Experiences

Greeting the Rising Sun from atop Haleakala Bundle up, fill a Thermos with hot java, and drive the 37 miles from sea level to 10,000 feet to witness the birth of yet another day. Breathing in the rarefied air and watching the first rays of light streak across the sky makes the Haleakala sunrise a mystical experience.

Watching for Whales No need to head out in a boat—in winter, you can see these majestic mammals breach and spy hop from shore. One of the best places is scenic McGregor Point, at mile marker 9 along Honoapiilani Highway, just outside Maalaea in south Maui. The humpbacks arrive as early as November, but the majority travel through Maui's waters from mid-December to mid-April.

Plunging Under the Sea (p. 286) **Atlantis Adventures** (✆ **800/548-6262**) takes the whole family down into the shallow coastal waters off Lahaina in a real sub. The kids will love seeing all the fish—maybe even a shark—and you'll stay dry the entire time.

Riding the Rails on the Sugarcane Train (p. 266) Passengers of all ages love the steam engine rides on **Lahaina/Kaanapali & Pacific Railroad** (✆ **808/667-6851**). The open-air cars travel through sugar cane fields between Lahaina and Kaanapali while the conductor sings and calls out the landmarks.

Looking for Stars The stars over Kaanapali shine big and bright—you can see them in all their glory at **Hyatt Regency Maui** (✆ **808/661-1234**), where the world's first recreational computer-driven telescope brings the rings of Saturn into crisp view nightly.

as its mascot. You can't miss it: A huge, almost life-size metal sculpture of a mother whale and two nursing calves greets you. A few more steps, and you're met by the looming, bleached-white bony skeleton of a 40-foot sperm whale; it's pretty impressive.

On the second floor of the mall is the **Whale Center of the Pacific** (✆ **808/661-5992**), a museum celebrating the "Golden Era of Whaling" (1825–60). Harpoons and scrimshaw are on display; the museum has even re-created the cramped quarters of a whaler's seagoing vessel. It's open daily from 9:30am to 10pm; admission is free. Children 6 and older should like it, and you should plan at least a half-hour to see everything.

SOUTH MAUI

Maalaea

Maui Ocean Center ★★★ All ages. This 5-acre facility houses the largest aquarium in Hawaii and features one of Hawaii's largest predators: the tiger shark. As you walk past the three dozen or so tanks and countless exhibits, you'll slowly descend from the "beach" to the deepest part of the ocean, without ever getting wet. Start at the surge pool, where you'll see shallow-water marine life such as spiny urchins and cauliflower coral, then move on to the reef tanks, turtle pool, "touch" pool (with starfish and urchins), and

Getting Up-Close and Personal with Sharks, Stingrays, and Starfish (p. 268) Hawaii's largest aquarium, the **Maui Ocean Center** (✆ **808/270-7000**), has a range of sea critters—from tiger sharks to tiny starfish—that are sure to fascinate kids of all ages. At this 5-acre facility in Maalaea, visitors can take a virtual walk from the beach down to the ocean depths via the three dozen tanks, countless exhibits, and the 100-foot-long main oceanarium.

Seeing the World from a Dragonfly's View (p. 265) Kids will think this is too much fun to be educational. Don a face mask and get the dizzying perspective of what a dragonfly sees as it flies over a mountain stream, or watch the tiny *oopu* fish climb a stream at the **Hawaii Nature Center** (✆ **808/244-6500**) in beautiful Iao Valley, where you'll find some 30 hands-on, interactive exhibits and displays of Hawaii's natural history.

Watching Windsurfers Ride the Waves at Hookipa Just off the Hana Highway past Paia is Hookipa Beach, known the world over as a windsurfing mecca. The great waves and consistent wind draw top windsurfers from around the globe. Watch spellbound as these colorful sailboarders ride, sail, and pirouette over the waves, turning into the wind and flipping into the air while rotating 360 degrees. It's the best free show in town.

Heading to Kula to Bid the Sun Aloha Harold Rice Park, just off Kula Highway, is the perfect vantage point for watching the sun set over the entire island: down the side of Haleakala, out across the isthmus, and over to the West Maui Mountains, with Molokai and Lanai in the distance. As the sun sinks, the light shifts from bright yellow to mellow red. Once the sun drops below the horizon, the sky puts on its own Technicolor show in a dazzling array of colors.

eagle-ray pool before you reach the star of the show: the 100 foot long, 600,000-gallon main tank featuring tiger, gray, and white-tip sharks, as well as tuna, surgeonfish, triggerfish, and numerous other tropicals. The most phenomenal thing about this tank is that the walkway goes right through it—so you'll be surrounded on three sides by marine creatures. A very cool place, and well worth at least a couple of hours.

Maalaea Harbor Village, 192 Maalaea Rd. (the triangle btw Honoapiilani Hwy. and Maalaea Rd.). ✆ **808/270-7000.** www.mauioceancenter.com. Admission $24 adults, $21 seniors, $17 children 3–12. Daily 9am–5pm (until 6pm July–Aug).

Kihei

Captain George Vancouver "discovered" Kihei in 1778, when it was only a collection of fishermen's grass shacks on the hot, dry, dusty coast. (Hard to believe, eh?) Even little kids will get a kick out of the **totem pole,** which stands today where he's believed to have landed, across from Maui Lu Resort, 575 S. Kihei Rd. Vancouver sailed on to "discover" British Columbia, where a great international city and harbor now bear his name.

West of the junction of Piilani Highway (Hwy. 31) and Mokulele Highway (Hwy. 350) is **Kealia Pond National Wildlife Preserve** (✆ **808/875-1582;** www.fws.gov/refuges), a 700-acre U.S. Fish and Wildlife wetland preserve where endangered Hawaiian stilts, coots, and ducks hang out and splash. There's something here for the entire family, from small kids to teenagers. You can walk the area in a half-hour, or spend the day on the beach here. These ponds work two ways: as bird preserves and as sedimentation basins that keep the coral reefs from silting from runoff. You can take a self-guided tour along a boardwalk dotted with interpretive signs and shade shelters, through sand dunes, and around ponds to Maalaea Harbor. The boardwalk starts at the outlet of Kealia Pond on the ocean side of North Kihei Road (near mile marker 2 on Piilani Hwy.). Among the Hawaiian water birds seen here are the black-crowned high heron, Hawaiian coot, Hawaiian duck, and Hawaiian stilt. There also are shorebirds such as sanderlings, Pacific golden plovers, ruddy turnstones, and wandering tattlers. From July to December, the hawksbill turtle comes ashore here to lay her eggs.

Wailea

The best way to explore this golden resort coast is to rise with the sun and head for Wailea's 1.5-mile **coastal nature trail ★**, stretching between the Kea Lani Hotel and the kiawe thicket just beyond the Renaissance Wailea. It's a great family walk, a serpentine path that meanders uphill and down past native plants, old Hawaiian habitats, and a billion dollars' worth of luxury hotels. You can pick up the trail at any of the resorts or from clearly marked SHORELINE ACCESS points along the coast and walk as little as you want (10–15 min.) or walk the entire 3-mile round-trip (at least 1 hr. with slower, younger children). The best time to go is when you first wake up; by midmorning, the coastal trail is too often clogged with pushy joggers, and it grows crowded with beachgoers as the day wears on. As the path crosses several bold black-lava points, it affords new vistas of islands and ocean; benches allow you to pause and contemplate the view across Alalakeiki Channel, where you may see jumping whales in season. Sunset is another good time to hit the trail.

HOUSE OF THE SUN: HALEAKALA NATIONAL PARK ★★★

At once forbidding and compelling, Haleakala ("House of the Sun") National Park is Maui's main natural attraction. More than 1.3 million people a year go up the 10,023-foot-high mountain to peer down into the crater of the world's largest dormant volcano. (Haleakala is officially considered active, even though it has not rumbled since 1790.) That hole could hold all of Manhattan.

The entire family will love this national park. There's more to do here than stare into a big black hole: Just going up the mountain is an experience. Where else on the planet can you climb from sea level to 10,000 feet in just 37 miles, or a 2-hour drive? The snaky road passes through big, puffy, cumulus clouds to offer magnificent views of the isthmus of Maui, the West Maui Mountains, and the Pacific Ocean.

Many drive up to the summit in predawn darkness to watch the **sun rise over Haleakala ★★★**; others coast down the 37-mile road from the summit on a bicycle with special brakes. (See "For the Active Family," later in this chapter.) Hardy adventurers hike and camp inside the crater's wilderness. (See "For the Active Family.") Those bound for the interior should bring their survival gear, because the terrain is raw, rugged, and punishing—not unlike the moon.

Just the Facts

Haleakala National Park extends from the summit of Mount Haleakala down the volcano's southeast flank to Maui's eastern coast, beyond Hana. There are actually two separate and distinct destinations within the park: **Haleakala Summit** and the **Kipahulu**

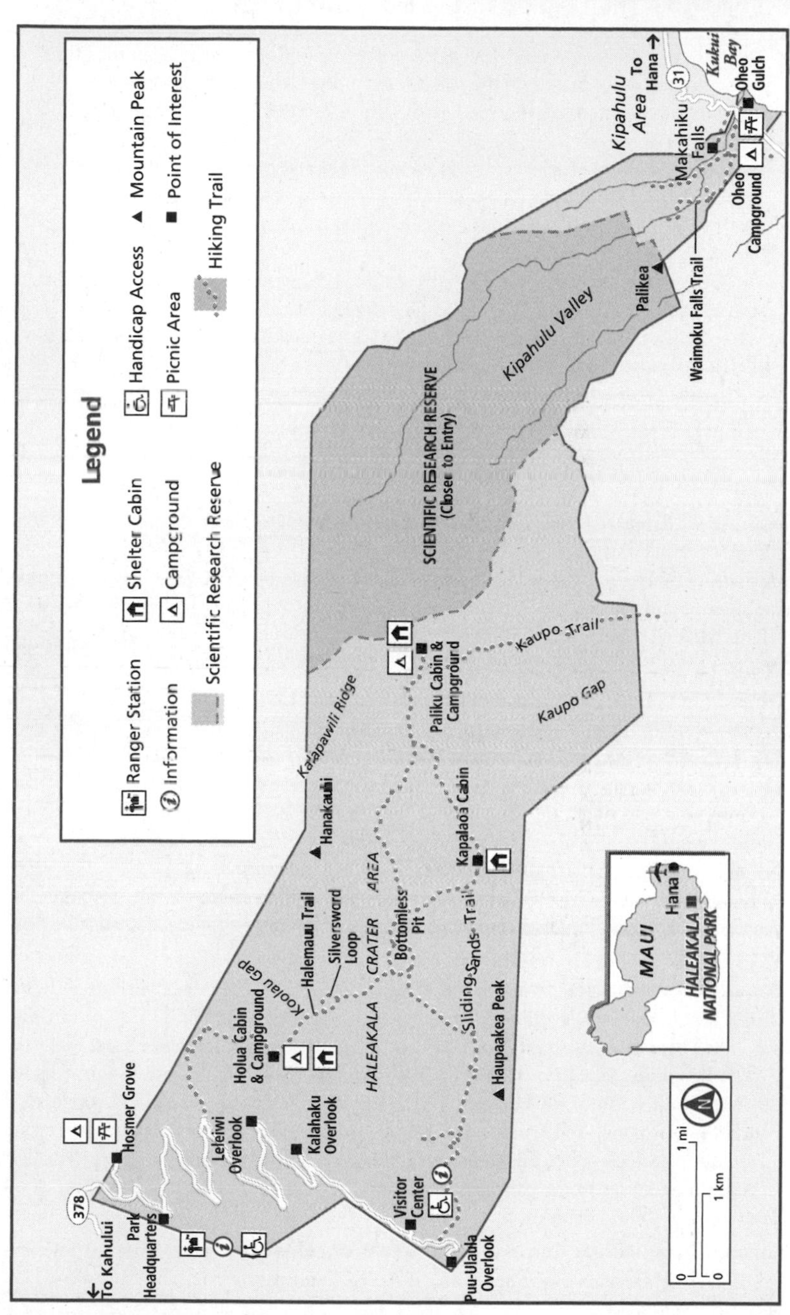
Legend
Ranger Station
Information
Shelter Cabin
Campground
Scientific Research Reserve
Handicap Access
Picnic Area
Hiking Trail
Mountain Peak
Point of Interest
To Kahului
378
Park Headquarters
Hosmer Grove
Leleiwi Overlook
Kalahaku Overlook
Visitor Center
Puu-Ulaula Overlook
Holua Cabin & Campground
Koolau Gap
Halemauu Trail
Silversword Loop
HALEAKALA CRATER AREA
Bottomless Pit
Sliding Sands Trail
Haupaakea Peak
Hanakauhi
Kapalaoa Cabin
Paliku Cabin & Campground
Kaupo Trail
Kaupo Gap
SCIENTIFIC RESEARCH RESERVE (Closed to Entry)
Kipahulu Valley
Palikea
Waimoku Falls Trail
Makahiku Falls
Oheo Campground
Oheo Gulch
Kipahulu Area
To Hana
31
Kukui Bay
MAUI
Hana
HALEAKALA NATIONAL PARK
0 1 mi
0 1 km

Fun Facts The Legend of the House of the Sun

According to ancient legend, Haleakala got its name from a very clever trick that the demigod Maui pulled on the sun. Maui's mother, the goddess Hina, complained one day that the sun sped across the sky so quickly that her tapa cloth couldn't dry.

Maui, known as a trickster, devised a plan. The next morning he went to the top of the great mountain and waited for the sun to poke its head above the horizon. Quickly, Maui lassoed the sun, bringing its path across the sky to an abrupt halt.

The sun begged Maui to let go, and Maui said he would on one condition: that the sun slow its trip across the sky to give the island more sunlight. The sun assented. In honor of this agreement, the Hawaiians call the mountain Haleakala, or "House of the Sun."

To this day, the top of Haleakala has about 15 minutes more sunlight than the communities on the coastline below.

coast. (See "Tropical Haleakala: Oheo Gulch at Kipahulu," later in this chapter.) The summit gets all the publicity, but Kipahulu draws crowds, too—it's lush, green, and tropical, and home to Oheo Gulch (also known as Seven Sacred Pools). No road links the summit and the coast; you have to approach them separately, and you need at least a day to see each place.

When to Go At the 10,023-foot summit, weather changes fast. With wind chill, temperatures can be freezing any time of year. Summer can be dry and warm; winter can be wet, windy, and cold. Before you go, get current weather conditions from the park (✆ **808/572-4400**) or the **National Weather Service** (✆ **808/871-5054**). Plan to spend the entire day here.

From sunrise to noon, the light is weak, but the view is usually free of clouds. The best time for photos is afternoon, when the sun lights the crater and clouds are few. Go on full-moon nights for spectacular viewing.

Remember, this is Mother Nature, not Disneyland, so there are no guarantees or schedules. Especially in winter, some mornings may be misty or rainy, and sunrise viewing may be obscured. It's the luck of the draw.

Access Points Haleakala Summit is 37 miles, or a 1½- to 2-hour drive, from Kahului. To get here, take Highway 37 to Highway 377 to Highway 378. For details on the drive, see "The Drive to the Summit," below. Pukalani is the last town for water, food, and gas.

The **Kipahulu** section of Haleakala National Park is on Maui's east end near Hana, 60 miles from Kahului on Highway 36 (Hana Hwy.). Due to traffic and rough road conditions, plan on 4 hours for the drive, one-way. For complete information, see "Tropical Haleakala: Oheo Gulch at Kipahulu," later in this chapter.

At both entrances to the park, the admission fee is $5 per person or $10 per car, good for a week of unlimited entry.

Information, Visitor Centers & Ranger Programs For information before you go, contact **Haleakala National Park,** Box 369, Makawao, HI 96768 (✆ **808/572-4400;** www.nps.gov/hale).

One mile from the park entrance, at 7,000 feet, is **Haleakala National Park Headquarters** (✆ **808/572-4400**), open daily from 7:30am to 4pm. Stop here to pick up information on park programs and activities, get camping permits, and occasionally see a Hawaiian nene bird. Restrooms, a pay phone, and drinking water are available.

The **Haleakala Visitor Center,** open daily from sunrise to 3pm, is near the summit, 11 miles past the park entrance. It offers a panoramic view of the volcanic landscape, with photos identifying the various features, and exhibits that explain the area's history, ecology, geology, and volcanology. Park staff members are often on hand to answer questions. Restrooms and water are available.

Rangers offer excellent, informative, and free **naturalist talks** at 9:30, 10:30, and 11:30am daily in the summit building. For information on **hiking** and **camping** possibilities, including wilderness cabins and campgrounds, see "For the Active Family," later in this chapter.

The Drive to the Summit

If you look on a Maui map, almost in the middle of the part that resembles a torso, there's a black, wiggly line that looks like this: WWWWW. That's **Highway 378,** also known as **Haleakala Crater Road**—one of the fastest-ascending roads in the world. This grand corniche has at least 33 switchbacks, passes through numerous climate zones; goes under, in, and out of clouds; takes you past rare silversword plants and endangered Hawaiian geese sailing through the clear, thin air; and offers a view that extends for more than 100 miles.

Driving to the summit takes 1½ to 2 hours from Kahului. No matter where you start out, you'll follow Highway 37 (Haleakala Hwy.) to Pukalani, where you'll pick up Highway 377 (aka Haleakala Hwy.), which you'll take to Highway 378. Along the way, expect fog, rain, and wind. You may encounter stray cattle and downhill bicyclists. Fill up your gas tank before you go—the only gas available is 27 miles below the summit at Pukalani. There are no facilities beyond the ranger stations—not even a coffee urn in sight. Bring your own food and water.

A word of warning: Remember, you're entering a high altitude wilderness area. Some people get dizzy due to the lack of oxygen; you might also suffer lightheadedness, shortness of breath, nausea, or worse: severe headaches, flatulence, and dehydration. People with asthma, pregnant women, heavy smokers, and those with heart conditions should be especially careful in the rarefied air. Bring water and a jacket or a blanket, especially if you go up for sunrise. Or you might want to go up to the summit for sunset, which is also spectacular. Although there are no posted age restrictions, this should be reserved for children over the age of 3.

At the **park entrance,** you'll pay an entrance fee of $10 per car (or $2 for a bicycle). About a mile from the entrance is **Park Headquarters,** where an endangered **nene,** or Hawaiian goose, may greet you with its unique call. With its black face, buff cheeks, and partially webbed feet, the gray-brown bird looks like a small Canada goose with zebra stripes; it brays out "nay-nay" (thus its name), doesn't migrate, and prefers lava beds to lakes. More than 25,000 nenes once inhabited Hawaii, but habitat destruction and predators (hunters, pigs, feral cats and dogs, and mongooses) nearly caused their extinction. By 1951, there were only 30 left. Now protected as Hawaii's state bird, the wild nene on Haleakala number fewer than 250—the species remains endangered.

Beyond headquarters are **two scenic overlooks** on the way to the summit; stop at Leleiwi on the way up and Kalahaku on the way back down, if only to get out, stretch, and get accustomed to the heights. Take a deep breath, look around, and pop your ears.

If you feel dizzy or drowsy, or get a sudden headache, consider turning around and going back down.

Leleiwi Overlook ★ is just beyond mile marker 17. From the parking area, a short trail leads you to a panoramic view of the lunar-like crater. When the clouds are low and the sun is in the right place, usually around sunset, you may experience a phenomenon known as the "Specter of the Brocken"—you can see a reflection of your shadow, ringed by a rainbow, in the clouds below. It's an optical illusion caused by a rare combination of sun, shadow, and fog that occurs in only three places on the planet: Haleakala, Scotland, and Germany.

Two miles farther along is **Kalahaku Overlook ★**, the best place to see a rare **silversword.** You can turn into this overlook only when you are descending from the top. The silversword is the punk of the plant world, its silvery bayonets displaying tiny, purple bouquets—like a spacey artichoke with attitude. This botanical wonder proved irresistible to humans, who gathered them in gunnysacks for Chinese potions, British specimen collections, and just for the sheer thrill of having something so rare. Silverswords grow only in Hawaii, take from 4 to 50 years to bloom, and then, usually between May and October, send up a 1- to 6-foot stalk with a purple bouquet of sunflower-like blooms. They're now very rare, so don't even think about taking one home.

Continue on, and you'll quickly reach **Haleakala Visitor Center,** which offers spectacular views. You'll feel as if you're at the edge of the earth, but the actual summit's a little farther on, at **Puu Ulaula Overlook ★★★** (also known as Red Hill), the volcano's highest point, where you'll find a mysterious cluster of buildings officially known as Haleakala Observatories, but unofficially called **Science City.** If you go up for sunrise, the building at Puu Ulaula Overlook, a triangle of glass that serves as a windbreak, is the best viewing spot. After the daily miracle of sunrise—the sun seems to rise out of the vast ocean (hence the name "House of the Sun")—you can see all the way across Alenuihaha Channel to the often snowcapped summit of Mauna Kea on the Big Island.

EAST MAUI & HEAVENLY HANA

Hana is paradise on Earth—or just about as close as you can get to it, anyway. In and around Hana, you'll find a lush tropical rainforest dotted with cascading waterfalls and sparkling blue pools, skirted by red- and black-sand beaches.

The Road to Hana ★★★

Car top down, sunscreen on, radio tuned to a little Hawaiian music on a Maui morning—it's time to head out to Hana along the Hana Highway (Hwy. 36), a wiggle of a road that runs along Maui's northeastern shore. The drive takes at least 3 hours from Lahaina or Kihei—but take all day. Going to Hana is about the journey, not the destination.

There are wilder roads, steeper roads, and more dangerous roads, but in all of Hawaii, no road is more celebrated than this one. It winds 50 miles past taro patches, magnificent seascapes, waterfall pools, botanical gardens, and verdant rainforests, and ends at one of Hawaii's most beautiful tropical places. Everyone in the family will find something along this magical road.

The outside world discovered the little village of Hana in 1926, when the narrow coastal road, carved by pickax-wielding convicts, opened. The mud-and-gravel road, often subject to landslides and washouts, was paved in 1962, when tourist traffic began to increase; it now sees 1,000 cars and dozens of vans a day, according to storekeeper Harry Hasegawa. Go at the wrong time, and you'll be stuck in a bumper-to-bumper rental-car parade—peak traffic hours are midmorning and midafternoon year-round, especially on weekends.

In the rush to "do" Hana in a day, most visitors spin around town in 10 minutes and wonder what all the fuss is about. It requires time to take in Hana, play in the waterfalls, sniff the tropical flowers, hike to bamboo forests, and view the spectacular scenery. Stay overnight if you can, and meander back in a day or two. If you really must do the Hana Highway in a day, go just before sunrise and return after sunset.

Tips: Practice aloha. Give way at one-lane bridges, wave at oncoming motorists, let the big guys in 4×4s have the right of way—it's just common sense, brah. If the guy behind you blinks his lights, let him pass. And don't honk your horn—in Hawaii, it's considered rude.

THE JOURNEY BEGINS IN PAIA Before you even start out, fill up your gas tank. Gas in Paia is expensive, and it's the last place for gas until you get to Hana, some 54 bridges and 600 hairpin turns down the road.

Paia was once a thriving sugar-mill town. The mill is still here, but the population shifted to Kahului in the 1950s when subdivisions opened there, leaving Paia to shrivel up and die. But the town refused to give up, and it has proven its ability to adapt to the times. Now chic eateries and trendy shops stand next door to the old ma-and-pa establishments. Plan to be here early, around 7am, when **Charley's ★**, 142 Hana Hwy. (**© 808/579-9453**), opens. Enjoy a big, hearty breakfast for a reasonable price.

WINDSURFING MECCA Just before mile marker 9 is **Hookipa Beach Park ★**, where top-ranked windsurfers come to test themselves against the forces of nature: thunderous surf and forceful wind. On nearly every windy day, after noon (the board surfers have the waves in the morning), you can watch dozens of windsurfers twirling and dancing in the wind like colored butterflies. To watch them, do not stop on the highway, but go past the park and turn left at the entrance on the far side of the beach. You can either park on the high grassy bluff or drive down to the sandy beach and park alongside the pavilion. Facilities include restrooms, a shower, picnic tables, and a barbecue area.

INTO THE COUNTRY Past Hookipa Beach, the road winds down into **Maliko Gulch** at mile marker 10. At the bottom of the gulch, look for the road on your right, which will take you out to **Maliko Bay.** Take the first right, which goes under the bridge and past a rodeo arena and on to the rocky beach. There are no facilities here except a boat-launch ramp. In the 1940s, Maliko had a thriving community at the mouth of the bay, but its residents rebuilt farther inland after a strong tidal wave wiped it out.

Back on the Hana Highway, for the next few miles, you'll pass through the rural area of **Haiku,** where you'll see banana patches, forests of guavas and palms, and avocados. Just before mile marker 15 is the **Maui Grown Market and Deli** (**© 808/572-1693**), a good stop for drinks or snacks for the ride.

At mile marker 16, the curves begin, one right after another. Slow down and enjoy the view of bucolic rolling hills, mango trees, and vibrant ferns. After mile marker 16, the road is still called the Hana Highway, but the number changes from Highway 36 to Highway 360, and the mile markers go back to 0.

A GREAT PLUNGE ALONG THE WAY A dip in a waterfall pool is everybody's tropical-island fantasy. A great place to stop is **Twin Falls ★**, at mile marker 2. Just before the wide, concrete bridge, pull over on the mountainside and park. There is a NO TRESPASSING sign on the gate. Although you will see several cars parked in the area and a steady line of people going up to the falls, be aware that this is private property and that trespassing is illegal in

 Hawaii. If you decide that you want to "risk it," you will walk about 3 to 5 minutes to the waterfall and pool, or continue on another 10 to 15 minutes to the second, larger waterfall and pool. (Don't go in if it has been raining.)

KOOLAU FOREST RESERVE After Twin Falls, the vegetation seems lusher, as though Mother Nature had poured Miracle-Gro on everything. This is the edge of the **Koolau Forest Reserve.** *Koolau* means "windward," and this certainly is one of the greatest examples of a lush windward area: The coastline here gets about 60 to 80 inches of rain a year, as well as runoff from the 200 to 300 inches that fall farther up the mountain. Here you'll see trees laden with guavas, as well as mangoes, java plums, and avocados the size of softballs. The spiny, long-leafed plants are hala trees, which the Hawaiians used for weaving baskets, mats, even canoe sails.

From here on out, there's a waterfall (and one-lane bridge) around nearly every turn in the road, so drive slowly and be prepared to stop and yield to oncoming cars.

DANGEROUS CURVES About a half-mile after mile marker 6, there's a sharp U-curve in the road, going uphill. The road is practically one-lane here, with a brick wall on one side and virtually no maneuvering room. Sound your horn at the start of the U-curve to let approaching cars know you're coming. Take this curve, as well as the few more coming up in the next several miles, very slowly.

Just before mile marker 7 is a forest of waving **bamboo.** The sight is so spectacular that drivers are often tempted to take their eyes off the road. Be very cautious. Wait until just after mile marker 7, at the **Kaaiea Bridge** and stream below, to pull over and take a closer look at the hand-hewn stone walls. Then turn around to see the vista of bamboo.

A GREAT FAMILY HIKE At mile marker 9, there's a small state wayside area with restrooms, picnic tables, and a barbecue area. The sign says KOOLAU FOREST RESERVE, but the real attraction here is the **Waikamoi Ridge Trail ★**, an easy .75-mile loop. The start of the trail is just behind the QUIET TREES AT WORK sign. The well-marked trail meanders through eucalyptus, ferns, and hala trees.

CAN'T-MISS PHOTO OPS Just past mile marker 12 is the **Kaumahina State Wayside Park ★**. This is not only a good pit stop (restrooms are available) and a wonderful place for a picnic (with tables and a barbecue area), but also a great vista point. The view of the rugged coastline makes an excellent shot—you can see all the way down to the jutting Keanae Peninsula.

Another mile and a couple of bends in the road, and you'll enter the Honomanu Valley, with its beautiful bay. To get to the **Honomanu Bay County Beach Park ★**, look for the turnoff on your left, just after mile marker 14, as you begin your ascent up the other side of the valley. The rutted dirt-and-cinder road takes you down to the rocky black-sand beach. There are no facilities here. Because of the strong rip currents offshore, swimming is best in the stream inland from the ocean. You'll consider the drive down worthwhile as you stand on the beach, well away from the ocean, and turn to look back on the steep cliffs covered with vegetation.

KEANAE PENINSULA & ARBORETUM At mile marker 17, the old Hawaiian village of **Keanae ★★★** stands out against the Pacific like a place time forgot. Here, on an old lava flow graced by an 1860 stone church and swaying palms, is one of the last coastal enclaves of native Hawaiians. They still grow taro in patches and pound it into poi, the staple of the old Hawaiian diet; and they still pluck *opihi* (limpet) from tide pools along the jagged coast and cast throw-nets at schools of fish.

At nearby **Keanae Arboretum,** Hawaii's botanical world is divided into three parts: native forest; introduced forest; and traditional Hawaiian plants, food, and medicine. You can swim in the pools of Piinaau Stream, or press on along a mile-long trail into Keanae Valley, where a lovely tropical rainforest waits at the end.

WAIANAPANAPA STATE PARK ★★★ On the outskirts of Hana, shiny black-sand Waianapanapa Beach appears like a vivid dream, with bright-green jungle foliage on three sides and cobalt blue water lapping at its feet. The 120-acre park on an ancient lava flow includes sea cliffs, lava tubes, arches, and that beach—plus a dozen rustic cabins. If you're interested in staying here, see "Family-Friendly Accommodations," earlier in this chapter. Also see "Beaches," below, and "For the Active Family," later in this chapter.

Hana ★★★

Green, tropical Hana, which some call heavenly, is a destination all its own, a small coastal village in a rainforest inhabited by 2,500 people, many part-Hawaiian. Beautiful Hana enjoys more than 90 inches of rain a year—more than enough to keep the scenery lush. Banyans, bamboo, breadfruit trees—everything seems larger than life, especially the flowers, such as wild ginger and plumeria. Several roadside stands offer exotic blooms for $1 a bunch. Just put money in the box. It's the Hana honor system.

The last unspoiled Hawaiian town on Maui is, oddly enough, the home of Maui's first resort, which opened in 1946. Paul Fagan, owner of the San Francisco Seals baseball team, bought an old inn and turned it into the **Hotel Hana-Maui,** which gave Hana its first and, as it turns out, last taste of tourism. Others have tried to open hotels and golf courses and resorts, but Hana, which is interested in remaining Hana, always politely refuses. There are a few B&Bs here, though; see "Family-Friendly Accommodations," earlier in this chapter.

A wood-frame 1871 building that served as the old Hana District Police Station now holds the **Hana Museum Cultural Center and Museum,** 4974 Uakea Rd. (✆ **808/248-8622;** www.hawaiimuseums.org). Children younger than 6 may get bored quickly here, but plan to spend at least 30 minutes to learn about the history of the area, and to look at excellent artifacts, memorabilia, and photographs. Also stop in at **Hasegawa General Store,** a Maui institution.

On the green hills above Hana stands a 30-foot-high white cross made of lava rock. The cross was erected by citizens in memory of Paul Fagan, who helped keep the town alive. The 3-mile hike up to **Fagan's Cross** provides a gorgeous view of the Hana coast, especially at sunset, when Fagan himself liked to climb this hill. Kids 8 and older should be able to do the uphill hike without a problem; allow an hour to climb up and don't wait too long after the sun has set, as it gets dark quickly in Hawaii.

Tropical Haleakala: Oheo Gulch at Kipahulu

If you're thinking about heading to the so-called Seven Sacred Pools, out past Hana at the Kipahulu end of Haleakala National Park, let's make this clear right now: There are more than seven pools—about 24, actually—and *all* water in Hawaii is considered sacred. It's all a PR campaign that has spun out of control. Folks here call it by its rightful name, **Oheo Gulch ★★★**, and visitors sometimes refer to it as Kipahulu, which is actually the name of the area where Oheo Gulch is located. No matter what you call it, it's beautiful. This dazzling series of pools and cataracts is so popular that it has its own roadside parking lot. Pack a picnic lunch and plan to spend a day hiking, swimming, and lazing around.

From the ranger station, it's just a short hike above the famous Oheo Gulch to two spectacular **waterfalls.** Check with park rangers before hiking up to or swimming in the pools, and always keep an eye on the water in the streams. The sky can be sunny near the coast; but flood waters travel 6 miles down from the Kipahulu Valley, and the water level can rise 4 feet in less than 10 minutes. It's not a good idea to swim in the pools in winter. The hike could be too strenuous for kids younger than 10.

Makahiku Falls is easily reached from the central parking area; the trailhead begins near the ranger station. **Pipiwai Trail** leads up to the road and beyond for a half-mile to the overlook. If you hike another 1.5 miles up the trail across two bridges and through a bamboo forest, you reach **Waimoku Falls.** It's a hard uphill hike, but press on to avoid the pool's crowd.

ACCESS POINTS Even though Oheo is part of Haleakala National Park, you cannot drive here from the summit. Oheo is about 30 to 50 minutes beyond Hana town, along Highway 31. The admission fee to enter is $5 per person or $10 per car. The Highway 31 bridge crosses some of the pools near the ocean; the others, plus magnificent 400-foot Waimoku Falls, are uphill, via an often-muddy but rewarding hour-long hike. Expect showers on the Kipahulu coast.

VISITOR CENTER The **Kipahulu Ranger Station** (✆ **808/248-7375**) is staffed from 9am to 5pm daily. Restrooms are available, but there's no drinking water. Here you'll find park-safety information, exhibits, and books. Rangers offer a variety of walks and hikes year-round; check at the station for current activities. Tent camping is permitted in the park; see "For the Active Family," later in this chapter, for details.

Beyond Oheo Gulch

A mile past Oheo Gulch on the ocean side of the road is **Lindbergh's Grave.** First to fly across the Atlantic Ocean, Charles A. Lindbergh (1902–74) found peace in the Pacific; he settled in Hana, where he died of cancer in 1974. The famous aviator is buried under river stones in a seaside graveyard behind the 1857 **Palapala Hoomau Congregational Church.** Kids younger than 10 may not be impressed by a graveyard, but it's worth a 10-minute stop.

Those of you who are continuing on around Maui to the fishing village of **Kaupo** and beyond should be warned that Kaupo Road, or Old Piilani Highway (Hwy. 31), is rough and unpaved, often full of potholes and ruts. There are no goods or services until you reach **Ulupalakua Ranch,** where there's a winery, a general store, and a gas station, which is likely to be closed. Before you attempt this journey, ask around about road conditions, or call the **Maui Public Works Department** (✆ **808/248-8254**) or the **Police Department** (✆ **808/248-8311**). This road frequently washes out in the rain. Most car rental companies forbid you from taking their cars on this road (they don't want to trek all the way out here to get you if your car breaks down), so you'd be better off retracing your route back through Hana. But if conditions are good, it can be a pretty drive in the spring. (It tends to be dry and boring in summer.)

6 BEACHES

WEST MAUI

Kaanapali Beach ★

Four-mile-long Kaanapali is one of Maui's best beaches, with grainy gold sand as far as the eye can see. The beach parallels the sea channel through most of its length, and a paved walk links hotels and condos, open-air restaurants, and the Whalers Village shopping center. Because Kaanapali is so long and broad, and because most hotels have adjacent swimming pools, the beach is crowded only in pockets—there's plenty of room to find seclusion. Summertime swimming is excellent. The best snorkeling is around Black Rock, in front of the Sheraton, where the water is clear, calm, and populated with clouds of tropical fish.

Facilities include outdoor showers; you can also use the restrooms at the hotel pools. Various beach-activities vendors line up in front of the hotels. There are no lifeguards. Parking is a problem, though. There are two public entrances: At the south end, turn off Honoapiilani Highway into the Kaanapali Resort, and pay for parking here; or continue on Honoapiilani Highway, turn off at the last Kaanapali exit at the stoplight near the Maui Kaanapali Villas, and park next to the beach signs indicating public acccss.

Kapalua Beach ★★★

This beach is the stuff of dreams: a golden crescent bordered by two palm-studded points. The sandy bottom slopes gently to deep water at the bay mouth; the water's so clear that you can see where the gold sands turn to green and then deep blue. Protected from strong winds and currents by the lava-rock promontories, Kapalua's calm waters are ideal for swimmers of all ages and abilities, and the bay is big enough to paddle a kayak around in without getting into the more challenging channel that separates Maui from Molokai. Waves come in just right for riding, and fish hang out by the rocks, making it great for snorkeling.

There are no lifeguards here; outdoor showers are stationed at both ends. Parking is limited to about 30 spaces in a small lot off Lower Honoapiilani Road, by Napili Kai Beach Club, so arrive early. Facilities include showers, restrooms, a rental shack, and plenty of shade.

SOUTH MAUI

Wailea's beaches may seem off-limits, hidden from plain view as they are by an intimidating wall of luxury resorts, but they're all open to the public by law. Look for the SHORELINE ACCESS signs along **Wailea Alanui Drive,** the resort's main boulevard.

Kamaole III Beach Park ★

Three beach parks—Kamaole I, II, and III—stand like golden jewels in the front yard of the funky seaside town of Kihei, which, all of a sudden, is sprawling with suburban blight. The beaches are the best thing about Kihei. These three are popular with local residents and visitors alike because they're easily accessible. On weekends, they're jam-packed with fishermen, picnickers, swimmers, and snorkelers. The most popular is Kamaole III, or "Kam-3." The biggest of the three beaches, with wide pockets of gold sand, it's the only one with a children's playground and a grassy lawn. Swimming is safe here, but scattered lava rocks are toe-stubbers at the waterline, and you should make sure

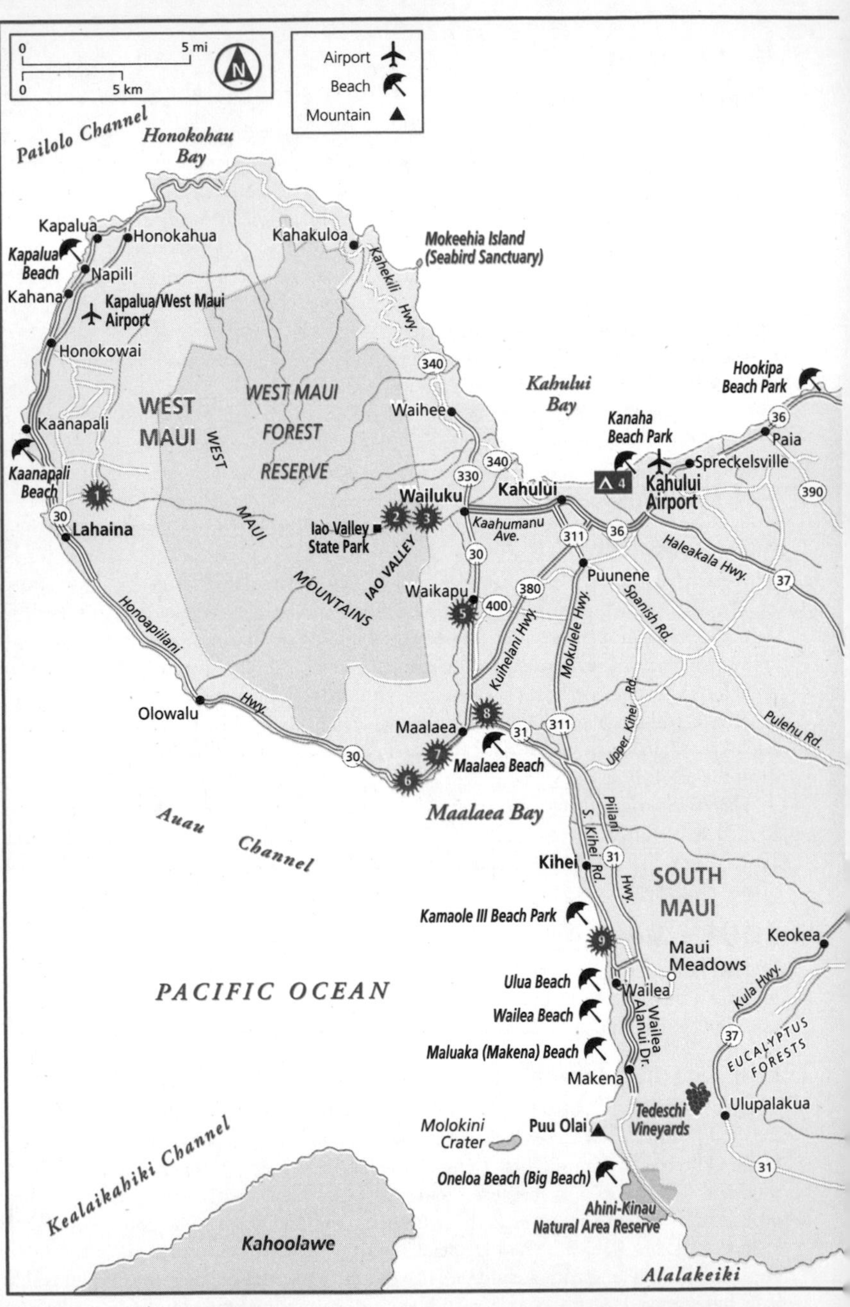

0
5 mi
0
5 km
N
Airport
Beach
Mountain
Pailolo Channel
Honokohau Bay
Kapalua
Honokahua
Kahakuloa
Mokeehia Island (Seabird Sanctuary)
Kapalua Beach
Napili
Kahana
Kapalua/West Maui Airport
Honokowai
Kahekili Hwy.
340
Kahului Bay
Hookipa Beach Park
WEST MAUI
WEST MAUI FOREST RESERVE
Waihee
Kaanapali
Kanaha Beach Park
36
Paia
Sprecklesville
Kaanapali Beach
WEST MAUI MOUNTAINS
330
Kahului
Kahului Airport
390
Wailuku
Lahaina
Iao Valley State Park
IAO VALLEY
Kaahumanu Ave.
311
Haleakala Hwy.
37
Puunene
Waikapu
400
380
Spanish Rd.
Honoapiilani Hwy.
Kuihelani Hwy.
Mokulele Hwy.
Upper Kihei Rd.
Pulehu Rd.
Olowalu
Maalaea
31
Maalaea Beach
Maalaea Bay
Auau Channel
Piilani Hwy.
S. Kihei Rd.
Kihei
SOUTH MAUI
Kamaole III Beach Park
Keokea
Maui Meadows
Kula Hwy.
PACIFIC OCEAN
Ulua Beach
Wailea
Wailea Beach
Wailea Alanui Dr.
EUCALYPTUS FORESTS
Maluaka (Makena) Beach
Makena
Tedeschi Vineyards
Ulupalakua
Molokini Crater
Puu Olai
Kealaikahiki Channel
Oneloa Beach (Big Beach)
Ahini-Kinau Natural Area Reserve
Kahoolawe
Alalakeiki

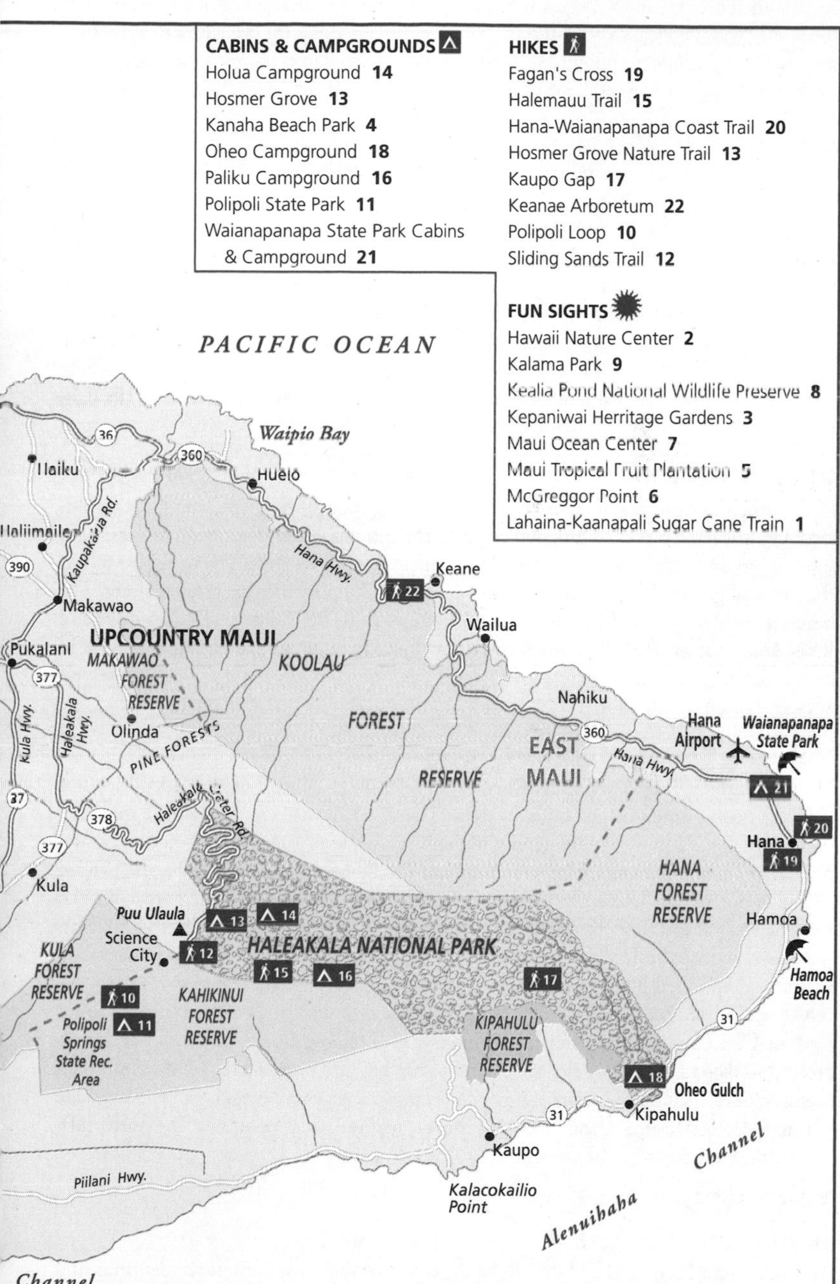
CABINS & CAMPGROUNDS
Holua Campground 14
Hosmer Grove 13
Kanaha Beach Park 4
Oheo Campground 18
Paliku Campground 16
Polipoli State Park 11
Waianapanapa State Park Cabins & Campground 21
HIKES
Fagan's Cross 19
Halemauu Trail 15
Hana-Waianapanapa Coast Trail 20
Hosmer Grove Nature Trail 13
Kaupo Gap 17
Keanae Arboretum 22
Polipoli Loop 10
Sliding Sands Trail 12
FUN SIGHTS
Hawaii Nature Center 2
Kalama Park 9
Kealia Pond National Wildlife Preserve 8
Kepaniwai Herritage Gardens 3
Maui Ocean Center 7
Maui Tropical Fruit Plantation 5
McGreggor Point 6
Lahaina-Kaanapali Sugar Cane Train 1
PACIFIC OCEAN
Waipio Bay
Haiku
Huelo
Haliimaile
Kaupakalua Rd.
Hana Hwy.
Keane
Makawao
Wailua
UPCOUNTRY MAUI
MAKAWAO FOREST RESERVE
KOOLAU FOREST RESERVE
Pukalani
Olinda
PINE FORESTS
Kula Hwy.
Haleakala Hwy.
Nahiku
EAST MAUI
Hana Airport
Waianapanapa State Park
Haleakala Crater Rd.
Hana
HANA FOREST RESERVE
Kula
Puu Ulaula
Science City
HALEAKALA NATIONAL PARK
Hamoa
Hamoa Beach
KULA FOREST RESERVE
KAHIKINUI FOREST RESERVE
Polipoli Springs State Rec. Area
KIPAHULU FOREST RESERVE
Oheo Gulch
Kipahulu
Kaupo
Piilani Hwy.
Kalacokailio Point
Alenuihaha Channel
Channel

your kids don't venture too far out, because the bottom slopes off quickly. Both the north and south shores are rocky fingers with a surge big enough to attract fish and snorkelers; the winter waves appeal to bodysurfers. Kam-3 is also a wonderful place to watch the sunset. Facilities include restrooms, showers, picnic tables, barbecue grills, and lifeguards. There's plenty of parking on South Kihei Road across from the Maui Parkshore condos.

Wailea Beach ★

Wailea is the best golden-sand crescent on Maui's sunbaked southwestern coast. One of five beaches within Wailea Resort, Wailea is big, wide, and protected on both sides by black-lava points. It's the front yard of the Four Seasons Wailea and the Grand Wailea Resort Hotel & Spa. From the beach, the view out to sea is magnificent, framed by neighboring Kahoolawe and Lanai and the tiny crescent of Molokini, probably the most popular snorkel spot in these parts. The clear waters tumble to shore in waves just the right size for gentle riding, with or without a board. From shore, you can see Pacific humpback whales in season (Dec–Apr) and surreal sunsets nightly. Facilities include restrooms, outdoor showers, and limited free parking at the blue SHORELINE ACCESS sign, which points toward Wailea Alanui Drive. No lifeguards.

Ulua Beach ★

One of the most popular beaches in Wailea, Ulua is a long, wide, crescent-shaped gold-sand beach between two rocky points. When the ocean's calm, Ulua offers Wailea's best snorkeling; when it's rough, the waves are excellent for bodysurfers. The ocean bottom is shallow and gently slopes down to deeper waters, making swimming generally safe. The beach is usually occupied by guests of nearby resorts. In high season (Dec 25–Mar and June–Aug), it's carpeted with beach towels and packed with sunbathers like sardines in cocoa butter. Facilities include showers and restrooms. Look for the blue SHORELINE ACCESS sign on South Kihei Road; nearby is a tiny parking lot. No lifeguards.

Maluaka Beach (Makena Beach) ★

On the southern end of Maui's resort coast, development falls off dramatically, leaving a wild, dry countryside of green kiawe trees. The Maui Prince sits in isolated splendor, sharing Makena Resort's 1,800 acres with only a couple of first-rate golf courses and a necklace of perfect beaches. The strand nearest the hotel is Maluaka Beach, often called Makena, notable for its beauty and its views of Molokini Crater, the offshore islet; and Kahoolawe, the so-called "target" island (it was used as a bombing target 1945–90). This is a short, wide, palm-fringed crescent of golden, grainy sand set between two black-lava points and bounded by big sand dunes topped by a grassy knoll. The swimming in this mostly calm bay is considered the best on Makena Bay, which is bordered on the south by Puu Olai Cinder Cone and historic Keawalai Congregational Church. The waters around Makena Landing, at the north end of the bay, are particularly good for snorkeling. Facilities include restrooms, showers, a landscaped park, lifeguards, and roadside parking. Along Makena Alanui, look for the SHORELINE ACCESS sign near the hotel, turn right, and head down to the shore.

EAST MAUI

Hookipa Beach Park ★

Two miles past Paia, on the Hana Highway, is one of the most famous windsurfing sites in the world. Because of its hard, constant wind and endless waves, Hookipa attracts top windsurfers and wave jumpers from around the globe. Surfers and fishermen also enjoy this small, gold-sand beach at the foot of a grassy cliff, which provides a natural amphitheater for spectators. Except when competitions are being held, weekdays are the best times to watch the daredevils fly over the waves. When waves are flat, snorkelers and divers explore the reef. Facilities include restrooms, showers, pavilions, picnic tables, barbecues, and parking. No lifeguards.

Waianapanapa State Park ★

Four miles before Hana, off the Hana Highway, is this beach park, which takes its name from the legend of the Waianapanapa Cave, where Chief Kaakea, a jealous and cruel man, suspected his wife, Popoalaea, of having an affair. Popoalaea left her husband and hid herself in a chamber of the Waianapanapa Cave. She and her attendant ventured out only at night for food. Nevertheless, a few days later, Kaakea was passing by the area and saw the shadow of the servant. Knowing he had found his wife's hiding place, Kaakea entered the cave and killed her. During certain times of the year, the water in the tide pool turns red, commemorating Popoalaea's death. (Scientists claim, less imaginatively, that the water turns red due to the presence of small red shrimp.)

Waianapanapa State Park's 120 acres contain 12 cabins (p. 252), a caretaker's residence, a beach park, picnic tables, barbecue grills, restrooms, showers, a parking lot, a shoreline hiking trail, and a black-sand beach. (The sand is actually small black pebbles.) This is a wonderful area for shoreline hikes (bring insect repellent—the mosquitoes are plentiful) and picnicking. Swimming is generally unsafe, though, due to strong waves and rip currents. Because Waianapanapa is crowded on weekends with local residents and their families, as well as tourists, weekdays are generally a better bet. No lifeguards.

7 FOR THE ACTIVE FAMILY

Snorkel Bob's (www.snorkelbob.com) has snorkel gear, boogie boards, and other ocean toys at three locations: 1217 Front St., Lahaina (✆ **808/661-4421**); Napili Village, 5425-C Lower Honoapiilani Hwy., Napili (✆ **808/669-9603**); and Kamaole Beach Center, 2411 S. Kihei Rd., Kihei (✆ **808/879-7449**). All locations are open daily from 8am to 5pm. If you're island-hopping, you can rent equipment from a Snorkel Bob's location on one island and return it to a branch on another.

IN THE WATER

Boating

Maui is big on snorkel cruises. The crescent-shaped islet called **Molokini** is one of the best snorkel and scuba spots in Hawaii. Trips to the island of **Lanai** (see chapter 8) are also popular for a day of snorkeling. Always remember to bring a towel, swimsuit, sunscreen, and hat on a snorkel cruise; everything else is usually included.

Maui Classic Charters ★★★ Ages 3 and up. Maui Classic Charters offers morning and afternoon **snorkel-sail cruises to Molokini** on *Four Winds II,* a 55-foot, glass-bottom catamaran, for $84 adults ($49 children 3–12 years) for the morning sail and $40 adults ($30 children) in the afternoon. *Four Winds* trips include a continental breakfast; a barbecue lunch; complimentary beer, wine, and soda; complimentary snorkeling gear and instruction; and sportfishing along the way.

Those looking for speed should book a trip on the fast, state-of-the-art catamaran, *Maui Magic.* The company offers a 5-hour snorkel journey to both Molokini and La

Pérouse for $99 for adults and $79 for children ages 5 to 12, including a continental breakfast; barbecue lunch; beer, wine, and soda; snorkel gear; and instruction. During **whale season** (Dec 22–Apr 22), the *Four Winds* has a whale-watch trip; a 3½-hour trip with beverages is $42 for adults and $30 for children ages 3 to 12.

Maalaea Harbor, slip 55 and slip 80. ✆ **800/736-5740** or 808/879-8188. www.mauicharters.com. Prices vary depending on cruise.

Pacific Whale Foundation **All ages.** This not-for-profit foundation supports its whale research by offering whale-watch cruises and snorkel tours, some to Molokini and Lanai. Families are welcome (even infants) on the fleet of large, roomy boats, from a 65-foot power catamaran to a 50-foot sailing catamaran. There are 15 daily trips to choose from, offered December to May, out of both Lahaina and Maalaea harbors.

101 N. Kihei Rd., Kihei. ✆ **800/942-5311** or 808/879-8811. www.pacificwhale.org. Trips from $23 adults, $17 children 7–12; free for children 6 and under. Snorkeling cruises from $30.

Trilogy ★★★ Kids Trilogy offers my favorite **snorkel-sail trips.** Hop aboard one of the fleet of custom-built catamarans, from 54 to 64 feet long, for a 9-mile sail from Lahaina Harbor to **Lanai's Hulopoe Beach,** a terrific marine preserve, for a fun-filled day of sailing, snorkeling, swimming, and **whale-watching** (in season, of course). This is the only cruise that offers a personalized ground tour of the island and the only one with rights to take you to Hulopoe Beach. The full-day trip costs $203 for adults, $101 for children ages 3 to 12. Ask about overnighters to Lanai.

Trilogy also offers snorkel-sail trips to **Molokini,** one of Hawaii's best snorkel spots. This half-day trip leaves from Maalaea Harbor and costs $118 for adults, $59 kids ages 3 to 12, including breakfast and a barbecue lunch. There's also a late-morning half-day snorkel-sail off Kaanapali Beach for the same price.

These are the most expensive sail-snorkel cruises on Maui, but they're worth every penny. The crews are fun and knowledgeable, and the boats comfortable and well equipped. All trips include breakfast (Mom's homemade cinnamon buns) and a very good barbecue lunch (shipboard on the half-day trip, on land on the Lanai trip). Note, however, that you will be required to wear a flotation device no matter how good your swimming skills are; if this bothers you, go with another outfitter.

Trilogy also offers sailing/snorkeling trips from Kaanapali to Honolua Bay, with lunch, for $118 and a host of other trips.

✆ **888/MAUI-800** (628-4800) or 808/TRILOGY (874-5649). www.sailtrilogy.com. Prices and departure points vary with cruise.

Day Cruises to Molokai

You can travel across the seas by ferry from Maui's Lahaina Harbor to Molokai's Kaunakakai Wharf on the ***Molokai Princess*** (✆ **800/275-6969** or 808/667-6165; www.mauiprincess.com). The 100-foot yacht, certified for 149 passengers, is fitted with the latest generation of gyroscopic stabilizers, making the ride smoother. The ferry makes the 90-minute journey from Lahaina to Kaunakakai daily; the round-trip cost is $85 adults and $43 children ages 3 to 12. Or you can choose to tour the island from two different package options: Cruise-Drive, which includes round-trip passage and a rental car for $191 for the driver, $76 per additional adult passenger, and $38 for children; or the Alii Tour, which is a guided tour in an air-conditioned van plus lunch for $191 for adults and $134 for children.

"Ocean" Camp

If you are lucky enough to be on Maui during the summer, your 6- to 12-year-old child can go to the **Pacific Whale Foundation's "Ocean Discovery Camp"** (✆ **808/244-8391** or www.pacificwhale.org), which has every ocean activity you can imagine: surfing lessons, windsurfing lessons, beach games, swimming, a visit to the Maui Ocean Center, and even a snorkel cruise to Molokini. Your day campers will be learning about marine life while having fun (such as making squid-ink tattoos—don't worry, they wash off). Held at the Ocean Science Discovery Center in Maalaea, next to the Maui Ocean Center, the 8:30am to 4pm weekday camp takes kids just for the day ($79) or for 5 days ($344).

Day Cruises to Lanai

In addition to **Trilogy** (see above), the following boats specialize in day trips to the island of Lanai.

Expeditions Lahaina-Lanai Ferry ★ Value All ages. The cheapest way to Lanai is the ferry, which runs five times a day, 365 days a year. It leaves Lahaina at 6:45 and 9:15am, and 12:45, 3:15, and 5:45pm; the return ferry from Lanai's Manele Bay Harbor leaves at 8 and 10:30am, and 2, 4:30, and 6:45pm. The 9-mile channel crossing takes between 45 minutes and an hour, depending on sea conditions. Reservations are strongly recommended. Baggage is limited to two checked bags and one carry-on. Call **Lanai City Service** (✆ **800/800-4000** or 808/565-7227) to arrange a car rental or bus ride when you arrive.

Boat: Lahaina Harbor. Office: 658 Front St., Suite 127, Lahaina, HI 96761. ✆ **800/695-2624** or 808/661-3756. www.go-lanai.com. Round-trip from Maui to Lanai $50 adult, $40 children 2–11, free for children 1 and under.

Bodyboarding & Bodysurfing

In winter, Maui's best bodysurfing spot is **Mokuleia Beach,** known locally as Slaughterhouse because of the cattle slaughterhouse that once stood here, not because of the waves—although these waves are for expert bodysurfers only. Take Honoapiilani Highway just past Kapalua Bay Resort; various trails will take you down to the pocket beach.

Good bodyboarding can be found at **Baldwin Beach Park,** just outside Paia. Storms from the south bring fair bodysurfing conditions and great bodyboarding to the lee side of Maui: **Oneloa Beach** (or Big Beach) in Makena, **Ulua** and **Kamaole III beaches** in Kihei, and **Kapalua Beach** are all good choices.

Ocean Kayaking

Gliding silently over the water, propelled by a paddle, seeing Maui from the sea the way the early Hawaiians did—that's what ocean kayaking is all about. One of Maui's best kayak routes is along the **Kihei Coast,** where there's easy access to calm water. Mornings are always best; the wind comes up around 11am, making seas choppy and paddling difficult.

For beginners, our favorite kayak-tour operator is **Makena Kayak Tours ★** (✆ **877/879-8426** or 808/879-8426; makenakyak@aol.com). Professional guide Dino Ventura is terrific with kids during the 2 1/2-hour trip from Makena Landing and loves taking first-timers over the secluded coral reefs and into remote coves. Kids 5 and older will probably enjoy this tour more than little ones; in fact, this could be a highlight of your vacation. It costs $55 a person, including refreshments and snorkel and kayak equipment.

Ocean Rafting

If you're semiadventurous and looking for a more intimate experience with the sea, try ocean rafting. The inflatable rafts hold 6 to 24 passengers. Tours usually include snorkeling and coastal cruising. One of the best (and most reasonable) outfitters is **Hawaiian Ocean Rafting** (✆ **888/677-RAFT** [677-7238] or 808/667-2191; www.hawaiioceanrafting.com), which operates out of Lahaina Harbor. The best deal is the 5-hour morning tour, which is $74 for adults and $53 for children ages 5 to 12. (Book online and save $11.) It includes three snorkeling stops and time spent searching for dolphins, not to mention continental breakfast and midmorning snacks.

Snorkeling

Snorkeling on Maui is easy—there are so many great spots where you can wade into the water with a face mask and look down to see tropical fish. Mornings are best; local winds kick in around noon. Maui's best snorkeling beaches include **Kapalua Beach;** along the Kihei coastline, especially at **Kamaole Beach Park III;** and along the Wailea coastline, particularly at **Ulua Beach.** For an off-the-beaten track experience, head south to **Makena Beach;** the bay is filled with clouds of tropical fish, and on weekdays, the waters are virtually empty.

The snorkeling at **Black Rock at Kaanapali** ★ is worth the inflated rates at the parking lots that buffer this beach. The prominent craggy cliff at the Sheraton Maui Hotel doesn't just end when it plunges into the ocean. Underwater, the sheer wall continues, creating one of the west side's best snorkeling areas: Turtles, rays, and a variety of snappers and goatfish cruise along the sandy bottom. In the crevices, ledges, and holes of the rock wall, you can find eels, shrimp, lobster, and a range of rainbow-hued tropical fish.

The number one snorkeling spot on Maui actually is offshore: **Molokini** ★★★. This sunken crater sits like a crescent moon fallen from the sky, almost midway between Maui and the uninhabited island of Kahoolawe. Molokini stands like a scoop against the tide and serves, on its concave side, as a natural sanctuary and marine-life preserve for tropical fish. Snorkelers commute daily in a fleet of dive boats. Molokini is accessible only by boat; see "Boating," above, for outfitters that can take you here. Expect crowds in the high season.

When the whales aren't around, **Captain Steve's Rafting** (✆ **808/667-5565;** www.captainsteves.com) offers 7-hour snorkel trips from Mala Wharf in Lahaina to the waters around **Lanai.** (You don't actually land on the island.) Rates of $150 for adults and $115 for children 12 and younger include breakfast, lunch, snorkel gear, and wet suits. I wouldn't recommend it for kids younger than 5 years old (too long a day and a little too bumpy).

Submarine Dives

Plunging 100 feet below the surface of the sea in a state-of-the-art, high-tech submarine is a great way to experience Maui's magnificent underwater world, especially if you're not a swimmer. **Atlantis Adventures** ★, 658 Front St., Lahaina (✆ **800/548-6262** or 808/667-2224; www.atlantisadventures.com), offers trips out of Lahaina Harbor every hour on the hour from 9am to 2pm. The fee is $80 for adults and $41 for children 11 and under. (Children must be at least 3 ft. tall.) Allow 2 hours for this underwater adventure. This is not a good choice if you're claustrophobic.

Surfing

Expert surfers visit Maui in winter, when the surf's really up. The best surfing beaches include **Honolua Bay,** north of the Kapalua Resort (the third bay past the Ritz-Carlton Kapalua, off the Honoapiilani Hwy., or Hwy. 30); **Lahaina Harbor** (in summer, there'll be waves just off the channel entrance with a south swell); **Maalaea,** just outside the breakwall of the Maalaea Harbor (a clean, world-class left); and **Hookipa Beach,** where surfers get the waves until noon (after that—in a carefully worked-out compromise to share this prized surf spot—the windsurfers take over).

Always wanted to learn to surf, but didn't know whom to ask? Call the **Nancy C. Emerson School of Surfing,** 358 Papa Place, Suite F, Kahului (✆ **808/244-SURF** [244-7873] or 808/662-4445; www.surfclinics.com). Nancy has been surfing since 1961, and has even been a stunt performer for various movies, including *Waterworld.* She's pioneered a new instructional technique called "Learn to Surf in One Lesson" you can, really. It's $85 per person for a 2-hour group lesson; private 2-hour classes are $175. Since all students must be able to float and be comfortable in the water, generally kids 5 and younger are too young.

In Hana, **Hana-Maui Sea Sports** (✆ **808/248-7711;** www.hana-maui-seasports.com) has 2-hour long-board lessons taught by a certified ocean lifeguard for $89.

Swimming

The following county beaches have lifeguards: Kahana Beach Park in Kahului; Kamaole I, II, and III beach parks in Kihei; D. T. Fleming and Hanakao'o beach parks in west Maui; H. A. Baldwin Beach Park in Paia; and, during summer, the Hana Beach Park in Hana.

For those kids intimidated by swimming in the ocean, the county has swimming pools at the Lahaina Recreation Center in Lahaina, the Kihei Community Center in Kihei, The War Memorial Complex in Wailuku, Kahului Community Park (Kokua Pool), Kahului (Kahului Pool), and Pukalani (Upcountry Pool).

Whale-Watching

The humpback is the star of the annual whale-watching season, which usually begins in December and can last until May.

WHALE-WATCHING FROM SHORE This is an activity the entire family can enjoy together. The best time to whale-watch is between mid-December and April: Just look out to sea. There's no best time of day, but it seems that when the sea is glassy and there's no wind, the whales appear. Once you see one, keep watching in the same vicinity; they may stay down for 20 minutes. Bring a book. And binoculars, if you can.

Some good whale-watching spots on Maui:

- **McGregor Point:** On the way to Lahaina, there's a scenic lookout at mile marker 9 (just before you get to the Lahaina Tunnel); it's a good viewpoint from which to scan for whales.
- **Wailea Marriott Resort:** On the Wailea coastal walk, stop at this resort to look for whales through the telescope installed as a public service by the Hawaii Island Humpback Whale National Marine Sanctuary.
- **Olowalu Reef:** Along the straight part of Honoapiilani Highway, between McGregor Point and Olowalu, you'll sometimes see whales leap out of the water. Their appearance can bring traffic to a screeching halt: People abandon their cars and run down to

the sea to watch, causing a major traffic jam. If you stop, pull off the road so others may pass.

- **Puu Olai:** It's a tough climb up this coastal landmark near the Maui Prince Hotel, but you're likely to be well rewarded: This is the island's best spot for offshore whale-watching. On the 360-foot cinder cone overlooking Makena Beach, you'll be at the right elevation to see Pacific humpbacks as they dodge Molokini and cruise up Alalakeiki Channel between Maui and Kahoolawe. If you don't see one, you'll at least have a whale of a view.

WHALE-WATCHING CRUISES For a closer look, take a whale-watching cruise. Just about all of Hawaii's snorkel and dive boats become whale-watching boats in season; some of them even carry professional naturalists onboard so you'll know what you're seeing. For the best options, see "Boating," earlier in this section.

ON THE LAND

Arts & Crafts

A great rainy-day activity is to head for Kapalua Resort to make a bowl from clay or paint a premade one, then fire it and take it home. The **Art School at Kapalua** (© **808/665-0007**), in a charming 1920s plantation building that was part of an old cannery operation, features local and visiting instructors and is open daily for people of all ages (except kids 4 and under, who are a little too young) and skill levels. This not-for-profit organization offers projects, classes, and workshops that highlight creativity in all forms, including photography, figure drawing, ceramics, landscape painting, painting on silk, and the performing arts (ballet, yoga, creative movement, Pilates). Classes are inexpensive. Call the school to see what's scheduled while you're on Maui.

Bicycling

For information on bikeways and maps, check out **www.bikehawaii.com** or get a copy of the *Maui County Bicycle Map,* which has information on road suitability, climate, mileage, elevation changes, bike shops, safety tips, and various bicycling routes. The map is available for $7.50 ($6.25 for the map and $1.25 for postage), paid for with bank checks or money orders only, from **Tri Isle R, C, and D Council,** Attn: Bike Map Project, 200 Imi Kala St., Suite 208, Wailuku, HI 96793.

If you want to bike on your own, **Haleakala Bike Company,** Haiku Market Place, Haiku (© **888/922-2453** or 808/575-9575; www.bikemaui.com), rents equipment from $45 a day (or $164 a week).

Hiking & Camping

In the past 3 decades, Maui has grown from a rural island to a fast-paced resort destination, but its natural beauty remains largely inviolate; there are still many places that can be explored only on foot. Those interested in seeing the backcountry—complete with virgin waterfalls, remote wilderness trails, and quiet, meditative settings—should head for Haleakala's upcountry or for the tropical Hana Coast.

Camping on Maui can be extreme (inside a volcano) or benign (by the sea in Hana). It can be wet, cold, and rainy; or hot, dry, and windy—often, all on the same day. If you're heading for Haleakala, remember that U.S. astronauts trained for the moon inside the volcano; bring survival gear. You'll need your swimsuit and rain gear if you're bound for Waianapanapa. Bring your own gear, as there are no places to rent camping equipment on Maui.

Moments Cruising Down a Volcano

It's not even close to dawn, but here you are, rubbing your eyes awake, riding in a van up the long, dark road to the top of Maui's dormant volcano. It's colder than you ever thought possible for a tropical island. The air is thin. You stomp your chilly feet while you wait, sipping hot coffee or chocolate. Then comes the sun, exploding over yawning Haleakala Crater, big enough to swallow Manhattan—a mystic moment you won't soon forget. Now you know why Hawaiians named the crater the House of the Sun. But there's no time to linger: Decked out in your screaming-yellow parka, you mount your mechanical steed and test its most important feature, the brakes—because you're about to coast 37 miles down a 10,000-foot volcano.

Cruising down Haleakala, from the lunar-like landscape at the top past flower farms, pineapple fields, and eucalyptus groves, is quite an experience—and just about anybody in the family 12 and older (and at least 5 ft. tall) can do it. This is a safe, no-strain bicycle trip that requires some stamina in the colder, wetter winter months but is fun for everyone in the warmer months—the key word being *warmer*. In winter and the rainy season, conditions can be harsh, especially at the top, with below-freezing temperatures and 40 mph winds.

Note: Not all tours go to the summit. If you want to start your bike ride at the summit, be sure to confirm. The cheapest trip starts at around the 6,500-foot level (about two-thirds up the mountain). After making sure you are secure on the bike, they will let you ride down by yourself at your own pace. Be sure to ask if your tour goes into the park and is escorted all the way down to the ocean.

Maui's oldest downhill company is **Maui Downhill** ★ (✆ **800/535-BIKE** [535-2453] or 808/871-2155; www.mauidownhill.com), which offers a sunrise safari bike tour, including continental breakfast and brunch, starting at $195. (Book online and save $50.) If it's all booked up, try **Maui Mountain Cruisers** (✆ **800/232-6284** or 808/871-6014; www.mauimountaincruisers.com), which has sunrise trips at $165 (book online and save); or **Mountain Riders Bike Tours** (✆ **800/706-7700** or 808/242-9739; www.mountainriders.com), with sunrise rides for $154 (book online to save $32). All rates include hotel pickup, transport to the top, bicycle, safety equipment, and meals. Wear layers of warm clothing—there may be a 30° change in temperature from the top of the mountain to the ocean. Generally, the tour groups will not take riders younger than 12, but younger children can ride along in the van that accompanies the groups. Pregnant women should also ride in the van.

For more information on Maui camping and hiking trails, and to obtain free maps, contact **Haleakala National Park,** P.O. Box 369, Makawao, HI 96768 (✆ **808/572-4400;** www.nps.gov/hale); and the **Hawaii Division of Forestry and Wildlife,** 54 S. High St., Wailuku, HI 96793 (✆ **808/984-8100;** www.dofaw.net). For information on trails, hikes, camping, and permits for state parks, contact the **Hawaii State Department of Land and Natural Resources,** State Parks Division, P.O. Box 621, Honolulu, HI 96809 (✆ **808/587-0300;** www.state.hi.us/dlnr); note that you can get information from the website but cannot obtain permits there. For Maui County Parks, contact the **Maui County Department of Parks and Recreation,** 1580-C Kaahumanu Ave., Wailuku, HI 96793 (✆ **808/243-7132;** www.mauimapp.com/information/campingcounty.htm).

GUIDED HIKES If you'd like a knowledgeable guide to accompany you on a hike, call **Maui Hiking Safaris** ★ (✆ **888/445-3963** or 808/573-0168; www.mauihikingsafaris.com). Owner Randy Warner takes visitors on half- and full-day hikes into valleys, rainforests, and coastal areas. Randy's been hiking around Maui for more than 25 years and is wise in the ways of Hawaiian history, native flora and fauna, and volcanology. His rates are $59 to $69 for a half-day and $105 to $139 for a full day and include day packs, rain parkas, snacks, water, and, on full-day hikes, sandwiches. He welcomes kids who can walk, and will suggest age-appropriate hikes.

Maui's oldest hiking guide company is **Hike Maui** ★ (✆ **808/879-5270;** www.hikemaui.com), headed by Ken Schmitt, who pioneered guided hikes on the Valley Isle. Hike Maui offers five different hikes a day, ranging from an easy 1-mile, 3-hour hike to a waterfall ($75), to a strenuous, full-day hike in Haleakala Crater ($150). Kids 6 and older are welcome on all hikes; the longer hikes are better for kids 8 and older. All prices include equipment and transportation.

For information on hikes given by the **Sierra Club, Hawaii Chapter** on Maui, call ✆ **808/573-4147** or check www.hi.sierraclub.org.

Haleakala National Park ★★★

For complete coverage of the national park, see "Exploring Maui with Your Kids," earlier in this chapter.

SLIDING SANDS & HALEMAUU TRAILS Hiking into Maui's dormant volcano is the best way to see it. The terrain inside the wilderness area of the volcano, which ranges from burnt-red cinder cones to ebony-black lava flows, is simply spectacular. There are some 27 miles of hiking trails, two camping sites, and three cabins.

Entrance to Haleakala National Park is $10 per car. The rangers offer free guided hikes, which are a great way to learn about the unusual flora and geological formations here. Everyone in the family will enjoy the briefing sessions on culture, history, and flora (daily at 10am, 11am, and noon) at the Summit Visitors Building, 11 miles up from the Visitor's Information Center. If your little ones can keep up (generally kids older than 6), there's a 2-hour, 2-mile guided cinder desert hike every Tuesday and Friday at 9am. (Meet at Sliding Sands Trail Head, next to the summit parking lot.) Every Monday and Thursday at 9am, there's a 3-hour, 3-mile guided Waikamoi Cloud Forest hike (meet at Hosmer Grove) to view rare native birds and plants. Although there are no posted age restrictions, rangers advise that this hike isn't appropriate for children younger than the age of 8. Wear sturdy shoes and be prepared for wind, rain, and intense sun. Bring water and a hat. Additional options include full-moon hikes and star program hikes. ***Warning:*** Always call in advance; the hikes and briefing sessions may be cancelled, so check first. For details, call the park at ✆ **808/572-4400** or visit www.nps.gov/hale.

Try to arrange to stay at least 1 night in the park; 2 or 3 nights will allow you more time to explore the fascinating interior of the volcano. (See below for details on the cabins and campgrounds in the wilderness area of the valley.) If you want to venture out on your own, the best route takes in two trails: into the crater along **Sliding Sands Trail,** which begins on the rim at 9,800 feet and descends into the belly of the beast to the valley floor at 6,600 feet; and back out along **Halemauu Trail.** Hardy hikers can consider making the 11-mile, one-way descent, which takes 9 hours, and the equally long return

A Word of Warning About the Weather

The weather at nearly 10,000 feet can change suddenly and without warning. Come prepared for cold, high winds; rain; and even snow in winter. Temperatures can range from 77°F (25°C) down to 26°F (–3°C), and high winds are frequent. Daytime temperatures can be 30° colder than at sea level. Sunrise and sunset temperatures average 30° to 40°F in winter (–1° to 4°C) and 40° to 50°F (4–10°C) in summer. Rainfall varies from 40 inches a year on the western end of the crater to more than 200 inches on the eastern side. Bring boots, waterproof gear, warm clothes, extra layers, and lots of sunscreen—the sun shines very brightly up here. For the latest weather information, call ✆ **808/871-5054.**

ascent in a day. The rest of us can extend this steep hike to 2 days. The descending and ascending trails aren't loops; the trailheads are miles (and several thousand feet in elevation) apart, so you'll need to make transportation arrangements in advance. Before you set out, stop at park headquarters to get camping and hiking updates.

The trailhead for Sliding Sands is well marked and the trail is easy to follow over lava flows and cinders. As you descend, look around: The view is breathtaking. In the afternoon, waves of clouds flow into the Kaupo and Koolau gaps. Vegetation is spare to nonexistent at the top, but the closer you get to the valley floor, the more vegetation you'll see: bracken ferns, pili grass, shrubs, even flowers. On the floor, the trail travels across rough lava flows, passing by rare silversword plants, volcanic vents, and multicolored cinder cones.

The Halemauu Trail goes over red and black lava and past vegetation, such as evening primrose, as it begins its ascent up the valley wall. Occasionally, riders on horseback use this trail. The proper etiquette is to step aside and stand quietly next to the trail as the horses pass.

Some shorter and easier hiking options include the half-mile walk down the **Hosmer Grove Nature Trail,** or the first mile or two down **Sliding Sands Trail,** which gives you a hint of what lies ahead. (Even this short hike is exhausting at the high altitude.) A good day hike is **Halemauu Trail** to Holua Cabin and back, an 8-mile, half-day trip.

STAYING IN THE WILDERNESS AREA Most people stay at one of two tent campgrounds, unless they get lucky and win the lottery—the lottery, that is, for one of the three wilderness cabins. For more information, contact **Haleakala National Park,** P.O. Box 369, Makawao, HI 96768 (✆ **808/572-4400;** www.nps.gov/hale).

Cabins It can get really cold and windy down in the valley (see "A Word of Warning About the Weather," above), so try for a cabin. They're warm, protected from the elements, and reasonably priced. Each has 12 padded bunks (but no bedding; bring your own), a table, chairs, cooking utensils, a two-burner propane stove, and a wood-burning stove with firewood. (You may also have a few cockroaches.) The cabins are spaced so that each one is an easy walk from the other: Holua Cabin is on the Halemauu Trail, Kapalaoa Cabin on Sliding Sands Trail, and Paliku Cabin on the eastern end by the Kaupo Gap. The rates are $55 a night for groups of 1 to 6, $110 a night for groups of 7 to 12.

The cabins are so popular that the National Park Service has a lottery system for reservations. Requests for cabins must be made 3 months in advance. (Be sure to request alternate dates.) You can request all three cabins at once; you're limited to 2 nights in one cabin and 3 nights total in the wilderness each month.

Campgrounds If you don't win the cabin lottery, all is not lost—there are three tent-camping sites that can accommodate you: two in the wilderness and one just outside at Hosmer Grove. There is no charge for tent camping.

Hosmer Grove, located at 6,800 feet, is a small, open, grassy area surrounded by a forest. Trees protect campers from the winds, but nights still get very cold; sometimes there's ice on the ground up here. This is the best place to spend the night in a tent if you want to see the Haleakala sunrise. Come up the day before, enjoy the park, take a day hike, then turn in early. The glass-enclosed summit building opens at sunrise for those who come to greet the dawn—a welcome windbreak. Facilities at Hosmer Grove include a covered pavilion with picnic tables and grills, chemical toilets, and drinking water. No permits are needed, and there's no charge—but you can stay for only 3 nights in a 30-day period.

The two tent-camping areas inside the volcano are **Holua,** just off Halemauu at 6,920 feet; and **Paliku,** just before the Kaupo Gap at the eastern end of the valley, at 6,380 feet. Facilities at both campgrounds are limited to pit toilets and nonpotable catchment water. Water at Holua is limited, especially in summer. No open fires are allowed inside the volcano, so bring a stove if you plan to cook. Tent camping is restricted to the signed area. No camping is allowed in the horse pasture. The inviting grassy lawn in front of the cabin is off-limits. Camping is free, but limited to 2 consecutive nights, and no more than 3 nights a month inside the volcano. Permits are issued at Park Headquarters, daily from 8am to 3pm, on a first-come, first-served basis on the day you plan to camp. Occupancy is limited to 25 people in each campground.

Polipoli State Park ★

One of the most unusual hiking experiences in the state can be found at Polipoli State Park, part of the 21,000-acre Kula and Kahikinui Forest Reserve on the slope of Haleakala. At Polipoli, it's hard to believe that you're in Hawaii: First of all, it's cold, even in summer, because the elevation is 5,300 to 6,200 feet. Second, this former forest of native koa, ohia, and mamane trees, which was overlogged in the 1800s, was reforested in the 1930s with introduced species: pine, Monterey cypress, ash, sugi, red adler, redwood, and several varieties of eucalyptus. The result is a cool area, with sunlight muted by towering trees.

For families with children ages 7 and older, the **Polipoli Loop** is an easy 5-mile hike that takes about 3 hours; dress warmly for it. Take the Haleakala Highway (Hwy. 37) to Keokea and turn right onto Highway 337; after less than a half-mile, turn on Waipoli Road, which climbs swiftly. After 10 miles, Waipoli Road ends at the Polipoli State Park campgrounds. The well-marked trailhead is next to the parking lot, near a stand of Monterey cypresses; the tree-lined trail offers the best view of the island.

Polipoli Loop is really a network of three trails: Haleakala Ridge, Plum Trail, and Redwood Trail. After a half-mile of meandering through groves of eucalyptus, blackwood, swamp mahogany, and hybrid cypress, you'll join the Haleakala Ridge Trail, which, about a mile into the trail, joins with the Plum Trail (named for the plums that ripen June–July). This trail passes through massive redwoods and by an old Conservation Corps bunkhouse and a run-down cabin before joining up with the Redwood Trail, which climbs through Mexican pine, tropical ash, Port Orford cedar, and—of course—redwood.

Camping is allowed with a $5-per-night permit from the **Hawaii Division of Forestry & Wildlife,** 54 S. High St., Room 101, Wailuku, HI 96793 (✆ **808/984-8109;** www.hawaiistateparks.org/camping/fees.cfm). There also is a 10-bunk cabin, in the park, available for $45 a night for one to four guests ($5 for each additional guest); it has a cold shower and a gas stove, but no electricity or drinking water (bring your own).

Kanaha Beach Park Camping

One of the few Maui County camping facilities on the island is Kanaha Beach Park, located next to the Kahului Airport. The county has two separate areas for camping: seven tent sites on the beach and an additional 10 tent sites inland. This well-used park is a favorite of windsurfers, who take advantage of the strong winds that roar across this end of the island. Facilities include a paved parking lot, portable toilets, outdoor showers, barbecue grills, and picnic tables. Camping is limited to no more than 3 consecutive days; the permit fee is $3 per adult and 50¢ per child, per night, and can be obtained from the **Maui County Parks and Recreation Department,** 700 Halia Nakoa St., Unit 2, Wailuku, HI 96793 (✆ **808/243-7389;** www.mauimapp.com/information/camping county.htm). The 17 sites book up quickly; reserve your dates far in advance. (The county will accept reservations a year in advance.). Occasionally the county closes the park for a cleanup, so reserve in advance

Walanapanapa State Park ★★★

Tucked in a tropical jungle, on the outskirts of the little coastal town of Hana, is Waianapanapa State Park, a black-sand beach set in an emerald forest.

The **Hana-Waianapanapa Coast Trail** is an easy 6-mile hike that takes you back in time. Allow 4 hours to walk this relatively flat trail, which parallels the sea along lava cliffs and a forest of lauhala trees, and make sure your kids can walk that long (generally kids 8 and older do best). The best time to take the hike is either early morning or late afternoon, when the light on the lava and surf makes for great photos. Midday is the worst time; not only is it hot (lava intensifies the heat), but also no shade or potable water is available.

There's no formal trailhead; join the route at any point along the Waianapanapa Campground and go in either direction. Along the trail, you'll see remains of an ancient *heiau* (temple), stands of lauhala trees, caves, a blowhole, and a remarkable plant, *naupaka,* that flourishes along the beach. Upon close inspection, you'll see that the naupaka have only half-blossoms; according to Hawaiian legend, a similar plant living in the mountains has the other half of the blossoms. One ancient explanation is that the two plants represent never-to-be-reunited lovers: As the story goes, the couple bickered so much that the gods, fed up with their incessant quarreling, banished one lover to the mountain and the other to the sea.

Waianapanapa has 12 cabins and a tent campground. Go for the cabins (see "Family-Friendly Accommodations," earlier in this chapter), as it rains torrentially here, sometimes turning the campground into a mud-wrestling arena. Tent-camping is $5 per night but limited to 5 nights in a 30-day period. Permits are available from the **State Parks Division,** 54 S. High St., Room 101, Wailuku, HI 96793 (✆ **808/984-8109;** www.hawaiistateparks.org/camping/fees.cfm). Facilities include restrooms, outdoor showers, drinking water, and picnic tables.

Moments A Different Viewpoint: Zipping over the Forest Canopy

For those looking for a different perspective on Haleakala, try **Skyline Eco-Adventures' Zipline Haleakala Tour** (P.O. Box 880518, Pukalani, HI 96788; ✆ **808/878-8400;** www.skylinehawaii.com), which blends a short hike through a eucalyptus forest with four "zipline" crossings. During the zipline crossing, you'll be outfitted with a seat harness and connected to a cable, then launched from a 70-foot-high platform to "zip" along the cable suspended over the slopes of Haleakala. From this viewpoint, you fly over treetops, valleys, gulches, and waterfalls at 10 to 35 mph. These bird's-eye tours operate daily and take riders from ages 12 and older, weighing between 80 and 300 pounds. The trip costs $89 ($80 if you book online).

Horseback Riding

Maui offers spectacular adventure rides through rugged ranchlands, into tropical forests, and to remote swimming holes. If you'd like to ride down into Haleakala's crater, contact **PonyExpress Tours** ★ (✆ **808/667-2200** or 808/878-6698; www.ponyexpresstours.com), which offers a variety of rides down to the crater floor and back up, from $169 to $195 per person. Shorter 1- and 2-hour rides are also offered at Haleakala Ranch, located on the beautiful lower slopes of the volcano, for $95 and $115. If you book via the Internet, you get 10% off. PonyExpress provides well-trained horses and experienced guides, and accommodates all riding levels. You must be at least 10 years old, weigh no more than 230 pounds, and wear long pants and closed-toe shoes.

WAY OUT WEST ON MAUI: RANCH RIDES For families with children ages 7 and older, I recommend riding with **Mendes Ranch & Trail Rides** ★, 3530 Kahekili Hwy., 4 miles past Wailuku (✆ **808/871-5222;** www.mendesranch.com). The 300-acre Mendes Ranch is a real-life working cowboy ranch that has the essential elements of an earthly paradise—rainbows, waterfalls, palm trees, coral-sand beaches, lagoons, tide pools, a rainforest, and its own volcanic peak (more than a mile high). The morning ride, which lasts 2 hours and ends with a barbecue back at the corral (the perfect ranch-style lunch after a morning in the saddle), is $110 plus $20 for BBQ; or pick the 2- to 2½-hour afternoon ride at $110.

Parks & Playgrounds

The best parks and playgrounds are located in Maui's beach parks—see "Beaches," earlier in this chapter. There are a few specialty parks listed below.

Playgrounds

The county has a range of playgrounds in the various county parks. In Lahaina, playgrounds can be found at the Lahaina Recreation Center, Shaw Street and Honoapiilani Highway; Paunau Park, Lahainaluna Road and Paunau Street; and Wahikuli Park, just before Kaanapali on Honoapiilani Highway. North of Lanaina in Honokowai, there's a playground in Honokowai Park, on Lower Honoapiilani Road. In Kihei, playgrounds can be found at Kalama Park and Kamaole Park III, both on South Kihei Road.

For more information, contact the **Maui County Parks Department** at ✆ **808/270-7230** or check www.co.maui.hi.us/youth/maui/leisure/facilities.htm.

Skateboard Parks

The **Maui YMCA** sponsors the use of two skate parks, Kalama Park in Kihei and Keopuolani Regional Park in Kahului, with trained monitors supervising the kids. Visitors are welcome to use the skateboard facilities (bring your own board) for a $5 daily fee. For more information, call the Maui YMCA at ✆ **808/242-9007.**

8 SHOPPING WITH YOUR KIDS

THE SHOPPING SCENE

The island of Maui is a shopaholic's dream as well as an arts center, with a large number of resident artists who show their works in dozens of galleries and countless gift shops. Maui is also the queen of specialty products, an agricultural cornucopia that includes Kula onions, upcountry proteas, Kaanapali coffee, world-renowned potato chips, and many other taste treats that are shipped worldwide.

Shopping on Maui involves relatively painless parking (except in Lahaina, where even the parking lots in shopping centers seem full all the time). Most stores are open from 10am to 5pm Monday through Saturday and from noon to 5 or 6pm on Sunday. Big chain stores and department stores are open late on Friday and Saturday. Be sure to call the store before you go. Sales tax in Hawaii is 4.16% on everything (even food), and most stores will happily ship items back home. (However, you may not be happy with the price of shipping from Hawaii, which is quite expensive if you want your purchases within 6 weeks.)

The Neighborhoods

Central Maui: Wailuku & Kahului

Central Maui is home to some first-rate boutiques: Wailuku has its own antiques alleys, and the Kaahumanu Center, in neighboring Kahului, is becoming more fashionable by the month.

Lahaina & West Maui

As with any popular visitor destination, you'll have to wade through bad art and mountains of trinkets, particularly in Lahaina, where touristy boutiques line the streets between rare pockets of treasures. If you shop in west Maui, expect to pay resort prices, clear down to a bottle of Evian or sunscreen.

Kihei & Wailea

Kihei can be a glut of one minimall after another, with a few finds hidden in the urban blight. Down the street from Kihei, The Shops at Wailea, a nearly 16½-acre upscale complex, features more than 50 shops, everything from Louis Vuitton to Gap, and five restaurants. This is resort shopping much in the vein of Whalers Village in Kaanapali, where shopping and restaurant activity is concentrated in a single oceanfront complex, livening up what was an arid retail landscape.

Upcountry Maui & Hana

Upcountry, Makawao's boutiques are worth seeking out, despite some attitude and high prices. The charm of shopping on Maui has always rested in the small, independent

Mall Rats

Maui's open-air malls, as well as its indoor malls, have the benefits of easy parking, lots of shops to choose from, plenty of food outlets, and easily accessible restrooms.

In Kahului, the once rough-around-the-edges **Maui Mall,** 70 E. Kaahumanu Ave. (✆ **808/877-7559**), is newly renovated. It's now bigger and better, and has retained some of our favorite stores while adding a 12-screen movie megaplex that features current releases as well as art house films. The mall is still a place of everyday good things, from Longs Drugs to Star Market to Tasaka Guri Guri, the decades-old purveyor of inimitable icy treats that are neither ice cream nor shave ice, but something in between.

Up the street, **Queen Kaahumanu Center,** 275 Kaahumanu Ave. (✆ **808/877-3369**), offers more than 100 shops, restaurants, and theaters. Its second-floor Plantation District offers home furnishings and accessories, and gift and accessories shops. Kaahumanu covers all the bases, from the arts and crafts to a Foodland Supermarket and everything in between: a thriving food court, the island's best beauty supply, standard department stores like Macy's and Sears, and great specialty shops such as Sharper Image.

What was formerly a big, belching pineapple cannery is now a maze of shops and restaurants at the northern end of Lahaina town, known as the **Lahaina Cannery Mall,** 1221 Honoapiilani Hwy. (✆ **808/661-5304**). Find your way through the T-shirt and sportswear shops to stores selling basic necessities, such as Longs Drugs and Safeway.

In Kaanapali, upscale **Whalers Village,** 2435 Kaanapali Pkwy. (✆ **808/661-4567**), offers everything from Waldenbooks to Prada and Ferragamo. It is home to the Whalers Village Museum with its interactive exhibits and 40-foot sperm whale skeleton, and sand castles are on perpetual display, built by artists of the shifting sands. However, shoppers come for the designer thrills and beachfront dining.

In south Maui, **The Shops at Wailea** is the big shopping boost that resort-goers have been awaiting for years. Chains still rule (Gap, Louis Vuitton, Banana Republic, Tiffany & Co.), but there is fertile ground for the inveterate shopper in the nearly 60 shops in the complex. The high-end resort shops sell expensive souvenirs, gifts, clothing, and accessories for a lifetime of perpetual vacations.

shops and galleries that crop up in surprising places. Out in Hana there are a couple of tiny roadside places and a terrific gallery, but that's about it for shopping.

THE GOODS A TO Z

Arts & Crafts

Hui No'eau Visual Arts Center Besides being a shopper's paradise, this two-story, 1917 Mediterranean-style stucco home on a sprawling 9 acres also houses the premier art center on Maui. Visiting artists offer lectures, classes, and demonstrations, all at reasonable

Moments A Night of Art in Lahaina

Lahaina's merchants and art galleries go all out from 7 to 9pm on Friday, when **Art Night** ★ brings an extra measure of hospitality and community spirit. The Art Night openings are usually marked with live entertainment and refreshments and a livelier-than-usual street scene. Kids younger than 12 may be antsy after you visit the first gallery, so you'll have to gauge your time on how much art (and entertainment) they can take. (***Hint:*** Feed 'em dinner first.)

prices, in basketry, jewelry making, ceramics, painting, and other media. Classes on Hawaiian art, culture, and history are also available. The exhibits here are drawn from a wide range of disciplines and multicultural sources. The gift shop, featuring many one-of-a-kind works by local artists and artisans, is worth a stop. 2841 Baldwin Ave., Makawao. ✆ **808/572-6560.**

Maui Crafts Guild Housing crafts of high quality and in all price ranges, from pit-fired raku to bowls of Norfolk pine and other Maui woods, fashioned by Maui hands, this artist-owned and -operated guild features works ranging from basketry, hand-painted fabrics, jewelry, beadwork, traditional Hawaiian stone work, copper sculpture, and pottery of all styles. Upstairs, sculptor Arthur Dennis Williams displays his breathtaking work in wood, bronze, and stone. Everything can be shipped. **Aloha Bead Co.** (✆ **808/579-9709**), in the back of the gallery, is a treasure-trove for beadworkers. 43 Hana Hwy., Paia ✆ **808/579-9697.**

Maui Hands Maui hands have made 90% of the items in this shop/gallery. Because it's a consignment shop, you'll find Hawaii-made handicrafts and prices that aren't inflated. The selection includes paintings, prints, jewelry, glass marbles, native-wood bowls, and tchotchkes for every budget. This is an ideal stop for made-on-Maui products and crafts of good quality. The original **Maui Hands** is in Makawao at the Courtyard, 3620 Baldwin Ave. (✆ **808/572-5194**); another Maui Hands can be found in Paia, at 84 Hana Hwy. (✆ **808/579-9245**).

Baby & Preschooler Clothes

Blue Ginger Kids Started by two women in Lahaina in 1983, this children's version of their popular store features easy-care clothing in tropical designs on cotton and rayon batik fabrics, not only for kids (matching outfits for babies and girls) but also for the entire family. Whalers Village, Lahaina. ✆ **808/661-1666.**

Books

Borders Books & Music One of the largest bookstores on Maui, Borders has an extensive selection of books, music, DVDs, videos, and a great cafe in which to sit and read. Maui Marketplace, 270 Dairy Rd., Kahului. ✆ **808/877-6160.**

Borders Express The store offers a great selection of titles for kids as well as adults. Queen Kaahumanu Center, Kahului. ✆ **808/871-6112.**

Compleat Comics Company If you have comics and game enthusiasts in your family, here's the store for them. Call ahead since they keep very odd hours. 333 Dairy Rd., Kahului. ✆ **808/873-7274.** www.compleatcomics.com.

Moments **An Inside Look at Lei Making**

If you are in Lahaina on the second or last Thursday of the month, stroll by the front lawn of the **Baldwin House,** 120 Dickenson St. (at Front St.), for a splendid look at lei making and an opportunity to meet the gregarious seniors of Lahaina. From 10am to 4pm, they demonstrate lei making, sell their own floral creations, and talk story about the old days in Hawaii.

Food

Down to Earth Natural Foods Come here for fresh organic produce, a bountiful salad bar, sandwiches, smoothies, vitamins and supplements, fresh-baked goods, chips, snacks, whole grains, and more. It's located close to the airport. 305 Dairy Rd., Kahului. ✆ **808/877-2661.**

Honolua Store Walk on the old wood floors peppered with holes from golf shoes and find your everyday essentials: bottled water, stationery, mailing tape, jackets, chips, wine, soft drinks, paper products, fresh fruit and produce, and aisles of notions and necessities. With picnic tables on the veranda and a takeout counter offering deli items—more than a dozen types of sandwiches, salads, and budget-friendly breakfasts—there are always long lines of customers. Golfers and surfers love to come here for the morning paper and coffee. 502 Office Rd. (next to the Ritz-Carlton Kapalua), Kapalua. ✆ **808/669-6128.**

Flowers

Sunrise Protea Farm Proteas are a Maui trademark and an abundant crop on Haleakala's rich volcanic slopes. They also travel well, dry beautifully, and can be shipped worldwide with ease. Sunrise offers a walk-through garden and gift shops, friendly service, and a larger-than-usual selection. Freshly cut flowers arrive from the fields on Tuesday and Friday afternoons. You can order individual blooms, baskets, arrangements, or wreaths for shipping all over the world. (Next door, the Sunrise Country Market offers fresh local fruit, snacks, and sandwiches, with picnic tables for lingering.). 16157 Haleakala Hwy., Kula. ✆ **808/876-0200.** www.sunriseprotea.com.

Galleries

Hana Coast Gallery **Finds** This gallery is a good reason to go to Hana: It's an aesthetic and cultural experience that informs as it enlightens. Tucked away in the posh hideaway hotel, the gallery is known for its high level of curatorship and commitment to the cultural art of Hawaii. The 3,000-square-foot gallery is devoted entirely to Hawaii artists, featuring sculptures, paintings, prints, feather work, stone work, and carvings in displays that are so natural they could well exist in someone's home. In the Hotel Hana-Maui. ✆ **808/248-8636.**

Lahaina Arts Society Galleries With its membership of more than 185 Maui artists, the nonprofit Lahaina Arts Society is an excellent community resource. Changing monthly exhibits in the Banyan Tree and Old Jail galleries offer a good look at the island's artistic well: two-dimensional art, fiber art, ceramics, sculpture, prints, jewelry, and more. In the shade of the humongous banyan tree in the square across from Pioneer Inn, "Art in the Park" fairs are offered every second and fourth weekend of the month. 648 Wharf St., Lahaina ✆ **808/661-3228.**

Gifts & Souvenirs

Sandell *Finds* Since the early 1970s, artist, illustrator, and cartoonist David Sandell has been commenting on Maui through this artwork. Don't miss the opportunity to stop by his shop and "talk story" with this talented artist, who watched Maui go from undiscovered to discovered. His artwork—from original oils to prints to T-shirts—makes excellent souvenirs to take home. 133 Market St. ✆ **808/249-0234.**

Totally Hawaiian Gift Gallery This gallery makes a good browse for its selection of Niihau shell jewelry, excellent Hawaiian CDs, Norfolk pine bowls, Hawaiian quilt kits, soaps, handcrafted dolls, and hundreds of other "finds." It's also in the Maui Marriott in Kaanapali (✆ **808/667-2171**). In the Lahaina Cannery Mall, 1221 Honoapiilani Hwy., Lahaina. ✆ **808/667-2558.**

Markets

Maui's produce has long been a source of pride for islanders. The farmers' markets are where you'll find a fresh, inexpensive selection of Maui-grown fruit, vegetables, flowers, and plants. Some farmers' markets also feature crafts and gourmet foods. The current farmers' markets are at Queen Kaahumanu Center in Kahului, on Tuesday, Wednesday, and Friday, from 8am to 2pm; Maui Mall, Kahului, Tuesday, Wednesday, and Friday, 8am to 5pm; and Upcountry at Eddie Tam Community Center, Makawao, Saturday, 6am to noon.

Maui Swap Meet The Maui Swap Meet is a large and popular event. After 17 years on a parcel of land next to the Kahului Post Office, the Maui Swap Meet finally outgrew its home. In November 2008 the Swap Meet moved to Maui Community College campus, in Kahului, in a bigger area (4.5 acres, enough for 300 vendors and plenty of parking). The colorful Maui specialties include vegetables from Kula and Keanae, fresh taro, plants, proteas, crafts, household items, homemade ethnic foods, and baked goods, including some fabulous fruit breads. Now at the Community College the students sell artwork and ceramics and the culinary arts program has prepared food for sale. Every Saturday from 7am to 1pm, vendors spread out their wares in booths and under tarps, in a festival-like atmosphere that is pure Maui with a touch of kitsch. Between the cheap Balinese imports and New Age crystals and incense, you may find some vintage John Kelly prints and 1930s collectibles. Admission is 50¢, and if you go early while the vendors are setting up, no one will turn you away. Maui Community College, Kahului (access via Wahine Pio Ave.). ✆ 808/877-3100.

Museum Stores

Bailey House Museum Shop For made-in-Hawaii items, Bailey House is a must-stop. It offers a thoroughly enjoyable browse through authoritative Hawaiiana, in a museum that's one of the finest examples of missionary architecture, dating from 1833. The shop packs a wallop with its selection of remarkable gift items, from Hawaiian music to exquisite woods; traditional Hawaiian games to pareus and books. Prints by the legendary Hawaii artist Madge Tennent, lauhala hats hanging in midair, hand-sewn pheasant hatbands, jams and jellies, Maui cookbooks, and an occasional Hawaiian quilt are some of the treasures to be found here. 2375-A Main St., Wailuku. ✆ **808/244-3326.**

Maui Ocean Center After wandering through this terrific aquarium, stop by their gift store, located in the heart of the center. Available at this huge (6,000-sq.-ft.) store are plush stuffed marine animals; nature books; an array of fine artwork, jewelry, and Hawaiiana created by some of the island's most prominent artists; and the usual great

Moments Roselani: Maui's Best Ice Cream

For the crowning culinary experience of your trip to Maui, try **Roselani Tropoics Ice Cream,** Maui's only made-from-scratch, old-fashioned ice cream. In fact, be sure to try it early in your trip so you can eat your way through this little bit of heaven at restaurants, scooping parlors, or your own stash from grocery stores. It's nearly impossible to find a restaurant, hotel, or scooping parlor that does not have Roselani Tropics Ice Cream, but accept no substitute—demand Roselani. For a list of hotels, restaurants, parlors, and grocery stores carrying Roselani, call ✆ **808/244-7951** or check www.roselani.com.

The difference between Roselani and ordinary ice cream? With one lick your taste buds will be cheering—this is the perfect rich, creamy ice cream (made from 12%–16% butter fat). After Roselani Tropics Ice Cream, all other ice creams pale in comparison.

souvenirs—T-shirts. Maalaea Harbor Village, 192 Maalaea Rd. (in the triangle between Honoapiilani Hwy. and Maalaea Rd.). ✆ **808/270-7000.**

Music

Borders Books Music & Café Yes, it's a chain, but it also is the number one source for Hawaiian music on Maui. Terrific selection, plus earphones for hearing the CDs before you buy. Maui Market Place, 270 Dairy Rd., Kahului. ✆ **808/877-6160.**

Shoes

Sandal Tree It's unusual for a resort shop to draw local customers on a regular basis, but the Sandal Tree attracts a flock of footwear fanatics who come here from throughout the islands for rubber thongs (aka "slippahs") and Top-Siders, sandals and dressy pumps, athletic shoes and hats, designer footwear, and much more. Prices are realistic, too. Also in Grand Wailea Resort, 3850 Wailea Alanui Dr., Wailea; and in the Hyatt Regency Maui, 200 Nohea Kai Dr., Kaanapali. Whalers Village, 2435 Kaanapali Pkwy., Kaanapali. ✆ **808/667-5330.**

Sports Stuff

Sports Authority Here you'll find Maui's largest selection of sporting goods and sportswear, for sports ranging from baseball to yoga. Maui Market Place, 270 Dairy Rd., Kahului. ✆ **808/871-2558.**

Sweets for the Sweet

Broke da Mouth Cookies Looking for the ultimate taste treat? These are not just any cookies, but mouthwatering, delicious, terrific cookies (less than $3 a bag) that range from chocolate mac-nut, oatmeal raisin, and shortbread to almond, peanut butter, and coconut crunch. While you are here, take a look at the other goodies (a chocolate-haupia pie to die for and a lilikoi cake that will make your taste buds stand up and applaud). ***Warning:*** These cookies are so good, you may eat half of your take-home gifts before you get home. 190 Alamaha St., Kahului. ✆ **808/873-9255.**

T. Komoda Store and Bakery For 6 decades, Komoda's has been "the place" for famous cream puffs. Old-timers know to come early, or they'll be sold out. Then the cinnamon rolls, doughnuts, pies, and chocolate cake take over. Pastries are just the beginning; poi, macadamia nut candies and cookies, and small bunches of local fruit keep the customers coming. 3674 Baldwin Ave., Makawao. ✆ **808/572-7261.**

Toys

KayBee Toys If (horrors!) you left your child's favorite toy or game at home and are in desperate need of replacing the "latest" whiz-bang, this is the place to go with everything from infant toys to electronic games. Queen Kaahumanu Center, 275 Kaahumanu Ave., Kahului. ✆ **808/871-0988.**

Maui Toy Works Here's a store designed for kids—your little ones could stay here for hours. The terrific collection has something for everyone on your list from Hawaiian dolls to stuffed animals, collectible cards, even an assortment of water toys. Lahaina Cannery Mall, 1221 Honoapiilani Hwy., Lahaina. ✆ **808/661-4766.**

9 ENTERTAINMENT FOR THE WHOLE FAMILY

THE BIG VENUES

The island's most prestigious entertainment venue is the $28-million **Maui Arts & Cultural Center** in Kahului (✆ **808/242-7469;** www.mauiarts.org). The center is as precious to Maui as the Met is to New York, with a visual-arts gallery, an outdoor amphitheater, offices, rehearsal space, a 300-seat theater for experimental performances, and a 1,200-seat main theater. Whether it's hula, Pearl Jam, Willie Nelson, *The Nutcracker,* or the Maui Symphony Orchestra, only the best appear here. The center's activities are well publicized locally, so check the center's website or *Maui News* or ask your hotel concierge what's going on during your visit. Half-price tickets are available for children ages 12 and younger.

THEATER

The buzz in Lahaina is **Ulalena ★**, Maui Myth and Magic Theatre, 878 Front St. (✆ **877/688-4800** or 808/661-9913; www.ulalena.com), a riveting evening of entertainment that everyone from preschoolers to your hard-to-please teenagers will enjoy. The multimedia show weaves Hawaiian mythology with drama, dance, and state-of-the-art multimedia capabilities in a multimillion-dollar theater. Polynesian dance, original music, acrobatics, and chant, performed by a local and international cast, combine to create an evocative experience that often leaves the audience speechless. Some special moments: the goddesses dancing on the moon, the white sail of the first Europeans, the wrath of the volcano goddess Pele, the labors of the field-worker immigrants. The story unfolds seamlessly; at the end, you'll be shocked to realize that not a single word of dialogue was spoken. Performances are Monday through Friday at 6:30pm. Tickets are $60 to $100 for adults and $40 to $70 for children 12 and under.

A very different type of live entertainment is **Warren & Annabelle's,** 900 Front St., Lahaina (✆ **808/667-6244;** www.warrenandannabelles.com), a magic/comedy cocktail show with illusionist Warren Gibson and "Annabelle," a ghost from the 1800s who plays the grand piano (even taking requests from the audience) as Warren dazzles you with his sleight-of-hand magic. Appetizers, desserts, and cocktails are available (either as a package or a la carte). Check-in is 5 and 7:30pm. Show-only price is $56; show with gourmet appetizers and dessert is $95. You must be 21 years old to attend.

A Night to Remember: Luau, Maui Style

Most of the larger hotels in Maui's major resorts offer luau on a regular basis. You'll pay about $85 to $96 to attend one. To protect yourself from disappointment, don't expect it to be a homegrown affair prepared in the traditional Hawaiian way. There are, however, commercial luau that capture the romance and spirit of the luau with quality food and entertainment in outdoor settings.

Maui's best luau is indisputably the nightly **Old Lahaina Luau** ★★★ (✆ **800/248-5828** or 808/667-1998; www.oldlahainaluau.com). Located just oceanside of the Lahaina Cannery, the Old Lahaina Luau maintains its high standards in food and entertainment, in an oceanfront setting that is peerless. Here's something the entire family from the youngest to the oldest can enjoy together. Local craftspeople display their wares only a few feet from the ocean. Seating is provided on lauhala mats for those who wish to dine as the traditional Hawaiians did, but there are tables for everyone else. This luau offers a healthy balance of entertainment, showmanship, authentic high-quality food, educational value, and sheer romantic beauty. (No watered-down mai tais, either; these are the real thing.)

The luau begins at sunset and features Tahitian and Hawaiian entertainment, including ancient hula, hula from the missionary era, modern hula, and an intelligent narrative on the dance's rocky course of survival into modern times. The food, which is served from an open-air thatched structure, is as much Pacific Rim as authentically Hawaiian: imu-roasted kalua pig, baked mahimahi in Maui onion cream sauce, guava chicken, teriyaki sirloin steak, lomi salmon, poi, dried fish, poke, Hawaiian sweet potato, sautéed vegetables, seafood salad, and the ultimate taste treat, taro leaves with coconut milk. The cost is $96 for adults, $65 for children 12 and younger, plus tax.

The **Kaanapali Beach Hotel** (p. 240) has a wonderful show called ***Kupanaha*** that is perfect for the entire family. It features the renowned magicians Jody and Kathleen Baran and their entire family, including child prodigy magicians Katrina and Crystal. The dinner show features magic, illusions, and the story of the Hawaii fire goddess, Pele, presented through hula and chant performed by the children of the Kano'eau Dance Academy. The shows are Tuesday through Saturday; tickets are $89 to $99 for adults, $57 for teens (ages 13–20), and $41 for children ages 6 to 12 (free for children 5 and under). Included in the ticket price is dinner (entree choices include Island fish, roasted stuffed chicken, steak and shrimp, or a vegetarian dish, with a children's menu available). For reservations and tickets, call ✆ **808/661-0011** or visit www.kbhmaui.com

Maui does have live community theater, at the **Historic Iao Theater,** 68 N. Market St. in Wailuku (✆ **808/244-8680** or 808/242-6969; www.mauionstage.com). The performances range from locally written productions and well-known plays to musicals to community events.

MOVIES

If your kids are clamoring for a movie, check the local newspapers to see what's playing at the other theaters around the island (or go to www.mauigateway.com/~rw/movie). Major cinemas include **Maui Mall,** 70 E. Kaahumanu Ave., Kahului (✆ 808/249-2222); **Kaahumanu Theatres,** in the Kaahumanu Center in Kahului (✆ 808/873-3133); **Kukui Mall Theatre,** 1819 S. Kihei Rd., Kihei (✆ 808/875-4533); **Wallace Theatres** (✆ 808/249-2222), in Lahaina at the **Wharf Cinema Center,** 658 Front St.; and **Front Street Theatres** at the Lahaina Center, 900 Front St., (✆ 808/661-5009).

The **Maui Film Festival** presents "Academy House" films for the movie buffs on Wednesday nights at the **Maui Art and Cultural Center,** 1 Cameron Way (just off Kahului Beach Rd.), Kahului (✆ **808/572-3456;** www.mauifilmfestival.com), usually followed by live music and poetry readings. In the summer, around Father's Day weekend in June, the Maui Film Festival also puts on nights of cinema under the stars in Wailea.

STORY HOURS

Maui's public libraries frequently have wonderful free programs for children. The **Kihei Public Library,** 35 Waimahaihai St. (✆ **808/875-6833**), has a Toddler's Story time on Thursday at 10:30am, featuring simple stories, songs, movement, and crafts for 2- and 3-year-olds. On Friday at 10:30am, the Kihei Library has a Preschool Story Time (ages 3–5); and on the last Tuesday of each month, also at the Kihei Library, at 7pm, is a Pajama Story Time (ages 2–8), where your kids can come in their PJs and fuzzy slippers, and holding their favorite stuffed animal to enjoy the storytelling. Also check out the **Lahaina Public Library,** 680 Wharf St. (✆ **808/662-3950**); the **Makawao Library,** 1159 Makawao Ave. (✆ **808/573-8785**); and the **Wailuku Library,** 251 High St. (✆ **808/243-5766**).

Borders Books & Music, in the Maui Marketplace at 270 Dairy Rd., Kahului (✆ 808/877-6160), also features storytelling and songs for kids; call for the latest schedule of events.

ARCADES

The Fun Factory, in the Kaahumanu Center in Kahului (✆ **808/877-5096**), has been expanded to 5,000 square feet of entertainment for kids of all ages. They'll play the video games, ride the kiddie cars, and join in the dozens of other activities here until they drop.

HAWAIIAN MUSIC

HAWAIIAN MUSIC The best of Hawaiian music can be heard every Wednesday night at the indoor amphitheater at the Napili Kai Beach Resort with the **"Masters of Hawaiian Slack Key Guitar Series"** (✆ **888/669-3858;** www.slackkey.com/masters.htm). The weekly shows present a side of Hawaii that few visitors ever get to see. Host George Kahumoku, Jr., introduces a new slack-key master every week. Not only is there incredible Hawaiian music and singing, but George and his guest also "talk story" about old Hawaii, music, and Hawaiian culture. Not to be missed.

HAWAIIAN HULA

Free hula shows are every Saturday and Sunday from 1 to 2pm at the **Maui Mall** in Kahului; every Wednesday 2:30pm and again on Friday at 3:30pm at the **Lahaina Center;** every Saturday and Sunday at 1pm and again every Tuesday and Thursday at 7pm at the **Lahaina Cannery Mall;** every Monday, Wednesday, and Saturday, 6:30 to 8pm at the **Whalers Village** in Kaanapali; and every night at the **Kaanapali Beach Hotel** from 6:30 to 7:30pm.

7

Molokai

Born of volcanic eruptions 1.5 million years ago, Molokai remains a time capsule on the dawn of the 21st century. It has no deluxe resorts, no stoplights, and no buildings taller than a coconut tree. Molokai is the least developed, most "Hawaiian" of all the islands, making it especially attractive to families looking to experience an older, slower Hawaii.

Those looking for swank accommodations, gourmet restaurants, and ready-made activities may not enjoy this island. At first brush, Molokai may seem too rural, too remote, too basic—but therein lies the "magic" of this island. If you want a unique vacation, with quiet time enjoying the gifts of Mother Nature, making an effort to get to know the residents who still live close to the earth, and letting the island reveal its secrets, then you will have a family trip that not only will linger in your memory, but quite possibly could change your life.

1 ORIENTATION

ARRIVING

BY PLANE Molokai has two airports, but you'll most likely fly into **Hoolehua Airport,** which everyone calls "the Molokai Airport." It's on a dusty plain about 6 miles from Kaunakakai town. Commuter airlines Pacific Wings started operating a discount airline, **PW Express** (✆ **888/866-5022** or 808/873-0877; www.pacificwings.com/pwexpress), with eight daily direct flights between Molokai and Honolulu, and three daily flights between Kahului, Maui, and Molokai. Another inexpensive air carrier is **go!** airlines (✆ **888/IFLYGO2** [435-9462]**;** www.iflygo.com), in conjunction with Mokulele Airlines, which provides services from Kona, Kahului, and Honolulu to Molokai under the name **go!Express.** Currently, go!Express offers the best rates and deals among Hawaii's airline carriers. Generally, go!Express and PW Express are substantially cheaper than **Island Air** (✆ **800/323-3345** from the mainland, or 800/652-6541 interisland; www.islandair.com), which has 8 to 10 direct flights a day from Honolulu. **George's Aviation** (✆ **866/834-2120,** 808/834-2120 from Honolulu, or 808/893-2120 from Maui; www.georgesaviation.com) has commuter flights on Monday, Friday, and Sunday from Honolulu and Maui to Molokai.

BY BOAT You can travel across the seas by ferry from Maui's Lahaina Harbor to Molokai's Kaunakakai Wharf on the ***Molokai Princess*** (✆ **800/275-6969** or 808/667-6165; www.mauiprincess.com). The 100-foot yacht, certified for 149 passengers, is fitted with the latest generation of gyroscopic stabilizers, making the ride smoother. The ferry makes the 90-minute journey from Lahaina to Kaunakakai daily; the round-trip cost is $85 adults and $43 children ages 3 to 12. Or you can choose to tour the island from two different package options: Cruise-Drive, which includes round-trip passage and a rental car for $191 for the driver, $76 per additional adult passenger, and $38 for children; or

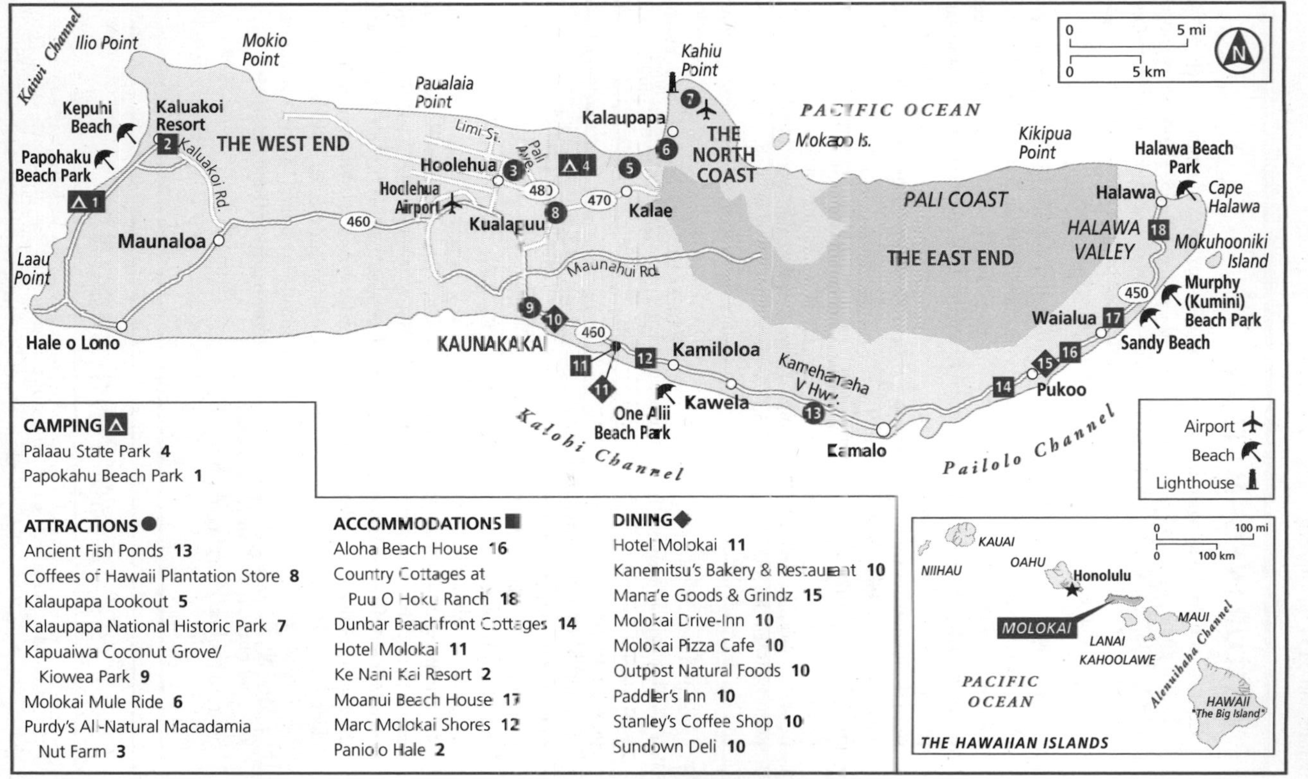

CAMPING
Palaau State Park 4
Papokahu Beach Park 1

ATTRACTIONS
Ancient Fish Ponds 13
Coffees of Hawaii Plantation Store 8
Kalaupapa Lookout 5
Kalaupapa National Historic Park 7
Kapuaiwa Coconut Grove/ Kiowea Park 9
Molokai Mule Ride 6
Purdy's All-Natural Macadamia Nut Farm 3

ACCOMMODATIONS
Aloha Beach House 16
Country Cottages at Puu O Hoku Ranch 18
Dunbar Beachfront Cottages 14
Hotel Molokai 11
Ke Nani Kai Resort 2
Moanui Beach House 17
Marc Molokai Shores 12
Paniolo Hale 2

DINING
Hotel Molokai 11
Kanemitsu's Bakery & Restaurant 10
Mana'e Goods & Grindz 15
Molokai Drive-Inn 10
Molokai Pizza Cafe 10
Outpost Natural Foods 10
Paddler's Inn 10
Stanley's Coffee Shop 10
Sundown Deli 10

 the Alii Tour, which is a guided tour in an air-conditioned van plus lunch for $191 for adults and $134 for children.

VISITOR INFORMATION

Contact the **Molokai Visitors Association,** P.O. Box 960, Kaunakakai, HI 96748 (✆ **800/800-6367** from the U.S. mainland and Canada, 800/553-0404 interisland, or 808/553-3876; www.molokai-hawaii.com), or stop by their office in The Moore Center, 2 Kamoi St., Suite 200, Kaunakakai. The staff can give you all the information you need on what to see and do while you're on Molokai.

KAUNAKAKAI ★

Once an ancient canoe landing, Kaunakakai was the royal summer residence of King Kamehameha V. The port town bustled when pineapple and sugar were king, but those days, too, are gone. With its Old West–style storefronts laid out in a 3-block grid on a flat, dusty plain, Kaunakakai is a town from the past. It also is the dividing point between the lush, green East End and the dry, arid West End.

THE NORTH COAST ★★

Upland from Kaunakakai, the land tilts skyward and turns green, with scented plumeria in yards and glossy coffee trees all in a row, until it blooms into a true forest—and then abruptly ends at a great precipice, falling 3,250 feet to the sea. The north coast is a remote, forbidding place, with a solitary peninsula—**Kalaupapa** ★★★—once the home of exiled lepers. (It's now a National Historical Park.) Unfortunately, entry to the area is restricted to children 16 and older.

THE WEST END ★

This end of the island, which was once home to **Molokai Ranch** (which closed in 2008), is miles of stark desert terrain, bordered by the most beautiful white-sand beaches in Hawaii. The rugged rolling land slopes down to Molokai's only destination resort, **Kaluakoi,** a cul-de-sac of condos clustered around a 3-decades-old seafront hotel (which closed in 2001) near 3-mile-long Papohaku, the island's biggest beach. On the way to Kaluakoi, you'll find **Maunaloa,** a 1920s-era pineapple-plantation town once slated to become a master-planned community; but after the Molokai Ranch and Molokai Lodge closed, Maunaloa turned into a ghost town. The West End is dry, dry, dry. It hardly ever rains, but when it does (usually in winter), expect a downpour and lots of red mud.

THE EAST END ★★★

The area east of Kaunakakai becomes lush, green, and tropical, with golden pocket beaches and a handful of cottages and condos that are popular with thrifty travelers. With this voluptuous landscape comes rain. However, most storms are brief (15-min.) affairs that blow in, dry up, and disappear.

2 GETTING AROUND

Getting around Molokai isn't easy if you don't have a rental car, and rental cars are often hard to find here. On holiday weekends—and remember, Hawaii celebrates different holidays than the rest of the United States (see "When to Go," in chapter 2)—car rental agencies simply run out of cars. Book before you go. There's no municipal transit or shuttle service, but a 24-hour taxi service is available. (See below.)

CAR RENTAL AGENCIES Rental cars are available from **Budget** (✆ **808/567-6877**) and **Dollar** (✆ **808/567-6156**); both agencies are located at the Molokai Airport.

TAXI & TOUR SERVICES **Molokai Off-Road Tours & Taxi** (✆ **808/553-3369;** www.molokai.com/offroad) offers regular taxi service and an airport shuttle ($29 for 1–3 people one-way to Kaunakakai).

Fast Facts Molokai

American Express There are no American Express offices on Molokai.

Babysitters Call **PATCH** (✆ **808/839-1988**), or your hotel can refer you to qualified babysitters.

Dentists If you need one, call **Dr. Chris Chow** in Kaunakakai (✆ **808/553-3602**).

Doctors & Hospitals **Molokai General Hospital** is in Kaunakakai (✆ **808/553-5331**).

Drugstores Molokai is such a rural community that there are no 24-hour pharmacies, but **Molokai Drugs** in Kaunakakai (✆ **808/553-5790**) is open Monday through Saturday.

Emergencies Call ✆ **911.** For nonemergencies, call the **police** at ✆ **808/553-5355** and the **fire department** at ✆ **808/553-5601.**

Internet Access The public libraries offer Internet access to the public; your other best bet is your hotel.

Libraries The library is in Kaunakakai (✆ **808/553-1765**). It's open Monday and Wednesday from noon to 8pm; and Tuesday, Thursday, and Friday from 9am to 5pm.

Post Office The post office is in downtown Kaunakakai (✆ **808/553-5845**).

Radio There are no local radio stations on Molokai, but you can pick up signals from Maui and Honolulu.

Restrooms Fast-food restaurants and beach parks are your best bets for restrooms. The ones at fast-food joints are likely to be cleaner than those at the beach, however.

Safety Molokai is generally a safe tourist destination; but visitors have been crime victims, so stay alert and use common sense. The most common crime against travelers is rental-car break-ins. Never leave any valuables in your car, not even in your trunk.

3 FAMILY-FRIENDLY ACCOMMODATIONS

Molokai is Hawaii's most affordable island, especially for hotels. And because the island's restaurants are few, most hotel rooms and condo units come with kitchens, which can save you a bundle on dining costs.

Tips More Than an Outfitter

You don't have schlep your car seat, jogging stroller, regular stroller, or portable crib to Molokai. **Molokai Outdoors Activities,** in the lobby of Hotel Molokai, just outside Kaunakakai (✆ **877/553-4477** or 808/553-4477; www.molokai-outdoors.com), has all that paraphernalia for rent at very reasonable daily and weekly rates.

There aren't a ton of accommodations options on Molokai—mostly B&Bs, condos, a few quaint oceanfront vacation rentals, an aging resort, and a very expensive lodge. For camping on Molokai, you have two options: the upscale tentalows offered by Molokai Ranch Beach Village or, for hardy souls, camping with your own tent at the beach or in the cool upland forest. (See "Camping," later in this chapter.) I've listed my top picks below; for additional options, contact **Molokai Visitors Association** (✆ **800/800-6367** from the U.S. mainland and Canada, or 808/553-3876; www.molokai-hawaii.com).

Note: Taxes of 11.42% will be added to your hotel bill. Parking is free.

KAUNAKAKAI

Hotel Molokai ★ Kids Since the 2008 closing of the Lodge at Molokai Ranch, this nostalgic Hawaiian motel-like complex has been the only hotel on the island. The modest hotel is composed of a series of modified A-frame units, nestled under coco palms along a gray-sand beach that has a great view of Lanai but isn't good for swimming. In 2006 the entire hotel underwent a $1-million renovation, from repaving the parking lot to redoing the kitchen. The interiors of all the rooms have been upgraded and look clean and new. This is a modest budget hotel—the rooms have all the necessities but aren't fancy. Be sure to ask for a room with a ceiling fan; most rooms have a lanai. The mattresses are on the soft side, the sheets thin, and the bath towels rough, but you're on Molokai. The kitchenettes have coffeemakers, toasters, pots, and a two-burner stove. The front desk is open only from 7am to 8pm; late check-ins or visitors with problems have to go to security.

Kamehameha V Hwy. (P.O. Box 1020), Kaunakakai, HI 96748. ✆ **808/553-5347.** Fax 800/477-2329. www.hotelmolokai.com. 45 units. $159–$219; $229 with kitchen; from $249 double suite. Children 17 and under stay free in parent's room. Cribs and rollaway beds $20 each. AE, DC, DISC, MC, V. **Amenities:** Fairly good, reasonably priced restaurant w/bar; outdoor pool; watersports equipment/rentals; bike rentals; activities desk; babysitting; coin-op laundry. *In room:* A/C, TV, dataport, kitchenette in some units, fridge, coffeemaker, hair dryer, iron, safe.

Marc Molokai Shores These condos are perfect for families—the units are basic but spacious, with kitchens and large lanais. The quiet complex of three-story Polynesian-style buildings faces a small gold-sand beach and is less than a mile from Kaunakakai. Alas, the beach is mostly for show (offshore, it's shallow mud flats underfoot); but your kids can jump in the swimming pool, and the barbecue area comes with an ocean view. The central location can be a plus, minimizing driving time from the airport or town, and it's convenient to the mule ride, as well as the lush East End countryside. There's no daily maid service. Check the website for Internet-only discounts.

Kamehameha V Hwy. (P.O. Box 1037), Kaunakakai, HI 96748. ✆ **800/535-0085** or 808/553-5954. Fax 808/553-5954. www.marcresorts.com. 102 units. $190–$210 1-bedroom apt (sleeps up to 4); $250 2-bedroom apt (up to 6). Children 17 and under stay free in parent's room. Cribs and rollaway beds $17 each.

Discounted rates for weekly and extended stays, plus corporate, military, and senior discounts. AE, DC, MC, V. **Amenities:** Putting green; salon; coin-op laundry. *In room:* TV, kitchen, fridge, coffeemaker, iron.

THE WEST END

Ke Nani Kai Resort ★ The large apartments are set up for families to spread out, with real kitchens, washer/dryers, VCRs, attractive furnishings, and breezy lanais. There's a huge pool, a volleyball court, tennis courts, and golf on the neighboring Kaluakoi course. These condos are farther from the sea than other local accommodations but are still just a brief walk from the beach. The two-story buildings are surrounded by parking and garden areas. The only downside: Maid service is every third day.

In the Kaluakoi Resort development, Kaluakoi Rd., off Hwy. 460 (P.O. Box 289), Maunaloa, HI 96770. ✆ **800/535-0085** or 808/552-2761. Fax 808/552-0045. www.kenanikai.com. 100 units. $95–$125 1-bedroom apt (sleeps up to 4); $120–$165 2-bedroom apt (up to 6). 3-night minimum. Children 17 and under stay free in parent's room. Cribs and rollaway beds $17. AE, DISC, DC, MC, V. **Amenities:** Outdoor pool; golf course; 2 tennis courts; Jacuzzi. *In room:* TV, kitchen, fridge, coffeemaker.

Paniolo Hale ★ (Finds) Tucked into a verdant garden on the dry West End, this condo complex has the advantage of being next door to a white-sand beach and a golf course. The two-story, Old Hawaii ranch-house design is airy and homey, with oak floors and walls of folding-glass doors that open to huge screened verandas, doubling your living space. The one- and two-bedrooms come with two bathrooms and will easily accommodate a big family with three or four children running around. Some units have hot tubs on the lanai. All are spacious, comfortably furnished, and well equipped, with full kitchens and washer/dryers.

Next door to Kaluakoi Resort, Lio Place, Kaulakoi, HI 96770. Reservations: Molokai Vacation Rentals, P.O. Box 1979, Kaunakakai, HI 96748. ✆ **808/553-8334.** Fax 808/553-3783. www.molokai-vacation-rental.com. 77 units. $105–$145 double studio; $130–$195 1-bedroom apt (sleeps up to 4); $225–$275 2-bedroom apt (up to 6). 3-night minimum; 1-week minimum Dec 20–Jan 5. Cribs $5. AE, MC, V. **Amenities:** Outdoor pool; nearby golf course. *In room:* TV, kitchen, fridge, coffeemaker, washer/dryers.

THE EAST END

Aloha Beach House ★★ (Finds) This is a great place to stay on Molokai. Nestled in the lush East End, this Hawaiian-style beach house sits right on the white-sand beach of Waialua. Perfect for families, the impeccably decorated, two-bedroom, 1,600-square-foot beach house has a huge open living/dining/kitchen area that opens onto an old-fashioned porch for meals or for sitting in the comfy chairs and watching the clouds roll by. It's fully equipped, from the complete kitchen (including a dishwasher) to a VCR (plus a library of videos) to all the beach toys you can think of. It's conveniently located close to the **Mana'e Goods and Grindz** (p. 312) in case you need to pick up something or feel like eating out.

Located just after MM 19. Reservations: c/o The Rietows, P.O. Box 79, Kilauea, HI 96754. ✆ **888/828-1008** or 808/828-1100. Fax 808/828-2199. www.molokaivacation.com. 1 house. $290 2-bedroom double plus $175–$225 cleaning fee. Extra person $20. 3-night minimum. No credit cards. *In room:* TV, Wi-Fi, kitchen, fridge, coffeemaker.

Country Cottage at Pu'u O Hoku Ranch ★ Escape to a working cattle ranch! *Pu'u O Hoku* ("Star Hill") Ranch, which spreads across 14,000 acres of pasture and forests, is the last place to stay before Halawa Valley—it's at least an hour's drive from Kaunakakai along the shoreline. Two acres of tropically landscaped property circle the ranch's rustic cottage, which boasts breathtaking views of rolling hills and the Pacific Ocean. The wooden cottage features comfortable country furniture, a full kitchen, two bedrooms (one with a double bed, one with two twin beds), two bathrooms, and a separate dining room on the enclosed lanai. TVs and VCRs are available on request. I recommend stargazing at night, watching the sunrise in the morning, and hiking, swimming, or a game of croquet in the afternoon. For larger groups, there's a four-bedroom, three-bathroom house (sleeps up to eight) on the property. Horseback riding is available at the ranch; see p. 321 for details.

Kamehameha V Hwy., at MM 25. Reservations: P.O. Box 1889, Kaunakakai, HI 96748. ✆ **808/558-8109.** Fax 808/558-8100. www.puuohoku.com. 2 units. $160 double. 2-night minimum. Extra person $20. No credit cards. **Amenities:** Pool. *In room:* TV/DVD/VCR, kitchen, fridge, coffeemaker.

Dunbar Beachfront Cottages ★★ This is one of the most peaceful, comfortable, and elegant properties on Molokai's East End, and the setting is simply stunning. Each of these two green-and-white plantation-style cottages sits on its own secluded beach (good for swimming)—you'll feel like you're on your own private island. The Puunana Cottage has a king bed and two twin beds, while the Pauwalu has a queen bed and two twin beds. Each has a full kitchen, VCR, ceiling fans, comfortable tropical furniture, a large furnished deck (perfect for whale-watching in winter), and views of Maui, Lanai, and Kahoolawe across the channel.

Kamehameha V Hwy., past mile marker 18. Reservations: c/o Matt and Genesis Dunbar, HC01, Box 738, Kaunakakai, HI 96748. ✆ **800/673-0520** or 808/558-8153. www.molokai-beachfront-cottages.com. 2 units. $170 cottage (sleeps up to 4), plus 1-time $75 cleaning charge. 3-night minimum. No credit cards. *In room:* TV, kitchen, fridge, coffeemaker, washer/dryer.

Moanui Beach House ★ If you're looking for a quiet, remote beach house, this is it. The genial Fosters, who have lived in the islands for many years, run this two-bedroom beach house, right across the street from a secluded white-sand cove beach. The A-frame has a shaded lanai facing the ocean, a screened-in lanai on the side of the house, a full kitchen, and an ocean view that's worth the price alone. The Fosters leave a "starter supply" of breakfast foods for guests (fruit basket, home-baked bread, tropical fruit juices, tea, and coffee).

Kamehameha V Hwy., at MM 20. Reservations: c/o Glenn and Akiko Foster, HC01, Box 300, Kaunakakai, HI 96748. ✆/fax **808/558-8236.** 1 unit. $150 2-bedroom double. 3-night minimum. Extra person $30. No credit cards. *In room:* TV, kitchen, fridge, coffeemaker, hair dryer, iron, washer/dryer.

4 FAMILY-FRIENDLY DINING

Molokai is strong on adventure, the outdoors, and the get-away-from-it-all feeling. No traffic lights and honking horns here, nor long lines at overbooked, self-important restaurants. But when it comes to dining, Molokai is not nirvana. Even with the first upscale hotel and dining room open in Maunaloa, Molokai's culinary offerings are spare. They are dominated by mom-and-pop eateries, nothing fancy, most of them fast-food or take-out places and many of them with a home-cooked touch.

Molokai's restaurants are inexpensive or moderately priced, and several of them do not accept credit cards. Regardless of where you eat, you certainly won't have to dress up. Nearly all of them welcome families (kids are well loved on Molokai) and are willing to go out of their way to make sure your finicky eaters are happy. In most cases, we've listed just the town rather than the street address because, as you'll see, street addresses are as meaningless on this island as fancy cars and sequins. Reservations are not accepted unless otherwise noted.

You'll find the restaurants reviewed below on the "Molokai" map on p. 305.

KAUNAKAKAI

Hotel Molokai ★ AMERICAN/ISLAND On the ocean, with a view of Lanai, torches flickering under palm trees, and tiny fairy lights lining the room and the neighboring pool area, the Hotel Molokai's dining room evokes the romance of a South Seas fantasy. It's a casual room and provides the only nightlife in Kaunakakai (see "Entertainment for the Whole Family," later in this chapter) and the most pleasing ambience on the island. Kids will gobble down the chocolate chip pancakes at breakfast and the giant burgers at lunch, and you'll love the easy-on-the-wallet prices. As the sun sets and the torches are lit for dinner, the menu turns to heavier meats, ribs, fish, and pasta. Try the fresh catch, Korean kalbi ribs, barbecued pork ribs, New York steak, coconut shrimp, or garlic chicken. Temper your expectations of culinary excellence, and you're sure to enjoy a pleasing dinner in an atmosphere that's unequaled on the island.

On Kamehameha V Hwy. ✆ **808/553-5347.** Kids' menu, highchairs, boosters. Reservations recommended for dinner. Main courses $8–$15 lunch, $15–$25 dinner; kids' menu $9–$12. AE, MC, V. Daily 7am–2pm and 6–9pm; bar until 10:30pm.

Molokai Drive-Inn AMERICAN/TAKEOUT It is a greasy spoon, but it's one of the rare drive-up places with fresh *akule* (mackerel), ahi (when available), and fried saimin, at budget-friendly prices. The honey-dipped fried chicken is a favorite among residents who also come here for the floats, shakes, and other artery-clogging choices. There's no kids' menu, but they'll love the burgers and the chicken. Don't expect much in terms of ambience: This is a fast-food takeout counter that smells like fried food—and it doesn't pretend to be otherwise.

Kaunakakai. ✆ **808/553-5655.** Most items less than $8–$9.25. No credit cards. Mon–Thurs 6am–9pm; Fri–Sun 6:30am–10:30pm.

Molokai Pizza Cafe ★ PIZZA It's been *the* in-spot for local families since it opened, with excellent pizzas and sandwiches that have made it a Kaunakakai regular as well as one of my favorite eateries on the island. Pasta, sandwiches, and specials round out the menu. (Next to pizza, chicken nuggets are the biggest hit among the younger-than-12 set.) Kids are not only welcome but catered to with coin-operated cars and a toy airplane, and adults should feel equally at home with the very popular barbecued baby back ribs plate and the fresh fish dinners. Children's art and letters in the tiled dining room add an entertaining and charming touch. Free delivery to Hotel Molokai is a welcome addition.

In Kahua Center, on the old Wharf Rd. ✆ **808/553-3288.** Kids' menu, highchairs, boosters, crayons. Large pizzas $18–$23; kids' menu $7. No credit cards. Sun 11am–10pm; Mon–Thurs 10am–10pm; Fri–Sat 10am–11pm.

Outpost Natural Foods ★ VEGETARIAN The healthiest and freshest food on the island is served at the lunch counter of this health food store, around the corner from the main drag on the ocean side of Kaunakakai town. The tiny store abounds in Molokai papayas, bananas, herbs, potatoes, watermelon, and other local produce, complementing its selection of vitamins, cosmetics, and health aids, as well as bulk and shelf items. But the real star is the closet-size lunch counter. The salads, burritos, tempeh sandwiches, vegetarian potpie, tofu-spinach lasagna, and mock chicken, turkey, and meatloaf (made from oats, sprouts, seeds, and seasonings) are testament to the fact that vegetarian food need not be boring. A must for health-conscious diners and shoppers. No tables—take it out to the beach instead.

70 Makaena Place. ✆ **808/553-3377.** Most items less than $12–$15. AE, DISC, MC, V. Mon–Thurs 9am–6pm; Fri 9am–4pm; Sun 10am–5pm.

Paddlers' Inn AMERICAN/LOCAL This local diner, with everything from burgers to steak, recently added breakfast ($6.75 for homemade sausage gravy and biscuits). If you want to meet local residents, come to this friendly place. Lunch is generally filled with hungry diners grinding on one-third-pound all-beef burgers, big sandwiches, or plate lunches. Vegetarians will find a few items here, but not a lot. Call ahead for dinner specials. Later in the evening, the small cafe becomes a hot spot for Molokai entertainment (see p. 325). Sunday brunch starts at 10:30am.

10 Mohala St. ✆ **808/553-5256.** www.paddlersinnmolokai.com. Highchair. Main courses under $12 breakfast, under $22 lunch, and under $30 dinner. DISC, MC, V. Mon–Fri 6:30am–9pm; Sat 9am–9:30pm; Sun 9am–9pm.

Stanley's Coffee Shop and Gallery COFFEE SHOP Breakfast, coffee, and sandwiches are on tap at this tiny cafe, located across the street from the Triangle Park and next door to St. Sophia Catholic Church. If you need an Internet connection or computer, they can supply that too (at $1 per minute). Upstairs is the small gallery, which also does framing. Lunch has a host of sandwiches (all under $5.25), and the strongest espresso coffee in Kaunakakai.

Ala Malama St. ✆ **808/553-9966.** Highchair. Breakfast under $6; lunch less than $9. MC, V (purchases over $20). Mon–Fri 6:30am–4pm; Sat 6:30am–2pm.

Sundown Deli ★ DELI This popular deli's offerings are home-cooked and healthful, with daily specials that include vegetarian quiche, vegetarian lasagna, and club sandwiches. The sandwiches (such as smoked turkey and chicken salad) and several salads (Caesar, Oriental, stuffed tomato) are served with a soup that changes daily (clam chowder, Portuguese bean, cream of broccoli). Vitamins, T-shirts, and snacks are also sold in this tiny cafe; most of the business here is takeout.

145 Puali St. (across the street from Veterans Memorial Park). ✆ **808/553-3713.** Sandwiches, soups, and salads $3.95–$7.50. AE, MC, V. Mon–Fri 7:30am–3:30pm.

THE EAST END

Mana'e Goods and Grindz ★ AMERICAN Formerly the Neighborhood Store, this place has a new name, but it's still the same quick-stop market/lunch counter. It's nothing fancy, and that's what I love about it. Near mile marker 16 in the Pukoo area en route to the East End, this tiny store appears like a mirage, complete with large parking area and picnic tables. The place serves omelets, Portuguese sausage, and other breakfast specials (brunch is very popular), then segues into sandwiches, salads, mahimahi plates, and varied over-the-counter lunch offerings, served on paper plates with plastic utensils. Favorites include the mahimahi plate lunch, the chicken katsu, and the Mexican plate, each one with a tried-and-true home-cooked flavor. There are daily specials, ethnic dishes, and some vegetarian options, as well as burgers (including a killer veggie burger), saimin, and legendary desserts. Made-on-Maui Roselani ice cream is a featured attraction. A Molokai treasure, this is the only grocery store on the East End (see "Shopping with Your Kids," p. 322).

Pukoo. ✆ **808/558-8498.** Most items less than $10; bento $8.75. Mon–Fri 8am–4pm; Sat–Sun 8am–5pm.

5 EXPLORING MOLOKAI WITH YOUR KIDS

There are a great number of sights that you and your family can enjoy on Molokai, but come prepared—there are no strollers for rent at any of the sights listed below. You'll find the following attractions on the "Molokai" map on p. 305.

Frommer's Favorite Molokai Family Experiences

Flying a Kite (p. 322) Not only can you get a guaranteed-to-fly kite at the **Big Wind Kite Factory** (✆ **808/552-2634**) in Maunaloa, but kite designer Jonathan Socher offers free kite-flying classes to kids, who'll learn how to make their kites soar, swoop, and, most important, stay in the air for more than 5 minutes.

Spending the Day at Murphy (Kumimi) Beach Park (p. 318) Just beyond Wailua on the East End is this small wayside park that's perfect for kids. You'll find safe swimming conditions, plenty of shade from the ironwood trees, and small pavilions with picnic tables and barbecue grills.

IN & AROUND KAUNAKAKAI

Kapuaiwa Coconut Grove/Kiowea Park ★ **All ages.** This royal grove—1,000 coconut trees on 10 acres planted in 1863 by the island's high chief Kapua'iwa (later, King Kamehameha V)—is a major roadside attraction. The shoreline park is a favorite subject of sunset photographers and visitors who delight in a hand-lettered sign that warns: DANGER: FALLING COCONUTS. In its backyard, across the highway, stands Church Row: seven churches, each a different denomination—clear evidence of the missionary impact on Hawaii. This is a great place to stop for a half-hour.

Along Maunaloa Hwy. (Hwy. 460), 2 miles west of Kaunakakai.

Post-A-Nut ★ **All ages.** The postmaster will help you say "Aloha" with a dried Molokai coconut. Just write a message on the coconut with a felt-tip pen, and she'll send it via U.S. mail over the sea. Coconuts are free, but postage is $11 for a mainland-bound, 2-pound coconut. You can post your nuts and be out of there in 10 minutes.

Hoolehua Post Office, Pu'u Peelua Ave. (Hwy. 480), near Maunaloa Hwy. (Hwy. 460). ✆ **808/567-6144.** Mon–Fri 7:30–11:30am and 12:30–4:30pm.

Purdy's All-Natural Macadamia Nut Farm (Na Hua O'Ka Aina) ★ Finds **All ages.** The Purdys have made macadamia nut buying an entertainment event, offering tours of the homestead and giving lively demonstrations of nutshell cracking in the shade of their towering trees. The tour of the 70-year-old nut farm explains the growth, bearing, harvesting, and shelling processes, so by the time you bite into the luxurious macadamia nut, you'll have more than a passing knowledge of its entire life cycle. Allow at least an hour to wander around and get the tour.

Lihi Pali Ave. (behind Molokai High School), Hoolehua. ✆ **808/567-6601.** www.visitmolokai.com. Free admission. Mon–Fri 9:30am–3:30pm; Sat 10am–2pm; closed on holidays.

THE NORTH COAST

Even if you don't get a chance to see Hawaii's most dramatic coast in its entirety—not many people do—you shouldn't miss the opportunity to glimpse it from the **Kalaupapa Lookout** at Palaau State Park. On the way, there are a few diversions (arranged here in geographical order).

Coffees of Hawaii **Ages 5 and up.** The defunct Del Monte pineapple town of Kualapuu is rising again—only this time, coffee is the catch, not pineapple. Located in the cool foothills, Molokai Coffee Company has planted coffee beans on 600 acres of former pineapple land. The plantation is irrigating the plants with a high-tech, continuous water and fertilizer drip system. You can see it all on the self-guided walking tour or the Morning Espresso Tour, which is led by a guide from the plantation and gives you a tour of the sorting facility and processing procedures. The less physically motivated should try the Mule Drawn Wagon tour, great for a family. The 2-hour tour is led by a guide and two mules (Moana and Leila or Lilo and Loke) through the coffee fields and around the reservoir. Afternoon hiking adventures include a 2½-hour hike through the coffee fields to the top of Kualapuu Hill for a terrific view of Molokai. The Plantation Store sells arts and crafts from Molokai. Stop by the Espresso Bar for a Mocha Mama, an intoxicating blend of coffee, ice cream, and chocolate that will keep you going all day—maybe even all night.

1630 Farrington Ave. (near the junction of Hwy. 470), Kualapuu. ✆ **877/322-FARM** (322-3276) or 808/567-9490, ext. 26. www.coffeesofhawaii.com. Mon–Fri 8am–5pm; Sat 8am–4pm; Sun 8am–2pm. Self-guided tour free. Morning Espresso Tour Mon–Fri 10am; $20 adults, $10 children 5–10, free for children 4 and under. Mule Drawn Wagon Tour Mon–Fri 8am and 1pm, Sat–Sun 8am; $35 adults, $10 children 5–10, free for children 4 and under. Afternoon Hiking Adventures daily 3–5:30pm; free.

Molokai Museum and Cultural Center En route to the California Gold Rush in 1849, Rudolph W. Meyer (a German professor) came to Molokai, married the high chieftess Kalama, and began to operate a small sugar plantation near his home. Now on the National Register of Historic Places, this restored 1878 sugar mill, with its century-old steam engine, mule-driven cane crusher, copper clarifiers, and redwood evaporating pan (all in working order) is the last of its kind in Hawaii. The mill also houses a museum that traces the history of sugar growing on Molokai and has special events, such as wine tastings, taro festivals, an annual music festival, and occasional classes in ukulele making, loom weaving, and sewing. Call for a schedule.

Meyer Sugar Mill, Hwy. 470 (just after the turnoff for the Ironwood Hills Golf Course and 2 miles below Kalaupapa Overlook), Kalae. ✆ **808/567-6436.** Admission $2.50 adults, $1 students. Mon–Sat 10am–2pm.

Palaau State Park ★ **All ages.** This 234-acre piney-woods park, 8 miles out of Kaunakakai, doesn't look like much until you get out of the car and take a hike. If your children are younger than 16, they can't actually enter Kalaupapa, so the **Kalaupapa Lookout ★★★** is the only place from which to see the former place of exile. The trail is marked, and historic photos and interpretive signs will explain what you're seeing. You can quickly walk in and out in a half-hour, but allow a couple of hours to wander through the park and gaze at the incredible view of Kalaupapa.

It's airy and cool in the ironwood forest, where camping is free at the designated state campground. You'll need a permit from the **Division of State Parks** (✆ **808/567-6618;** www.hawaiistateparks.org). Not many people seem to camp here, probably because of the legend associated with the **Phallic Rock ★**. Six feet high, Molokai's famous Phallic Rock is a legendary fertility tool that appears to be working today. According to Hawaiian legend, a woman who wishes to become pregnant need only spend the night near the rock and *voilà!* It's probably a coincidence, of course, but Molokai does have a growing number of young pregnant women. Supposedly, the rock belonged to Nanahoa, a demigod who quarreled with his wife, Kawahuna, over a pretty girl. In the tussle, Kawahuna was thrown over the cliff, and both husband and wife were turned to stone.

At the end of Hwy. 470.

The Legacy of Father Damien: Kalaupapa National Historic Park ★★★

An old tongue of lava that sticks out to form a peninsula, Kalaupapa became infamous because of man's inhumanity to victims of a formerly incurable contagious disease. King Kamehameha V sent the first lepers—nine men and three women—into exile on this lonely shore, at the base of ramparts that rise like temples against the Pacific, on January 6, 1866. By 1874, more than 11,000 lepers had been dispatched to die in one of the world's most beautiful—and lonely—places. They called Kalaupapa "The Place of the Living Dead."

Leprosy is actually one of the world's least contagious diseases, transmitted only by direct, repetitive contact over a long period. It's caused by a germ, *Mycobacterium leprae,* that attacks the nerves, skin, and eyes, and is found mainly, but not exclusively, in tropical regions. American scientists found a cure for the disease in the 1940s.

Kalaupapa is now a National Historic Park (✆ **808/567-6802;** www.nps.gov/kala) and one of Hawaii's richest archaeological preserves, with sites that date from A.D. 1000. About 60 former patients chose to remain in the tidy village of whitewashed houses with statues of angels in their yards. The original name for their former affliction, leprosy, was officially banned in Hawaii by the state legislature in 1981. The name used now is "Hansen's disease," for Dr. Gerhard Hansen of Norway, who discovered the germ in 1873. The few remaining residents of Kalaupapa still call the disease leprosy, although none are too keen on being called lepers.

You must be at least 16 years old to venture into Kalaupapa. The best way to see this haunting place is by riding a mule. Contact **Molokai Mule Ride ★★★**, 100 Kalae Hwy., Suite 104, on Highway 470, 5 miles north of Highway 460 (✆ **800/567-7550** or 808/567-6088; www.muleride.com). Advance reservations (at least 2 weeks ahead) are required. Cost is $165 per person.

SEEING KALAUPAPA BY PLANE The fastest and easiest way to get to Kalaupapa is by hopping on a plane and zipping to Kalaupapa airport. From here, you can pick up the same Kalaupapa tour that the mule riders and hikers take. **Molokai Mule Ride** (see above) will pick you up at the Kalaupapa airport and take you to some of the area's most scenic spots, including Kalawao, where Father Damien's church still stands, and the town of Kalaupapa. The package includes round-trip airfare from Honolulu, hotel pickup, guided mule tour, entry permits, Historical Park tour, and a picnic lunch for $319 per person, two-person minimum.

If you are coming from Maui, your choices are either by ferry (where you will hike in and back out in 1 day or take the mule ride, but you will have to overnight due to the ferry's schedule), or by plane (call them and they can help set up a charter plane).

If you are on Molokai and want to fly directly into Kalaupapa, Molokai Mule Ride will book you from the Molokai Airport to Kalaupapa and include entry permits, Historical Park tour with Damien Tours, and a light picnic lunch for $130 per person, two-person minimum.

SEEING KALAUPAPA BY FERRY/HIKING From Maui, take the ***Molokai Princess*** ferry to Molokai (✆ **800/275-6969** or 808/667-6165; www.mauiprincess.com), where you are met and transported by van to the top of the 1,700-foot sea cliffs. Here you hike down the 3-mile trail to the Kalaupapa National Historic Park; at the park, you are met by Damien Tours and given a van tour of the peninsula, during which you'll visit Father Damien's St. Philomena Church, see his early gravesite, and hear the stories of struggle and courage of the residents of Kalaupapa. The only catch is you have to hike back up the 1,700-foot cliffs, where you are picked up by the van and returned to the ferry dock for the trip back to Maui. This fabulous experience really should be undertaken only by the physically fit (it will take about an hour hiking down and another 90 min. to hike back up). Cost for ferry, transportation, tour, and lunch is $277 (participants must be 16 years and older).

THE EAST END

The East End is a cool and inviting green place that's worth a drive to the end of King Kamehameha V Highway (Hwy. 450). Unfortunately, the trail that leads into the area's greatest natural attraction, Halawa Valley, is now off-limits.

En Route to Halawa Valley

No visit to Molokai is complete without at least a passing glance at the island's **ancient fishponds,** a singular achievement in Pacific aquaculture. With their hunger for fresh fish and lack of ice or refrigeration, Hawaiians perfected aquaculture in A.D. 1400, before Christopher Columbus "discovered" America. They built gated, U-shaped stone and coral walls on the shore to catch fish on the incoming tide; they would then raise them in captivity. The result: a constant, ready supply of fresh fish.

The ponds, which stretch for 20 miles along Molokai's south shore and are visible from Kamehameha V Highway (Hwy. 450), offer insight into the island's ancient population. It took close to a thousand people to tend a single fishpond, and more than 60 ponds once existed on this coast. All the fishponds are named; a few are privately owned. Some are silted in by red-dirt runoff from south coast gulches; others have been revived by folks who raise fish and seaweed.

The largest, 54-acre **Keawa Nui Pond,** is surrounded by a 3-foot-high, 2,000-foot-long stone wall. **Alii Fish Pond,** reserved for kings, is visible through the coconut groves at One Alii Beach Park (p. 318). From the road, you can see **Kalokoeli Pond,** 6 miles east of Kaunakakai on the highway.

Our Lady of Sorrows Catholic Church, one of five built by Father Damien on Molokai and the first outside Kalaupapa, sits across the highway from a fishpond. Park in the church lot (except on Sun) for a closer look.

St. Joseph's Catholic Church The afternoon sun strikes St. Joseph's Church with such a bold ray of light that it looks as if God is about to perform a miracle. This little 1876 wood-frame church is one of four Father Damien built "topside" on Molokai. Restored in 1971, the church stands beside a seaside cemetery, where feral cats play under the gaze of a Damien statue amid gravestones decorated with flower leis.

King Kamehameha V Hwy. (Hwy. 450), just after mile marker 10.

Smith Bronte Landing Site In 1927 Charles Lindbergh soloed the Atlantic Ocean in a plane called *The Spirit of St. Louis* and became an American hero. That same year, Ernie Smith and Emory B. Bronte took off from Oakland, California, on July 14, in a single-engine Travelair aircraft named *The City of Oakland,* headed across the Pacific

Moments Halawa Valley: A Hike Back in History

"There are things on Molokai, sacred things, that you may not be able to see or may not hear, but they are there," said Pilipo Solotario, who was born and raised in Halawa Valley, and survived the 1946 tsunami that barreled into the ancient valley. "As Hawaiians, we respect these things."

If people are going to "like Molokai," Solotario feels it is important that they learn about the history and culture that are parts of the secret of appreciating the island, he said.

"I see my role, and I'm 65 years old, as educating people, outsiders on our culture, our history," he said at the beginning of one of his cultural hikes into his family property in Halawa Valley. "To really appreciate Molokai you need to understand and know things so that you are *pono,* you are right with the land and don't disrespect the culture. Then, then you see the real Molokai."

Solotario, and his family, who own the land in the valley, are the only people allowed to hike into Halawa. They lead daily tours, great for the family from ages 8 and older, which begin at the County Park pavilion with a history of the valley, a discussion of Hawaiian culture, and a display of the fruits, trees, and other flora you will be seeing in the valley. As you hike through the valley, Solotario stops to point out historical and cultural aspects, including chanting in Hawaiian before entering a sacred *heiau* (temple). At the falls, after another brief chant, visitors can swim in the brisk waters of the waterfall. The cost of the 4-hour tour is $75. Contact **Molokai Fish & Dive** (✆ **808/553-5926;** www.molokaifishanddive.com). Bring insect repellent, water, a snack, and a swimsuit. Don't forget your camera.

Note that if you venture away from the county park into the valley on your own, you are trespassing and can be prosecuted.

Ocean for Honolulu, 2,397 miles away. The next day, after running out of fuel, they crash-landed upside down in a kiawe thicket on Molokai, but emerged unhurt to become the first civilians to fly to Hawaii from the U.S. mainland. The 25-hour, 2-minute flight landed Smith and Bronte a place in aviation history—and a roadside marker on Molokai.

King Kamehameha V Hwy. (Hwy. 450), at mile marker 11, on the *makai* (ocean) side.

Halawa Valley ★

Of the five great valleys of Molokai, only Halawa, with its two waterfalls, golden beach, sleepy lagoon, great surf, and offshore island, is easily accessible. Unfortunately, the trail through fertile Halawa Valley (which was inhabited for centuries) and on to the 250-foot Moaula Falls has been closed for some time. There is one operator who conducts hikes to the falls; see "Halawa Valley: A Hike Back in History," below.

You can spend a day at the county beach park (described under "Beaches," below), but do not venture into the valley on your own. In a kind of 21st-century *kapu* (ancient law), the private landowners in the valley, worried about slip-and-fall lawsuits, have posted NO TRESPASSING signs on their property.

To get to Halawa Valley, drive north from Kaunakakai on Highway 450 for 30 miles along the coast to the end of the road, which descends into the valley past Jersalema Hou Church. If you'd just like a glimpse of the valley on your way to the beach, there's a scenic overlook along the road: After Pu'u O Hoku Ranch at mile marker 25, the narrow two-lane road widens at a hairpin curve, and you'll find the overlook on your right. It's 2 miles more to the valley floor.

6 BEACHES

With imposing sea cliffs on one side and lazy fishponds on the other, Molokai has little room for beaches along its 106-mile coast. Still, a big gold-sand beach flourishes on the West End, and you'll find tiny pocket beaches on the East End. The emptiness of Molokai's beaches is both a blessing and a curse: The seclusion means no lifeguards at any of the beaches.

See the "Molokai" map on p. 305 for locations of these beaches.

KAUNAKAKAI

One Alii Beach Park

This thin strip of sand, once reserved for the *alii* (chiefs), is the oldest public beach park on Molokai. You'll find One Alii Beach Park (*One* is pronounced *o-nay,* not *won*) by a coconut grove on the outskirts of Kaunakakai. Safe for swimmers of all ages and abilities, it's often crowded with families on weekends, but it can be all yours on weekdays. Facilities include outdoor showers, restrooms, and free parking.

THE WEST END

Papohaku Beach ★★

Nearly 3 miles long and 100 yards wide, gold-sand Papohaku Beach is one of the biggest in Hawaii (17-mile-long Polihale Beach on Kauai is the biggest). It's great for walking, beachcombing, picnics, and year-round sunset watching. The big surf and riptides make swimming risky except in summer, when the waters are calmer. Go early in the day when the tropic sun is less fierce and the winds are calm. The beach is so big that you may never see another soul except at sunset, when a few people gather on the shore in hopes of spotting the elusive green flash, a natural wonder that takes place when the horizon is cloud free. Facilities include outdoor showers, restrooms, picnic grounds, and free parking.

THE EAST END

Sandy Beach ★

Molokai's most popular swimming beach—ideal for families with small kids—is a roadside pocket of gold sand protected by a reef, with a great view of Maui and Lanai. You'll find it off the King Kamehameha V Highway (Hwy. 450) at mile marker 20. There are no facilities—just you, the sun, the sand, and the surf.

Murphy Beach Park (Kumimi Beach Park)

In 1970, the Molokai Jaycees wanted to create a sandy beach park with a good swimming area for the children of the East End. They chose a section known as Kumimi Beach, which was owned by the Pu'u O Hoku Ranch. The beach was a dump, literally. The ranch owner, George Murphy, immediately gave his permission to use the site as a park;

the Jaycees cleaned it up and built three small pavilions, plus picnic tables and barbecue grills. Officially, the park is called the George Murphy Beach Park (shortened to Murphy Beach Park over the years), but some old-timers still call it Kumimi Beach and, just to make things real confusing, some people call it Jaycees Park.

No matter what you call it, this is a small park shaded by ironwood trees that line a white-sand beach. It's generally a very safe swimming area. On calm days, snorkeling and diving are great outside the reef. Fishermen are also frequently spotted here looking for papio and other island fish.

Halawa Beach Park ★

At the foot of scenic Halawa Valley is this beautiful black-sand beach with a palm-fringed lagoon, a wave-lashed island offshore, and a distant view of the West Maui Mountains across the Pailolo Channel. The swimming is safe in the shallows close to shore, but where the waterfall stream meets the sea, the ocean is often murky and unnerving. A winter swell creases the mouth of Halawa Valley on the north side of the bay and attracts a crowd of local surfers. Facilities are minimal; bring your own water and snacks. To get here, take King Kamehameha V Highway (Hwy. 450) east to the end.

7 FOR THE ACTIVE FAMILY

The best place to rent beach toys (snorkels, boogie boards, beach chairs, fishing poles, and more) is **Molokai Rentals and Tours,** Kaunakakai (✆ **800/553-9071** or 808/553-5663; www.molokai-rentals.com). Another good place to check out is **Molokai Fish & Dive,** Kaunakakai (✆ **808/553-5926;** www.molokaifishanddive.com). You can rent snorkeling gear, fishing gear, even ice chests here. This is also a hot spot for fishing news and tips on what's running where.

IN THE WATER

BODYBOARDING & BODYSURFING Molokai has only three beaches that offer ridable waves for bodyboarding and bodysurfing: Papohaku, Kepuhi, and Halawa. Even these beaches are only for experienced bodysurfers, due to the strength of the rip currents and undertows. You can rent boogie boards with fins for just $5 a day or $20 a week at **Molokai Outdoors Activities** (✆ **877/553-4477** or 808/553-4477; www.molokai-outdoors.com).

OCEAN KAYAKING During the summer months, when the waters on the north shore are calm, Molokai offers some of the most spectacular kayaking in Hawaii. You can paddle from remote valley to remote valley, spending a week or more exploring the exotic terrain. However, most of Molokai is for the experienced kayaker only. You must be adept at paddling through open ocean swells and rough waves. **Molokai Outdoors Activities** (✆ **877/553-4477** or 808/553-4477; www.molokai-outdoors.com) has a "downwinder" tour: six miles of Molokai's reef as you paddle downwind ($89, plus $10 for lunch per person). They also rent kayaks; rates start at $26 a day.

SNORKELING When the waters are calm, Molokai offers excellent snorkeling; you'll see a wide range of butterfly fish, tangs, and angelfish. Good snorkeling can be found—when conditions are right—at many of Molokai's beaches. **Molokai Outdoors Activities** (✆ **877/553-4477** or 808/553-4477; www.molokai-outdoors.com) has the best prices

Molokai's Best Snorkel Spots

Most Molokai beaches are too dangerous for snorkeling in winter, when big waves and strong currents are generated by storms that sweep down from Alaska. From mid-September to April, stick to Murphy Beach Park (also known as Kumimi Beach Park) on the East End. In summer, roughly May to mid-September, the Pacific Ocean turns into a flat lake, and the whole west coast of Molokai opens up for snorkeling. Mike Holmes, of Molokai Ranch & Fun Hogs Hawaii, says the best spots are as follows:

Kawaikiunui, Ilio Point, and **Pohaku Moiliili** (West End) These are all special places seldom seen by even those who live on Molokai. You can reach Kawaikiunui and Pohaku Moiliili on foot after a long, hot, dusty ride in a four-wheel-drive vehicle, but it's much easier and quicker to go by sea. See above for places to rent a kayak and get advice. It's about 2 miles as the crow flies from Pohaku Moiliili to Ilio Point.

Kapukahehu (Dixie Maru) Beach (West End) This gold-sand family beach is well protected, and the reef is close and shallow. The name *Dixie Maru* comes from a 1920s Japanese fishing boat stranded off the rocky shore. One of the Molokai Ranch cowboys hung the wrecked boat's nameplate on a gate by Kapukahehu Beach, and the name stuck. To get here, take Kaluakoi Road to the end of the pavement, and then take the footpath 300 feet to the beach.

Murphy (Kumimi) Beach Park ★ (East End) This beach is located between mile markers 20 and 21, off Kamehameha V Highway. The reef here is easily reachable, and the waters are calm year-round.

on snorkel gear rentals ($6 a day for fins, mask, and snorkel or $24 a week). Molokai Outdoors also offers snorkel/kayak tours for $69 per person.

For snorkeling tours on a boat, contact Walter Naki of **Molokai Action Adventures** (© **808/558-8184**), who offers leisurely snorkeling, diving, and swimming trips in his 21-foot Boston whaler for $50 per person for a 4- to 6-hour custom tour.

SURFING Depending on the time of year and the wave conditions, Molokai can offer some great surfing for the beginner, as well as the expert. **Molokai Outdoors Activities** (© **877/553-4477** or 808/553-4477; www.molokai-outdoors.com) not only will know where the waves are, but also rent gear: soft surfboards ($13 a day). Good surfing spots include Kaunakakai Wharf in town, Hale O Lono Beach and Papohaku Beach on the West End, and Halawa Beach on the East End.

ON THE LAND

BICYCLING Molokai is a great place to see by bicycle. The roads are not very busy and there are great places to pull off the road and take a quick dip.

Molokai Bicycle, 80 Mohala St., Kaunakakai (© **808/553-3931;** www.bikehawaii.com/molokaibicycle/), offers bike rentals for $15 a day, or $70 a week, including a complimentary helmet and lock. Owner Phillip Kikukawa is a schoolteacher, so call him in late afternoon when he's in the show.

CAMPING Bring your own camping equipment, as none is available for rent on the island.

One of the best year-round places to camp on Molokai is **Papohaku Beach Park ★**, on the island's West End. This drive-up seaside site makes a great getaway. Facilities include restrooms, drinking water, outdoor showers, barbecue grills, and picnic tables. Groceries and gas are available in Maunaloa, 6 miles away. Kaluakoi Resort is a mile away. Get camping permits by contacting **Maui County Parks Department,** P.O. Box 526, Kaunakakai, HI 96748 (✆ **808/553-3204;** www.co.maui.hi.us/parks/permits/parks permits.htm). Camping is limited to 3 days, but if nobody else has applied, the time limit is waived. The cost is $3 a person per night.

For a change, you can camp in an ironwood forest. At the end of Highway 470 is the 234-acre piney woods known as **Palaau State Park ★★**, home to the Kalaupapa Lookout (the best vantage point for seeing the historic leper colony). Camping is free, but you'll need a permit from the **Division of State Parks** (✆ **808/567-6618;** www.hawaii stateparks.org/camping/maui.cfm). For more on the park, see p. 314.

HIKING Molokai's most awesome hike is the **Pepeopae Trail ★★**, which takes you back a few million years. On the cloud-draped trail (actually a boardwalk across the bog), you'll see mosses, sedges, native violets, knee-high ancient ohia, and lichens that evolved in total isolation over eons. Eerie intermittent mists blowing in and out will give you an idea of this island at its creation.

The narrow boardwalk, built by volunteers, protects the bog and keeps you out of the primal ooze. Don't venture off it; you could damage this fragile environment or get lost. The 3-mile round-trip takes about 90 minutes to hike—but first you have to drive about 20 miles from Kaunakakai, deep into the Molokai Forest Reserve on a four-wheel-drive road. ***Warning:*** Don't try this with a regular rental car. Plan a full day for this outing. Better yet, go on a guided nature hike with the **Nature Conservancy of Hawaii,** which guards this unusual ecosystem. For information, write to the Nature Conservancy at 1116 Smith St., Suite 201, Honolulu, HI 96817. No permit is required for this easy hike. Call ahead (✆ **808/537-4508** or 808/553-5236; www.nature.org) to check on the condition of the ungraded, four-wheel-drive, red-dirt road that leads to the trailhead and to let people know that you'll be up there.

To get here, take Highway 460 west from Kaunakakai for 3½ miles and turn right before the Maunawainui Bridge onto the unmarked Molokai Forest Reserve Road (sorry, there aren't any road signs). The pavement ends at the cemetery; continue on the dirt road. After about 2 to 2½ miles, you'll see a sign telling you that you are now in the Molokai Forest Reserve. At the Waikolu Lookout and picnic area, which is just over 9 miles on the Molokai Forest Reserve Road, sign in at the box near the entrance. Continue on the road for another 5 miles to a fork in the road with the sign PUU KOLEKOLE pointing to the right side of the fork. Do not turn right; instead, continue straight at the fork, which leads to the clearly marked trailhead. The drive will take about 45 minutes.

HORSEBACK RIDING One of the most scenic places to go riding on Molokai is **Pu'u O Hoku Ranch** (✆ **808/558-8109;** www.puuohoku.com), about 25 miles outside Kaunakakai on the East End. Guided trail rides pass through green pasture on one of the largest working ranches on Molokai, then head up into the high mountain forest. Don't forget your camera: There are plenty of scenic views of waterfalls, the Pacific Ocean, and the islands of Maui and Lanai in the distance. Rates are $55 for an hour-long ride, $75 for a 2-hour ride, and $120 for a beach adventure. Riders should be at least 10 years old; family discounts are given (three riders get a 5% discount; five riders, a 10% discount).

8 SHOPPING WITH YOUR KIDS

Molokai is not a shopping mecca. In fact, shopping here consists mainly of getting the basics—food, clothing—though a handful of shops offer some specialty items. Below are my picks.

FOOD

Friendly Market Center Friendly's has an especially good selection of produce and healthy foods—from local poi to blue-corn tortilla chips. Soy milk, organic brown rice, a good selection of pasta sauces, and Kumu Farms macadamia nut pesto (the island's stellar gourmet food) are among the items that surpass standard grocery-store fare. In Kaunakakai. ✆ **808/553-5595.**

Kualapuu Market This market, in its third generation, is a stone's throw from the Coffees of Hawaii store. It's a scaled-down, one-stop shop with wine, food, and necessities—and a surprisingly presentable, albeit small, assortment of produce, from Molokai sweet potatoes to Ka'u navel oranges in season. The shelves are filled with canned goods, propane, rope, hoses, paper products, and baking goods, reflecting the uncomplicated, rural lifestyle of the area. In Kualapuu. ✆ **808/567-6243.**

Mana'e Goods and Grindz Formerly the Neighborhood Store 'N Counter, the only grocery on the East End sells batteries, film, aspirin, cookies, beer, Molokai produce, candies, paper products, and other sundries. There's good food pouring out of the kitchen for the breakfast and lunch counter, too. See p. 312 for the restaurant review. In Pukoo. ✆ **808/558-8498.**

Misaki's Grocery and Dry Goods Established in 1922, this third-generation local legend is one of Kaunakakai's two grocery stores. Some of its notable items: chopped garlic from Gilroy, California; fresh luau leaves (taro greens); fresh okra; Boca Burgers; large Korean chestnuts in season; gorgeous bananas; and an ATM. The fish section includes akule and ahi, fresh and dried, but the stock consists mostly of meats, produce, baking products, and a humongous array of soft drinks. Liquor, stationery, candies, and paper products round out the selection of this full-service grocery. In Kaunakakai. ✆ **808/553-5505.**

Molokai Wines & Spirits This is your best bet on the island for a decent bottle of wine. The shop offers 200 labels, including Caymus, Silver Oak, Joseph Phelps, Heitz, Bonny Doon, and a carefully culled European selection. *Wine Spectator* reviews are tacked to some of the selections and the snack options include imported gourmet cheeses, salami, and Carr's biscuits. In Kaunakakai. ✆ **808/553-5009.**

GIFTS & SOUVENIRS

Big Wind Kite Factory & the Plantation Gallery ★★ Jonathan and Daphne Socher, kite designers and inveterate Bali-philes, have combined their interests in a kite factory/import shop that dominates the commercial landscape of Maunaloa, the reconstituted plantation town. Maunaloa's naturally windy conditions make it ideal for kite-flying classes, which are offered free for all ages when conditions are right. The adjoining Plantation Gallery features local handicrafts such as milo-wood bowls, locally made T-shirts, Hawaii-themed sandblasted glassware, baskets of lauhala and other fibers, and Hawaiian-music CDs. There are also many Balinese handicrafts, from jewelry to clothing and fabrics. In Maunaloa. ✆ **808/552-2364.**

The Perfect Molokai Souvenir

It's small, it's easy to pack and take back home, and it's made only on Molokai. It's Molokai salt. The Hawaii Kai Corporation (www.hawaiikaico.com) has two product lines featuring Molokai salt: the gourmet **Soul of the Sea** ($18 for 12 oz.) and the **Palm Island Gourmet** ($6 for 8 oz.). Soul of the Sea salt is hand-harvested from some of the cleanest ocean water in the state, hand-processed and hand-packed on Molokai. It comes in three varietals: Papohaku White, Kilauea Black, and Haleakala Red. While making Soul of the Sea salt, Hawaii Kai Corporation got a byproduct they call Ocean Essence, which they blend with Molokai salt and restore trace minerals lost in the heating process. The result is Palm Island Gourmet, which comes in White Silver, Red Gold, or Black Lava.

Coffees of Hawaii Plantation Store and Espresso Bar This is a fairly slick—for Molokai—combination coffee bar, store, and gallery for more than 30 artists and craftspeople from Hawaii. Sold here are the Malulani Estate and Muleskinner coffees that are grown, processed, and packed on the 500-acre plantation surrounding the shop. (See p. 314 for details on plantation tours.) The gift items are worth a look: pikake and plumeria soaps from Kauai, perfumes and pure beeswax candles from Maui, koa bookmarks and hair sticks, pottery, woods, and baskets. Hwy. 480 (near the junction of Hwy. 470), Kualapuu. © **800/709-BEAN** (709-2326) or 808/567-9023.

Imamura Store Wilfred Imamura, whose mother founded this store, recalls the old railroad track that stretched from the pier to a spot across the street. "We brought our household things from the pier on a hand-pumped vehicle," he recalls. His store, appropriately, is a leap into the past, a marvelous amalgam of precious old-fashioned things. Rubber boots, Hawaiian-print tablecloths, Japanese tea plates, ukulele cases, plastic slippers, and even coconut bikini tops line the shelves. But it's not all nostalgia: The Molokai T-shirts, jeans, and palaka shorts are of good quality and inexpensive, and the pareu fabrics are a find. In Kaunakakai. © **808/553-5615.**

Molokai Fine Arts Gallery ★★ Finds If you only go shopping in one store in Kaunakakai, this is the one you should see. Featuring the very best of Molokai artists and craftspersons, this expanded gallery (they recently moved to a much bigger and better space) has a visitor-friendly layout that allows you to spend as much time as you want perusing the myriad forms of art, from exquisite handmade jewelry (from contemporary gold earrings, necklaces, and rings to Molokai shell leis), scenic paintings, batik on wood, and photos to etched glass, carved bowls and even feather leis. 2 Kamoi St., Suite 300, Kaunakakai. © **808/553-8520.** www.molokaifinearts.com.

A Touch of Molokai ★ Even though the Kaluakoi Hotel is closed, this fabulous shop remains open. It is well worth the drive. The surf shorts and aloha shirts sold here are better than the norm, with attractive, up-to-date choices by Jams, Quiksilver, and other name brands. Tencel dresses, South Pacific shell necklaces (up to $400), and a magnificent, hand-turned milo bowl also caught our attention. Most impressive are the wiliwili, kamani, and soap-berry leis and a handsome array of lauhala bags, all made on Molokai. At Kaluakoi Hotel & Golf Club. © **808/552-0133.**

Moments The Hot Bread Run

For years, local residents have lined up waiting for Molokai Bread to be taken from the oven. Molokai's well-known and well-loved export, Molokai Bread—developed in 1935 in a cast-iron, kiawe-fired oven—is the signature product at **Kanemitsu's Bakery,** 79 Ala Malama St. (✆ **808/553-5855**). Flavors range from apricot-pineapple to mango (in season), but the classics remain the regular white, wheat, cheese, sweet, and onion-cheese breads. Kanemitsu's is part of Molokai's nightlife, too. Whenever anyone on Molokai mentions "hot bread," he's talking about the hot-bread run at Kanemitsu's, the surreal late-night ritual for die-hard bread lovers. Those in the know line up at the bakery's back door beginning at 10:30pm, when the bread is whisked hot out of the oven and into waiting hands. You can order your fresh bread with butter, jelly, cinnamon, or cream cheese, and the bakers will cut the hot loaves down the middle and slather on the works so it melts in the bread. The cream-cheese-and-jelly bread makes a fine substitute for dessert.

MUSEUM STORES

Molokai Museum Gift Shop The restored 1878 sugar mill sits 1,500 feet above the town of Kualapuu. It's a considerable drive from town, but a good cause for those who'd like to support the museum and the handful of local artisans who sell their crafts, fabrics, cookbooks, quilt sets, and other gift items in the tiny shop. There's also a modest selection of cards, T-shirts, coloring books, and, at Christmas, handmade ornaments made of lauhala and koa. Meyer Sugar Mill, Hwy. 470 (just after the turnoff for the Ironwood Hills Golf Course, and 2 miles below Kalaupapa Overlook), Kalae. ✆ **808/567-6436.**

SPORTS SHOP

Molokai Fish & Dive Here you'll find the island's largest selection of T-shirts and souvenirs, crammed in among fishing, snorkeling, and outdoor gear that you can rent or buy. Find your way among the fish nets, boogie boards, diving equipment, bamboo rakes, beach towels, postcards, juices and soft drinks, disposable cameras, and staggering miscellany of this chockablock store. One entire wall is lined with T-shirts, and the selection of Molokai books and souvenirs is extensive. The staff is happy to point out the best snorkeling spots of the day. In Kaunakakai. ✆ **808/553-5926.**

SWEETS FOR THE SWEET

Kamoi Snack-N-Go The Kamoi specialty: sweets and icy treats. Ice cream made by Dave's on Oahu comes in flavors such as green tea, lychee sherbet, *ube* (a brilliant purple color, made from Okinawan sweet potato), haupia, mango, and many other tropical—and traditional—flavors. Schoolchildren and their parents line up for the cones, shakes, sundaes, and popular Icee floats served at this tiny snack shop. If the ice cream doesn't tempt you, maybe something in the aisles full of candies will. It's takeout only; no tables. In Kamoi Professional Center. ✆ **808/553-3742.**

9 ENTERTAINMENT FOR THE WHOLE FAMILY

Molokai is a very family-oriented place. The babies, the teenagers, even the grandparents go everywhere together. Your troops will be warmly welcomed everywhere. There aren't a lot of entertainment options on this rural island, though; families generally make their own entertainment with beach picnics, children's baseball games, backyard music, and the offerings below.

Hotel Molokai, in Kaunakakai (✆ **808/553-5347**; www.hotelmolokai.com), offers live entertainment by local musicians poolside and in the dining room every night. On Friday from 4 to 6pm is Aloha Fridays Night, when the musicians of Molokai who have been performing here for decades show you why people love their music and hula. With its South Seas ambience and poolside setting, it has become the island's premier venue for local and visiting entertainers.

The **Paddlers' Inn** (✆ **808/553-5256**), also in Kaunakakai, recently has become a nightspot for live Hawaii music, comedy acts, and other entertainment (Karaoke on Tues, Mon-night football, and so on).

8

Lanai

Lanai (pronounced lah-nigh-ee) is not an easy place to reach. There are no direct flights from the mainland. This quiet, gentle oasis is a place where families come looking for dramatic beauty, quiet, solitude, and an experience with nature. There is a wealth of activities for you and your kids: snorkeling and swimming in the marine preserve known as Hulopoe Bay; hiking on 100 miles of remote trails; talking story with the friendly locals; and beachcombing and whale-watching along stretches of otherwise deserted sand. For the adventurous, there's horseback riding in the forest, scuba diving in caves, or renting a four-wheel-drive vehicle for the day and discovering wild plains where spotted deer run free.

1 ORIENTATION

ARRIVING

BY PLANE No matter where you're coming from, you'll have to make a connection in Honolulu or Kahului (on Maui), where you catch a plane for the 25-minute flight to Lanai's airport. You'll touch down in Puuwai Basin, once the world's largest pineapple plantation; it's about 10 minutes by car to Lanai City and 25 minutes to Manele Bay.

Commuter airlines Pacific Wings started operating a discount airline, **PW Express** (✆ **888/866-5022** or 808/873-0877; www.pacificwings.com/pwexpress), with daily nonstop flights between Lanai and Honolulu. Another inexpensive air carrier, **go!** Airlines (✆ **888/IFLYGO2** [435-9462]**;** www.iflygo.com), provides services from Kahului, Maui, and Honolulu to Lanai, under the name **go!Express,** on their new fleet of Cessna Grand Caravan 208B planes. Currently, go!Express offers the best rates and deals among Hawaii's airline carriers. Also offering service to Lanai is **Island Air** (✆ **800/652-6541** or 808/565-6744; www.islandair.com) with daily flights from Honolulu.

BY BOAT A round-trip journey on **Expeditions Lahaina/Lanai Passenger Ferry** (✆ **808/661-3756**) takes you between Maui and Lanai for $25 adults and $20 children, each way. The ferry runs five times a day, 365 days a year, between Lahaina and Lanai's Manele Bay harbor. The 9-mile channel crossing takes 45 minutes to an hour, depending on sea conditions. Reservations are strongly recommended—call or book online. Baggage is limited to two checked bags and one carry-on.

VISITOR INFORMATION

Lanai Visitors Bureau, P.O. Box 631436, Lanai City, HI 96763, or 431 Seventh St., Suite A, Lanai City (✆ **800/947-4774** or 808/565-7600; fax 808/565-9316; www.visitlanai.net), and the **Hawaii Visitors and Convention Bureau** (✆ **800/GO-HAWAII** (464-2924) or 808/923-1811; www.gohawaii.com) provide brochures, maps, and island guides. For a free *Road and Site Map* of hikes, archaeological sites, and other attractions, contact the **Castle and Cooke Resorts,** P.O. Box 310, Lanai City, HI 96763 (✆ **808/565-3000;** www.lanai-resorts.com).

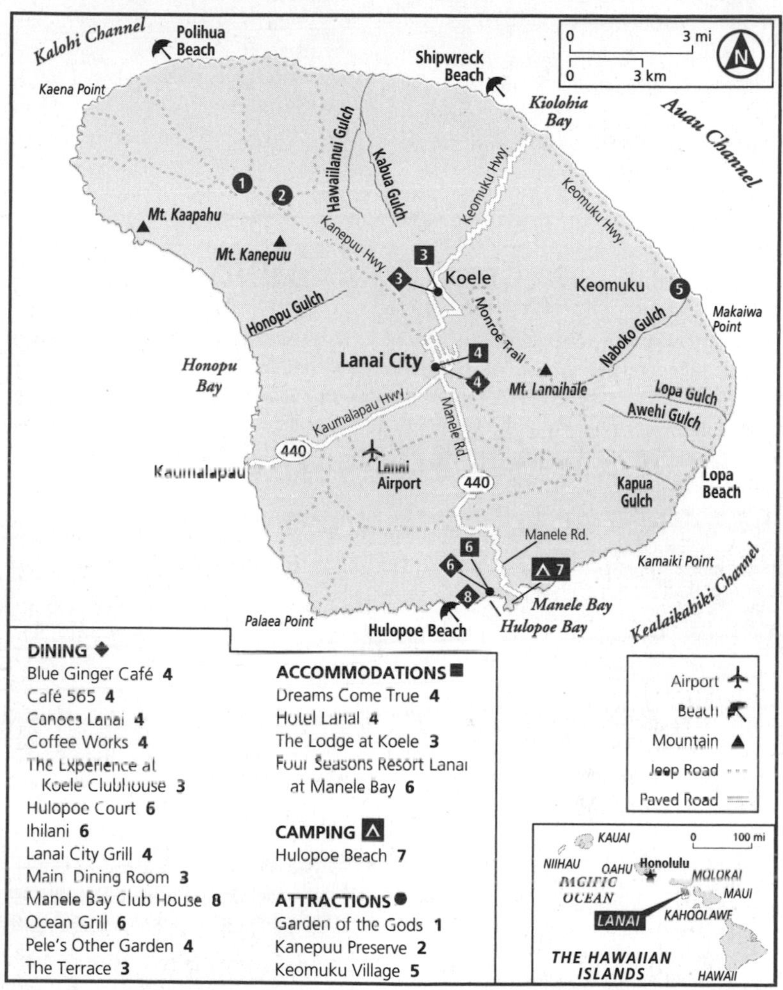

LANAI IN BRIEF

Inhabited Lanai is divided into three parts—Lanai City, Koele, and Manele—and two distinct climate zones: hot and dry, and cool and misty.

Lanai City (pop. 3,000) sits at the heart of the island at 1,645 feet above sea level. It's the only place on the island where you'll find services, and if you're on a budget, this is where you should stay. Built in 1924, this plantation village is a tidy grid of quaint, tin-roofed cottages in bright pastels, with roosters penned in tropical gardens of banana, lilikoi, and papaya. The town centers around Dole Park Square, a charming village square lined with towering Norfolk and Cook

Island pines, and with plantation buildings which house general stores selling basic necessities.

In the nearby cool upland district of Koele is The Lodge at Koele, standing alone on a knoll overlooking pastures and the sea at the edge of a pine forest, like a grand European manor.

The other bastion of indulgence, the Four Seasons Resort Lanai at Manele Bay, is on the sunny southwestern tip of the island at Manele. You'll get more of what you expect from Hawaii here—beaches, swaying palms, mai tais, and the like.

2 GETTING AROUND

With so few paved roads here, you'll need a four-wheel-drive vehicle if you plan to explore the island's remote shores, its interior, or the summit of Mount Lanaihale. Even if you have only a day on Lanai, rent one and see the island. Both cars and four-wheel-drive vehicles are available at the **Dollar Rent-A-Car** desk at **Lanai City Service/Lanai Plantation Store,** 1036 Lanai Ave. (✆ **800/588-7808** for Dollar reservations, or **808/565-7227** for Lanai City Service). Expect to pay about $135 a day for a four-wheel-drive Jeep.

The Lodge at Koele, The Four Seasons Resort Lanai at Manele Bay, and Hotel Lanai provide transportation for their guests; others can call the **Lanai Plantation Store** (✆ **808/565-7227**) for transportation from Lanai City to Hulopoe Beach for $15 per person one-way.

Fast Facts Lanai

American Express There are no American Express offices on Lanai.

Babysitters Call **PATCH** (✆ **808/839-1988**), or your hotel can refer you to qualified babysitters.

Dentists For emergency dental care, call **Dr. James Sagawa** (✆ **808/565-6418**).

Doctors & Hospitals If you need a doctor, contact the **Lanai Family Health Center** (✆ **808/565-6423**) or the **Lanai Community Hospital** (✆ **808/565-6411**).

Drugstores Lanai's only pharmacy is at the **Lanai Community Hospital,** 628 Seventh Ave. (✆ **808/565-9650**).

Emergencies Call the police, fire department, or ambulance services at ✆ **911,** or the **Poison Control Center** at ✆ **800/362-3585.**

Internet Access Besides your hotel, the best place for Internet access is Lanai's public library (see below).

Libraries The library is on Fraser Avenue in Lanai City (✆ **808/565-7920**). It's open Monday through Wednesday and Friday from 9am to 4:30pm and Thursday from 2 to 8pm.

Post Office The post office is at 731 Lanai Ave., in Lanai City (✆ **808/565-6517**). It's open Monday through Friday from 9am to 4pm and Saturday from 11:30am to 1:30pm.

Radio Lanai doesn't have any local radio stations, but you can pick up the signals from Maui and Oahu.

Restrooms Fast-food joints and beach parks are the best spots for restrooms when your kids can't wait.

Safety Lanai is generally safe; but crimes against travelers aren't unheard of, so stay alert and use the same common sense you'd use in a big city.

Useful Telephone Numbers For a weather report, call the **National Weather Service** at ✆ **808/565-6033.**

3 FAMILY-FRIENDLY ACCOMMODATIONS

The majority of the accommodations are located "in the village," as residents call Lanai City, with the exception of Manele Bay Hotel or tent camping under the stars at the park. Don't forget to add 11.42% in taxes to all accommodation bills. Assume that parking is free unless otherwise noted. You'll find the hotels reviewed below on the map on p. 327.

VERY EXPENSIVE

Four Seasons Resort Lanai, The Lodge at Koele ★★ The luxury resort chain Four Seasons has come to Lanai. In 2005, the Four Seasons took over the management of the Lodge's sister property, the former Manele Bay Hotel, now the Four Seasons Resort Lanai at Manele Bay (see below). In 2006, this well-known luxury chain totally renovated and remodeled this 102-room inn. This elegant lodge resembles a grand English country estate. It's located in the cool mist of the mountains in a 21-acre grove of Norfolk Island pines at 1,700 feet above sea level, 8 miles inland from any beach. Most people look at it as a romantic retreat, but The Lodge does accommodate children. There's no additional charge for children 17 and younger, and there are plenty of activities for them in the resort's complimentary "Kids for All Seasons" program. Personally, I think you and the kids might be happier on the beach at the sister property, Four Seasons Resort, listed below.

P.O. Box 630310, Lanai City, HI 96793. ✆ **800/321-4666** or 808/565-7300. Fax 808/565-4561. www.fourseasons.com/koele. 102 units. $445–$1,145 double; $1,200–$7,000 suites. Numerous packages available. Extra person $100. Children 17 and under stay free in parent's room. Cribs and rollaway beds free. AE, DC, MC, V. Airport shuttle $35 round-trip. **Amenities:** 2 restaurants; bar (w/quiet live music, hula, and occasional talks by celebrities); outdoor pool; golf at the Experience at Koele, an 18-hole championship Greg Norman/Ted Robinson–designed course, and executive putting green; tennis courts; health club; Jacuzzi; watersports equipment/rentals at sister hotel Four Seasons Resort Lanai at Manele Bay; bike rentals; children's program; game room; concierge; activities desk; car rental desk; business center; shopping arcade; room service; massage; babysitting; laundry service; dry cleaning. *In room:* A/C, TV, dataport, minibar, fridge, coffeemaker, hair dryer, iron, safe.

Four Seasons Resort Lanai at Manele Bay ★★★ The well-known luxury hotel chain Four Seasons took over management of this 250-unit resort after a multimillion-dollar makeover. We visited the resort just months after the change in management, and, at the time, the resort was still in the growing pains of bringing the staff up to Four Seasons' level of impeccable service. There were some dropped balls, but we chalked it up to the "settling-in stage" and are very confident that by the time you are reading this review, all problems will be ironed out and that this will become a jewel in the Four Seasons' chain. It's located on a sun-washed southern bluff overlooking fabulous Hulopoe Beach, one of Hawaii's best stretches of golden sand just a short 2-minute walk away. This resort is much less formal than The Lodge up the hill. It attracts more families, and because it's warmer here, people wander through the lobby in shorts and T-shirts. They offer the same complimentary children's program (ages 5–12) that The Lodge does, with most of the activities focused more on the beach and ocean. Teens can participate in the Surf Shack Teen Center with activities and entertainment suited for the 13- to 18-year-old set, such as a cybercafe with video games, pool table, and lounge area, and off-property programs such as a beach party and a fishing expedition. Room service, and all the dining outlets here and at the Lodge at Koele, has a kids' menu for ages 5 to 12; kids 5 and younger eat free with their parents. If you are vacationing during school breaks, there are evening programs for kids which include dinner, games, and prizes.

P.O. Box 630310, Lanai City, HI 96793. ✆ **800/321-4666** or 808/565-7700. Fax 808/565-2483. www.fourseasons.com/manelebay. 250 units. $345–$645 double; $750–$1,500 suite. Numerous packages available. Additional person $100. Children 16 and under stay free in parent's room. Cribs and rollaway beds free. AE, DC, MC, V. Airport shuttle $35 round-trip. **Amenities:** 3 restaurants; bar w/breathtaking views; large outdoor pool; golf at the Jack Nicklaus–designed Challenge at Manele; tennis courts; health club; small spa; Jacuzzi; watersports equipment/rentals; children's program; game room; concierge; activities desk; business center; shopping arcade; salon; room service; massage; babysitting; laundry service; dry cleaning. *In room:* A/C, TV, dataport, minibar, coffeemaker, hair dryer, iron, safe.

MODERATE

Hotel Lanai ★ This hotel lacks the facilities of the two resorts described above, but it's perfect for families who can't afford to spend $400 (and up) per night. This clapboard plantation-era relic has retained its quaint character and lives on as a country inn. The guest rooms are extremely small (some rooms can handle another person, some are too small), but they are clean and newly decorated with Hawaiian quilts, wood furniture, and ceiling fans (but no air-conditioning or televisions). The most popular are the lanai units, which feature a lanai shared with the room next door. I recommend the small one-bedroom cottage with a TV and bathtub, perfect for a small family.

828 Lanai Ave. (P.O. Box 630520), Lanai City, HI 96763. ✆ **800/795-7211** or 808/565-7211. Fax 808/565-6450. www.hotellanai.com. 11 units. $139 double; $159 Premium Rooms; $209 cottage double. Rates include continental breakfast. Extra person $30. Children 8 and under stay free in parent's room. Rollaway beds (in 2 units only) $30. AE, MC, V. Airport shuttle $36 round-trip. **Amenities:** Excellent restaurant; intimate bar; access to 2 resort golf courses on the island and 9-hole golf course in town; nearby tennis courts; free use of snorkeling equipment.

INEXPENSIVE

Dreams Come True Bed & Breakfast ★ Finds In addition to their quaint plantation bed-and-breakfast, where two of the four bedrooms feature four-poster canopied beds, with additional single beds (perfect for small families), they also rent a nearby four-bedroom home for $580 a night. No cribs or rollaway beds are available here. Sleeps 10 to 12 comfortably.

547 12th St. (P.O. Box 525), Lanai City, HI 96763. ✆ **800/566-6961** or 808/565-6961. Fax 808/565-7056. http://circumvista.com/dreamscometrue.html. 4 units. $145 double. Rates include continental breakfast. Extra person $35. AE, DISC, MC, V. *In room:* No phone.

4 FAMILY-FRIENDLY DINING

Your children will be welcome in Lanai's restaurants, which are a curious mix of innocence and sophistication, with strong cross-cultural elements that liven up the culinary offerings. You can dine like a sultan on this island, but be prepared for high prices. The tony hotel restaurants require deep pockets (or bottomless expense accounts), and there are only a handful of options.

You'll find the restaurants reviewed below on the map on p. 327.

VERY EXPENSIVE

Ihilani ★★ MEDITERRANEAN Here's a place that's probably best for an adult night out, although accommodations are made for children. A number of top Hawaii chefs (such as Philippe Padovani and Edwin Goto) have each added their style of melding Mediterranean with Island cuisine during their tenure here. The result is Lanai's top gourmet restaurant in a formal atmosphere with inspiring food. The latest incarnation of this classy restaurant, overlooking the resort and the ocean beyond, is traditional Italian cuisine. Appetizers include tender fried calamari and marinara sauce, Chardonnay-steamed mussels, and sirloin carpaccio with white truffle oil. Main courses range from inspiring risottos (from Puna goat cheese with pine nuts and baby vegetables to lobster) to fresh fish (ahi caponata with eggplant), veal, chicken, and beef. The kids, if you bring them, will be happy with the grilled mahimahi or the turkey sandwich.

In the Four Seasons Resort Lanai at Manele Bay. ✆ **808/565-2296.** Kids' menu, highchairs, boosters, crayons. Reservations strongly recommended. Jackets requested for men. Main courses $31–$50; set menu $106 without wine, $160 with wine; kids' menu $4–$11. AE, DC, MC, V. Tues–Sat 6–9:30pm.

Main Dining Room ★★ NEW AMERICAN Get a sitter for the kids and enjoy this romantic setting: a roaring fire, bountiful sprays of orchids, sienna-colored walls, and well-dressed women in pearls sitting across from men in jackets, with wine buckets tableside. The menu highlights American favorites with intense flavors. The Dining Room is known for its use of fresh herbs, vegetables, and fruit grown on the island, harvested just minutes away. It's extremely pricey and not really appropriate for children younger than 12, although they do have a kids' menu with grilled cheese sandwiches, hamburgers, or mac and cheese.

In The Fours Seasons Resort Lanai, The Lodge at Koele. ✆ **808/565-4580.** Kids' menu, highchairs, boosters. Reservations required. Entrees $50–$65; kids' menu $3–$8.50. AE, DC, MC, V. Daily 6–9:30pm.

EXPENSIVE

Hulopoe Court ★ HAWAIIAN REGIONAL The main dining room at The Four Seasons Resort, which offers fresh, local ingredients in their breakfast and dinner items, is very kid-friendly. (They get their own menu and crayons to play with until the food arrives.) The kids' menu has a breakfast buffet ($12) or a la carte ($4–$8.50) and dinner and lunch menus featuring hot dogs to mahimahi ($4.50–$7). The staff goes out of their way to make sure even your pickiest eater will be happy, which is great because at these prices you certainly don't want to see food go to waste. It's somewhat formal (collared shirts on men), so make sure your kids are wearing something more than bathing suits. (Shorts and T-shirts are okay, though.)

In the Four Seasons Resort Lanai at Manele Bay. ✆ **808/565-2290.** Kids' menu, highchairs, boosters, crayons. Reservations recommended. Collared shirt required for men. Breakfast entrees $19–$23, buffet $31; dinner main courses $31–$41; kids' menu $6.50–$10. AE, MC, V. Daily 7–11am and 6–9:30pm.

Ocean Grill ★ SEAFOOD The former Pool Grille has been remodeled and expanded, and is open for lunch and dinner. Located just off the pool, the casual, open-air, Hawaii-style bistro serves interesting lunches like wraps and sandwiches (such as a veggie wrap with portobello mushrooms, red bell peppers, provolone cheese, avocado, and roasted garlic hummus), a great selection of salads (including a yummy calamari salad), and a range of entrees such as *kalua* pork and cheese quesadilla, or mahimahi fish and chips. At dinner, watch the sun set and the stars come out as you dine on fresh local fish, steak, free-range chicken, or small-plate entrees such as Hawaiian kampachi, crab cakes, lobster, and red curry chowder.

In the Four Seasons Resort Lanai at Manele Bay. ✆ **808/565-2092.** Kids' menu, high chairs, boosters. Lunch $15–$20; dinner $35–$50; kids' menu $4.50–$9. AE, MC, V. Daily 11am–5pm and 5:30–9pm.

The Terrace ★ AMERICAN The main dining room for The Lodge at Koele, situated between the 35-foot-high Great Hall and a wall of glass looking out over prim English gardens, the Terrace is far from your typical hotel dining room. The menu may be fancy for comfort food, but it does indeed comfort. Expect hearty breakfasts and American classics for dinner. The chicken tenders from the kids' menu is the usual favorite, but there are a host of other offerings from peanut butter and jelly (with a tropical twist, sliced bananas) to kosher hot dogs.

In The Fours Seasons Resort Lanai, The Lodge at Koele. ✆ **808/565-4580.** Kids' menu, highchairs. Reservations recommended. Main courses $16–$27 breakfast, $14–$25 lunch; dinner entrees $28–$40; kids' menu $6–$10. AE, DC, MC, V. Daily 6am–9:30pm.

MODERATE

The Experience at Koele Clubhouse AMERICAN This tiny diner overlooks the verdant, rolling hills of the Experience at Koele Golf Course. Soups, salads, and sandwiches rule here. You'll find that most of your fellow diners have just finished a round of golf; you can join them at one of a handful of tables inside or on the lanai overlooking the pastoral view. Oversized sandwiches range from a delicious portobello mushroom on toasted focaccia bread to open-faced chicken salad (with a yummy mango-avocado salsa), smoked turkey club, or a charbroiled cheddar burger.

The Experience at Koele Golf Course. ✆ **808/565-4605.** Lunch $10–$19. AE, DC, MC, V. Daily 10:30am–4:30pm.

Lanai City Grill ★★ PACIFIC RIM Celebrated Maui chef Bev Gannon (Haliimaile General Store, Joe's Restaurant) redesigned the menu in this cute eatery, where the decor consists of pine-paneled walls, chintz curtains, and a fireplace. The menu sticks to whatever is in season and fresh that day with fish, seafood, meats, and rotisserie chicken. They are happy to fix something that will make your kids happy.

In the Hotel Lanai, 828 Lanai Ave., Lanai City. ✆ **808/565-7211.** www.hotellanai.com. Highchairs, boosters. Main courses $14–$38. MC, V. Daily 5:30–9pm.

Manele Bay Clubhouse ★ PACIFIC RIM The view from the alfresco tables here may be the best on the island, encompassing Kahoolawe, Haleakala on Maui, and, on an especially clear day, the peaks of Mauna Kea and Mauna Loa on the Big Island. You can lunch on lighter fare: Asian tuna salad with grilled ahi, turkey club sandwich, clubhouse burgers with caramelized onions and cheese, or more substantial entrees, ranging from fish and chips to Kalbi barbeque beef. Kids can order from their own menu. The clubhouse is casual, the view of the ocean is awe-inspiring, and it's a great gathering place.

In the Challenge at Manele Clubhouse. ✆ **808/565-2230.** Reservations recommended. Kids' menu, high chairs. Main courses $16–$20; kids' menu $4–$8.50. AE, DC, MC, V. Daily 10:30am–4:30pm lunch only.

INEXPENSIVE

Blue Ginger Cafe COFFEE SHOP An inexpensive alternative to the pricey resorts, this down-home cafe is extremely casual, and although there is no kids' menu, they welcome families. The kids generally order the chicken katsu, the teriyaki chicken, or the very popular fried saimin, all priced around $7.50. The offerings are solid, no-nonsense, everyday fare: tasty French toast made with homemade bread, very popular hamburgers on homemade buns, and mahimahi with capers in a white-wine sauce.

409 Seventh Ave. (at Ilima St.), Lanai City. ✆ **808/565-6363.** Highchairs, boosters. Breakfast and lunch items under $13; dinner under $16. No credit cards. Daily 6am–8pm.

Café 565 PIZZA/SUB SANDWICHES Kids will love this colorful pizzeria, which spills out of an old house into the front yard with its umbrella tables. Hot and cold sub sandwiches, daily plate lunch specials, and great salads complete the menu. Right now they have a limited kids' menu (but they plan to expand it), and the most popular item is the pizza sub—basically a pizza sandwich on a baguette.

408 Eighth St. (at Ilima St.), Lanai City. ✆ **808/565-6622.** Limited kids' menu, highchairs, boosters. Subs $5–$10; pizza $14–$20; kids' menu $1–$3.50. AE, DISC, MC, V. Mon–Sat 10am–3pm; Mon–Fri 5–8pm.

Canoes Lanai LOCAL Formerly Tanigawa's, this ma-and-pa eatery may have changed its name, but it still remains the landmark that it has been since the 1920s. In those days, the tiny storefront sold canned goods and cigarettes; the 10 tables, hamburgers, and Filipino food came later. This hole in the wall is a local institution, with a reputation for serving local-style breakfasts. The fare—fried rice, omelets, short stack, and simple ham and eggs—is more greasy spoon than gourmet, but it's budget-friendly.

419 Seventh St., Lanai City. ✆ **808/565-6537.** High chairs. Main courses under $8.50 breakfast; sandwiches $2.50–$8.50; burgers $2–$5. No credit cards. Thurs–Tues 6:30am–1pm.

Coffee Works ★ COFFEE SHOP A menu of espresso coffees and drinks, ice cream (including local brands), and a small selection of pastries make Lanai City's new gathering place a must stop in your tour of Lanai City. Just a tiny cafe with tables and benches on a pleasing wooden deck a stone's throw from Dole Park, this is a good replenishing stop, with plenty of items for your kids to slurp and munch on. Formerly a plantation house, the structure fits in with the surrounding plantation homes in the heart of Lanai City. There are some nice gift items available, including T-shirts, tea infusers, Chai, teapots, cookies, and gourmet coffees.

604 Ilima, Lanai City (across from the post office). ✆ **808/565-6962.** Most items under $5. AE, DC, DISC, MC, V. Mon–Sat 6am–4pm; Sun 6am–noon.

Pele's Other Garden ★★ DELI/BISTRO This popular Lanai City eatery has added a patio with umbrella tables outside and expanded the kitchen in the back, so there's a lot more seating than there used to be—and a fuller menu to match. Owners Mark and Barbara have turned Pele's Other Garden from a small sandwich shop to a full-scale deli and bistro. Daily soup and menu specials, excellent pizza, fresh organic produce, and special items such as top-quality black-bean burritos, roasted red peppers, and stuffed grape leaves make Pele's Other Garden a Lanai City must. Sandwiches are made with wraps or whole-wheat, rye, sourdough, or French bread, all baked on the island and delivered fresh daily. In the evening, you dine on china at cloth-covered tables, and the menu expands to include pastas (bow-tie pasta with butterflied garlic shrimp, fettuccine with smoked salmon), pizza, and salads. Beer and wines by the glass (from $4.25) and a full bar (happy hour 4:30–6:30pm Mon–Fri) are available.

 Dole Park, 811 Houston St., Lanai City. ✆ **808/565-9628.** www.pelesothergarden.com. Lunch items less than $8; pizza from $7; dinner items $17–$20. AE, DISC, MC, V. Mon–Fri 10am–2pm and 5–8pm.

5 EXPLORING LANAI WITH YOUR KIDS

You'll need a four-wheel-drive vehicle to reach all the sights listed below. Renting a Jeep is an expensive proposition on Lanai—about $135 a day—so we suggest that you rent one just for the day (or days) you plan on sightseeing. Otherwise, it's easy enough to get to the beach and around Lanai City without your own wheels. For details on vehicle rentals, see "Getting Around," earlier in this chapter.

You'll find the following attractions on the map on p. 327.

GARDEN OF THE GODS ★

Whether you have a curious 2-year-old or a worldly 16-year-old, they'll find few experiences in Hawaii more thrilling than a four-wheel drive into the country. A dirt road leads

Frommer's Favorite Lanai Family Experiences

Snorkeling Hulopoe Beach (p. 335) Crystal-clear waters teem with brilliant tropical fish off one of Hawaii's best beaches. There are tide pools to explore, waves to play in, and other surprises such as a pod of spinner dolphins that often makes a splashy entrance.

Discovering the Garden of the Gods (above) Eroded by wind, rain, and time, these geologic badlands are worth visiting at sunrise or sunset, when the low light plays tricks on the land—and your mind.

Four-Wheeling It (p. 328) Four-wheeling is a way of life on Lanai because there are only 30 miles of pavement. Plenty of rugged trails lead to deserted beaches, abandoned villages, and valleys filled with wild game.

Camping Under the Stars (p. 337) The campsites at Hulopoe Beach Park are about as close to the heavens as you can get. The crashing surf will lull you to sleep at night, and chirping birds will wake you in the morning. If you're into roughing it, this is a great way to experience Lanai.

Watching the Whales at Polihua Beach Located on the north shore, this beach—which gets its name from the turtles that nest here—is a great place to watch for whales during the winter months.

Exploring Tide Pools An entire world of marine life lives in the tide pools on the eastern side of Hulopoe Bay. Everything in the water, including the tiny fish, is small—kid-size. After examining the wonders of the tide pool, check out the larger swimming holes in the lava rock, perfect for children.

Listening to Storytellers (p. 341) Check with the **Lanai Library,** Fraser Avenue near Fifth Street, Lanai City (✆ **808/565-6996**), to see if any storytelling or other children's activities are scheduled. The events are usually free and open to everyone.

out of Lanai City, through the now-uncultivated pineapple fields, past the Kanepuu Preserve (a dry-land forest preserve teeming with rare plant and animal life), to the so-called Garden of the Gods, on Lanai's north shore. This place has little to do with gods, Hawaiian or otherwise. It is, however, the ultimate rock garden: a rugged, barren, beautiful place full of rocks strewn by volcanic forces and shaped by the elements into a variety of shapes and colors—brilliant reds, oranges, ochers, and yellows. Allow at least an hour to get here, and don't forget your camera, snacks, and drinks (once you leave Lanai City, there's nothing but wilderness).

OFF THE TOURIST TRAIL: KEOMOKU VILLAGE

If the kids are feeling restless, take a drive to Keomoku Village, on Lanai's east coast. You'll really be off the tourist trail. All that's in Keomoku—a ghost town since the mid-1950s—is a 1903 clapboard church in disrepair, an overgrown graveyard, an excellent view across the 9-mile Auau Channel to Maui's crowded Kaanapali Beach, and some very empty beaches that are perfect for a picnic or some snorkeling. This former ranching and fishing village of 2,000 was the first non-Hawaiian settlement on Lanai, but it dried up after droughts killed off the Maunalei Sugar Company. The village, such as it is, is a great little escape from Lanai City. Follow Keomoku Road for 8 miles to the coast, turn right on the sandy road, and keep going for 5¾ miles. Everyone in the family should enjoy this trip; allow a couple of hours for exploring.

6 BEACHES

If you like big, wide, empty, gold-sand beaches and crystal-clear, cobalt-blue water full of bright tropical fish—and who doesn't?—go to Lanai. With 18 miles of sandy shoreline, Lanai has some of Hawaii's least crowded and most interesting beaches. One spot in particular is perfect for swimming, snorkeling, and watching spinner dolphins play: Hulopoe Beach, Lanai's best.

HULOPOE BEACH ★★★

In 1997, Dr. Stephen Leatherman of the University of Maryland (a professional beach surveyor who's also known as "Dr. Beach") ranked Hulopoe the best beach in the United States. It's easy to see why. This palm-fringed, gold-sand beach is bordered by black-lava fingers, protecting swimmers from the serious ocean currents that sweep around Lanai. In summer, Hulopoe is perfect for swimming, snorkeling, or just lolling about; the water temperature is usually in the mid-70s. Swimming is usually safe, except when swells kick up in winter. The bay at the foot of the Four Seasons Resort/Manele Bay is a protected marine preserve, and the schools of colorful fish know it. So do the spinner dolphins that come here to play, as well as the humpback whales that cruise by in winter. Hulopoe is also Lanai's premier beach park, with a grassy lawn, picnic tables, barbecue grills, restrooms, showers, and ample parking. You can camp here, too.

HULOPOE'S TIDE POOLS Some of the best lava-rock tide pools in Hawaii are found along the south shore of Hulopoe Bay. These miniature Sea Worlds are full of strange creatures: asteroids (sea stars) and holothurians (sea cucumbers), not to mention spaghetti worms, Barber Pole shrimp, and Hawaii's favorite local delicacy, the opihi, a tasty morsel also known as the limpet. Kids enjoy swimming in the enlarged tide pool at the eastern edge of the bay.

SHIPWRECK BEACH ★

This 8-mile-long windswept strand on Lanai's northeastern shore—named for the rusty ship *Liberty* stuck on the coral reef—is a sailor's nightmare and a beachcomber's dream. The strong currents yield all sorts of flotsam, from Japanese handblown-glass-fish floats and rare pelagic paper nautilus shells to lots of junk. It's not a place for swimming, but it's fun to walk the beach with the kids and help them search for buried treasure. The road to the beach is paved most of the way, but you really need a four-wheel-drive vehicle to get down here.

POLIHUA BEACH ★

So many sea turtles once hauled themselves out of the water to lay their eggs in the sun-baked sand on Lanai's northwestern shore that Hawaiians named the beach here *Polihua,* or "egg nest." Although the endangered green sea turtles are making a comeback, they're seldom seen here now. There are no facilities except fishermen's huts and driftwood shelters, so bring water and sunscreen. Beware of the strong currents, which make the water unsafe for swimming. This strand is ideal for beachcombing, fishing, or relaxing on the sand.

7 FOR THE ACTIVE FAMILY

IN THE WATER

Lanai has Hawaii's best water clarity because it lacks major development, because it has low rainfall and runoff, and because its coast is washed clean daily by the sea current known as "The Way to Tahiti." But the strong sea currents pose a threat to swimmers, and there are few good surf breaks. Most of the aquatic adventures—swimming, snorkeling, scuba diving—are centered on the somewhat protected south shore, around Hulopoe Bay.

The only outfitter for watersports is **Trilogy Lanai Ocean Sports** ★ (✆ **888/MAUI-800** [628-4800] or 808/565-9303; www.visitlanai.com).

SAILING & SNORKELING **Ages 3 and up.** Trilogy, which has built a well-deserved reputation as the leader in sailing/snorkeling cruises in Hawaii, has a morning snorkel/sailing trip along Lanai's protected coastline, which includes sailing past hundreds of spinner dolphins into some of the best snorkeling sites in the world. The entire family will enjoy this: the price is $203 (half-price for children 3–15) and includes lunch, sodas, snorkel gear, and instruction.

SURFING **Ages 8 and up.** If you have ever wanted to learn how to surf, then let instructor Nick Palumbo, a surfing champion, take you on a 4×4 surfing safari to a secluded surf spot where he will have you up and riding the waves in no time. His **Lanai Surf School & Surf Safari** (✆ **808/306-9837;** lanaisurfsafari@hotmail.com) features a package of a 2½-hour lesson with surfboard, 4×4 transportation, refreshments, and "a really good time" for $185 per person for two people and $155 per person for groups of three or more. So long as your kids can swim, Nick can teach them how to surf.

WHALE-WATCHING **All Ages.** Year-round, **Trilogy** offers 1½-hour adventures on a 32-foot, 26-passenger, rigid-hulled inflatable boat. From late December to April, they are on the lookout for whales, but the remainder of the year, schools of spinner dolphins are

Perfect for a Rainy Day: Lanai Art Center

A perfect activity for a rainy day in Lanai City is the **Lanai Art Center,** 333 Seventh St., located in the heart of the small town. They have programs for everyone from preschoolers to teenagers, as well as adults. Frequently, top artists from across Hawaii visit this home-grown art program and teach a variety of classes including raku (Japanese pottery), silk-printing, silk-screening, pareu making (creating your own design on this islanders' wrap), gyotaku (printing a real fish on your own T-shirt), watercolor drawing, and a variety of other island crafts. The cost is usually in the $25 range for the 2- to 3-hour classes plus the cost of materials; parents usually stick around to enjoy the class with their child. For more information, call ✆ **808/565-7503** or visit www.lanaiart.org.

featured on this Blue Water Marine Mammal Watch. The cost is $75 (half-price for children 3–15).

ON THE LAND

BICYCLING **Ages 8 and up.** The **Lodge at Koele** (✆ **808/565-7300**) has mountain bikes to rent. You get a backpack and lunch with a 4-hour ($35) or 8-hour ($55) rental. For general information about bike trails, go to www.bikehawaii.com.

CAMPING **All ages.** There is only one legal place to camp on Lanai: Hulopoe Beach Park, which is owned by Castle & Cooke Resorts. To camp in this exquisite beach park, with its crescent-shaped, white-sand beach bordered by kiawe trees, contact **Hulopoe Beach Park,** Castle & Cooke Resorts, P.O. Box 630310, Lanai City, HI 96763 (✆ **808/565-3000**). There's a $20 registration fee, plus a charge of $5 per person, per night. Hulopoe has six campsites; each can accommodate up to six people. Facilities include restrooms, running water, showers, barbecue areas, and picnic tables.

HIKING **All ages.** Take the entire family on the self-guided nature trail in the Kanepuu Preserve. It's an easy walk (everyone in the family can do it), and exploring the eight stations takes about 10 to 15 minutes. Interpretive signs explain the natural or cultural significance of what you're seeing.

The **Four Seasons Resort Lanai/The Lodge at Koele** (✆ **808/565-7300;** www.fourseasons.com/koele) has a 2½-hour Koloiki Ridge Nature hike through 5 miles of the upland forests of Koele at 11am daily. The fee is $15.

The **Four Seasons Resort Lanai at Manele Bay** (✆ **808/565-2000;** www.fourseasons.com/manalebay) offers a 1½-hour fitness hike along an old fisherman's trail at 9am Tuesday and Friday, led by Joe West, wildlife and outdoor photographer extraordinaire. Bring your camera and ask Joe for picture-taking tips. The fee is $15.

The 3-hour self-guided **Koele Nature Hike** starts by the reflecting pool in the backyard of The Lodge at Koele and takes you on a 5-mile loop through Norfolk Island pines, into Hulopoe Valley, past wild ginger, and up to Koloiki Ridge, with its panoramic view of Maunalei Valley and of Molokai and Maui in the distance. You're welcome to take the hike even if you're not a guest at The Lodge. The path isn't clearly marked—ask the concierge for a free map. I suggest doing this hike in the morning; by afternoon the clouds usually roll in, marring visibility at the top and increasing your chance of being caught in a downpour. Best for ages 8 and up.

The **Munro Trail,** a tough 11-mile (round-trip) uphill climb through the groves of Norfolk pines, is a lung-buster, but if you reach the top, you'll be rewarded with a breathtaking view of Molokai, Maui, Kahoolawe, the peaks of the Big Island, and—on a really clear day—Oahu in the distance. Figure on 7 hours. The trail begins at Lanai Cemetery along Keomoku Road (Hwy. 44) and follows Lanai's ancient caldera rim, ending up at the island's highest point, Lanaihale. Go in the morning for the best visibility. After 4 miles, you'll get a view of Lanai City. The weary retrace their steps from here, while the more determined go the last 1¼ miles to the top. Die-hards head down Lanai's steep south-crater rim to join the highway to Manele Bay. Best for ages 12 and up.

This self-guided nature trail in the **Kanepuu Preserve** (see p. 337) is about a 10- to 15-minute walk through eight stations, with interpretive signs explaining the natural or cultural significance of what you're seeing. The trailhead is clearly marked on the Polihua Road on the way to the Garden of the Gods. Kanepuu is one of the last remaining examples of the type of forest that once covered the dry lowlands throughout the state. There are some 49 plant species here that are found only in Hawaii. The **Nature Conservancy** (✆ **808/565-7430**) conducts guided hikes every month; call for details.

HORSEBACK RIDING **Ages 9 and up.** Horses can take you to many places in Lanai's unique landscape that are otherwise unreachable. The **Four Seasons Lanai Resort's Stables at Koele** (✆ **808/565-4424**) offers various daily rides (9am and 1:30pm), including slow, gentle group rides starting at $95 for a 1½-hour **Paniolo Trail Ride,** which takes you into the hills surrounding Koele. You'll meander through guava groves and ironwood trees; catch glimpses of axis deer, quail, wild turkeys, and Santa Getrudis cattle; and end with panoramic views of Maui and Lanai. Private rides can be arranged for $160 per person for 2 hours. Kids will love the 15-minute pony rides and you'll love the $10-per-person price. Sunset rides (1½ hours) are available for $190 per person. Long pants and closed-toe shoes (like running shoes) are required, and safety helmets are provided. Bring a jacket—the weather is chilly and rain is frequent. Children must be at least 9 years old and 4 feet tall, and riders cannot weigh more than 225 pounds.

TENNIS **All ages.** Public courts, lit for night play, are available in Lanai City at no charge; call ✆ **808/565-6979** for reservations. If you are a guest at The Lodge or at Manele Bay, The Lodge offers three new Premiere Cushion outdoor hard courts. The tennis courts offer complimentary use of Wilson racquets, balls, and bottled ice water for guests. Guests are also invited to experience the tennis center at Four Seasons Resort Lanai at Manele Bay, which offers a full Pro Shop, use of a ball machine, and weekly tennis mixers and tournaments. Courts are $20 per person for hotel guests (not open to nonguests). For information, call ✆ **808/565-2072.**

8 SHOPPING WITH YOUR KIDS

Amazingly there is shopping on this tiny island. Okay, it's not in big department stores; in fact, there aren't any brand-name chain stores here, just small ma-and-pa general stores and a few boutiques. Allow at least a half-day to wander around Dole Square checking out the shops listed below.

ARTS & CRAFTS

Lanai Art Center ★ Finds This wonderful center was organized in 1989 to provide a place where both residents and visitors could come to create art. The center offers classes and studio time in ceramics, painting and drawing, calligraphy, woodworking, photography, silk and textile painting, watercolor, and glass. Plus there's an impressive schedule of visiting instructors, who teach everything from writing to folk arts (quilting, lei making, and instrument making) to oil painting. One of the center's prime focuses is to teach children. In addition, their gallery features the work of Lanai residents at excellent prices. Check out the center's reasonably priced classes, generally in the $25 range, or browse in the gallery for excellent deals. 333 Seventh St. ✆ **808/565-7503.** www.lanaiart.org.

CHILDREN'S CLOTHES

Gifts with Aloha ★ This store of treasures offers everything from children's clothing, books, and toys to swimwear, ukuleles, and locally made cards for every occasion. Dole Park, 363 Seventh St. (at Ilima St.). ✆ **808/565-6589.** www.giftswithaloha.com.

The Local Gentry ★★ Finds This one-of-a-kind boutique has great children's, women's, and men's clothes at excellent prices. There are also great T-shirts, swimwear, jewelry, bath products, picture frames, jeans, chic sunglasses, and offbeat sandals. 363 Seventh St. (behind Gifts with Aloha, facing Ilima St.). ✆ **808/565-9130.**

FOOD

Central Bakery ★ Finds This is the mother lode of the island's baked delights. If you've noshed on the fantastic sandwiches at The Lodge at Koele's The Terrace or any of the stellar desserts at its Main Dining Room or at Four Seasons Resort Lanai at Manele Bay, you've enjoyed goodies from Central Bakery. The bakery supplies all breads, all breakfast pastries, specialty ice creams and sorbets, all banquet desserts, and restaurant desserts on the island. Although it's not your standard retail outlet, you can call in advance, place your order, and pick it up. They prefer as much notice as possible (preferably 48 hr.) but, in a pinch, will take a 24-hour order. Breads (most $4.50) range from walnut onion to roasted potato bacon to olive onion. They also have cookies (chocolate chip, oatmeal, coconut—all for 50¢), brownies, muffins, croissants (including chocolate croissants), and scones, plus an assortment of breakfast pastries (pineapple turnover, hazelnut roll, mascarpone apricot Danish, pistachio chocolate roll, and others). 1311 Fraser Ave., Lanai City. ✆ **808/565-3920.**

Pine Isle Market A local landmark for two generations, Pine Isle specializes in locally caught fresh fish, but you can also find fresh herbs and spices, canned goods, electronic games, ice cream, toys, *zoris* (sandals), diapers, paint, cigars, and other basic essentials of work and play. 356 Eighth St. ✆ **808/565-6488.**

Richard's Shopping Center The Tamashiros' family business has been on the square since 1946; not much has changed over the years. This "shopping center" is, in fact, a general store with a grocery section, paper products, ethnic foods, meats (mostly frozen), liquor, toys, film, cosmetics, fishing gear, sunscreens, clothing, kitchen utensils, T-shirts, and other miscellany. 434 Eighth St. ✆ **808/565-6047.**

GALLERIES

Heart of Lanai Art Gallery Denise Hennig, the resident artist at Hotel Lanai, displays her own photographs and watercolors of landscapes, people, and the lifestyle of Lanai's plantation past, as well as the work of other local Lanai artists, at her afternoon teas, Tuesday through Saturday, from 2:30 to 4:30pm. Drop by and enjoy a cup of tea with her as she shows you the art she is displaying that week. Her home/gallery is located behind the hospital in a bright yellow house. 758 Queens St. ✆ **808/565-7815.** www.lanaionline.com/Merchants/heart_of_lanai.htm.

Mike Carroll Gallery If he is on the island, you'll find Mike Carroll at work here on his original oil paintings, which generally depict Lanai's landscape. After a successful 22-year career as a professional artist in Chicago, Carroll moved to Lanai and has been painting the beauty and the lifestyle of the island ever since. You'll find an extensive selection of his original work, some limited editions, prints, and notecards, plus a dozen or so of Maui and Lanai's top artists and even some locally made, one-of-a-kind jewelry. 443 Seventh St. ✆ **808/565-7122.** www.mikecarrollgallery.com.

GIFTS & SOUVENIRS

Dis 'N Dat ★★ Finds Don't miss this outrageously whimsical shop with an eclectic assortment that includes unusual (but finely crafted) teak and exotic wood sculptures and carvings, mobiles, wind chimes, handmade jewelry, and stained glass. The shop carries the biggest collection of Hawaii slipper necklaces, earrings, anklets, and bracelets. You'll also find T-shirts, pottery, ceramics, batik scarves, hula lamps, whimsical dragonfly lamps, woven baskets, and even waterfalls. 418 Eighth St. (at Kilele St.). ✆ **866/DIS-N-DAT** (347-6328) or 808/565-9170. www.suzieo.com.

Gifts with Aloha ★ Phoenix and Kimberly Dupree's store of treasures has blossomed since they moved to a larger location on the other side of Dole Park. They are now shipping minigardens and lamps to the mainland, and are selling fabulously stylish hats, locally made clothing, T-shirts, swimwear, quilts, Jams World dresses, children's clothes, toys, Hawaii-themed CDs, DVDs, music, books, art by local artists (including some of the most beautiful jewelry in the islands), and more. The sumptuous honey from the Big Island is available here, as are jams and jellies by Lanai's Fabrao House. The made-on-Maui soaps and bath products—in gardenia, pikake, and plumeria fragrances—make great gifts. Dole Park, 363 Seventh St. (at Ilima St.). ✆ **808/565-6589.**

MARKETS

Lanai Marketplace Everyone on Lanai, it seems, is a backyard farmer. From 7 to 11am on Saturday, they all head to this shady square to sell their dewy-fresh produce, home-baked breads, plate lunches, and handicrafts. This is Lanai's version of the farmers' market: petite in scale (like the island) but charming, and growing. Dole Square.

9 ENTERTAINMENT FOR THE WHOLE FAMILY

The only regular nightlife venues are the Lanai Playhouse, at the corner of Seventh and Lanai avenues in Lanai City, and the two Four Seasons resorts, The Lodge at Koele and Manele Bay.

The **Lanai Playhouse** (✆ **808/565-7500**) is a historic 1920s building that has won awards for its renovations. When it opened in 1993, the 150-seat venue stunned residents by offering first-run movies with Dolby sound—quite contemporary for anachronistic Lanai. Lanai Playhouse usually, but not always, shows two movies each evening from Friday to Tuesday (also Wed in summer), at 6:30 and 8:30pm, with occasional Sunday and Monday matinees; if a 3-hour movie is on, it's shown at 7:30pm. Tickets are $8 for adults and $5 for kids and seniors. The playhouse is also the venue for occasional special events.

The **Lanai Art Center** features the "Stars Under the Stars" (www.visitlanai.net) free screening of classic films (plus a cartoon) outdoors in the Dole Park on a 20-foot screen. Films begin at sunset, the first Thursday of the month; bring your own blankets, beach chairs, and a picnic dinner.

The Four Seasons Resort Lanai, The Lodge at Koele has stepped up its live entertainment. In the lodge's Great Hall, in front of its manorial fireplaces, local artists serenade listeners—who sip port and fine liqueurs while sinking into plush chairs—with contemporary Hawaiian, classical, and other genres of music. The special programs are on weekends, but throughout the week some form of nightly entertainment takes place from 7 to 10pm.

Occasionally, special events will bring in a few more nightlife options. During the annual **Pineapple Festival,** generally the first weekend in July, some of Hawaii's best musicians arrive to show their support for Lanai (see "Kids' Favorite Hawaii Events," in chapter 2). Other special events include the **Aloha Festival** (www.alohafestivals.com), which takes place either at the end of September or the first week in October, and the **Christmas Festival,** the first Saturday in December (contact **Lanai Visitors Bureau,** P.O. Box 631436, Lanai City, HI 96763, or 431 Seventh St., Suite A, Lanai City; ✆ **800/947-4774** or 808/565-7600; fax 808/565-9316; www.visitlanai.net).

Listening to Storytellers and other children's activities are regular features at the Lanai Library, Fraser Avenue near Fifth Street, Lanai City (✆ **808/565-6996**). The events include programs for preschoolers, kids ages 6 to 8, and kids ages 9 to 12; they're usually free and open to everyone.

9

Kauai

Kauai is a magical land. This is where "Puff, the Magic Dragon" played in Hanalei, where tiny mythical people performed great feats under the cover of darkness, where kings roamed in valleys, and giants slept in mountains. What child wouldn't want to come here to play?

On any list of the world's most spectacular islands, Kauai ranks right up there with Bora Bora, Huahine, and Rarotonga. All the elements are here: moody rainforests, majestic cliffs, jagged peaks, emerald valleys, palm trees swaying in the breeze, daily rainbows, and some of the most spectacular golden beaches you'll find anywhere. Soft tropical air, sunrise bird song, essence of ginger and plumeria, golden sunsets, sparkling waterfalls—you don't just go to Kauai, you absorb it with every sense. It may get more than its fair share of tropical downpours, but that's what makes it so lush and green—and creates an abundance of rainbows.

Kauai is essentially a single large shield volcano that rises 3 miles above the sea floor. The island lies 90 miles across the open ocean from Oahu, but it seems at least a half-century removed in time.

Kauai's beauty has played a supporting role in more than 40 Hollywood films, from *South Pacific* to *Jurassic Park.* But this island is not just another pretty face: Its raw wilderness is daunting, its seas are challenging, its canyons are forbidding—two-thirds of the island is impenetrable. This is the place for an active family: There are watersports galore, and miles of trails through rainforests and along ocean cliffs for hikers, bikers, and horseback riders.

But Kauai is also great for families looking to relax. Here you'll find miles of sandy beaches and quiet spots in the forest where you can listen to the rain dance on the leaves, as well as an endless supply of laid-back, lazy days that end with the sun sinking into the Pacific in a blaze of glorious tropical color.

1 ORIENTATION

ARRIVING

The final approach to Lihue Airport is dramatic; try to sit on the left side of the aircraft, where passengers are treated to an excellent view of the Haupu Ridge, Nawiliwili Bay, and Kilohana Crater. **United Airlines** (✆ **800/225-5825;** www.ual.com) offers direct service to Kauai, with daily flights from Los Angeles and San Francisco. **American Airlines** (✆ **800/433-7300;** www.aa.com) has direct flights from Los Angeles. **SunTrips** (✆ **800/514-5194;** www.suntrips.com) has a charter from San Francisco or Oakland once a week that is direct. **Pleasant Holidays** (✆ **800/742-9244;** www.pleasantholidays.com), one of Hawaii's largest travel companies offering low-cost airfare and package deals, has two weekly nonstop flights from Los Angeles and San Francisco using American Trans Air. All other airlines land in Honolulu, where you'll have to connect to a 30-minute interisland flight to Kauai's Lihue Airport. Among the two interisland jet carriers— **go!** (✆ **888/IFLYGO2** [435-9462]; www.iflygo.com), and **Hawaiian Airlines**

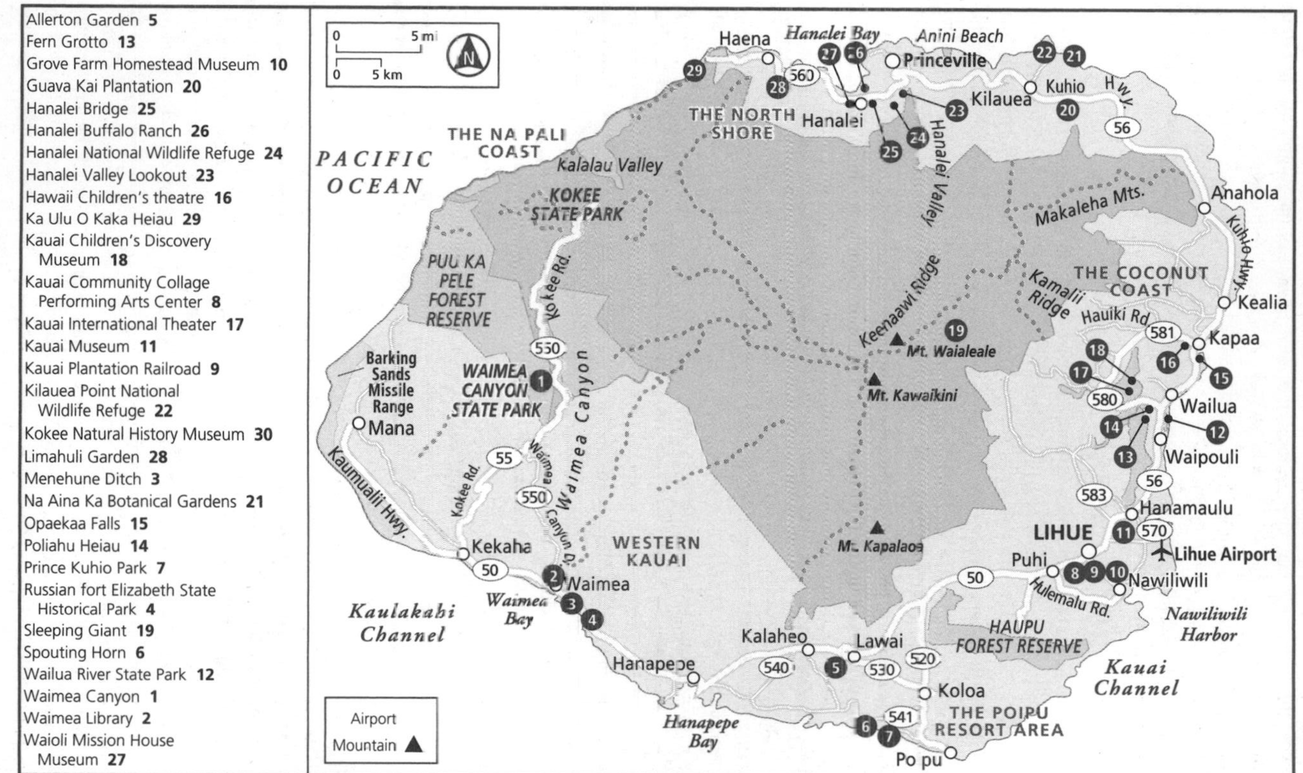
Allerton Garden 5
Fern Grotto 13
Grove Farm Homestead Museum 10
Guava Kai Plantation 20
Hanalei Bridge 25
Hanalei Buffalo Ranch 26
Hanalei National Wildlife Refuge 24
Hanalei Valley Lookout 23
Hawaii Children's theatre 16
Ka Ulu O Kaka Heiau 29
Kauai Children's Discovery Museum 18
Kauai Community Collage Performing Arts Center 8
Kauai International Theater 17
Kauai Museum 11
Kauai Plantation Railroad 9
Kilauea Point National Wildlife Refuge 22
Kokee Natural History Museum 30
Limahuli Garden 28
Menehune Ditch 3
Na Aina Ka Botanical Gardens 21
Opaekaa Falls 15
Poliahu Heiau 14
Prince Kuhio Park 7
Russian fort Elizabeth State Historical Park 4
Sleeping Giant 19
Spouting Horn 6
Wailua River State Park 12
Waimea Canyon 1
Waimea Library 2
Waioli Mission House Museum 27
0 5 mi
0 5 km
N
PACIFIC OCEAN
THE NA PALI COAST
Kalalau Valley
KOKEE STATE PARK
PUU KA PELE FOREST RESERVE
Kokee Rd.
Barking Sands Missile Range
WAIMEA CANYON STATE PARK
Mana
Kaumualii Hwy.
Waimea Canyon
Waimea Canyon Dr.
Kekaha
Waimea
Waimea Bay
Kaulakahi Channel
WESTERN KAUAI
Hanapepe
Hanapepe Bay
Kalaheo
Lawai
Koloa
Po pu
THE POIPU RESORT AREA
HAUPU FOREST RESERVE
Hulemalu Rd.
Puhi
LIHUE
Nawiliwili
Nawiliwili Harbor
Kauai Channel
Lihue Airport
Hanamaulu
Waipouli
Wailua
Kapaa
Kealia
Hauiki Rd.
THE COCONUT COAST
Kamalii Ridge
Makaleha Mts.
Anahola
Kuhio Hwy.
Kuhio Hwy.
Kilauea
Anini Beach
Princeville
Hanalei Bay
Haena
Hanalei
THE NORTH SHORE
Hanalei Valley
Keenaawi Ridge
Mt. Waialeale
Mt. Kawaikini
Mt. Kapalaoa
Airport
Mountain

 (✆ **800/367-5320,** 808/245-1813, or 808/838-1555; www.hawaiianair.com)—there is a flight at least every hour to Lihue.

You'll land at the Lihue Airport, located 3 miles outside of the county seat of Lihue. There's a county visitor information kiosk located next to each baggage claim area. All of the major car rental companies have branches at Lihue Airport; see "Getting Around," below, and "Getting Around Hawaii," in chapter 2, for details on renting in Hawaii. If you're not renting a car (although you should be), call **Kauai Taxi Company** (✆ **808/246-9554**) for airport pickup.

VISITOR INFORMATION

The **Kauai Visitors Bureau** is located on the first floor of the Watumull Plaza, 4334 Rice St., Suite 101, Lihue, HI 96766 (✆ **808/245-3971;** www.kauaidiscovery.com). For a free official *Kauai Vacation Planner* or recorded information, call ✆ **800/262-1400.** The **Poipu Beach Resort Association,** P.O. Box 730, Koloa, HI 96756 (✆ **888/744-0888** or 808/742-7444; www.poipu-beach.org), will send you a free guide to accommodations, activities, shopping, and dining in the Poipu Beach area.

KAUAI IN BRIEF

Lihue & Environs

Lihue is where most visitors first set foot on the island. This red-dirt farm town, the county seat, is a plain and simple place, with used-car lots and mom-and-pop shops. It's also the source of bargains: inexpensive lodging, great deals on dining, and some terrific shopping buys. And there's a beach kids will love: **Kalapaki Beach** ★★. Next door is **Nawiliwili,** the island's main harbor.

The Poipu Resort Area

POIPU BEACH ★★★ On Kauai's sun-soaked south shore, this is a pleasant if sleepy resort destination of low-rise hotels set on gold-sand pocket beaches. It's a great place for watersports, and a good base from which to tour the rest of Kauai. The only drawback is that the North Shore is about 1 to 1½ hours away.

Western Kauai

You must take your kids to one of Hawaii's most spectacular natural wonders, **Waimea Canyon** ★★★ (the "Grand Canyon of the Pacific"), and, farther upland and inland, one of its best parks, **Kokee State Park** ★★.

HANAPEPE For a quick trip back in time, turn off Highway 50 at Hanapepe, once one of Kauai's biggest towns. Founded by Chinese rice farmers, this picturesque town has unusual shops and bargain restaurants. Nearby is **Salt Pond Beach Park** ★, where the kids can watch Hawaiians dry a reddish sea salt in shallow, red-clay pans.

WAIMEA This little coastal town, the original capital of Kauai, seems to have quit the march of time. This was the spot where, in 1778, British explorer Capt. James Cook dropped anchor and discovered a sleepy village of grass shacks.

The Coconut Coast

The eastern shore of Kauai, north of Lihue, is a jumble of commerce and condos strung along the coast road named for Prince Kuhio, with several small beaches beyond. Almost anything you need, and a lot of stuff you can live without, can be found along this coast, which is known for its hundreds of coconut trees waving in the breeze. It's popular with budget travelers because of the affordable hotels and condos to choose from, and it offers great restaurants and the island's major shopping areas.

KAPAA ★ The center of commerce on the east coast and the capital of the Coconut Coast condo-and-hotel district, this restored plantation town looks just like an antique. False-front wooden stores line both sides of the highway; it looks as though they've been here forever—until you notice the fresh paint and new roofs and realize that everything has been rebuilt since Hurricane Iniki smacked the town flat in 1992.

The North Shore

Kauai's North Shore may be the most beautiful place in Hawaii. There's only one road in and out, and only two towns, Hanalei and Kilauea—the former by the sea, the latter on a lighthouse cliff that's home to a bird preserve.

KILAUEA ★ This village is home to an antique lighthouse, tropical-fruit stands, little stone houses, and Kilauea Point National Wildlife Refuge, a wonderful seabird preserve. The village itself has its charms: The 1892 Kong Lung Company, Kauai's oldest general store, sells antiques, art, and crafts; and you can order a jazzy Billie Holiday Pizza to go at Kilauea Bakery and Pau Hana Pizza.

PRINCEVILLE ★ A little overwhelming for Kauai's wild North Shore, Princeville Resort is Kauai's biggest project, an 11,000-acre development set on a high plain overlooking Hanalei Bay. This resort community includes a luxury Sheraton hotel, 10 condo complexes, new timeshare units, and cliffside access to pocket beaches.

HANALEI ★★★ Picture-postcard Hanalei is the laid-back center of North Shore life and an escapist's dream; it's also the gateway to the wild Na Pali Coast. At **Hanalei Bay,** sloops anchor and surfers play year-round. The 2-mile-long crescent beach, the biggest indentation on Kauai's coast, is ideal for kids in summer, when the wild surf turns placid. On either side of two-lane Kuhio Highway, you'll find just enough shops and restaurants to sustain you for a week's visit—unless you're a hiker, surfer, or sailor, or you have some other preoccupation that just might keep you here the rest of your life.

HAENA ★★ Emerald-green Haena isn't a town or a beach but an ancient Hawaiian district, a place of exceptional natural beauty and the gateway to the Na Pali Coast. This idyllic, 4-mile coast has lagoons, bays, great beaches, spectacular snorkeling, a botanical garden, and more for your family to explore.

The Na Pali Coast ★★★

The road comes to an end, and now it begins: the Hawaii you've been dreaming about. Kauai's Na Pali Coast (*na pali* means "the cliffs") is a place of extreme beauty and Hawaii's last true wilderness. Its majestic splendor will forever remain unspoiled because no road will ever traverse it. You can enter this state park only on foot or by sea. Those of us who aren't up to the arduous trek on razor-thin cliff trails can explore the wild coast in an inflatable rubber Zodiac, a billowing sailboat, a high-powered catamaran, or a hovering helicopter, which will take your kids for the ride of their lives.

Niihau: The Forbidden Island

Just 17 miles across the Kaulakahi Channel from Kauai lies the arid island of Niihau, "The Forbidden Island." Visitors are not allowed on this privately owned island, which is a working cattle and sheep ranch with about 200 residents living in the single town of Puuwai.

In 1864, after an unusually wet winter that turned the dry scrubland of the small island (18×6 miles) into green pasture, Eliza Sinclair, a Scottish widow, decided to buy Niihau and move her family here. King Kamehameha IV agreed to sell the island for $10,000. The next year, normal weather returned, and the green pastures withered into sparse semidesert vegetation.

Today, Sinclair's great-great-grandson, Bruce Robinson, continues to run the ranching operation and fiercely protects the privacy of the island residents. From the outside, life on Niihau has not changed much in 140 years: There's no running water, indoor plumbing, or electrically generated power. The Hawaiian language is still spoken. Most of the men work for the ranch when there is work, and fish and hunt when there is no work. The women specialize in gathering and stringing *pupu Niihau,* prized, tiny seashells (found only on this island), into Niihau's famous leis, which fetch prices in the thousands of dollars.

2 GETTING AROUND

BY CAR

You need a car to see and do everything on Kauai. Luckily, driving here is easy. However, there really is only one major road that circles the island, and during rush hour, from about 6 to 9am and 3 to 6pm, this road turns into a giant parking lot. A trip from the airport to Poipu could be as quick as 30 to 45 minutes during non-rush-hour times or as much as 1½ hours during rush hour.

From Lihue Airport, turn right and you'll be on Kapule Highway (Hwy. 51), which eventually merges into Kuhio Highway (Hwy. 56) a mile down. This road will take you to the Coconut Coast and through the North Shore before reaching a dead end at Kee Beach, where the Na Pali Coast begins.

If you turn left from Lihue Airport and follow Kapule Highway (Hwy. 51), you'll pass through Lihue and Nawiliwili. Turning on Nawiliwili Road (Hwy. 58) will bring you to the intersection of Kaumualii Highway (Hwy. 50), which will take you to the south and southwest sections of the island. This road doesn't follow the coast, however, so if you're heading to Poipu (and most people are), take Maluhia Road (Hwy. 520) south.

Kaumualii Highway (Hwy. 50) continues to Waimea, where it then dwindles to a secondary road before reaching a dead end at the other end of the Na Pali Coast.

To get to Waimea Canyon, take either Waimea Canyon Road (Hwy. 550), which follows the western rim of the canyon and affords spectacular views, or Kokee Road (Hwy. 55), which goes up through Waimea Canyon to Kokee State Park (4,000 ft. above sea level); the roads join up about halfway.

CAR RENTALS All of the major car rental agencies are represented on Kauai; for a complete list, as well as tips on insurance and driving rules, see "Getting Around Hawaii," in chapter 2. The rental desks are just across the street from Lihue Airport, but you must go by van to collect your car. For deep discounts on weekly car rental rates, call **Hookipa Haven Vacation Services** (✆ **800/398-6284;** www.hookipa.com). Rates in low season (Jan, Apr 16–June, and Aug 21–Dec 18) are $143 a week ($28 a day); they jump up to $162 a week ($35 a day) in high season.

OTHER TRANSPORTATION OPTIONS

Kauai Taxi Company (✆ **808/246-9554**) offers taxi, limousine, and airport shuttle service. **Kauai Bus** (✆ **808/241-6410;** www.kauai.gov) operates a fleet of 15 buses that serve the entire island. Taking the bus may be practical for day trips if you know your way around the island, but you can't take anything larger than a shopping bag aboard, and the buses don't stop at any of the resort areas. However, they do serve more than a dozen coastal towns between Kekaha, on the southwest shore, all the way to Hanalei. Buses run more or less hourly from 5:30am to 6pm. The fare is $1.50, or 75¢ for children ages 7 to 18. (Kids 6 and younger ride free.)

Fast Facts Kauai

American Express There's no local office on the island.

Babysitters Call **PATCH** (✆ **808/839-1988**), or your hotel can refer you to qualified babysitters.

Dentists Emergency dental care is available from **Dr. Mark A. Baird,** 4-9768 Kuhio Hwy., Kapaa (✆ **808/822-9393**); and from **Dr. Michael Furgeson,** 4347 Rice St., Lihue (✆ **808/246-6960**).

Doctors Walk-ins are accepted at **Kauai Medical Clinic,** 3-3420 Kuhio Hwy., Suite B, Lihue (✆ **808/245-1500,** or 808/245-1831 after hours). You can also try the **North Shore Clinic,** Kilauea and Oka roads, Kilauea (✆ **808/828-1418**); **Koloa Clinic,** 5371 Koloa Rd. (✆ **808/742-1621**); **Eleele Clinic,** 3292 Waialo Rd. (✆ **808/335-0499**); or **Kapaa Clinic,** 3-1105 Kuhio Hwy. (✆ **808/822-3431**).

Drugstores There are no 24-hour pharmacies on Kauai. On the south side of the island, try the **Southshore Pharmacy,** 5330 Koloa Rd., Koloa (✆ **808/742-7511**); on the north side, **Northshore Pharmacy,** 2460 Oka, Kilauea (✆ **808/828-1844**); and between them, **Longs Drugs,** 4-831 Kuhio Hwy., Lihue (✆ **808/822-4915**).

Emergencies Dial ✆ **911** for police, fire, and ambulance service. The **Poison Control Center** can be reached at ✆ **800/362-3585.**

Hospitals **Wilcox Health System,** 3420 Kuhio Hwy., Lihue (✆ **808/245-1100**), has emergency services available around the clock.

Internet Access To get online in the Poipu area, go to **Koloa Country Store,** 5356 Kolo Rd. (✆ **808/742-1255**); in Waimea, **Na Pali Explorer,** 9935 Kaumualii Hwy. (✆ **808/338-9999**); in Kapaa, **Business Support Services,** 4-1191 Kuhio Hwy. (✆ **808/822-5504**); and in Hanalei, **Bali Ha'i Photo,** 5-5190 Kuhio Hwy. (✆ **808/826-9181**), or **Akamai Computer Technology,** 5-4280 Kuhio Hwy. (✆ **808/826-1042**). The public library (see below) offers free Internet access.

Libraries There are six branches of the public library on Kauai; for the location nearest you and hours of operation, check www.librarieshawaii.org. The Lihue branch, 4344 Hardy St. (✆ **808/241-3222**), is open Monday and Wednesday from 11am to 7pm, and Tuesday, Thursday, and Friday from 9am to 4:30pm.

Newspapers The *Garden Island* is the island's daily paper. The *Honolulu Advertiser* and the *Honolulu Star Bulletin* are circulated statewide.

Police For nonemergencies, call ✆ **808/245-9711.**

Post Office The main post office is at 4441 Rice St., Lihue. To find the branch office nearest you, call ✆ **800/ASK-USPS** (275-8777).

Radio The most popular stations are **KHPR** (88.1 or 90.7 FM), the National Public Radio station; **KONG** (570 AM), news, talk, sports; **KUAI** (720 AM), Hawaiian and contemporary music, surf reports, sports; **KKCR** (91.9 and 90.9 FM), nonprofit community radio with various formats; **KONG** (93.5 FM), contemporary music; **KSRF** (95.9 FM), surf and contemporary Hawaiian music; **KFMN** (96.9 FM), adult contemporary; **KITH** (98.9 FM), travel host, island music, commercial travel information; **KTOH** (99.9 FM), oldies music from the 1950s on; and **KSHK** (103.3 FM), classic rock.

Restrooms In a pinch, fast-food joints and beach parks are your best bets.

Safety Kauai is generally safe, but use the same common sense you would in a big city.

Useful Telephone Numbers For current weather conditions, call ✆ **808/245-6001.** For marine conditions, call ✆ **808/245-3564.**

3 FAMILY-FRIENDLY ACCOMMODATIONS

To avoid long drives every day, be sure to review "Kauai in Brief," earlier in this chapter, to choose the location that best fits your vacation needs.

Taxes of 11.42% are added to all hotel bills. Parking is free unless otherwise noted.

LIHUE & ENVIRONS

If you need to stay overnight near the airport, try the **Garden Island Inn** (p. 350).

Very Expensive

Kauai Marriott Resort & Beach Club ★★ If your tykes love the water (they go in at 8am and reluctantly leave only for bathroom breaks and lunch), this is your place. Water is everywhere throughout the resort: lagoons, waterfalls, fountains, a 5-acre circular swimming pool (the largest on the island), and a terrific stretch of beach out front. The lagoons are home to six islands that serve as an exotic minizoo; they lend an air of fantasy to the place, and, along with the enormous pool and children's program, make the resort popular with families.

Guest rooms are fairly large and comfortable, with fabulous views of gold-sand Kalapaki Beach. Amenities such as free meals for kids 11 and younger, a complimentary shuttle to the airport (only a mile away), cultural activities, a children's pool, and a great kids' program ($45 per child for a full day) with plenty to do (ukulele and hula lessons, pottery painting classes, and more) add up to a great place to stay.

Kalapaki Beach, Lihue, HI 96766. ✆ **800/220-2925** or 808/245-5050. Fax 808/246-5148. www.marriott hawaii.com. 356 units. $359–$555 double; from $694 suite. Extra person $40. Children 17 and under stay free in parent's room (4 maximum). Cribs free; rollaway beds free for children 17 and under. AE, DC, DISC, MC, V. Valet parking $12; self-parking $9. Free airport shuttle. **Amenities:** 4 restaurants; 2 bars; the largest pool on the island; 36-hole Jack Nicklaus golf course; 8 tennis courts; state-of-the-art health club; 5 Jacuzzis; watersports equipment/rentals; children's program; concierge; activities desk; car rental desk; business center; shopping arcade; salon; room service; massage; babysitting; coin-op laundry; laundry service; dry cleaning. *In room:* A/C, TV/VCR, dataport, fridge, coffeemaker, hair dryer, iron, safe.

Expensive

Hilton Kauai Beach Resort First, the property—formerly the Radisson Kauai—underwent a $7-million renovation in 2006 to convert it to a condo-hotel (which means a portion of the rooms in the hotel are privately owned). Then, in late 2006, Hilton took over the management of the property and spent another $14 million to renovate and add such amenities as a 24-hour business center, an executive club floor, Hilton's bedding and bath items, and an expanded fitness center. The result? The 25-acre beachfront property, located 4 miles north of Lihue, is a now a great choice for families. To start, there's a 3-mile stretch of the beach next door to a top-ranked municipal golf course; next there is a complimentary airport shuttle; and then there are the four-pool complex, a 12-foot waterfall cascading into the main pool, and a flume and lava tube water slide at the sand-bottom pool. The best deal for a family is the Family and Friends Program, in which the second room is 50% off. The rooms have all been renovated and updated with plush new carpeting, a Balinese-style wood entry door, marble bathroom and floors, top-of-the-line bedding, and high-speed wireless Internet. The Hilton also added a new whirlpool spa in a stone grotto surrounded by ferns and a waterfall. The location is good, about equidistant from both North- and South-shore activities, and also close to the Wailua River and its kayaking, water-skiing, river tours, historic sites, and waterfalls. The only problems here are the windy conditions and the lack of safe swimming on the beautiful white-sand beach. Another caveat: no children's program, but there is a playground and a kids' menu in the dining room.

4331 Kauai Beach Dr., Lihue, HI 96766. ✆ **800/HILTONS** (445-8667) or 808/245-1955. Fax 808/246-9085. www.hilton.com. 350 units. $179–$399 double; from $1,500 suite. Daily resort fee $11 for nightly sunset cocktail party and Polynesian dance show, coffee/tea service 6–7am, use of the Alolani Spa and Fitness Center, in-room coffee and tea service, in-room safe, local phone calls, in-room wireless access, shuttle service to airport, and parking. Numerous packages available, including car rentals, senior rates, and more. Extra person $20. Children 12 and under stay free in parent's room. Cribs free. AE, DC, DISC, MC, V. Parking included in daily resort fee. **Amenities:** Restaurant; bar; 4 outdoor pools; tennis courts; fitness room; spa; Jacuzzi; watersports equipment/rentals; concierge; activities desk; car rental desk; business center; shopping arcade; salon; massage; babysitting; coin-op washer/dryers; laundry service; dry cleaning. *In room:* A/C, TV, dataport, Wi-Fi, fridge, coffeemaker, hair dryer, iron, safe.

Moderate

Kauai Beach Villas These beachfront condos are a good option for families seeking more space and privacy than they'd get elsewhere in Lihue. The only drawback is the unsafe swimming conditions at the beautiful but windy white-sand beach; the kids should content themselves with the pools spread across the property. Each unit is outfitted with a fully equipped kitchen, a washer/dryer, and a lanai big enough for two lounge chairs, a table, and four chairs. Each two-bedroom unit has a lanai off each bedroom, too. The immaculately landscaped grounds feature tennis courts, barbecue areas, and a volleyball court. The Wailua Municipal golf course is next door.

4330 Kauai Beach Dr., Lihue. Reservations c/o Kauai Vacation Rentals, 3-3311 Kuhio Hwy, Lihue, HI 96766. ✆ **800/367-5025** or 808/245-8841. Fax 808/246-1161. www.kauaivacationrentals.com. 150 units. $162–$250 1-bedroom for 4; $119–$350 2-bedroom for 6. 3-night minimum. AE, DISC, MC, V. **Amenities:** 4 outdoor pools; tennis courts; access to nearby health club; 2 Jacuzzis; activities desk; coin-op washer/dryers; laundry; dry cleaning. *In room:* A/C (in bedrooms), TV/VCR, dataport, kitchen, fridge, coffeemaker, hair dryer, iron, safe, washer/dryer, answering machine.

Inexpensive

Garden Island Inn ★ Finds This bargain hunter's delight is located 2 miles from the airport, 1 mile from Lihue, and within walking distance of shops and restaurants. The spacious rooms have a variety of bedding, including the family-friendly room with a queen bed and two twin beds. Each unit contains a fridge, microwave, wet bar, TV, and coffeemaker; some have private lanais, and the suites have sitting areas; all have ocean views. Owner Steve Layne offers friendly service, lots of advice on activities (the entire staff happily uses their connections to get you discounts), and even complimentary use of beach gear, golf clubs (a course is nearby, as are tennis courts), and coolers. ***Warning:*** The inn is located close to the airport and harbor, plus daytime street traffic can make this property noisy.

3445 Wilcox Rd. (across the street from Kalapaki Beach, near Nawiliwili Harbor), Lihue, HI 96766. ✆ **800/648-0154** or 808/245-7227. Fax 808/245-7603. www.gardenislandinn.com. 21 units. $99–$180 double. Extra person $10. Children 17 and under stay free in parent's room. Cribs and rollaway beds $10 each. AE, DC, MC, V. **Amenities:** Complimentary watersports equipment; activities desk. *In room:* A/C, TV, free Wi-Fi, fridge, microwave, coffeemaker, hair dryer, iron, wet bar.

THE POIPU RESORT AREA

Very Expensive

Grand Hyatt Kauai Resort and Spa ★★★ Kids Hard to believe that this luxury hotel (one of Hawaii's best) can get "grander," but the new multimillion-dollar renovations of this already "grand" resort has taken the level of casual elegance to a new level. This is one of Hawaii's best luxury hotels and one of the top-ranked tropical resorts in *Condé Nast Traveler*'s annual readers' poll. The four-story resort, built into the oceanside bluffs, spreads over 50 acres that overlook Shipwreck Beach (which is too rough for most swimmers) at the end of the road in Poipu. The $250-million Hyatt uses the island architecture of the mid-1920s to recapture the old Hawaii of the Matson Line steamship era.

The airy atmosphere replicates the casual elegance of a grand plantation overlooking the sea. The result is a comfortable, modest place for everyone from children to grandparents. Your 3-year-old will probably want to try the 150-foot water slide (a 47-sec. ride through a stream of warm water) before you are unpacked. Camp Hyatt offers the perfect activities for your 3- to 12-year-olds ($70 for a full day and $55 for a half-day with lunch), including night camp (4–10pm, costing $10 an hour per child). The more mature preteen ladies can spend the day with their moms at the **ANARA Spa ★★★**, the best spa on Kauai. For infants, the staff will handle everything from cribs with bumpers and mobiles to a refrigerator for formula. Other pluses include kiddie menus and "color me" place mats at every restaurant, and kids 5 and younger eat free at the buffet breakfast at the Ilima Terrace. All this, and a concierge who will make sure your family's vacation is perfect.

1571 Poipu Rd., Koloa, HI 96756. ✆ **800/55-HYATT** (554-9288) or 808/742-1234. Fax 808/742-1557. www.kauai.hyatt.com. 602 units. $480–$810 double; from $910 Grand Club; from $1,600 suite. Resort fee

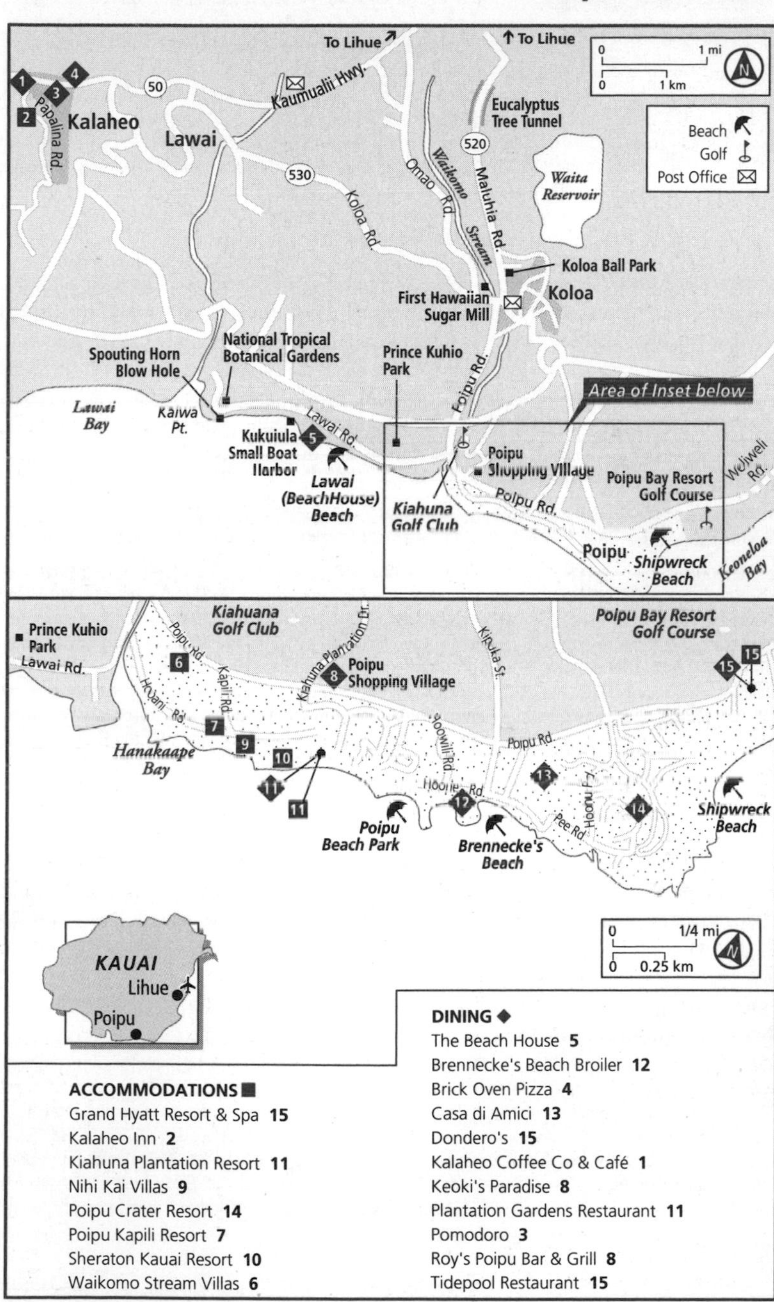
To Lihue
To Lihue
0 1 mi
0 1 km
Beach
Golf
Post Office
Kalaheo
Papalina Rd.
Lawai
50
Kaumualii Hwy.
530
Koloa Rd.
Omao Rd.
Waikomo Stream
520
Maluhia Rd.
Eucalyptus Tree Tunnel
Waita Reservoir
Koloa Ball Park
Koloa
First Hawaiian Sugar Mill
National Tropical Botanical Gardens
Spouting Horn Blow Hole
Prince Kuhio Park
Poipu Rd.
Area of Inset below
Lawai Bay
Kaiwa Pt.
Kukuiula Small Boat Harbor
Lawai Rd.
Lawai (BeachHouse) Beach
Kiahuna Golf Club
Poipu Shopping Village
Poipu Rd.
Poipu Bay Resort Golf Course
Weliweli Rd.
Poipu
Shipwreck Beach
Keoneloa Bay
Prince Kuhio Park
Lawai Rd.
Kiahuana Golf Club
Poipu Rd.
Kapili Rd.
Hoonani Rd.
Kiahuna Plantation Dr.
Poipu Shopping Village
Kiploka St.
Poipu Bay Resort Golf Course
Hanakaape Bay
Hoowili Rd.
Poipu Rd.
Hoone Rd.
Hoonu Rd.
Pee Rd.
Poipu Beach Park
Brennecke's Beach
Shipwreck Beach
0 1/4 mi
0 0.25 km
KAUAI
Lihue
Poipu
DINING
The Beach House 5
Brennecke's Beach Broiler 12
Brick Oven Pizza 4
Casa di Amici 13
Dondero's 15
Kalaheo Coffee Co & Café 1
Keoki's Paradise 8
Plantation Gardens Restaurant 11
Pomodoro 3
Roy's Poipu Bar & Grill 8
Tidepool Restaurant 15
ACCOMMODATIONS
Grand Hyatt Resort & Spa 15
Kalaheo Inn 2
Kiahuna Plantation Resort 11
Nihi Kai Villas 9
Poipu Crater Resort 14
Poipu Kapili Resort 7
Sheraton Kauai Resort 10
Waikomo Stream Villas 6

$15 for local calls, self- and valet parking, 1 hr. at the tennis court, access to the spa and classes, and 10% discount in various shops on property. Packages available. Extra person $50. Children 17 and under stay free in parent's room. Cribs and rollaway beds free. AE, DC, DISC, MC, V. **Amenities:** 6 restaurants (see Dondero's on p. 366); 6 bars (the partially open-air Stevenson's Library has mellow jazz Thurs–Sat nights); an elaborate freshwater fantasy pool complex, plus 2 more pools and 5 acres of saltwater swimming lagoons w/islands and a man-made beach; 4 tennis courts; one of the best health clubs on the island; 25,000-sq.-ft. ANARA Spa w/lava-rock shower gardens, 10-headed Swedish shower, and indoor-outdoor treatment rooms offering everything from Hawaiian massage to seaweed body wraps; 3 Jacuzzis; watersports equipment/rentals; bike rentals; extensive Camp Hyatt kids' program; game room; concierge; activities desk; car rental desk; business center; shopping arcade; salon; room service; massage; babysitting; free use of laundry facilities; same-day laundry service/dry cleaning; concierge-level rooms. *In room:* A/C, TV/VCR, dataport, high-speed Internet access ($15/day), minibar, fridge, coffeemaker, hair dryer, iron, safe.

Sheraton Kauai Resort ★★ This Sheraton has the feeling of Old Hawaii and a dynamite location on one of Kauai's best beaches. This family-friendly hotel features two children's pools and a very safe beach for swimming (not to mention sandcastle building, Frisbee throwing, or just plain digging). Kids ages 12 and younger eat free at the Shells Restaurant (off the *keiki,* or children's, menu for breakfast and dinner), and at the poolside restaurant they can get a kids' "lunch in a pail." Coin-operated laundry facilities, board games to take back to the rooms, and special discount rates for families needing a second room all add up to one value-packed deal. The Kaui Keiki Aloha Program (for ages 3–12 years) features arts and crafts, storytelling, pool play, and other activities for $50 for a full day and $35 for a half-day with lunch.

2440 Hoonani Rd., Koloa, HI 96756. ✆ **800/782-9488** or 808/742-1661. Fax 808/742-4041. www.sheraton-kauai.com. 413 units. $420–$720 double (maximum 4 in room); from $800–$1,600 suite for 4. Resort fee of $18 for sunset mai tai punch hour (Sun, Mon, Wed, Fri) with a torch-lighting ceremony, parking, Internet access, guest library with daily newspapers and 4 computers with Internet access, and use of fitness center and tennis courts. Extra person $60. Children 17 and under stay free in parent's room. Cribs free; rollaway beds $55. AE, DC, DISC, MC, V. **Amenities:** 3 restaurants; extraordinary bar; 2 outdoor pools (1 w/water playground, 1 for children); 3 tennis courts (2 lighted); health club facing the ocean (one of the most scenic places to work out on Kauai); small spa; Jacuzzi; watersports equipment/rentals; children's program; game room; concierge; activities desk; shopping arcade; salon; room service; babysitting; coin-op laundry; same-day laundry service and dry cleaning. *In room:* A/C, TV/VCR, dataport, fridge, coffeemaker, hair dryer, iron, safe.

Expensive

Outrigger Kiahuna Plantation ★★ This complex consists of several plantation-style buildings, loaded with Hawaiian style and scattered throughout a 35-acre garden setting with lagoons, lawns, and a gold-sand beach. Golf, shopping, and restaurants are within easy walking distance. All condo units are spacious, with full kitchens, daily maid service, and lanais. Guests can send their children to the Sheraton Kauai Resort's Kauai Keiki Aloha Program (see above).

2253 Poipu Rd., Koloa, HI 96756. ✆ **800/OUTRIGGER** (688-7444) or 808/742-6411. Fax 808/742-1689. www.outrigger.com. 207 units. $249–$479 1-bedroom apt (sleeps up to 4); $385–$525 2-bedroom apt (sleeps up to 6). Packages available, including 5th night free, car packages, senior rates, and more. Children 17 and under stay free in parent's room. Cribs $5 per day or $25 per week; rollaway beds $15 per day. AE, DC, DISC, MC, V. **Amenities:** Restaurant (see Plantation Gardens on p. 366); bar; outdoor pool; tennis courts; watersports equipment/rentals; children's program; activities desk; shopping arcade nearby; coin-op laundry. *In room:* TV/VCR, kitchen, fridge, coffeemaker, hair dryer, iron, safe.

Moderate

Poipu Kapili Resort ★★ This quiet, upscale, oceanfront cluster of condos is outstanding in every area. We like the home-away-from-home comforts and special touches:

(Value) The King of Condos

One of the easiest ways to find lodging in the Poipu Beach area is to contact **Parrish Collection Kauai** (formerly Grantham Resorts), 3176 Poipu Rd., Koloa, HI 96756 (✆ **800/325-5701** or 808/742-2000; fax 808/742-9093; www.parrishkauai.com). Parrish handles more than 100 "handpicked" rental units for 12 different condo developments, plus dozens of vacation homes, ranging from quaint cottages to elite resort homes. Parrish Kauai has high standards for their rental units and offers extremely fair prices. If the properties are not maintained to their standards, they have no problem taking the units (and, in one case, an entire condominium project) out of their selected rentals. The condos start at $105 for a spacious one-bedroom, gardenview unit in low season, and vacation cottages start at $235 and go up to $1,695 for exquisite multimillion-dollar ocean estates. There's a 5-night minimum for condos and a 7-night minimum for homes. All rentals are well equipped (full kitchen, washer/dryer, wet bar, TV/DVD, and phone).

If you're staying on Kauai for 5 days, ask Parrish Kauai about the **"Frommer's Preferred Guest Discount"** (see the reviews for Nihi Kai Villas, Poipu Crater Resort, and Waikomo Stream Villas below). There's not a better deal on Kauai. Kudos to Parrish Kauai for these fabulous vacation bargains.

a video and book library, a spacious pool, several barbecues, tennis courts lit for night play, and an herb garden. (You're welcome to take samples if you're cooking.) A golf course is also nearby. The apartments are large (one-bedroom/two-bathroom units are 1,150 sq. ft.; two-bedroom/three-bathroom units are 1,820 sq. ft.) and have fully equipped kitchens, tropical furnishings, ceiling fans, and private lanais. The oceanfront two-story town houses are our favorites because they catch the trade winds. The two-bedroom units also have washer/dryers. (Common laundry facilities are available on the property as well.) Upon check-in, kids ages 5 to 12 get an "Island Explorer Kit," with backpack, coloring book, sunglasses, and binoculars. Although the Pacific is right outside your window, the nearest sandy beach is a block away (which can be a blessing because it means more privacy), but there is a swimming pool with a children's area and slide on the property.

2221 Kapili Rd., Koloa, HI 96756. ✆ **800/443-7714** or 808/742-6449. Fax 808/742-9162. www.poipukapili.com. 60 units. $230–$345 1-bedroom apt (sleeps up to 4); $345–$465 2-bedroom apt (up to 6). Discounts for longer stays; 7th night free May 1–Dec 20. Rates include Fri continental breakfast by the pool. Packages available. Children 17 and under stay free in parent's room. Cribs $15 per day; rollaway beds $16 per day. MC, V. **Amenities:** Oceanside pool; championship lighted tennis courts; activities desk; coin-op laundry. *In room:* TV/VCR/DVD, dataport, free high-speed Internet, kitchen, fridge, coffeemaker, hair dryer (upon request), iron.

Inexpensive

Kalaheo Inn ★ (Value) What a deal! Located in the town of Kalaheo, a 12-minute drive from world-famous Poipu Beach, a 5-minute drive from the Kukuiolono Golf Course, and within walking distance of restaurants, the inn is a comfortable 1940s motel totally remodeled in 1999 and converted into apartment units with kitchenettes. It's

Chickens & Roosters

One of the first things that visitors notice about Kauai is that there seems to be an unusually large number of *moa* (wild chickens). Kauai has always had a history of having more than its fair share of chickens and roosters running about, but after Hurricane Iniki picked up and scattered the fowl all over the island in 1992, they have been populating at a prodigious rate. Generally, a few chickens scratching around in the dirt is quaint and downright picturesque. However, the "dark side" of the chicken population explosion is the increase in the number of roosters. There are roosters everywhere. In fact, a new industry has cropped up: Rooster Eradicators. Mainly resorts hire these Rooster Eradicators to remove the birds from the well-manicured grounds because the large number of these male birds has lead to, well, a sort of crowing contest. Generally roosters will crow as the sun comes up. But on Kauai, with the population increase, the roosters crow all day long and throughout the night in some places. Be warned that part of the charm of Kauai is the rooster population. So if you are not a rooster "affectionado," bring earplugs.

perfect for families (especially the two-bedroom units that also have a sofa bed for just $123). Owners Chet and Tish Hunt couldn't be friendlier, handing out complimentary beach towels, beach toys, and even golf clubs to guests. (Links are nearby.) They love families and have a storeroom full of games to keep the kids entertained. This is a must-stay for vacationers on a budget.

444 Papaline Rd. (just behind the Kalaheo Steakhouse), Koloa, HI 96756. ✆ **888/332-6023** or 808/332-6023. Fax 808/742-6432. www.kalaheoinn.com. 14 units. $83 double studio; $93–$103 1-bedroom; $123 2-bedroom; $183 3-bedroom with full kitchen. Children 17 and under stay free in parent's room. Cribs and futons free. MC, V. **Amenities:** Complimentary watersports equipment; children's games; Internet, coin-op laundry. *In room:* TV, kitchen or kitchenette, fridge, coffeemaker, iron.

Nihi Kai Villas ★ Value Johnathan Parrish is a marketing genius. His Parrish Collection Kauai (see p. 353) is offering the deal of the decade for families on these large, two-bedroom units just 600 feet from the beach. If you stay 7 nights, the rate for these well-equipped oceanview apartments starts at an unbelievable $145 a night. You may not be getting new carpet, new furniture, new drapes, or a prime beachfront location, but you *are* getting a clean, well-cared-for unit with a full kitchen, washer/dryer, and TV/VCR, all at an unbeatable price. The property is a 2-minute walk from world-famous Brennecke's Beach (great for bodysurfing) and a block from Poipu Beach Park. On-site amenities include an oceanfront swimming pool, tennis and paddle courts, and a barbecue and picnic area. Within a 5-minute drive are two great golf courses, several restaurants, and loads of shopping.

1870 Hoone Rd., Poipu. Reservations: c/o Parrish Collections, 3176 Poipu Rd., Suite 1, Koloa, HI 96756. ✆ **800/325-5701** or 808/742-2000. Fax 808/742-9093. www.parrishkauai.com. 70 units. $145–$195 1-bedroom double; $159–$279 2-bedroom for 4; $300–$500 3-bedroom for 6. 5-night minimum. Futons $5 per night. DC, DISC, MC, V. From Poipu Rd., turn toward the ocean on Hoowili Rd., then left on Hoone Rd.; Nihi Kai Villas is just past Nalo Rd. on Hoone Rd. **Amenities:** Outdoor pool; nearby golf course; tennis courts; Jacuzzi; concierge; activities desk. *In room:* TV/DVD/CD, dataport, high-speed Internet, kitchen, coffeemaker, iron, washer/dryer.

Poipu Crater Resort (Value) Here's a deal travelers on a budget can't beat: two-bedroom gardenview units from just $119 a night. This resort (part of the Parrish Collection Kauai; see p. 353) consists of 15 duplexes in a tropical garden setting. Each unit is about 1,500 square feet with living area, kitchen, large lanai, bathroom, and guest bedroom downstairs and master bedroom and bathroom upstairs. Each has a full kitchen (with microwave), as well as a washer/dryer and VCR. The complex has a swimming pool, tennis and paddle ball courts, sauna, Ping-Pong tables, and barbecues. Poipu Beach is about a 10-minute walk away, and the entire Poipu Beach resort area (offering everything from restaurants to golf courses) is within a 5-minute drive. The only caveats are no maid service and no air-conditioning.

2330 Hoohu Rd., Poipu. Reservations: c/o Parrish Collections, 3176 Poipu Rd., Suite 1, Koloa, HI 96756. ✆ **800/325-5701** or 808/742-2000. Fax 808/742-9093. www.parrishkauai.com. 30 units. $119–$139 2-bedroom gardenview. 5-night minimum. Futons $5 per night. DC, DISC, MC, V. From Poipu Rd., turn toward the ocean on Hoowili Rd., then left on Hoone Rd.; continue on Hoone Rd., past the bends, where the road is now called Pee Rd.; turn left off Pee Rd. onto Hoohu Rd. **Amenities:** Outdoor pool; nearby golf course; tennis courts; sauna; barbecue area. *In room:* TV/VCR, CD player, kitchen, coffeemaker, iron, washer/dryer.

Waikomo Stream Villas ★ (Value) The Parrish Collection Kauai (see p. 353) has one more fabulous deal: these 1,000-square-foot one-bedroom apartments, which comfortably sleep four; and larger two-bedroom units, which sleep six. Tucked into a lush tropical garden setting, the spacious, well-decorated units have everything you could possibly need on your vacation: full kitchen, VCR, washer/dryer, and private lanai. The complex—which has both adults' and children's pools, tennis courts, and a barbecue area—is adjacent to the Kiahuna Golf Club and just a 5-minute walk from restaurants, shopping, and Poipu's beaches and golf courses.

2721 Poipu Rd. (just after entry to Poipu, on ocean side of Poipu Rd.), Poipu. Reservations: c/o Grantham Resorts, 3176 Poipu Rd., Suite 1, Koloa, HI 96756. ✆ **800/325-5701** or 808/742-2000. Fax 808/742-9093. www.grantham-resorts.com. 60 units. $105–$159 1-bedroom for 4; $135–$189 2-bedroom for 6. 5-night minimum. Futons $5. DC, DISC, MC, V. **Amenities:** 2 outdoor pools (1 for children); complimentary tennis courts; Jacuzzi; concierge; activities desk. *In room:* TV/VCR, dataport, kitchen, fridge, coffeemaker.

WESTERN KAUAI

Kokee Lodge (Value) This is an excellent choice for families, especially if you want to do some hiking in Waimea Canyon and Kokee State Park. There are two types of cabins here: The older ones have dormitory-style sleeping arrangements (and resemble a youth hostel), while the new ones have two separate bedrooms each. Both styles sleep six and come with cooking utensils, bedding, and linens. We recommend the newer units, which have wood floors, cedar walls, and more modern kitchen facilities. (Some are wheelchair accessible as well.) There are no phones or TVs in the units, but there is a pay phone at the general store. You can purchase firewood for the cabin stove at Kokee Lodge, where a restaurant is open for continental breakfast and lunch every day. There's also a cocktail lounge, a general store, and a gift shop. ***Warning for light sleepers:*** This area is home to lots of roosters, which crow at dawn's first light (see "Chickens & Roosters" box, p. 354).

P.O. Box 819, Waimea, HI 96796. ✆ **808/335-6061.** 12 units. $65 double. 5-night maximum. Cleaning fee $20. Extra person $5 for ages 6 and over. DC, DISC, MC, V. *In room:* Kitchen, fridge, no phone.

Waimea Plantation Cottages ★ This beachfront vacation retreat is like no other in the islands: Among 27 acres of towering coco palms sit clusters of restored sugar-plantation cottages dating from the 1880s to the 1930s, and bearing the names of their original plantation-worker dwellers. The lovely cottages have been transformed into cozy, comfortable guest units with period rattan and wicker furniture and fabrics from the 1930s, sugar's heyday on Kauai. Each has a furnished lanai and a fully equipped modern kitchen and bathroom; some units are oceanfront. Facilities include an oceanfront pool, tennis courts, and laundry. The seclusion of the village makes it a nice place for kids to wander and explore, away from traffic. The only downsides: the black-sand beach, which is lovely but not conducive to swimming (the water is often murky at the Waimea River mouth), and the location, at the foot of Waimea Canyon Drive—its remoteness can be very appealing, but the North Shore is 2 hours away. Golf courses and tennis courts, however, are much closer.

9400 Kaumualii Hwy. (P.O. Box 367), Waimea, HI 96796. ✆ **800/992-4632** or 808/338-1625. Fax 808/338-2338. www.waimea-plantation.com. 48 units. $220–$360 1-bedroom double; $275–$425 2-bedroom (sleeps up to 4); $325–$475 3-bedroom (up to 5); $400–$525 4-bedroom (up to 8); $600–$800 5-bedroom (up to 9). Children 16 and under stay free in parent's room. AE, DC, DISC, MC, V. **Amenities:** Restaurant; bar; large outdoor pool; activities desk; Wi-Fi in lobby; coin-op laundry; dry cleaning. *In room:* Cable TV, kitchen, fridge, coffeemaker, iron, safe.

THE COCONUT COAST

Expensive

Outrigger at Lae Nani ★ The Lae Nani ("beautiful promontory point") offers a quiet, relaxing setting right on a very swimmable beach, next door to a shopping complex with numerous eateries. The one- and two-bedroom units are roomy, with large living rooms, separate dining rooms, complete kitchens, and generous lanais. The two-bedroom/two-bathroom units can easily fit a family of six. Maid service is provided daily. Extras include a swimming pool, a lava-rock-protected swimming area, barbecue facilities, tennis courts, and self-service laundry facilities.

410 Papaloa Rd., Kapaa, HI 96746. ✆ **800/OUTRIGGER** (688-7444) or 808/822-4938. Fax 808/822-1022. www.outrigger.com. 54 units. $259–$355 1-bedroom for 4; $279–$425 2-bedroom for 6. 2-night minimum. Cribs and rollaway beds $20. AE, DC, DISC, MC, V. **Amenities:** Oceanfront outdoor pool; complimentary tennis courts; coin-op washer/dryers. *In room:* TV, dataport, kitchen, fridge, coffeemaker, iron.

ResortQuest Kauai Beach at Makaiwa ★ After 18 months and more than $23 million in renovations, the old Kauai Coconut Beach Resort reopened as the Courtyard by Marriott Kauai-Waipouli Beach in 2005. One year later, ResortQuest took over this centrally located property, just 10 minutes from Lihue Airport, in the town of Waipouli. The 311-room resort, which sits on 11 acres nestled between a coconut grove and a white-sand beach, is now completely updated and remodeled. The convenient location is close to shopping and visitor attractions along the Coconut Coast, and also is centrally positioned on the island for easy access to the North Shore and the Poipu Beach area on the south shore.

The resort features a new swimming pool, hot tub, day spa, business center, fitness center, tennis courts, jogging paths, lounge (with nightly entertainment), and restaurant. The resort has kept the award-winning Hawaiian luau by Tihati Productions, with dinner and show Tuesday through Sunday evenings. Patrons of the old Kauai Coconut Beach Resort will hardly recognize the new, enlarged lobby and entryway. The large guest rooms have been gutted and redecorated with a Hawaiian theme, and include such amenities as hardwood furniture and a 27-inch television.

4-484 Kuhio Hwy., Kapaa, HI 96746. ✆ **866/774-2924** or 808/822-3455. Fax 808/822-1830. www.resortquesthawaii.com. 311 units. $259–$429 double (online rates start at $180). Extra person $25. Children 17 and under stay free in parent's room. Valet parking $7; self-parking $6. AE, DC, DISC, MC, V. **Amenities:** Full-service restaurant; bar; outdoor pool; golf nearby; tennis nearby; Jacuzzi; activities desk; room service;

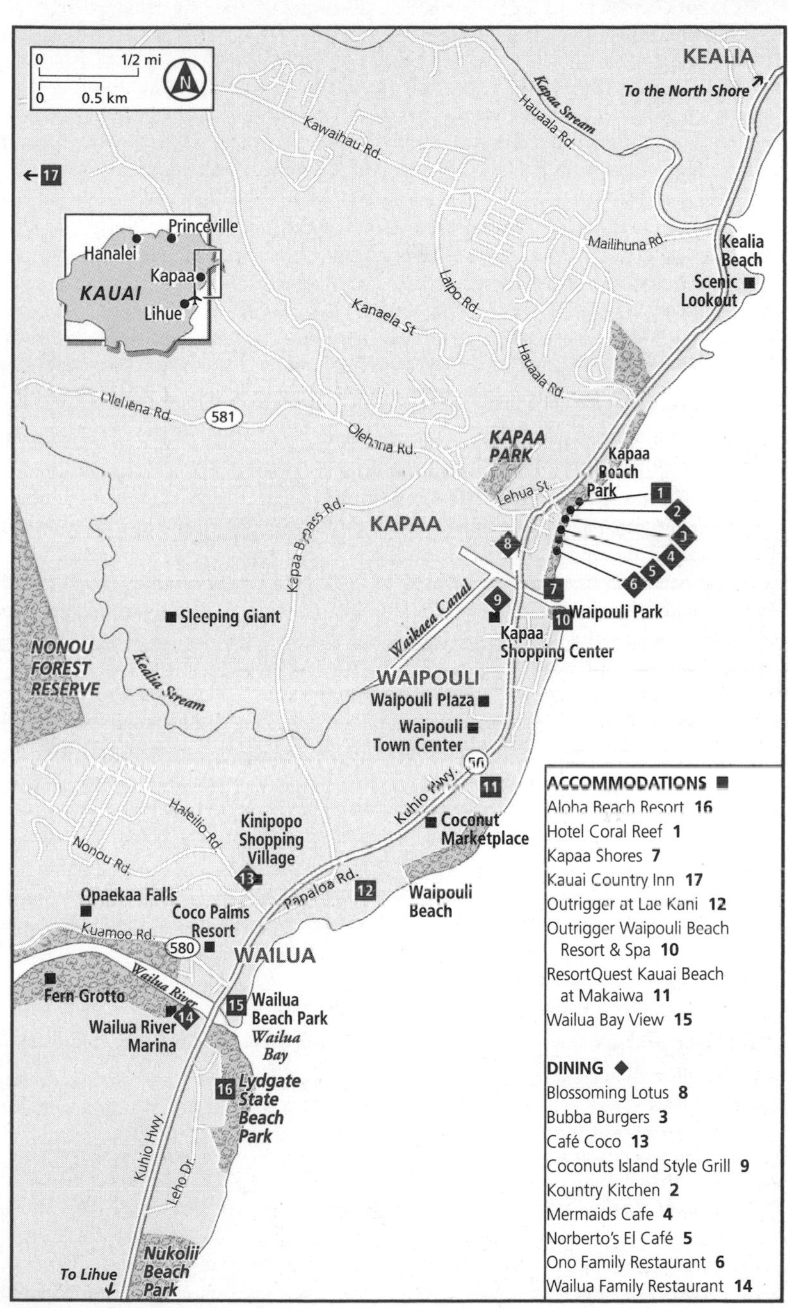
0 1/2 mi
0 0.5 km
N
KEALIA
To the North Shore
Kapaa Stream
Hauaala Rd.
Kawaihau Rd.
17
Princeville
Hanalei
Kapaa
KAUAI
Lihue
Mailihuna Rd.
Kealia Beach
Scenic Lookout
Laipo Rd.
Kanaela St
Hauaala Rd.
Olehena Rd.
581
Olehena Rd.
KAPAA PARK
Kapaa Beach Park
Lehua St.
KAPAA
Kapaa Bypass Rd.
Waikaea Canal
Sleeping Giant
Waipouli Park
Kapaa Shopping Center
NONOU FOREST RESERVE
Kealia Stream
WAIPOULI
Waipouli Plaza
Waipouli Town Center
56
Kuhio Hwy.
Haleilio Rd.
Kinipopo Shopping Village
Coconut Marketplace
Nonou Rd.
Papaloa Rd.
Waipouli Beach
Opaekaa Falls
Coco Palms Resort
Kuamoo Rd.
580
WAILUA
Wailua River
Fern Grotto
Wailua River Marina
Wailua Beach Park
Wailua Bay
Lydgate State Beach Park
Kuhio Hwy.
Leho Dr.
Nukolii Beach Park
To Lihue
ACCOMMODATIONS
Aloha Beach Resort 16
Hotel Coral Reef 1
Kapaa Shores 7
Kauai Country Inn 17
Outrigger at Lae Kani 12
Outrigger Waipouli Beach Resort & Spa 10
ResortQuest Kauai Beach at Makaiwa 11
Wailua Bay View 15
DINING
Blossoming Lotus 8
Bubba Burgers 3
Café Coco 13
Coconuts Island Style Grill 9
Kountry Kitchen 2
Mermaids Cafe 4
Norberto's El Café 5
Ono Family Restaurant 6
Wailua Family Restaurant 14

 coin-op washer/dryers; laundry; dry cleaning; jogging path. *In room:* A/C, TV/VCR, dataport, Wi-Fi (fee $12/day), fridge, coffeemaker, hair dryer, iron, safe.

Moderate

Aloha Beach Resort Kauai Formerly the SunSpree Resorts, a division of Holiday Inn that emphasizes moderate rates and lots of free activities for families, the resort is now under new ownership. The result is a family-friendly choice located right next door to Lydgate Beach Park (with Kamalani Playground for the kids) and convenient to nearby golf. The rooms are typical of the former owner, Holiday Inn: clean and functional, but nothing spectacular, just standard moderate hotel rooms. No special family packages, but there is a kids' menu and the resort has an extensive cultural program, including activities specifically for kids such as Keiki Crafts and several storytelling sessions.

3-5920 Kuhio Hwy., Kapaa, HI 96746. ✆ **888/823-5111** or 808/823-6000. Fax 808/823-6666. www.alohabeachresortkauai.com. 216 units. $119–$295 double; $171–$405 1-bedroom cottages for 4. Check the Web for incredible savings. Extra person $30. Children 17 and under stay free in parent's room. Cribs free; rollaway beds $15. AE, DC, DISC, MC, V. **Amenities:** Restaurant and deli takeout; bar; 2 outdoor pools; tennis courts; small health club; Jacuzzi; complimentary snorkel gear; children's program; game room; activities desk; babysitting; coin-op laundry; laundry service; dry cleaning. *In room:* A/C, TV, dataport, fridge, coffeemaker, hair dryer, iron, safe.

Outrigger Waipouli Beach Resort & Spa ★★ Kids This luxurious beach resort opened at the very end of December 2006 on 13 acres between the historic towns of Wailua and Kapaa. The resort features six hotel rooms and 190 high-end condo units (153 two-bedroom/three-bath units and 37 one-bedroom/two-bath units), of which 130 units are in the rental pool (75% are the two-bedroom units). Each unit is furnished with the top-of-the-line materials like granite countertops; stainless steel appliances by Sub-Zero, Wolf, and Fisher/Paykel; a double dishwasher; a full-sized Whirlpool washer and dryer; whirlpool bathtubs in the master bathrooms; and 37-inch flatscreen TVs. The two-bedroom units are 1,300 square feet with floor-to-ceiling windows and two lanais.

The resort includes a long list of amenities like a 4,000-square-foot Aveda spa, a fitness center, and a 300,000-gallon heated saltwater fantasy pool, with flowing river, garden, dual serpentine waterslides, sand-bottom children's pool, and three sand-bottom whirlpool tubs. Plus, the entire property, all the guest rooms, and the common areas are nonsmoking.

The location, across the street from the Kauai Village Shopping Center and the Waipouli Town Center, means guests are within walking distance of restaurants and shops and, more important, just across the street from a Safeway grocery store and a Longs Drug Store and pharmacy.

4-820 Kuhio Hwy., Kapaa, HI 96746 ✆ **800/OUTRIGGER** (688-7444) or 808/823-8300. Fax 808/823-8301. www.outrigger.com. 196 units. $175–$205 hotel double; $309–$335 1-bed/2-bath for 4; $369–$629 2-bed/3-bath for 6. 2-night minimum. AE, DC, DISC, MC, V. **Amenities:** 2 restaurants; bar; huge oceanside outdoor pool; 3 outdoor whirlpools; nearby golf course; nearby tennis courts; fitness center; spa; activities desk; laundry service; dry cleaning. *In room:* A/C, TV/DVD, high-speed Wi-Fi, full kitchen (condos only), fridge, coffeemaker, hair dryer, iron, safe, full-size washer and dryer (condos only).

Inexpensive

Hotel Coral Reef Value Here's a budget choice right on the beach. This small, unpretentious hotel faces a grassy lawn, coconut trees, and a white-sand beach. It offers economical rooms and friendly service in an ideal location, within walking distance of shops, restaurants, golf, and tennis, and just 100 feet away from good swimming and snorkeling. There's even an 8-mile bike path that starts right on the grounds. This is a budget hotel, not the Ritz, so expect clean but well-worn carpets, drapes, and furniture. For families they recommend either a room with two double beds or the oceanfront suite with a queen in the bedroom and a queen-size sofa bed in the living room for younger kids. Mike and Melonie Harris, owner and gracious hostess of this quaint hotel, are always happy to give you pointers on how to stretch your budget and still have a good time on Kauai.

1516 Kuhio Hwy. (at the northern end of Kapaa, btw mile markers 8 and 9), Kapaa, HI 96746. ✆ **800/843-4659** or 808/822-4481. Fax 808/822-7705. www.hotelcoralreef.com. 19 units. $125–$289 double; from $209 suite. Extra person $25. Children 12 and under stay free in parent's room. Room/car packages available. AE, MC, V. **Amenities:** Pool; activities desk; coin-op washer/dryers. *In room:* A/C, TV, fridge, coffeemaker, safe (in some oceanfront rooms).

Kapaa Shore Resort ★ These apartments are located right on the beach in the heart of Kapaa. Even the budget units have a partial view of the ocean, but oceanfront units are available for a bit more money. The one-bedrooms can comfortably sleep four, while the two-bedrooms can sleep as many as six. (The sofa in each unit pulls out into a queen-size bed.) All units are in excellent shape and come with fully equipped modern kitchens and large lanais where you can enjoy a sunrise breakfast or sunset cocktails. On-site amenities include a large pool, a tennis court, a family-size hot tub, a shuffleboard court, laundry facilities, and barbecues. Golf courses, restaurants, and bars are nearby.

900 Kuhio Hwy. (btw MM 7 and 8). Reservations: c/o Garden Island Properties, 4-928 Kuhio Hwy., Kapaa, HI 96746. ✆ **800/801-0378** or 808/822-4871. Fax 808/822-7984. www.kauaiproperties.com. 81 units. $120–$165 1-bedroom; $140–$210 2-bedroom. 5-night minimum. Cribs $42–$75 per week; rollaway beds $75 per week. MC, V. **Amenities:** Outdoor pool; tennis courts; Jacuzzi; salon; coin-op laundry. *In room:* Cable TV, DVD, dataport, Wi-Fi, kitchen, fridge, coffeemaker, iron.

Kauai Country Inn ★★ Finds Book this place! It's hard to believe that, nestled in the rolling hills behind Kapaa, this old-fashioned country inn exists. Hosts Mike and Martina Hough, refugees from life in the fast lane (they used to run an international advertising agency in Los Angeles), have taken their considerable creative talents and produced a slice of paradise on 2 acres. Each of the four suites is uniquely decorated in Hawaiian Art Deco with a touch of humor, complete with hardwood floors, a kitchen or kitchenette, your own computer with high-speed Internet connection, and lots of little amenities. Everything is top-drawer, from the furniture to the Sub-Zero refrigerator. They recently added a two bedroom country cottage for families with young children. The grounds are immaculate, and you can pick as much organic fruit as you want from the abundance of mango, guava, lilikoi, star fruit, orange, and lemon trees. Beatles fans take note: Mike has been collecting memorabilia for decades and has the only private Beatles Museum in the state (including a Mini Cooper S car owned by Beatles manager Brian Epstein, original paintings by John Lennon, and a host of books, records, movies, tapes, and T-shirts, among other items). Annie, the house golden retriever, personally greets each guest like her long-lost friend. Although it's about a half-hour drive from the beach, it's in a relaxing rural neighborhood and there's plenty of room on the property for the kids to run around.

6440 Olohena Rd., Kapaa, HI 96746. ✆ **808/821-0207.** www.kauaicountryinn.com. 5 units. $99–$159 1- and 2- bedroom suites double; $229–$250 2-bedroom cottage for 6. 4-night minimum suites; 4-night minimum cottage. Extra person in suites $20. Discount car rentals available. AE, MC, V. **Amenities:** Hot tub, laundry facilities. *In room:* TV/VCR/DVD, computer w/high-speed Internet, kitchen or kitchenette, fridge, coffeemaker, hair dryer, iron.

Wailua Bay View ★ (Value) Located right on the ocean, these spacious one-bedroom apartments offer excellent value for families of four. All units have ceiling fans, full kitchens (including microwave and dishwasher), washer/dryers, and large lanais. Some have air-conditioning as well. The bedrooms are roomy, and the sofa bed in the living room allows you to sleep a couple of kids. Some of the $125 garden units are close to the road and can be noisy; ask for one with air-conditioning, which generally drowns out the street sounds. The oceanview units are more expensive but still a great deal. On-site facilities include a pool and barbecue area. Restaurants, bars, shopping, golf, and tennis are nearby.

320 Papaloa Rd., Kapaa, HI 96746. ✆ **800/882-9007.** Fax 425/391-9121. www.wailuabayview.net. 45 units. $155 double. 7th night free. One-time cleaning fee $95. Discount car rentals available. MC, V. **Amenities:** Small outdoor pool; coin-op laundry. *In room:* A/C (most units), TV/VCR, dataport, kitchen, fridge, coffeemaker, iron.

THE NORTH SHORE

Want to rent a rock star's treehouse? How about coochy-coochy entertainer Charo's beachfront estate? **Hanalei North Shore Properties** (✆ **800/488-3336** or 808/826-9622; www.kauai-vacation-rentals.com) handles all kinds of weekly rentals—from beachfront cottages and condos to romantic hideaways and ranch houses—along the North Shore. Renting a home is a great way to enjoy the area's awesome nature, especially for those who like to avoid resorts and fend for themselves. Shopping, restaurants, and nightlife are abundant in nearby Hanalei. The company does not accept credit cards.

If you are looking for a more "country" setting, consider **North Country Farms** (✆ **808/828-1513;** www.northcountryfarms.com), a private, handcrafted, redwood cottage on a 4-acre organic farm. It's a great place for families ($130 for two; children 14 and younger stay free with parents).

You'll find the following accommodations on the map "Kauai's North Shore: Princeville & Hanalei," on p. 382.

Very Expensive

Princeville at Hanalei ★★★ This resort is the jewel in the Sheraton crown, a palace full of marble and chandeliers. It enjoys one of the world's finest settings, between Hanalei Bay and Kauai's steepled mountains. Nearby are outstanding surfing and windsurfing areas, as well as a wonderful reef for snorkeling. The panoramic view from the lobby has to be the most dramatic vista from any hotel in the state. The Princeville is Kauai's most popular setting for weddings; more than 300 a year are performed outdoors by the pool.

In the spring of 2009, this hotel will be rebranded a St. Regis (the hotel's most exclusive brand). This grand hotel steps down a cliff; the entrance is actually on the ninth floor, and you take elevators down to your room and the beach. Each opulent room has such extras as a door chime, dimmer switches, bedside control panels, a safe, original oil paintings, an oversize bathtub, and a "magic" bathroom window, which the kids will love: a liquid-crystal shower window that you can switch in an instant from clear to opaque. There are no lanais, but oversize windows allow you to admire the awesome view from your bed.

In addition to a great children's program (fees for a full day of activities run $65 per child), this property has oodles of activities not only for children, but for the entire family, from horseback riding to adventures exploring the island. The hotel grounds are a fantasy land for children (and some adults), with a huge swimming pool next to a sandy beach.

Other great amenities here: twice-daily fresh towels, daily newspaper, complimentary resort shuttle, comprehensive Hawaiiana program, riding stables, in-house cinema, arts program (from photography to painting), and a wealth of outdoor activities.

5520 Kahaku Rd. Reservations: c/o P.O. Box 3069, Princeville, HI 96722-3069. ✆ **800/826-4400** or 808/826-9644. Fax 808/826-1166. www.princeville.com. 252 units. $600–$875 double; $1,000–$5,800 suite. Extra person $80. Children 17 and under stay free in parent's room. Cribs free; rollaway beds $80. AE, DC, DISC, MC, V. Valet or self-parking $15. **Amenities:** 3 restaurants (1 w/excellent nightly entertainment; also see La Cascata on p. 374); 3 bars; huge oceanside outdoor pool; outstanding golf on 2 courses; 25 tennis courts; first-rate health club and spa; 3 outdoor Jacuzzis (including a really palatial one); watersports equipment/rentals; bike rentals; children's program; game room; concierge; activities desk; car rental desk; business center; shopping arcade; salon; 24-hr. room service; massage; babysitting; same-day laundry service and dry cleaning. *In room:* A/C, TV/VCR, dataport, minibar, fridge, coffeemaker, hair dryer, iron, safe, complimentary coffee and tea in room.

Expensive

Hanalei Bay Resort ★★ This 22-acre resort is just up the street from ritzy Princeville Resort (see above), overlooking the fabled Bali Ha'i cliffs and Hanalei Bay. It has the same majestic view, but for as little as half the price. The place recaptures the spirit of Old Hawaii, especially in the three-story stucco units that angle down the hill to the gold-sand, palm fringed beach it shares with its neighbor. Units range from hotel rooms to one-bedroom suites and overlook the bay, the lush grounds, and the distant mountains. Shuttle service is available for those who may have problems walking on steep hillsides. The suites have either kitchenettes or complete kitchens. Other family pluses include three swimming pools, barbecue facilities, and laundry facilities. Also, the on-site restaurant has children's menus. No cribs, but you can arrange a rental.

5380 Honoiki St. (P.O. Box 220), Princeville, HI 96722. ✆ **800/827-4427** or 808/826-6522. Fax 808/826-6680. www.hanaleibayresort.com. 236 units. $215–$305 double; $260 studio with kitchenette (up to 4); $380–$420 1-bedroom suite (up to 4). Rates for suites include full breakfast and afternoon cocktails. AE, DC, DISC, MC, V. **Amenities:** Restaurant; bar; 2 inviting outdoor freshwater pools; complimentary shuttle to Princeville Resort's top-ranked golf courses; 8 tennis courts, pro shop, and tennis school; Jacuzzi; concierge; activities desk; salon; massage; babysitting; coin-op laundry (apts have washer/dryers in units); laundry service; dry cleaning. *In room:* A/C, TV, dataport, kitchenette, fridge, coffeemaker, hair dryer, iron, safe.

Moderate

Hanalei Colony Resort and Spa ★ Picture this: A perfect white-sand beach just steps from your door, with lush tropical gardens, jagged mountain peaks, and fertile jungle serving as its backdrop. Welcome to Haena, Kauai's northernmost town and gateway to the famous Na Pali Coast, with miles of hiking trails, fabulous sunset views, and great beaches. This 5-acre resort is the place to stay if you're looking to experience the magic of the enchanting North Shore. The units are unbelievably spacious—6 people could sleep in the two-bedroom units comfortably—making them great for families. In 2006, the property upgraded the interiors of all the two-bedroom units with new, custom-made tropical furnishings throughout, and is nearly finished with converting all the two-bedroom units to two bathrooms. Both the one- and the two-bedroom units have a private lanai (the less-expensive budget units face the garden), a full kitchen, a dining area, a living room, and ceiling fans. (The area is blessed with cooling trade winds, so air-conditioning isn't necessary.) The atmosphere is quiet and relaxing: no TVs, stereos, or phones. (However, the common area has a TV and complimentary computer use.) The property has a large pool, laundry facilities, and a barbecue and picnic area. Guests have access to complimentary beach mats and towels, a lending library, and children's toys, puzzles, and games (plus badminton and croquet for the entire family). During the summer months, the resort features a weekly schedule of activities for kids at $20 each (discount for the second child).

5-7130 Kuhio Hwy. Reservations: c/o P.O. Box 206, Hanalei, HI 96714. ✆ **800/628-3004** or 808/826-6235. Fax 808/826-9893. www.hcr.com. 48 units. $240–$420 2-bedroom apt for 4. Rate includes continental breakfast once a week. 5-night minimum May 1–Sept 30 and Dec 12–Jan 4. 7th night free. Extra person $15. Children 18 and under stay free in parent's room. Cribs free; rollaway beds $15. AE, MC, V. **Amenities:** Good-size outdoor pool; Jacuzzi; coin-op laundry. *In room:* Kitchen, fridge, coffeemaker, no phone.

4 FAMILY-FRIENDLY DINING

Kauai's best dining spots ring the shores: Poipu on the south, Kapaa on the east, and Hanalei on the north. And that's a good thing, because on Kauai, street names seem irrelevant and locations are determined by trees, erstwhile mom-and-pop stores, and other landmarks of rural life. Follow the winding road and you'll find the tried-and-true temples of Hawaiian Regional Cuisine amid plate-lunch palaces and a new, post-hippie breed of affordable, top-quality eateries that cook healthful, fresh, and tasty cuisine.

On your jaunt across the island, you'll find affordable choices for everyone in your family, from hamburger joints to busy neighborhood diners. So long as you don't expect filet mignon on a fish and chips budget, it shouldn't be difficult to please both your kids' palate and your pocketbook. But if you're looking for lobster, rack of lamb, or risotto to write home about, you'll find those pleasures, too.

For condo dwellers who are preparing their own meals, we've featured a variety of markets and shops around Kauai—including some wonderful green markets and fruit stands—where you can pick up the island's best foodstuffs. These are listed in "Shopping with Your Kids," later in this chapter. If you're looking for fresh island fruit, also see the box "Fruity Smoothies & Other Exotic Treats," on p. 403.

In the listings below, reservations are not required unless otherwise noted.

LIHUE & ENVIRONS

Expensive

Gaylord's ★★ CONTINENTAL/PACIFIC RIM You might want to get a sitter and come without the kids to this romantic restaurant in a 1930s plantation manager's estate on a 1,700-acre sugar plantation. The private dining room has a lavish table, always elegantly set, as if Queen Liliuokalani is expected at any minute; another room accommodates private parties. The main dining room, which winds around a flagstone courtyard overlooking rolling lawns and purple mountains, serves American classics (New York steak, rack of lamb, prime rib), along with pasta, fresh seafood, and lavish desserts.

At Kilohana, 3-2087 Kaumualii Hwy., Lihue. ✆ **808/245-9593.** Some kids' menu items, highchairs, crayons. Reservations recommended. Main courses $13–$16 lunch, $24–$50 dinner. AE, DC, DISC, MC, V. Mon–Sat 8–10am (breakfast buffet) and 11am–2:30pm; daily 5:30–9pm; Sun 9:30am–2pm (brunch).

JJ's Broiler ★ AMERICAN Kids will love this open-air restaurant right on the water. The kids' menu has the usual favorites, from burgers to grilled cheese. Adults will be drawn to the Slavonic steaks, herb-crusted ahi, and the Lazy Susan of salad greens that's brought to your table. The coconut shrimp and Manila clams are big sellers, and the Mauna Kea scallops (which look like a mountain on a heap of rice with nori) are an imaginative twist on seafood. Lunchtime appetizers include potato skins, calamari rings, quesadillas, and wontons—the United Nations of pupu! The high ceilings, two-story dining, Kenwood Cup posters, and nautically designed rooms are enhanced by stellar views of the bay.

3416 Rice St., Nawiliwili. ✆ **808/246-4422.** Kids' menu, highchairs, crayons. Reservations recommended for dinner. Lunch sandwiches $10–$12; dinner main courses $18–$25; kids' menu $9 lunch, $11 dinner. DISC, MC, V. Daily 11am–10pm.

Moderate

Duke's Canoe Club ★ SEAFOOD/STEAK It's hard to go wrong at Duke's. Part of a highly successful restaurant chain, this oceanfront oasis is the hippest spot in town, with a winning combination of great views, affordable menu, attractive salad bar, popular music, and a very happy happy hour. The noontime best-seller is stir-fried cashew chicken, but the fresh mahi burger and the grilled-chicken quesadilla are front-runners, too. No kids' menu at lunch, but the inexpensive fish tacos are a major attraction. At dinner, adults may eye the five or six varieties of fresh catch a night, but the kids probably will order the shrimp scampi or ribs off their own menu. Hawaiian musicians serenade diners nightly, while downstairs in the Barefoot Bar, traditional and contemporary Hawaiian music adds to the cheerful atmosphere.

In the Kauai Marriott Resort & Beach Club, 3610 Rice St., Nawiliwili. ✆ **808/246-9599.** Kids' menu (dinner only), highchairs, boosters. Reservations recommended for dinner. Lunch $7–$11; dinner $11–$32; kids' menu $7.95 average. Taco Tuesday 4–6pm, with $2.50 fish tacos and $3.25 draft beer. AE, DISC, MC, V. Barefoot Bar daily 11am–11:30pm; main dining room daily 5–10pm.

Inexpensive

Hanamaulu Cafe CHINESE/JAPANESE/SUSHI For a cultural experience, take your family to this serene Japanese garden restaurant, with a tatami-floored teahouse. You can dine at the sushi bar, American-style, or in the teahouses for lunch or dinner (but you must call ahead for teahouse dining). At lunch, enter a world of chop suey, wontons, teriyaki chicken, and sukiyaki (less verve than value), with many other choices in budget-friendly Japanese and Chinese plate lunches. No kids' menu, but dishes are served family-style and everyone can partake.

3-4291 Kuhio Hwy., Hanamaulu. ✆ **808/245-2511.** Boosters, sassy seats. Reservations recommended. Main courses $9–$20. MC, V. Tues–Fri 10am–1pm; daily 4:30–8:30pm.

Kalapaki Beach Hut AMERICAN Tricky to find, but what a savings for your wallet! (*Hint:* Look for the anchor chain in front of the green building.) This "hut" has window service and a few tables downstairs and more upstairs (with an ocean view out the screen windows). Basic fare is served on paper plates with plastic cutlery at cheap, cheap prices. Breakfasts are hearty omelets, pancakes, and numerous egg dishes. Lunches are heavy on the hamburgers (prepared 10 different ways), lots of sandwiches, a few healthy salads, and fish and chips. The kids get their own menu (smaller sized). This casual restaurant welcomes people in their bathing suits and slippers.

3474 Rice St., Nawiliwili. ✆ **808/246-6330.** Kids' menu, boosters. Breakfast $4.75–$7.75; lunch $4.50–$7.75; kids' menu $4.50 all-inclusive. AE, DISC, MC, V. Daily 7am–8pm.

THE POIPU RESORT AREA

You'll find the restaurants in this section on the "Poipu Resort Area" map on p. 351.

Expensive

The Beach House ★★★ HAWAIIAN REGIONAL The Beach House remains the south shore's premier spot for sunset drinks, appetizers, and dinner—a treat for all the

Plate-Lunch Pointers

If you haven't yet come face to face with the local phenomenon called *plate lunch,* Kauai is a good place to start. Like saimin, the plate lunch is more than a gastronomic experience—it's a part of the local culture. Lihue is peppered with affordable plate-lunch counters that serve this basic dish: two scoops of rice, potato or macaroni salad, and a beef, chicken, fish, or pork entree—all on a single plate to take out. Although heavy gravies are usually de rigueur, some of the less traditional purveyors have streamlined their offerings to include healthier touches, such as lean grilled fresh fish. At its best, a plate lunch can be a marvel of flavors, a saving grace after a long hike; at its worst, it's a plate-size fried-grease bomb. With the increasing popularity of such diets as Atkins and South Beach, many plate lunch places are now happy to replace all those starches with a mixed green salad if you request.

The following are the best plate-lunch counters on Kauai. How fortunate that each is on a different part of the island!

The **Koloa Fish Market ★**, 5482 Koloa Rd. (© **808/742-6199**), is in southern Kauai, on Koloa's main street. A tiny corner stand with plate lunches (no kids' menu), prepared foods, and two stools on a closet-size veranda, it sells excellent fresh fish poke, Hawaiian-food specials, and seared ahi to go. It's gourmet fare masquerading as takeout.

On the Hanamaulu side of Lihue, across the street from Wal-Mart, look for the prim gray building that reads **Fish Express ★**, 3343 Kuhio Hwy. (© **808/245-9918**). It's astonishing what you'll find here for less than $10: Cajun-style grilled ahi with guava basil, fresh fish grilled in a passion-orange-tarragon sauce, fresh fish tacos in garlic and herbs, and many other delectables, all served with rice, salad, and vegetables (no kids' menus but a great selection of items). The Hawaiian plate lunch (laulau or kalua pork, lomi salmon, ahi poke, rice or poi) is a top seller, as are the several varieties of smoked fish, everything from ahi to swordfish.

senses. The oceanfront room is large, accented with oversize sliding-glass doors, with Old Hawaiian Regional favorites on the menu. Families are welcome; kids get their own menus and crayons to color with until dinner arrives. (If you come at sunset, you might be able to see a turtle or two bobbing in the waves.) Menus change daily and include Kauai asparagus salad, seared crusted macadamia nut mahimahi, sea scallops with lemon grass and kaffir lime, and the Beach House crab cake with mint sambal butter sauce and grilled tomato compote. Desserts shine, too, especially the molten chocolate desire—a chocolate tart that arrives warm and wonderful—and the Kahlúa taro cheesecake, tangy with lilikoi crème fraîche.

5022 Lawai Rd., Poipu. © **808/742-1424.** Kids' menu, highchairs, crayons. Reservations recommended. Main courses $22–$36; kids' menu $12–$14. AE, MC, V. Daily 5:30–9:30pm (hours may vary during the summer).

In east Kauai's Kapaa town, the indispensable **Pono Market,** 4-1300 Kuhio Hwy. (✆ **808/822-4581**), has similarly enticing counters of sashimi, poke, Hawaiian food, sushi, and a diverse assortment of takeout fare. It's known for its flaky *manju* (sweet potato and other fillings in a baked crust), apple turnovers, sandwiches, excellent boiled peanuts, pork and chicken *laulau,* and plate lunches—shoyu chicken, sweet-and-sour spareribs, pineapple-glazed chicken, teriyaki fish, and so on.

At **Mark's Place,** 1610 Haleukana St. in Puhi Industrial Park (✆ **808/245-2722**), just southwest of Lihue, island standards (Korean-style chicken, teriyaki beef, beef stew, chicken katsu) come with brown rice (or white) and salad for $6 or $8.50.

Lihue, the island's county and business seat, is full of ethnic eateries serving inexpensive plate lunches, everything from bentos to Hawaiian, Korean, and Chinese food. **Local Boy's Restaurant & Deli,** 3204 Kuhio Hwy. (just past the old Lihue Theater, ✆ **808/246-8898**), is a budget bonanza and a popular stop for jumbo-size appetites (kid-size plates $3–$4.75). They also are open for breakfast, where you are hard-pressed to find anything over $5. For a box lunch for kids (just $3.75), go to **Po's Kitchen,** 4100 Rice St. (✆ **808/246-8617**), which offers Japanese specials: cone sushi, chicken katsu, teriyaki beef plates, and bentos. One block away, **Garden Island BBQ,** 4252-A Rice St. (✆ **808/245-8868**), is the place for Chinese plate lunches and local staples such as barbecued or lemon chicken and teriyaki steak, as well as a kids' menu (lemon chicken $5.25).

In the Kukui Grove Center, at Kaumualii Highway (Hwy. 50) and Old Nawiliwili Road, **Joni-Hana** (✆ **808/245-5213**) is famous for its specials—nearly 20 a day! The tiny counter serves fried noodles, lemon-shoyu ono (wahoo), teriyaki everything, and many other local dishes.

Casa di Amici ★★ INTERNATIONAL/ITALIAN This storybook restaurant has fairy lights, high ceilings, beveled glass, and a generous open deck where you can dine among palms and heliotropes. (There's live classical music Sat 6:30–9:30pm on the baby grand piano.) Worth seeking out, it's the third left turn past Brennecke's Beach, not more than 2 minutes from Poipu Beach Park, in an enclave of condos and vacation rentals. The memorable Italian food has strong Mediterranean and cross-cultural influences. You'll find organic greens from Kilauea, several risotto choices, black tiger prawns with ravioli of lobster thermidor, chicken angelica, and surprises such as Thai lobster bisque and duck kalua carbonara. No kids' menu, but if your bambinos are not happy with the selections, the kitchen will make buttered pasta or pasta topped with a red sauce.

2301 Nalo Rd., Poipu. ✆ **808/742-1555.** Highchairs. Reservations recommended. Main courses $18–$27. DC, MC, V. Daily 6pm–closing.

Dondero's ★★★ ITALIAN If you are looking for a romantic dinner under the stars, overlooking the ocean, or tucked away at an intimate table surrounded by inlaid marble floors, ornate imported floor tiles, and Franciscan murals, this is the place for you. You get all this atmosphere at Dondero's, plus the best Italian cuisine on the island, served with efficiency. It's hard to have a bad experience here. This is a grown-ups' night-out type of place, so to really enjoy the experience, get the kids a sitter. Our recommendations for a meal to remember: Start with either the fresh mozzarella cheese with tomatoes and roasted peppers or the warm goat cheese, roasted eggplant, cannellini beans, and fried basil leaves. Then move on to the black ink linguine with scallops, shrimp, mussels, salmon, clams, and lobster; the risotto with porcini mushrooms and taleggio cheese; or the grilled snapper with roasted vegetables and balsamic glaze. Save room for dessert, especially the chocolate crème brûlée with fresh berries. If you bring the kids, they have their own Italian menu ranging from penne pasta to fettuccine to linguine to pizza. Dinners are pricey, but worth every penny.

Grand Hyatt Kauai Resort and Spa, 1571 Poipu Rd., Poipu. © **808/742-1234.** Kids' menu, highchairs, boosters, crayons and coloring book pages. Reservations required. Main courses $24–$42; kids' menu $15. AE, DC, DISC, MC, V. Daily 6–10pm.

Plantation Gardens Restaurant ★★ HAWAIIAN REGIONAL Bring the kids and eat here. That's as plain as we can make it. A mix of irresistible garden ambience and a well-executed menu (plus a kids' menu) fashioned around fresh local ingredients, and a respect for island traditions, make this place a winner. The fish and shellfish are from local waters and many of the fruits, herbs, and vegetables are grown on the restaurant premises. Try the shrimp and wasabi ravioli, made with fresh local shrimp, ricotta cheese, goat cheese, kaffir lime, and lemon grass. The historic architecture includes a generous veranda and gracious details of a 1930s estate that belonged to the manager of Hawaii's first sugar plantation. If the kids get restless, send them outside to the koi ponds, under coconut and hau trees, with orchids, bromeliads, and a cactus/succulent garden on the lush grounds.

In Kiahuna Plantation Resort, 2253 Poipu Rd. © **808/742-2216.** Kids' menu, highchairs, boosters, crayons. Reservations recommended. Main courses $18–$30; kids' menu $8.95–$13. AE, DC, MC, V. Daily 5:30–10pm dinner; from 5pm for pupu and cocktails.

Roy's Poipu Bar & Grill ★★ EURASIAN This is a loud, lively room with ceiling fans, marble tables, works by local artists, and a menu tailor-made for foodies (plus one for the children). The signature touches of Roy Yamaguchi (of Roy's restaurants) are abundantly present: an excellent, progressive, and affordable wine selection; fresh local ingredients prepared with a nod to Europe, Asia, and the Pacific; and service so efficient it can be overbearing. Because appetizers such as nori-seared ahi with black-bean sauce, spinach-shiitake ravioli, and crisp shrimp cakes with butter sauce are a major part of the menu, you can sample Roy's legendary fare without breaking the bank. The three dozen nightly specials invariably include eight fresh-fish dishes prepared at least five or six ways.

In Poipu Shopping Village, 2360 Kiahuna Plantation Dr. © **808/742-5000.** www.roysrestaurant.com. Kids' menu, highchairs, boosters, crayons. Reservations recommended. Main courses $28–$40; kids' menu $13. AE, DC, DISC, MC, V. Daily 5:30–9:30pm.

Tidepool Restaurant ★★ SEAFOOD Here's another ultraromantic restaurant at the Grand Hyatt (see also Dondero's, above). A cluster of Polynesian-looking thatched bungalows overlooks the lagoon in a dreamy open-aired restaurant with tiki torches flickering in the moonlight. The atmosphere would be enough to book a table, but the cuisine is outstanding, a definite do-not-miss. Their specialty is fresh fish, and they prepare it in a number of ways (the signature dish is macadamia nut–crusted mahimahi with a Kahlúa, lime, and ginger butter sauce), but they also have juicy steaks and ribs, as well as entrees for vegetarians. Kids have a three-course set menu: appetizer, choice of entree (mahimahi, chicken, pizza, pasta, or fish), and a sundae for dessert. Book early, and ask for a table overlooking the water.

Grand Hyatt Kauai Resort and Spa, 1571 Poipu Rd., Poipu. ✆ **808/742-1234.** Kids' set menu, highchairs, boosters, crayons and coloring book pages. Reservations a must. Main courses $23–$43; kids' 3-course menu $15. AE, DC, DISC, MC, V. Daily 5:30–10pm.

Moderate

Brennecke's Beach Broiler ★ AMERICAN/SEAFOOD Cheerful petunias in window boxes and second-floor views of Poipu Beach are pleasing touches at this seafood-burger house, a terrific family restaurant. The view alone is worth the price, but it helps that the best hamburgers on the south shore are served here, as well as excellent vegetarian selections. It's so casual that you and the kids can drop in before or after the beach and dine on nachos, fresh-fish sandwiches, kiawe-broiled fish and kabobs, prime rib, pasta, build-your-own gourmet burgers, and the salad bar.

2100 Hoone Rd. (across from Poipu Beach Park). ✆ **808/742-7588.** www.brenneckes.com. Kids' menu, highchairs, crayons. Main courses $9–$38; kids' menu $7–$13. AE, DC, DISC, MC, V. Daily 11am–10pm (streetside deli takeout daily 8am–9pm).

Keoki's Paradise SEAFOOD/STEAK Keoki's Paradise is sprawling and lively, and your kids will be welcomed and catered to (kids' menu, crayons to entertain them, and waitstaff to joke with them). Lunch favorites include a fresh ahi sandwich, fresh-fish tacos, Thai shrimp sticks, and chicken Caesar salad—all good and affordable. In the evenings, regulars tout the fresh fish crusted in lemon grass, basil, and bread crumbs. When it's time for dessert, the original Hula pie from Kimo's in Lahaina is an ever-sinful presence. The cafe in the bar area serves lighter fare and features live Hawaiian music daily except Tuesday and Saturday.

In Poipu Shopping Village, 2360 Kiahuna Plantation Dr. ✆ **808/742-7534.** Kids' menu, highchairs, boosters, crayons. Reservations recommended. Main courses $6–$14 lunch, $18–$55 dinner; kids' menu $6–$9.95. AE, DC, DISC, MC, V. Daily 5–10pm in the main dining room; cafe menu daily 11am–11pm.

Pomodoro ★ ITALIAN Pomodoro is the Italian magnet of the west side, a small, casual, and intimate second-floor dining room with a bar, potted plants, soft lighting, and pleasing Italian music. It's a warm, welcoming place for families, where Hawaiian hospitality meets European flavors: homemade garlic focaccia, homemade mozzarella, chicken saltimbocca, and homemade pastas (cannelloni, manicotti, and excellent lasagna, the house specialty). Whether you order the veal, chicken, scampi, calamari, or very fresh organic green salads, you'll appreciate the wonderful home-style flavor and the polite, efficient servers, and the kids will be happy with spaghetti and meatballs.

In Rainbow Plaza, Kaumualii Hwy. (Hwy. 50), Kalaheo (inland from Poipu). ✆ **808/332-5945.** Kids' menu, highchairs, boosters. Reservations recommended. Main courses $14–$24; kids' menu $10. MC, V. Daily 5:30–10pm.

Inexpensive

Brick Oven Pizza PIZZA A Kalaheo fixture for more than 25 years, Brick Oven is the quintessential mom-and-pop business, serving pizza cooked directly on the brick hearth, brushed with garlic butter, and topped with fresh cheeses and long-simmering sauces. This is the real thing! You have a choice of whole-wheat or white crust, plus many toppings. The seafood-style pizza-bread sandwiches are big at lunch, and the "Super Pizza" with everything on it—that's *amore.* No kids' menu, but they'll be too busy with the family pizza. Plus, they give the kids pizza dough to play with while the pizza is being cooked.

2-2555 Kaumualii Hwy. (Hwy. 50), Kalaheo (inland from Poipu). ✆ **808/332-8561.** Highchairs, boosters. Sandwiches less than $10; pizzas $10–$30. Mon 4–10pm; Tues–Sun 11am–10pm.

Kalaheo Coffee Co. & Cafe COFFEE SHOP/CAFE This coffeehouse (with a worldwide selection of coffee beans) also serves masterful breakfasts: burritos, veggie omelets with sun-dried tomatoes and mushrooms, Belgian waffles, and bagels. At lunch, the fabulous grilled-turkey burgers are the headliner on a list of winners. Fresh-from-the-garden salads brighten up the day. The tasty, inexpensive soup changes daily. The cinnamon "knuckles" (baked fresh daily), lilikoi cheesecake, and fresh apple pie and carrot cake are more reasons to stop by. No kids' menu, but there's plenty for them to choose from, plus there are small toys to entertain the tots.

2-2436 Kaumualii Hwy. (Hwy. 50), Kalaheo (inland from Poipu). ✆ **808/332-5858.** Highchairs. Most items less than $13. DISC, MC, V. Mon–Sat 6:30am–2:30pm; Sun 6:30am–2pm.

WESTERN KAUAI

Hanapepe Cafe ★★ GOURMET VEGETARIAN/ITALIAN It's worth the drive to bring the kids to this small gourmet delight. At lunch they elevate the garden burger to gourmet status: You can top yours with sautéed mushrooms, grilled onions, pesto, fresh-grated Parmesan, and other choices. Other lunch notables: fresh rosemary home fries, a great grilled vegetable sandwich, and whole roasted garlic heads. Kids have their own menu (pastas and sandwiches). On the Friday-night dinner menu, the Italian specialties shine: Southwestern-style lasagna or lasagna quattro formaggi with spinach, mushrooms, and four cheeses; crepes; and the nightly special with the cafe's famous marinara sauce—terrific choices all. There's no liquor license, so if you want wine, bring your own (corkage fee $5). As we went to press, they just opened a bakery shop and are now serving a light breakfast.

3830 Hanapepe Rd., Hanapepe. ✆ **808/335-5011.** Kids' menu, highchairs, boosters, crayons. Reservations recommended for dinner. Breakfast items $8; lunch entrees $6–$12; dinner entrees $16–$28. MC, V. Mon–Thurs 7:30am–3pm; Fri 7:30am–2pm and 6–9pm.

Shrimp Station SHRIMP Looking for a picnic lunch to take up to Waimea Canyon? Stop at this roadside eatery, which is nothing more than a kitchen with a few picnic tables outside. The shrimp cooking inside, however, makes up for the lack of ambience. The shrimp is cooked a variety of ways from shrimp taco to a shrimp burger, but the star attraction is their shrimp plates (choice of garlic shrimp, Cajun, Thai, or sweet chili garlic). Your kids can get as dirty as they like since the Shrimp Station offers a sink with soap to clean up after chowing down. If you decide to take out, make sure you have plenty of wipes to clean up after munching these tasty but messy shrimp dishes.

9652 Kaumualii Hwy., Waimea. ✆ **808/338-1242.** Shrimp platters $11–$12. MC, V. Daily 11am–5pm.

Toi's Thai Kitchen AMERICAN/THAI A west Kauai staple, Toi's has gained a following for its affordable, authentic Thai food in a casual atmosphere, perfect for the family on a budget. Tucked into a corner of a small shopping complex (blindfold your kids and look for the McDonald's on the highway), Toi's serves savory dishes utilizing fresh herbs and local ingredients, many of them from the owner's garden. No kids' menu, but you can share the dishes family-style. Popular items include the house specialty, Toi's Temptation (homegrown herbs, coconut milk, lemon grass, and your choice of seafood, meat, or tofu); the vegetable curries; shrimp satay; and ginger-sauce nua (your choice of seafood, meat, or tofu in a fresh ginger stir-fry). Most of the rice, noodle, soup, curry, and main-course selections allow you to choose from among pork, chicken, seafood, beef, or vegetarian options. Buttered garlic nua, peanut-rich satays, and stir-fried Basil Delight are among Toi's many tasty preparations. All dishes come with green-papaya salad, dessert, and a choice of jasmine, sticky, or brown rice.

In the Eleele Shopping Center, Eleele. ✆ **808/335-3111.** Highchairs, boosters. Main courses $10–$17. AE, MC, V. Mon–Sat 10:30am–2pm and 5:30–9pm.

Wrangler's Steakhouse STEAK Good service and pleasant veranda seating are among the pluses of this family-run operation. A combination of cowboy, plantation, and island traditions, Wrangler's serves steak, and lots of it—big, hand-selected cuts—and adds some island touches, from vegetable tempura to ahi with penne pasta. Families like Wrangler's because of its multicourse dinners that won't break the bank and a kids' menu that features burgers.

9852 Kaumualii Hwy., Waimea. ✆ **808/338-1218.** Kids' menu, highchairs, boosters, crayons. Lunch $8–$12; dinner main courses $17–$30; kids' menu $6.50. AE, MC, V. Mon–Thurs 11am–8:30pm; Fri 11am–9pm; Sat 5–9pm.

THE COCONUT COAST

You'll find the restaurants in this section on the "Coconut Coast" map on p. 357.

Moderate

Caffè Coco ★★ GOURMET BISTRO This gets our vote for the most charming ambience on Kauai, with gourmet fare cooked to order at cafe prices, and special attention paid to the kids. Caffè Coco appears just off the main road at the edge of a cane field in Wailua, with a backyard that kids will love: shaded by pomelo, avocado, mango, tangerine, lychee, and banana trees, with a view of the Sleeping Giant Mountain. Not only do the trees create the experience of eating in an enchanted garden, but they also provide many of the ingredients for the muffins, chutneys, salsas, and fresh-squeezed juices that Ginger Carlson whips up in her kitchen. Seats are indoors (beyond the black-light art gallery) or on the gravel-floored back courtyard, where tiki torches flicker at night. The food is excellent, with vegetarian and other healthful delights such as spanakopita, Greek salad, fish wraps, macadamia nut and black sesame ahi with wasabi cream, and an excellent tofu-and-roast-veggie wrap. The kids' menu features items such as quesadillas and penne pasta.

4-369 Kuhio Hwy., Wailua. ✆ **808/822-7990.** Kids' menu, highchairs. Reservations recommended. Main courses $7–$21; specials usually less than $20; kids' menu $5.50–$7.75. MC, V. Tues–Sun 5–9pm.

Coconuts Island Style Grill ★ AMERICAN/ECLECTIC Kauai's newest sensation is right on the highway, next to Taco Bell, where fans line up for the happy hour pupu and affordable, tasty fare. Coconuts is upbeat and busy, with a cheerful tropical dining room with bamboo ceilings and coconut everything: bar floor, fixtures, furniture, and lights. There are lots of wines by the glass, good beers on tap, and a wide-ranging menu, including the best-selling teriyaki-dipped salmon. An excellent seafood chowder, grilled polenta with herb pesto and braised spinach, a burger with house-made potato chips, and shrimp cakes are also popular. The appetizer menu—nine items, from baby back ribs to lobster ravioli—is a hit from the time the doors open at 4pm. Kids will love the tasty burger with homemade crispy chips.

4-919 Kuhio Hwy. © **808/823-8777.** Kids' menu, highchairs, boosters. Reservations accepted only for 5 or more. Main courses $12–$29; kids' menu $6.50–$11. AE, DC, MC, V. Daily 4–9pm.

Wailua Family Restaurant AMERICAN/LOCAL The salad bars, efficient service, and family-friendly feeling here are legendary. Seniors and kids get discounts on the huge menu and a cross-cultural salad bar that includes a Mexican bar, pasta bar, sushi section, homemade soups, and ethnic samplings from Korean, Japanese, Filipino, and Hawaiian traditions. Everything, from the menu to the servings to the budget-friendly prices, winds up generous and big at Wailua Family Restaurant. The papaya is always freshly sliced at breakfast (there's a breakfast buffet Sat–Sun), the corn bread is good, and the eggs Benedict comes with a choice of ham or turkey. You can also order mahimahi or ono with the eggs for a high-protein start. The all-you-can-eat buffet (soup, salad, pasta, taco, and desserts) is a steal for $12; and seafood, sandwiches, stir-fries, teriyaki steak, and seafood combos are among the American and ethnic classics on the menu. There is outdoor seating now, too.

4361 Kuhio Hwy., across from Kinipopo Shopping Village. © **808/822-3325.** Kids' menu, highchairs, boosters. Breakfast $6–$15; main courses less than $8 lunch, $9–$44 dinner; kids' menu $4–$6. MC, V. Sun–Tues and Thurs 6:30am–9pm; Fri–Sat 6:30am–9:30pm; closed Wed.

Inexpensive

Blossoming Lotus ★★ VEGETARIAN This vegetarian restaurant has become so popular that they had to move into larger quarters just around the corner. In a tranquil atmosphere with plenty of light from the two-story dining room, stone flooring, wooden tables, and muted music, this organic gourmet vegan restaurant even has carnivores raving about the incredible food. Appetizers include spring rolls filled with fresh garden veggies served with a Thai dipping sauce, and a cosmic corn bread packed with cilantro and chiles. Entrees range from a coconut curry to a daily pizza. Lots of salads, wraps/sandwiches, and sinful-looking (but healthy) desserts round out the always-changing menu. No kids menu, but this is a great place to share dishes with the entire family. There's live entertainment every night and a terrific vegan brunch on Saturday and Sunday. If you want a quick drink or snack, the **Lotus Root** (4-1384 Kuhio Hwy., the previous location for this restaurant; © **808/823-6658**) offers just-baked goods, ice cream, juices, and smoothies.

Dragon Building, 4504 Kukui St., Kapaa. © **808/822-7678.** www.blossominglotus.com. Highchairs, boosters. Dinner main courses $12–$19; brunch $6–$15. AE, DISC, MC, V. Daily 5–9pm.

Bubba Burgers AMERICAN Here at the house of Bubba, they dish out humor, great T-shirts, and burgers nonpareil, along with tempeh burgers for vegetarians. Grilled fresh-fish sandwiches cater to the sensible, fish and chips to the carefree, and fish burgers to the undecided. But old-fashioned hamburgers are still the main attraction. No kids' menu, but the kids will be more interested in the Slopper (open-faced with chili), the half-pound Big Bubba (three patties), the Hubba Bubba (with rice, hot dog, and chili—a Bubba's plate lunch), and old-fashioned burgers. For a burger joint, it's big on fish too, with a daily trio of fresh-fish specials, fish burgers, and fish and chips. There's a second location in Hanalei Center, on the town's main road (© **808/826-7839**), where all items are less than $8.

4-1421 Kuhio Hwy., Kapaa. © **808/823-0069.** Boosters. All items less than $8. MC, V. Daily 10:30am–8pm in the winter and 10:30am–10pm in the summer (June 1 to Labor Day weekend).

Kountry Kitchen AMERICAN Forget counting calories when you sit down to the brawny omelets here. Kids can choose their own omelet fillings from several possibilities. Sandwiches and American dinners (steak, fish, and chicken) are standard coffeehouse fare, but sometimes fresh-fish specials stand out. The kids' menu features everything from pancakes to grilled cheese sandwiches. ***Warning:*** Sit as far away from the grill as possible; the smell of grease travels—and clings to your clothes.

1485 Kuhio Hwy., Kapaa. ✆ **808/822-3511.** Kids' menu, highchairs, boosters. Breakfast and lunch entrees $6–$17; kids' menu $4.50 breakfast, $5.75 lunch. MC, V. Daily 6am–1:30pm.

Mermaids Cafe ★ ISLAND STYLE Here's the place to pick up healthy food for the kids without dipping into their college fund. This tiny sidewalk cafe, with brisk takeout and a handful of tables on Kapaa's main drag, serves up health food in gourmet sauces: tofu or chicken satay, chicken coconut curry plate, and seared ahi wrap (made with the chef's special blend of garlic, jalapeño, lemon grass, kaffir lime, basil, and cilantro, then wrapped in a spinach tortilla)—all fabulous. The fresh-squeezed lemonade is made daily, and you can choose white or organic brown rice. Because of the limited seating, it's best to get takeout for the beach.

1384 Kuhio Hwy., Kapaa. ✆ **808/821-2026.** Main courses less than $11. DC, DISC, MC, V. Mon–Sat 11am–9pm.

Norberto's El Café MEXICAN *¡Olé!* Finally there's an inexpensive, healthy Mexican restaurant where the kids will be welcome. The lard-free, home-style fare here includes top-notch chiles rellenos with homemade everything, vegetarian selections by request, and, if you're lucky, fresh-fish enchiladas. All of the sauces are made from scratch, and the salsa comes red-hot with homegrown chile peppers fresh from the chef's garden. Norberto's signature is the spinachy Hawaiian taro-leaf enchiladas, a Mexican version of laulau, served with cheese and taro or with chicken. Kids' plates include entree plus soup, beans, and rice.

4-1373 Kuhio Hwy., Kapaa. ✆ **808/822-3362.** Highchairs, boosters, crayons. Reservations recommended for parties of 6 or more. Main courses $4.75–$9.45; complete dinners $14–$18; kids' plate $11. MC, V. Mon–Sat 5:30–9pm.

Ono Family Restaurant AMERICAN Breakfast at this small coffee shop is a big deal, with eggs Florentine (two poached eggs, blanched spinach, and hollandaise sauce) leading the pack, and eggs Canterbury (much like eggs Benedict, but with more ingredients) following close behind. Steak and eggs; banana, coconut, and macadamia nut pancakes; and dozens of omelet choices also attract throngs of loyalists. Lunch is no slouch either, with scads of fish, veggie, steak, tuna, and turkey sandwiches to choose from, and Ono beef or buffalo burgers with various toppings highlighting the menu. The gourmet hamburger with fries and soup demands an after-lunch siesta. The most popular item on the kids' menu is keiki burgers with fries.

4-1292 Kuhio Hwy., Kapaa. ✆ **808/822-1710.** Kids' menu, highchairs, boosters, crayons. Most items less than $12; kids' menu $5.25. AE, DC, DISC, MC, V. Daily 7am–2pm.

En Route to the North Shore

Duane's Ono-Char Burger BURGERS This roadside burger stand has been serving up hefty, all-beef burgers for generations. (And now there are Boca burgers, for vegetarians.) The teriyaki sauce and blue cheese are only part of the secret of Duane's beefy, smoky, and legendary ono-char burgers, which come in several styles: teriyaki, mushroom, cheddar, barbecue, and the Special, with grilled onions, sprouts, and two cheeses. The broiled-fish sandwich (another marvel of the seasoned old grill) and the marionberry ice-cream shake, a three-berry combo, are popular as well. The kids' menu and outdoor seating at picnic tables make this a must-stop as you drive to the North Shore.

On Kuhio Hwy., Anahola. ✆ **808/822-9181.** Kids' menu. Hamburgers $6–$7.25; kids' menu $3.75–$4.65. MC, V. Mon–Sat 10am–6pm; Sun 11am–6pm.

A Hawaiian Feast: The Luau

Originally, an ancient Hawaiian feast was called a *pa'ina* or *'aha'aina,* but in 1856, the *Pacific Commercial Advertiser* (the newspaper of the day) started referring to the feast as a "luau," a name referring to the young taro tops always served at the feast. Try to take in a luau while you're on Kauai. A luau today can range from a backyard affair to a commercial production at a major resort. The best ones are put on by local churches, schools, or hula *halau* (schools). However, most visitors won't have the opportunity to see these truly authentic feasts. Several commercial luau listed below will provide a taste and a feel for them.

Most luau are fixed in price, generally $68 to $99 for adults, less for children. A variety of traditional foods and entertainment is provided. The luau usually begins at sunset and features Polynesian and Hawaiian entertainment, which can range from lavish affairs with flaming knives or torches being juggled, to performances of ancient hula, missionary-era hula, and modern hula, as well as narration of the stories and legends portrayed by the dances. The food always includes imu-roasted kalua pig, lomi salmon, dried fish, poke (raw fish cut into small pieces), poi (made from taro), laulau (meat, fish, and vegetables wrapped in ti leaves), Hawaiian sweet potato, sautéed vegetables, salad, and the ultimate taste treat, a dessert called *haupia* (coconut pudding). Don't worry; if you've never heard of these items (and can't pronounce them either), most luau will also have more common preparations of fish, chicken, and roast beef, as well as easily recognizable salads and standard desserts like cake.

The mainstay of the feast is the imu, a hot earthen pit in which the pig and other items are cooked. The preparations for the feast actually begin in the morning, when the luau master layers hot stones and banana stalks in the pit to get the temperature up to 400°F. The pig, vegetables, and other items are lowered into the pit and cooked all day. The water in the leaves steams the pig and roasts the meat to a tender texture.

One of the larger commercial luau in the island is **Smith's Tropical Paradise Garden Lu'au,** in the Tropical Paradise Gardens on the Wailua River (© **808/821-6895** or 821-6896; www.smithskauai.com), every Monday, Wednesday, and Friday at 5pm (during the popular summer months it is 5 days a week

THE NORTH SHORE

You'll find the restaurants in this section on the map "Kauai's North Shore: Princeville & Hanalei" on p. 382.

Expensive

Bar Acuda ★★★ TAPAS Plan a quiet evening for just the two of you, leave the kids with a sitter, and enjoy the culinary wizardry of Chef Jim Moffat. After two successful restaurants in San Francisco (The Slow Club and 42°), Moffat up and moved to the tiny town of Hanalei and opened this sleek, romantic restaurant specializing in his favorite tapa dishes from the Southern European regions along 42° latitude (Southern France,

Mon–Fri). Luau prices are $75 for adults, $30 for children 7 to 13, and $19 for children 3 to 6 (***budget tip:*** book online and save 10%); or you can come for just the entertainment at 7:30pm and pay $15 for adults, $7.50 for children ages 3 to 12 and no charge for infants ages 2 and under.

The **Sheraton Kauai,** Poipu Beach (© **808/742-8200;** www.sheratonkauai.com), claims the island's only oceanfront luau. The Surf to Sunset Luau is held on Monday and Friday, beginning at 6pm with a shell lei greeting and a mai tai. Photos with Poipu Beach serving as the background are offered, and guests can wander among the local artisans who teach lei making, lauhala weaving, and coconut frond weaving. After the feast, and before Pilah's Royal Polynesian Revue begins the entertainment, there is a pareu (sarong) fashion show that teaches visitors several techniques for tying this island cloth into a variety of types of clothing. Costs for adults range from $75 for the buffet dinner and entertainment to $99 for premier seating, table service, and professional photos. Children, ages 6 to 12 years, are $37 and $49.

The luau at the **ResortQuest Kauai Beach,** Kapaa (© **808/823-0311;** Tues–Sun) begins at 5:30pm with an imu ceremony in which the pig is removed from the pit, followed by entertainment featuring ancient and modern hula performances. The cost is $65 for adults, $62 for seniors, $42 for teenagers 13 to 18, $32 for children 3 to 12, and free for children 2 and under.

The Princeville Resort puts on a beachside luau called **Pa'ina O' Hanalei,** 5520 Kahaku Rd., Princeville (© **800/826-4400** or 808/826-9644; www.princeville.com), Monday and Thursday at 6pm. Under a canopy of stars, a full feast is served and a Polynesian revue performs. The cost is $99 for adults, $90 for seniors, $45 for children 5 to 12, free for children 4 and under.

On the south coast, check out **Tihati Production's "Havaiki Nui,"** in the Grand Hyatt Kauai Resort & Spa, 1571 Poipu Rd., Poipu (© **800/55 HYATT** [554 9288] or 808/240-6456; www.kauai-hyatt.com), every Sunday and Thursday. They have not only an elaborate buffet but also a very professional Polynesian show. The cost is $94 for adults, $84 for teens 13 to 20, and $57 for children 5 to 12; children 4 and under are free.

Italy, Spain, and Portugal). In an atmosphere of candlelight and exotic mouthwatering aromas coming from the open exhibition kitchen, the creative dishes range from Hawaiian *onaga* (a deep-water snapper) baked in papillote with pineapple, lime, chilies, and vanilla ($27) to a whole roasted tomato bruschetta with leeks, balsamic, and grilled bread ($8.50) to a grilled rib-eye steak with salsa verde and steak fries ($28). The excellent wine selection includes some 50 handpicked, estate-bottled wines, mainly from Italy, France, Spain, Oregon, and California (with an emphasis on Rohne-style grapes). Half of the wines are available by the glass. Great for adults; might be too sophisticated for kids.

5-5161 Kuhio Hwy., Hanalei. © **808/826-7081.** www.restaurantbaracuda.com. Tapas $6–$28. MC, V. Tues–Sun 6–9pm.

 La Cascata ★★★ MEDITERRANEAN/SOUTHERN ITALIAN The North Shore's special-occasion restaurant is sumptuous—a Sicilian spree in Eden. Although they accommodate kids, make this one an adults' night out. Try to get here before dark so that you can enjoy the views of Bali Ha'i, the persimmon-colored sunset, and the waterfalls of Waialeale, all an integral part of the feast. Click your heels on the terra-cotta floors, take in the trompe l'oeil vines, train your eyes through the concertina windows, and pretend you're being served on a terrazzo in Sicily. The dazzling menu offers Mediterranean-inspired food made with fresh local ingredients. Polenta, charred peppers, Kauai asparagus, organic Kauai vegetables, risottos, ragouts, grilled fresh fish, and vegetable napoleons are colorful and tasty, and beautifully presented.

In the Princeville Resort, 5520 Ka Haku Rd. ✆ **808/826-9644.** Highchairs, boosters, crayons. Reservations recommended for dinner. Main courses $28–$48; 3-course prix-fixe dinner $65. AE, DC, DISC, MC, V. Daily 6–10pm.

Lighthouse Bistro Kilauea ★★ CONTINENTAL/ITALIAN/PACIFIC RIM Even if you're not on your way to the legendary Kilauea Lighthouse, this bistro is so good it's worth bringing the family for a special trip. The charming green-and-white wooden building next to Kong Lung Store has open sides, old-fashioned plantation architecture, open-air seating, trellises, and high ceilings. The ambience is wonderful and the food is excellent: an eclectic selection that highlights local ingredients in everything from fresh-fish tacos and fresh-fish burgers to mac nut–crusted ahi. The kids' menu ranges from linguine to quesadillas.

In Kong Lung Center, Kilauea Rd. (off Hwy. 56 on the way to the Kilauea Lighthouse), Kilauea. ✆ **808/828-0481.** Kids' menu, highchairs, boosters, crayons. Reservations recommended. Lunch $7–$15; dinner main courses $11–$39; kids' menu $4.95–$7.95. MC, V. Daily noon–2:30pm and 5:30–9pm.

Moderate

Hanalei Dolphin Restaurant & Fish Market ★ SEAFOOD Hidden behind a gallery called Ola's are this fish market and adjoining steak-and-seafood restaurant, on the banks of the Hanalei River. Particularly inviting are the fresh-fish sandwiches, served under umbrellas at the river's edge. Most appealing (besides the river view) are the appetizers (such as ceviche fresh from the fish market, with a jaunty dash of green olives), the view, and the family-friendly amenities.

5144 Kuhio Hwy., Hanalei. ✆ **808/826-6113.** Kids' menu, highchairs, boosters, crayons. Main courses $20–$34; kids' menu $6–$12. MC, V. Daily 11am–9pm (fish market daily 11am–7pm).

Hanalei Gourmet AMERICAN Send the kids to school, the old (1926) Hanalei School, that is, where wood floors, wooden benches, and blackboards of yesteryear now are a haven for today's Hanalei hipsters noshing on the Tu Tu Tuna (far-from-prosaic tuna salad with green beans, potatoes, niçoise olives, and hard-boiled eggs); fresh grilled ahi sandwiches; roasted eggplant sandwiches; chicken-salad boats (in papaya or avocado, with macadamia nuts and sans mayonnaise); and other selections. This is an informal cross-cultural tasting, from stir-fried veggies over udon to Asian ahi-pasta salad to artichoke hearts fried in beer batter. The kids' menu has a great burger selection. No matter how noisy or rambunctious your kids get, no one will notice. (The music on the sound system can be almost deafening.) Nightly live music adds to the fun.

In the Old Hanalei Schoolhouse, 5-5161 Kuhio Hwy., Hanalei. ✆ **808/826-2524.** Kids' menu, highchairs, crayons. Main courses $7–$23; kids' menu $7. DC, DISC, MC, V. Sun–Thurs 8am–10:30pm; Fri–Sat 8am–11:30pm.

Kilauea Bakery & Pau Hana Pizza ★ BAKERY/PIZZA When owner, baker, and avid diver Tom Pickett spears an ono and smokes it himself, his catch appears on the

Billie Holiday pizza, guaranteed to obliterate the blues with its brilliant notes of Swiss chard, roasted onions, Gorgonzola-rosemary sauce, and mozzarella. And the much-loved bakery puts out guava sourdough; Hanalei poi sourdough; fresh chive, goat-cheese, and sun-dried-tomato bread; blackberry–white chocolate scones; and other fine baked goods. The breads go well with the soups and hot lunch specials, and the pastries with the new full-service espresso bar, which serves not only the best of the bean, but also blended frozen drinks and such up-to-the-minute voguish things as iced chai and Mexican-chocolate smoothies (with cinnamon). The Picketts have added a small dining room, and the few outdoor picnic tables under umbrellas are as inviting as ever. The macadamia nut–butter cookies and lilikoi fruit Danishes are sublime.

In Kong Lung Center, Kilauea Rd. (off Hwy. 56 on the way to the Kilauea Lighthouse), Kilauea. ✆ **808/828-2020.** Highchairs. Pizzas $11–$31. MC, V. Daily 6:30am–9pm.

Sushi & Blues ★ PACIFIC RIM/SUSHI This second-floor oasis has a large picture window for gazing at the Hanalei waterfalls and, most important, chefs who know their sushi. Traditional sushi, fusion sushi, and hot Pacific Rim dishes for those who aren't sushi lovers please diners of every stripe. The kids' menu features a range of items, including a popular teriyaki chicken meal ($5.95). Big hits on the main menu: eight types of fresh fish prepared in fusion flavorings involving mango, garlic, sake, sesame, coconut, passion fruit, and other Pacific Rim preparations. The action fires up Wednesday, Thursday, Saturday, and Sunday from 8:30pm and later, with live music from Hawaiian to blues and jazz to rock 'n' roll.

In Ching Young Village, Hanalei. ✆ **808/826-9701.** www.sushiandblues.com. Kids' menu, highchairs, boosters, crayons. Reservations recommended for parties of 6 or more. Main courses $18–$23; sushi rolls from $4; kids' meal $6. MC, V. Tues–Sun 6–10pm.

Inexpensive

Kilauea Fish Market ★ HEALTHY PLATE LUNCH This is the perfect place to get a picnic takeout lunch or an easy dinner to go to take back and watch the sunset. Coriena Rogers not only has healthy, yummy meals made with just-caught fish, but also has a deli section with fresh fish for those looking to cook it themselves. Located just off the road to the Kilauea Lighthouse, this tiny hole in the wall has a few tables outside in a garden setting, but generally people pick up and go. Vegetarians will be happy with the daily specials. She has options of brown or white rice and she insists on using organic greens in her salads. Some of the best prices on the north shore.

4270 Kilauea Lighthouse Rd., Kilauea. ✆ **808/828-6244.** Most items less than $15. MC, V. Mon–Sat 11am–8pm.

Tropical Taco ★ MEXICAN For more than a quarter of a century, Roger Kennedy has been making tacos and burritos in Hanalei. For years, you could find him working out of his green "taco wagon" parked along the road. But recently, Roger has come up in the world and he now has a "regular" restaurant (with wood floors and seating along the outside lanai, where you can people-watch) in the Hanalei Building. He's still serving his tasty assortment of tacos and burritos, plus his signature "fat Jack" (a 10-in. tortilla deep-fried with cheese, beans, and beef or fish). No kids' menu per se, but the keiki will love everything that Roger offers; and he even warns everyone that his tasty treats are "not to be consumed 1 hour before surfing!" Just as with his taco wagon, Roger still offers "anything you want to drink, as long as it's lemonade."

Hanalei Building, 5-5088 Kuhio Hwy., Hanalei. ✆ **808/827-TACO** (827-8226). www.tropicaltaco.com. Most items less than $10. No credit cards. Mon–Sat 11am–5pm.

5 EXPLORING KAUAI WITH YOUR KIDS

No matter how much time you have on Kauai, make it a priority to see the entire island. It's small enough that with proper planning and mapping out the things you want to experience, you and your kids will build memories that will last a lifetime.

LIHUE & ENVIRONS

Grove Farm Homestead **All ages.** Your family can experience a day in the life of an 1860s sugar planter on a visit to Grove Farm Homestead, which shows how good life was (for some, anyway) when sugar was king. Plan to spend an hour in Hawaii's best remaining example of a sugar-plantation homestead. Founded in 1864 by George N. Wilcox, a Hanalei missionary's son, Grove Farm was one of the earliest of Hawaii's 86 sugar plantations. A self-made millionaire, Wilcox died a bachelor in 1933, at age 94. His estate looks much like it did when he lived here, complete with period furniture, plantation artifacts, and Hawaiiana.

4050 Nawiliwili Rd. (Hwy. 58) at Pikaka St. (2 miles from Waapa Rd.), Lihue. ✆ **808/245-3202.** www.hawaiimuseums.org. Requested donation $10 adults, $5 children 11 and under. Tours offered Mon and Wed–Thurs at 10am and 1pm; reservations required.

Kauai Museum ★ **All ages.** The history of Kauai is kept safe in an imposing Greco-Roman building that once served as the town library. This great little museum is worth at least an hour-long stop before you set out to explore the island. It contains a wealth of historical artifacts and information tracing the island's history from the beginning of time through Contact (when Capt. James Cook "discovered" Kauai in 1778), the monarchy period, the plantation era, and the present. You'll hear tales of the menehune (the mythical elflike people who were said to build massive stoneworks in a single night) and see old poi pounders and idols, relics of sugar planters and *paniolos,* a nice seashell collection, old Hawaiian quilts, feather leis, a replica of a plantation worker's home, and much more—even a model of Cook's ship, the HMS *Resolution,* riding anchor in Waimea Bay.

4428 Rice St., Lihue. ✆ **808/245-6931.** www.kauaimuseum.org. Admission $10 adults, $8 seniors, $3 students 13–17, $1 children 6–12; free for children 5 and under. Free guided tours (with admission) Tues–Fri 10:30am (make reservations). Open Mon–Fri 9am–4pm; Sat 10am–4pm. First Sat of every month is "Family Day," when admission is free.

Kauai Plantation Railway ★ **All ages.** The first new railroad to be built in Hawaii in 100 years opened in 2007 after 5 years of work, 6,000 ties, 30,000 hand-driven spikes, and 480,000 pounds of iron rail. The Kauai Plantation Railway is part scenic tour, part-cultural tour, part agricultural tour, part educational tour, and 100% fun for the family. The train, consisting of two refurbished diesel engines and four custom (hardwood floors) passenger cars, travels along a 3-mile figure-eight track through the grounds of Kilohana (see below). The 40-minute tour is narrated by very knowledgeable guides (all dressed in green "palaka" print shirts) who not only weave in Kauai's history but also point out the more than 50 different crops which have been planted along the train route (everything from Hawaii crops like sugar, pineapple, and taro to fruit trees to fragrant plants (ginger, gardenia, plumeria), vegetable plants, and even hardwood trees (milo, koa). The train stops briefly at the "animal farm," where some pigs, goats, sheep, chickens, and cows are available for petting.

Kilohana, 3-2087 Kaumualii Hwy., Lihue. ✆ **808/245-RAIL** (245-7245). www.kauaiplantationrailway.com. Admission $19 adults, $15 children 2–12, free for children 1 and under. Mon–Sat 10am–2pm.

Fun Facts The Legendary Little People

According to ancient Hawaiian legend, among Kauai's earliest settlers were the menehune, a race of small people who worked at night to accomplish magnificent feats. Above Nawiliwili Harbor, the **Menehune Fish Pond**—which at one time extended 25 miles—is said to have been built in just 1 night, with two rows of thousands of menehune passing stones hand to hand. The menehune were promised that no one would watch them work, but one person did. When they discovered the spy, the menehume stopped working immediately, leaving two gaps in the wall. From Nawiliwili Harbor, take Hulemalu Road above Huleia Stream; look for the HAWAII CONVENTION AND VISITORS BUREAU marker at a turnoff in the road, which leads to the legendary fishpond. Kayakers can paddle up Huleia Stream to see it up close.

THE POIPU RESORT AREA

No Hawaii resort has a better entrance: On Maluhia Road, eucalyptus trees planted in 1911 as a windbreak for sugar cane fields now form a monumental **tree tunnel.** The leafy green, cool tunnel starts at Kaumualii Highway; you'll emerge at the golden-red beach.

Allerton Garden of the National Tropical Botanical Garden ★ Ages 12 and above. Discover an extraordinary collection of tropical fruit and spice trees, rare Hawaiian plants, and hundreds of varieties of flowers at the 186-acre preserve known as **Lawai Gardens,** said to be the largest collection of rare and endangered plants in the world. Adjacent **McBryde Garden,** a royal home site of Queen Emma in the 1860s, is known for its formal gardens, a delicious kind of colonial decadence. It's set amid fountains, streams, waterfalls, and European statuary. Endangered green sea turtles can be seen here. (Their home in the sea was wiped out years ago by Hurricane Iniki.) The 2½-hour tours are fascinating for green thumbs and novices alike.

Visitor Center, Lawai Rd. (across the street from Spouting Horn), Poipu. ✆ **808/742-2623.** www.ntbg.org. Admission $35 adults, $20 children 6–12. Guided 2½-hr. tours by reservation only Mon–Sat at 9am, 10am, 1pm, and 2pm; Sun 10am and 1pm. Self-guided tours of McBryde Garden Mon–Sat 9am–4pm, $20 adults and $10 children 6–12, free for children 5 and under (trams into the valley leave once an hour on the half-hour, last tram 2:30pm); guided tour of Allerton Garden Mon–Sat 9am, 10am, 1pm, and 2pm, $40 adults, $20 children 10–12. Reserve a week in advance in peak months of July–Sept.

Prince Kuhio Park All ages. This small roadside park, the birthplace of Prince Jonah Kuhio Kalanianaole, the "People's Prince," whose March 26 birthday is a holiday in Hawaii, is worth a 10-minute stop. He opened the beaches of Waikiki to the public in 1918 and served as Hawaii's second territorial delegate to the U.S. Congress. What remains here are the foundations of the family home, a royal fishpond, and a shrine where tributes are still paid in flowers.

Lawai Rd., Koloa. Just after MM 4 on Poipu Rd., veer to the right of the fork in the road; the park is on the right side.

Spouting Horn ★ All ages. This natural phenomenon is second only to Yellowstone's Old Faithful. It's quite a sight—big waves hit Kauai's south shore with enough force to send a spout of funneled saltwater 10 feet or more up in the air; in winter, the water can get as high as six stories. Plan about a half-hour here; the kids will be thrilled every time the spout blows.

Frommer's Favorite Kauai Family Experiences

Surfing with an Expert (p. 394) If seven-time world champ Margo Oberg, a member of the Surfing Hall of Fame, can't get your kid—or you—up on a board riding a wave, nobody can. She promises same-day results, even for klutzes.

Paddling up the Huleia River (p. 393) Indiana Jones ran for his life up this river to his seaplane in *Raiders of the Lost Ark*. You and the kids can venture down it yourself in a kayak. The picturesque Huleia winds through tropically lush Huleia National Wildlife Refuge, where endangered species such as great blue herons and Hawaiian gallinules take wing. It's ideal for everyone.

Climbing the Wooden Jungle Gyms at Lydgate State Park (p. 399) This unique playground has a maze of jungle gyms for children of all ages. You can whip down slides, explore caves, hang from bars, and climb all over. It's a great place to spend the afternoon.

Cooling Off with a Shave Ice (p. 367) On a hot, hot day, stop by **Brennecke's Beach Broiler,** across from Poipu Beach Park (✆ **808/742-7588**), and order a traditional Hawaiian shave ice. This local treat consists of crushed ice stuffed into a paper cone and topped with a tropical-flavored syrup. If you can't decide on a flavor, go for the "rainbow"—three different flavors in one cone.

Exploring a Magical World (p. 386) **Na Aina Kai Botanical Gardens** on some 240 acres, sprinkled with some 70 life-size (some larger than life-size) whimsical bronze statues, lies hidden off the beaten path of the North Shore. It is opening a tropical children's garden featuring a gecko hedge maze, a tropical jungle gym, a treehouse in a rubber tree, and a 16-foot-tall Jack-and-the-Beanstalk giant with a 33-foot wading pool below. It's open only 4 days a week, so book before you leave the mainland for Hawaii so that you won't be disappointed.

Experiencing a Hands-On Learning Adventure (p. 381) The **Kauai Children's Discovery Museum,** located in Kapaa (✆ **808/823-8222;** www.kcdm.org), arose out of a grass-roots community effort to have a fun place where kids could learn about science, culture, arts, technology, and nature. In addition to the exhibits, there are Keiki Camps where you can leave the kids all day, and they will be taken on various outings to the beach and to points of interest.

Spouting Horn is different from other blowholes in Hawaii in that it has an additional hole that blows air that sounds like a loud moaning. According to Hawaiian legend, this coastline was once guarded by a giant female lizard (Mo'o); she would gobble up any intruders. One day, along came Liko, who wanted to fish in this area. Mo'o rushed out to eat Liko. Quickly, Liko threw a spear right into the giant lizard's mouth. Mo'o then chased Liko into a lava tube. Liko escaped, but legend says Mo'o is still in the tube, and the moaning sound at Spouting Horn is her cry for help.

At Kukuiula Bay, beyond Prince Kuhio Park (see above).

WESTERN KAUAI

Waimea Town

If you'd like to take a self-guided tour of this historic town, stop at the **Waimea Library,** at mile marker 23 on Highway 50, to pick up a map and guide to the sites.

Kiki a Ola (Menehune Ditch) **All ages.** Hawaiians were expert rock builders, able to construct elaborate edifices without using mortar. They formed long lines and passed stones hand over hand, and lifted rocks weighing tons with ropes made from native plants. Their feats gave rise to fantastic tales of menehune, elflike people hired by Hawaiian kings to create massive stoneworks in a single night—reputedly for the payment of a single shrimp. (See "The Legendary Little People," above.) It'll take just a couple of minutes to examine the remaining 2-foot-high portion of the wall; the rest of the marvelous stonework is buried under the roadbed.

From Hwy. 50, go inland on Menehune Rd.; a plaque marks the spot about 1 1/2 miles up.

Russian Fort Elizabeth State Historical Park **All ages.** To the list of those who tried to conquer Hawaii, add the Russians. In 1815, a German doctor tried to claim Kauai for Russia. He even supervised the construction of a fort in Waimea, but he and his handful of Russian companions were expelled by Kamehameha I a couple of years later. Now a state historic landmark, the ruins of Russian Fort Elizabeth (named for the wife of Russia's Czar Alexander I) is on the eastern headlands overlooking the harbor, across from Lucy Kapahu Aukai Wright Beach Park. You can take a free, half-hour, self-guided tour of the site, which affords a keen view of the west bank of the Waimea River, where Captain Cook landed, and of the island of Niihau across the channel.

Hwy. 50 (on the ocean side, just after MM 22), east of Waimea.

The Grand Canyon of the Pacific: Waimea Canyon ★★★

The great gaping gulch known as Waimea Canyon is quite a sight. This valley, known for its reddish lava beds, reminds everyone who sees it of the Grand Canyon. Kauai's version is bursting with ever-changing color, just like its namesake, but it's smaller—only a mile wide, 3,567 feet deep, and 12 miles long. A massive earthquake sent all the streams flowing into a single river that ultimately carved this picturesque canyon. Today, the Waimea River—a silver thread of water in the gorge that's sometimes a trickle, often a torrent, but always there—keeps cutting the canyon deeper and wider, and nobody can say what the result will be 100 million years from now.

The Drive Through Waimea Canyon & Up to Kokee

By car, there are two ways to visit Waimea Canyon and reach Kokee State Park, 20 miles up from Waimea. From the coastal road (Hwy. 50), you can turn up Waimea Canyon Drive (Hwy. 550) at Waimea town; or you can pass through Waimea and turn up Kokee Road (Hwy. 55) at Kekaha. The climb is very steep from Kekaha, but Waimea Canyon Drive, the rim road, is narrower and rougher. A few miles up, the two merge into Kokee Road.

The first good vantage point is **Waimea Canyon Lookout,** located between mile markers 10 and 11 on Waimea Canyon Road. From here, it's another 6 miles to Kokee. There are a few more lookout points along the way that also offer spectacular views, such as **Puu Hina Hina Lookout,** between mile markers 13 and 14, at 3,336 feet; be sure to pull over and spend a few minutes pondering this natural wonder. (The giant white object that looks like a golf ball and defaces the natural landscape is a radar station left over from the Cold War.)

Kokee State Park

It's only 16 miles from Waimea to Kokee, but the park is a whole different world because it is 4,345 acres of rainforest. You'll enter a new climate zone, where the breeze has a bite and trees look quite continental. You're in a cloud forest on the edge of the Alakai Swamp, the largest swamp in Hawaii, on the summit plateau of Kauai. Days are cool and wet, with intermittent bright sunshine, not unlike Seattle on a good day. Bring a sweater and, if you're staying over, be sure you know how to light a fire. (Overnight lows dip into the 40s.)

Right next to Kokee Lodge (which lies on the only road through the park, about a mile before it ends) is the **Kokee Natural History Museum ★** (✆ **808/335-9975;** www.kokee.org), open daily from 10am to 4pm (free admission). This is the best place to learn about the forest and Alakai Swamp before you set off hiking in the wild. The museum shop has great trail information and local books and maps, including the official park trail map. I recommend getting the *Pocket Guide on Native Plants on the Nature Trail for Kokee State Park* and the *Road Guide to Kokee and Waimea Canyon State Park.*

A **nature walk** is the best intro to this rainforest; it starts behind the museum at the rare Hawaiian koa tree. This easy, self-guided walk of about .25 mile takes about 20 minutes if you stop and look at all the plants identified along the way.

Two miles above Kokee Lodge is **Kalalau Lookout ★**, the spectacular climax of your drive through Waimea Canyon and Kokee. When you stand at the lookout, below you is a work in progress that began at least 5 million years ago. It's hard to stop looking; the view is breathtaking, especially when light and cloud shadows play across the red-and-orange cliffs.

There's lots more to see and do up here: Anglers fly-fish for rainbow trout, and hikers tackle the 45 trails that lace the Alakai Swamp. (See "For the Active Family," later in this chapter.) That's a lot of ground to cover, so you might want to plan on staying over. If pitching a tent is too rustic for you, the wonderful **cabins** set in a grove of redwoods are one of the best lodging bargains in the islands. (See "Family-Friendly Accommodations," earlier in this chapter.) The restaurant at the **Kokee Lodge** (p. 355) is open for continental breakfast and lunch, daily from 9am to 3:30pm.

For advance information, contact the **Division of State Parks,** P.O. Box 1671, Lihue, HI 96766 (✆ **808/335-5871**); and the **Kokee Lodge Manager,** P.O. Box 819, Waimea, HI 96796 (✆ **808/335-6061**). The park is open daily year-round. The best time to go is early in the morning, to see the panoramic view of Kalalau Valley from the lookout at 4,000 feet, before clouds obscure the valley and peaks.

Helicopter Rides over Waimea Canyon & the Na Pali Coast ★★★

Don't leave Kauai without seeing it from a helicopter. It's expensive but worth the splurge. You can take home memories of the thrilling ride up and over the Kalalau Valley on Kauai's wild North Shore and into the 5,200-foot vertical temple of Mount Waialeale, the most sacred place on the island and the wettest spot on earth. (In some cases, you can even take a video of your ride home.) All flights leave from Lihue Airport. Even your youngest kids will enjoy this trip. Allow at least an hour for flying time, plus another hour for check-in and flight instructions.

Air Kauai Helicopters ★ Since 1988, Chuck DiPiazza has been flying visitors over Kauai without incident. He flies custom-designed, huge-windowed (37% larger than most helicopter windows), A-Star helicopters with high-back leather seats, and has moved the pilot over to the left side of the helicopter (instead of the usual position on

Kauai Children's Discovery Museum

This is every parent's dream: an enthralling, hands-on learning adventure to take kids to on rainy days. (Hey, it's so much fun, the kids will beg to come back even on sunny days.) The **Kauai Children's Discovery Museum,** located under the Whale Tower in the Kauai Village Shopping Center in Kapaa (✆ **808/823-8222;** www.kcdm.org), offers hands-on, interactive exhibits that range from playing with Hawaiian musical instruments to participating in virtual reality television to hiding out in a "magic treehouse" and reading a book. (There's even a baby area for kids 4 and younger.) Not only is it thrilling for kids, but it's also a great place for them to interact and meet children from Kauai. The 7,000-square-foot play center is open Tuesday to Saturday from 9am to 5pm; during school breaks they also are open on Monday from 7am to 5pm. Admission is $4 for kids (ages 1–17 years) and $5 for adults.

the right), which allows not only a better view, but more legroom. Another plus: All his helicopters have Bose Acoustic Noise Canceling Stereo Headsets, which helps in those noisy birds. If possible, ask for Captain Chuck; his commentaries are informative and down-to-earth. He welcomes questions and loves to show off his multi-CD player, combining the "right" music with the tour.

3651 Ahukini Rd., Lihue, HI 96766. ✆ **800/972-4666** or 808/246-4666. www.airkauai.com. 60-min. tour $219 per person.

Blue Hawaiian Helicopters★★★ Blue Hawaiian has been the Cadillac of helicopter tour companies on Maui and the Big Island for more than a decade, and recently they have expanded their operations to Kauai. I strongly recommend that you try to book with them first. Their operation is first-class, and the equipment is the most state-of-the-art in Hawaii: American Eurocopter ECO-Star, which reduces noise in the helicopter by 50% and allows 23% more interior room. Plus the craft has individual Business Class–style seats, two-way communication with the pilot, and expansive glass for incredible views. The 50-minute flights first journey to Hanapepe Valley, then continue on to Mana Waiapuna, commonly referred to as "Jurassic Park Falls." Next it's up the Olokele Canyon, then on to the Waimea Canyon, the famed "Grand Canyon of the Pacific." Most of the flight then will be along the Na Pali Coast, before heading out to the Bali Ha'i Cliffs, and the pristine blue waters of Hanalei Bay and the Princeville Resort area. If the weather gods are on your side, you'll get to see the highest point on Kauai: Mount Waialeale, the wettest spot on earth, with an average rainfall of 450 to 500 inches annually. Your flight will take you right into the center of the crater with its 5,000-foot walls towering above and its 3,000-foot waterfalls surrounding you, something you will remember forever.

Harbor Mall staging area, 3501 Rice St., Lihue; take off from the Lihue Airport. ✆ **800/745-2583** or 808/245-5800. www.bluehawaiian.com. 50-min. tour $274 ($241 if you book online).

Jack Harter Helicopters ★ The pioneer of helicopter flights on Kauai, Jack was the one who started the sightseeing-via-helicopter trend. On the 60-minute tour, he flies a four-passenger Bell Jet Ranger Model 204 (with "scenic view" windows), a six-seater A-Star, or a Eurocopter AS350BA A-Star. The 90-minute tour (in the Bell Jet Ranger

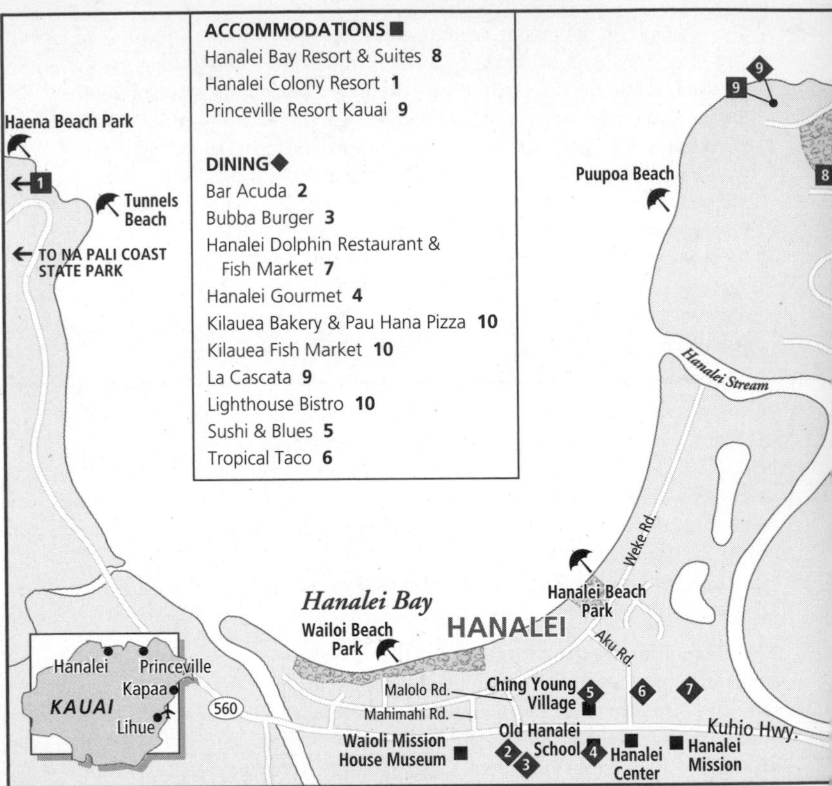

only) hovers over the sights a bit longer than the 60-minute flight, so you can get a good look; but we found the shorter tour sufficient.

4231 Ahukini Rd., Lihue. ✆ **888/245-2001** or 808/245-3774. www.helicopters-kauai.com. 60- to 65-min. tour $229; 90- to 95-min. tour $384 (book on the Internet and save $40).

Sunshine Helicopters The 60-minute flight starts in Lihue and takes you through Waimea Canyon, along the Na Pali Coast, and over Waialeale Crater and the two sets of waterfalls that appeared in *Fantasy Island.* Will's A-Star six-passenger 'copter has side-by-side seats (nobody sits backward and everybody gets a window seat) and enlarged windows. A veteran pilot, Will has flown several thousand hours over Kauai since 1984 and knows the island, its ever-changing weather conditions, and his 'copters.

3222 Kuhio Hwy., Lihue. ✆ **888/245-4354** or 808/245-8881. www.helicopters-hawaii.com. $269–$349 per person ($230–$310 if you book online).

THE COCONUT COAST

Fern Grotto **All ages.** This is one of Kauai's oldest (since 1946) and most popular tourist attractions. Several times daily a 157-passenger motorized barge takes people up

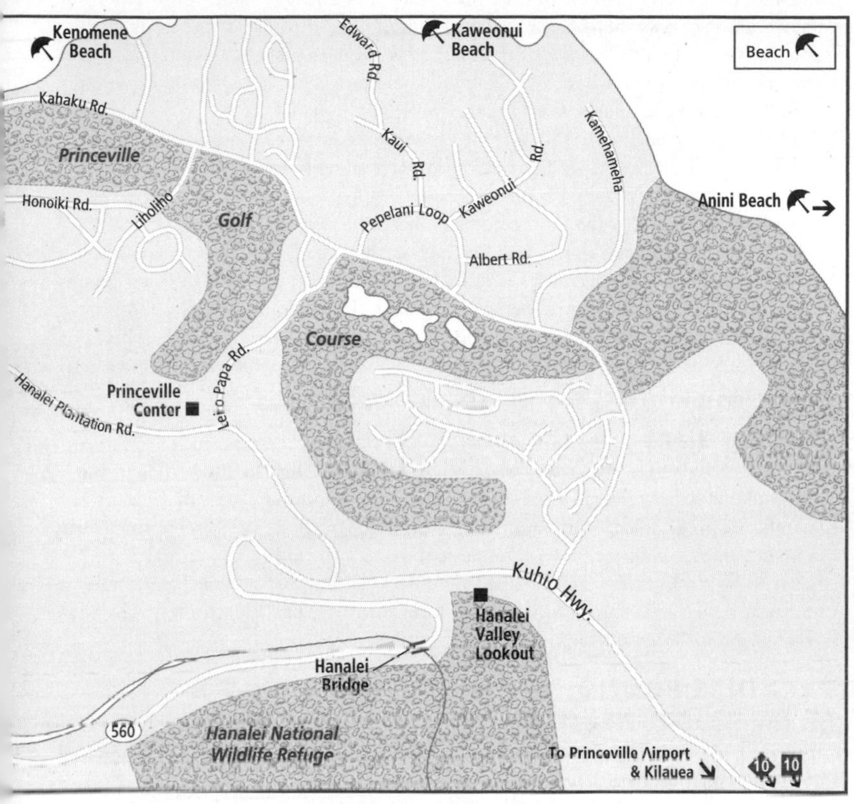

and down the river on a 90-minute, 2½-mile river trip to a natural amphitheater filled with ferns. A steady flow of water from a plantation created a reservoir above the cavern that keeps them happy and growing. The drought of the past few years, coupled with the closing of the plantation (which cut off the supply of water), made the place dry up. But the Hawaii Tourism Authority and Kauai County are spending $440,000 to refurbish the Fern Grotto. The grotto is the source of many Hawaiian legends and a popular site for weddings. The Smith family now has a monopoly on the tours (a circuit court judge evicted the Waialeale Boat Tours from the river because the company had not paid rent for use of the state-owned marina and Fern Grotto State Park for more than 4 years).

Contact Smith's Motor Boats for tours. ✆ **808/821-6892.** www.smithskauai.com. Reservations recommended. Admission $20 adults, $10 children 2–12. Daily 9am–3:30pm. Wailua Marina, at the mouth of the Wailua River; turn off Kuhio Hwy. (Hwy. 56) into Wailua Marine State Park.

Wailua River State Park

Ancients called the Wailua River "the river of the great sacred spirit." Seven temples once stood along this 20-mile river, which is fed by 5,148-foot Mount Waialeale, the wettest spot on earth. You can go up Hawaii's biggest navigable river by boat or kayak (see "For the Active Family," later in this chapter). You can also drive Kuamoo Road (Hwy. 580, sometimes called King's Hwy.), which goes inland along the north side of the river from Kuhio Highway (Hwy. 56)—from the northbound lane, turn left at the stoplight just before the ruins of Coco Palms Resort. Kuamoo Road goes past the *heiau* (temple) and historical sites to Opaekaa Falls and Keahua Arboretum, a Hawaii Division of Forestry & Wildlife attempt to reforest the watershed with native plants.

There's a nice overlook view of 40-foot **Opaekaa Falls ★★**, 1$^1/_2$ miles up Highway 580. This is probably the best-looking drive-up waterfall on Kauai. With the scenic peaks of Makaleha mountains in the background and a restored Hawaiian village on the riverbanks, these falls are what the tourist-bureau folks call an "eye-popping" photo op.

Near Opaekaa Falls overlook is **Poliahu Heiau,** the large lava-rock temple of Kauai's last king, Kaumualii, who died on Oahu in 1824 after being abducted by King Kamehameha II. If you stop here, you'll notice two signs. The first, an official 1928 bronze territorial plaque, says that the royal heiau was built by menehunes, which it explains parenthetically as "Hawaiian dwarves or brownies." A more recent, hand-painted sign warns visitors not to climb on the rocks, which are sacred to the Hawaiian people.

Sleeping Giant

If you squint your eyes just so as you pass the 1,241-foot-high Nounou Ridge, which forms a dramatic backdrop to the coastal villages of Wailua and Waipouli, you can see the fabled Sleeping Giant. On Kuhio Highway, just after mile marker 7, around the minimall complex Waipouli Town Center, look *mauka* (inland) and you may see what appears to be the legendary giant named Puni who, as the story goes, fell asleep after a great feast. If your kids don't see him at first, help them visualize him this way: His head is Wailua and his feet are Kapaa.

PARADISE FOUND: THE NORTH SHORE ★★★

On the Road to Hanalei

The first place everyone should go on Kauai is Hanalei. The drive along **Kuhio Highway** (Hwy. 56, which becomes Hwy. 560 after Princeville to the end of the road) displays Kauai's grandeur at its absolute best. Just before Kilauea, the air and the sea change, the light falls in a different way, and the last signs of development are behind you. Now there are roadside fruit stands, a little stone church in Kilauea, two roadside waterfalls, and a long, stiltlike bridge over the Kalihiwai Stream and its green river valley.

If you don't know a guava from a mango, stop in Kilauea at the cool, shady **Guava Kai Plantation,** at the end of Kuawa Road (✆ **808/828-6121**), for a refreshing, free treat. After you take a walk through the orchards and see what a guava looks like on the tree, you can sample the juice of this exotic pink tropical fruit (which also makes a great jam or jelly—sold here, too). The plantation is open daily from 9am to 5pm.

Birders might want to stop off at **Kilauea Point National Wildlife Refuge,** a mile north of Kilauea, and at **Hanalei National Wildlife Refuge,** along Ohiki Road, at the west end of the Hanalei River Bridge. (For details, see "For the Active Family," later in this chapter.) In the Hanalei Refuge, along a dirt road on a levee, you can see the **Hariguchi Rice Mill,** now a historic treasure.

Now the coastal highway heads due west and the showy ridgelines of Mount Namahana create a grand amphitheater. The two-lane coastal highway rolls through pastures of grazing cattle and past a tiny airport and the luxurious Princeville Hotel.

Five miles past Kilauea, just past the Princeville Shopping Center, is **Hanalei Valley Lookout.** Big enough for a dozen cars, this lookout attracts crowds of people who peer

Bridge Etiquette: Showing Aloha on Kauai's One-Lane Bridges

Unlike the aggressive drivers you see on the mainland, Hawaii's drivers are much more laid-back and courteous than most. Hanalei has a series of one-lane bridges where not only is it proper etiquette to be courteous, but it is the law. When you approach a one-lane bridge, slow down and *yield* if a vehicle, approaching in the opposite direction, is either on the bridge or just about to enter the bridge. (This is not a contest of chicken.) If you are in a long line of vehicles approaching the bridge, don't just join the train crossing the bridge. The local "rule of thumb" is to let about seven to eight cars over the bridge, then yield and give the cars waiting on the other side of the bridge a chance to come across.

over the edge into the 917-acre Hanalei River Valley. So many shades of green: rice green, taro green, and green streams lace a patchwork of green ponds that back up to green-velvet Bali Ha'i cliffs. Pause to catch the first sight of taro growing in irrigated ponds; maybe you'll see an endangered Hawaiian black-necked stilt. Don't be put off by the crowds; this is definitely worth a look.

Farther along, a hairpin turn offers another scenic look at Hanalei town, and then you cross the **Hanalei Bridge.** The Pratt truss steel bridge, prefabbed in New York City, was erected in 1912; it's now on the National Registry of Historic Landmarks. If it ever goes out, the nature of Hanalei will change forever; currently, this rusty, one-lane bridge (which must violate all kinds of Department of Transportation safety regulations) isn't big enough for a tour bus to cross.

You'll drive slowly past the **Hanalei River banks** and Bill Mowry's **Hanalei Buffalo Ranch,** where 200 American bison roam in the tropic sun; you may even see buffalo grazing in the pastures on your right. The herd is often thinned to make buffalo patties. (You wondered why there was a buffalo burger on the Ono Family Restaurant menu, didn't you?)

Just past Tahiti Nui, turn right on Aku Road before Ching Young Village, then take a right on Weke Road. **Hanalei Beach Park,** one of Hawaii's most gorgeous, is a half-block ahead on your left. Swimming is excellent here year-round, especially in summer, when Hanalei Bay becomes a big, placid lake. For details, see "Beaches," below.

If this exquisite, 2-mile-long beach doesn't meet your expectations, head down the highway, where the next 7 miles of coast yield some of Kauai's other spectacular beaches, including **Lumahai Beach,** of *South Pacific* movie fame, as well as **Tunnels Beach** (p. 390), where the 1960s puka-shell necklace craze began, and **Haena Beach Park** (p. 390), a fabulous place to kick back and enjoy the waves, particularly in summer. Once you've found your beach, stick around until sundown, then head back to one of the North Shore's restaurants for a fresh seafood dinner. (See "Family-Friendly Dining," earlier in this chapter.) Another perfect day in paradise.

Attractions Along the Way

Ka Ulu O Laka Heiau **Ages 4 and up.** On a knoll above the boulders of **Kee Beach** (p. 391) stands a sacred altar of rocks, often draped with flower leis and ti-leaf offerings, dedicated to Laka, the goddess of hula. It may seem like a primal relic from the days of idols, but it's very much in use today. Often, dancers (men and women) of Hawaii's hula halau climb the cliff, bearing small gifts of flowers. In Hawaiian myths, Lohiau, a handsome chief, danced here before the fire goddess Pele; their passion became *Haena,* which means "the heat." Sometimes, in a revival of the old Hawaiian ways (once banned by missionaries), a mother of a newborn will deposit the umbilical cord of her infant at this sacred shrine. The site is filled with what Hawaiians call *mana,* or power. Plan a half-hour to hike to the heiau and back.

From the west side of Kee Beach, take the footpath across the big rocks almost to the point; then climb the steep grassy hill.

Limahuli Garden and Preserve of the National Tropical Botanical Garden ★ Ages 4 and up. Out on Kauai's far North Shore, beyond Hanalei and the last wooden bridge, there's a mighty cleft in the coastal range where ancestral Hawaiians lived in what can only be called paradise. Carved by a waterfall stream known as Limahuli, the lush valley sits at the foot of steepled cliffs that Hollywood portrayed as Bali Ha'i in the film classic *South Pacific.* Allow a couple of hours to tour this small, almost secret garden. It appeals not just to green thumbs but to all who love Hawaii's great outdoors. Here botanists hope to save Kauai's endangered native plants. You can take the self-tour to view the plants, which are identified in Hawaiian and English. From taro to sugar cane, the mostly Polynesian imports tell the story of the people who cultivated the plants for food, medicine, clothing, shelter, and decoration. In addition, Limahuli's stream is sanctuary to the last five species of Hawaiian freshwater fish.

Visitor Center, 1/2 mile past MM 9 on Kuhio Hwy. (Hwy. 560), Haena. ✆ **808/826-1053.** Fax 808/826-1053. www.ntbg.org. Admission self-guided tours $15 adults, free for children 12 and under; guided tours $25 adults, $15 teenagers 13–18, free for children 12 and under. Tues–Sat 9:30am–4pm. Advance reservations required for 2 1/2-hr. guided tours Tues–Sat 10am. During peak months of July–Sept, book at least a week ahead.

Na Aina Kai Botanical Gardens ★★★ Finds All ages. Do not miss this incredible, magical garden on some 240 acres, populated by about 70 life-size (some larger than life-size) whimsical bronze statues. Hidden off the beaten path of the North Shore, this is the place both for avid gardeners and for people who think they don't like botanical gardens. The gardens have everything: waterfalls, pools, arbors, topiaries, colonnades, gazebos, a maze you will never forget, a lagoon with spouting fountains, a Japanese teahouse, and an enchanting path along a bubbling stream to the ocean. The imaginative, fairy tale creativity that has gone into these grounds will be one of your fondest memories of Kauai. A host of different tours are available for adults and kids 13 and older which range from 1 1/2 hours ($30) to 5 hours ($75) long, and from casual guided strolls, to a ride in the covered CarTram, to treks from one end of the gardens to the ocean. However, the younger crowd (13 and younger) will just flip over the "Under the Rainbow" Children's Garden Family Tour. Your kids will love the 16-foot Jack-and-the-Beanstalk statue, at the entryway to the garden, followed by the splashing-wading pool, a hopscotch through a gecko-shaped maze, a giant treehouse in a jungle, and lots of playground equipment, sculptures, and magical things for kids. The 2-hour tour costs $30 for adults and $20 for kids, Tuesday through Friday only.

4101 Wailapa Rd. (write: P.O. Box 1134), Kilauea, HI 96754. ✆ **808/828-0525.** Fax 808/828-0815. www.naainakai.org. Tues–Fri 8am–5pm. Tours vary. Advance reservations strongly recommended. To get here from Lihue, drive north past MM 21 and turn right on Wailapa Rd. At the road's end, drive through the iron gates. From Princeville, drive south 6½ miles and take the 2nd left past MM 22 on Wailapa Rd. At the road's end, drive through the iron gates.

Waioli Mission House Museum **All ages.** If you time your visit just right, you can visit this 150-year-old mission house, which serves today as a living museum that retains its sense of what life was like for the New England missionaries who came to Kauai to convert the "heathens" to Christianity. Plan to spend an hour on this walk back in history.

Kuhio Hwy. (Hwy. 560), just behind the green Waioli Huia Church, Hanalei. ✆ **808/245-3202.** Free admission (donations gratefully accepted). Tours Mon and Wed–Thurs 10am and 1pm. Reservations required.

The End of the Road

The real Hawaii begins where the road stops. This is especially true on Kauai—for at the end of Highway 56, the spectacular **Na Pali Coast** begins. To explore it, you have to set out on foot, by boat, or by helicopter. For details on experiencing this region, see "Helicopter Rides over Waimea Canyon & the Na Pali Coast," earlier in this section; and "For the Active Family," later in this chapter.

6 BEACHES

Eons of wind and rain have created this geological masterpiece of an island, with its fabulous beaches, like Hanalei, Kee, and Kalapaki. All are accessible to the public, as stipulated by Hawaii law, and many have facilities.

LIHUE'S BEST BEACH

Kalapaki Beach ★

This graceful half-moon of golden sand, which sits at the foot of the Marriott Resort & Beach Club, is 50 yards wide and a quarter-mile long. It's protected by a jetty and patrolled by lifeguards, making it very safe for kids and neophyte swimmers. The waves are good for surfing when there's a winter swell, and the view from the sand—of the steepled, 2,200-foot peaks of the majestic Haupu Ridge that shields Nawiliwili Bay—is awesome. Kalapaki is the best beach not only in Lihue but on the whole east coast. From Lihue Airport, turn left onto Kapule Highway (Hwy. 51) to Rice Street; turn left and go to the entrance of the Marriott; pass the hotel's porte cochere and turn right at the SHORELINE ACCESS sign. Facilities include lifeguards, free parking, restrooms, and showers; food and drink are available nearby.

THE POIPU RESORT AREA

Mahaulepu Beach ★★

Mahaulepu is the best-looking unspoiled beach in Kauai and possibly in the whole state. Its 2 miles of reddish-gold, grainy sand line the southeastern shore at the foot of 1,500-foot-high Haupu Ridge, just beyond the Hyatt Regency Poipu and McBryde sugar cane fields, which end in sand dunes and a forest of casuarina trees. Almost untouched by modern life, Mahaulepu is a great escape from the real world. It's ideal for beachcombing and shell hunting, but swimming can be risky, except in the reef-sheltered shallows 200 yards west of the sandy parking lot. There's no lifeguard, no facilities—just great natural beauty everywhere you look. (This beach is where George C. Scott portrayed

Ernest Hemingway in the movie *Islands in the Stream.*) While you're here, see if you can find the Hawaiian petroglyph of a voyaging canoe carved in the beach rock.

To get here, drive past the Hyatt Regency Poipu 3 miles east on a red-dirt road, past the golf course and stables. Turn right at the T-intersection; go 1 mile to the big sand dune, turn left, and drive a half-mile to a small lot under the trees.

Poipu Beach Park ★

Big, wide Poipu is actually two beaches in one; it's divided by a sandbar, called a *tombolo.* On the left, a lava-rock jetty protects a sandy-bottom pool that's perfect for children; on the right, the open bay attracts swimmers, snorkelers, and surfers. And everyone likes to picnic on the grassy lawn graced by coconut trees. You'll find excellent swimming, small tide pools for exploring, great reefs for snorkeling and diving, good fishing, nice waves for surfers, and a steady wind for windsurfers. Poipu attracts a daily crowd, but the density seldom approaches Waikiki levels, except on holidays. Facilities include restrooms, showers, picnic areas, **Brennecke's Beach Broiler** nearby (p. 367), and free parking in the red-dirt lot. To get here, turn onto Poipu Beach Road, then turn right at Hoowili Road.

WESTERN KAUAI

Salt Pond Beach Park

Hawaii's only salt ponds still in production are at Salt Pond Beach, just outside Hanapepe. Generations of locals have come here to swim, fish, and collect salt crystals that are dried in sun beds. The tangy salt is used for health purposes and to cure fish and season food. The curved reddish-gold beach lies between two rocky points and features a protected reef, tide pools, and gentle waves. Swimming here is excellent, even for children; this beach is also good for diving, windsurfing, and fishing. Amenities include a lifeguard, showers, restrooms, camping area, picnic area, pavilion, and parking lot. To get here, take Highway 50 past Hanapepe and turn on Lokokai Road.

Polihale State Park ★

This mini-Sahara at the western end of the island is Hawaii's biggest beach: 17 miles long and as wide as three football fields. This is a wonderful place to get away from it all, but don't forget your flip-flops—the midday sand is hotter than a lava flow. The golden sands wrap around Kauai's northwestern shore from Kekaha plantation town, just beyond Waimea, to where the ridgebacks of the Na Pali Coast begin. The state park includes ancient Hawaiian heiau and burial sites, a view of the "forbidden" island of Niihau, and the famed **Barking Sands Beach,** where footfalls sound like a barking dog. (Scientists say that the grains of sand are perforated with tiny echo chambers, which emit a "barking" sound when they rub together.) Polihale also takes in the Pacific Missile Range Facility, a U.S. surveillance center that snooped on Russian subs during the Cold War; and Nohili Dune, which is nearly 3 miles long and 100 feet high in some places.

Be careful in winter, when high surf and rip currents make swimming dangerous. The safest place to swim is **Queen's Pond,** a small, shallow, sandy-bottom inlet protected from waves and shore currents. There are facilities for camping, as well as restrooms, showers, picnic tables, and pavilions. To get here, take Highway 50 past Barking Sands Missile Range and follow the signs through the sugar cane fields to Polihale. Local kids have been known to burgle rental cars out here, so don't leave tempting valuables in your car.

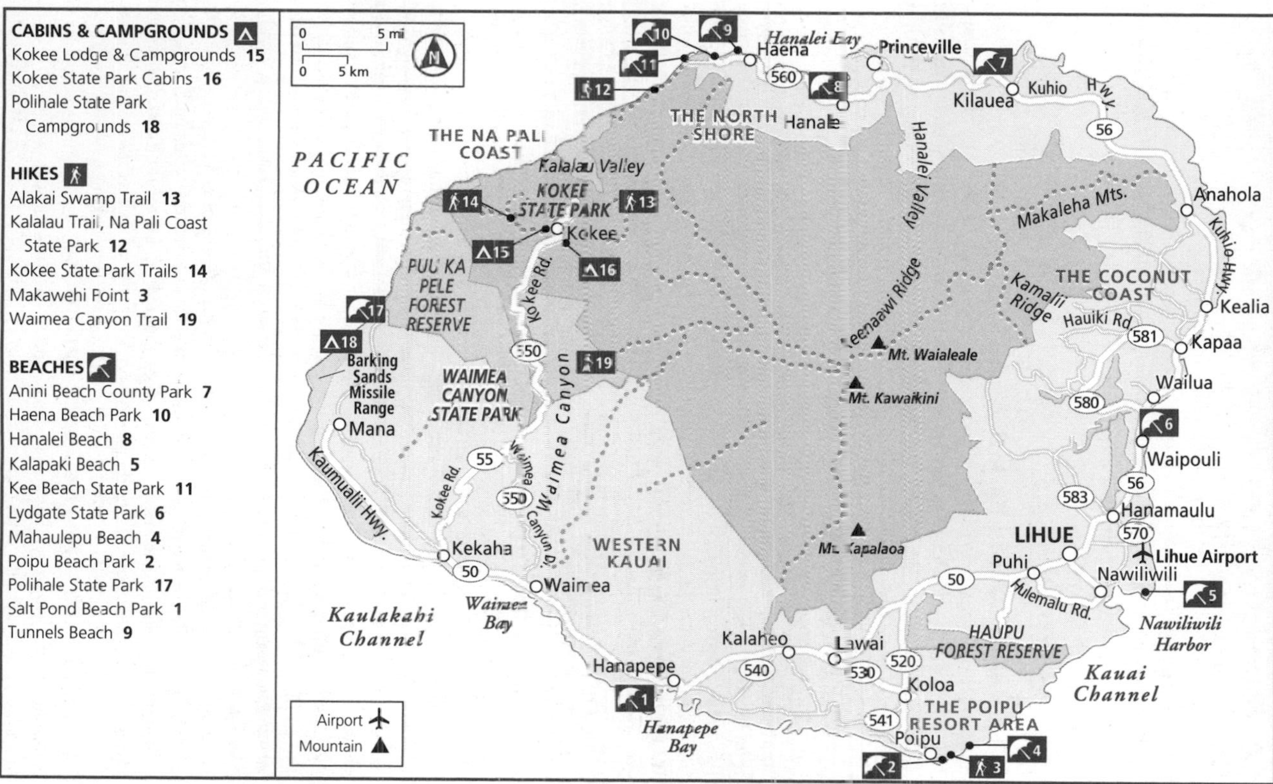

CABINS & CAMPGROUNDS
Kokee Lodge & Campgrounds 15
Kokee State Park Cabins 16
Polihale State Park Campgrounds 18
HIKES
Alakai Swamp Trail 13
Kalalau Trail, Na Pali Coast State Park 12
Kokee State Park Trails 14
Makawehi Point 3
Waimea Canyon Trail 19
BEACHES
Anini Beach County Park 7
Haena Beach Park 10
Hanalei Beach 8
Kalapaki Beach 5
Kee Beach State Park 11
Lydgate State Park 6
Mahaulepu Beach 4
Poipu Beach Park 2
Polihale State Park 17
Salt Pond Beach Park 1
Tunnels Beach 9
0 5 mi
0 5 km
PACIFIC OCEAN
THE NA PALI COAST
Kalalau Valley
KOKEE STATE PARK
Kokee
PUU KA PELE FOREST RESERVE
Kokee Rd.
Barking Sands Missile Range
Mana
WAIMEA CANYON STATE PARK
Waimea Canyon
Kaumualii Hwy.
Waimea Canyon Dr.
Kekaha
Waimea
Waimea Bay
Kaulakahi Channel
WESTERN KAUAI
Hanapepe
Hanapepe Bay
Kalaheo
Lawai
Koloa
Poipu
THE POIPU RESORT AREA
HAUPU FOREST RESERVE
Hulemalu Rd.
Puhi
LIHUE
Nawiliwili
Nawiliwili Harbor
Kauai Channel
Lihue Airport
Hanamaulu
Waipouli
Wailua
Kapaa
Kealia
Anahola
Kuhio Hwy.
Hauiki Rd.
THE COCONUT COAST
Kamalii Ridge
Makaleha Mts.
Mt. Waialeale
Mt. Kawaikini
Hanalei Valley
THE NORTH SHORE
Hanalei Bay
Haena
Princeville
Kilauea
Kuhio Hwy.
Airport
Mountain

THE COCONUT COAST

Lydgate State Park ★

This seacoast park has a rock-wall fishpond that blunts the open ocean waves and provides the only safe swimming and the best snorkeling on the eastern shore. The 1-acre beach park, near the mouth of the Wailua River, is a great place for a picnic or for kite flying on the green. It also contains **Kamalani Playground** for the kids. It's 5 miles north of Lihue on Kuhio Highway (Hwy. 56); look for the turnoff just before the Kauai Resort Hotel. Facilities include a pavilion, restrooms, outdoor showers, picnic tables, barbecue grills, lifeguards, and parking.

THE NORTH SHORE

Anini Beach County Park ★★

Anini is Kauai's safest beach for swimming and windsurfing. It's also one of the island's most beautiful: It sits on a blue lagoon at the foot of emerald cliffs, looking more like Tahiti than almost any other strand in the islands. This 3-mile-long, gold-sand beach is shielded from the open ocean by the longest, widest fringing reef in Hawaii. With shallow water, 4 to 5 feet deep, it's also the very best snorkel spot on Kauai, even for children and beginners. On the northwest side, a channel in the reef runs out to the deep blue water with a 60-foot drop that attracts divers. Anini has a park, a campground, picnic and barbecue facilities, and a boat-launch ramp. Follow Kuhio Highway (Hwy. 56) to Kilauea; take the second exit, called Kalihiwai Road (the first exit dead-ends at Kalihiwai Beach), and drive a half-mile toward the sea; turn left on Anini Beach Road.

Hanalei Beach ★

Gentle waves roll across the face of half-moon Hanalei Bay, running up to the wide area of golden sand; sheer volcanic ridges laced by waterfalls rise to 4,000 feet on the other side, 3 miles inland. Is there any beach with a better location? Celebrated in song and hula and featured on travel posters, this beach owes its natural beauty to its age—it's an ancient sunken valley with post-erosional cliffs. Hanalei Bay indents the coast a full mile inland and runs 2 miles point to point, with coral reefs on either side and a patch of coral in the middle—plus a sunken ship that belonged to a king, so divers love it. Swimming is excellent year-round, especially in summer, when Hanalei Bay becomes a big, placid lake. The aquamarine water is also great for bodyboarding, surfing, fishing, windsurfing, canoe paddling, kayaking, and boating. (There's a boat ramp on the west bank of the Hanalei River.) The area known as **Black Pot,** near the pier, is particularly good for swimming, snorkeling, and surfing. Facilities include a pavilion, restrooms, picnic tables, and parking. This beach is always packed with both locals and visitors, but you can usually find your own place in the sun by strolling down the shore; the bay is big enough for everyone.

To get here, take Kuhio Highway (Hwy. 56), which becomes Highway 560 after Princeville. In Hanalei town, make a right on Aku Road just after Tahiti Nui, then turn right again on Weke Road, which dead-ends at the parking lot for the Black Pot section of the beach; the easiest beach access is on your left.

Tunnels Beach & Haena Beach Park ★★

Postcard-perfect, gold-sand Tunnels Beach is one of Hawaii's most beautiful. When the sun sinks into the Pacific along the fabled peaks of Bali Ha'i, there's no better-looking beach in the islands: You're bathed in golden rays that butter up the blue sky, bounce off

Moments **Stargazing**

Any Kauai beach is great for stargazing, almost any night of the year. Once a month, on the Saturday nearest the new moon, when the skies are darkest, the **Kauai Educational Association for the Study of Astronomy** sponsors a star watch at Kaumakani, at the softball field (follow Hwy. 50 west past Hanapepe; after mile marker 18, look for K.E.A.S.A. signs on the right for parking and the star-watch location. There's a monthly meeting at 6pm followed by the public star watch at sunset. For information on the next star watch, contact K.E.A.S.A., P.O. Box 161, Waimea, HI 96796 (✆ **808/332-STAR** [332-7827]; www.keasa.org). Video presentations start at 6pm, with stargazing to follow.

the steepled ridges, and tint the pale clouds hot pink. Catch the sunset from the pebbly sand beach or while swimming in the emerald-green waters, but do catch it. Tunnels is excellent for swimming nearly year-round and is safe for snorkeling because it's protected by a fringing coral reef. (The waters can get rough in winter, though.) The long, curvy beach is sheltered by a forest of ironwoods that provides welcome shade from the tropic heat.

Around the corner is grainy-gold-sand Haena Beach Park, which offers excellent swimming in summer and great snorkeling amid clouds of tropical fish. But stay out of the water in winter, when the big waves are dangerous. Haena also has a popular grassy park for camping. Noise-phobes will prefer Tunnels.

Take Kuhio Highway (Hwy. 56), which becomes Highway 560 after Princeville. Tunnels is about 6 miles past Hanalei town, after mile marker 8 on the highway (look for the alley with the big wood gate at the end), and Haena is just down the road. Tunnels has no facilities, but Haena has restrooms, outdoor showers, barbecue grills, picnic tables, and free parking (no lifeguard, though).

Kee Beach State Park ★★

Where the road ends on the North Shore, you'll find a dandy little reddish-gold beach almost too beautiful to be real. Kee (*hay* ay) is on a reef-protected cove at the foot of fluted volcanic cliffs. Swimming and snorkeling are safe inside the reef but dangerous outside; those North Shore waves and currents can be killers. This park has restrooms, showers, and parking—but no lifeguard. To get here, take Kuhio Highway (Hwy. 56), which becomes Highway 560 after Princeville; Kee is about 7½ miles past Hanalei.

7 FOR THE ACTIVE FAMILY

For the family that wants to get out and enjoy the island's beauty and natural resources, you will fall in love with Kauai. Below are my picks of the best places to go, things to do, and outfitters to hire.

IN THE WATER

Several outfitters on Kauai not only offer equipment rentals and tours, but also give out expert information on weather forecasts, sea and trail conditions, and other important matters for hikers, kayakers, sailors, and other backcountry adventurers. For watersports questions and equipment rental, contact **Kayak Kauai Outbound,** 1 mile past Hanalei Bridge on Hwy. 560, in Hanalei (✆ **800/437-3507** or 808/826-9844; www.kayakkauai.com), the outfitters' center in Hanalei. They also have their own private dock (the only one on Kauai) for launching kayaks and canoes. In Kapaa, contact **Kauai Water Ski & Surf Co.,** Kinipopo Shopping Village, 4-356 Kuhio Hwy. (on the ocean side of the highway), Kapaa (✆ **808/822-3574**). In the Lihue and Poipu areas, go with **Snorkel Bob's Kauai** at 4-734 Kuhio Hwy. (just north of Coconut Plantation Marketplace), Kapaa (✆ **800/262-7725** or 808/823-9433; www.snorkelbob.com), and in Koloa at 3236 Poipu Rd. (just south of Poipu Shopping Village), near Poipu Beach (✆ **808/742-2206**).

Boating

One of Hawaii's most spectacular natural attractions is Kauai's **Na Pali Coast.** Unless you and the kids are willing to make an arduous 22-mile hike, there are only two ways to see it: by helicopter (see "Helicopter Rides over Waimea Canyon & the Na Pali Coast," earlier in this chapter) or by boat. Picture yourself cruising the rugged Na Pali coastline in a 42-foot ketch-rigged yacht under full sail, watching the sunset as you enjoy a tropical cocktail, or speeding through the aquamarine water in a 40-foot trimaran as porpoises play off the bow.

When the Pacific humpback whales make their annual visit to Hawaii from December to March, they swim right by Kauai. In season, most boats on Kauai—including sail and powerboats—combine whale-watching with their regular adventures.

Capt. Andy's Sailing Adventures ★ Ages 2 and up. Captain Andy operates a 55-foot, 49-passenger catamaran out of two locations on the south shore. The **snorkel/picnic cruise,** a 5½-hour cruise to the **Na Pali Coast,** from May to October, costs $139 for adults and $99 for children 2 to 12, and includes a deli-style lunch, snorkeling, and drinks. There's also a 4-hour Na Pali Coast **dinner sunset cruise** that sets sail for $105 for adults and $80 for children, and a 2-hour pupu cocktail sunset sail with drinks and pupu for $69 adults and $50 children. They also offer a 6-hour Na Pali Zodiac cruise on inflatable boats for $139 to $159 adults and $99 to $109 children 5 to 12 years old. ***Hot tip:*** Book on their website for 20% off!

Kukuiula Small Boat Harbor, Poipu; and Port Allen, Eleele. ✆ **800/535-0830** or 808/335-6833. www.napali.com. Prices vary depending on trip.

Liko Kauai Cruises ★ Ages 4 and up. Liko offers more than just a typical whale-watching cruise; this is a 5-hour combination Na Pali Coast snorkeling tour that includes a historical lecture, whale-watching (in season), snorkeling, and lunch. It all happens on a 49-foot power catamaran (with only 24 passengers). In addition to viewing the whales, you'll glimpse sea caves, waterfalls, lush valleys, and miles of white-sand beaches; you'll also make stops along the way for snorkeling.

Kekaha Small Boat Harbor, Waimea. ✆ **888/SEA-LIKO** (732-5456) or 808/338-0333. Fax 808/338-1327. www.liko-kauai.com. Na Pali trips $140 adults, $95 children 4–12 (lunch included).

Bodyboarding & Bodysurfing

The best places for bodysurfing and boogie boarding are **Kalapaki Beach** (near Lihue) and **Poipu Beach.** In addition to the rental shops listed above, one of the most inexpensive places to rent boogie boards is **Snorkel Bob's** (see above), which charges just $15 a week.

Kayaking

Kauai is made for kayaking. You can take the Huleia River into **Huleia National Wildlife Refuge** (located along the eastern portion of the Huleia Stream where it flows into Nawiliwili Bay). It's the last stand for Kauai's endangered birds, and the only way to see it is by kayak. The adventurous can head to the Na Pali Coast, featuring majestic cliffs, empty beaches, open-ocean conditions, and monster waves. Or you can paddle around Hanalei Bay.

Kayak Kauai Outbound ★, a mile past Hanalei Bridge on Highway 560, in Hanalei (✆ **800/437-3507** or 808/826-9844; www.kayakkauai.com), has a range of tours for independent souls. They're probably best for kids 9 or 10 and older. The shop's experts will be happy to take you on a guided kayaking trip or to tell you where to go on your own. Equipment rental starts at $28 for a one-person kayak and $52 for a two-person ocean kayak per day. Kayak lessons are $50 per person per hour. Tours (some including snacks) start at $115 per person and include transportation and lunch for the all-day excursion. Kayak Kauai also has its own private dock (the only one on Kauai) for launching kayaks and canoes.

Rick Haviland, who gained fame after he was mentioned in Paul Theroux's book *The Happy Isles of Oceania*, is the owner of **Outfitters Kauai ★**, 2027A Poipu Rd. (in Poipu Plaza, a small five-shop mall before the road forks to Poipu/Spouting Horn), Poipu (✆ **888/742-9887** or 808/742-9667; www.outfitterskauai.com). There are various kayaking tours, including one that takes you up a jungle stream and involves a short hike to waterfalls and a swimming hole. Although children as young as 5 are allowed, it may be a bit too strenuous for younger children. The cost is $98 for adults and $78 for children ages 5 to 14, including lunch, snacks, and drinks. Outfitters Kauai also rents river kayaks by the day, for $40.

The best places to rent kayaks are **Kauai Water Ski & Surf Co.,** Kinipopo Shopping Village, 4-356 Kuhio Hwy. (on the ocean side), Kapaa (✆ **808/822-3574**); or **Pedal 'n Paddle,** Ching Young Village Shopping Center, Hanalei (✆ **808/826-9069;** www.pedalnpaddle.com).

Snorkeling

See the intro to this section for locations of **Snorkel Bob's.**

For great shoreline snorkeling, try the reef off **Kee Beach/Haena Beach Park,** located at the end of Highway 560. **Tunnels Beach,** about a mile before the end of Highway 560 in Haena, has a wide reef that's great for poking around in search of tropical fish. Be sure to check ocean conditions—don't go if the surf is up or if there's a strong current. **Anini Beach,** located off the northern Kalihiwai Road (between mile markers 25 and 26 on Kuhio Hwy., or Hwy. 56), just before the Princeville Airport, has a safe, shallow area with excellent snorkeling. **Poipu Beach Park** has some good snorkeling to the right side of Nukumoi Point—the tombolo area, where the narrow strip of sand divides the ocean, is best. If this spot is too crowded, wander down the beach in front of the old Waiohai resort; if there are no waves, this place is hopping with marine life. **Salt Pond Beach Park,** off Highway 50 near Hanapepe, has good snorkeling around the two rocky points, home to hundreds of tropical fish.

Surfing

Hanalei Bay's winter surf is the most popular on the island, but it's for experts only. **Poipu Beach** is an excellent spot to learn to surf; the waves are small and—best of all—nobody laughs when you wipe out. Check with the local surf shops or call the **Weather Service** (✆ **808/245-3564**) to find out where surf's up.

Surf lessons are available from the **Margo Oberg Surf School,** at the Nukumoi Surf Shop, across from Brennecke's Beach (✆ **808/742-8019;** www.surfonkauai.com). Margo charges $65 for 1½ hours of group instruction, including surfboard and leash; she guarantees that by the end of the lesson, you'll be standing and catching a wave. She also offers semiprivate lessons (for two to four people) for $90 per person and private one-on-one lessons for $125 for 2 hours. Children must be able to swim; generally, by the time kids are 7 they will be able to paddle and learn how to surf without a problem.

Equipment is available for rent (ranging from $5 an hour or $20 a day for "soft" beginner boards to $7.50 an hour or $30 a day for hard boards) from **Nukumoi Surf Co.,** across from Brennecke's Beach, Poipu Beach Park (✆ **888/384-8810** or 808/742-8019; www.nukumoisurf.com/surfshophawaii.html); **Hanalei Surf Co.,** 5-5161 Kuhio Hwy. (across from Zelo's Beach House Restaurant in Hanalei Center), Hanalei (✆ **808/826-9000**); and **Pedal 'n Paddle,** Ching Young Village Shopping Center, Hanalei (✆ **808/826-9069**).

Tubing

Back in the days of the sugar plantations, on really hot days, if no one was looking, local kids would grab inner tubes and jump into the irrigation ditches crisscrossing the cane fields for an exciting ride. Today you can enjoy this (formerly illegal) activity by "tubing" the flumes and ditches of the old Lihue Plantation through **Kauai Backcountry Adventures** (✆ **888/270-0555** or 808/245-2506; www.kauaibackcountry.com). Passengers are taken in four-wheel-drive vehicles high into the mountains above Lihue to look at vistas generally off-limits to the public. At the flumes, you will be outfitted with a giant tube, gloves, and headlamp (for the long passageways through the tunnels). All you do is jump in the water, and the gentle gravity-feed flow will carry you through forests, into tunnels, and finally to a mountain swimming hole, where a picnic lunch is served. The 3-hour tours are $100 and appropriate for anyone older than the age of 5 (minimum height 43 in.). Swimming is not necessary, as all you do is relax and drift downstream.

Water-Skiing

Hawaii's only freshwater water-skiing is on the Wailua River. Ski boats launch from the boat ramp in Wailua River State Park, directly across from the marina. **Kauai Water Ski & Surf Co.,** Kinipopo Shopping Village, 4-356 Kuhio Hwy., Kapaa (✆ **808/822-3574**), rents equipment and offers lessons and guided tours; you can take a 15-minute ski for $45, or for $75 you get a half-hour trip and for $140 you get an hour. Kids should be able to swim well; children older than 7 make good beginning water-skiers.

ON THE LAND

Biking

There are a couple of great places on Kauai for two-wheeling: the **Poipu area,** which has wide, flat roads and several dirt-cane roads (especially around Mahaulepu); and the cane road (a dirt road used for hauling sugar cane) between **Kealia Beach** and **Anahola,** north of Kapaa.

For a great selection of high-quality mountain bike rentals at reasonable prices, it's worth the drive to **Pedal 'n Paddle,** in Hanalei (✆ **808/826-9069;** www.pedalnpaddle.com), which has not only high-grade Kona mountain bikes with Shimano components but also bikes with front-end suspension systems. Rentals start at $12 to $20 a day or

A Warning About Flash Floods

When it rains on Kauai, the waterfalls rage and rivers and streams overflow, causing flash floods on roads and trails. If you're hiking, avoid dry streambeds, which flood quickly and wash out to sea. Before going hiking, camping, or sailing, especially in the rainy season (Nov–Mar), check the weather forecast by calling © **808/245-6001.**

$50 to $80 a week and include helmet, bike lock, and car rack. The shop also has kids' 20-inch BMX bikes. The knowledgeable folks here are more than happy to provide you with free maps and tell you about the best biking spots on the island.

GUIDED BIKE TOURS **Outfitters Kauai ★** (© **808/742-9667;** www.outfitterskauai.com) offers a fabulous downhill bike ride from Waimea Canyon to the ocean. The 12-mile trip (mostly coasting) begins at 6am, when the van leaves the shop in Poipu and heads up to the canyon. By the time you've scarfed down the fresh-baked muffins and coffee, you're at the top of the canyon, just as the sun is rising over the rim—it's a remarkable moment. The tour makes a couple of stops on the way down for short, scenic nature hikes. You'll be back at the shop around 10am. The sunset trip follows the same route. Both tours cost $98 for adults, $78 for children 12 to 14.

Hiking

Kauai is an adventurer's delight. The island's greatest tropical beauty isn't easily reachable; you've got to head out on foot and find it. For more information on Kauai's hiking trails, contact the **Division of State Parks,** P.O. Box 1671, Lihue, HI 96766 (© **808/274-3446**); the **Hawaii Division of Forestry & Wildlife,** P.O. Box 1671, Lihue, HI 96766 (© **808/274-3077**); **Kauai County Parks and Recreation,** 4193 Hardy St., Lihue, HI 96766 (© **808/241-6670**); or the **Kokee Lodge Manager,** P.O. Box 819, Waimea, HI 96796 (© **808/335-6061**).

Kayak Kauai Outbound ★, a mile past Hanalei Bridge on Highway 560 in Hanalei (© **800/437-3507** or 808/826-9844; www.kayakkauai.com), is the premier all-around outfitter on the island. It's staffed by local experts who keep track of weather forecasts and sea and trail conditions; they have a lot of pertinent information that hikers, campers, and other backcountry adventurers need to know. Plus they have guided hiking tours starting at $84 per person. If you don't plan to bring your own gear, you can rent it here or at **Pedal 'n Paddle,** in Hanalei (© **808/826-9069;** www.pedalnpaddle.com). If you want to buy camping equipment, head for **Ace Island Hardware,** at Princeville Shopping Center (© **808/826-6980**).

GUIDED HIKES You can join a guided hike with Kauai's **Sierra Club, Hawaii Chapter,** P.O. Box 3412, Lihue, HI 96766 (© **808/246-8748;** www.hi.sierraclub.org), which offers four to seven different hikes every month, varying from an easy family moonlit beach hike, to a moderate 4-mile trip up some 1,100 feet, to 8-mile-plus treks for serious hikers only. The club also does guided hikes of Kokee State Park (see below), usually on weekends. Because there's no staffed office, the best way to contact the chapter is to check the website; outings are usually listed 3 to 6 months in advance, with complete descriptions of the hike, the hike leader's phone number, and what to wear and bring. You can also check the daily newspaper, the *Garden Island,* for a list of hikes in the

Community Calendar section. Generally, the club asks for a donation of $5 per person per hike for nonmembers, $1 for children 17 and younger and Sierra Club members. The club also does service work (clearing trails, picking up trash) on the hikes, so you may spend an hour doing service work, then 2 to 3 hours hiking. Last year, the club took three service-work trips along the Na Pali Coast trail to help maintain it.

Other options for guided hikes include **Princeville Ranch Adventures** (✆ **808/826-7669;** www.kauai-hiking.com), which offers various hikes on 2,000 acres of private property, such as a 4-hour hike to a waterfall (plus another hour swimming) for $79; and **Kauai Nature Tours** (✆ **888/233-8365** or 808/742-8305; www.kauainaturetours.com), which offers a geological-history excursion, a tour of Kauai's environments from the mountain to the ocean, and a Mahaulepu coast hike, all of which are led by scientists and cost $129 for adults and $89 for children ages 5 to 10.

The Poipu Resort Area

MAKAWEHI POINT ★ Like a ship's prow, Makawehi Point juts out to sea on the east side of Keoneloa Beach (known locally as Shipwreck Beach), which lies in front of the Hyatt Regency Poipu. This 50-foot-high sand-dune bluff attracts a variety of people: pole fishers, whale-watchers, those who just like the panoramic views of the Pacific, and daredevils who test their courage by leaping off the cliff into the waves. (Don't try it.)

The trailhead begins on the east end of Shipwreck Beach, past the Hyatt. It's an easy 10-minute walk up to Makawehi Point; after you take in the big picture, keep going uphill along the ridge of the sand dunes (said to contain ancient Hawaiian burial sites), past the coves frequented by green sea turtles and endangered Hawaiian monk seals, through the coastal pine forest, and past World War II bunkers to the very top. Now you can see Haupu Ridge and its 2,297-foot peak, the famously craggy ridgeline that eerily resembles Queen Victoria's profile, and, in the distance, Mahaulepu Beach, one of the best looking in Hawaii. Inland, three red craters dimple the green fields; the one in the middle, the biggest, Pu'u Huni Huni, is said to have been the last volcano to erupt on Kauai—but it was so long ago that nobody here can remember when.

Western Kauai

WAIMEA CANYON TRAILS On a wet island like Kauai, a dry hike is hard to find. But in the desert-dry gulch of Waimea Canyon, known as the "Grand Canyon of the Pacific" (once you get here, you'll see why—it's pretty spectacular), you're not likely to slip and slide in the muck as you go.

Canyon Trail You want to hike Hawaii's Grand Canyon, but you don't think you have the time or it's too much for the kids? Well, then, take the Canyon Trail to the east rim for a breathtaking view into the 3,000-foot-deep canyon. Park your car at the top of Halemanu Valley Road. It's located between mile markers 14 and 15 on Waimea Canyon Road, about a mile down from the museum. Walk down the not very clearly marked trail on the 3.5-mile round-trip, which takes 2 to 3 hours and leads to Waipoo Falls (as does the hike below) and back. We suggest going in the afternoon, when the light is best.

KOKEE STATE PARK At the end of Highway 550, which leads through Waimea Canyon to its summit, lies a 4,640-acre state park of high-mountain forest wilderness (3,600–4,000 ft. above sea level). The rainforest, bogs, and breathtaking views of the Na Pali coastline and Waimea Canyon are the draw at Kokee. This is the place for hiking—among the 45 miles of maintained trails are some of the best hikes in Hawaii. Official maps of all the park's trails are for sale for 50¢ at the **Kokee Natural History Museum** (✆ **808/335-9975**).

A few words of advice: Always check current trail conditions; up-to-date trail information is available on a bulletin board at the Kokee Natural History Museum. Stay on established trails; it's easy to get lost here. Get off the trail well before dark. Carry water and rain gear—even if it's perfectly sunny when you set out—and wear sunscreen.

For complete coverage of the state park, see p. 380.

Halemanu-Kokee Trail This trail takes you on a pleasant, easy-to-moderate 2.5-mile round-trip walk through a native koa and ohia forest inhabited by native birds. The trailhead is near mile marker 15; pick up the Faye Trail, which leads to this one. The Halemanu-Kokee links Kokee Valley to Halemanu Valley (hence the name); along the way, you'll see a plum orchard, valleys, and ridges.

Alakai Swamp Trail ★ If you want to see the "real" Hawaii, this is it—a big swamp that's home to rare birds and plants. The trail allows you a rare glimpse into a wet, cloud-covered wilderness preserve where 460 inches of rainfall a year is common. This 7-mile hike used to take 5 hours of sloshing through the bog, with mud up to your knees. Now a boardwalk protects you from the shoe-grabbing mud. Come prepared for rain. (The only silver lining is that there are no mosquitoes above 3,000 ft.)

The trailhead is off Mohihi (Camp 10) Road, just beyond the Forest Reserve entrance sign and the Alakai Shelter picnic area. From the parking lot, the trail follows an old World War II four-wheel-drive road. Stick to the boardwalk; this is a fragile eco-area (not to mention the mud). At the end of the 3.5-mile slog, if you're lucky and the clouds part, you'll have a lovely view of Wainiha Valley and Hanalei from Kilohana Lookout.

Cabins & Tent Campgrounds Camping facilities include state campgrounds, one private tent area, and the **Kokee Lodge** (p. 355), which has 12 cabins for rent at very reasonable rates. At 4,000 feet, the nights are cold, particularly in winter. Because no open fires are permitted at Kokee, the best deal is the cabins. The **Kokee Lodge Restaurant** is open daily from 9am to 3:30pm for continental breakfast and lunch. Groceries and gas aren't available in Kokee, so stock up in advance, or you'll have to make the long trip down the mountain.

The **state campground** at Kokee allows tent camping only. Permits can be obtained from a **Division of State Parks** office on any island; on Kauai, it's at 3060 Eiwa St., Room 306, Lihue, HI 96766 (✆ **808/274-3444**). The permits are $5 per night; the time limit is 5 nights in a single 30-day period. Facilities include showers, drinking water, picnic tables, a pavilion with tables, restrooms, barbecues, sinks for dishwashing, and electric lights.

Tent camping at **Camp Sloggett,** owned by the Kauai YWCA, 3094 Elua St., Lihue, HI 96766 (✆ **808/335-6060;** www.campingkauai.com), is available for $10 per person per night. (Children 4 and younger stay free.) The sites are on 1½ acres of open field, with a covered pit for fires and a barbecue area, plus volleyball and badminton nets. There's also a hostel-style accommodation at the **Weinburg Bunkhouse,** with bunk beds, separate toilets, showers, and kitchenettes ($25 per person). There also is a caretaker's cottage, where rates are $85 during the week and $120 on weekends (2 nights minimum and $100 cleaning deposit), and the Sloggett Lodge, which sleeps 15 in two bedrooms, available for $25 a night per person (plus $100 cleaning fee). To get here, continue on the highway past park headquarters and take the first right after the Kokee Lodge. Follow the dirt road and look for the wooden CAMP SLOGGETT sign; turn right and follow the bumpy road past the state cabins into a large clearing.

BEACH CAMPING AT POLIHALE STATE PARK Polihale holds the distinction of being the westernmost beach in the United States. The beach is spectacular—some 300 feet wide in summer, with rolling sand dunes (some as high as 100 ft.), and the islands of Niihau and Lehua just offshore. Bordered by a curtain of Na Pali Coast cliffs on the north, razor-sharp ridges and steep valleys to the east, and the blue Pacific on the south and west, this is one of the most dramatic camping areas in the state.

The campgrounds for tent camping are located at the south end of the beach, affording privacy from daytime beach activities. There's great swimming in summer (even then, be on the lookout for waves and rip currents—there are no lifeguards), some surfing (the rides are usually short), and fishing. Camping is on sand, although there are some kiawe trees for shade. (***Warning:*** Kiawe trees drop long thorns, so make sure you have protective footwear.) Facilities include restrooms, showers, picnic tables, barbecues, and a spigot for drinking water. You can purchase supplies about 15 miles away in Waimea.

Permits, which are $5 per night, are available through the **Division of State Parks,** 3060 Eiwa St., Lihue, HI 96766 (✆ **808/274-3445;** www.hawaiistateparks.org/parks/kauai). You're limited to 5 nights in any 30-day period. To reach the park from Lihue, take Highway 50 west to Barking Sands Pacific Missile Range. Bear right onto the paved road, which heads toward the mountains. There will be small signs directing you to Polihale; the second sign will point to a left turn onto a dirt road. Follow this for about 5 miles; at the fork in the road, the campgrounds are to the left and the beach park is to the right.

The North Shore

NA PALI COAST STATE PARK Simply put, the Na Pali Coast is the most beautiful part of the Hawaiian Islands. Hanging valleys open like green-velvet accordions, and waterfalls tumble to the sea from the 4,120-foot-high cliffs; the experience is both exhilarating and humbling. Whether you hike in, fly over, or take a boat cruise past, be sure to see this park.

Established in 1984, Na Pali Coast State Park takes in a 22-mile stretch of fluted cliffs that wrap around the northwest shore of Kauai between Kee Beach and Polihale State Park. Volcanic in origin, carved by wind and sea, "the cliffs" (*na pali* in Hawaiian), which heaved out of the ocean floor 200 million years ago, stand as constant reminders of majesty and endurance. Four major valleys—Kalalau, Honopu, Awaawapuhi, and Nualolo—crease the cliffs.

Unless you boat or fly in (see "Boating," earlier in this chapter; or "Helicopter Rides over Waimea Canyon & the Na Pali Coast," on p. 380), the park is accessible only on foot—and it's not easy. An ancient footpath, the **Kalalau Trail,** winds through this remote, spectacular, 6,500-acre park, ultimately leading to Kalalau Valley. Of all the green valleys in Hawaii, and there are many, only Kalalau is a true wilderness—probably the last wild valley in the islands. No road goes here, and none ever will. The remote valley is home to long-plumed tropical birds, golden monarch butterflies, and many of Kauai's 120 rare and endangered species of plants. The hike into the Kalalau Valley is grueling and takes most people 6 to 8 hours one-way.

Despite its inaccessibility, this journey into Hawaii's wilderness has become increasingly popular since the 1970s. Overrun with hikers, helicopters, and boaters, the Kalalau Valley was in grave danger of being loved to death. Strict rules about access have been adopted. The park is now open to hikers and campers only on a limited basis, and you must have a permit (though you can hike the first 2 miles, to Hanakapiai Beach, without a permit). Permits are $10 per night and are issued in person at the **Kauai State Parks**

Office, 3060 Eiwa St., Room 306, Lihue, HI 96766 (✆ **808/274-3445;** www.hawaii stateparks.org/parks/kauai). You can also request one by writing **Kauai Division of State Parks,** at the address above. For more information, contact **Hawaii Department of Land and Natural Resources,** 1151 Punchbowl St., Room 130, Honolulu, HI 96813 (✆ **808/587-0320**).

HIKING THE KALALAU TRAIL ★★ The trailhead is at Kee Beach, at the end of Highway 560. Even if you only go as far as Hanakapiai, bring water. Hiking the Kalalau is the most difficult and challenging hike in Hawaii, and one you'll never forget. Even the Sierra Club rates the 22-mile round-trip into Kalalau Valley and back as "strenuous"— this is serious backpacking.

The first 2 miles of the hike will take you to **Hanakapiai Beach.** Do not attempt this hike unless you have adequate footwear (closed-toe shoes at least; hiking shoes are best), water, a sun visor, insect repellent, and adequate hiking clothes (shorts and T-shirt are fine; your bikini is not). Your kids must be able to hike continuously for 3 to 4 hours on uneven and steep surfaces. It's only 2 miles to Hanakapiai Beach, but the first mile is all uphill. This tough trail takes about 2 hours one-way and dissuades many. Day hikers love this initial stretch, so it's usually crowded. The island of Niihau and Lehua Rock are often visible on the horizon. At mile marker 1, you'll have climbed from sea level to 400 feet; now it's all downhill to Hanakapiai Beach. Sandy in summer, the beach becomes rocky when winter waves scour the coast. There are strong currents and no lifeguards, so swim at your own risk. You can also hike another 2 miles inland from the beach to **Hanakapiai Falls,** a 120-foot cascade. Allow an additional 3 hours for that stretch.

Horseback Riding

Only in Kauai can you ride a horse across the wide-open pastures of a working ranch under volcanic peaks and rein up near a waterfall pool. Near the Poipu area, **CJM Country Stables,** 1731 Kelaukia St. (2 miles beyond the Hyatt Regency Kauai), Koloa (✆ **808/742-6096;** www.cjmstables.com), offers both 2- and 3-hour escorted Hidden Valley beach rides. You'll trot over Hidden Valley ranch land, past secluded beaches and bays, along the Haupu Ridge, across sugar cane fields, and to Mahaulepu Beach; it's worth your time and money just to get out to this seldom-seen part of Kauai. The Scenic Valley Beach Ride costs $98 for the 2-hour ride. The 3-hour Secret Beach Ride is $125. There's also a 3½-hour swim/beach/picnic ride for $115. Kids should be at least 8 years old to participate.

Princeville Ranch Stables, Highway 56 (just after the Princeville Airport), Hanalei (✆ **808/826-6777;** www.princevilleranch.com), has a variety of outings. The 1½-hour ocean-bluff ride takes in views of the mountains and the vista of the ocean and costs $80. The 4-hour Waterfall Picnic Ride crosses ranch land, takes you on a short (but steep) hike to swimming pools at the base of waterfalls, and then feeds you a picnic lunch for $135 ($125 for the 3-hour ride). Riders must be in good physical shape and at least 8 years old. Don't forget to put your swimsuit on under your jeans. The Princeville Ranch Stables also offers other adventures, ranging from the less strenuous wagon rides to a cattle-drive ride.

Playgrounds

Located at the north end of Lydgate Park, near the Aloha Beach Resort in Wailua, is the **Kamalani Playground.** Built by 7,000 volunteers in 1994, the playground features a volcano slide, swings, mazes, a Japanese garden, a labyrinth, and lots of artwork by Kauai children.

Tennis

The **Kauai County Parks and Recreation Department,** 4444 Rice St., Suite 150, Lihue (✆ **808/241-6670**), has a list of the nine county tennis courts around the island, all of which are free and open to the public. Private courts open to the public include the **Princeville Tennis Club,** Princeville Hotel (✆ **808/826-3620;** www.princeville.com), which has six courts available for $18 per person ($12 for guests) for 90 minutes. On the south side, try **Grand Hyatt Kauai Resort and Spa,** Poipu Resort (✆ **808/742-1234**), which has four courts, available for $30 an hour; and **Kiahuna Swim and Tennis Club,** Poipu Road (just past the Poipu Shopping Village on the left), Poipu Resort (✆ **808/742-9533**), which has 10 courts renting for $10 per person per hour.

Workshops

The **Garden Island Arts Council** (www.gardenislandarts.org) periodically has a series of community art workshops for children and adults ranging from watercolors, ceramic relief tiles, and papermaking to life drawing. Check the website for information on current workshops and classes.

8 SHOPPING WITH YOUR KIDS

Shopping with your kids can be an adventure on this island. Where else can you browse vintage Hawaiiana practically in a cane field, buy exquisite home accessories in an old stone building built in 1942, and get a virtual agricultural tour of the island through city-sponsored green markets that move from town to town throughout the week, like a movable feast? At Kauai's small, tasteful boutiques, you can satisfy your shopping ya-yas in concentrated spurts around the island. This is a bonanza for the boutique shopper—particularly the one who appreciates the thrill of the hunt.

THE SHOPPING SCENE

Lihue

Downtown Lihue is not a shopping paradise. I suggest you drive out to the **Kukui Grove Center,** at Kaumualii Highway (Hwy. 50) and Old Nawiliwili Road. The best store here is the **Kauai Products Store** (✆ **808/246-6753**), a fount of local handicrafts (about 60% Kauai artists) and a respectable showcase for made-on-the-island products, such as soaps, paintings, clothing, coffee, Kukui guava jams, fabrics, and Niihau shell leis.

Poipu

Expect mostly touristy shops in Poipu, the island's resort mecca; here you'll find T-shirts, souvenirs, black pearls, jewelry, and the usual quota of tired marine art and trite hand-painted silks. The formerly characterless **Poipu Shopping Village,** at 2360 Kiahuna Plantation Dr., is shaping up to be a serious shopping stop. **Hale Mana** (✆ **808/742-1027**) is a glorious collection of hard-to-find gift items of excellent taste (antique picture frames, beaded bags, unique candles, pillows, Hawaiian handmade paper, and more). Tiny **Bamboo Lace** (✆ **808/742-1450**) lures the fashionistas with its resort wear and accessories. Across the courtyard, **Sand People** (✆ **808/742-2888**) is great for understated resort wear, while the newly renovated **Overboard** (✆ **808/742-1299**) rides the wave of popularity in aloha wear and surf stuff.

Ultimate Kauai Souvenir: The Red-Dirt Shirt

If you are looking for an inexpensive, easy-to-pack souvenir or gift, check out the red-dirt shirt. The shirts were born out of turning a bad situation into a positive one. The "legend" is that **Paradise Sportswear** in Hanapepe (✆ **808/335-5670;** www.dirtshirt.com) lost the roof of their warehouse during Hurricane Iniki in 1992. After the storm passed, employees returned to the building to find all their T-shirts covered with Kauai's red soil. Before throwing out their entire inventory as "too soiled to sell," someone had an idea: sell the shirts as a Kauai "red-dirt shirt." Fast forward a dozen years and the shirts have numerous outlets on Kauai.

The best prices on the red-dirt shirts can be found at the factory by the Port Allen Small Boat Harbor, open daily from 9am to noon and 1 to 4pm. You can watch the silk-screen process or purchase a few shirts from the retail shop, which has T-shirts for infants to XXXXL. The deals are on the factory seconds and discontinued designs.

Hanapepe

Hanapepe Road (the main road through the town) is lined with gift shops and galleries, including our very favorite Hanapepe store, **Banana Patch Studio,** 3865 Hanapepe Rd. (✆ **808/335-5944;** www.bananapatchstudio.com), which has the best prices on the island for tropical plates and cups, hand-painted tiles, artwork, handmade soaps, pillows with tropical designs, and jewelry. They will pack and ship your purchases anywhere. Hanapepe's gallery owners and artists recently instituted the **Friday Night Art Walk** every Friday from 6 to 9pm. Gallery owners take turns hosting this informal event along Hanapepe Road.

The Coconut Coast: Kapaa

"Downtown" Kapaa continues to flourish. On the main strip, across from Sunnyside Market, you'll find the recently expanded **Kela's Glass Gallery** (✆ **808/822-4527**), the island's showiest place for handmade glass in all sizes, shapes, and prices, with the most impressive selection in Hawaii. Go nuts over the vases and studio glass pieces. Then stroll along this strip of storefronts to **Kebanu Gallery** (✆ **808/823-6820**), **Hula Girl** (✆ **808/822-1950**), and **South China Sea Trading Company** (✆ **808/823-8655**), and see if you can resist their wares.

North Shore

Hanalei, touristy as it is, is still a shopping destination. Anticipate a handful of great shops, a few art galleries and boutiques, and several minimalls—not much to distract you from an afternoon of hiking or snorkeling.

Save your time, energy and, most of all, discretionary funds, for this end of the island. Starting in Kailua, don't miss **Kong Lung,** in a 1942 Kilauea stone building (the last to be built on the Kilauea Plantation) off Highway 56 on Kilauea Road (✆ **808/828-1822**). Kong Lung is a showcase of design, style, and quality, from top-of-the-line dinnerware and bath products to aloha shirts, jewelry, ceramics, women's wear, stationery, and personal and home accessories. The book selection is fabulous. It's expensive, but browsing here is a joy. Directly behind Kong Lung is newcomer **Lotus Gallery** (✆ **808/828-9898**), a showstopper for lovers of antiques and designer jewelry.

In Hanalei, at **Ola's,** by the Hanalei River on the Kuhio Highway (Hwy. 560), after the bridge and before the main part of Hanalei town (© **808/826-6937**), Sharon and Doug Britt, an award-winning artist, have amassed a head-turning assortment of American and island crafts, including Doug's paintings and the one-of-a-kind furniture that he makes out of found objects, driftwood, and used materials. From health foods to groceries to Bakelite jewelry, the **Ching Young Village Shopping Center,** in the heart of Hanalei, covers a lot of bases. It's more funky than fashionable, but Hanalei, until recently, has never been about fashion. Next door to Ching Young Village is **On the Road to Hanalei** (© **808/826-7360**), worth your time to wander around and check out the unusual T-shirts (great gifts to take home because they don't take up much suitcase space), scarves, pareus, jewelry, and other unique gifts. Across the street in the **Hanalei Center,** the standout boutique is the **Yellowfish Trading Company** ★ (© **808/826-1227**), where owner Gritt Benton's impeccable eye and zeal for collecting are reflected in the 1920s to 1940s collectibles: menus, hula-girl nodders, hula lamps, rattan and koa furniture, vases, bark-cloth fabric, retro pottery and lamp bases, must-have vintage textiles, and wonderful finds in books and aloha shirts.

THE GOODS A TO Z

Aloha Wear

As you make your way from Lihue to the North Shore, you'll pass **Bambulei** (© **808/823-8641**), bordering the cane field in Wailua next to Caffè Coco. Watch for the sign just past the Wailua intersection, across from Kintaro's Restaurant. Bambulei houses a charming collection of 1930s and 1940s treasures—everything from jewelry to exquisite vintage aloha shirts. If it's not vintage, it will look vintage, and it's bound to be fabulous. Vintage muumuu are often in perfect condition, and dresses go for $20 to $2,000.

Baby & Preschooler Clothes

In the heart of Poipu is the best place for unique keiki clothes: **Sand Kids** in the Poipu Shopping Center (© **808/742-7123**). In Kapaa, set back from the main road across from Foodland supermarket, **Marta's Boat** (© **808/822-3926**) is one of the island's more appealing boutiques for children's clothes.

Books

For the biggest selection of books, go to **Borders,** 4305 Nawiliwili Rd., Lihue (© **808/246-0862**), for beach-reading material and a great selection of all things Hawaiian, plus music. Two great new and used bookstores are **Hanalei Book Store,** 4489 Aku Rd. (© **808/826-2568**); and **Tin Can Mailman Books and Antiques,** Kinipopo Shopping Village, 4-356 Kuhio Hwy., Wailua (© **808/822-3009**).

Flowers & Leis

Every Friday is "Aloha Friday" at the **free lei-making workshops** at the **West Kauai Technology and Visitors Center,** 9565 Kaumualii Hwy., Waimea (© **808/338-1332**), where from 9:30 to 11am they have free lei-making classes; be sure to reserve in advance.

You can take paradise home with you—well, at least the outrageously beautiful flowers. The best place to order flowers sent home is **Tropical Flowers of Hawaii,** 3465 Lawailoa Lane, Koloa (© **800/699-7984** or 808/332-7984; www.a-tropical-flower.com). Not only is the owner, Charles, a flower genius (who grows a range of tropical flowers, including some very rare and unusual varieties), but his hardy blooms and his

Fruity Smoothies & Other Exotic Treats

Fruit stands have sprouted on this island, and smoothies are gaining ground as the milkshake of the new millennium. Joe Halasey and his wife, Cynthia, run **Banana Joe's** (✆ **808/828-1092**), the granddaddy of Kauai's roadside fruit-and-smoothie stands, a Kilauea landmark since it opened in 1986 at 52719 Kuhio Hwy., between mile markers 23 and 24 heading north, on the mauka (mountain) side of the street. Sapodilla, star apple (round, purple, and sweet, like a creamy Concord grape), macadamia nuts, Anahola Granola, and home-made breads—such as banana and mango-coconut—are among Banana Joe's attractions.

Mango Mama's, 4660 Hookui St. (✆ **808/828-1020**), is another favorite on the Kilauea roadside. Recently expanded, it's now a full-service cafe serving espresso, smoothies, fresh-squeezed juices, sandwiches, bagels, coffee, coffee smoothies, and fresh fruit. The Kauai Breeze (fresh mango, pineapple, passion fruit, and guava) is a big winner here.

At the north end of Kapaa town, **Killer Juice Bar,** 4-1586 Kuhio Hwy. (✆ **808/821-1905**), is a sight for sore eyes after a drive through commercial Kapaa. Smoothies are $2.50 to $5.50, fresh juices are $1.25 (wheat grass) to $5 (carrot)—and they're good! An attractive selection of fresh fruit—gemlike tomatoes, atemoyas, star fruit, papayas—is displayed in the front. Queen of the smoothies is the Amazing Mango Memory, made with fresh local mangoes in season or, when they're not available, with fresh mangoes from Mexico. The Killer Bars, chocolate chip squares for $1.50, live up to their name.

On the Coconut Coast, just before you reach the center of Kapaa town heading north on Kuhio Highway, keep an eye out to the left for **Sunnyside Farmers' Market,** 4-1345 Kuhio Hwy. (✆ **808/822-0494**). Here you can always find realistically priced Sunrise papayas, pineapples, local bananas, tomatoes, and other Kauai produce. You can also get preinspected Sunrise papayas for travel out of state, local apple bananas, coconuts, mangoes in season, and pineapples from Maui and Kauai.

Near the Lihue Airport, Pammie Chock at **Kauai Fruit & Flower** (✆ **808/245-1814**) makes a pineapple–passion fruit smoothie that gets my vote as the best on the island.

skill at packing means that your little bit of Kauai will live for a long, long time. All this and extremely reasonable prices. (Bouquets start at just $15.)

Food

The taste treat of Kauai is lavender-colored taro chips, sliced and cooked just like potato chips. The best place to get these chips is the source, **Taro Ko Chips Factory,** located in an old green plantation house at 3940 Hanapepe Rd. (✆ **808/335-5586**). Cooking in a tiny, modest kitchen at the east end of town, these famous taro chips are handmade by the farmers who grow the taro in a nearby valley. Despite their breakable nature, the chips make great gifts. To really impress them back home, get the li hing mui–flavored chips.

 To get to the factory from Lihue, turn right off Highway 50 onto Hanapepe Road, in Hanapepe, the town just after Eleele.

Markets

The county of Kauai sponsors regular weekly **Sunshine Markets** throughout the island. The biggest market is at **Kapaa New Town Park,** in the middle of Kapaa town, on Wednesday at 3pm. The Sunshine Market in **Lihue,** held on Friday at 3pm at the Vidhina Stadium Parking Lot, is close in size and extremely popular. The schedule for the other markets: **Koloa Ball Park,** Monday at noon; **Kalaheo Neighborhood Center,** Tuesday at 3pm; **Hanapepe Park,** Thursday at 3pm; **Kilauea Neighborhood Center,** Thursday at 4:30pm; and **Kekaha Neighborhood Center,** Saturday at 9am. For more information on Sunshine Markets, call ✆ **808/241-6390,** or go to www.kauai.gov. Especially at the Koloa Market, which draws hundreds of shoppers, go early and shop briskly.

On the North Shore, Kilauea is the agricultural heart of the island, with two weekly green markets: the county-sponsored **Sunshine Market,** Thursday at 4:30pm at the Kilauea Neighborhood Center; and the private Kilauea Quality Farmers' Association (mostly organic growers) **Farmers' Market,** Saturday from 11:30am to 1:30pm behind the Kilauea Post Office. Also on the North Shore, about a quarter-mile past Hanalei in an area called Waipa, the **Hawaiian Farmers of Hanalei**—anywhere from a dozen to 25 farmers—gather along the main road with their budget-friendly, just-picked produce. This market is held every Tuesday at 2pm.

On the south shore, closer to the resorts, in Poipu, with a view across asparagus fields and the chiseled ridges of Haupu Mountain, the **Poipu Southshore Market** sells produce, some of it by Haupu Growers, daily from 10am to 6pm on Koloa Bypass Road. Haupu Growers is the major supplier of Kauai asparagus, and this is where you'll find it. Asparagus season begins in October.

Museum Gift Shops

The gift shop of the **Kauai Museum,** 4428 Rice St. (✆ **808/245-6931;** www.kauaimuseum.org), is your best bet for made-on-Kauai arts and crafts, from Niihau shell leis to woodwork, lauhala and coconut products, and more.

Up in Kokee State Park, the gift shop of the **Kokee Natural History Museum** (✆ **808/335-9975;** www.kokee.org) is *the* stop for botanical, geographical, historical, and nature-related books and gifts, not only on Kauai, but on all the islands. Audubon bird books, hiking maps, and practically every book on Kauai ever written line the shelves.

Music

For a variety of music, try **Borders,** 4305 Nawiliwili Rd., Lihue (✆ **808/246-0862**). If you are looking for a variety of authentic, traditional Hawaiian music, check out **Hawaiian Paradise Music,** 5-4280 Kuhio Hwy., Kapaa (✆ **808/826-0245;** www.hawaiianparadisemusic.com), for a terrific selection of contemporary island music, traditional falsetto, hula music, ancient Hawaiian chants, Tahitian music, Hawaiian Christmas music, island reggae, and Hawaiian slack-key guitar. DVDs and videos are available, too.

Surf & Sports

Across the street from Poipu Beach, **Nukumoi Surf Co.,** 2080 Hoone Rd. (✆ **808/742-8019;** www.nukumoisurf.com/surfshophawaii.html), is a pleasant surprise. They offer an

Niihau Shell Lei: The Island's Most Prized Artwork

Because Kauai is so close to Niihau, the "Forbidden Island" just offshore, it's the best place in the state to buy the exquisite Niihau shell lei. There is nothing that can match the craftsmanship and the tiny shells in this highly sought-after and highly prized jewelry. The shells are hand-picked from the beach, then sorted according to size and color; some 80% of the shells are thrown out because they are chipped, cracked, discolored, or otherwise imperfect. The best shells are the tiny ones, and the best colors (the shells can be white, yellow, blue, red, or gold) are white or the rare gold. A necklace can take anywhere from hours to years to complete. Each shell is strung with very small and very intricate knots. Predictably, the leis are not cheap; they range from several hundred to several thousand dollars, depending on the length, the shells used, and the intricate work involved.

You can find Niihau shell leis at numerous locations on Kauai. My two favorite places are **Hawaiian Trading Post,** Koloa Road and Kaumualii Highway in Lawai (✆ **808/332-7404**), which carries a range of items from junky souvenirs to an excellent selection of Niihau leis (you have to ask them to bring out the "good stuff" from the back); and the website **www.niihau.us/leis1.htm**, which is owned and operated by Niihau residents (so you can buy direct, so to speak).

excellent selection of sunglasses, swimwear, surf equipment, and watersports regalia, and not just for the younger-than-20 crowd.

Sweets for the Sweet

Popo's Cookies, 971 E. Kuhio Hwy., Kapaa (✆ **808/822-6911**), is the *ne plus ultra* of store-bought cookies on the island. Popo's chocolate chip, macadamia nut, chocolate–macadamia nut, chocolate-coconut, almond, peanut butter, and other varieties of butter-rich cookies are among the most sought-after food items to leave the island.

Toys

Marta's Boat, 770 Kuhio Hwy., Kapaa (✆ **808/882-3926**), is one of the island's more unusual boutiques for not only children's and women's clothing, but also a tangle of accessories, toys (from infants up), and unusual gift items.

9 ENTERTAINMENT FOR THE WHOLE FAMILY

Kauai is known for lots of things: the most beautiful beaches in the state, the magnificent Na Pali cliffs jutting into the ocean, the incredible rainforests, the wide panoramas of the Waimea Canyon. But it is not known for a vibrant nightlife. Local families seek out their own entertainment; below are their favorite options.

THEATER

Occasionally the **Kauai Community College Performing Arts Center,** 3-1901 Kaumualii Hwy., Lihue (✆ **808/245-8270;** www.lcc.hawaii.edu/org/th/kccpac.html), is a venue for professional productions, cultural events, concerts, and even films. For arts and culture, local residents generally rely on the plays put on by the nonprofessional group **Kauai Community Players;** call ✆ **808/245-7700,** or go to www.kauaicommunity players.org, to find out what the latest production is and where it will be performed. It's not Broadway (or off-Broadway), but it is energetic community theater at its best.

The **Kauai International Theater** performs at the intimate 62-seat theater in the Kauai Village Shopping Center. Calling itself "The Farthest Off Off Off Broadway in the Country," the small theater stages musicals, comedies, dramas, and local and international plays year-round. For information on the next production, call ✆ **808/821-1588.**

The **Hawaii Children's Theatre,** 5726 Noni Place, Kapaa (✆ **808/246-8985;** www. hawaiichildrenstheatre.com), has periodic performances of kids' theater; call for details about their next production.

HAWAIIAN MUSIC & HULA

There are several places you can take your family to watch the hula for free. The **Poipu Shopping Village** (✆ **808/742-2831**) offers free hula performances every Tuesday and Thursday at 5pm in the outdoor courtyard.

Closer to Lihue, the **Harbor Mall,** 3501 Rice St. (✆ **808/245-6255**), has a free hula show every Wednesday at 12:15pm.

The Coconut Coast of Wailua, Waipouli, and Kapaa offer sunset torch-lighting ceremonies, music, and other evening entertainment, but the real action takes place after dark. Starting at 5pm, the **Coconut Marketplace,** 4-484 Kuhio Hwy. (✆ **808/822-3641**), features a free hula show Wednesdays, performed by local residents ranging in age from a keiki hula troop of tiny dancers who still don't have their permanent teeth, to lithe young women and men gracefully performing this ancient Hawaiian art, to grandmothers who have been dancing for decades.

Western Kauai has **Hanapepe Art Night,** every Friday night starting at 6pm, for which the town's nine boutique galleries and shops open their doors for an artistic evening with live entertainment, refreshments, and a chance to meet Kauai's top artists.

To listen to Hawaiian music, head for the North Shore. The **Hanalei Gourmet,** in the Old Hanalei Schoolhouse, 5-5161 Kuhio Hwy. (✆ **808/826-2524**), has live music every night. Down the road, in the **Hanalei Bay Resort,** 5380 Honoiki St. (✆ **808/826-6522;** www.hanaleibayresort.com), is a music lover's gem: the **Happy Talk Lounge,** which features contemporary Hawaiian music Monday through Saturday from 6:30 to 9:30pm and jazz on Sunday. At **Princeville Resort Kauai,** 5520 Kahaku Rd. (✆ **808/826-9644;** www.princeville.com), in the main lobby, the **Living Room** (filled with comfy, overstuffed furniture) has a range of nightlife activities such as a Hawaiian chanting ceremony, Hawaiian dancing, and an entertaining talk on Hawaiian culture, from 6:30pm on Tuesday, Thursday, and Sunday. On the other nights, island-related entertainment takes place from 7 to 11pm. Still farther north, the **Mediterranean Gourmet** at the **Hanalei Colony Resort** (✆ **808/826-9875**) has live Hawaiian music on Monday, Tuesday, and Friday from 6:30 to 8:30pm.

On the south shore, the **Kauai Marriott Resort & Beach Club,** 3610 Rice St., Nawiliwili (✆ **808/246-9599**), has a host of nightlife activities. Every Monday and Thursday, at 5:30pm, is a sunset hula and torch-lighting ceremony on the beach. At

Kukui's Restaurant (✆ **808/245-5050**), in the resort, they have Hawaiian contemporary music on Friday and Saturday starting at 5pm and during Sunday brunch from 10:30am.

The **Grand Hyatt Kauai Resort and Spa** (✆ **808/245-5050**) has a torch-lighting ceremony every Tuesday and Saturday at 6pm that includes a keiki hula show with Hawaiian musicians. On Sunday, Monday, Wednesday, Thursday, and Friday, live Hawaiian music takes place from 6pm.

The **Hilton Kauai Beach Resort,** 4331 Kauai Beach Dr., Lihue (✆ **808/245-1955**), has free nightly entertainment, depending on the night, ranging from jazz to Hawaii, in the Shutters Lounge from 6pm.

MOVIES

If the kids are up for a movie, Kauai's two mainstream theaters, the **Kukui Grove Cinemas,** in the Kukui Grove Shopping Center, 4368 Kukui Grove St. (✆ **808/245-5055**), and **Coconut Market Place Cinema 1 and 2** (✆ **808/821-2324**) feature the latest films. Film buffs will love the old-fashioned **Historic Waimea Theater** in Waimea (✆ **808/338-0282;** www.waimeatheater.com), which shows a wide range of movies from the current popular films to art films.

STORY HOURS

Storytelling and read-aloud programs are offered by the various public libraries, ranging from magic shows for preschoolers to storytelling for the older children, with puppets, magic, and juggling. For information on these and other storytelling programs, contact the **Hawaii State Public Library** (✆ **808/241-3222;** www.librarieshawaii.org).

Appendix: Fast Facts, Toll-Free Numbers & Websites

1 FAST FACTS: THE HAWAIIAN ISLANDS

AMERICAN EXPRESS For 24-hour traveler's check refunds and purchase information, call © **800/221-7282.** For local offices, see the "Fast Facts" sections in the individual island chapters.

AREA CODE All the Hawaiian Islands are in the **808** area code. Note that if you're calling one island from another, you'll have to dial 1-808 first.

ATM NETWORKS See "Money & Costs," p. 34.

AUTOMOBILE ORGANIZATIONS Auto clubs will supply maps, suggested routes, guidebooks, accident and bail-bond insurance, and emergency road service. The **American Automobile Association (AAA)** is the major auto club in the United States. If you belong to an auto club in your home country, inquire about AAA reciprocity before you leave. You may be able to join AAA even if you're not a member of a reciprocal club; to inquire, call AAA (© **800/222-4357**). AAA is actually an organization of regional auto clubs, so look under "AAA Automobile Club" in the White Pages of the telephone directory. AAA has a nationwide emergency road-service telephone number (© **800/AAA-HELP [222-4357]**).

BUSINESS HOURS Most offices are open Monday through Friday from 8am to 5pm. Bank hours are Monday through Thursday from 8:30am to 3pm and Friday from 8:30am to 6pm; some banks are open on Saturday as well. Shopping centers are open Monday through Friday from 10am to 9pm, Saturday from 10am to 5:30pm, and Sunday from noon to 5 or 6pm.

CAR RENTALS See "Getting Around Hawaii," p. 51.

DRINKING LAWS The legal drinking age in Hawaii is 21. Bars are allowed to stay open daily until 2am; places with cabaret licenses are able to keep the booze flowing until 4am. Grocery and convenience stores are allowed to sell beer, wine, and liquor 7 days a week. Proof of age is required and often requested at bars, nightclubs, and restaurants, so it's always a good idea to bring ID when you go out.

Do not carry open containers of alcohol in your car or any public area that isn't zoned for alcohol consumption. The police can fine you on the spot. And nothing will ruin your trip faster than getting a citation for DUI ("driving under the influence"), so don't even think about driving while intoxicated.

DRIVING RULES See "Getting Around Hawaii," p. 51.

ELECTRICITY Like Canada, the United States uses 110 to 120 volts AC (60 cycles), compared to 220 to 240 volts AC (50 cycles) in most of Europe, Australia, and New Zealand. Downward converters that change 220–240 volts to 110–120 volts are difficult to find in the United States, so bring one with you.

EMBASSIES & CONSULATES All embassies are located in the nation's capital, Washington, D.C. Some consulates are located in major U.S. cities, and most nations have a mission to the United Nations in New York City. If your country isn't listed below, call for directory information in Washington, D.C. (✆ **202/555-1212**), or log on to **www.embassy.org/embassies.**

The embassy of **Australia** is at 1601 Massachusetts Ave. NW, Washington, DC 20036 (✆ **202/797-3000;** www.austemb.org). There are consulates in New York, Honolulu, Houston, Los Angeles, and San Francisco.

The embassy of **Canada** is at 501 Pennsylvania Ave. NW, Washington, DC 20001 (✆ **202/682-1740;** www.canadianembassy.org). Other Canadian consulates are in Buffalo (New York), Detroit, Los Angeles, New York, and Seattle.

The embassy of **Ireland** is at 2234 Massachusetts Ave. NW, Washington, DC 20008 (✆ **202/462-3939;** www.irelandemb.org). Irish consulates are in Boston, Chicago, New York, San Francisco, and other cities. See the website for complete listing.

The embassy of **New Zealand** is at 37 Observatory Circle NW, Washington, DC 20008 (✆ **202/328-4800;** www.nzembassy.com. New Zealand consulates are in Los Angeles, Salt Lake City, San Francisco, and Seattle.

The embassy of the **United Kingdom** is at 3100 Massachusetts Ave. NW, Washington, DC 20008 (✆ **202/588-7800;** www.britainusa.com). Other British consulates are in Atlanta, Boston, Chicago, Cleveland, Houston, Los Angeles, New York, San Francisco, and Seattle.

EMERGENCIES Dial ✆ **911** for police, fire, or ambulance.

GASOLINE (PETROL) At press time, in the U.S., the cost of gasoline (also known as gas, but never petrol), is abnormally high. Taxes are already included in the printed price. One U.S. gallon equals 3.8 liters or .85 imperial gallons. Fill-up locations are known as gas or service stations.

HOLIDAYS See "Kids' Favorite Hawaii Events," p. 23.

HOSPITALS For information on doctors, dentists, and hospitals, see the "Fast Facts" sections in the individual island chapters.

INSURANCE **Medical Insurance:** Although it's not required of travelers, health insurance is highly recommended. Most health insurance policies cover you if you get sick away from home—but check your coverage before you leave.

International visitors to the U.S. should note that unlike many European countries, the United States does not usually offer free or low-cost medical care to its citizens or visitors. Doctors and hospitals are expensive, and in most cases will require advance payment or proof of coverage before they render their services. Good policies will cover the costs of an accident, repatriation, or death. Packages such as **Europ Assistance's "Worldwide Healthcare Plan"** are sold by European automobile clubs and travel agencies at attractive rates. **Worldwide Assistance Services, Inc.** (✆ **800/777-8710;** www.worldwideassistance.com) is the agent for Europ Assistance in the United States. Though lack of health insurance may prevent you from being admitted to a hospital in nonemergencies, don't worry about being left on a street corner to die: The American way is to fix you now and bill the daylights out of you later.

If you're ever hospitalized more than 150 miles from home, **MedjetAssist** (✆ **800/527-7478;** www.medjetassistance.com) will pick you up and fly you to the hospital of your choice in a medically equipped and staffed aircraft 24 hours day, 7 days a week. Annual memberships are $225 individual, $350 family; you can also purchase short-term memberships.

Canadians should check with their provincial health plan offices or call **Health Canada** (✆ **866/225-0709;** www.hc-sc.gc.ca) to find out the extent of their coverage and what documentation and receipts they must take home in case they are treated in the United States.

Travelers from the U.K. should carry their European Health Insurance Card (EHIC), which replaced the E111 form as proof of entitlement to free/reduced-cost medical treatment abroad (✆ **0845 606 2030;** www.ehic.org.uk). Note, however, that the EHIC covers only "necessary medical treatment," and for repatriation costs, lost money, baggage, or cancellation, travel insurance from a reputable company should always be sought (www.travelinsuranceweb.com).

Travel Insurance: The cost of travel insurance varies widely, depending on the destination, the cost and length of your trip, your age and health, and the type of trip you're taking, but expect to pay between 5% and 8% of the vacation itself. You can get estimates from various providers through InsureMyTrip.com. Enter your trip cost and dates, your age, and other information, for prices from more than a dozen companies.

U.K. citizens and their families who make more than one trip abroad per year may find that an annual travel insurance policy works out cheaper. Check www.moneysupermarket.com, which compares prices across a wide range of providers for single- and multitrip policies.

Most big travel agents offer their own insurance and will probably try to sell you their package when you book a holiday. Think before you sign. **Britain's Consumers' Association** recommends that you insist on seeing the policy and reading the fine print before buying travel insurance. **The Association of British Insurers** (✆ **020/7600-3333;** www.abi.org.uk) gives advice by phone and publishes Holiday Insurance, a free guide to policy provisions and prices. You might also shop around for better deals: Try **Columbus Direct** (✆ 0870/033-9988; www.columbusdirect.net).

Trip-Cancellation Insurance: Trip-cancellation insurance will help retrieve your money if you have to back out of a trip or depart early, or if your travel supplier goes bankrupt. Trip cancellation traditionally covers such events as sickness, natural disasters, and State Department advisories. The latest news in trip-cancellation insurance is the availability of expanded hurricane coverage and the "any-reason" cancellation coverage—which costs more but covers cancellations made for any reason. You won't get back 100% of your prepaid trip cost, but you'll be refunded a substantial portion. **TravelSafe** (✆ **888/885-7233;** www.travelsafe.com) offers both types of coverage. Expedia also offers any-reason cancellation coverage for its air-hotel packages. For details, contact one of the following recommended insurers: **Access America** (✆ **866/807-3982;** www.accessamerica.com); **Travel Guard International** (✆ **800/826-4919;** www.travelguard.com); **Travel Insured International** (✆ **800/243-3174;** www.travelinsured.com); and **Travelex Insurance Services** (✆ **888/457-4602;** www.travelex-insurance.com).

INTERNET ACCESS See the "Fast Facts" sections in the individual island chapters.

LEGAL AID If you are "pulled over" for a minor infraction (such as speeding), never attempt to pay the fine directly to a police officer; this could be construed as attempted bribery, a much more serious crime. Pay fines by mail or directly into the hands of the clerk of the court. If accused of a more serious offense, say and do nothing before consulting a lawyer. Here the burden is on the state to prove a person's guilt beyond a reasonable doubt, and everyone has the right to remain silent, whether he or she is suspected of a crime or actually arrested. Once arrested, a person can make one telephone call to a party of his or her choice. International visitors should call their embassy or consulate.

LOST & FOUND Be sure to tell all of your credit card companies the minute you discover your wallet has been lost or stolen, and file a report at the nearest police precinct. Your credit card company or insurer may require a police report number or record of the loss. Most credit card companies have an emergency toll free number to call if your card is lost or stolen; they may be able to wire you a cash advance immediately or deliver an emergency credit card in a day or two. Visa's U.S. emergency number is ✆ **800/847-2911** or 410/581-9994. American Express cardholders and traveler's check holders should call ✆ **800/221-7282.** MasterCard holders should call ✆ **800/307-7309** or 636/722-7111. For other credit cards, call the toll-free number directory at ✆ **800/555-1212.**

If you need emergency cash over the weekend when all banks and American Express offices are closed, you can have money wired to you via **Western Union** (✆ **800/325-6000;** www.westernunion.com).

MAPS See "Visitor Information & Maps" p. 16.

MEASUREMENTS See the chart on the inside front cover of this book for details on converting metric measurements to U.S. equivalents.

MEDICAL CONDITIONS If you have a medical condition that requires **syringe-administered medications,** carry a valid signed prescription from your physician; syringes in carry-on baggage will be inspected. Insulin in any form should have the proper pharmaceutical documentation. If you have a disease that requires treatment with **narcotics,** you should also carry documented proof with you—smuggling narcotics aboard a plane carries severe penalties in the U.S.

For **HIV-positive visitors,** requirements for entering the United States are somewhat vague and change frequently. For up-to-the-minute information, contact **AIDSinfo** (✆ **800/448-0440** or 301/519-6616 outside the U.S.; www.aidsinfo.nih.gov) or the **Gay Men's Health Crisis** (✆ **212/367-1000;** www.gmhc.org).

NEWSPAPERS & MAGAZINES See the "Fast Facts" sections in the individual island chapters.

PASSPORTS **For Residents of Australia:** You can pick up an application from your local post office or any branch of Passports Australia, but you must schedule an interview at the passport office to present your application materials. Call the **Australian Passport Information Service** at ✆ **131-232,** or visit the government website at www.passports.gov.au.

For Residents of Canada: Passport applications are available at travel agencies throughout Canada or from the central **Passport Office,** Department of Foreign Affairs and International Trade, Ottawa, ON K1A 0G3 (✆ **800/567-6868;** www.ppt.gc.ca). ***Note:*** Canadian children who travel must have their own passport. However, if you hold a valid Canadian passport issued before December 11, 2001, that bears the name of your child, the passport remains valid for you and your child until it expires.

For Residents of Ireland: You can apply for a 10-year passport at the **Passport Office,** Setanta Centre, Molesworth Street, Dublin 2 (✆ **01/671-1633;** www.irlgov.ie/iveagh). Those under age 18 and over 65 must apply for a 3-year passport. You can also apply at 1A South Mall, Cork

(✆ **021/272-525**), or at most main post offices.

For Residents of New Zealand: You can pick up a passport application at any New Zealand Passports Office or download it from their website. Contact the **Passports Office** at ✆ **0800/225-050** in New Zealand or 04/474-8100, or log on to www.passports.govt.nz.

For Residents of the United Kingdom: To pick up an application for a standard 10-year passport (5-yr. passport for children 15 and under), visit your nearest passport office, major post office, or travel agency, or contact the **United Kingdom Passport Service** at ✆ **0870/521-0410** or search its website at www.ukpa.gov.uk.

POLICE Dial ✆ **911** for police.

SMOKING It's against the law to smoke in public buildings, including airports, shopping malls, grocery stores, retail shops, buses, movie theaters, banks, convention facilities, and all government buildings and facilities. There is no smoking in restaurants, bars, and nightclubs. Most bed-and-breakfasts prohibit smoking indoors, and more and more hotels and resorts are becoming nonsmoking even in public areas. Also, there is no smoking within 20 feet of a doorway, window, or ventilation intake (no hanging around outside a bar to smoke—you must go 20 ft. away).

TAXES The United States has no value-added tax (VAT) or other indirect tax at the national level. Every state, county, and city may levy its own local tax on all purchases, including hotel and restaurant checks and airline tickets. Hawaii state general excise tax is 4%; the city and county of Honolulu adds an additional .005% on anything purchased there. Hotel tax is 11.4%. These taxes will not appear on price tags.

TELEGRAPH, TELEX & FAX **Telegraph and telex services** are provided primarily by Western Union. You can telegraph money, or have it telegraphed to you, very quickly over the Western Union system, but this service can cost as much as 15% to 20% of the amount sent.

Most hotels have **fax machines** available for guest use (be sure to ask about the charge to use it). Many hotel rooms are even wired for guests' fax machines. A less expensive way to send and receive faxes may be at stores such as **The UPS Store** (formerly Mail Boxes Etc.).

TIME The continental United States is divided into **four time zones:** Eastern Standard Time (EST), Central Standard Time (CST), Mountain Standard Time (MST), and Pacific Standard Time (PST). Alaska and Hawaii have their own zones. For example, when it's 9am in Los Angeles (PST), it's 7am in Honolulu (HST), 10am in Denver (MST), 11am in Chicago (CST), noon in New York City (EST), 5pm in London (GMT), and 2am the next day in Sydney.

Daylight saving time is in effect from 1am on the second Sunday in March to 1am on the first Sunday in November, except in Arizona, Hawaii, the U.S. Virgin Islands, and Puerto Rico. Daylight saving time moves the clock 1 hour ahead of standard time.

TIPPING Tips are a very important part of certain workers' income, and gratuities are the standard way of showing appreciation for services provided. (Tipping is certainly not compulsory if the service is poor!) In hotels, tip **bellhops** at least $1 per bag ($2–$3 if you have a lot of luggage) and tip the **chamber staff** $1 to $2 per day (more if you've left a disaster area for him or her to clean up). Tip the **doorman** or **concierge** only if he or she has provided you with some specific service (for example, calling a cab for you or obtaining difficult-to-get theater tickets). Tip the **valet-parking attendant** $1 every time you get your car.

In restaurants, bars, and nightclubs, tip **service staff** 15% to 20% of the check, tip **bartenders** 10% to 15%, tip **checkroom attendants** $1 per garment, and tip **valet-parking attendants** $1 per vehicle.

As for other service personnel, tip **cab drivers** 15% of the fare; tip **skycaps** at airports at least $1 per bag ($2–$3 if you have a lot of luggage); and tip **hairdressers** and **barbers** 15% to 20%.

TOILETS You won't find public toilets or "restrooms" on the streets in most U.S. cities, but they can be found in hotel lobbies, bars, restaurants, museums, department stores, railway and bus stations, and service stations. Large hotels and fast-food restaurants are often the best bet for clean facilities. If possible, avoid the toilets at parks and beaches, which tend to be dirty; some may be unsafe. Restaurants and bars in resorts or heavily visited areas may reserve their restrooms for patrons.

USEFUL PHONE NUMBERS

U.S. Dept. of State Travel Advisory: ✆ 202/647-5225 (manned 24 hr.).

U.S. Passport Agency: ✆ 202/647-0518.

U.S. Centers for Disease Control International Traveler's Hotline: ✆ 404/332-4559.

VISAS For information about U.S. visas, go to **http://travel.state.gov** and click on "Visas." Or go to one of the following websites:

Australian citizens can obtain up-to-date visa information from the **U.S. Embassy Canberra,** Moonah Place, Yarralumla, ACT 2600 (**✆ 02/6214-5600**), or by checking the U.S. Diplomatic Mission's website at **http://usembassy-australia.state.gov/consular**.

British subjects can obtain up-to-date visa information by calling the **U.S. Embassy Visa Information Line** (**✆ 0891/200-290**) or by visiting the "Visas to the U.S." section of the American Embassy London's website at **www.usembassy.org.uk**.

Irish citizens can obtain up-to-date visa information through the **Embassy of the USA Dublin,** 42 Elgin Rd., Dublin 4, Ireland (**✆ 353/1-668-8777**), or by checking the "Consular Services" section of the website at **http://dublin.usembassy.gov**.

Citizens of **New Zealand** can obtain up-to-date visa information by contacting the **U.S. Embassy New Zealand,** 29 Fitzherbert Terrace, Thorndon, Wellington (**✆ 644/472-2068**), or get the information directly from the website at **http://wellington.usembassy.gov**.

2 TOLL-FREE NUMBERS & WEBSITES

MAJOR U.S. AIRLINES

(*flies internationally as well)

Alaska Airlines
✆ 800/252-7522 (in U.S. and Canada)
www.alaskaair.com

American Airlines*
✆ 800/433-7300 (in U.S. and Canada)
✆ 020/7365-0777 (in U.K.)
www.aa.com

Continental Airlines*
✆ 800/523-3273 (in U.S. and Canada)
✆ 084/5607-6760 (in U.K.)
www.continental.com

Delta Air Lines*
✆ 800/221-1212 (in U.S. and Canada)
✆ 084/5600-0950 (in U.K.)
www.delta.com

go!
✆ 888/435-9462
www.iflygo.com
(interisland Hawaii only)

Hawaiian Airlines*
✆ 800/367-5320 (in U.S. and Canada)
www.hawaiianair.com

Northwest Airlines
✆ 800/225-2525 (in U.S.)
✆ 870/0507-4074 (in U.K.)
www.flynaa.com

United Airlines*
✆ 800/864-8331 (in U.S. and Canada)
✆ 084/5844-4777 in U.K.
www.united.com

US Airways*
✆ 800/428-4322 (in U.S. and Canada)
✆ 084/5600-3300 (in U.K.)
www.usairways.com

MAJOR INTERNATIONAL AIRLINES

Air France
✆ 800/237-2747 (in U.S.)
✆ 800/375-8723 (U.S. and Canada)
✆ 087/0142-4343 (in U.K.)
www.airfrance.com

Air New Zealand
✆ 800/262-1234 (in U.S.)
✆ 800/663-5494 (in Canada)
✆ 0800/028-4149 (in U.K.)
www.airnewzealand.com

Air Tahiti Nui
✆ 877/824-4846 (in U.S. and Canada)
www.airtahitinui-usa.com

Alitalia
✆ 800/223-5730 (in U.S.)
✆ 800/361-8336 (in Canada)
✆ 087/0608-6003 (in U.K.)
www.alitalia.com

British Airways
✆ 800/247-9297 (in U.S. and Canada)
✆ 087/0850-9850 (in U.K.)
www.british-airways.com

China Airlines
✆ 800/227-5118 (in U.S.)
✆ 022/715-1212 (in Taiwan)
www.china-airlines.com

Delta Air Lines
✆ 800/221-1212 (in U.S. and Canada)
✆ 084/5600-0950 (in U.K.)
www.delta.com

Hawaiian Airlines
✆ 800/367-5320 (in U.S. and Canada)
www.hawaiianair.com

Japan Airlines
✆ 012/025-5931 (international)
www.jal.com

Korean Air
✆ 800/438-5000 (in U.S. and Canada)
✆ 0800/413-000 (in U.K.)
www.koreanair.com

Quantas Airways
✆ 800/227-4500 (in U.S. and Canada)
✆ 084/5774-7767 (in U.K.)
✆ 13 13 13 (in Australia)
www.quantas.com

Philippine Airlines
✆ 800/I-Fly-Pal (435-9725) (in U.S. and Canada)
✆ 632/855-8888 (in Philippines)
www.philippineairlines.com

Virgin Atlantic Airways
✆ 800/821-5438 (in U.S. and Canada)
✆ 087/0574-7747 (in U.K.)
www.virgin-atlantic.com
www.westjet.com

CAR RENTAL AGENCIES

Alamo
✆ 800/GO-ALAMO (462-5266) (in U.S. and Canada)
www.alamo.com

Avis
✆ 800/331-1212 (in U.S. and Canada)
✆ 084/4581-8181 (in U.K.)
www.avis.com

Budget
✆ 800/527-0700 (in U.S.)
✆ 087/0156-5656 (in U.K.)
✆ 800/268-8900 (in Canada)
www.budget.com

Dollar
✆ 800/800-4000 (in U.S.)
✆ 800/848-8268 (in Canada)
✆ 080/8234-7524 (in U.K.)
www.dollar.com

Enterprise
✆ 800/261-7331 (in U.S.)
✆ 514/355-4028 (in Canada)
✆ 012/9360-9090 (in U.K.)
www.enterprise.com

Hertz
✆ 800/645-3131
✆ 800/654-3001 (for international reservations)
www.hertz.com

National
✆ 800/CAR-RENT (227-7368) (in U.S. and Canada)
www.nationalcar.com

Rent-A-Wreck
✆ 800/535-1391
www.rentawreck.com

Thrifty
✆ 800/367-2277
✆ 918/669-2168 (international)
www.thrifty.com

MAJOR HOTEL & MOTEL CHAINS

Best Western International
✆ 800/780-7234 (in U.S. and Canada)
✆ 0800/393-130 (in U.K.)
www.bestwestern.com

Doubletree Hotels
✆ 800/222-TREE (222-8733) (in U.S. and Canada)
✆ 087/0590-9090 (in U.K.)
www.doubletree.com

Embassy Suites
✆ 800/EMBASSY (362-2779)
http://embassysuites1.hilton.com

Four Seasons
✆ 800/819-5053 (in U.S. and Canada)
✆ 0800/6488-6488 (in U.K.)
www.fourseasons.com

Hilton Hotels
✆ 800/HILTONS (445-8667) (in U.S. and Canada)
✆ 087/0590-9090 (in U.K.)
www.hilton.com

Holiday Inn
✆ 800/315-2621 (in U.S. and Canada)
✆ 0800/405-060 (in U.K.)
www.holidayinn.com

Hyatt
✆ 888/591-1234 (in U.S. and Canada)
✆ 084/5888-1234 (in U.K.)
www.hyatt.com

Marriott
✆ 877/236-2427 (in U.S. and Canada)
✆ 0800/221-222 (in U.K.)
www.marriott.com

Radisson Hotels & Resorts
✆ 888/201-1718 (in U.S. and Canada)
✆ 0800/374-411 (in U.K.)
www.radisson.com

Sheraton Hotels & Resorts
✆ 800/325-3535 (in U.S.)
✆ 800/543-4300 (in Canada)
✆ 0800/3253-5353 (in U.K.)
www.starwoodhotels.com/sheraton

Westin Hotels & Resorts
✆ 800/937-8461 (in U.S. and Canada)
✆ 0800/3259-5959 (in U.K.)
www.starwoodhotels.com/westin

Wyndham Hotels & Resorts
✆ 877/999-3223 (in U.S. and Canada)
✆ 050/6638-4899 (in U.K.)
www.wyndham.com

INDEX

General Index

M

A Guide for Every Type of Traveler

Frommer's Complete Guides

For those who value complete coverage, candid advice, and lots of choices in all price ranges.

Pauline Frommer's Guides

For those who want to experience a culture, meet locals, and save money along the way.

MTV Guides

For hip, youthful travelers who want a fresh perspective on today's hottest cities and destinations.

Day by Day Guides

For leisure or business travelers who want to organize their time to get the most out of a trip.

Frommer's With Kids Guides

For families traveling with children ages 2 to 14 seeking kid-friendly hotels, restaurants, and activities.

Unofficial Guides

For honeymooners, families, business travelers, and others who value no-nonsense, *Consumer Reports*–style advice.

For Dummies Travel Guides

For curious, independent travelers looking for a fun and easy way to plan a trip.

Visit Frommers.com

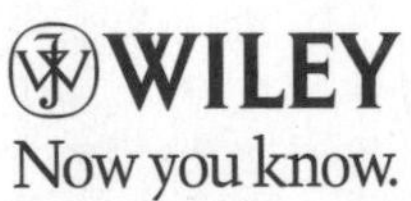